Computer Technology Innovators

Computer Technology Innovators

The Editors of Salem Press

SALEM PRESS
A Division of EBSCO Publishing
Ipswich, Massachusetts

GREY HOUSE PUBLISHING

Cover photo: Computer pioneer and Apple Computer cofounder Steve Wozniak. (Getty Images)

Computer Technology Innovators, 2013, published by Grey House Publishing, Inc., Amenia, NY, under exclusive license from EBSCO Publishing, Inc.

∞ The paper used in these volumes conforms to the American National Standard for Permanence of Paper for Printed Library Materials, Z39.48 1992 (R1997).

Library of Congress Cataloging-in-Publication Data

Computer technology innovators / the editors of Salem Press.
  pages cm
 Includes bibliographical references and index.
 ISBN 978-1-4298-3805-4 (hardcover)
 1. Computer scientists--Biography. 2. Computer science--Technological innovations. I. Salem Press..
 QA76.2.A2C66 2013
 004.092'2--dc23
 [B]

2012045266

ebook ISBN: 978-1-4298-3806-1

CONTENTS

Appendixes

Indexes

PUBLISHER'S NOTE

Computer Technology Innovators profiles the most innovative and influential individuals in the development of computer technology and the evolution of the Internet, many who have never been covered in any Salem Press set before. From the genesis of the World Wide Web in 1989 as a way to organize and manage data to the founding of the world's largest Internet retailer, Amazon.com, in 1994, to the first documented tweet in 2006, the history of the Internet is immeasurably rich, with milestones that have revolutionized our society. This new title examines those individuals most responsible for the technology and strategies behind the Internet today, from the pioneering community of engineers and intellectuals who worked to realize a vision of shared networks and research, to the dot-com founders and leaders driving business and commerce today.

SCOPE OF COVERAGE

Computer Technology Innovators features more than 120 biographies of individuals who have had a significant influence on the development of computer technology, culminating with the advent of the Internet and beyond, with an emphasis on early pioneers such as inventors and engineers and influential founders and executives of computer companies. Each essay has been written specifically for this set; biographies represent a strong, global, cross-gender focus, with accompanying sidebars describing the company, organization, online service, or website with which that individual is most often associated. Among the editors' criteria for inclusion in the set was an individual's historical significance, whether through their respective company's influence in the Internet world or their role in the development and evolution of the Internet itself; his or her relevance to academic curriculum; and his or her appeal to high school and undergraduate students and general readers.

ESSAY LENGTH AND FORMAT

Each essay is approximately 2,000 words in length and displays standard reference top matter offering easy access to the following biographical information:

- The name by which the subject is best known.
- A succinct description of each individual's nationality and occupation.

- The most complete birth and death dates, followed by the most precise locations of those events available.
- The areas of achievement, including primary field and specialty, with which the subject is often most closely identified. This latter is an all-encompassing categorical list and includes: mathematics and logic; physics and engineering; computer software; computer hardware; computer programming; security; Internet; management, executives, and investors; marketing; commerce; social media; content and data; applications; news and entertainment; and ethics and policy.
- The primary company or organization with which the individual has been associated in a meaningful way.
- A synopsis of the individual's historical importance in relation to computer technology and the evolution of the Internet, indicating why the person is or should be studied today.

Each essay concludes with a byline for the contributing writer. The bodies of the essays are divided into the following parts:

- Early Life provides facts about the individual's upbringing. Where little is known about the person's early life, historical context is provided.
- Life's Work, the heart of the article, consists of a straightforward, generally chronological account of how the individual gained recognition in his or her chosen primary field (applied science; computer science; business and commerce; and Internet), emphasizing the most significant endeavors and achievements—and failures—of the figure's life and career.
- Personal Information provides closing remarks on the person, including post–achievement activities or positions, family life, and topics of general interest.

Each essay also includes an annotated Further Reading section that provides a starting point for additional research.

SPECIAL FEATURES

Several features distinguish this series as a whole from other biographical reference works. The back matter includes the following aids, appendices, and indexes:

- Timeline: presents a comprehensive time line of milestone events that represent a concise history of the Internet, both theoretical and commercial in scope.
- General Bibliography: offers an extensive list of resources relevant to the study of the history of computer technology and the Internet.
- Biographical Directory: an annotated and concise listing of those individuals featured in the volume.
- Category Index: profiles figures by area of primary field or specialty.
- Company Index: lists the individuals associated or affiliated with a company or organization, in many capacities.
- Index: provides a comprehensive index including personages, scientific and computer-related

concepts and discoveries, technologies, terms, principles, and other topics of discussion.

Other features include:
- Sidebars: A highlight of this publication and key feature of every essay, the sidebars describe the company, organization, online service, or website for which each profiled person is best known. Sidebars also describe why the organization or company was influential within a particular field.
- Images: More than eighty illustrations appear with the essays.

CONTRIBUTORS

Salem Press would like to extend its appreciation to all involved in the development and production of this work. The essays have been written and signed by writers and scholars of history, the sciences, and other disciplines related to the essays' topics.

CONTRIBUTORS

John H. Barnhill

Sarah Boslaugh

Lena Brandis

Marcella Bush Trevino

Justin Corfield

Jason A. Helfer

Bill Kte'pi

Christopher Leslie

Vytautas Malesh

Jamal A. Nelson

Trish Popovitch

Pilar Quezzaire

Wylene Rholetter

Elizabeth Rholetter Purdy

Stephen T. Schroth

Lloyd L. Scott Jr.

Robert N. Stacy

Melvin E. Taylor Jr.

Claire C. Turner

Rachel Wexelbaum

Gavin Wilk

Kin Vong

Computer Technology Innovators

HOWARD H. AIKEN

Designer of the Harvard Mark I computer

Born: March 8, 1900; Hoboken, New Jersey
Died: March 14, 1973; Palo Alto, California
Primary Field: Computer science
Specialty: Computer hardware
Primary Company/Organization: IBM

INTRODUCTION

In the late 1930s, college professor Howard H. Aiken sold International Business Machines (IBM) on developing the digital computer he had designed. Although other claimants exist, Aiken, according to historians, has the strongest claim of any of the contenders to the title of inventor of the digital computer. His Automatic Sequence Controlled Calculator was the progenitor if not the prototype of the modern computer.

EARLY LIFE

Born in Hoboken, New Jersey, to Daniel and Margaret Emily Mierisch Aiken, Howard Hathaway Aiken grew up in Indianapolis, Indiana. To help support his family he took a night job as a switchboard operator for the local utility. The school superintendent, Milo Stewart, hearing that Aiken was working the twelve-hour-shift night job as well as attending school, allowed Aiken to test out of classes to cover a shortage of credits and graduate early. He graduated from Arsenal Tech's first graduating class. Stewart also wrote recommendations to every public utility in the university town of Madison, Wisconsin, where Aiken found a job as a telephone operator. He moved there with his mother, establishing her in her own apartment while he roomed with two or three others. In 1919, Aiken began attending the University of Wisconsin, graduating in electrical engineer-

ing in 1923. After graduation, he took a job at an electric plant and worked in Madison, Chicago, and Detroit until 1932. Graduate work at the University of Chicago and Harvard University came later; Aiken received an A.M. from Harvard in 1937 and his Harvard doctorate in physics in 1939. His mother traveled to Cambridge with him and remained there while Aiken was on the faculty, even after his postwar marriage. She prepared a

Howard H. Aiken.

hot lunch for him every day. Aiken said it was a good way to guarantee that she had at least one meal a day. Aiken became assistant professor and naval lieutenant commander in 1941.

Life's Work

In graduate school, Aiken became aggravated by the time it took to do the computations involved in differential equations integral to his electronics studies. Thinking that he and other scientists could better spend their time on real problems than on simple arithmetic, Aiken decided to invent a machine to handle the simple tasks. It was a bit harder than merely collecting parts and putting them together, however.

Aiken read the work of Charles Babbage and used it as the basis for his design. Aiken began working on the machine in 1935, when he joined the Harvard staff as instructor in physics and communications engineering. The machine required two years of theoretical work and six years of construction. Aiken was a naval reserve officer on leave to Harvard for the project.

In 1937, he developed a way to identify numbers in binary code using the on/off characteristic of electrical relays. Beginning work in 1939, Aiken made his machine as simple as he could while getting it to use positive and negative numbers, sines and other mathematical functions, and common mathematical sequences. Operation had to be automatic in what IBM labeled the Automatic Sequence Controlled Calculator, more familiarly the Mark I.

Aiken's colleagues thought the calculator would be far too expensive to build and directed him to IBM, a major manufacturer of accounting machines, tabulators, calculators, and other office machines. IBM used punch card technology, accumulated data, and transferred data across devices as accounting tools. IBM was the only company in the world that had the expertise and components that Aiken needed. Later machines—for instance ENIAC (the Electronic Numerical Integrator and Computer)—would be created through custom parts, but Aiken took IBM's experience and parts and used them for his new device.

Aiken met with James Bryce, holder of more than 500 patents, and the two broached the idea of the ASCC to IBM president Thomas Watson. IBM agreed to fund two-thirds of the bill, and the government financed the other third of the half-million-dollar project. IBM took on a project well beyond anything it had attempted before. It required new engineering and design, not just assembly from off-the-shelf parts. Aiken was more

attuned to broader concepts, and he had no particular interest in the nuts and bolts.

There were few mechanical calculators in existence in 1943, when, as a Harvard professor, Aiken contacted IBM. His Automatic Sequence Controlled Calculator (ASCC) had no keyboard or screen. It was powered by electricity and used punch cards to give commands and magnetic switches to perform the computations at speeds impossible for humans. The ASCC debuted in 1943. Called the Mark I, it added, subtracted, divided, and multiplied to 23 decimal places and referred back to its earlier results. It gave access to multiple users simultaneously (at least two). It weighed 35 tons, stood 8 feet tall, and required 500 miles of wire and most of the space in a laboratory at Harvard. It had 750,000 parts, was 5 inches thick, and had 3,000 relays that clicked noticeably, making the Mark I in operation sound like a knitter's convention. Operations entailed working with 1,400 switches and running four punched paper tapes, but the machine could add or subtract 23-digit numbers in 0.3 second, multiply in 4 seconds, and divide in 12 seconds. Aiken and several IBM employees shared the patent.

Although journalists called it an electronic brain, the Mark I had no electronics but was instead an electromechanical device. Slow by modern standards, the Mark I nevertheless began the modern computing industry and made the United States its world leader.

Later designs—the Mark II, III, and IV computers—were more streamlined. The Mark series enabled the U.S. Navy to calculate trajectories for bombs and missiles during and after World War II. It appeared to be a mechanical brain, a threat to humanity, but it did relieve human beings of massive amounts of drudge work.

The Mark II's data relay switch failed because of a dead moth between two contacts. After that, any correction to a computer was referred to as "debugging."

Bryce was the only person at IBM whom Aiken respected and for whom he had no harsh words. Watson had a deep respect for the Ivy League and a strong commitment to using his company for the betterment of humanity. However, as head of IBM, a major business, Watson was not inclined to bend to Aiken, who also was not inclined to compromise. According to Ralph Niemann, who worked with Aiken in Dahlgren, Virginia, Aiken was "fiercely independent and dynamic." Working at IBM's labs in Endicott, New York, he encountered friction: Aiken and IBM each regarded the other as taking too much credit for the machine.

Aiken was also practical, however, asking interviewee mathematicians if they knew how to handle a

Affiliation: IBM

IBM is commonly defined as the brainchild of Thomas J. Watson, Sr., in 1914, but arguably its roots go back to the 1870s, when Herman Hollerith found a solution to the long-standing problem of counting census data. Hollerith's punch card equipment debuted in the 1890 census. By 1911 Hollerith was ready to sell his company, and the firm merged with two others to form IBM, with Watson coming on as head of the new business in 1914. Watson took a small entrepreneurial company and made it into a vertically integrated behemoth dominating business machines through aggressive research and development in business areas through the Depression and World War II. After the war, computing shifted to from electromechanical to electronic technologies, and IBM found itself struggling until Thomas Watson Jr., brought out the company's first electronic machine, with the System 360 dominating from the 1960s through the 1980s. Complacency and difficulties turning the *Queen Mary* of computing companies led IBM to struggle in the 1980s and later as small and innovative start-ups moved faster into new technologies.

screwdriver. He was available night and day for workers who encountered problems and understood the importance of what he was doing in pioneering large-scale computers. He considered himself not only a designer but also a teacher and molder of people. He initially believed that the computer would be suited only for mathematical uses, but he came to recognize that it had business applications as well. Aiken's Mark II, known as the Aiken Relay Computer, was developed for the Naval Surface Weapons Center in Dahlgren. The Mark II and Mark III were built at a combined cost of $2 million. When designing computers Aiken sought to balance the speed of the calculator with the capacity of the input-output devices.

When Harvard opened a new computer facility, later named for Aiken, Aiken was its first director. He was also instrumental in establishing university-level computer science. Courses in computer science began at Columbia in 1946–47, the year before they did at Harvard. In 1947, Aiken established the first master's program focusing on computing machines, a precursor to the computer science program. Many of Aiken's students went on to become key figures in the development of computing.

The ASCC was known in Nazi Germany, and in the 1950s preparers of lineages and family trees of computing commonly gave the ASCC a prominent position as the first, with Aiken as the inventor. When he received the initial Harry Goode Memorial Award for Outstanding Achievement in the Field of Computing, it recognized his major impact on the field, as did the 1965 renaming of the Harvard center for him.

PERSONAL LIFE

Aiken's personality clash with Watson led him to deny Watson's involvement in the development of the ASCC. When he retired, he moved to Fort Lauderdale, where he received a distinguished professorship from the University of Miami. He developed the university's computer center and computer science program. He became a consultant, founding Howard Aiken Industries Incorporated, and specialized in taking over and reviving struggling businesses and then selling them. He also consulted for Lockheed Missiles and Monsanto. He developed a method of encrypting data for information security.

Aiken had married Lousie Mancill in 1939. After they divorced in 1942, he married Agnes Montgomery, a Latin teacher. He divorced Agnes and married his final wife, Mary McFarland. He had two children: Rachel Ann by his first wife and Elizabeth (Betsy) by his second.

Aiken was 6 feet, 4 inches tall with a large head and an intimidating presence. He had a quick temper and could be difficult to work with. Isaac Auerbach tells the story of how, while taking a course at Harvard with Aiken, he sought summer employment with J. Presper Eckert and John Mauchly's Electronic Control Company in Philadelphia. Aiken had a with-us-or-with-the-enemy attitude and apparently a jealousy of Eckert and Mauchly because their ENIAC was competing successfully with his Mark I. From that point Auerbach was a pariah, shunned by Aiken on contact, until finally Auerbach moved to Burroughs, at which point Aiken renewed his friendship with Auerbach.

Aiken also had a soft side, however, and was regarded by many as affable, sociable, and generous. When John Harr was a graduate student in mathematics, Aiken initially turned him down for a job as a programmer because he preferred not to work with graduate students and others who could not commit to programming full time. Aiken relented after Harr returned and, not mentioning graduate school, said he needed work and would study as time permitted. Harr got the job and the degree and worked for Aiken for eight years.

While on a business trip to St. Louis, Aiken died on March 14, 1973. He was seventy-three years old.

John H. Barnhill

FURTHER READING

Bonasia, J. "Aiken, the Computer Master." *Investor's Business Daily* 18 July 2008: n. pag. *Business Source Complete*. Web. 30 Apr. 2012. A brief overview of Aiken's invention of the Automatic Sequence Controlled Calculator.

Cohen, I. Bernard. *Howard Aiken: Portrait of a Computer Pioneer*. Boston: MIT, 2000. Print. Biography of Aiken by a colleague at Harvard acknowledges Aiken's contributions but also indicates that the development of the digital computer was more than a one-person effort.

Cohen, I. Bernard, Gregory W. Welch, and Robert V. D. Campbell, eds. *Makin' Numbers: Howard Aiken and the Computer*. Boston: MIT, 1999. Print. Full of Aiken's work, including the technical element.

Esmenger, Nathan L. "*Howard Aiken/Makin' Numbers*." *Business History Review* 73.4 (1999): 761. Print. Reviews Cohen's biography as well as the companion piece, Cohen's coedited collection of essays *Makin' Numbers*. The focus is on technical development of the ASCC, the Harvard Mark I, and Aiken's role in developing computer science as a discipline.

Karwatka, Dennis. "Howard Hathaway Aiken." *Tech Directions* 55.9 (1996): 12. *Business Source Complete*. Web. 27 Apr. 2012. Profiles Aiken's career.

Pugh, Emerson. *Building IBM: Shaping an Industry and Its Technology*. Boston: MIT, 1995. Print. Traces the history of the company through the 1990s.

FRANCES E. ALLEN

First woman to win the A. M. Turing Award

Born: August 4, 1932; Peru, New York
Died: -
Primary Field: Computer science
Specialty: Computer programming
Primary Company/Organization: IBM

INTRODUCTION

Frances E. Allen, an American computer research scientist and pioneer in computing, spent nearly half a century working on compilers and high-performance computing systems. Her work led to technologies that formed the foundation for the theory of program optimization and contributed to the use of high-performance computers in weather forecasting, DNA matching, and national security-code breaking. Allen was among the first women recognized for her role in the technical aspect of computing. Her many awards include being named an IBM Fellow and winning the A. M. Turing Award; she was the first woman to be so honored with both titles.

EARLY LIFE

Frances Elizabeth "Fran" Allen was born August 4, 1932, in Peru, New York, a few miles south of the Canadian border. The oldest of six children, four boys and

Frances E. Allen.

two girls, Allen grew up on the family dairy farm without electricity, plumbing, or central heating. Her parents encouraged their children to read and emphasized the value of an education. An excellent student overall, Allen was first interested in English and writing, but, inspired by a mathematics teacher, she decided to become a math teacher. She received a B.S. degree from the New York State Teachers' College at Albany (now State University of New York at Albany) in 1954 and returned to teach mathematics in Peru at the high school from which she had graduated.

After two years of teaching, she decided to pursue the advanced degree that New York required for full certification of teachers. She attended Columbia University for one summer, but, eager to complete her studies, she entered graduate school at the University of Michigan. At Michigan she was introduced to computing through an elective offered in the school of engineering, a decade before computer science as a discipline existed. The course required her to program complex mathematical calculations on a room-size IBM 650, a project she found fascinating. She earned a master's degree in mathematics in 1957 and accepted a job with IBM, which was actively recruiting women at that time. Allen found great satisfaction in teaching and intended to work for IBM for only one year in order to pay off student loans before resuming her career as a high school math teacher.

LIFE'S WORK

Joining IBM's T. J. Watson Research Center on July 15, 1957, Allen was first assigned the task of teaching Fortran (which stands for "formula translation"), the first high-level programming language, developed by IBM and released in the spring of 1957. Its purpose was to allow scientists and engineers to write programs and thus increase the number of people who could program for computers. Allen found the scientists who were her students resistant to learning Fortran and skeptical of its promise, but a 500 percent increase in the speed with which programs could be written eventually persuaded them of the program's value. A few years later, Allen helped to design Alpha, another high-level programming language, designed for the top-secret Stretch-Harvest computer. So secret was the work that its funding fell under the so-called Bureau of Ships, and only later was the actual sponsoring agency, the National Security Agency, made public knowledge. Allen's contribution helped to increase the efficiency of intelligence gathering from intercepted communications around the world.

At one point the computer, with its output available only to government officials, scanned more than 7 million messages in less than four hours.

Allen worked closely during her early years at IBM with John Cocke, the research scientist and innovator who was the primary designer of the microprocessor, which simplified computer hardware and made faster computation possible. Colleagues say that it was Allen, a strong supporter of sharing IBM's innovations in her field, whose published papers and speeches in academic settings were largely responsible for the dissemination of Cocke's ideas. For fifteen years, from 1980 to 1995, Allen served as head of IBM's research team working on compiler software for multiprocessor computers. Her work with the Parallel TRANslation Group (PTRAN), which she founded in the early 1980s, is one of her most notable achievements. In 1989, Allen became the first woman to be named an IBM Fellow. The appointed position, the highest honor the company bestows, recognizes an honoree's history of significant achievement and his or her potential for future accomplishments. The fellowship also gave Allen greater freedom to pursue her particular research interests.

In 2000, Allen became technical adviser on IBM's Blue Gene Project. The first stage of the project had the goal of building a parallel computer massive enough to handle the immense number of mathematical calculations needed to study biomolecular phenomena such as protein folding. Allen saw in the requirement for extraordinarily fast and powerful computer capabilities and in the need for problem-solving software a return to the projects that had consumed her during her first years in the field.

In 2002, Allen retired after forty-five years at IBM. That year she received the Augusta Ada Lovelace Award, named in honor of the first computer programmer, from the Association for Women in Computing. Four years later, she became the first woman to receive the prestigious A. M. Turing Award, named for British mathematician Alan M. Turing. The award, presented by the Association for Computing Machinery (ACM), has been given annually since 1966 to computer scientists and engineers who have made significant contributions of enduring importance to computing. Often called the Nobel Prize of computing, the award carried a cash prize of $100,000 and an invitation to deliver a lecture at ACM's annual meeting.

At various times in her career, during sabbaticals from IBM, Allen has returned to teaching as an adjunct professor or visiting lecturer. From 1970 to 1973, she was a visiting professor at New York University. In 1988–89, she served as the Chancellor's Distinguished Lecturer and Mackay Lecturer at the University of California, Berkeley. In 1997, she was Regents Lecturer at the University of California, San Diego.

Perhaps because she remembers her own isolation during periods of her career, Allen has been a longtime advocate for women in computing. When she began at IBM, the company employed women in considerable numbers as programmers because women were considered more detail-oriented than men, and their attention to detail was thought to be an advantage. However, by the mid-1960s, IBM required degrees, and most of the degree holders were men. Allen recalls being the only woman among forty IBM scientists working on a project in the 1960s. An early award included a tie clip and cuff links, and even the document naming her an IBM Fellow recognizes Frances E. Allen for "his" contributions.

Allen committed early to encouraging young women to enter the field, and she felt a particular responsibility to women in computer technology at IBM. Formal and informal mentoring became part of her daily routine. She focused on helping women build networks, believing them to be key in gaining promotions, opportunities, and recognition. Acknowledging her contributions as mentor to women within the company in 2000, IBM instituted the Frances E. Allen IBM Women in Technology Mentoring Award and made Allen herself the first recipient. In retirement, she became an IBM Fellow Emerita, serving on the advisory board of the Anita Borg Institute for Women and Technology and continuing her commitment to foster the role of women in computing through her active involvement in professional organizations such as the American Philosophical Society, the National Academy of Engineers, the American Academy of Arts and Sciences, the Association for Computing Machinery, and the Institute of Electrical and Electronics Engineers.

PERSONAL LIFE

In 1972, Allen married Jacob Theodore "Jack" Schwartz, a mathematician and founder of the computer science department at New York University, which he chaired from 1964 to 1980. The two met when Schwartz was working on the program optimization that Allen and Cocke had pioneered. Allen and Schwartz later divorced, but they remained friendly and supportive of each other professionally until Schwartz's death in 2009.

An avid mountain climber since the 1970s and a member of the American Alpine Club and the Alpine Club of Canada, Allen has participated in expeditions to the Arctic, where she was part of teams that made six first ascents, mapping uncharted mountains on Baffin Island (the largest island in the Arctic archipelago), and established a new route across Ellesmere, another island. Other adventures include climbing Mexico's 17,802-foot Popocatépetl and participating in an exploratory expedition on the Chinese-Tibetan border. In April 2006, four years after she retired, she climbed a 14,000-foot peak in the Himalayas. Allen has noted that computer research and mountain climbing are not as different as they may seem. Both offer new challenges

---

Affiliation: IBM

In 1952, Thomas J. Watson Jr., succeeded his father as president of IBM and led the company into a new age with a focus on developing and marketing computer technologies. In 1957, Frances E. Allen became part of the first generation of women employed in IBM Research. Beginning with her initial assignment to teach a new computer programming language to IBM scientists, Allen's achievements over more than forty years reflect changes in the company. IBM's AN/FSQ-7 was the fastest-operating computer of the 1950s, but during the 1960s, the IBM 7030, known as Stretch, tripled that speed. A compiler is that part of a computer that translates software written by programmers into signals the computer's hardware can understand. Allen worked to develop a compiler for the Stretch.

The 1980s saw the introduction of the original IBM PC, the business computer that became the industry standard. Allen continued research on compiler software for parallel computers. The Parallel TRANslator (PTRAN), a system for automatically restructuring sequential Fortran programs for execution on parallel architectures, was founded by Allen in the early 1980s. She continued to work on improving efficiency for computer programming for multiprocessing systems throughout much of her career. Transitioning from traditional mainframe computers into microprocessor-based parallel computers was a significant factor in IBM's survival, and the work of Allen and her team was crucial to that transition.

and opportunities to explore new ideas and solve new problems. However, she has also noted that her half century in computer research has been the greatest adventure of her life.

Wylene Rholetter

FURTHER READING

Allen, Frances E. "An Interview with Frances E. Allen." Interview by Guy L. Steele Jr. *Communications of the ACM* 54.1 (2011): 39–45. Print. A lengthy interview with Allen that provides a detailed account of her long career with IBM, with particular attention to her work on the IBM Stretch and her collaboration with John Cocke.

"First Woman Selected for Top Computer Science Award." *Diverse Issues in Higher Education* 24.4 (2007): 51. Print. An announcement of Allen's winning the 2006 Turing Award that recounts her accomplishments that led to that recognition. The chair of the Turing Award Committee that selected Allen is quoted.

Lohr, Steve. "Scientist at Work: Frances Allen; Would-Be Math Teacher Ended Up Educating a Computer Revolution." *New York Times* 6 Aug. 2002: 3. Print. An overview of Allen's life and career published the week after her retirement from IBM. Includes information about her personal life and her professional achievements.

Misa, Thomas J., ed. *Gender Codes: Why Women Are Leaving Computing*. New York: Wiley-IEEE Computer Society Press, 2010. Print. Allen is among the women programmers, systems analysts, managers, and information technology executives of the 1960s and 1970s whose achievements are celebrated. The accomplishments of women of this period are contrasted to the diminishing number of women entering computer science in the twenty-first century.

PAUL ALLEN

Cofounder of Microsoft

Born: January 21, 1953; Seattle, Washington
Died: -
Primary Field: Computer science
Specialty: Computer software
Primary Company/Organization: Microsoft

INTRODUCTION

Known by the public as a cofounder of the software giant Microsoft, Paul Allen played an active role in the company until 1983, when his role ended for health reasons. Since that time, he has become a major player in a number of venues by investing in computer technologies, medical research, space and oceanic exploration, entertainment, and sports. Allen and his sister Jody founded the Paul G. Allen Family Fund to promote community projects in the Pacific Northwest. He also built the Paul G. Allen School for Global Animal Health at Washington State University. Allen owns the Seattle Seahawks football team and the Portland Trail Blazers basketball team and is part owner of the Seattle Sounders soccer team. He also owns a yacht, the Octopus which he sails annually to the Cannes Film Festival, where he hosts lavish parties for celebrities.

Paul Allen.

EARLY LIFE

Paul Gardner Allen was born on January 21, 1953, in Seattle, Washington, to Kenneth Allen and Edna Faye Gardener. He attended Lakeside, a private boy's preparatory school in Seattle. When Allen was thirteen, a new student by the name of Bill Gates arrived at Lakeside. The two became fast friends. Gates was a mathematical whiz kid, and Allen was fascinated with electronics. Both boys were addicted to books, and Allen particularly enjoyed science fiction and books that explained how things worked. He read the periodical *Popular Mechanics* with fervor. Because his father was an associate director at the University of Washington library, Allen was exposed to a wide variety of books. Unlike Gates, who has generally been described as "nerdy" at this age, Allen was considered "cool." He sported a Fu Manchu mustache and aviator sunglasses and always carried a briefcase.

Along with Richard Weiland and Kent Evans, Gates and Allen discovered the PDP-10 computer. Since computers were so new at the time, Lakeside teachers knew very little about them. Thus, the boys were left alone to learn how they worked. The four friends founded the Lakeside Programmers Group and attempted to find ways to use computers to make money. Over time, the group did make money, but it also spent a good deal by using excessive computer time, for which the school and their parents were expected to pay. The boys eventually won free computer time in exchange for finding bugs in the system.

When Allen entered Washington State University in 1971 to study computer science, Gates still had two more years at Lakeside. The two friends continued to work on Traf-O-Data, a program they had created to assist cities in Washington with tracking traffic. Although they eventually made around $20,000 from the project, it became obsolete when the federal government began providing a similar service for free. Allen dropped out of Washington State in 1974. He moved to Boston and took a job with Honeywell, a technology innovator. Since Gates was also in Boston attending Harvard University, the two continued to work together on computer projects.

LIFE'S WORK

In February 1975, Allen and Gates began work on advancing Beginner's All-Purpose Symbolic Instruction Code (BASIC) for use in the Altair computer, owned by Albuquerque-based Micro Instrumentation and Telemetry Systems (MITS). BASIC was a computer language that had been developed by two Dartmouth professors in 1964, John Kemeny and Thomas Kurtz. Gates stopped going to class, and Allen camped out in Harvard's computer room for eight weeks as they created Microsoft (MS) BASIC. Allen concentrated on technical aspects while Gates wrote code.

When they finished their version of BASIC, Allen flew the program to New Mexico, writing an overlooked loading program on the way. At the time, MITS was near collapse and was putting all its hopes in the success of the Altair. The company offered Allen a job as software director, and he remained in Albuquerque. Gates soon joined him there. They founded Microsoft on April 4, 1975. In October, MITS released a version of MS-BASIC for use in 4K and 8K computers.

In July 1976, Microsoft released an improved version of MS-BASIC and began selling it to companies such as General Electric, NCR, and Citibank. Allen resigned from MITS in November 1976 to devote his full attention to Microsoft. Two months later, Gates dropped out of Harvard to do the same. Apple had been using Microsoft's BASIC, but by the time the Apple II was released in 1977, Apple was using its own operating system. Allen responded by creating the SoftCard, making it possible for Apple computers to run Microsoft programs. Some 20,000 SoftCard units sold in the first year.

In 1980, Microsoft convinced Bell Laboratories to grant the company a Unix license. Even more important for the fledgling company was a 1981 deal with IBM to provide an operating system for their microcomputer. Gates licensed Tim Paterson's 86-DOS (DOS stood for "disk operating system"), polishing it and then licensing it to IBM after Digital Research dragged its feet on sale of its C/PM operating system to IBM. IBM machines running MS-DOS became the computer of choice for most American businesses. IBM asked Microsoft to develop programs using Fortran, COBOL, and Pascal in addition to BASIC. By the age of thirty, Allen had become a billionaire.

Allen left Microsoft in 1983 for health reasons: He had been diagnosed with Hodgkin's lymphoma. He would continue to serve as a consultant and as a member of the board of directors until 2000. His Microsoft shares continued to contribute to his growing wealth. In 1987, *Forbes* listed him as the eighty-seventh richest person in the world. Gates was ranked twenty-ninth.

After successful treatment, Allen made a name for himself quite apart from Gates and Microsoft in the worlds of business, research, and philanthropy. He

Affiliation: Microsoft

Bill Gates and Paul Allen founded Microsoft in 1975. From the beginning, Allen was considered the "idea man," while Gates was the one with the ability to put ideas into action. Both were determined that Microsoft would succeed in putting a desktop computer running Microsoft software in every home.

During the early days as Microsoft continued to grow, Allen insisted that the key to successful growth was recruiting talented individuals who had an aptitude for the job and who were enthusiastic about computers and Microsoft. In 1981, after negotiating a contract with IBM to provide an operating system for its computers, Microsoft continued to expand its use of computer languages and its development of computer software. Since IBM clones also used MS-DOS, Microsoft began amassing major profits. Within two years, more than sixty computer systems were operating on MS-DOS.

By the end of 1982, Microsoft had 200 employees and was garnering $34 million in annual sales. In February 1983, Microsoft created its first publishing division and subsequently signed a deal with Simon and Schuster to distribute Microsoft publications. In April, Microsoft Word was introduced. When Microsoft went public in 1986, Allen owned 6 million shares to Gates's 11 million. By the mid-1980s, half of all Microsoft revenue was generated from sales of MS-DOS. By the end of the decade, 30 million computers were using the program. In 2003, *Forbes* identified Allen as the fourth-richest man in the world and Gates as the richest.

founded Asymetrix Learning Systems in 1984. Steve Wood, who had worked closely with him at Microsoft, served as the new company's vice president. Asymetrix created development tools used by other companies, including Microsoft. The company went public in 1998 and became SumTotal Systems in 2004.

In 1986, Allen established Vulcan Ventures, a holding company that manages all his various projects. In 1992, he set up Internal Research, a think tank that drew some of the brightest minds of Silicon Valley. The following year, Allen spent $243 million to purchase a controlling interest in Ticket Master but later sold more than half of that stock to the Home Shopping Network.

With the goal of helping to make the Internet more accessible to the public, Allen began investing in companies that developed hardware and wireless communication technologies. In 1998, he purchased Marcus Cable and bought 90 percent of Charter Communications, which placed him seventh on the list of top cable companies in the United States. The following year,

Allen expanded his cable interests by investing almost $2 billion in RCN Corporation. That same year, he signed on to become a partner in a new enterprise being put together by Ron Howard and Brian Grazer of Imagine Entertainment and Steven Spielberg, Jeffrey Katzenberg, and David Geffen of DreamWorks to distribute short films over the Internet. Although the project was never fully initiated, Allen continued to invest in media enterprises such as Oprah Winfrey's Oxygen Media, which specializes in women's programming.

In 2000, Allen and his sister, Jo Lynn (Jody) Allen, launched the Experience Music Project (EMP), a Seattle-based interactive rock-and-roll museum. Jody serves as the museum's executive director. Paul also takes a more active role in the music world by playing a guitar for the Seattle-based group Grown Men. In 2004, he realized a long-held dream by building the Science Fiction Experience in the south wing of EMP.

PERSONAL LIFE

Allen continued to serve as a senior strategy adviser for Microsoft and to own several million shares of the company's stock. With a personal fortune estimated at $30 billion, he remains one of the richest men in the world. He has never married and has pledged to leave most of his fortune to various charities. Allen lives on Lake Washington near Seattle.

The early years of the twenty-first century were a time of both illness and widening horizons for Allen. In 2004, he became the sole investor in Burt Rutan's commercial spacecraft project. Their *Space Ship One* won the $10 million Ansari X Prize for the first private manned spaceflight. In both 2007 and 2008, *Time* magazine identified Allen as one of its 100 Most Influential People. In 2009, Allen was diagnosed with another serious condition, this time non-Hodgkin's lymphoma, but the disease went into remission with treatment. In 2010, he founded the Allen Human Brain Atlas (www.brain-map.org), devoted to charting the human brain.

In 2011, Allen published his memoir *Idea Man: A Memoir by the Co-founder of Microsoft*. While he insists that his account of Microsoft's founding is neutral and was never meant as a criticism of Gates, with whom he has remained friends, the media treated the book as an attack on Allen's cofounder. Allen responded by noting that people describe events according to their own perspectives and suggested that he and Gates simply remember the same events differently.

In 2012, the *Chronicle of Philanthropy* named Allen as "the most charitable living American" as a result of the $372.6 million he had contributed to various charities in 2011. Also in 2012, Allen invested $13.2 billion to establish Stratolaunch Systems and subsequently announced that the company would be building a jet with a wingspan of 385 feet with the capability of launching light rockets into space from high altitudes. Stratolaunch's first unmanned test is scheduled for 2016.

Elizabeth Rholetter Purdy

FURTHER READING

Allen, Paul. *Idea Man: A Memoir by the Co-founder of Microsoft*. New York: Penguin, 2011. Print. Allen's somewhat controversial autobiography about the founding of Microsoft. Illustrated.

Gillies, James, and Robert Cailliau. *How the Web Was Born: The Story of the World Wide Web*. New York: Oxford UP, 2000. Print. An extremely detailed examination of the development of the Internet that traces the roles played by key individuals. Includes a time line, a comprehensive bibliography, and an index.

Ichbiah, Daniel, and Susan L. Knepper. *The Making of Microsoft: How Bill Gates and His Team Created the World's Most Successful Software Company*. Rocklin: Prima, 1991. Print. Examines the development of Microsoft in considerable detail. Includes key dates, a glossary, and an index.

Kirby, Jason. "Microsoft Cofounder Paul Allen in Conversation with Jason Kirby." *Maclean's* 9 May 2011: 15–16. Print. Written in question-answer format.

Wainwright, Geoff. "Bill Gates: Perfect Vision." *Remembering the Future: Interviews from Personal Computer World*. Ed. Wendy M. Grossman. New York: Springer, 1997. 31–36. Print. Based on interviews from the 1990s as Microsoft continued its meteoric rise. Includes illustrations.

Wallace, James. *Overdrive: Bill Gates and the Race to Control Cyberspace*. New York: Wiley, 1997. Print. Written as an update to Wallace and Erickson's co-authored work *Hard Drive*, a chronicle of the rise of the Internet and important Microsoft milestones such as the launch of Windows 95. Includes illustrations and index.

Wallace, James, and Jim Erickson. *Hard Drive: Bill Gates and the Making of the Microsoft Software Empire*. New York: Wiley, 1992. Print. The authors use stories that previously appeared in the *Seattle Post-Intelligencer*, supplemented by interviews with current and former employees. Subsequently used against Microsoft in an antitrust suit. Includes illustrations and index.

JOHN VINCENT ATANASOFF

Cocreator of the first electronic digital computer

Born: October 4, 1903; Hamilton, New York
Died: June 15, 1995; Frederick, Maryland
Primary Field: Computer science
Specialty: Computer hardware
Primary Company/Organization: Iowa State College

INTRODUCTION

One of the fathers of the computer, John Vincent Atanasoff was an Iowa State College professor whose work in the 1930s and 1940s culminated in the first electronic digital computer: the Atanasoff-Berry Computer (ABC), designed with his student Clifford E. Berry. The ABC included numerous features that would become synonymous with computing, although it lacked a central processing unit (CPU). ABC's significance was not immediately recognized; it was only through a later patent case, showing that the patent sought actually derived from Atanasoff's work, that Atanasoff's seniority in the burgeoning field was established. Atanasoff was later placed in charge of designing a large-scale computer for the Naval Ordnance Laboratory and designed systems for the Navy's Operation Crossroads, a series of atomic bomb tests at Bikini Atoll.

EARLY LIFE

John Vincent Atanasoff was born in Hamilton, New York, on October 4, 1903, to John Atanasoff and Iva Lucena Atanasoff (née Purdy). The elder Atanasoff's name had been anglicized from Ivan Atanasov at Ellis Island when he had emigrated from Bulgaria in 1889. After studying philosophy at Colgate College, the elder Atanasoff married Purdy, an English teacher, and took a job as an industrial engineer. The family relocated to Brewster, Florida, after John's birth, where his father had accepted a job as an electrical engineer. The Atanasoffs encouraged John's education and intellectual development, indulging his fascination with diverse subjects and his gift for mathematics. His mother introduced him to number bases, while his father gave him a slide rule, which helped John with mathematical studies beyond what the local school offered, including differential calculus.

Atanasoff finished high school at fifteen, although he waited until shortly before his eighteenth birthday to begin college at the University of Florida in 1921. He was interested in theoretical physics, but the school did not offer a physics major; he therefore majored in electrical engineering instead, the most theory-heavy offering. Graduating with straight As in 1925 led to fellowship offers from numerous graduate programs, including Harvard's. He chose Iowa State College on the strength of its engineering and science programs. While working on his master's degree in mathematics and teaching, he met his future wife, Lura Meeks of Oklahoma, through the Dixie Club, an organization for southern students. They married in 1926, shortly after he finished his degree; two years later they relocated to Madison, where John pursued his Ph.D. in theoretical physics from the University of Wisconsin. It was in Madison that he first worked with a computer. Computing fascinated him and would become a large part of his work when he returned to Iowa in 1930 as a member of the faculty: assistant professor in mathematics and physics.

LIFE'S WORK

The significance of Atanasoff's work is sometimes lost on laypersons because of the distinctions involved; Atanasoff did not invent the first computing machine (machines in the nineteenth century, if not earlier devices, could lay claim to that title), nor did he coin the term *digital computer*. He differentiated instead between the analog computers to which he had been exposed in Madison, and which represented the field at the time, and "proper computing machines" that would be free of the flaws he perceived in analog devices. He started by trying to improve analog computing devices. In 1936, he and Iowa State College physics professor Glen Murphy built the Laplaciometer, which calculated the geometry of surface areas. Although it was no worse than other machines of its time, the Laplaciometer frustrated Atanasoff with its limited accuracy.

John Vincent Atanasoff.

The leap in his computer designs came in 1937. By his account, he drove aimlessly for miles, consumed in thought, and finally pulled over 200 miles later at a roadhouse, where he drank bourbon and Coca-Cola and brainstormed ideas on cocktail napkins. The core innovations of the Atanasoff-Berry Computer (ABC) project were developed that night, including the use of a binary numeric system for its computational processes, electrical rather than mechanical power, and what Atanasoff later called regenerative memory, similar in functionality to today's dynamic random access memory (DRAM). With a grant from the college, Atanasoff purchased parts and hired Clifford E. Berry, an electrical engineering student. The two worked on their new computer from 1939 to 1941, although the work was frequently interrupted as Atanasoff began work for the Naval Ordnance Laboratory in Washington, D.C., in the fall of 1939. The United States' entrance into World War II at the end of 1941 ended work on the ABC. Atanasoff and Berry had succeeded in its design and construction, but a patent application was never submitted, perhaps because they had intended to continue refining it.

At the Naval Ordnance Laboratory—established for the research and development of technology for the Navy—Atanasoff was placed in charge of developing

Affiliation: Iowa State College

Iowa State University of Science and Technology was known as Iowa State College of Agriculture and Mechanic Arts when John Vincent Atanasoff and Clifford E. Berry were there. It was founded as a coeducational institution in 1858 and became the first land-grant college after the passage of the 1862 Morrill Act, which sought improvements to agricultural education. From the start, the college had a strong focus in engineering, offering courses in civil, electrical, mechanical, and mining engineering. In the later nineteenth century, the school added the country's first courses in domestic economy (a combination of home economics and consumer science) and the first state-run veterinary college. The VEISHA (pronounced VEE-shah) festival—for veterinary medicine, engineering, industrial science, home economics, and agriculture—was founded in 1922 and has become the largest student-run festival in the country, celebrating the school and its faculty. Significant alumni of the school include astronauts, economists, and engineers, while faculty have included Pulitzer-winning novelist Jane Smiley, Nobel-winning chemist Dan Shechtman, statisticians George Snedecor and Wayne Arthur Fuller, and computer pioneer John Vincent Atanasoff.

With engineering student Berry, Atanasoff designed and constructed a prototype electronic digital computer between 1939 and 1941. The first of its kind, the Atanasoff-Berry Computer (ABC) was designed to solve linear equations, but more important than the tasks it performed was its implementation of the design concepts Atanasoff and Berry had developed. The ABC was the first computer to use binary arithmetic, parallel processing, and regenerative capacitor memory—the same kind of memory used in dynamic random access memory (DRAM) today. Moreover, it relied not on ratchets and mechanical components for its computing but on electronics. Memory and computing were handled as separate functions by distinct components, in order to address aspects of analog computing that had left Atanasoff dissatisfied. While later general-purpose machines occupied entire rooms, the ABC was the size of a couch or recliner. By today's standards, however, it was huge, weighing hundreds of pounds and employing 280 vacuum tubes and thirty-one gas-filled tubes called thyratrons, which functioned as electrical switches. It was neither programmable nor fully automated, and there was a margin of error in the system's results that Atanasoff and Berry did not have time to correct before the ramp-up of World War II called them to disparate defense jobs.

Although the ABC was a precursor to later digital computers rather than a fully realized vision, the leap forward from analog computing that it represented was arguably more significant, involving more numerous innovations, than the improvements made by later computers that incorporated its approach.

a large-scale general-purpose computer for the Navy. When the war ended with the detonation of nuclear devices over Hiroshima and Nagasaki, Japan, atomic bombs became a higher priority, and Atanasoff was assigned to work designing systems in support of Operation Crossroads, the code name used for both atmospheric and underwater nuclear tests at Bikini Atoll in the Marshall Islands. Other government projects in which Atanasoff was involved included long-range explosive detection and seismography. In 1949, he left the Naval Ordnance Laboratory to work for the Army Field Forces for a year, returning to the Naval Ordnance Laboratory in 1950 to direct the Navy Fuse Program for a year. Despite his original intentions of returning to Iowa State College (now Iowa State University) to teach after his military work, he transitioned to the private defense sector instead, founding the Ordnance Engineering Corporation in 1952. The company was soon sold to

Aerojet General Corporation, for which he worked from 1957 to 1960, first as Atlantic division manager and later as vice president. Upon his "retirement" in 1961, he founded Cybernetics Incorporated, which he oversaw for the next twenty years.

The ABC's fame and acknowledgment of Atanasoff's and Berry's roles as the fathers of the digital computer came about because of the patent application filed by J. Presper Eckert and John Mauchly for their Electronic Numerical Integrator and Computer, ENIAC, the first electronic digital general-purpose computer. (The ABC was designed specifically to solve linear equations.) ENIAC was built during World War II, and its patent was held by the Sperry Rand Corporation, which in 1967 sued the Honeywell Corporation for infringing that patent, simultaneous with Honeywell's countersuit for fraud and antitrust violations. Among other claims, Honeywell maintained that the ENIAC patent was invalid because the work was not unique. Mauchly had earlier examined the ABC.

The patent was eventually ruled invalid, though for more technical reasons relating to patent law rather than the originality or lack thereof of Mauchly and Eckert's design. However, based on the testimony of Atanasoff, after a six-year legal battle the U.S. District Court ruled in 1973 that the ABC had been the first electronic digital computer. Furthermore, because the ENIAC patent was invalid, the electronic digital computer itself (general-purpose or otherwise) was deemed to be in the public domain. This conclusion had the long-term salutary impact of accelerating the development of the computer industry.

PERSONAL LIFE

Atanasoff and his wife Lura met when she was majoring in home economics at Iowa State College. She briefly taught in Montana in the fall of 1926 to save money toward finishing her degree, but she broke her contract in order to return to her husband and soon gave birth to Elsie, their eldest child. The younger children, Joanne and John, were born after the family's relocation to Madison, where John Sr. earned his doctorate.

Atanasoff's long separation from his family during World War II and the postwar years, while working for the Naval Ordnance Laboratory in Washington, D.C., as the family remained in Ames, Iowa, took a toll on his relationship. In 1949, he and Lura divorced, and he married Alice Crosby, moving with her to Fort Monroe, Virginia, to take the chief scientist job for the Army Field Forces. Lura and the children moved to Denver.

Atanasoff and Alice moved to New Market, Maryland, in 1961, ostensibly retiring, although Atanasoff continued to work for another twenty years, albeit at a slower pace than in the previous decades. He died of a stroke in 1995.

Bill Kte'pi

FURTHER READING

Atanasoff, John V. "Advent of the Electronic Digital Computing." *IEEE Annals of the History of Computing* 6.3 (1984): 229–82. Print. Atanasoff's own account of the ABC, problems encountered, reasons for the design choices he and Berry made, and the later patent cases in which he testified.

Burks, Alice Rowe. *Who Invented the Computer? The Legal Battle That Changed Computing History.* New York: Prometheus, 2003. Print. An account of the *Honeywell v. Sperry Rand* case, which established Atanasoff and Berry as the fathers of the digital computer.

Gleick, James. *The Information: A History, a Theory, a Flood.* New York: Pantheon, 2011. Print. A history of the information revolution, placing Atanasoff's work in a broader context.

Mooers, Calvin N. "The Computer Project at the Naval Ordnance Laboratory." *IEEE Annals of the History of Computing* 23.2 (2001): 51–67. Print. Focuses on the Naval Ordnance Laboratory's abandoned large-scale computer project.

Smiley, Jane. *The Man Who Invented the Computer: The Biography of John Atanasoff, Digital Pioneer.* New York: Doubleday, 2010. Print. An engaging biography of Atanasoff by the acclaimed fiction writer.

CHARLES BABBAGE

Mathematician and designer of the difference and analytical engines

Born: December 26, 1791; London, England
Died: October 18, 1871; London, England
Primary Field: Applied science
Specialty: Mathematics and logic
Primary Company/Organization: Cambridge University

INTRODUCTION

Charles Babbage was the inventor of the difference and analytical engines, which became the forerunners of the modern computer. The difference engine employed the first example of computer language on record. Because his funding came partly from the British government and often fell prey to political maneuvering, Babbage failed to obtain support for some of his designs. He believed that technical progress was dependent on science. He was considered a major voice in the school of thought that sought to apply scientific methods to commerce during the Industrial Revolution, and his ideas were implemented in the development of tools and in manufacturing and engineering techniques. His work on calculus led to reforming notations used in calculus throughout England and other parts of Europe. Although Babbage was recognized as a mathematical genius during his lifetime, his work failed to win him widespread fame. He often suffered ridicule at the hands of his contemporaries because he was so far ahead of his time. It was not until the computer age, during the last quarter of the twentieth century and nearly a century after his death, that Babbage was finally given his due as the creator of the first mechanical computer. As a result, he is now alternately known as the father, the grandfather, and the godfather of modern computing.

EARLY LIFE

Charles Babbage was born the day after Christmas in 1791, near London. His father was Benjamin Babbage, a wealthy London banker and merchant, and his mother was born Elizabeth (Betsy) Plumleigh. A number of childhood illnesses interrupted Babbage's studies, and he was often tutored at home. At other times, he attended Enfield School, where the headmaster, the Reverend

Charles Babbage.

Stephen Freeman, was an ardent amateur astronomer. The school had a large library, and Babbage spent hours there studying mathematics on his own. He had taught himself to solve algebraic equations, and when he could not sleep, young Charles often stayed up all night working algebra problems.

When he was a young boy, Babbage's mother took him to visit a technical exhibition. For the first time, he saw machines that mimicked human behavior. At that exhibition, he was given a private demonstration by an exhibitor named Merlin of a beautiful silver dancer holding a bird that flapped its wings and opened and closed its beak. Babbage retained a lifelong fascination with the dancer and later purchased it at auction. According to Herbert Klein, repairing the dancer marked a watershed in Babbage's life because it demonstrated the point at which Babbage forsook creative inspiration in favor of a systemic method of planning each step of the process involved in repairing the dancer.

By 1810, Babbage was ready for college. He entered Trinity College at Cambridge University but chose to transfer to Peterhouse in 1812. Often ahead of his Cambridge tutors, Babbage grew frustrated at their inability to answer his questions about mathematics. He became one of the cofounders of the Cambridge Analytical Society.

LIFE'S WORK

After completing college, Babbage remained dependent on his father. The £300 he received from his father and the £150 he garnered from various property rentals meant that he and his family lived moderately well. Although he attempted to find a teaching post, Babbage was turned down for political reasons. He continued to work on his various inventions, spending most of his time on analytical work and electrical research. Babbage spent considerable time thinking about the how to use mathematics in practical applications and about ways to eliminate human error in calculations. This led to his notion of performing calculations by machine. Eventually, his ideas coalesced into the design of the difference engine.

Babbage also began publishing papers and giving lectures. In 1815, he gave a series of twelve lectures on the subject of astronomy at the Royal Institution in London. He was named a Fellow of the institution the following year. In 1820, Babbage was one of a group of men who met at Freemason's Tavern in Lincoln's Inn Fields on January 12 to establish the Astronomical Society. The following year, Babbage met John Herschel,

---

Affiliation: British Museum

After Charles Babbage's death in 1871, many of his machines eventually found a home in the British Museum. Working with a group of scholars, historians, and computer experts, the Science Museum of the British Museum determined to build a working model of Babbage's second difference machine, using Babbage's original design from notebooks that had been discovered in 1937. The project, which began in 1985, was set to be completed in 1991 on the 200th anniversary of Babbage's birth. Curator and electronics engineer Doron Swade was assigned to lead the project.

When it was completed on time in 1991 at a cost of $500,000, the difference engine contained four thousand parts. The machine, which was 11 feet long, 7 feet tall, and weighed 3 tons, was operated by a handle. The cost of building a printing machine was considered prohibitive, but Nathan Myhrvold of Microsoft agreed to fund the building of the printing apparatus in return for an identical machine being erected at his home in Seattle, Washington. The printer was finally completed in 2000. It also contained four thousand parts and it weighed 2.5 metric tons.

---

with whom he began working closely on the performance of astronomical calculations. Babbage also worked closely with his friend Augusta Ada Lovelace, the Countess of Lovelace. She was the daughter of the poet George Gordon, Lord Byron. Lovelace and Babbage collaborated on designing machines that could play games such as chess and tick-tack-toe or predict horseraces. When others made fun of his inventions, Lovelace never wavered in her support for Babbage's abilities.

In 1821, at the age of thirty, Babbage began work on his difference engine, which could perform addition, subtraction, multiplication, and division. It became the first successful automatic calculator ever built. Babbage programmed the difference engine to set up tables of repeated operations and print the calculations onto punch cards. Such cards had first been used in Jacquard looms to control the printing of patterns. In Babbage's machine, a human operator was necessary to shift gears for various operations. Because no tools existed to build the various gears, wheels, and cranks he needed for his machine, Babbage helped to design and build them.

By 1834, Babbage was working on his second major invention, the analytical engine, which was more sophisticated than the difference engine. The analytical engine contained processing and memory units and was made up of the *store*, which held the numbers used in calculations, and the *mill*, which performed the mathematical calculations. Calculations were printed via a printing mechanism. Although he had raised significant funds for the project, Babbage began arguing with the engineer employed to build it. Ultimately, the analytical engine was never completed. In 1846, Babbage began working on an improved difference engine.

Babbage's work was not confined to early computer models. When asked to work on railway safety, he designed a railway and built a railway carriage. He was also asked to develop a system by which wins at roulette were guaranteed. Babbage's interests were diverse. In addition to projects involving mathematics, he worked on projects involving electricity and magnetism, astronomical instruments, a speedometer, cryptology, and diving bells. He was also interested in religion, archaeology, and oceanic navigation.

In 1826, in preparation for a job that failed to materialize, Babbage wrote a well-received book on life insurance (or *assurance*, as it was called by the British) for the public, *A Comparative View of the Various Institutions for the Assurance of Lives*. The following year, Babbage published *Tables of Logarithms of the Natural Numbers from 1 to 108,000*, on the use of logarithms in his computers. In 1830, he published *Reflections of the Decline of Science in England* and followed it up two years later with *On the Economy of Machinery and Manufactures*. For the latter work, Babbage conducted extensive research in workshops and factories throughout Europe and drew heavily on his own experience in building machines and on manufacturing reports generated by the House of Commons. In 1837, Babbage produced *Ninth Bridgewater Treatise*, a response to the eight treatises on theology and science recently published by the Earl of Bridgewater. By 1828, Babbage had been named Lucasian Professor of Mathematics at Cambridge. He would hold that position until 1839.

Babbage died in 1871 at the age of seventy-nine. Many of the details of his personal life chronicled by biographers have been garnered from his memoir, *Passages from the Life of a Philosopher* (1864). He continues to be a subject of studies in fields that range from religion to the history of technology.

PERSONAL LIFE

While he was in college at Cambridge, Babbage met Georgina Whitmore, who became the abiding love of his life. Despite his father's disapproval, he and Georgina married on July 2, 1814, after Babbage completed his work at Cambridge. Their family comprised at least eight children born between 1815 and 1827, but only three or four (sources differ) grew to adulthood. Upon the death of his father in 1827, Babbage inherited some £100,000. That year, Georgina and a son also died. Babbage was inconsolable after Georgina's death and was unable to look after his surviving children for months afterward.

Babbage was a liberal reformer, and he knew virtually all of the other liberal reformers of his day. Enamored of the nineteenth-century social scene, he moved in scientific and literary social circles that included such luminaries as the natural scientist Charles Darwin, author Charles Dickens, and the Duke of Wellington.

After Babbage's death, his son Henry belatedly expressed interest in carrying on his father's work. In 1910, Henry built the mill of his father's analytical engine and eventually built six operational models of the difference engine. One of his engines was sent to the United States and placed on display at Harvard University, where Howard Aiken, the creator of the Mark I, the first American computer, was able to examine it closely.

Other scientists and computer experts in the United States are also well aware of the debt that they owe to Charles Babbage. He was honored by the University of Minnesota, which erected the Charles Babbage Institute, in 1978. It continues to serve as an archive and research center that focuses on the history of information technology and promotes new research in the field.

In 2011, John Graham-Cumming, the author of *The Geek Atlas: 128 Places Where Science and Technology Come Alive*, announced plans to build Babbage's analytical engine. While it is dependent on obtaining funding, Graham-Cumming's project is scheduled to be completed by October 18, 2021, the 150th anniversary of Charles Babbage's death.

Elizabeth Rholetter Purdy

FURTHER READING

Babbage, Charles. *Passages from the Life of a Philosopher*. 1864. New York: Kelley, 1969. Print. Babbage's own view of his life and work. Illustrations include original designs of the analytical engine.

Geary, Frank, and Renee Prendergast. "Philosophers and Practical Men: Charles Babbage, Irish Merchants, and the Economics of Information." *European Journal of the History of Economic Thought* 15.4 (2008): 571–94. Print. With a focus on *The*

Economics of Machinery and Manufacture, the authors examine Babbage's influence on the formation of industrial firms. Includes a bibliography.

Hyman, Anthony. *Charles Babbage: Pioneer of the Computer*. Princeton: Princeton UP, 1982. Print. Examines Babbage's life and work through his correspondence, lectures, and professional papers. Includes illustrations of Babbage's designs and excerpts from his memoir as well as other illustrations, a bibliography, and an index.

Klein, Herbert. "From Romanticism to Virtual Reality: Charles Babbage, William Gibson, and the Construction of Cyberspace." *Interdisciplinary Humanities* 24.1 (2007): 36–50. Print. Examines the impact of forward thinkers such as Babbage on the development of modern technology. Includes a notes section.

North, John, ed. *Mid-nineteenth Century Scientists*. New York: Pergamon, 1969. Print. Details the major changes in science between the late eighteenth and early twentieth centuries, including Babbage's role in that development. Includes illustrations and charts.

Richards, Joan. "God, Truth, and Mathematics in Nineteenth-Century England." *Theology and Science* 9.1 (2011): 54–74. Print. Looks at the role of religion in the lives of Babbage and other philosophical and scientific thinkers of the period. Includes separate endnotes and biographical notes sections.

Swade, Doron. *The Difference Engine: Charles Babbage and the Quest to Build the First Computer*. New York: Viking, 2001. Print. Biographical sources used in the work include the growing body of new material on Babbage as well as previously published material. Includes illustration and index.

JOHN BACKUS

Developer of the Fortran programming language

Born: December 3, 1924; Philadelphia, Pennsylvania
Died: March 17, 2007; Ashland, Oregon
Primary Field: Computer science
Specialty: Computer programming
Primary Company/Organization: IBM

INTRODUCTION

John Backus's work at IBM revolutionized computer programming. In the 1950s, he assembled and led the team that developed Fortran, the first high-level programming language, one rigorous enough to remain in use today. In the course of doing so, he also introduced the first optimizing compiler, in order to encourage Fortran's adoption. Later in the same decade he introduced the Backus-Naur Form (BNF), a notation technique for context-free grammar, a metalinguistic approach to describing languages. Such notation techniques—of which BNF remains one of the two standards—make it easier to discuss and describe programming languages. Backus used it in developing programming languages in the ALGOL family, but he continued to look for better ways to program. His function-level programming language, FP, never caught on, but his introduction of it did raise interest in functional programming as a general area of research.

EARLY LIFE

John Warner Backus was born on December 3, 1924, in Philadelphia, Pennsylvania. A poor student from a wealthy family, he graduated from the Hill School, a boarding school in Pottstown (northwest of Philadelphia), in 1942 but was expelled from the University of Virginia before finishing his freshman year. His expulsion left him vulnerable to the draft, and he entered the U.S. Army, where he served at Fort Stewart, Georgia. His poor academic performance may have been due to apathy or inattention, because his military aptitude tests were strong, and while still in the Army he sampled several academic programs in rapid succession: engineering at the University of Pittsburgh, premedical courses at Haverford, and the Flower and Fifth Avenue Medical School in New York City. He dropped out of medical school for lack of interest but designed his own metal plate to replace a cranial bone tumor in his skull.

In 1946, he was discharged honorably from the Army and remained in New York City, working as a radio technician long enough to develop an interest in mathematics. Finally he found a program he could stick with: mathematics at Columbia University, from which he graduated in 1949. Shortly before his graduation, while touring the Selective Sequence Electronic Calculator (SSEC) at IBM's Computing Center, he mentioned

John Backus.

an interest in the SSEC to his tour guide and was soon hired as a programmer.

LIFE'S WORK

The SSEC operated from 1948 to 1952 and had been constructed when IBM was dissatisfied with the lack of credit it received for its involvement in the construction of the Harvard Mark I (a computer at Harvard University formally known as the Automatic Sequence Controlled Calculator). The construction in 1946 of the Electronic Numerical Integrator and Computer (ENIAC), a fully electronic computer, further motivated IBM to make its mark. The SSEC was deliberately installed on a ground-floor room with a large display window, formerly occupied by a shoe store, so that pedestrians could get a good look at it. The computer used both electromechanical relays and more than twelve thousand vacuum tubes to perform its operations. Its first application was a program called Ephemeris, which in seven minutes could calculate the position of Earth's moon and the planets. This helped to demonstrate the SSEC's computing power; paying customers such as General Electric and the Atomic Energy Commission followed.

Backus worked on the SSEC for three years, developing techniques that were later adopted for use in the National Aeronautics and Space Administration's Apollo program. However, from the start, Backus's real contribution was his approach to the art of programming itself, not just its end products. Programming at the time was done in assembly language, a low-level programming language with a one-to-one correspondence between each programming statement and a machine instruction. Assembly language is specific to a particular model of computer—though this was not yet a limitation in the 1940s and 1950s. Backus's first innovation was a high-level programming language that acted as a programmer's aid: Speedcoding, which made it easier for programmers to handle floating-point number operations. Given the laborious nature of programming in assembly language, any shortcut saved considerable time and money. Unlike low-level programming languages, high-level languages are more abstract, no longer focused on a one-to-one correlation with machine instructions. By today's standards, Speedcoding—the first high-level programming language for an IBM computer—was not very abstract, and although it made programming easier and reduced errors, its programs ran much more slowly (as much as twenty times more slowly) as those written in assembly language.

Backus's experience with Speedcoding led him to propose the IBM Mathematical Formula Translating System (which became Fortran) in 1954. Backus said that his interest in simplifying the programming experience came from his own laziness and boredom: He did not like the tedious work of assembly language. On some level, regardless of how much it contributed to his motivation, he must have realized the gains that could be realized and the sophisticated programs that could be written if the man-hours required to write a program were substantially reduced. The team assembled to develop Fortran, personally chosen by Backus, was eclectic almost to the point of eccentricity and included a researcher from the Massachusetts Institute of Technology (MIT), a cryptographer, a chess champion, and a young woman who had just graduated from Vassar. Long workdays were interrupted by snowball fights outside the offices.

Fortran was not intended as a programming language with special applications, as such, but because of the nature of the work done by computers when Backus developed it, it is especially suited for scientific and engineering work. It became more popular than Speedcoding had ever been and remains one of the most popular languages in disciplines that depend on number crunching—fields like meteorology, computational sciences,

Affiliation: IBM

The International Business Machines Corporation, later IBM, was founded in 1911 by the merger of three manufacturers, and it originally sold devices such as tabulating machines and time clocks to businesses. Early IBM culture was shaped by Thomas J. Watson, Sr., hired away in 1914 from the National Cash Register Company. Although Watson is best remembered today for the probably apocryphal statement that there would never be a market for more than five computers, the more significant quote was his motto for the company, "Think." Fourteen years before IBM even trademarked the name IBM, it trademarked Think as a name for a periodical—the monthly magazine distributed to employees. Think was the motivational slogan Watson plastered IBM's headquarters with, putting it on walls, stationery, notepads, and even matchbooks; it was the reason the company later named its notebook computer the ThinkPad.

Under Watson, IBM marshaled its resources and considerable workforce to offer business solutions other companies were not equipped to provide. It custom-made early computers for large businesses and governments, leaving small-scale business customers to companies like National Cash Register (NCR). As the modern computing industry developed during and immediately following World War II, IBM was determined to become a big part of it. John Backus's development of the Fortran programming language in the 1950s was a large component of IBM's success in computers; it was the first high-level programming language to become popular enough that competing manufacturers offered compilers for it in order to attract or retain customers. IBM was instrumental in supporting the National Aeronautics and Space Administration, introducing general-purpose computers for nonscientific applications, developing the Universal Product Code, and popularizing personal computers, although its personal computer business was sold to Lenovo in 2005.

and fluid dynamics. Of course, the Fortran used today has considerably evolved, with the most recent version having been released in 2010. However, there is no doubt that it is the descendant of Backus's initial work.

Although Fortran soon eclipsed Speedcoding in popularity, the Speedcoding experience and its effect on programs' running time made users reluctant to adopt Fortran at first. Fortran was released in 1956—containing more than twenty-five thousand lines of assembly language—but use of Fortran increased the following spring, when the Fortran compiler was released. A compiler is the go-between that translates a programming language into machine instructions; Fortran's was an optimizing compiler, assuring that the program would perform at speeds roughly the same as assembly language. A revised and improved version of the language, Fortran II, followed in 1958, adding user-defined subroutines that made procedural programming possible. By the start of the 1960s, Fortran had become popular enough that it was available for four different models of IBM computers, and other manufacturers were including Fortran compilers in order to remain competitive. Programmers used Fortran on dozens of different models, making it the first programming language to be so widely used. Because the language has remained in use from the early modern computing era until the present day, its evolution and that of its compilers has developed in parallel with the state of computing as a whole. Today, Fortran is the language used for comparing the performance of high-end supercomputers.

By 1958, there were two different proposals for a universal programming language, one of which was supported by Backus and the Association for Computing Machinery (ACM). A joint meeting was held with members of the ACM and the Society of Applied Mathematics and Mechanics in Germany (GAMM) from May 27 to June 2, 1958, in Zurich. At the meeting, Backus and others hammered out the proposal for the International Algebraic Language (IAL), an ambitious programming language. No one liked the IAL acronym, and it was replaced with ALGOL the following year. Although Backus contributed to its conception, the original version of ALGOL, ALGOL 58, was not widely implemented at IBM because of the focus on Fortran. ALGOL 58 nevertheless introduced many important programming language concepts, some of which would later be adopted by versions of Fortran, as well as numerous other languages.

It was his work on the Backus-Naur Form (BNF) that led to Backus's Turing Award (bestowed in 1977). The BNF was formulated as a context-free grammar that could be used to describe ALGOL 58 (and its successor, ALGOL 60), both to make it easier for computer scientists to communicate with one another about programming languages and to make them easier to teach.

The BNF name is not Backus's; computer scientist Peter Naur, in writing about ALGOL 60, simplified the character set Backus had used and referred to the style of notation Backus introduced as the Backus Normal Form. Because of Naur's contributions, this soon became the Backus-Naur Form. The BNF has also been of interest to information theorists and linguists, whose interest in programming languages is purely theoretical.

When Backus accepted his Turing Award, he delivered a lecture—as is the custom—choosing the topic "Can Programming Be Liberated from the von Neumann Style?" In the lecture, he described not only a new programming language, FP, but also a new approach to programming languages, a function-level language that lacks the variables of value-level programming languages such as Fortran. While FP did not become as popular as Backus might have hoped, he did catalyze a growth in research into function-level languages. Backus retired from IBM in 1991.

PERSONAL LIFE

Backus was married twice, his marriage to Marjorie Jamison ending in divorce in 1966. His second wife, Barbara Stannard, died in 2004; they had married in 1968. Backus died in 2007 in Ashland, Oregon, survived by two daughters, Karen and Paula.

Bill Kte'pi

FURTHER READING

Ceruzzi, Paul E. *A History of Modern Computing*. 2nd ed. Cambridge: MIT, 2012. Print. A narrative history of the computer industry from 1945 to 1995, including the spread of Fortran and the evolution of programming languages.

Ensmenger, Nathan L. *The Computer Boys Take Over: Computers, Programmers, and the Politics of Technical Expertise*. Cambridge: MIT, 2010. Print. Like the Ceruzzi book, an account of the personalities and development of the computer industry, including Backus and his contemporaries.

Lohr, Steve. *Go To: The Story of the Math Majors, Bridge Players, Chess Wizards, Maverick Scientists, and Iconoclasts—The Programmers Who Created the Software Revolution*. New York: Basic, 2001. Print. Although there is no book-length biography of Backus, he is featured in the chapter on Fortran.

Mitchell, John C. *Concepts in Programming Languages*. New York: Cambridge UP, 2002. Print. A conceptual introduction to computer programming languages, including Fortran.

Rajaraman, V., and Priti Shankar. "John Backus—Inventor of Fortran." *Resonance* 12.8 (2007): 3–5. Print. A review of Backus's major contributions after his death.

RALPH H. BAER

Developer of early home video game technology

Born: March 8, 1922; Rodalben, Germany
Died: -
Primary Field: Computer science
Specialty: Computer hardware
Primary Company/Organization: Sanders Associates

INTRODUCTION

Ralph H. Baer fled Nazi Germany to become an engineer in the United States after serving in military intelligence during World War II. Among the first to earn a degree in television engineering, he was interested in advancing the possibilities of television technology beyond passive viewing. While working for a defense contractor, he led a small team designing the first home video game console, a device intended to make home television sets interactive: the Magnavox Odyssey, soon followed by the Odyssey2, which preceded the Atari and other well-known brands, as well as including a keyboard for input at a time when personal computers were still largely unheard of. His later work included the popular handheld game Simon.

EARLY LIFE

Ralph Henry Baer was born on March 8, 1922, in Rodalben in the Palatinate region of Germany, the son of a factory worker. As a young Jewish boy in Nazi Germany, he was expelled from his school in 1933 and forced to enroll in an all-Jewish school. His family left Germany for the United States in 1938 as the anti-Jewish pogroms began in Europe. Newly immigrated to New York City at the age of sixteen, he helped support his family by working in a factory, took correspondence

Ralph H. Baer.

courses from the National Radio Institute to become certified as a radio service technician, and worked servicing home and car radios, FM radios, and early television sets. Drafted in 1943, he served in France in U.S. Army intelligence.

After the war, Baer attended Chicago's American Television Institute of Technology and graduated with a bachelor of science degree in television engineering in 1949, the first in the world to receive a television engineering degree. Unable to find a job related to the new technology fresh out of college, he took a variety of engineering jobs before joining the newly formed defense contractor Sanders Associates in Nashua, New Hampshire, in 1956.

LIFE'S WORK

Baer was hired as the staff engineer to the manager of the Equipment Design Division at Sanders Associates and initially worked building surveillance systems for use in West Berlin, as well as aircraft radar systems. In 1958, he was made division manager and chief engineer for equipment design, with the authority to direct his own projects. Expenditures eventually had to be justified, but the costs of the usual work the company did—custom-designed and custom-manufactured circuitry for the military and the National Aeronautics and Space Administration, high-end medical equipment, and other specialized technology—were high enough, with direct labor costs close to $10 million per year, that smaller projects could be pursued during free time without impacting the company's overhead. Some of these projects were dead-ends; some led to improved products; some led to innovations that might or might not have commercial applications. Letting employees pursue projects they are passionate about is a technique that many companies have used since—either by looking the other way, as Sanders did, or by actively encouraging such pursuits, as Google does—in order to keep employees engaged with their work and developing potentially profitable ideas that might not be discovered otherwise.

What Baer wanted to do was keep the television revolution moving rather than settle for a device that could be used only by passively watching it. He wrote a four-page paper in 1966, accompanied by a diagram for a two-player game that used the television set as its display. Much of the work was conducted in a small workshop in Sanders's Canal Street building, a 10- by 20-foot former library. Baer and his team envisioned a set-top box—the first video game console—which would do the processing and act as an interface for input devices, while the customer's television would function as the display device. Video games were not the only intended use, although the first stand-alone arcade games (supplementing mechanical midway games and pinball games) were being released at the time, including the light gun game *Duck Hunt* and the first-person racer *Grand Prix*, both of which were electromechanical rather than fully electronic. Unlike the console Baer developed—first called the Brown Box and later the Odyssey—these games contained their own displays. However, a home console that could "piggyback" on the customer's existing television set could be sold at a lower price point. Furthermore, unlike arcade games or the home version of *Pong*, which came later, the Odyssey could play multiple games, and the customer could purchase more games and peripheral devices later, at a substantially lower cost than the console.

A working prototype was finished in 1968. The work was done a little at a time, in spare moments. When others at Sanders heard about the project, Baer's team began making short black-and-white movies to demonstrate their work and convince executives to let them keep developing the Brown Box. These videos, from the late 1960s and early 1970s, demonstrate various applications for the Brown Box: playing video

Ping-Pong on the television screen; making impulse purchases of products seen in television commercials (with the advantage, Baer points out, that the customer does not risk forgetting the product name, make, model, or other details) with a Brown Box equipped with a modem developed at Sanders; and online education. (Having taken radio technician correspondence courses, Baer was surely in a position to understand the advances to classroom-free education that could be made through the use of electronics and telecommunications.) As some of these applications demonstrate, Baer was not just inventing the first home video game system; he actually had in mind innovations that would not be implemented by the industry for years to come. He demonstrated online gaming decades before today's massively multiplayer online role-playing games (MMORPGs), for instance, with proof-of-concept demonstrations of video games played over cable with TelePrompTer Corporation in 1968 and Warner Cable in 1973.

The Brown Box was demonstrated to numerous American television set manufacturers, including RCA, GE, Zenith, Sylvania, Sears, and Magnavox. RCA originally licensed the console but soon canceled it. A year later, in 1971, Magnavox agreed to produce the console that would be known as the Magnavox Odyssey. It premiered exactly twelve months later, in March 1972. Games for the Odyssey included basic sports games—baseball, handball, hockey, table tennis, soccer—and the game *Shooting Gallery*, which used a light gun that detected light from the television set to identify whether a target had been hit. Games were produced on removable printed circuit boards that were inserted into a slot.

The Odyssey generated a lot of what would now be called buzz but fared poorly financially. Too many customers assumed it would work only on Magnavox televisions. Others may not have realized that they would not need to purchase a new console for each individual game. However, in particular, the Odyssey was simply ahead of its time; the demand for video games did not yet exist, nor did the brand-name "killer app" games like *Donkey Kong* or *Pac-Man*, which would drive much of the demand for later generations of consoles.

Two months after the Magnavox Odyssey's premiere, Nolan Bushnell attended a demonstration of the console and played the Ping-Pong game designed for it. Not long after, he hired Allan Alcorn to design a coin-operated Ping-Pong video game for arcades, which became *Pong*, the first major arcade game. A home version of *Pong* followed, and Bushnell later became president of Atari, the first successful home video game company.

Further models of the Odyssey were introduced. In 1978, the Odyssey^2 was a significant leap forward; while Odyssey consoles from 1975 to 1977 had added sound, four-player games, and improvements to game play, the Odyssey^2 came with a small keyboard much like that of a laptop computer. The Odyssey^2 was Sanders's entry in what is now called the second generation of video games, contemporary with the Atari 2600, Intellivision, ColecoVision, and Vectrex but generally superior in design. A speech synthesis unit sold separately greatly enhanced the sound available to games, helping to popularize *Quest for the Rings*, an early role-playing game. The Odyssey^2 game line included versions (or "ports") of *Frogger*, *Popeye*, and *Q*Bert*, the *Pac-Man*-like *K. C. Munchkin,* and *Pick Axe Pete,* a popular action game.

Over a ten-year period, Baer testified in numerous patent infringement cases in which Magnavox or Sanders was the plaintiff, defending his video game innovations from the many copycats of the era. Nearly $100 million was awarded to the two companies. Atari settled an infringement case over *Pong* out of court.

Baer continued working on video games at Sanders. In 1975, he developed interactive games using videocassette recorders (VCRs), which like console video games were an opportunistic technology taking advantage of the fact that consumers already owned the television. Data would be nested in the video signal in order to allow for interaction between the player, a microprocessor, and video footage. In the late 1970s, he led a Sanders group contracted to video game producer Coleco, to develop video games for that firm—including *Telstar*, *Arcade*, and *Combat*—which led to Coleco's production in 1978 of *KidVid*, a video game system for preschoolers, and a video disc interface for Coleco's ColecoVision console and Adam home computer.

In the late 1970s, Baer began developing electronic toys, the component parts having become cheap enough to make this a quickly accelerating field. In 1978, he invented the *Simon* handheld electronic game, which became an iconic game known for its four-section circular design of green, red, blue, and yellow buttons. Later games and toys included interactive Teddy bears building on the VCR game technology Baer had pioneered, interactive books for Golden Books, and in 2000 the line of Talking Tools for Hasbro. Although he retired from Sanders in 1987, Baer continued to work as a consultant for the company until 1990. From 1990 to his retirement in 2001, he devoted himself full time to R. H. Baer Consultants, which he had originally founded for afterhours work in 1975.

Affiliation: Sanders Associates

Sanders Associates was founded in 1951 by Royden Sanders Jr., and ten other former employees of defense contractor Raytheon. Briefly based in Waltham, Massachusetts, it relocated in 1952 to Nashua, New Hampshire, a former textile industry hub surrounded by dairy farms. Principally a defense contractor, Sanders focused on the design and manufacture of electronic systems such as surveillance, navigation, intelligence, imaging, and targeting systems. Its expertise in printed and flexible circuitry led to numerous private-sector clients as well, such as medical equipment and aerospace technology manufacturers. In 1986, Sanders was bought by the Lockheed Corporation, which in 2000 sold the unit that had absorbed it, Lockheed Martin Aerospace Electronic Systems, to BAE. Today it is part of BAE Systems Electronics and Integrated Solutions.

It may seem unusual that a high-tech defense contractor developed the first home video game console, preceding the home version of *Pong* by two years. If not for Ralph Baer, it would not have happened. Most of the projects at Sanders in the late 1960s and early 1970s were so expensive that no one particularly minded the engineers tinkering with other projects on the side, a practice that could take the form of brainstorming and thus a way to generate ideas that could then find commercial applications. The project that became the Odyssey video game console began exactly that way, in fits and starts, because of Baer's desire to make television interactive: He envisioned educational applications, many of which would eventually be realized by the introduction of personal computers and later the Internet.

After his retirement, Baer published *Videogames: In the Beginning*, his memoir of the early video game era. In a nod to the amount of time he spent testifying in patent infringement cases, the book has a "Plaintiff's Exhibit" sticker on the cover. He also points out in the book that after Lockheed purchased Sanders, inventors were guaranteed a share of the profits generated by their inventions—a rule that went into effect much too late to help Baer.

PERSONAL LIFE
Baer married Dena Whinston in 1952 while living in New York, and they remained married until her death in 2006. Their son James Whinston Baer was born in New York; Mark Whinston Baer and Nancy Doris Baer were born in Manchester, New Hampshire, after Baer relocated to work for Sanders. In 2004, President George W. Bush awarded Baer the National Medal of Technology "for inventing the first video game console."

Bill Kte'pi

FURTHER READING
Baer, Ralph H. *Videogames: In the Beginning*. Springfield: Rolenta, 2005. Print. Baer's own account of the Magnavox Odyssey and the first generation of video games, of the patent infringement cases in which he testified, and of his later work.
Dillon, Roberto. *The Golden Age of Video Games: The Birth of a Multibillion Dollar Industry*. New York: CRC, 2011. Print. A general history of video games from their early days to the rise of PC gaming and the Commodore bankruptcy.
Donovan, Tristan. *Replay: The History of Video Games*. East Lewes: Yellow Ant, 2010. Print. Not quite an oral history, this video game history is nevertheless informed by numerous interviews, including one with Baer.

STEVE BALLMER
CEO of Microsoft

Born: March 24, 1956; Detroit, Michigan
Died: -
Primary Field: Business and commerce
Specialty: Management, executives, and investors
Primary Company/Organization: Microsoft

INTRODUCTION
As the chief executive officer (CEO) of software giant Microsoft Corporation since 2000, Steve Ballmer is considered one of the more influential technology executives. Microsoft initially rose to prominence on

the strength of its operating systems, MS-DOS and later Microsoft Windows. Microsoft has expanded its product line from operating systems to include a suite of office productivity software, Internet search engines, gaming devices, and other products. After Bill Gates stepped down as Microsoft CEO at the end of 1999, Ballmer stepped into that role to lead Microsoft.

EARLY LIFE

Steven Anthony "Steve" Ballmer was born in 1956 and grew up in the community of Farmington Hills, Michigan, a suburb of Detroit. Ballmer's father, Frederic Henry Ballmer, a Swiss immigrant, was a manager for the Ford Motor Company, while his mother, Beatrice Dworkin, was born into a family that owned a Detroit auto parts business. Ballmer attended Detroit County Day School (DCDS), a private, secular preparatory school located in Beverly Hills, Michigan, from which he was graduated in 1973. While enrolled at DCDS, Ballmer was also enrolled in engineering classes at what was then known as the Lawrence Institute of Technology. Ballmer excelled in his studies, earned a perfect score of 800 on the mathematics portion of the Scholastic Aptitude Test (SAT), and enrolled as a freshman at Harvard University. Ballmer double-majored in mathematics

Steve Ballmer.

and economics. He also worked as a writer and editor of *The Harvard Crimson*, the university's daily student-run newspaper. Ballmer also worked for *The Harvard Advocate*, a well-regarded literary journal, and served as the student manager of the Harvard varsity football team. During his sophomore year, Ballmer lived down the hall from his classmate and later business partner Bill Gates. Although the partygoing Ballmer was much more extroverted than Gates, the two became fast friends and sometimes studied together for classes and tests. Ballmer graduated with an A.B. degree in 1977, magna cum laude.

Immediately upon graduation from Harvard, Ballmer found employment at Procter & Gamble, where he worked as an assistant product manager. During the time that Ballmer worked for Procter & Gamble, he was officemates with Jeffrey R. Immelt, who later became chairman of the board and CEO of General Electric Company (GE). In 1979, Ballmer entered the Stanford Graduate School of Business, a professional school of Stanford University, although in 1980 he left without graduating to join Microsoft Corporation.

LIFE'S WORK

Although Ballmer enjoyed his time at the Stanford Graduate School of Business, when his old friend Gates approached him to join Microsoft, Ballmer agreed to join the then small company. Ballmer joined Microsoft as its first business manager for a salary of $50,000 per year, which was augmented by an ownership stake in the company. When Microsoft formally incorporated the year after Ballmer joined the company, this state was translated into 8 percent of Microsoft's stock. When the company had its initial public offering of stock in 1986, this stake made Ballmer a multimillionaire before he had turned thirty. Estimated to be worth more than $15 billion today, Ballmer retains a 4 percent stake in Microsoft, making him one of the corporation's largest shareholders.

Standing 6 feet, 5 inches tall and weighing more than 200 pounds, Ballmer's imposing physical presence and exuberant, outgoing personality made him an immediate leader in Microsoft's operations. During the early 1980s, Ballmer was named to head several Microsoft divisions, including operating systems development, sales and support, and operations. Microsoft originally was established to sell software programs that used the Beginner's All-purpose Symbolic Instruction Code (BASIC) to program the Altair 8800 computer, an early microcomputer popular with hobbyists. In 1981,

Affiliation: Microsoft

When Steve Ballmer joined Microsoft Corporation, founded by Bill Gates and Paul Allen, in 1980 as its business manager, Microsoft had only a couple dozen employees. Under Ballmer's leadership, Microsoft has grown to become one of the world's largest corporations, with more than ninety thousand employees and multiple products.

Microsoft first became known for supplying the operating system MS-DOS, which helped popularize the IBM PC. As Microsoft built upon the success of this product by developing its Windows operating system, office productivity applications, an Internet browser, software developer tools, entertainment devices, and other products, Ballmer helped to guide its sales strategy. During the late 1980s and early 1990s, Microsoft's revenues increased by more than $1 billion per year.

Ballmer has long been regarded as Microsoft's emotional leader, even before he took over as CEO from founder Gates. Known for his energetic style and motivational abilities, Ballmer has worked with Gates for more than thirty years to keep Microsoft one of the most significant software and technology firms in the world.

however, International Business Machines Corporation (IBM) approached Microsoft to see if it would create an operating system for its machines that used an Intel Corporation 8086 central processing unit (CPU). IBM planned to use the 8086 CPU in its IBM personal computer (PC), but it had been unable to devise an operating system that would run its PCs. To remedy this problem, IBM turned to Microsoft to produce an operating system for the IBM PC. Microsoft purchased what was known as the "quick and dirty operating system" (QDOS) from Seattle Computer Products for $75,000 in an effort to meet this need. QDOS was also known as 86-DOS. QDOS/86-DOS was renamed MS-DOS (for Microsoft DOS) and offered for sale as part of the IBM PC beginning in 1982. MS-DOS was an improvement over previous operating systems and proved highly popular with consumers.

MS-DOS was licensed to IBM, which produced a version known as PC-DOS, as well as versions available from other vendors. Microsoft received a royalty on all versions of DOS produced, however, which was to prove very lucrative. When MS-DOS version 1.0 was released, the IBM PC, and thus Microsoft, had many competitors. These competitors included Apple Computer's Apple II, Commodore International's Commodore 64, and others. The IBM PC was very popular with

businesses. As a result, many who had used the IBM PC at work chose an IBM PC, or a clone, for home use. This greatly increased Microsoft's share of the operating system market, as a copy of MS-DOS was included with each PC sold.

In the mid-1980s, IBM and Microsoft began to work jointly to devise an operating system to succeed MS-DOS. This operating system was known as Operating System/2 (OS/2). After several years of development, OS/2 version 1.0 was released in December 1987. This initial release of OS/2 operated only in text mode and lacked a graphical user interface (GUI). Despite this, OS/2 received strong reviews and achieved modest sales. OS/2 version 1.1, with a GUI, was released in October 1988. While engaged in developing OS/2 with IBM, Microsoft, under Ballmer's leadership, was also working on an operating system known as Windows.

Windows was a 16-bit operating system employing a GUI. Microsoft had first released it in 1985. Ballmer was promoted to head of Microsoft's systems software group in 1984. Windows became popular only upon the release of version 3.0 in May 1990. Windows 3.0 and later versions allowed icons to be dragged and dropped, better video and audio, and multitasking. Because Windows and MS-DOS were packaged with all PCs, while OS/2 was available only as a pricey stand-alone software package, the solo Microsoft project was much more successful than the partnership with IBM. Some accused Ballmer and Microsoft of engaging in the OS/2 project with IBM only to divert attention from the development of Windows. Nonetheless, Windows proved to be the operating system of choice for most global users, while OS/2 and other rivals were soon forgotten.

Under Ballmer's oversight, Microsoft also became the leader in office productivity software. Since the advent of microcomputer popularity in the mid-1980s, a variety of productivity programs had been used by office workers and others to assist them in their tasks. These productivity programs included word processors, which allowed for the production of textual documents, including drafting, editing, formatting, and printing. Popular word-processing programs for early PCs included WordStar, WordPerfect, Ami Pro, Xy-Write, and others. Other popular productivity software included spreadsheets and presentation applications.

Early leaders in the spreadsheet category included VisiCalc, Lotus 1-2-3, and Borland's Quattro. Presentation software made it possible for almost anyone to create professional looking slides that included type-setting and graphics, originally in slide form but later as overheads and via LCD projectors. Popular presentation software programs included Harvard Graphics, Lotus Freelance Graphics, Adobe Persuasion, and Novell Presentations. Ballmer and Gates recognized the importance of word processors and other productivity software and set about to increase Microsoft's share of the market for these applications. The applications that led the market at this time—WordPerfect Corporation's WordPerfect and Lotus Development Corporation's Lotus 1-2-3—were well entrenched, but Microsoft developed its own word processor, Word, and its own spreadsheet program, Excel, to attempt to gain market share. Microsoft's aggressive pricing and continually upgraded product features began to chip away at the older products' dominance. When Microsoft was able to bring Windows-ready versions of its applications to market before its rivals, however, it was able to become the market leader for the first time. Some have suggested that WordPerfect's and Lotus's failure to have Windows versions of their products ready for market was in part based on Microsoft's failure to share necessary source code with its rivals.

Ballmer continued to play a leading role in Microsoft's operations, serving as executive vice president of sales and support as of 1992. After Gates's "Internet Tidal Wave" memo of May 1995, Microsoft began to develop and market products aggressively in order to take advantage of the market for browser software for Internet use. To that end, Microsoft created Internet Explorer, a web browser that became the market leader in the late 1990s, dethroning Netscape Navigator. To achieve this, it is estimated that Microsoft employed more than one thousand programmers at a time and spent more than $100 million per year to support the more technologically sophisticated features available on the Internet.

In 2000, Gates stepped down as CEO of Microsoft in favor of Ballmer, who had served as president since July 1998. Ballmer continued as president and CEO until February 2001, at which point he stepped down from that position. Ballmer also was responsible for the .NET Framework development, a software framework including a large library and language interoperability across several programming languages.

PERSONAL LIFE

Ten years after he began working at Microsoft, Ballmer married Connie Snyder, a public relations executive who worked for Microsoft when the couple met. The parents of three sons, Ballmer and Snyder live in Bellevue, a suburb of Seattle. One of Ballmer's and Snyder's neighbors is recording artist and saxophone player Kenny G.

Ballmer enjoys participating in several sports, including jogging, golf, and basketball. A lifelong Detroit Pistons fan, Ballmer was part of the group that attempted to purchase the Seattle SuperSonics before the National Basketball Association (NBA) franchise relocated to Oklahoma City. As someone who grew up near the heart of the United States' automobile industry, Ballmer has a preference for American cars, especially Lincolns.

Stephen T. Schroth and Jason A. Helfer

FURTHER READING

Allen, Paul. *Idea Man: A Memoir by the Co-founder of Microsoft*. New York: Penguin, 2011. Print. Allen's autobiography, at times controversial, with the focus on the founding of Microsoft. Illustrated.

Christakis, N. A., and J. H. Fowler. *Connected: The Surprising Power of Our Social Networks and How They Shape Our Lives*. Boston: Little, Brown, 2009. Print. Looks at how collaboration and participation in social networking enhance an individual's effectiveness.

Mane, S., and P. Andrews. *Gates: How Microsoft's Mogul Reinvented an Industry—And Made Himself the Richest Man in America*. New York: Touchstone, 1994. Print. Explores Gates's and Microsoft's quest to move from being a software company to a provider of office machines and home entertainment devices.

Maxwell, F. A. *Bad Boy Ballmer: The Man Who Rules Microsoft*. New York: HarperCollins, 2002. Print. Delves into the background of Gates's best friend and his transition from a behind-the-scenes manager to leader of one of the globe's largest corporations.

Turow, J. *The Daily You: How the New Advertising Industry Is Defining Your Identity and Your Worth*. New Haven: Yale UP, 2011. Print. Investigates how data about today's consumers are collected and how consumer power is affected by the customized media environment.

Wallace, J., and J. Erickson. *Hard Drive: Bill Gates and the Making of the Microsoft Empire*. New York: Wiley, 1992. Print. Examination of the business practices that transformed Microsoft from a start-up technology company into an industry giant.

CLIFFORD E. BERRY

Cocreator of the first electronic digital computer

Born: April 19, 1918; Gladbrook, Iowa
Died: October 30, 1963; New York, New York
Primary Field: Computer science
Specialty: Computer hardware
Primary Company/Organization: Iowa State College

INTRODUCTION

Clifford E. Berry was the cocreator of the Atanasoff-Berry Computer (ABC), the first electronic digital computer while a graduate student at Iowa State College from 1939 to 1941. Although later computers such as the Electronic Numerical Integrator and Computer (ENIAC) were better known, the ABC introduced numerous innovations critical to the advent of modern computing, including several still in use today—such as regenerative capacitator memory, parallel processing, the separation of memory and computing as distinct functions, the use of binary (base 2) arithmetic for computing, and the move away from using mechanical parts such as ratchets and gears. Little known for decades, the importance of Berry's work was recognized ten years after his death when the U.S. District Court acknowledged the primacy of the ABC.

EARLY LIFE

Clifford Edward Berry was born on April 19, 1918, in Gladbrook, Iowa, to Fred Berry and Grace Strohm Berry. He was the oldest of four children and quickly picked up his father's interest in electrical projects. Fred owned an electrical appliance store and repair service, and he built the town's first radio, just as radios began to experience their boom in popularity. Radios were the first devices young Clifford tinkered with, his father instructing him. His excellence in school led to his skipping the fourth grade; grade skipping was more common at the time, when there were few to no programs for accelerated students.

In 1929, the Berrys moved to the town of Marengo, where Fred managed the local office of the Iowa Power Company. Clifford built his first ham radio and continued in his studies. In Clifford's second year of high school, his father was fatally shot by a fired employee; the family remained in Marengo long enough for Clifford to finish high school and then relocated to Ames in order to be near Clifford while he attended Iowa State College (ISC). Now Iowa State University, ISC had started as a land-grant college and had an excellent program in engineering; it attracted numerous out of state students and skilled professors. It was the school Fred had suggested for his son. Clifford graduated with a bachelor of science degree in electrical engineering in 1939.

LIFE'S WORK

One of Berry's professors was Harold Anderson, a close friend of John Vincent Atanasoff. Atanasoff had earned his master's degree at ISC and returned there to teach after finishing his Ph.D. at the University of Wisconsin. While at Wisconsin, he had had his first experiences with computers and found them both fascinating and frustrating. He wanted to build something better and discussed his ideas and frustrations with Anderson. When he asked Anderson to recommend a student to assist him, Berry was a few months away from graduating and intended to enter the school's graduate program in physics. He impressed Atanasoff as much as he had Anderson, and a stipend was arranged for him so that he

Clifford E. Berry.

Affiliation: Iowa State College

The institution known today as the Iowa State University of Science and Technology was still the Iowa State College of Agriculture and Mechanic Arts when John Vincent Atanasoff and Clifford E. Berry were there. It was founded as a coeducational institution in 1858 and became the first land-grant college after the passage of the 1862 Morrill Act, which sought improvements to agricultural education. From the start, ISC had a strong focus in engineering, offering courses in civil, electrical, mechanical, and mining engineering. In the later nineteenth century, the school added the country's first domestic economy college courses (a combination of home economics and consumer science) and the first state-run veterinary college. The VEISHA festival (pronounced VEE-shah, for veterinary medicine, engineering, industrial science, home economics, and agriculture), which was founded in 1922, has become the largest student-run festival in the country, celebrating the school and its faculty. Significant alumni of the school include astronauts, economists, and engineers, while faculty have included Pulitzer-winning novelist Jane Smiley, Nobel-winning chemist Dan Shechtman, statisticians George Snedecor and Wayne Arthur Fuller, and John Vincent Atanasoff.

As an engineering student, Berry helped Atanasoff design and construct a prototype electronic digital computer from 1939-1941. The first of its kind, the Atanasoff-Berry Computer (ABC) was designed to solve linear equations, but more important than the tasks it performed was its implementation of the design concepts Atanasoff and Berry had developed. The ABC was the first computer to use binary arithmetic, parallel processing, and regenerative capacitor memory (the same kind of memory used in DRAM today). Further, it relied not on ratchets and mechanical components for its computing, but on electronics. Memory and computing were handled as separate functions by distinct components, to address aspects of analog computing that had left Atanasoff dissatisfied. While later general-purpose machines occupied entire rooms, the ABC was the size of a couch or recliner, weighing hundreds of pounds and employing 280 vacuum tubes and 31 gas-filled tubes called thyratrons which functioned as electrical switches. It was not programmable, nor fully automated, and there was a margin of error in the system's results which Atanasoff and Berry did not have time to correct before the ramp-up of World War II called them to disparate defense jobs. The ABC was a precursor to later digital computers, more than a fully realized vision; but the leap forward from analog computing that it represented was arguably more significant, involving more numerous innovations, than the improvements made by later computers that incorporated its approach.

could assist in Atanasoff's research instead of teaching or finding work outside the university.

The two began their work in 1939, building on ideas Atanasoff had brainstormed the previous year. Atanasoff had a good sense of how he wanted to achieve his vision but needed help fully implementing it. While the terms *analog computer* and *digital computer* were not yet widely used, existing computers were what we now call analog: computing devices that stored or manipulated quantities by moving parts into different positions. Slide rules and abacuses are common examples of analog computers—simple in construction but requiring constant operator involvement to use and a bit of training to understand. Analog computers could be automated and could be built to solve complex problems, but the mechanical actions were prone to error and inefficient. Atanasoff sought what he then called a "proper computing device" and would later be called a digital computer. The project was initially funded with an $850 grant from the college

(through the agronomy department, which hoped to benefit from better economic analyses made possible by faster computation) and an additional $5,000 from the New York City–based Research Corporation.

Atanasoff took a job at the Naval Ordnance Laboratory later in 1939, reducing the amount of time he and Berry worked together on the project face to face. Numerous engineers around the country found themselves pursued for defense jobs as the nation anticipated the possibility of war with Germany and Japan. Berry assisted Atanasoff in drafting a thirty-five-page manuscript describing their designs, entitled "Computing Machines for the Solution of Large Systems of Linear Algebraic Equations," and in 1940 it was given to a patent attorney hired by the college in order to protect the ABC's invention. Because of interruptions to the work, the patent was never filed. In later years, the patent on the ENIAC computer would be challenged in court by a rival corporation seeking to invalidate the patent in order to bring digital computers into the public domain. The U.S. District Court invalidated ENIAC's patent in 1973, ten years after Berry's death, on the justification that it derived too heavily from the ABC. Berry was posthumously acknowledged as one of the fathers of the digital computer.

Atanasoff was always quick to credit Berry as the catalyst for the breakthrough. The elder scientist had worked for several years on his ideas; it was the assistance of Berry, as much as the funding, that made it possible to turn cocktail-napkin ideas into a working prototype. Berry was instrumental in moving the ABC's design further away from the norms of analog computing; Atanasoff pointed out that Berry removed any references to the abacus from their notes in order to keep it from shackling their attempt at innovation.

Although the ABC was not programmable—the major difference between it and its immediate successors—and was designed to handle only linear equations, it was the first of its kind. It implemented many innovations that have become synonymous with modern computing: the use of binary (base-two) digits to represent data for computation, electronic calculation rather than the inefficiencies of mechanical parts, and segregated systems for computation and memory. The system used regenerative capacitor memory, the same kind of memory used by dynamic random access memory (DRAM) today, using sixty-four bands of fifty capacitors to represent data as 50-bit binary numbers. The bands were contained by a pair of drums that rotated once per second. Arithmetic was conducted by vacuum tubes, of which there were 280, as well as 31 thyratrons. The input-output mechanism was entirely Berry's work and was the subject of his thesis.

Berry completed his master's degree in 1941 and work on the ABC, which lacked some refinements, was put on hold. He continued his studies in ISC's physics department but did so from afar, relocating to California to take a defense job at Pasadena's Consolidated Engineering Corporation (CEC), founded by the son of Herbert Hoover. The military draft was going strong at the time—the Draft Board was not willing to excuse him from the draft for working on the ABC but instead wanted him to work more directly on defense in another matter, which accounts for ISC's flexibility in allowing him to move across country while still enrolled as a graduate student. Berry completed his Ph.D. in 1948 with a dissertation entitled *Effects of Initial Energies on Mass Spectra*. His rise in CEC was rapid: In 1949 he became chief physicist; in 1952, assistant director of research; and in 1959, technical director and director of engineering of the analytical and control division. He remained

with CEC until 1963, when he relocated to Plainview, New York, to become manager of advanced development at Vacuum Electronics Corporation. In his professional work, Berry patented thirty different inventions: eleven related to vacuums and electronics and nineteen to mass spectrometry.

PERSONAL LIFE

While working on the ABC, Berry met Martha Jean Reed, Atanasoff's secretary and a fellow graduate of ISC, who had a slight limp left after surviving polio. Like Berry, Reed had lost her father at a young age. They were married in 1942, a year after Berry completed his master's degree in physics, and moved to Pasadena, California, for Berry's Consolidated Engineering Corporation job. They had two children, Carol and David. Unbeknownst to Berry, Atanasoff had deep reservations about the relationship; long after Berry's death, Atanasoff confessed that he had wished something had intervened to prevent the marriage and that he distrusted his secretary's influence on his assistant. According to Atanasoff, when he visited them in Pasadena in the 1950s, the Berrys both drank more heavily than had been their earlier habit.

Berry left Pasadena for New York in October 1963. He died the same month, before his family relocated, of suffocation. His death was ruled a suicide, but both Atanasoff and members of the Berry family suspected foul play.

Bill Kte'pi

FURTHER READING

Atanasoff, John V. "Advent of the Electronic Digital Computing." *IEEE Annals of the History of Computing* 6.3 (1984): 229–82. Print. Atanasoff's own account of the ABC, problems encountered, reasons for the design choices he and Berry made, and the later patent cases in which he testified.

Burks, Alice Rowe. *Who Invented the Computer? The Legal Battle That Changed Computing History*. New York: Prometheus, 2003. Print. An account of the *Honeywell v. Sperry Rand* lawsuit, which established Atanasoff and Berry as the fathers of the digital computer.

Gleick, James. *The Information: A History, a Theory, a Flood*. New York: Pantheon, 2011. Print. A history of the information revolution, putting the ABC in a broader context.

McCartney, Scott. *ENIAC: The Triumphs and Tragedies of the World's First Computer*. New York: Walker,

1999. Print. McCartney, as the title indicates, takes the position that ENIAC, pioneered by John Mauchly and J. Presper Eckert, was the first digital computer, playing up the improvements ENIAC made on the ABC, but even in so doing he covers Berry and Atanasoff's work in depth.

Smiley, Jane. *The Man Who Invented the Computer: The Biography of John Atanasoff, Digital Pioneer.* New York: Doubleday, 2010. Print. An engaging biography of Atanasoff by the acclaimed fiction writer. Although there is no book-length biography of Berry, he is featured here.

ANITA BORG

Founder of the Institute for Women and Technology

Born: January 17, 1949; Chicago, Illinois
Died: April 6, 2003; Sonoma, California
Primary Field: Internet
Specialty: Ethics and policy
Primary Company/Organization: Anita Borg Institute for Women and Technology

INTRODUCTION

Anita Borg, an American computer scientist, is best known for her advocacy for the inclusion of women in technological and scientific fields. She founded Systers, an electronic mailing list made up of women computer professionals, and, with computer scientist Telle Whitney, founded the Grace Hopper Celebration of Women in Computing, a technical computer science conference inspired by the legacy of Navy admiral Grace Murray Hopper. Most notably, Borg founded the Institute for Women and Technology (IWT), a nonprofit research and development organization with a dual focus on increasing the number and influence of women in technology and increasing the positive effects of technology on the lives of women. She served as the first president of IWT. Shortly after her death, the institute was renamed the Anita Borg Institute for Women and Technology in her honor.

EARLY LIFE

Anita Borg Naffz was born on January 17, 1949, in Chicago, Illinois, to a housewife and a salesman. She spent most of the first twelve years of her life in Palatine, a small town about thirty-five miles outside Chicago. Her parents moved with their two daughters for a year to Hawaii, where Borg attended fifth grade in a racially diverse school, an experience that enlarged her ten-year-old view of the world. The Naffz family returned to the Chicago area briefly but later moved to Mukilteo, Washington, near Seattle. Borg credited her mother with

teaching her that mathematics could be fun and her father with fostering her spirit of adventure.

Borg entered the University of Washington in 1967 but quit after two years. She married and followed her first husband to New York, where he enrolled in graduate school. The young couple's straitened finances made it necessary for her to find a job. She worked as a "girl Friday" in the data-processing department of a small insurance company. It was during her tenure with the insurance company that her interest in computer science developed. She taught herself Common Business-Oriented Language (COBOL) and started doing programming

Anita Borg.

for the company. When her marriage ended in divorce two years later, scholarships enabled her to enroll in New York University, where a new computer science department had recently emerged from the mathematics department. Borg saw a degree in computer science as a means to financial independence. She entered the Ph.D. program in 1973 with plans to leave once she had a master's degree, but she soon found her studies a welcome challenge. She received her Ph.D. in computer science from the Courant Institute at New York University in 1981.

LIFE'S WORK

Borg's first job after completing her degree was for Auragen Systems, a small start-up company in New Jersey. She was assigned to a team charged with creating a fault-tolerant operating system. The work was far removed from the theoretical work of graduate school, but she found working on the operating system challenging and exciting. However, the project was still incomplete in 1985, when Auragen failed.

Borg was hired by Nixdorf, a German corporation and an Auragen investor with rights to the company's technology. She spent a year in Germany working on the computer system that eventually became Nixdorf's TARGON (the acronym for a German joke, translated as "A Thousand Users Go Together: Oh Nixdorf"). In 1986, she accepted a job with Digital Equipment Corporation's (DEC's) Western Research Laboratory in Palo Alto, California, where she remained for the next twelve years developing tools related to the performance of microprocessor memory systems.

A year after she joined DEC, Borg attended the Symposium on Operating System Principles, an Association for Computing Machinery conference. She was struck by the small number of women among the roughly four hundred conferees. Borg left the conference with about twenty e-mail addresses of women who shared her concerns. That list became the foundation of Systers, the first e-mail community for women in computing.

The name combined "sisters" and "systems," referencing its founding as a community for women working with operating systems, but the group soon expanded to include women working in all fields of technical computing. Within a decade, the group had grown to twenty-three hundred. By 2012, Systers' membership had reached thirty-four hundred women in fifty-eight countries. More than a quarter century after its founding, Systers continues to fulfill Borg's dream of a safe place for women in computer technology to discuss problems and issues relevant to women in their profession.

During her years at DEC, Borg also conceived the idea of a conference for women in technical computing that would match the industry's best conferences in quality but would be structured with the needs and interests of women in mind. The result was the Grace Hopper Celebration of Women in Computing, the brainchild of Borg and Telle Whitney, then with Actel. The first conference was held in Washington, D.C., June 9–11, 1994, with more than 450 women in attendance. Named in tribute to Rear Admiral Grace Murray Hopper, a pioneer of computer programming, the conference has historically featured women leaders in industry, academia, and government as speakers and has offered a forum for researchers to present their work. At the same time, it has addressed common interests such as networking, mentoring, and greater recognition for the achievements of women in computing. The 2011 conference, held in Portland, Oregon, attracted almost three thousand participants from thirty-four countries.

In 1997, Borg read *The Futures of Women: Scenarios for the 21st Century* (1996), by Pamela McCorduck and Nancy Ramsey, and their ideas prompted her to consider what women in general (not only those working in technical fields) want from technology and what they can bring to it. From these ideas came the concept for the Institute for Women and Technology. Later that year, Borg left DEC for the Xerox Palo Alto Research Center (PARC). She was frustrated by DEC's lack of interest in her idea for an institute that would combine an initiative to attract women to computing with the creation of technology driven by women's real-life experiences. PARC was much more receptive to the idea and agreed to support Borg's development of an independent, nonprofit institute.

The Institute for Women and Technology (IWT) was officially founded in 1997, with Borg as its founding director and president. Systers and the Grace Hopper Celebration of Women in Computing became programs within the institute. During her years as president of IWT, Borg oversaw the creation of "virtual development centers," collaborations between the institute and universities such as Purdue, Texas A&M, and Carnegie Mellon in which undergraduates, faculty, and community residents work together to brainstorm ideas for technology projects for which students then create prototypes. She also promoted the international scope and influence of the institute through such projects as a partnership between IWT and the Pacific Institute for Women's Health in order to find ways for technology to be used to connect women's organizations in Africa. In addition to early support from Xerox, Borg won IWT sponsorship from Hewlett-Packard, Sun Microsystems, Microsoft, and dozens of other corporations. She persuaded the deans of engineering at Princeton University and the University of California at Berkeley to serve on WIT's board of trustees. Ill health forced Borg to resign as IWT president in 2002, but her role as founder of the institute that has born her name since 2003 has assured her place in the history of women in computing.

Borg was recognized as a visionary and leader many times. Her awards include the Pioneer Award from the Electronic Frontier Foundation and the Augusta Ada Lovelace Award from the Association for Women in Computing, both granted in 1995. In 1996, she was named a Fellow of the Association for Computing Machinery, and in 1998, she was inducted into the Women in Technology International Hall of Fame. U.S. president Bill Clinton appointed Borg to the Commission on the Advancement of Women and Minorities in Science, Engineering, and Technology in 1999. Three years later, Borg was the recipient of the $250,000 Heinz Award in Technology, the Economy, and Employment. Perhaps the most fitting tribute is the Google Anita Borg Scholarship program, established in 2004 to honor Borg's work by encouraging young women to excel in computer science and related fields. More than two hundred women have been awarded this honor since the program's inauguration, and the program has been expanded to include women students not only in the United States but also in Canada, Australia, New Zealand, Europe, North Africa, and the Middle East.

PERSONAL LIFE

As far back as her graduate school days, when she insisted that her weekends be free for motorcycle trips, Borg exhibited the adventurous spirit that her parents had fostered in her youth. This would be reflected in Borg's leisure activities as well as in her professional life. Licensed to pilot a small plane, she also enjoyed mountain biking, scuba diving, and sailing. Fond of a T-shirt that proclaimed "Well-Behaved Women Rarely Make History," Borg found driving her Porsche Boxster, a birthday gift, a great way to relieve stress.

In 2000, shortly after Borg was diagnosed with brain cancer, she married Winfried Wilcke, physicist and computer architect, who shared her interest in flying and sailing. Friends said the marriage was motivated by Wilcke's desire to be with Borg during treatment and to empower him to make legal decisions concerning her health. Borg died at the Sonoma home of her mother,

---

Affiliation: Anita Borg Institute for Women and Technology

The Institute for Women and Technology, a nonprofit research and development organization, was founded in 1997 by Anita Borg, a computer scientist passionate about expanding the role of women in technology. Borg served as president of the institute from its founding until 2002. After her death in 2003, the institute was renamed the Anita Borg Institute for Women and Technology (ABI). The institute's purpose is to encourage women to enter and provide leadership in technical computing professions and to involve women in the ways in which technology is designed and implemented.

Companies such as Hewlett-Packard, Google, Microsoft, and nearly two dozen others partner with the institute to fulfill its mission. In 2010, the Anita Borg Institute generated overall revenue and support of almost $5 million. More than ten programs fall under the umbrella of the ABI. Among these are Systers, the world's largest e-mail community of women in computing; the Grace Hopper Celebration of Women in Computing, inspired by computer pioneer Rear Admiral Grace Murray Hopper and cofounded by Anita Borg and Telle Whitney, president and CEO of ABI since 2002; and TechWomen, a professional mentorship and exchange program for women in technology from the Middle East and North Africa funded by the U.S. Department of State's Bureau of Educational and Cultural Affairs.

Beverley Naffz, on April 7, 2003. In addition to her husband and mother, she was survived by her sister, Lee Naffz, of Leavenworth, Washington.

Wylene Rholetter

FURTHER READING

Camp, Jean L. "We Are Geeks, and We Are Not Guys: The Systers Mailing List." *Wired Women: Gender and New Realities in Cyberspace.* Ed. Lynn Cherny and Elizabeth Reba Weise. Seattle: Seal, 1996. 114–25. Print. An essay about the e-mail community of women in technical computing founded by Anita Borg in 1987. Focus is on ways these women challenge the stereotype of the geek as male.

Edwards, Cliff. "Scientist Works to Give Women a Voice in the Cyberworld." *Black Issues in Higher Education* 17.5 (2000): 64. Print. Provides details of Borg's work in her role as founder and president of the Institute for Women and Technology to increase participation of women and minorities in technology. Includes biographical data and quotations from Borg.

Hafner, Katie. "Anita Borg, 54, Trailblazer for Women in Computer Field." *New York Times* 10 Apr. 2003: A25. Print. This obituary gives an overview of Borg's life and professional achievements. Quotes colleagues paying tribute to her commitment and influence in computing.

Klawe, Maria, Telle Whitney, and Caroline Simard. "Women in Computing—Take 2." *Communications of the ACM* 52.2 (2009): 68–76. Print. This follow-up to a 2005 article focuses on changes, positive and negative, in women in computing. Notes strategies employed by the Anita Borg Institute for Women and Technology, with which two of the authors are affiliated. Photographs, illustration.

Misa, Thomas J., ed. *Gender Codes: Why Women Are Leaving Computing*. New York: Wiley-IEEE Computer Society Press, 2010. Print. Borg is referenced among the women programmers, systems analysts, managers, and IT executives whose achievements are recognized. The accomplishments of women in technology during the 1960s and 1970s are contrasted with the diminishing number of women entering computer science in the twenty-first century.

PAUL BRAINERD

Founder of Aldus

Born: 1947; Medford, Oregon
Died: -
Primary Field: Computer science
Specialty: Computer software
Primary Company/Organization: Aldus

INTRODUCTION

Programmer and philanthropist Paul Brainerd is one of the cofounders of Aldus, the software company that introduced desktop publishing (a term Brainerd coined). PageMaker, Aldus's flagship product, was a software package that allowed for total manipulation of each page to be printed, from text to layout, including images, charts, and graphs. In 1985, this was a revolutionary step forward in publishing, which until that time had benefitted only slightly from word processors, machines that offered only a slight advance over typewriters, and was still dominated by typesetting. As the industry shifted from typesetting to desktop publishing, PageMaker remained the major program for more than a decade, and when Aldus was purchased by competitor Adobe, Brainerd used his share of the sale proceeds to fund the philanthropic organizations to which he later devoted his career.

EARLY LIFE

Paul Brainerd was born in 1947 in Medford, Oregon, the son of Phil and Vernatta Brainerd. After high school, he attended the University of Oregon. He developed an interest in publishing while editing the student paper, the *Oregon Daily Emerald*, which introduced him to the technical and financial aspects of publishing. Under his editorship, the *Daily Emerald* cut its production cost in

Paul Brainerd.

half by switching to offset printing by borrowing the press of a local newspaper in the off-hours. He later attended the University of Minnesota, where he worked on the student paper and earned his degree in journalism. After college he worked as a journalist, imagining a time when computer software would be better designed to answer the needs of journalists and publishers, just as early computers had answered the needs of scientists and statisticians. He worked as an assistant at the *Minneapolis Star Tribune*, where he was introduced to the products of Boston-based Atex, which made software that streamlined the newspaper production process.

This led to a job with Atex and a move back to the Northwest to work in Atex's research center in Redmond, Washington. The Redmond center was closed in 1984, when Kodak bought Atex out. Brainerd turned down Kodak's offer of a job back in Boston. Instead, he decided the time was right to start his own company, taking advantage of the availability of the recently introduced Macintosh computer and the forthcoming LaserWriter printer.

LIFE'S WORK

Brainerd cofounded the Seattle-based software company Aldus in February 1984, with Jeremy Jaech, Mark Sundstrom, Mike Templeman, and Dave Walter. Brainerd served as the company's chairman. The company was named for Aldo Manuzio, better known as Aldus Manutius, the Renaissance Italian publisher who invented italic print, the comma, and a small-format book that was the antecedent to the mass-market paperback.

Aldus's flagship product was Aldus PageMaker, the first desktop publishing software, released in 1985. PageMaker used Adobe PostScript, a programming language for printers that had been introduced the previous year and that shipped with Apple LaserWriter printers in 1985. PostScript was a page description language developed at the Xerox Palo Alto Research Center (PARC) for laser printers. (Adobe Systems was founded by its developer, John Warnock, when his bosses at Xerox would not market PostScript.) PostScript and the LaserWriter made desktop publishing a possibility; PageMaker made it happen, beginning the desktop publishing revolution that flourished for years, principally on Macintosh systems until PC-compatible computers caught up with the Mac's publishing capabilities in the early 1990s. The Mac was primitive in many other respects, especially in the 1980s; the first desktop publishers were constrained by the Mac's 1-bit 512 {multi} 342 screen and inconsistencies in letter spacing. Letter-spacing issues would

be corrected in later versions of PageMaker, which gave users control over kerning (the ability to adjust spacing between individual characters). Furthermore, the combination of the Macintosh and LaserWriter printer cost nearly $9,000—more than many new cars.

Unlike later Mac and Windows systems, the early Mac systems also lacked what-you-see-is-what-you-get (WYSIWYG, pronounced WIH-zee-wihg) functionality—referring to consistency between the appearance of a document on the screen and the appearance of a document in print. Early desktop publishing required numerous trial-and-error printouts, and occasionally files would print out differently on different printers, requiring adjustments if the file were transferred somewhere else before printing. In addition, desktop publishing was memory-intensive by the standards of available hardware, because of the amount of image manipulation required; as a result, software was prone to frequent crashing. PostScript made strides in addressing this problem, because it included scalable fonts stored not in the computer's memory but in the printer's read-only memory (ROM).

Despite all these limitations, even the first generation of desktop publishing was an enormous leap forward, and Aldus sold $12 million in software its first year. From a printing and publishing perspective, computers until 1985 were little more than typewriters, though using the desktop typesetting package TeX, released in 1978, at least made them very good typewriters. PageMaker received a number of awards, and the competing Ventura Publisher was released in 1986 for MS-DOS (PC) computers, which Aldus countered by releasing a Windows version of PageMaker in 1987. Future versions of the PC release came with a Windows runtime file that allowed MS-DOS users to use the program without needing to purchase Windows. Support for OS/2, with its multithreading capabilities, was added with version 3.01.

Many of the features offered by early versions of PageMaker have been folded into modern word processors, but mid-1980s word processors did little more than arrange text in various fonts and sizes, possibly adding columns; adding images or effects more complicated than bold or italics was laborious at best, and few adjustments were possible. Nor did most word processors have effective tools for making charts and graphs, an area where image programs were also weak. PageMaker allowed drag-and-drop placement of many page elements, including both text and graphics; a vast array of possible page layouts; simple drawing tools as well

Affiliation: Aldus

Paul Brainerd was one of the founders and the chairman of Aldus. Aldus Corporation was the first desktop publishing software company, especially known for its flagship product, Aldus PageMaker, which took advantage of the new capabilities of advanced printers and the PostScript programming language to introduce desktop publishing for the first time. For many years, desktop publishing was all but synonymous with a trinity of software programs used in tandem: PageMaker (1984), Illustrator (1987), and Photoshop (1990), the latter two released by Adobe, the company that released PostScript and would eventually acquire Aldus. Aldus offered its own vector graphics program, Freehand, which competed with Illustrator for years (and was not included with the Aldus acquisition, so continued its competition until after Adobe acquired it in its 2005 purchase of Macromedia). Aldus also developed PhotoStyler, a bitmap editor; the SuperPaint painting program; Digital Darkroom, a Photoshop competitor; the SuperCard multimedia authoring program; database programs such as Fetch and TouchBase Pro; and the tagged image file format (TIFF), which was the standard image file format for the publishing industry and desktop publishers for years.

= During the attempted Communist coup in Russia in 1991, magazines and newspapers were shut down. Access to the Internet was not yet widespread enough for anyone to think to shut it down as well. Russians networking online used PageMaker to distribute political pamphlets throughout the country, keeping the free press alive during the short-lived coup.

PageMaker began desktop publishing, and by 1994, it remained the most significant desktop publishing application not owned by Adobe, which had laid the foundation for the field but still failed to offer an application competing with PageMaker. This was the principal motivation behind Adobe's acquisition of Aldus in 1994. Eventually PageMaker was eclipsed by rival QuarkXPress and Adobe's new program InDesign, and although the product is still available, it is no longer developed.

Twenty-two different businesses were formed by "Aldusians," former Aldus employees, many of whom used their profits from the sale to Adobe to fund a new business venture. They are often affectionately called the Baby Pauls, in honor of Brainerd.

---

as the capacity to import graphics; and the PostScript compatibility that, once the kinks of the earliest versions were worked out, achieved WYSIWYG results. It was desktop publishing, more than word processing, that drove the demand for fonts, both free and especially commercial, and which resulted in the explosive growth of the clip art and vector graphics cottage industries. Laser printers were expensive, heavier than most furniture, noisy, and hot, but with PageMaker they offered the user a world of options beyond conventional dot-matrix printers, and stationery and office-supply stores began offering special laser printer paper, with features ranging from foil overlays to T-shirt iron-ons that the user could design in PageMaker. Later versions of the software made editing files easier, integrated more seamlessly with the other desktop publishing programs that had developed (such as line art programs, photomanipulation programs, and databases), and added better text-manipulation features that made text as customizable as images.

Desktop publishing not only forced the printing and publishing industry to become computer literate but also allowed the computer literate to become publishers. Small businesses could produce their own pamphlets, brochures, manuals, and other printed material for customers, as well as increasing the quality of in-house publications such as corporate newsletters. Anyone with free time and access to the voter registration rolls could wallpaper a neighborhood with political fliers. Others started fanzines, special-interest newsletters or magazines, or produced catalogs for home businesses of used or specialized goods during this pre-eBay, pre-Amazon marketplace age.

Aldus had a somewhat odd relationship with Adobe, since on one hand it was dependent on or complemented by many Adobe products, notably PostScript but also the vector graphics program Illustrator and the photomanipulation program Photoshop. The latter two programs, in conjunction with PageMaker, formed the desktop publisher's toolkit upon Photoshop's release in 1990. Aldus offered competing products in both categories—FreeHand and Digital Darkroom (acquired in the 1990 purchase of Silicon Beach Software), respectively—but neither had the same level of success. However, Adobe was unable to eclipse Aldus; PageMaker remained the product leader until well into the 1990s, when QuarkXPress gained ground on it.

Brainerd took two years off from the day-to-day operations of Aldus to focus on the company's long-term strategizing, but he returned when the company began posting losses. The quest for new management to free him up for other concerns led to meetings with rivals and colleagues at Adobe.

PERSONAL LIFE
Adobe acquired Aldus in 1994. In 1995, using one-third of his proceeds from the sale, Brainerd founded the Brainerd Foundation, a philanthropic foundation, through which he and his family awarded grants promoting environmental interests and good environmental citizenship in Brainerd's native Pacific Northwest.

In 1997, Brainerd deepened his commitment to philanthropy by starting Social Venture Partners (SVP). While the Brainerd Foundation's focus was specific, SVP's was broader. It consisted of one hundred partners, each of whom committed $5,000 to a pool and then voted as a group on which projects to fund from that pool. The organization was specifically formed in order to get investors more involved with and aware of the programs they funded, rather than encouraging mindless check writing. Brainerd also thought this approach would encourage philanthropy among the many newly wealthy of the Pacific Northwest, where high-tech fortunes had been made. By personally meeting with representatives of programs to be funded and discussing programs as a group, partners could get a sense of how charitable donations worked and what their money was actually used for. The organization prioritized educational and children's needs programs at the start.

One of the Brainerd Foundation's programs was the construction of IslandWood, a 255-acre environmental learning center on Bainbridge Island. Brainerd married Debbi Brainerd, who with him had cofounded Island-Wood. His sister Sherry is a member of the board of directors of the Brainerd Foundation, as well as its vice president.

Bill Kte'pi

FURTHER READING
Brainerd, Paul. "Social Venture Partners: Engaging a New Generation of Givers." *Nonprofit and Voluntary Sector Quarterly*, 1999. Print. Brainerd's account of his transition from software to philanthropy.

Levy, Steven. *Insanely Great: The Life and Times of Macintosh, the Computer That Changed Everything*. New York: Penguin, 2000. Print. An account of the Macintosh's early success, despite significant design problems and a staggering retail price for its first model. Includes information on Aldus and PageMaker's role in making the Mac the computer of choice for desktop publishing.

Loxley, Simon. *Type: The Secret History of Letters*. New York: I. B. Tauris, 2006. Print. A history of typesetting, including desktop publishing and Brainerd's involvement in it.

"Our History." Brainerd Foundation, n.d. Web. 1 Aug. 2012.

Sandler, Michael R. *Social Entrepreneurship in Education: Private Ventures for the Public Good*. New York: R&L Education, 2010. Print. A recent overview of the role of social entrepreneurship such as that of Brainerd's Social Venture Partners in education.

URSULA BURNS
Chairman and CEO of Xerox

Born: September 20, 1958; New York, New York
Died: -
Primary Field: Business and commerce
Specialty: Management, executives, and investors
Primary Company/Organization: Xerox

INTRODUCTION
Ursula Burns is an American success story. Raised by a single mother in a New York City housing project, she became the first African American woman to lead a Fortune 500 company, Xerox. Beginning as an intern in the summer of 1980, she steadily rose through the ranks at Xerox to become chief executive officer (CEO) in July 2009, succeeding Anne Mulcahy. The transition from Mulcahy to Burns marked the first transfer of power from one female CEO to another female CEO. On May 20, 2010, Burns became chair of the company.

EARLY LIFE
Ursula M. Burns was born on September 20, 1958, the second of three children. She grew up in New York City in the Baruch Houses, a public housing project on

Ursula Burns.

Delancey Street inhabited by Jewish immigrants, Hispanics, and African Americans. The common factor within such ethnic diversity, according to Burns, was poverty. Both of her parents were Panamanian immigrants, but her father had no part in Burns's upbringing. Her mother, Olga, ran a day-care center in her home and took in ironing to support her family, trading cleaning services to a doctor in exchange for free health care for her children. Believing a parochial school would provide a stronger and safer educational experience, she managed to see that her children attended Catholic schools. Ambitious for her children, she reminded them that they were not defined by their circumstances and encouraged them to succeed academically.

Burns graduated from Cathedral High School, a Catholic all-girls school on East 56th Street. She was still in high school when she researched top-paying jobs that would utilize her abilities in mathematics and science and set her sights on a degree in mechanical engineering. A scholarship through the New York Higher Education Opportunity Program allowed her to enter the Polytechnic Institute (now Polytechnic University) in Brooklyn. She graduated in 1980 with a B.S. degree in mechanical engineering. The summer after graduation, she took a position with Xerox as an intern. The

following year, a Xerox initiative to encourage minorities to pursue graduate work allowed her to enroll in Columbia University, where she earned a master's degree in mechanical engineering.

LIFE'S WORK
Degree in hand, Burns became a full-time employee of Xerox. Her intelligence and work ethic as a product developer and manager earned her rapid promotion in the company, but it was her outspokenness and authenticity that caught the attention of Wayland R. Hicks, then Xerox's executive vice president of marketing and customer operations. In 1989, Burns was invited to participate in a work-life discussion. When someone asked whether Xerox's policy on diversity was leading to the hiring of unqualified people, Burns found Hicks's response too mild and had no hesitation in saying so. Hicks was impressed with her honesty and courage and made her his executive assistant in 1990, a move that marked Burns early in her career as on the rise. A similar boldness in speaking her mind, this time relating to the gap between decisions made and actions implemented, led Paul A. Allaire, then CEO and chairman, to make her his executive assistant the following year.

The lessons Burns learned in those positions, the need to combine honesty with diplomacy among them, stood Burns in good stead during the years that followed as she was given increasingly greater responsibilities. She led several business teams, including the company's color business and office network printing business. In 1995, she was named the vice president and general manager of Xerox's work-group copier-business unit. In 1997, she became vice president and general manager of the departmental business unit, a job that charged her with overseeing development, construction, sales, and service of large work-group digital copiers and light lens copiers. She was named vice president of global manufacturing in 1999. A year later, she decided to leave the company.

Xerox was facing tough times, and Burns had lost faith in its leadership. However, Anne Mulcahy, who became CEO in 2001, persuaded Burns to remain and help the company recover. Later that year, Burns was named senior vice president of corporate strategic services, heading up manufacturing and supply-chain operations. Burns worked with Mulcahy to restructure the company as a leader in color technology and document services. Research and development were strategic in the company's rescue operations, and in her new role Burns led Xerox's global research and product development, along with marketing and delivery. While Mulcahy was visibly engaged as the public face of Xerox, holding meetings with concerned stockholders and corporate clients, Burns was the inner core of the company, negotiating with unions, hiring an outside contractor, and reducing the workforce by nearly 40 percent. Her actions reportedly saved the company, which had been teetering on the brink of bankruptcy, $2 billion over the next few years.

In April 2007, Burns became president of Xerox, making her Xerox's highest-ranking African American and second only to CEO Mulcahy in the company hierarchy. She also joined the board of directors. Mulcahy praised Burns for her knowledge and experience and the vital part her technology strategy had played in the company's survival. The new title Burns had acquired added corporate strategy, human resources, marketing operations, and global accounts to the responsibilities she had held in her previous office and required her to establish a second office at the company's headquarters in Stamford, Connecticut. The new appointment also signaled that she was in line for the company's highest position.

Burns was named CEO in July 2009, a personal achievement and a historic moment in the history of American business. Not only was Burns the first African American woman to be named CEO of a major company, but the passing of the title from Mulcahy to Burns also marked the first time that one female CEO of a major corporation had handed the reins of leadership to another woman. A few weeks later, Burns announced the $6.4 billion purchase of Affiliated Computer Services, an outsourcing firm. It was the largest acquisition in Xerox's long history and communicated the company's switch from defensive to offensive strategy. For the next year, Burns and Mulcahy worked together closely to make the transition of power a smooth one. On May 20, 2010, Burns was named chairman of Xerox. An African American girl from New York's public housing projects had become the leader of a Fortune 500 company that employed 140,000 people and served clients in more than 160 countries.

Under her watch, Xerox, once famous as the document company, transformed itself into a company that earns half its revenue from services such as managing electronic ticket transactions, road tolls, and parking meters. In addition to her work at Xerox, Burns serves on the boards of American Express; Boston Scientific, a manufacturer of medical devices; the Center on Addiction and Substance Abuse (CASA); the University

---

Affiliation: Xerox

Founded in 1906 in Rochester, New York, Xerox began as the Haloid Company, a manufacturer of photographic paper. In 1949, Haloid announced the first xerographic copier. Ten years later, the Xerox 914, the first plain-paper xerographic copier, launched a new industry. In 1961, the company became the Xerox Corporation. The following year, it was a Fortune 500 company and the leader in a growing global photocopying market. By the end of the decade, annual sales topped $1 billion.

The 1980s saw Xerox steadily losing market shares to Japanese firms. Problems multiplied in the 1990s. Cheaper desktop printers were decimating sales of the company's iconic stand-alone copiers; mounting debt, falling stocks, and a Securities and Exchange Commission investigation of accounting irregularities had pundits declaring the situation terminal. When Anne Mulcahy took over as CEO in 2001, Xerox had posted a $94 million loss.

Mulcahy, ably assisted by her second-in-command Ursula Burns, downsized the company and revamped product lines. When Mulcahy passed the mantle of leadership to Burns, who in 2009 became CEO and the first African American woman to lead a Fortune 500 company, Xerox was well on its way to transitioning to a service-based company. By 2012, service revenues, led by business-process outsourcing, exceeded projections. According to Burns, more than half the company's total revenue came from services, a trend she expected to grow as Xerox continued to distance itself from its history as a company whose products revolved around paper.

---

of Rochester; For Inspiration and Recognition of Science and Technology (FIRST), a nonprofit organization founded by the inventor Dean Kamen to inspire students to pursue engineering and technology studies; and the National Association of Manufacturers. In 2009, President Barack Obama appointed Burns to the White House Committee on Science, Technology, Engineering, and Math (STEM) Education, and in 2010, he appointed her a vice chair of the President's Export Council. In 2011, Burns held the eighth position on *Fortune* magazine's list of the fifty most powerful women in business.

Burns is particularly vocal in her advocacy of STEM education, working references into her frequent speeches whenever possible. More than most, she is aware of the difference education can make in a life, the difference between a child with no place to go and nothing to look forward to and one who can aim for and reach the top of a professional mountain.

PERSONAL LIFE

Shortly after she began working full-time for Xerox, Burns began dating Lloyd F. Bean, a Xerox scientist twenty years her senior. The couple married in 1988. They have two children, a son, Malcolm, born in 1989, and a daughter, Melissa, born in 1992. Despite her demanding career, Burns has made a practice of reserving weekends for her family. Even after her husband retired and theoretically freed Burns to extend her work hours, she remained adamant about the importance of family time. She also takes time for physical activity, rising early to run for thirty-five minuted on most days and working with a personal trainer twice a week.

Burns speaks candidly the influence of her mother, Olga Burns, in her life. Despite a seven-figure annual income, she still shops for her own groceries, often does laundry, and has a housekeeper only one day per week. Her mother's lessons concerning honesty and humility, she says, stay with her. When she acknowledged the contributions of mentors throughout her career at a *Fortune* Most Powerful Women dinner, she recognized her mother as her most significant mentor. Olga, who died in 1983, did not live to see her daughter's historic achievements, but Burns says she still feels her mother's encouragement. A sign on her office wall reads "Don't do anything that wouldn't make your Mom proud!"

Wylene Rholetter

FURTHER READING

Burns, Ursula. "Ursula Burns." Interview by Geoff Colvin. *Fortune* 161.6 (2010): 96–102. Print. An interview with Burns in which she discusses Xerox's acquisition of Affiliated Computer Services. She also expresses concerns about the poor level of study and teaching of mathematics and science in the United States, a problem she sees as both economic and social. Color photographs, graph.

Deutsch, Claudia H. "An Apparent Heir at Xerox." *New York Times* 1 June 2003: BU2. Print. A look at Burns's journey to become Xerox's ranking African American executive and speculations about her being named CEO, published six months after she was named company president.

Kolakowski, Nicholas. "Ursula Burns: Focused on the Core." *Eweek* 29.3 (2012): 10–13. Print. In her position as CEO, Burns talks about changes at Xerox, including redefining the company as a provider of services and the need to streamline business processes.

Mulcahy, Anne. "Why Succession Shouldn't Be a Horse Race." *Harvard Business Review* 88.10 (2010): 47–51. Print. Mulcahy discusses the work of choosing and grooming her successor and the way she and Burns worked as a team to effect a smooth transition when Burns replaced her as CEO. Photographs.

Zweigenhaft, Richard L., and G. William Domhoff. *The New CEOs: African American, Latino, and Asian American Leaders of Fortune 500 Companies.* Lanham: Rowman, 2011. Print. An exploration of the elements that led to the success of women and minorities leading Fortune 500 companies, including their influence on business and the larger culture.

VANNEVAR BUSH

Electrical engineer and developer of analog computers

Born: March 11, 1890; Everett, Massachusetts
Died: June 28, 1974; Belmont, Massachusetts
Primary Field: Computer science
Specialty: Computer hardware
Primary Company/Organization: U.S. Office of Scientific Research and Development

INTRODUCTION

American scientific researcher and electrical engineer Vannevar Bush is known for his pioneering work in the fields of analog computing, automated human memory, and information storage and retrieval. Bush served as dean of engineering and vice president of the Massachusetts Institute of Technology (MIT), president of the Carnegie Institution, and director of the U.S. government's Office of Scientific Research and Development during his lengthy career. He is known for his foresight in predicting the commercial and personal household uses of electronic devices. Bush's differential analyzer was one of the most powerful analog computers. During

World War II, he emerged as a leading force behind the mobilization of the partnership between the government, scientific, and business communities, making him an architect of what came to be known as the military-industrial complex. His groundbreaking 1945 Atlantic Monthly *article "As We May Think" introduced the hypothetical information storage and retrieval machine known as the memex, which facilitated information retrieval through the use of associative linking—a theoretical forerunner of the Internet and hypertext.*

Early Life

Vannevar Bush was born March 11, 1890, in Everett, Massachusetts, to a Universalist minister, the Reverend Richard Perry Bush, formerly of Provincetown, Rhode Island, and Emma Linwood Paine. He had two sisters. He endured numerous childhood illnesses but excelled in his school, with a particularly strong aptitude for mathematics. Bush's strong-willed, self-confident personality emerged at an early age and would become a recognized character trait throughout his life and career. He came from a long line of sea captains, which he sometimes credited for his leadership abilities.

Bush attended Tufts College in Massachusetts on a partial scholarship, working as a mathematics tutor

Vannevar Bush.

and assistant to cover the remainder of his educational expenses. He earned both his bachelor of science and master of science degrees in engineering by 1913. Bush was credited with his first invention while pursuing his master's at Tufts. The "profile tracer" was a land-surveying device that could automatically calculate and map land elevations and measure distances on uneven terrain. Bush believed that the profile tracer's commercial failure taught him the importance of the political side of the scientific and business worlds.

Bush was first employed in the test department at General Electric. He was laid off shortly after beginning work, however, because of a plant fire. In 1914, he briefly taught mathematics at Clark University in Massachusetts, where he was offered a 1915 doctoral fellowship to study acoustics with renowned professor Arthur Webster. He instead left for the MIT, where he was free to choose his field of specialization. He was awarded Ph.D.s in engineering from both Harvard and MIT in 1916.

Life's Work

Bush returned to Tufts as an assistant professor of electrical engineering after earning his Ph.D.s, remaining until 1919. He became interested in the role of the scientific community in the national war effort after the United States entered World War I in 1917. Like-minded scientists had formed the National Research Council (NRC) in 1916 to further the development of military technology. Bush presented the NRC with an initially well-received plan for a magnetic field-based submarine detector. The U.S. Navy successfully tested Bush's submarine detector, but its failure in actual use, combined with Bush's controlling personality and lack of political skills, ultimately led to the abandonment of the project. During his early career, Bush also helped found what became Raytheon Corporation in 1922.

Bush left his teaching position at Tufts after a short stay to join the faculty of the Department of Electrical Engineering at MIT in 1919, rising to dean of engineering and vice president in 1932. He would remain at MIT for twenty-five years. While there, he developed and built one of the most successful differential analyzers, a machine capable of solving differential equations, by 1931. The prestigious Rockefeller Foundation had provided the funding. He patented the Rockefeller differential analyzer in 1935, and the U.S. military would later use it to calculate its ballistics tables during World War II.

Bush's most pioneering work at MIT involved analog computers. These large machines, the forerunners of electronic digital computers, relied on mechanical parts to perform calculations. While at MIT, Bush also became interested in the potential for machines to process and store large amounts of information. He envisioned a machine called a rapid selector that could store, quickly retrieve, and project information on microfilm. Although several rapid selectors were built at MIT in the mid- to late 1930s, technical problems prevented their successful use. The digital computers developed in the 1940s would replace analog computers.

Bush left MIT to become president of the Carnegie Institution, a position he held from 1939 to 1955. The position provided him with prestige, funding, and an informal scientific advisory role with the U.S. government. In 1940, Bush won approval from President Franklin Roosevelt to form the National Defense Research Committee (NDRC). The NDRC was a cooperative measure between science, government, military, and business leaders on an unprecedented scale. Bush served as NDRC chairman. He then became director of the Office of Scientific Research and Development (OSRD) in 1941, which absorbed the NDRC. Both organizations sought to increase U.S. military preparedness after the outbreak of World War II.

MIT established its prominent role in government-funded scientific research through Bush's association with both MIT and the OSRD, a connection that would continue long after Bush's leadership. The OSRD introduced improved microwave-based radar systems, the proximity fuse, and new tactics deployed against submarines; it was also involved in the secret Manhattan Project, which developed the first atomic bomb.

Bush presented his position in favor of permanent government involvement in scientific research in a 1944 report entitled *Science, the Endless Frontier*. His report is credited as one of the primary motivations for the 1950 establishment of the National Science Foundation. Bush would later be recognized as one of the creators of the modern military-industrial complex that emerged in the postwar period, although he had personally become concerned with the militarization of science.

Bush's best-known publication was the article "As We May Think," which originally appeared in the *Atlantic Monthly* magazine in 1945 but has been reprinted numerous times. The article contained a description of a hypothetical machine, called a memex, that would allow rapid processing of large amounts of information. The automation of human memory was a field Bush felt was being overlooked by the scientists of his day. Other devices described in the article included a Cyclops Camera, worn on the forehead; a Vocoder, which would type the spoken word; and a thinking machine, which worked in a way similar to the modern calculator.

Bush's theoretical memex represented the potential next step to follow his earlier work with the differential analyzer, an early version of a computer designed to augment human memory. It included a desk, keyboard, and microfilm storage unit and was operated with buttons and levers. It had the capacity to store documents on microfilm and easily retrieve them later through the utilization of associative links, which Bush termed associative trails. The retrieved information was then displayed on screens. Many later pioneers of the digital

Affiliation: Massachusetts Institute of Technology

The Massachusetts Institute of Technology (MIT) traces its history back to the 1861 approval of natural scientist William Barton Rogers's 1859 charter to found the Massachusetts Institute of Technology and Boston Society of Natural History. The institute's philosophy centered on useful knowledge, practical experience, and the integration of the professional and liberal arts at the undergraduate level.

The first classes were held in a rented space in the city of Boston. The Boston Technology building was completed in the city's Back Bay neighborhood in 1866, but the Institute soon outgrew its facilities. Kodak founder George Eastman anonymously awarded the institute a sizable donation, which was used to purchase land in Cambridge adjacent to the Charles River. The new facility, designed by William Welles Bosworth, opened in 1916.

During World War II, MIT gained renown for its prominent role in defense-related research. Then MIT vice president Vannevar Bush was also the head of the U.S. Office of Scientific Research and Development. MIT's notable products for the U.S. military included the development of the first real-time digital computer, the first electronic navigation system, the electronic air defense system known as the Semi-Automatic Ground Environment (SAGE) through Project Whirlwind, and the long-range navigation system (LORAN). After the war, MIT continued its prominent connection to the military-industrial complex through its work within Cold War military technology and the space race. MIT has maintained its reputation as one of the country's leading institutionso of higher education in the fields of science, technology, and engineering.

computer and information age cited Bush as one of the main influences on their work, including Ted Nelson, who coined the word *hypertext*.

PERSONAL LIFE

Bush served on the board of directors of several companies in his later career, including AT&T. He also served as chairman of the MIT Corporation from 1957 to 1959 and as honorary chairman from 1959 to 1971. He was granted numerous honorary degrees from universities, including Columbia, Princeton, Yale, and Johns Hopkins. He held honorary degrees from Cambridge and Trinity College and was dubbed a Knight Commander of the civilian division of the Most Excellent Order of the British Empire in 1948.

In addition to these honors, Bush received numerous awards, including the Franklin Institute's Louis Edward Levy Medal (1928), the American Society of Mechanical Engineers' Holley Medal (1943), the Roosevelt Memorial Association's Distinguished Service Medal (1945), the National Academy of Sciences' Marcellus Hartley Public Welfare Medal (1945), the Hoover Medal (1946), the National Medal of Merit (1948), the Medal of the Industrial Research Institute (1949), and the National Medal of Science (1964).

Bush married Phoebe Davis on September 5, 1916. The couple had two sons, Richard Davis Bush and John Hathaway Bush. Vannevar Bush died on June 28, 1974. Technological developments since his death, including the global popularization of the Internet, have solidified his place as a visionary in computer science and information technology.

Marcella Bush Trevino

FURTHER READING

Bush, Vannevar. *Science: The Endless Frontier*. Washington, DC: US GPO, 1945. Charleston: NABU, 2011. E-book. Bush's classic treatise detailing his belief in the need for continued federal government funding of scientific research in the post–World War II era.

Bush, Vannevar, James M. Nyce, and Paul Kahn. *From Memex to Hypertext: Vannevar Bush and the Mind's Machine*. Boston: Academic, 1991. Print. A collection of Bush's lifetime writings on the memex as well as discussions from leading historians and computer science researchers tracing the development and impact of his work.

Greenberg, Daniel S. "Vannevar Bush and the Myth of Creation." In *Science, Money, and Politics: Political Triumph and Ethical Erosion*. Chicago: U of Chicago P, 2001. Print. Greenberg discusses Bush's role in U.S. government funding of scientific research within a larger discussion of the influence of politics and special interests on the field.

Mahoney, Matt. "77 Years Ago in TR Future Perfect Vannevar Bush Gave Depression-Era Readers a Preview of Future Technologies." *Technology Review* Dec. 2010: 96. Print. Discusses Bush's writings of future technology and their relation to the technological developments of the decades that followed his work.

Zachary, G. Pascal. *Endless Frontier: Vannevar Bush, Engineer of the American Century*. Cambridge: MIT, 1999. Print. Classic biography that covers Bush's life, education, career, writings, and impact, including his 1945 *Atlantic Monthly* article "As We May Think."

NOLAN BUSHNELL

Cofounder of Atari

Born: February 5, 1943; Clearfield, Utah
Died: -
Primary Field: Business and commerce
Specialty: Management, executives, and investors
Primary Company/Organization: Atari

INTRODUCTION

Legendary entrepreneur Nolan Bushnell has been involved in the computer industry since its advent, working to produce hardware, software, and games that have proven highly popular over time. Bushnell has also served as a mentor, consultant, and guiding force to many young entrepreneurs, making him highly influential in several generations of technology, restaurant, and gaming pioneers. As someone who has initiated more than twenty start-up businesses, Bushnell has been one of the foremost innovators and visionaries of his generation.

EARLY LIFE

Nolan Key Bushnell was born on February 5, 1943, in Clearfield, Utah, located near Ogden. His family, which included three sisters, were members of the Church of Jesus Christ of Latter-day Saints. Bushnell's father ran a family-owned concrete business. When Bushnell was in the third grade, his teacher assigned him a unit on electricity. This so excited him that he experimented with various lamps and small appliances at home and then decided that he wanted to be an engineer. Bushnell eventually assumed the management of this business when his father died when Nolan was fifteen; he also enrolled at Utah State University in Logan, Utah. Bushnell soon transferred to the University of Utah in Salt Lake City, where he studied at its College of Engineering. He graduated with a degree in electrical engineering in 1968. While a student at Utah, Bushnell was a member of the social fraternity Pi Kappa Alpha.

From the age of nineteen and continuing throughout college, Bushnell had a summer job working at Lagoon Amusement Park in Farmington, Utah. He was especially fond of working on the park's midway arcade, where a variety of games were available to customers who wished to try their luck at winning a prize. After several years working at Lagoon Amusement

Nolan Key Bushnell.

Park, Bushnell was promoted to a supervisory position in the games section of the park. While enrolled at Utah, Bushnell had access to the university's Digital Equipment Corporation (DEC) PDP-1 computer. Using the PDP-1, he began playing *Spacewar!,* one of the earliest computer games, devised by students at the Massachusetts Institute of Technology (MIT). *Spacewar!* is played with two participants, each of whom controls a spaceship and tries to destroy the other. The University of Utah then boasted one of the pioneering computer science departments in the United States, and its students' expertise in designing computer graphics led to a variety of *Spacewar!* imitators, including Bushnell.

LIFE'S WORK

Upon graduating from the University of Utah, Bushnell and his friend Ted Dabney began working for Nutting Associates, an early manufacturer of coin-operated arcade games. While at Nutting, Bushnell and Dabney worked to design a clone of *Spacewar!* that they would try to make commercially available to arcades. By 1971, Nutting was producing its product, *Computer Space,* which ultimately was a commercial failure because it was technically too complex to be produced using the technology available during the early 1970s. Despite this, *Computer Space* set many precedents that influenced the industry for decades to come. The game was coin-operated and available only on a machine that was dedicated to providing that gaming experience to users. During the development of *Computer Space,* Bushnell and Dabney worked repairing broken pinball games in order to generate money to keep their project afloat. Although it generated sales of more than $3 million and sold between five hundred and one thousand units, Computer Space was unable to sustain itself; Bushnell blamed Nutting Associates for not promoting it well. Bushnell determined that although it had been poorly implemented, his concept for video games was sound.

Bushnell and Dabney next formed Syzygy Engineering to produce their own video games. Initially Syzygy planned to produce a driving game, but Bushnell decided that would be too complicated for their limited resources. In early 1972, Bushnell had seen a demonstration of the Magnavox Odyssey, the first video game console available for home use. The Odyssey had contained a tennis game, and Bushnell decided that Syzygy would produce an arcade version of a tennis game named *Pong*. While the machine was in development, Bushnell received a cease-and-desist letter informing him that the name Syzygy was already in use by a California corporation. Needing to change the company's name, Bushnell decided on the term *atari*, which came from the Chinese game Go. Syzygy was rebranded Atari, Inc., just in time for the launch of *Pong*. After piloting the machine in a Sunnyvale, California, bar, where customers lined up to play the game, Bushnell realized he had a hit. After Nutting Associates declined an offer to produce *Pong*, Bushnell decided that Atari would produce the game itself. Atari was almost instantly successful as a company that designed and produced arcade games, and it produced a variety of other successful games, including *Space Race, Rebound, Gotcha, QuadraPong, Tank,* and *Gran Trak 10.*

By 1975, Bushnell was working on a game console that, hooked up to a television, could replicate the Atari arcade game experience at home. Similar to the problems with *Computer Space*, the main problem was that the available technology was not adequate to support the product he envisioned. This changed when MOS Technology, Inc., introduced the MOS Technology 6502, an 8-bit microprocessor that was powerful

---

Affiliation: Atari

At the time Bushnell founded the company that would become Atari, his ideas were more advanced than the available technology of the day could support. As more advanced, less expensive, and smaller microprocessors were developed, however, Atari was able to place its coin-operated machines in stores, restaurants, bars, and arcades, where they proved phenomenally successful. As available technology continued to improve, Atari was able to offer the Atari 2600, a home console that permitted its arcade games to be played on a television. Wildly successful, the Atari 2600 sold millions of units.

Although Bushnell sold Atari to Warner Communications in 1976, he remained at the company for several more years. During this time he helped develop the Atari 800/400, a home computer that also permitted games to be played from it. After Bushnell left Atari in 1979, it struggled with the downturn in video game sales that occurred in 1983. Warner Communications sold Atari to the founder of Commodore International in 1984, where it operated successfully as Atari Corporation for the rest of the decade. The arcade games division, which Warner Communications had retained, was sold in 1985 to Namco Ltd., a Japanese game developer.

---

enough to provide a good gaming experience yet inexpensive enough to be practicable. Bushnell proceeded with the Atari 2600, a revolutionary machine at the time. In 1976, Bushnell was approached by Warner Communications, Inc., which offered to purchase Atari for $30 million. Although Bushnell was confident that the then-unreleased Atari 2600 would be successful, he accepted the offer and agreed to stay on at Atari. The Atari 2600 proved to be one of the most successful game consoles ever released upon its debut the following year. Bushnell next began the development of the Atari 800, an 8-bit home computer that would compete with the Apple II, the Commodore PET, and the Atari 400, a lower-powered version. Although the Atari 800/400 was designed to replace the Atari 2600, it also had a keyboard and a proprietary disk operating system (DOS) that featured a drop-down menu that was quite advanced for the time. While the Atari 800/400 was highly successful upon its release in 1979, selling more than 4 million units over the next five years, Bushnell left the company the same year and company infighting led to Atari's contraction and ultimate sale to Jack Tramiel, the founder of Commodore International.

In 1977, Bushnell had purchased Pizza-Time Theater from Warner, which had originally been conceptualized as a place where children could play video games while eating pizza. After leaving Atari Bushnell refined the concept, renaming it Chuck E. Cheese's Pizza-Time Theater, with an animatronic show and rides added. Although the enterprise was very successful, Bushnell turned over its operations to a new hire with extensive restaurant experience.

Bushnell next focused on his newest venture, Catalyst Technologies Venture Capital Group, one of the first business incubators designed to help new technology businesses get started. Although Catalyst had shut down most services by 1986, it nurtured several innovative firms and served as a model for future business incubators. Bushnell invested in Sente Technologies, an arcade game producer founded by former Atari workers. He later purchased Sente and used it to supply his Pizza-Time Theater stores with games, until in turn selling Sente to Bally Manufacturing Corporation, the parent of Bally-Midway.

During the 1990s, Bushnell became involved with a small game developer as a consultant. Later he worked with uWink, the developer of bistro software, and, after that, a small California restaurant chain that combined food with entertainment: Using touch screens, customers could both place their orders and play games while they waited for their food to arrive. Although none of these endeavors proved as successful as Atari or Pizza-Time Theater, they were innovative and received a certain amount of positive publicity. In 2010, Bushnell was named to the Atari board of directors. He remains involved in the industry with a software company, Brainrush, and its antiaging games, which provide on-line games that are intended to assist users in improving concentration, focus, and memory.

PERSONAL LIFE

Although raised in a Mormon household, Bushnell considers himself a former member of the church. He married Paula Rochelle Nelson in 1966; the couple had two daughters and a son, but the marriage ultimately ended in divorce. Bushnell later remarried; with his second wife, Nancy, he would have five children. Bushnell has stated that he has enjoyed tinkering with electronic devices since he childhood and claims that as a youngster he nearly burned down his parents' garage during one of his "experiments." He enjoys a variety of hobbies, including games such as Go (either in its original format or on a computer), and he played tournament-level chess while enrolled in college. Recently, Bushnell has learned to rollerblade and snowboard.

Upon his sale of Atari to Warner Communications, Bushnell purchased the Folger mansion in Woodside, California, which sat on sixteen acres of land. Bushnell eventually settled in Los Angeles, where he owns a boat he has named *Charlie*, which was his father's name. Although known for being gregarious, Bushnell draws a great deal of inspiration from solitude, which he finds in his "cave," a converted garage that is a combination office, library, and workshop. In honor of his many contributions to a variety of fields, Bushnell has been inducted into the Video Game Hall of Fame and the Consumer Electronics Association Hall of Fame. He has also received the British Academy of Film and Television Arts (BAFTA) fellowship in recognition of his pioneering role in the video games industry and was recognized by *Newsweek* magazine as one of fifty individuals who changed America.

Stephen T. Schroth and Jason A. Helfer

FURTHER READING

Bagnall, B. *Commodore: A Company on the Edge*. 2nd ed. Winnipeg: Variant, 2010. Print. Account of how the superior programming of Atari and Commodore computers failed to result in the expected market success because of high turnover and poor decisions.

Bissell, T. *Extra Lives: Why Video Games Matter*. New York: Vintage, 2010. Print. Explores the popularity of video games, investigating the aesthetic and psychological appeal of many of the most popular games.

Cohen, S. *Zap: The Rise and Fall of Atari*. New York: McGraw-Hill, 1987. Print. An appraisal of Atari's journey from Bushnell's start-up and its evolution to a $2 billion corporation within the span of a decade and its subsequent decline.

Donovan, T. *Replay: The History of Video Games*. Lewes: Yellow Ant, 2010. Print. Looks at the commercial processes that transformed the video game from a diversion created by technophiles to a multibillion-dollar business run by multinational corporations.

Kent, S. L. *The Ultimate History of Video Games: From Pong to Pokemon—The Story Behind the Craze That Touched Our Lives and Saved the World*. New York: Three Rivers, 2001. Print. Examines the founding of the video game industry, led by Bushnell's *Pong*, and how it has evolved over time.

C

ROD CANION

Cofounder and former CEO of Compaq

Born: January 19, 1945; Houston, Texas
Died: -
Primary Field: Computer science
Specialty: Computer hardware
Primary Company/Organization: Compaq

INTRODUCTION

Trained as an electrical engineer and known for his soft voice, khakis, and sports shirts, Texan Rod Canion has spent much of his life defining new technologies. As a cofounder and the first chief executive officer (CEO) of the Compaq Computer Corporation, Canion led the company in breaking records during the early days of the computer revolution in the late twentieth century. Under his guidance, Compaq rose to become one of the most trusted names in home computing. The company initiated the trend in cloning the personal computer (PC) and originated the first "luggable" computer by removing the boundaries that restricted computer use to offices, allowing users to work while at home or traveling. During his time with the company, Compaq broke a number of records and set high standards for the technology companies that followed it. After being fired from the company in 1991, Canion created a new company in partnership with his old friend and Compaq cofounder Jim Harris.

EARLY LIFE

Joseph "Rod" Canion was born on January 19, 1945, three months before the end of World War II. Thus, he grew up in a rapidly changing world that ultimately saw the technology revolution of the late twentieth and early twenty-first centuries. Canion developed a love of tinkering as a child, and he spent much of his teen years building hot rods. Canion spent most of his early life in Houston, Texas, and he received a bachelor's degree in science from the University of Houston in 1966. Two years later, he completed his master's degree in electrical engineering with an emphasis on computer science at the same institution. After graduating from college, Canion moved to Dallas to work for Texas Instruments,

Rod Canion.

which was generating cutting-edge technology at the time. For this reason, Texas Instruments was widely known as the "electronics Titan."

Canion's work ethic was formed during his early years at Texas Instruments. While there, he worked with James (Jim) M. Harris, a fellow engineer, and William (Bill) H. Murto, a vice president of sales, and the three became fast friends. Except for a brief period when Canion was lured away from Texas Instruments with the promise of better compensation, he spent thirteen years on his first job.

LIFE'S WORK

In the early 1980s, Canion designed an IBM clone, inviting Harris and Murto to work with him on turning the design into a model. In 1982, the three friends established Gateway Technologies, financing their initial efforts through an investment of $1,000 each. Their plan was to form a company that would build hard drives and peripherals, and none of them was really interested in building entire computers. However, financier Ben Rosen was convinced that their PC clone was capable of rivaling IBM's PC, and he persuaded them to manufacture computers. After investing heavily in the company that had become Compaq Computer Corporation, Rosen agreed to serve as chairman of the board of the new company.

The Compaq Computer Corporation was officially founded in 1982 by Canion, Harris, and Murto. The fortune of the company was initially tied to a single computer, which weighed 28 pounds and was roughly the size of a large briefcase or a small suitcase. The first Compaq computer ran the MS-DOS operating system as developed by Bill Gates and Paul Allen of Microsoft. Sporting a nine-inch screen and a folding keyboard, it was dubbed a "luggable" computer. Some reviews of the computer suggested that it was a viable companion to the IBM office computer rather than a rival product. Compaq promoted the model as both more powerful and more versatile than the IBM PC.

Canion raised $25 million in venture capital and decided that it was in Compaq's best interests to sell through dealers rather than directly to customers. Upon becoming Compaq's first CEO, Canion devised a savvy financial strategy that emphasized marketing of the product. He launched a series of television commercials hawking the Compaq computer. During its first year in business, Compaq shipped fifty-three thousand personal computers to consumers. Canion led the company to becoming the first in American history to generate more than $100 million in sales during its first year of operation. Under his guidance, Compaq subsequently rose to Fortune 500 status faster than any company had ever done, went public faster than any other company, and became the first American company to reach $1 billion in sales.

Eschewing competitiveness within the company, as CEO of Compaq Canion chose to emphasize consensus building and was adamant about maintaining the small-company atmosphere as Compaq continued to expand. He instituted the practice of holding quarterly meetings at a local church in Houston that lasted for four days. Canion's purpose was to promote a sense of both personal and combined responsibility for the company's success. As Compaq's fortunes continued to rise, Canion's personal lifestyle appeared to be little affected by the company's enormous success. Alison S. Weintraub of *Inter@ctive Week* reported that

---

Affiliation: Compaq

Started in 1982 and offering only one computer model, Compaq quickly became a name to be reckoned with in the emerging computer industry. It was outranked only by the industry giant, IBM. The following year, Compaq went public, raising $67 million. The lion's share of the money raised was poured back into the company. During its second year, Compaq shipped 150,000 units to dealers and generated profits of $329 million.

By the mid-1980s, computer prices were beginning to drop in the United States with the introduction of PC "clones" made of cheaper Asian models and components. Some American companies opted to reduce quality to remain competitive, but Rod Canion refused to allow Compaq to follow the trend. The wisdom of that decision was demonstrated by increasing sales, which rose to $503 million in 1985. The following year, Compaq was designated as a Fortune 500 company. In 1987, Compaq reported $1 billion in sales, and its sales doubled in 1988.

Over the next few years, the market for laptop computers continued to expand, and Compaq introduced its first traditional laptop in October 1988. Subsequently, Compaq rose to second place in the laptop market, outranked only by the Japan-based Toshiba. By 1989, global sales had climbed to $3 billion. Canion was forced out of the company in 1991. In 2002, Compaq was merged into Hewlett-Packard, which had been founded by William Hewlett and David Packard in 1939. Hewlett-Packard continues to sell the Compaq Presario.

---

he continued to drive a Chevy Blazer, wear a $29 Casio watch, and use a 29-cent Bic pen.

By 1983, Compaq was being publicly traded, and Canion poured much of the money raised back into the company. It was then that Compaq began manufacturing its first desktop computer. Within a year, Compaq had begun marketing a Desk Pro model that used Intel's 8086 chip. By December, Compaq had shipped out 150,000 units and had generated $329 million in annual sales. By 1987, Compaq had reached the billion-dollar mark. Over the course of the next three years, Compaq became the first company to sell a 386 PC and the first to offer a 20-megahertz machine. Joining the laptop market in 1988, Compaq was generating sales of more than $3 billion by 1989.

However, 1991 brought a reversal of fortune. Other dealers began opting to sell directly to customers. At the same time, a recession hit the United States, and foreign sales began to slide. For the first time in its history, Compaq reported a loss. Admitting that losses had risen to approximately $71 million, the company was forced to lay off fourteen hundred workers.

Amid mounting rumors of internal strife at Compaq, reports surfaced that Canion and Rosen were arguing about the advisability of moving Compaq operations overseas to save on production costs. Allegedly, Rosen supported the move while Canion opposed it. Despite the fact that Canion considered him a close friend and mentor, Rosen forced him out of the company that he had cofounded, setting him adrift. Murto had already left the company in 1987 to produce religious films, but Harris, who was serving as vice president of engineering, handed in his resignation and opted to continue to work with Canion rather than remain with Compaq.

Canion benefited financially from his dismissal from Compaq, receiving a $3 million severance package and selling off $10 million in Compaq stock. He later noted that he spent the next few months with his family considering his options for the future.

In 1992, Canion and Harris founded Insource Technology, a consulting firm that specialized in providing services in the fields of finance, technology, and the Internet. Their contracts with Compaq prevented competing with their former employer by manufacturing computers. By the twenty-first century, Insource was recording $20 million in revenue and a 49 percent compound annual growth rate. Even while continuing his ties with Insource, Canion took on new challenges by investing in new technology companies and becoming involved in making them successful.

In 1998, Canion signed on as an executive with Tricord Systems and led the company in developing computer storage devices. That year, Canion invested in GK Intelligent, a company involved in using artificial intelligence to develop a web-based training program for businesses. He abruptly left the company when rumors of illegal financial dealings emerged, refusing to become involved in illegal activities. The executives he had brought with him to Tricord also left the company.

In 1999, Canion decided to invest in the start-up Questia Media after hearing its young founder, Troy Williams, and becoming enthusiastic about the concept of facilitating online research for college students. Canion and Harris each invested $400,000 in the company, and Canion agreed to serve as chairman of the board. By 2001, Questia's employee base had swelled to 145 employees.

Personal Life

Canion married, but he and his wife were divorced in 1987. He was remarried, to a real estate broker, the following year. Together, Canion and his second wife had two sons and three daughters.

Canion has repeatedly been recognized for his contributions to technological innovation. In 1988, he was named Houston's International Executive of the Year and was designated as the CEO of the decade by Financial News Net. He also received awards from the University of Texas and Southern Methodist University. Canion has served on the boards of a number of companies, including AMVESCAP, Blue Arc, YoungLife, and Health, Inc. He also serves on the board of advisers for Sternhill Partners and is director emeritus of the Houston Technology Center. He continues to pursue his passion for flying.

Elizabeth Rholetter Purdy

Further Reading

Bridges, Linda. "The 15 Most Influential." *PC Week* 16.9 (1999): 69–72. Print. Profiles Canion as one of the most influential people involved in the development of the computer industry.

Canion, Rod. "Consensus, Continuity, and Common Sense: An Interview with Compaq's Rod Canion." Interview by Alan M. Webber. *Harvard Business Review* 68 (1990): 114–23. Print. Canion traces the rise of Compaq and discusses leadership of the company.

Ceruzzi, Paul E. *Computing: A Concise History*. Cambridge: MIT, 2012. Print. Part of MIT's Essential

Knowledge Series, this volume examines the development of the computer industry. Illustrated.

Jones, Kathryn. "Rod Canion." *Texas Monthly* 29.9 (2001): 76–103. Print. Examines the creation of Compaq Computer Corporation, with a focus on Canion's role in the company's success.

"Joseph R. 'Rod' Canion." *Entrepreneur* 10 Oct. 2008; n. pag. Print. Profile of Canion.

McWilliams, Gary. "Is Something Fishy at GK Intelligent?" *Business Week* 3595 (1998): n. pag. Print. Brief look at Canion's distancing himself from suspected misdealings at GK Intelligent.

Weintraub, Alison S. "Flying with New Ventures." *Inter@ctive Week* 7.38 (2000): n. pag. Print. This profile emphasizes Canion's life after he left Compaq.

SAFRA A. CATZ

President, CFO, and board member of Oracle

Born: December 13, 1961; Holon, Israel
Died: -
Primary Field: Business and commerce
Specialty: Management, executives, and investors
Primary Company/Organization: Oracle

INTRODUCTION

Safra A. Catz became president of Oracle Corporation, an enterprise software company, in 2004. In 2011, for the second time, she was named the company's chief financial officer as well. Generally considered the person most responsible for Oracle's financial performance, she became a member of the firm's board of directors in 2001. In 2008, she became a member of the board of directors for HSBC Holdings plc, one of the world's largest banking and financial services organizations. Fortune *magazine ranked her the eleventh most powerful woman in business in 2011, and* Time *included her on its 2012 list of the ten most influential women in technology. With total compensation in 2011 of more than $42 million, she topped* Fortune*'s list of the highest-paid women in business for that year.*

EARLY LIFE

Safra Ada Catz was born in Holon, Israel, on December 13, 1961, the elder of two daughters born to Leonard Catz, a nuclear physicist, and his wife, Judith, a speech therapist and a Holocaust survivor. Leonard fought in the Six-Day War in June 1967; Judith and the couple's young daughters took refuge in an air-raid shelter. The Catz family immigrated to the United States the same year. Safra was six. Her father accepted a position with the physics department at the Massachusetts Institute of Technology, and her mother worked in the Boston public school system. Catz graduated from Brookline High School, a public high school in Brookline, Massachusetts. She attended the University of Pennsylvania, where she was on the school's fencing team. In 1983, she graduated from the Wharton School of the University of Pennsylvania with a B.A. in business. She remained at the University of Pennsylvania to attend law school, transferring to Harvard University for her final year. She received a J.D. degree from the University of Pennsylvania's law school in 1986.

Safra A. Catz.

That year, in what Catz terms the best decision she ever made, she bypassed practicing law and chose instead to accept a job with Donaldson, Lufkin and Jenrette, a global investment bank, which later merged with Credit Suisse First Boston. She represented clients such as Softbank, Symantec, and Oracle. She was not immediately recognized as one of the rising stars in investment banking, but she established a reputation for a willingness to work hard, a strong commitment to her clients, and persistence that was sometimes interpreted as pushiness. By 1994, she was a senior vice president, and in 1997, she became managing director, a position she held until she left the company in 1999.

LIFE'S WORK

Recruited by Larry Ellison, Oracle's colorful chief executive officer (CEO), Catz, who was looking to cut back on the travel her work with Donaldson, Lufkin and Jenrette required, joined Oracle in April 1999 as senior vice president. Within months, she was named an executive vice president. An admitted numbers cruncher, Catz was concerned about Oracle's stalled margins. She thought the company was too fragmented and set about centralizing control. With little patience for those who were more interested in protecting their turf than in the company's welfare, she eliminated those unwilling to accept new policies. By the end of her first year at Oracle, the company had cut $1.2 billion from its operating expenses. Margins increased from 22 percent to 35 percent over the next year, and the increase continued climbing for the rest of the decade. In 2001, she was named to the board of directors, an indication of how quickly she had become a powerful player at Oracle.

On June 6, 2003, with Catz directing the moves, Oracle announced a takeover bid to acquire PeopleSoft, a human resources and business applications software company. Four days earlier, the acquisition of the J. D. Edwards Company made PeopleSoft the second-largest enterprise application software vendor. On June 13, PeopleSoft filed a lawsuit to block Oracle's takeover bid and claimed that Oracle had engaged in unfair trade practices. On January 12, 2004, Catz and Charles Phillips were named copresidents of Oracle. Almost exactly a month later, the U.S. Justice Department notified Oracle and PeopleSoft that the department's lawyers had recommended blocking the takeover on antitrust grounds. On February 26, 2004, the Department of Justice, joined by seven states, filed suit to block the takeover on antitrust grounds. Oracle rejected the usual response to the government's decision to block the

takeover. Rather than withdrawing, the company prepared to fight. As Oracle's manager of mergers and acquisitions strategy, Catz devoted much of her time to the case. In September 2004, a federal judge, Vaughn R. Walker, ruled in favor of Oracle, stating that the plaintiffs had failed to prove that the merger violated antitrust laws. A month later the decision was echoed in one from the European Commission. In December 2004, after an eighteen-month battle, Oracle announced that it had signed a definitive merger agreement to acquire PeopleSoft for approximately $10.3 billion. Oracle CEO Ellison praised Catz for overseeing the takeover from initial idea to final purchase.

Over the next six years, with Catz continuing as chief strategist for mergers and acquisitions, Oracle completed more than eighty acquisitions valued at more than $43 billion. It was her push to grow the company's hardware business that led to the purchase of Sun Microsystems in 2009. Within Oracle, she is known as the enforcer and gatekeeper of Ellison's ideas and the executive Ellison is most likely to heed. In addition to serving as copresident, she assumed the role of chief financial officer (CFO) in April 2011, a position she had also held concurrently with her copresidency from 2005 to 2008. The promotion to CFO placed her in an elite company. Less than 10 percent of Fortune 500 companies have a woman in the CFO position. In June 2011, Catz reported the company's first $10 billion quarter.

When rumors that Oracle executive vice president Keith Block, head of North American sales since 2002, would be pushed out (following the disclosure of e-mail messages in which he savagely criticized Oracle's purchase of Sun and the management decisions of copresident Mark Hurd) sent the value of Oracle shares down, it was Catz, as CFO, who responded with a surprising early announcement that Oracle had an increase in net income that exceeded analysts' predictions. Almost immediately, the price of Oracle shares not only recovered but also rose by almost 3 percent.

Ellison on several occasions suggested that Catz is heir apparent to his office, but Catz herself persistently denied any desire to become CEO, evidently committed to her role as chief strategist in Oracle's aggressive efforts to consolidate the software industry, a move she and Ellison agree is inevitable. Oracle has the reputation of eliminating executives who become too ambitious. Catz has outlasted a number of Oracle executives who may have harbored thoughts of becoming CEO. Intensely private by all accounts, she shuns the media spotlight, deflecting attention to Ellison. Insiders

Affiliation: Oracle

Oracle Corporation, based in Redwood City, California, is one of the world's largest software companies. The company was founded in 1977 by Lawrence J. Ellison, who created a prototype of a relational database and sold the idea to the Central Intelligence Agency. Adopting the name Oracle, Ellison went on to make sales to Navy Intelligence and the National Security Agency. In 1986, Oracle went public. The company suffered a severe blow in the early 1990s, when a reputation for selling software before it was ready to be released and poor customer service led to a $36 million loss and a domestic workforce reduction of 10 percent.

Ray Lane joined the company in 1992, first as a consultant and later as president. He focused on restructuring and increasing sales while Ellison led Oracle into Web-based data storage software before Microsoft recognized the potential of the Internet. The move improved the company's profile. A prolonged, hostile takeover of PeopleSoft, a maker of business software, begun in 2003, signaled Oracle's push to become the market leader for software used by corporations. The next nine years saw a frenzy of acquisitions by Oracle, most of them engineered by Safra A. Catz, a company copresident since 2004. The purchase of Sun Microsystems in 2009 positioned Oracle as IBM's chief competitor in the lucrative market for corporate computing.

suggest that regardless of her title, Catz's greatest responsibility is putting in place the policies that Ellison sets. She rarely grants interviews and has been known to resist photo opportunities set up by her own company. Friends and colleagues are reluctant to comment on her.

Catz often hosts political fund-raisers, but she shrewdly does so in a bipartisan manner. She oversees Oracle's philanthropic efforts, and, in a rare moment of personal revelation, admitted at a Women's High-Tech Coalition conference held in May 2005 that women in the business world must be better—more persistent, harder working, and more aggressive than men—in order to succeed. By all accounts, Catz's financial acuity, professional discipline, and assertiveness have made her one of the most successful women in corporate America. Insiders acknowledge that she is a force to be reckoned with and that her day-to-day operational decisions free Ellison to spend a large part of his life away from Oracle's offices. A low profile outside the business, power within it, and compensation that places her among the most highly paid women in the business world appear to be exactly what Catz wants.

PERSONAL LIFE

Catz is married to Gal Tirosh, a soccer coach. They have two sons, Daniel and Jonathan. The family resides in Los Altos, California. Catz has described her husband as secure in his role as primary caretaker for their children, acknowledging that his being on call for their sons has contributed to her success. Her mother, whom Catz called her greatest inspiration, died of breast cancer in 2004. Her father retired from his position as chairman of the Physics Department at the University of Massachusetts–Boston in 2005. Her sister, Sarit, is a stand-up comedian and television writer/producer.

Catz served as a global ambassador for the Susan G. Komen for the Cure foundation in 2009–10. She is also a lecturer at the Stanford Graduate School of Business, teaching a course titled "Mergers and Acquisitions: Accounting, Regulatory, and Governance Issues." She draws on her experience with the merger and acquisitions deals on which she has advised during her more than two decades in business.

Wylene Rholetter

FURTHER READING

Ferguson, Renee Boucher. "What's Next?" *Eweek* 1 Nov. 2004: 20–24. Print. Reports on the decisions of the U.S. Department of Justice and the European Commission that Oracle's proposed hostile takeover of PeopleSoft did not violate fair competition concerns. Also considers the effects of the merger on PeopleSoft's customers. Two color photographs.

Ghaffari, Elizabeth. "Ladder Climbers: The Corporate Path." *Outstanding in Their Field: How Women Corporate Directors Succeed*. Santa Barbara: Praeger/ABC-CLIO, 2009. 165–77. Print. Based on research and interviews, this book looks at how women have attained positions on boards of directors in corporate America. Catz is briefly referenced as one who has skillfully negotiated a difficult path.

Lashinsky, Adam. "The Enforcer." *Fortune* 28 Sept. 2009: 116–24. Print. Profiles Catz, examining her role as president of Oracle and devoting particular attention to her relationship with company founder and CEO Larry Ellison and the strategies that led to her being added to *Fortune*'s annual list of the most powerful women in business.

Pfeffer, Jeffrey. "How—and Why—People Lose Power." *Power: Why Some People Have It—And Others Don't*. New York: HarperCollins, 2010. 198–12. Print. The author, a professor at Stanford, uses examples and research from psychology and other social sciences to examine what separates winners from losers. Catz is one of the examples.

Symonds, Matthew. *Softwar: An Intimate Portrait of Larry Ellison and Oracle*. New York: Simon, 2004. Print. The author, political editor at *The Economist*, provides an authorized, mostly favorable account of Ellison's history with Oracle. Includes frequent references to Catz, particularly in the commentary on Ellison's management style.

John T. Chambers

Chairman and CEO of Cisco

Born: August 23, 1949; Cleveland, Ohio
Died: -
Primary Field: Business and commerce
Specialty: Management, executives, and investors
Primary Company/Organization: Cisco Systems

Introduction

In the dot-com boom of the 1990s, John T. Chambers's effort to grow Cisco by promoting it as an example of e-business led to his being called an Internet evangelist and introduced as "Mr. Internet." Showing how digital technology could help improve productivity and how a company can work effectively with government to provide Internet solutions, Chambers was a visionary of the dot-com era. After the dot-com crash, eyes turned to his leadership at Cisco for guidance on how companies could refocus themselves as customer-centric organizations.

Early Life

John T. Chambers was born to John "Jack" Turner Chambers, an obstetrician/gynecologist, and June Chambers, a psychiatrist, in Cleveland, Ohio. His family moved to Charleston, West Virginia, soon after his birth. Chambers graduated from Charleston High School in 1967.

Chambers studied electrical engineering at Duke University from 1967 to 1968, but he returned to West Virginia without a degree because maintaining a long-distance relationship with his high school sweetheart, Elaine Prater, was too difficult; they would marry four years later. Chambers earned a bachelor of science degree in economics (1971) and a law degree (1974) from West Virginia University, where Elaine was studying to become a speech therapist, and a master's of business administration in 1975 from Indiana University.

Although he had not intended to become a salesperson, an IBM recruiter persuaded him that by working for IBM he would help businesses transform their infrastructure. He accepted the position, and he and Elaine moved to New York. From 1976 to 1982, he sold million-dollar computers for IBM at a time when large, mainframe computers were dominant. In these years before Silicon Valley start-ups, IBM's mission to sell business machines enhanced its sales of computing technology. As smaller companies began to offer personal computers, IBM tried to introduce low-cost, portable computers, and Chambers noted how the traditional company was initially unsuccessful because its business culture could not adapt to changing circumstances.

John T. Chambers.

In 1982, Chambers moved to Lowell, Massachusetts, to work for Wang Laboratories, which had become the leader in office equipment designed for word processing. He started as the vice president for U.S. operations but also worked as senior vice president of America/Asia-Pacific operations. In January 1983, *Time* magazine named the microcomputer the machine of the year, and as these smaller and more versatile machines (soon called personal computers) began to make their way onto desks, the market for Wang's dedicated word processors declined. Mostly because of this change, Wang showed a net loss in 1989, and its other business lines were faltering. Chambers reported that planning the layoffs of five thousand employees made him ill. After founder An Wang's death in 1990, Chambers left the company.

LIFE'S WORK

Chambers's job search led him to contact a former colleague from Wang, who was then head of sales at Cisco. Chambers joined Cisco in January 1991 as senior vice president of worldwide sales and operations, the same year in which Tim Berners-Lee publicly announced his World Wide Web application for making documents sharable over the transmission-control protocol/Internet protocol (TCP/IP) Internet. Three years later, Chambers was promoted to executive vice president, becoming second in command of the business; that year, the first version of a commercial web browser, Netscape Navigator, was released. Chambers was named chief executive officer (CEO) of Cisco in 1995, the same year in which Netscape's profitable initial public offering (IPO) brought public attention to the money being made via Internet start-ups. Chambers took the challenge offered by new media to transform the business.

When Chambers joined Cisco, the company had $70 million in annual revenue and was known for selling routers. When he became president and CEO in 1995, the company was selling $1.2 billion, and he made sure that the company was focused on the customer, not the technology, and engaged in initiatives to reduce the cost of doing business. Chambers insisted that the company should move to a paperless environment because tracking information both on paper and electronically was redundant and digital technology could be used to enhance productivity. In 1994, the company began moving its human resources operations online, creating Cisco Employee Connection. In 1996, the company launched an external website, Cisco Connection Online (CCO), that gave employees, suppliers, and customers access to Cisco's information and systems. The site offered technical documents, allowed users to sign up for seminars, provided information about new products and solutions, and, perhaps most important, took sales orders. Using CCO, a customer could define the solution, price products for it, reach an agreement with suppliers, and receive automated customer support. This service made Cisco a node in a network of various operations.

In fact, it has been claimed that Cisco's extraordinary success in using the Internet to build business-to-business sales led people to say that the rules of conducting the business had changed. Chambers had abandoned the direct sales method, telling people that Cisco went from one thousand to twenty-six thousand employees in ten years by the productivity of digital systems. For those twenty-six thousand people, he

---

Affiliation: Cisco Systems

Cisco is a worldwide leader in networking solutions based in San Jose, California. It was founded in 1984 by a Stanford University couple, Sandy Lerner and Leonard Bosack. They met in graduate school at Stanford University and subsequently worked as managers for computer labs. Although both labs used Ethernet to create a network, each lab used a different kind of computer, so messages could not be sent between them. When a router was designed to negotiate between these networks, Lerner and Bosack decided that the device had commercial potential. They derived the name Cisco from the nearby city of San Francisco, and the company's logo resembles the Golden Gate Bridge. They sold their first routers in 1986 to universities and research centers, and after securing venture capital, the company went public on February 16, 1990. Lerner and Bosack left the company shortly thereafter. James Gillies and Robert Cailliau credit the company for helping introduce transmission-control protocol/Internet protocol (TCP/IP) to Europe: Cisco's routers were "the Trojan horses of the protocol wars" because they supplied translation between the TCP/IP-based Usenet and the networks running X.25 in Europe. One of the consequences of this is that the European Organization for Nuclear Research (CERN) was connected to the TCP/IP Internet, and there a few years later Tim Berners-Lee would develop the World Wide Web application based on TCP/IP protocols.

would report, only two handled travel expenses. He sold his company on the idea that it was a "virtual" global plant, with thirty-two plants worldwide, all enabled by network technology: Most products were made and delivered to customers without a single Cisco person handling the physical product. His products provided his company with better profit margins, and with interactive systems his managers could monitor the business in real time. This provided a compelling case for customers to follow his lead.

Thanks in large part to these systems, Cisco's market value went beyond $450 billion, surpassing Microsoft and GE, and at its height in March 2000, Cisco became the most valuable company in the world at $555 billion, with $906 million in earnings for the second quarter of 2000. Chambers was one of the first to sound the alarm that the dot-com bubble was about to burst when, in January 2001, he announced that corporate spending on information technology was slackening, and in April of that year he cautioned his providers that they would need to change with a changing market. From March 2000 to April 2001, the period known as the dot-com bust or collapse, the company's value decreased by 78 percent, and the company could not unload its inventory, worth $2 billion. As telecommunications companies and Internet service providers ran into financial difficulties, Cisco was hit hard. In March 2001, Chambers had to lay off eight-five hundred employees. Chambers is credited for turning the company around after the dot-com bust, rethinking its product strategies and internal organization so that within two more months, the company's outlook was improving. Cisco recovered more quickly and took the initiative to break into telecommunication equipment as Lucent and Nortel were still recovering. Chambers took a salary of $1 per year until the recovery was evident; he earned $3 this way before the board of directors restored his salary.

In addition to being Cisco's CEO, in November 2006 Chambers was named chairman of the board. Chambers charted a new vision for the company. Until that point, Chambers said, Cisco was operating behind the scenes. He announced in 2007 that the company was done with being only the "plumbers" of the Internet; while he said he was proud to be a plumber—it is great work and earns money—he wanted the company to enter the consumer electronics market. Making the Internet work means helping people share photos, seek medical advice, and stay in touch with friends and families. For businesses, this means connecting people on different continents with video conferencing. In both cases, the goal is to supply the parts of intelligent networks that help people view video, television, and entertainment, wherever they are. This vision seeks to destroy "digital silos," allowing customers to see content anywhere. Also important to the new strategy has been what Chambers calls "spin-ins": In contrast to forming a spin-off company, Cisco gets involved with start-up companies at an early stage, hoping that eventually the group can be brought into Cisco when its technology matures.

As CEO, Chambers has directed Cisco to undertake philanthropic initiatives. In the spring of 2009, for instance, he set up a network for Kosovo refugees, connecting refugee camps to each other and also to the Internet and World Wide Web, helping relatives find one another via a database of people displaced by the conflict. He led the Cisco board to donate $6 million to the September 11 disaster relief fund. He joined a public-private partnership to rebuild health care and education in the Sichuan, China, region after the May 2008 earthquake. He led the 21st Century Schools Initiative to improve education in the Gulf Coast region affected by Hurricane Katrina.

Chambers has received many accolades for his leadership. He was named one of *Time* magazine's 100 Most Influential People and made *Barron's* list of top CEOs in 2008. He was given the first Global Citizen Award by the Clinton Global Initiative in 2007, twice won an award from the U.S. Department of State for corporate responsibility (2005 and 2010), and earned an award for corporate citizenship by the Woodrow Wilson International Center for Scholars of the Smithsonian Institution in 2004.

PERSONAL LIFE

Chambers is married with a son, also named John, and a daughter, Lindsay. A committed member of the Republican Party, in June 2000 he hosted a fund-raiser for the GOP in his Los Altos, California, home and made substantial contributions to the House and Senate GOP campaign funds that year. He was one of the national cochairs of John McCain's campaign in 2008.

Chambers states that the turning point in his career was overcoming dyslexia and getting high grades in high school regardless of that learning disorder. In the 1990s as CEO, he attended a "take your child to work" day and a girl stumbled on her question, stating that she had a learning disability. Coming to her aid, Chambers said that he had one as well, for the first time publicly revealing his dyslexia.

Christopher Leslie

FURTHER READING

Chambers, John T. "The Boss: Speaking Up About Dyslexia." *The New York Times* 16 May 2001: n. pag. Print. Chambers takes a very candid and personal look at what having a learning disability means to him.

Gillies, James, and Robert Cailliau. *How the Web Was Born: The Story of the World Wide Web*. New York: Oxford UP, 2000. N. pag. Print. This examination of the development of the Internet traces the roles played by key individuals, and is by two of them. Includes a time line, a comprehensive bibliography, and an index.

Howcroft, Debra. "After the Goldrush: Deconstructing the Dotcom Market." *Journal of Information Technology* 16 (2001): 195–204. Print. Considers Internet-based enterprises after the dot-com crash, noting that although investors have "almost turned off from funding this sector," it is more interesting to consider why so many investors were drawn it in the first place. Aims to focus on "the concept of business-to-consumer commerce and uses mythology for providing some explanation as to why so many investors were lured into participating in the dot-com share bubble."

Sidhu, Inder. *Doing Both: How Cisco Capture's Today's Profit and Drives Tomorrow's Growth*. Upper Saddle River: FT Press, 2010. Print. Cisco senior vice president Sidhu's explanation of how his company increased revenue, profits, and earnings per share in an unstable global economy.

Waters, John K. *John Chambers and the Cisco Way: Navigating through Volatility*. New York: Wiley, 2002. Print. One of the few volumes that focuses specifically on Chambers and his pioneering company.

TIM COOK

CEO of Apple

Born: November 1, 1960; Robertsdale, Alabama
Died: -
Primary Field: Computer science
Specialty: Computer hardware
Primary Company/Organization: Apple

INTRODUCTION

Tim Cook represents the second generation of leadership in innovative businesses such as Apple and computers in general. After visionaries such as Steve Jobs created a reality to match their visions, people such as Cook—managers and nuts-and-bolts businessmen—transformed the somewhat unstable corporation into a stable venture able to adapt to changing circumstances while holding on to what made the founder's era so distinct. If Jobs and Steve Wozniak were Apple's prophets, Cook became the disciplined leader who preserved the legend.

EARLY LIFE

Tim Cook is the second of three sons of a shipyard worker and a housewife in Robertsdale, Alabama, a farm town near the Gulf Coast. At Robertsdale High School, he was a member of the high school marching band, graduated second in his class, and was voted "most studious." After high school he attended Auburn University, majoring in engineering. His professors recall him as a quiet and reserved student. After graduating from Auburn in 1982, he took a job at IBM in North Carolina. Working days and attending college at night, he earned a master's of business administration degree from Duke University in 1988.

At IBM, Cook developed a reputation for reliability and geniality, volunteering to work over Christmas so the company could fill its orders by the end of the year. He rose to be director of North American fulfillment, with responsibility for manufacturing and distribution of IBM personal computers in the Americas. In 1994, he left IBM for Intelligent Electronics, an electronics wholesaler, starting in the computer reselling division and rising to chief operating officer before Intelligent Electronics was sold to Ingram Micro. He moved to Compaq in 1997. After six months at Compaq, Cook was receptive to recruitment by Apple.

LIFE'S WORK

Apple sales had declined between 1997 and 1998; the company lost $1 billion the year before Cook arrived. When Cook joined Apple, Jobs had recently returned to the company after leaving it for several years, and Apple was renewing itself and consistently becoming more successful. Apple recruited Cook from Compaq

Tim Cook.

in 1998, just as the brightly colored iMac personal computer was revitalizing sales. Jobs had persuaded Cook to ignore those who said Compaq had a brighter future than Apple. Cook signed with Apple as senior vice president of worldwide operations.

Apple was having problems managing the supply chain and inventory. It had more components than it could use, more computers on hand than it could sell quickly. Cook regarded inventory as "fundamentally evil" and believed that it cost money to maintain that instead could be made into profit. He wanted computers as a product to be handled like milk: to flow as directly from the cow as feasible. Therefore, Cook closed warehouses, shrank inventory, and shipped products directly from factory to consumer as often as possible. He reduced inventory from a month's supply to a week's worth, tightened distribution channels, and cut costs markedly.

Cook also had Apple discontinue manufacture of components, relying on external partners instead. By establishing a profitable and tight relationship with eternal makers of components, he had these companies locked into Apple products, which locked out rivals. He began closing factories, cutting inventory, and renegotiating deals with suppliers around the world. He had Apple in the black within a year.

Cook got rid of the manufacturing component of the business, leaving Jobs free to concentrate on the company's strengths: industrial design and software. By fiscal 1999, Apple's gross margins were 28 percent compared to 19 percent in 1997, and the company made a $600 million profit despite continuing declines in sales.

Cook became head of Macintosh in 2004 and led the division through the switch from PowerPC to Intel chips. By using the program Boot Camp to run Windows, Apple attracted millions of computer users who wanted both Windows and a Mac.

In 2007, Cook replaced Jon Rubinstein as chief operating officer. As COO, Cook was responsible for worldwide sales, operations, service, and support and head of the Macintosh division. He did not deal with design, but Apple had Jonathan (Jony) Ive as senior vice president of industrial design, responsible for the iMac, iPod, and many other Apple products.

Cook balanced Jobs. Jobs was the intellectual who lectured Apple devotees on the ways that technology and liberal arts worked together; Cook was the nuts-and-bolts man. Jobs was the public face and had final say on design and positioning of products; Cook ran the company on a day-to-day basis. Thus, Cook was known to be skilled at running the company if not particularly adept at marketing and design.

As head of Macintosh in 2004, Cook for the first time became interim CEO, while Jobs underwent pancreatic surgery and recuperation. Cook was interim CEO again in 2009 during Jobs's liver transplant. By 2009, Cook was member of the board, a key player in Apple's success. He became interim CEO for the third time in 2011, when Jobs went on extended medical leave. Cook's total interim experience was over a year.

When Jobs resigned as CEO and Cook replaced him for the final time, Apple investors remained calm: Both Jobs and Cook were remaining on board, fifty-year-old Cook in the position in which he had served many times before and fifty-six-year-old Jobs as chairman of the board. Insiders figured that Cook was hot property and it was time to give him the title rather than keep him as an "acting" CEO or else run the risk that he would leave Apple—a risk that seemed real when the Apple board of directors began to discuss with recruiters possible successors to Jobs, whose health problems had been acknowledged to be of long duration.

Cook assumed leadership at Apple upon the death of Jobs in October 2011. Although determined to preserve Jobs's legacy at Apple—which had become the world's most creative and valuable company—Cook

Affiliation: Apple

On August 9, 2011, Apple became the world's largest company, surpassing Exxon/Mobil. By then Apple was without founders Steve Jobs and Steve Wozniak. It had Tim Cook, a CEO in the IBM mold. Cook was the sort who sought to fit the product line on a single conference room table. In 1997, Apple was down to two desktops and two portables. The iMac comes in four versions—two screen sizes, two processors—a marked departure from the plethora of PCs offered by Dell, Hewlett-Packard, and other computer companies. Cook is the discipline that holds the line at four rather than scattergunning options at every potential niche market.

Apple is today a hands-on family devoted to the vision of Jobs but efficient in the style of Cook. Jobs argued that the corporation should not be generous but should instead grow, make the employees rich, and give them the opportunity to be philanthropists if they chose. One of Cook's first acts as CEO was to implement corporate matching funds for employee-identified philanthropic opportunities.

quickly proved his ability by making significant changes in policy and direction while maintaining record growth and acknowledging that the excellence of Apple is due to the excellence of its people. He established his leadership style immediately, a style formed in the Apple culture, managing the labyrinthine inner workings of the firm and bringing out new technology and design.

By replacing Jobs with Cook, Apple kept potential competitors from stealing the man who was the natural successor to Jobs, the man who streamlined Apple and allowed delivery of product at lower prices while raising profits. In contrast to the mercurial and demanding Jobs, Cook was calm and undemonstrative, even in tense situations. Over the years, he had developed the ability to figure out what Jobs would do then put that plan into place with solid business principles to make it work. He has prepared for several years for the leadership role at Apple.

Cook works long hours, e-mailing at 4:00 A.M., holding Sunday night conference calls, and chairing long meetings. While Jobs could scream in such situations, Cook can embarrass subordinates by asking questions they cannot answer or presenting toilet plungers to underperforming sales personnel. Reportedly during an early meeting at Apple about problems in China, Cook mentioned that someone should be in China fixing the problem. Half an hour later, he looked at the operations manager and asked why he was still in the meeting. The operations manager was on board next flight to China.

Apple gave Cook nearly $400 million in stock options his first year as CEO, with half vesting in 2016 and the other half in 2021. The options for a million shares appreciated from $376 million upon award to $422 million a year later. Cook also received a 2011 salary of $900,000, an increase from $800,000 in 2010. Jobs was famous for accepting only a token dollar per year, but Jobs had more than 5.5 million shares of Apple stock at his death, whereas Cook had fewer than fourteen thousand—a $6 million asset compared to Jobs's $1 billion. Cook also has stock awards that vested in March 2012 and were valued at $100 million. Even before the new options for ever-more-valuable stock, Cook ranked fifty-eighth on *Forbes'* Most Powerful People list, and expectations were that he would soon be ranked in the *Forbes* 400.

Cook is humble but driven. Expectations are that he will be the caretaker of Apple even if he stays CEO for a decade. He unveiled the updated iPhone on October 4, 2011, the day before Jobs died. He wore jeans, a button-down shirt, and Nike runners (he is on Nike's board of directors). He told a couple of jokes. He did not, however, attempt to mimic Jobs's rousing speeches about how the technology would alter the future. He left the "gee whiz" presentations to other executives. His message was about the company and how he was proud to be a part of it; there would be no cult of personality to replace that of Jobs.

PERSONAL LIFE

Soft-spoken, Cook retains a hint of his southern drawl. Highly ethical, he is noted as calm, thoughtful, and as tough as a particular situation requires. He is disciplined, maintaining a high level of physical activity and long work hours.

Cook is a fitness fanatic, sleeping little, working out a lot, and eating mostly energy bars. His house in Palo Alto is modest, near Apple headquarters, and his vacation preference is hiking or cycling. He admires Robert Kennedy, is a devoted Auburn football fan, and enjoys the music of Bob Dylan. In 2012, he ranked first in Out.com's list of the most powerful lesbian, gay, bisexual, and transgender people.

Cook said in 2004, when Jobs's health problems became public, that Jobs was irreplaceable. Upon Jobs's death, while mourning, he committed to continue building Apple in the spirit of its founder.

John H. Barnhill

FURTHER READING

"Apple CEO Tim Cook: The One That Didn't Get Away." *Forbes.com* 26 Aug. 2011: 3. *Business Source Complete*. Web. 1 May 2012. More on Cook as an invaluable Apple asset, including rumors that Cook might jump ship.

Brownlee, John. "Who Is Apple's New CEO Tim Cook?" *Cult of Mac*. 25 Aug. 2011. Cultomedia Corp. Web. 1 May 2012. This website, devoted to Apple followers, provides a reliable short biography.

Carlton, Jim. Apple: *The Inside Story of Intrigue, Egomania, and Business Blunders*. New York: Random House, 1997. Print. Corporate history of Apple, now dated but valuable for its early insights.

Gatehouse, Jonathon. "Apple's Most Humble Servant." *Maclean's* 124.41 (2011): 52. *Academic Search Complete*. Web. 1 May 2012. A biography that covers early Cook's life, personal preferences, and a bit of the Apple experience.

Gore, Al. "Tim Cook." *Time* 179.17 (2012): 113. *Academic Search Complete*. Web. 1 May 2012. A brief overview of the accession of Cook to the helm of Apple after the death of Jobs.

Hesseldahl, Arik. "Tim Cook: A Steady Go-to Guide for Apple." *Businessweek Online* 15 Jan. 2009: 3. *Business Source Complete*. Web. 1 May 2012. Cook is credited with turning around Apple after the company had a bad year.

Lashinsky, Adam. *Inside Apple*. New York: Business Plus, 2012. Print. This journalistic interpretation contains much old information as well as much speculation, but it provides a good look at Apple.

New Word City editors. "How Steve Jobs Saved Apple." n.p.: New Word City, 2010. EPUB file. A seventeen-page digital resource on Jobs and Apple, available for the Kindle e-book reader.

Solomon, Brian. "For Apple CEO Tim Cook, a $376 Million Cherry On Top." *Forbes.com* 10 Jan. 2012: 51. *Business Source Complete*. Web. 1 May 2012. An overview focusing on Cook's Apple experience and his stock options as CEO.

SEYMOUR CRAY

Designer of supercomputers and founder of Cray Research

Born: September 28, 1925; Chippewa Falls, Wisconsin
Died: October 5, 1996; Colorado Springs, Colorado
Primary Field: Computer science
Specialty: Computer hardware
Primary Company/Organization: Cray Research

INTRODUCTION

Seymour Cray is acknowledged in the history of computer science as the father of supercomputing and the founder of the supercomputer industry. Without him, it is quite possible that we would not have the type of computers or the electronic devices we use to this day. Joel Birnbaum famously stated that "Many of the things that high performance computers now do routinely were at the farthest edge of credibility when Seymour envisioned them." Cray led a private life away from the computer science industry until his tragic and unexpected death in 1996 as the result of a traffic accident.

EARLY LIFE

Seymour Roger Cray was born on September 28, 1925, in the northwest of Wisconsin in Chippewa Falls. His father was a civil engineer. With his father's occupation and Cray's fascination with radios, motors, and electrical circuits, Cray developed an interest and talent in engineering and science. This passion led his parents to allow Cray to use the basement of their house as a laboratory for his studies and research. Cray's love of inventions was manifested early, and throughout his life he enjoyed tinkering with machines that could assist him or others.

When Cray was a young boy, he rigged a Morse code connection between his bedroom and that of his sister so that they could talk after lights were out. His father discovered the late-night clicking and told Cray to shut down the system because it was bothering the rest of the family. Cray's response to his father's request was to convert the clickers to lights and to continue talking with his sister. Cray composed this device out of Erector Set components that converted punched paper tape passed through it into Morse code signals.

Cray attended grade school and high school in Chippewa Falls. He completed high school in 1943 and was then drafted into the U.S. Army to serve in World War II.

LIFE'S WORK

Cray's technical abilities gave him the opportunity to become a radio operator for the U.S. Army. Once he had received his training, Cray was assigned to Europe and, although he served on the front lines, did not sustain any injuries. Cray was later transferred to the Pacific theater, where he worked on breaking coded messages that the Japanese were sending. At the conclusion of the war, he returned to the United States.

Once at home, Cray decided to attend the University of Minnesota, where he majored in electrical engineering. In 1949, he received his bachelor of science degree and then studied applied mathematics, receiving his master of science degree in 1951. After receiving his master's, Cray he joined Engineering Research Associates (ERA) in Saint Paul, Minnesota, at the suggestion of one of his university instructors. ERA was located in

Seymour Cray.

a renovated and restructured wooden glider factory. At ERA, Cray worked on digital computers, which were cutting-edge at the time. ERA was formed out of a former U.S. Navy laboratory that had devised and manufactured code-breaking machines. ERA specialized in computer technology but also developed a wide variety of projects that utilized basic engineering. During his tenure at ERA, Cray became known as an expert on digital technology. He was one of the leading designers of the ERA 1103, which became one of the first successful computers for scientific purposes.

In 1955, ERA was acquired by Remington Rand Company, a maker of business machines, which was then in turn acquired by Sperry Corporation to form Sperry Rand Corporation. All remaining staff from ERA were placed in Sperry Rand's scientific computing division, including Cray. Two years later, in 1957, the scientific division was closed and Cray and four other employees sought work at the Control Data Corporation (CDC). The other four were hired, but Cray was denied employment by CDC's chief executive officer (CEO), William Norris, until Cray finished a project that he had begun for the Navy. Norris had a good relationship with the Navy and wanted that relationship to remain intact. The project, the Naval Tactical Data System, was finished early 1958; thereafter, CDC hired Cray.

While at CDC, Cray became the lead designer of the next product after the ERA 1103, the CDC 1604. This product allowed CDC to become a major computer manufacturer. The CDC 1604 became one of the first, if not the first, computer to replace vacuum tubes with smaller transistors. Before the product shipped for sale, Cray set to work on the next version, the CDC 6600. The CDC 6600 was the computer first dubbed a *supercomputer*. The 6600 debuted as a hugely powerful machine, largely because of Cray's work on optimizing the system, and it outperformed everything else on the market at that time. In response to feeble attempts by competitors to outdo the 6600, Cray designed the CDC 7600, which proved to be five times faster than the 6600. The last system that Cray completed at CDC was the 8600. He began work on it in 1968 and realized that the enhanced clock speed would not allow him to reach his goals. Recognizing the need to enhance the design, Cray designed the 8600 with four processors, all sharing the same memory.

By 1970, Cray had become responsible for systems that would shape the high-performance computer industry for years to come. Around this period, Cray became exasperated with interference by CDC's upper management and lobbied for a laboratory to be built in his hometown of Chippewa Falls. He got his wish, and CDC built a new laboratory on land that Cray owned.

Upon his departure from CDC, Cray founded his own company, Cray Research, Inc., with the single goal of building the fastest computers on the globe. Norris invested $300,000 in start-up money for Cray's company. Research and development, as well as manufacturing, were based in Chippewa Falls, while the firm's business headquarters were in Minneapolis. When he started Cray Research, Cray shelved the 8600 design, primarily because at that time he believed that the software problems were too great for the company and industry to handle. Cray's company did not have the money to design a new computer, but after a couple of business meetings with Wall Street investment bankers, it was able to gain enough funding to continue work on new products. Upon approaching investors on Wall Street, Cray was surprised to find that his reputation had preceded him and that venture capitalists were delighted and willing to lend him the money he needed.

Three years after those meetings, Cray Research debuted the Cray-1, the first in Cray Research's line of supercomputers. The Cray-1 could perform more than 200 million calculations per second. It was released in 1976 and was used to solve large-scale scientific problems. It was sold to government and university laboratories. The Cray-1 outperformed every other computer on the market at that time. While designing the Cray-1, Cray made sure that the entire Cray-1 computer ran at a fast speed. In the past, only the processor had run; now other systems in the computer could keep up.

While Cray worked on the Cray-2, other teams in his corporation delivered the two-processor Cray X-MP, which was a huge success and was then followed by the four-processor X-MP. When the Cray-2 was finally released after six years of development, it was only marginally faster than the X-MP, largely because of the latter's very fast and large main memory. As a result, the Cray-2 sold in much smaller numbers. The Cray-2 processed at 250 megahertz (MHz) with a much deeper pipeline, making it more difficult to code than the short-pipe X-MP. The X-MP was also the first computer ever to provide a huge increase in central memory size. For the next few years, Cray's company came out with more products that had higher computing speed.

In 1980, Cray resigned as chairman and CEO of his growing firm to work in a new laboratory in Colorado Springs, Colorado. Cray stated that he had been distracted by day-to-day tasks and wanted to focus more

---

Affiliation: Cray Research

Cray Research was founded by Seymour Cray in 1972 to build supercomputers, beginning with the Cray-1. Faster than all other computers available at the time, the Cray-1 was highly successful when first released, especially with research centers, universities, and government laboratories, which could afford its then astronomical price of $8.8 million.

After its initial success with the Cray-1, Cray Research developed a number of other supercomputers, including the Cray X-MP, the Cray-2, the Cray-3, the Cray Y-MP, the Cray C90, and the Cray T90. Cray continued to enjoy great success with its supercomputers through the early 1990s; its machines were seen as the best available and had little competition. Despite this success, Cray was not able to develop a successful mini-supercomputer, a failure that limited the company's success

Once massively parallel computers came on the market in the late 1980s, Cray struggled to maintain its hold on its customer base. Although its machines were still the fastest, they were not significantly faster than massively parallel computers to justify the premium price Cray Research charged. In 1996, Cray Research merged with Silicon Graphics, Inc. (SGI) in an attempt to revitalize both businesses. After Seymour Cray died in an automobile accident later that year, SGI sold off its supercomputer business.

---

fully on design. He became an independent contractor, designing even faster machines than those at his laboratory in Chippewa Falls. He took the Cray-3 design with him to his new laboratory. Cray later named his new facility the Cray Computer Corporation. Because Cray was unwilling to use new state-of-the-art technology, the Cray-3 was not commercially successful, although it displayed reliable operation at a 500 MHz clock speed. When Cray's last system, the Cray-4, was almost completed, it operated at a clock rate of 1 gigahertz (GHz), a clock rate that no one else to date had achieved. However, with Cray products declining in sales and market share as the Cold War wound down in the late 1980s and early 1990s, and with the lowered revenues that made it difficult to provide new development funds, Cray Computer Corporation ran out of money. It filed for Chapter 11 bankruptcy on March 24, 1995. Cray then established a new company named SRC Computers, designing massively parallel machines. The new design concentrated on communications and memory performance, two problems that had shelved previous attempts at parallel designs.

Cray liked to use simple tools when working on his inventions, usually only a piece of paper and a pencil. However, he admitted that some of his work required more sophisticated devices. One day, someone told Cray that the Apple Computer company had purchased a Cray computer and was planning to simulate the next Apple computer design using the Cray computer. Cray expressed amusement, as he had been using an Apple to simulate the Cray-3. Cray's selection of people for his projects also reflected fundamentals. Once asked why he often hired new college graduates, he replied that they did not know that what he was asking them to do was impossible, so they tried.

No one in Cray's field has accomplished the constant success that he achieved during his lifetime. He dedicated his entire professional career to the designs and development of large-scale, high-performance systems. He often said that he was put on earth to do that job. Cray died at the age of seventy-one; he had sustained head and neck injuries in a traffic accident on September 22, 1996. Although he underwent emergency surgery to alleviate his injuries, he succumbed to those injuries two weeks after the crash.

SRC Computers continued development after Cray's death and now specializes in reconfigurable computing. The Computer Society of the Institute of Electrical and Electronics Engineers honored Cray with the Seymour Cray Computer Engineering Award. Established in late 1997, the award includes a crystal memento, an illuminated certificate, and a $10,000 honorarium; it is awarded to recognize innovative contributions to high-performance computing systems that best display the creative spirit shown by Seymour Cray.

PERSONAL LIFE

Cray and his first wife, Verene, had three children, including a son and two daughters. After his marriage to Verene ended in divorce, Cray married Gerri M. Harman in 1976.

Cray valued his time away from his work, although he had little time to enjoy many of his favorite activities because of his dedication to his company. An avid sportsman, Cray enjoyed skiing, tennis, windsurfing, and hiking. He also enjoyed fishing and traveling. He was known both for his down-to-earth demeanor and his unusual hobbies, such as digging a tunnel beneath his home. Although this activity might have been regarded as somewhat eccentric, Cray claimed that his ideas often came to him while he was digging.

Stephen T. Schroth and Melvin E. Taylor Jr.

FURTHER READING

Ceruzzi, Paul E. *A History of Modern Computing.* 2nd ed. Cambridge: MIT, 2012. Print. A narrative history of the computer industry from 1945 to 1995, including Cray in chapters headed "From Mainframe to Minicomputer" and "The Go-Go Years."

Murray, C. J. *The Supermen: The Story of Seymour Cray and the Wizards Behind the Supercomputer.* New York: Wiley, 1997. Print. The primary biography of the supercomputer pioneer, wherein the supercomputer itself is as much the focus as Cray—from its origins during World War II to its modern applications in climate modeling. The result provides a solid context for the history of modern computing generally. Includes Cray's final interview.

Scientific American, ed. *Understanding Supercomputing.* New York: Byron Preiss Visual, 2002. Print. A collection of fifteen articles published in *Scientific American* between 1995 and 2001 that together provide basic grounding in the technology of supercomputers.

Slater, R. "The Hermit of Chippewa Falls and His 'Simple, Dumb Things.'" *Portraits in Silicon.* Cambridge: MIT, 1989. 195–206. Print. A brief biography of Cray in this collection of sketches on pioneers in computer science.

Worthy, J. C. *William C. Norris: Portrait of a Maverick.* New York: Ballinger, 1987. Print. Biography of the founder of Control Data Corporation, where Cray designed the CDC 1604 and which he left to form his own company.

D

TED DABNEY

Cofounder of Atari

Born: 1943; Utah
Died: -
Primary Field: Computer science
Specialty: Computer hardware
Primary Company/Organization: Atari

INTRODUCTION

With Nolan Bushnell, Ted Dabney cofounded both Syzygy Engineering (in 1971) and Atari, Inc. (in 1972). The latter became the first major success of the newborn video game industry. Dabney and Bushnell created the first coin-operated arcade game, Computer Space, *based on Steve Russell's* Spacewar! *game—just as Atari's successful* Pong *was an adaptation of the table tennis game included with the Magnavox Odyssey home video game console. With the passage of time, Bushnell's legend has been magnified, in part through his own efforts, leaving Dabney in the shadows of the footlights.*

EARLY LIFE

Ted Dabney was born in 1943 in Utah. While in the Marine Corps he was given electronics courses as part of his training, which began his interest in engineering. He studied electrical engineering at the University of Utah, where he met Bushnell, his future business partner. After college, the two worked together at the engineering firm Ampex, which had been involved both in the space program and in early video recording technology. Dabney worked on the firm's military products for six years before transferring to the Video File unit in Sunnyvale, California. Video File was an Ampex technology that allowed recording of images and video to rhodium discs, providing fast access to visual information often used by law enforcement and hospitals, such as fingerprints, mug shots, and medical records. Los Angeles County was one of the major clients in Dabney's day. Some law enforcement agencies continue to use descendants of the original Video File system. Soon Dabney and Bushnell went into business together, forming the engineering firm Syzygy in 1971 and releasing the first coin-operated video game: *Computer Space.*

Ted Dabney.

LIFE'S WORK

Computer scientist Steve Russell invented *Spacewar!* in 1962. Although it was not the first game run on a computer—it was the third—it was the first to become well known in the computer field, and it was the result of hundreds of hours of labor to write code for a game inspired by the space-opera science fiction of E. E. "Doc" Smith. The result was a two-player game in which each player maneuvered a spaceship while trying to fire photon torpedoes on the opposing player's the sun.

spaceship and avoid the dangerous gravitational pull of The game was never made commercial; instead, Digital Equipment Corporation (DEC)—which had provided the PDP-1 computer for which it was written to the Massachusetts Institute of Technology in the hope that the school would find marketable applications for it—included *Spacewar!* with its computers as a diagnostic program. Russell later transferred to Stanford University, where he met Bushnell and introduced him to *Spacewar!*

Affiliation: Atari

Atari has had a varied corporate history and identity, but it began as Atari, Inc., in 1972, making arcade games and some of the first home video game consoles. The company was founded by Ted Dabney and Nolan Bushnell, partners in Syzygy who had developed *Computer Space*, the first arcade video game. For a dozen years, it developed both home and arcade video games, before splitting in 1984 into the Atari Corporation—which produced consumer electronics, including home video games, owned by Tramel Technology Limited—and Atari Games, Inc., which made arcade games. The Atari Corporation passed hands several times, notably purchased by Hasbro Interactive in 1998, at a time when board game publisher Hasbro was acquiring numerous game companies (including strategy board game publisher Avalon Hill, a division of Wizards of the Coast, owners of the collectible card game *Magic: The Gathering* and former TSR properties such as *Dungeons and Dragons*). Hasbro Interactive, a division of Hasbro, was in turn bought by IESA in 2001 and was renamed Atari Interactive 2003. That year, Atari Games was shut down by owner Midway Games, following a prolonged slump in the arcade industry. Atari Games had spent much of the late 1980s manufacturing both arcade games and game cartridges for the Nintendo Entertainment System. In 2009, Midway's intellectual property, including many Atari Games properties, was sold to Warner Bros. Entertainment.

The Atari 2600, released in 1977, was one of the most successful and significant video game consoles in history. Although some competing consoles had superior technology in some features, Atari benefited from the marketing and self-promotion savvy of Bushnell (Dabney was already beginning to be pushed out of the limelight) and the inclusion of several iconic game titles. *Pac-Man*, a Japanese game, was imported to the

United States and became the first megahit in the American video game industry, both at arcades and in consoles. The console version sold more than 5 million copies. The Atari 2600 was not officially discontinued until 1993, enjoying a remarkably long life in such a fast-paced industry.

Today, the Atari brand is owned by Atari, Inc., a subsidiary of Atari SA, a French holding company. Atari SA was formerly called Infogrames Entertainment, having changed to the Atari brand in 2009. Bushnell, an original Atari cofounder, joined Atari SA's board of directors in 2010. Other Atari SA holdings include Atari London Studio and Eden Games, the game development studio behind Test Drive Unlimited.

Atari, Inc. is based in New York City and is the corporate descendant of GT Interactive, a video game publisher founded by Good Times Home Video in 1993 in response to the popularity of *Doom*. This incarnation of Atari has produced three versions of the Atari Flashback console, a television console that plays classic video games and comes programmed with the games rather than requiring cartridges. The initial Atari Flashback shipped with mostly Atari 2600 games—*Adventure, Air-Sea Battle, Battlezone, Breakout, Canyon Bomber, Crystal Castles, Gravitar, Haunted House, Millipede, Saboteur, Sky Diver, Solaris, Sprintmaster, Warlord,* and *Yars' Revenge*—as well as a limited number of Atari 7800 games: *Asteroids, Centipede, Desert Falcon, Charley Chuck's Food Fight,* and *Planet Smashers.* The Flashback 2 increased the lineup to forty games, two of them—*Pitfall!* and *River Raid*—having originally been published by Activision. The joysticks were much more similar to the Atari 2600 joysticks. The Flashback 3 was licensed to Legacy Engineering and included sixty games, using a different style of hardware from that of the previous Flashbacks.

Bushnell and Dabney adapted *Spacewar!* for an arcade game by creating a custom-made computer using a black-and-white television as its display device. *Computer Space* was hard-wired into logic circuits rather than existing as a program running on a computer. The game was a little simpler than *Spacewar!* (the gravity hazard was omitted, and it was played as a single-player game with UFOs as targets instead of an opposing second player) and was built using small-scale integrated circuits on printed circuit boards. *Computer Space* also added a few features the *Spacewar!* lacked, mainly a sound circuit developed by Dabney, which added sound effects using Zener diodes, and a "win screen" consisting of the player's spaceship being "sent into hyperspace" (which was accomplished by inverting the video, another addition by Dabney).

Computer Space was released by Nutting Associates, a Mountain View, California, arcade game manufacturer that had previously released coin-operated trivia games. Fewer than two-thirds of the units manufactured were sold, although the game made a memorable splash in the industry and appeared in the movie *Soylent Green*. Dabney and Bushnell formed their own company, Syzygy Engineering, and sought the right game to develop for commercial potential. Discarding the idea of a driving game as too complex for players under driving age, Bushnell decided on an arcade version of the Magnavox Odyssey's table tennis game, which they marketed as *Pong*, using the same motion circuitry that Dabney had developed for *Computer Space*. By the time Pong was released, Syzygy had reorganized as Atari, Inc., a name Dabney suggested, because an unrelated company was already doing business under the name Syzygy. Pong was released to great success, though Atari was forced to pay a licensing fee after the makers of the Magnavox Odyssey sued for intellectual property infringement.

In order to circumvent the exclusive contracts that some venues wanted, Bushnell created a separate company, Kee Games, which was a wholly owned subsidiary of Atari but posed as a competitor. This way, whether a venue insisting on an exclusive contract signed with Atari or Kee, the business was still Atari's. In a dispute over the ethics and pragmatics of this arrangement, Dabney wound up leaving the company in 1978. Bushnell left later that year.

PERSONAL LIFE

An avid game player, Dabney's favorite game is Go (from which the name Atari originates). He worked part-time repairing pinball machines in Atari's early days and returned to that work after Bushnell bought out his share of the company. He is rarely in the public eye since, although in the twenty-first century he has participated in some message board threads about the golden age of video games, sometimes sparring with his former partner Bushnell.

Bill Kte'pi

FURTHER READING

Dillon, Roberto. *The Golden Age of Video Games: The Birth of a Multibillion Dollar Industry*. New York: CRC, 2011. Print. This history of video games virtually begins with Atari and thus gives the company ample coverage.

Montfort, Nick, and Ian Bogost. *Racing the Beam: The Atari Video Computer System*. Cambridge: MIT, 2009. Print. A much more technically informed and literate look at Atari than provided by histories more concerned with the cultural impact or entertainment value of the games.

Ramsay, Morgan. *Games at Work: Stories Behind the Games People Play*. New York: Apress, 2012. Print. An interview-based history of video games, including an interview with Dabney's partner at Atari, Bushnell.

WEILI DAI

Cofounder of Marvell Technology Group

Born: 1972; Shanghai, China
Died: -
Primary Field: Computer science
Specialty: Computer hardware
Primary Company/Organization: Marvell Technology Group

INTRODUCTION

Weili Dai, born in China and educated in the United States, is the cofounder of Marvell Technology Group Ltd., a leading semiconductor manufacturer. One of the most successful female technology entrepreneurs in the world, Dai is also noted for her philanthropy and her championing of women's greater participation in leadership and in business and technical fields.

EARLY LIFE

Weili Dai was born in Shanghai, China; her father was an engineer and her mother a nurse. She played badminton and junior semiprofessional basketball in China, and she credits the experience with giving her self-confidence and a passion for winning. The family moved to the United States in 1979, when Dai was seventeen; although she knew little English, she attended Abraham Lincoln High School in San Francisco for one year before enrolling at the University of California at Berkeley. She received her bachelor's degree in computer science from that institution, where she also met her husband. After graduation, she worked as a software engineer while supporting her husband in his graduate studies and taking care of her two young children.

LIFE'S WORK

Dai cofounded Marvell Technology Group in 1995, with her husband, Sehat Sutardja, and his brother, Pantas Sutardja. According to Dai, the company was planned around her kitchen table. Marvel Technology Group began with investments from friends and family

Weili Dai.

plus $200,000 they had earned from licensing a chip design; after two years, Diosdado Banatao, an electrical engineer just starting on a new career as a venture capitalist, invested $1 million in the company. Marvell first worked in the field of data storage, with its first large customer being the Yellow Pages. Its first major project was designing an analog chip for disk drives; the resulting chip operated 20 percent less expensively than a rival chip manufactured by Texas Instruments. By 2000, the company had landed such customers as Seagate Technology and Samsung Electronics. That year, the company boasted revenues of $88 billion.

On June 26, 2000, Marvell Technology Group held an initial public offering (IPO); the initial stock price of $15 per share rose to $21.93 by the end of 2000. From 2001 to 2005, the company's shares returned 38 percent annually. As of 2006, the three cofounders owned 22 percent of the company, and all three had become billionaires. That year, Marvell bought Intel's mobile phone chip business, bringing the company publicity at a time when it was not well known. As of 2011, Dai said Marvell had a 70 percent share of the silicon chip market and supplied chips for some of the best-known technology companies in the world, including Microsoft, Cisco, and Sony. Also as of 2011, Marvell had approximately six thousand employees, half in the United States and half overseas, and thirteen research and design centers—the most in the United States—with six in Asia and six in Europe as well. Each of these centers focuses on a particular facet of the company, an example of Dai's philosophy that different people have different talents and should focus on what they do well in order to contribute to the company.

In 2006, Marvell was investigated by the Securities and Exchange Commission (SEC) for backdating stock options, a practice whereby the option's purchase date is changed to an earlier date when the price was lower. In May 2007, a panel concluded that Marvell had in fact backdated stock options and lacked a system of internal controls, noting that it was unusual for a married couple to be the only members of the committee that awards stock options, as was the case with Marvell. As part of the settlement, Sutardja relinquished his post as chairman of Marvell, chief financial officer George Hervey resigned, and Dai relinquished her position as chief operating officer. In addition, Dai was stripped of financial responsibility and barred from serving as a director or officer of the company for five years, and the company paid a $10 million fine. Sutardja remained with the company as chief executive

Affiliation: Marvell Technology Group

Weili Dai cofounded Marvell Technology Group in 1995 with her husband, Sehat Sutardja, and his brother, Pantas Sutardja. Today, Marvell is a leading fabless semiconductor company (meaning that it does not have in-house manufacturing facilities) that ships more than a billion chips annually. The company is traded on the NASDAQ stock exchange (stock symbol MRVL) and grew every quarter from 2000 to 2006; it had revenues of $3.4 billion for fiscal year 2012. The company's corporate headquarters are in Bermuda, while its U.S. headquarters are in Santa Clara, California. Marvel employs approximately fifty-seven hundred people worldwide and has international design centers in Asia, Europe, the United States, and the Middle East.

Marvell's key markets are mobile and wireless devices (including laptops, smart phones, and gaming devices), storage solutions, cloud services and infrastructure, consumer solutions, and green technology (including low-power lighting solutions and energy-efficient management of AC/DC power). The company's growth has been facilitated by the seventy-eight patents held by Sehat Sutardja. Marvell's success is based on designing chips that are superior to their competition. Their first major success was a disk drive chip that operated 20 percent faster than a chip manufactured by Texas Instruments; created in 1998 for Seagate, this product helped Marvell capture 90 percent of the market for corporate disk drives as of 2006. In 2000, Marvell released an Ethernet chip that moved data ten times as fast as rival chips. In 2005, Marvell created a Wi-Fi chip for handheld devices that was smaller and used less power than other chips on the market.

Marvell has won numerous industry and other awards. In 1997, the company won the Seagate Strategic Supplier Award, and in the years 1997–99 Marvell was honored by the Fabless Semiconductor Association for outstanding financial performance. In 2000, Marvell won the Fujitsu Top Supplier Award and the Hitachi Excellent Partner Award, and in 2001 it won the Fujitsu Distinguished Partner Award. In 2002, Semiconductor Insights selected Marvell's Gigabit Switch as its Product of the Year. In 2004, Marvell's founders won the Ernst and Young Entrepreneur of the Year Award, and Marvell Asia was named one of the fastest-growing companies by DP Information Network Group. In 2005, *Forbes* magazine named Marvell one of America's best-managed companies. In 2007, Marvell was named an Intel Preferred Quality Supplier, won the Insight Award from Semiconductor Insights, and won the EDN Innovation Award for the Marvell Digital Video Format Converter. In 2008, Marvell's digital PFC controllers were named one of the greenest semiconductor applications, and Marvell's digital Video Format Converter was given the Secrets of Home Theater Best Video Award. In 2009, Marvell won an EDN Innovation Award, and its Mobile Hotspot was selected as the best mobile product of 2009 by the Mobile Excellence Awards. In 2010, the Marvell Moby was selected as Best Tablet by *LAPTOP Magazine*, and the Marvell ARMADA 1000 HD Media Processor SoC won the EDN Innovation Award. In 2011, Cisco named Marvell its Supplier of the Year.

officer, and Dai retained the title Director Strategic Marketing and Business Development.

PERSONAL LIFE

Dai married her husband, Sehat Sutardja, an immigrant from Indonesia, shortly after her graduation from college; she worked as a software engineer while he pursued his master's degree and Ph.D. in electrical engineering at the University of California, Berkeley. They two sons, Christopher and Nicholas; both are also electrical engineers. Dai and Sutardja have a reputation for being devoted to work, not taking vacations, and demanding the same kind of dedication from their employees.

Dai has argued that the varied demands placed on women make them experts at time management and multitasking (citing her own experiences working full time while raising her family) and also force them to develop both leadership and caretaking skills. Dai is involved in several philanthropic ventures and has served as a mentor to women from other countries.

Sarah Boslaugh

FURTHER READING

Balconi, Margherita, and Roberto Fontana. "Entry and Innovation: An Analysis of the Fabless Semiconductor Business." *Small Business Economics* 37.1 (2011): 87–106. Print. An analysis of the fabless semiconductor industry from 1984 to 2005, looking at the influence of human capital on the performance of these businesses.

Herel, Suzanne. "An Ex-Nerd, Chipmaker Is First of All a Team Player." *San Francisco Chronicle* 6 June 2011: D1. Print. A profile of Dai, focusing on her experiences as a child in China, her education in the United States, and her work with Marvell Technology Group.

Hurtate, Jeorge S., Evert A. Wolsheimer, and Lisa M. Tafoya. *Understanding Fabless IC Technology.* Burlington: Elsevier, 2007. Print. An overview of the fabless silicon chip business, with an emphasis on practical issues such as the design process, communications between the design company and the foundry (where the chips are actually made), and the use of e-commerce, information technology, and management information systems in the fabless business model.

Whelan, David. "Meet Marvell." *Forbes* 178.3 (2006): 58–62. Print. A profile of Marvell Technology Group on the occasion of its purchase of Intel's mobile phone chip business, focusing on the company culture and financial performance.

MICHAEL DELL

Founder, chairman, and CEO of Dell

Born: February 23, 1965; Houston, Texas
Died: -
Primary Field: Business and commerce
Specialty: Management, executives, and investors
Primary Company/Organization: Dell

INTRODUCTION

Michael Dell is one of the most successful entrepreneurs of his time, revolutionizing the manufacture and creation of the personal computer (PC) during the 1980s. While computers had previously been marketed and sold in an impersonal and distant manner, Dell made the decision to extract the middleman from the process. As a result his company, Dell Computer Corporation, served as the manufacturer and seller of the PCs it made and was able to customize products to better meet consumers' needs. This approach was highly successful, and Dell PCs became popular with corporate and higher-education users in addition to consumers. As Dell has grown, it has added product lines and services, including servers, data storage systems, and information technology support services. Dell remains one of the top sellers of PCs in the United States.

EARLY LIFE

Michael Saul Dell was born on February 23, 1965, in Houston, Texas, the son of an orthodontist and a stockbroker. Dell enrolled at Gary L. Herod Elementary School in Houston, and while a top student, even then he had dreams of being an entrepreneur. At the age of eight, Dell attempted to register for the General

Educational Development (GED) test, which if passed would confer the equivalent of a high school diploma, so that he could leave school and start his own business. Dell had a variety of part-time jobs even as a child, and this enabled him to purchase his first calculator at the age of seven. While enrolled in junior high school, Dell

Michael Dell.

came across a teletype machine for the first time and after-school hours programming it. At the age of fifteen, after seeing computers in a local RadioShack store, Dell became determined to purchase his own computer. Shortly thereafter, Dell purchased his first computer, an Apple II, which he took apart so that he could determine how it worked.

Dell attended Memorial High School in Hedwig Village, Texas. Memorial High School drew its students from a variety of wealthy neighborhoods in Houston and offered Dell a variety of competitive classes, including those in computer science and economics. Dell obtained a summer job, where he was responsible for selling subscriptions to the *Houston Post*, a local newspaper, by telephone. After noticing that newly married couples and those who had recently purchased a home were most likely to purchase a subscription, Dell targeted these groups, obtaining the names of those who had recently received a marriage license or filled out a mortgage application. As a result, Dell was able to earn more than $18,000 per year, better than the salary a beginning teacher would make at his high school.

Upon graduation from high school, Dell enrolled at the University of Texas at Austin, where he intended to be a premedical student. While a freshman living in the private Dobie Center residential complex, Dell began a business assembling computers from kits, as well as selling upgrade equipment for those who already owned a PC. Dell also was able to obtain a vendor license that allowed him to bid on contracts with the state of Texas, which he was successful in doing because he was not burdened by the overhead of most of his rivals.

LIFE'S WORK

By January 1984, Dell was so confident that a manufacturer selling PCs directly to the consumer could be successful that began his own computer company, initially known as PCs Limited. Beginning with an initial capitalization of $1,000, Dell operated his company out of a rented condominium and was quickly successful in selling IBM-compatible PCs built from stock parts. As a result of this success, Dell's family provided him with $300,000 in expansion capital and he dropped out of the University of Texas to devote all his efforts to his company, which he later renamed Dell Computer Corporation. Having outgrown the condominium, Dell moved operations to a business center located in nearby North Austin, where he was joined by a telephone sales staff and three people who served as his manufacturing group.

In 1985, Dell produced the first computer the company had designed itself, the Turbo PC. The Turbo PC was built using an Intel 8088 microprocessor, the same as the original IBM PC. The Turbo PC, with a price tag of $795, was offered for sale directly to consumers, who were made aware of the machine through advertisements Dell placed in national computer magazines. Consumers who saw the ads would call Dell and select the configuration they wanted from a variety of options. Dell would then assemble the computer and ship the completed machine directly to the consumer. This arrangement not only allowed Dell to offer lower prices than available in retail stores but also permitted the customers a degree of customization that was rare in the industry. In its first year in operation, Dell grossed more than $70 million in sales, constituting the sale of more than sixty thousand computers.

Dell quickly began to expand his company to take advantage of the many opportunities available during the technology boom of the 1980s. In 1987, the company established its first overseas presence, in Ireland, which would soon be followed by eleven more international locations. In June 1988, Dell made its initial public offering (IPO) of stock and saw the value of its shares double during their first month on the market. In an effort to allay the concerns of customers about the lack of brick-and-mortar stores to act as service centers, Dell established its on-site service program. Pursuant to this program, Dell would dispatch a technician to the office or home of a customer whose computer was malfunctioning.

In 1990, Dell experimented with altering its sales model. Dell entered into agreements with a variety of warehouse club and computer superstores that permitted its computers to be sold in store, much as its rivals did. Although this venture attracted a great deal of attention at the time, it was ultimately unsuccessful, and Dell refocused on its direct-to-consumer model of sales. Dell's traditional telephone ordering system was augmented in 1996, when it allowed consumers to purchase its machines over the Internet for the first time.

Michael Dell served as chief executive officer (CEO) of the company from its inception until 2004, when he resigned from that position while remaining chairman of the board of directors. From 1997 through 2004, the company enjoyed a tremendous growth in sales, allowing it to surpass Compaq Computer Corporation to become the largest maker of PCs in 1999. There were multiple reasons for this success. According to national magazines such as *Consumer Reports* and

PC Magazine, Dell had the reputation for the best customer service, reliability, and technical support of any PC maker. Dell also was able to make inroads in selling its products to corporate users, which gave it a reliable sales base while influencing home purchase decisions of workers who were familiar with Dell machines from their place of employment.

This reputation for quality, however, began to change after 2002. At that time, Dell had begun moving call centers overseas, which displeased many customers. Simultaneously, Dell's rapid growth caused its on-site service program to become inadequate. Finally, a problem Dell was having with faulty components resulted in negative publicity stemming from well-publicized reports of Dell laptops catching fire. As a result of these problems, Dell's sales slowed considerably in 2005, and the value of its stock price declined by 25 percent. By 2006, Dell's growth was slower than that of the industry as a whole, the first time this had occurred.

Michael Dell returned as CEO in 2007, replacing Kevin Rollins, who had succeeded him three years earlier. After returning to the helm of the company he had founded, Dell oversaw its expansion into several new markets. In 2008, Dell purchased EqualLogic to gain a share of the Internet small computer system interface (iSCSI) market, a means of linking storage systems. In 2009, the company purchased Perot Systems, renaming it Dell Services, a provider of information technology services. As a CEO, Dell was criticized by some, who noted that he used outsourcing (thus eliminating staff jobs) and generous government tax breaks to enrich his company and himself. Dell's stock price improved, however, after he returned as CEO.

PERSONAL LIFE

Dell settled in Austin, Texas, with his wife, Susan, and the family's four children. The Dells' 33,000-square-foot house was reported to be the most expensive domestic building ever erected in Texas. The Dells also own other homes, including one in Hawaii, a vacation home in the Caribbean, and the 6D Ranch, located outside Austin, where Dell raises Arabian horses. In 1999, the Dells founded the Michael and Susan Dell Foundation, which focuses on children who live in urban communities, both in the United States and in India. Since its inception, the foundation has distributed more than $600 million to assist with education and health initiatives.

Dell has also provided the University of Texas with a new computer science building and helped fund the Dell Children's Medical Center, the Dell Pediatric

---

Affiliation: Dell, Inc.

Founded in a condominium, Dell has grown to become one of the largest manufacturers of PCs in the world. Using a direct-to-consumers sales strategy, Dell has been able to build strong sales while retaining a great deal of customer loyalty. Although other vendors had tried this strategy before, Dell became its most successful exemplar because it realized that customers needed on-site service to reassure those customers who were reluctant to purchase a computer over the telephone or online.

Dell has expanded beyond its initial capacity as the manufacturer of PCs to engage in a variety of other areas. Dell provides laptops, printers, high-definition televisions, and other products to the consumer market while making available servers, storage solutions, cloud computing, consulting services, and other products and services to businesses, government agencies, and other organizations. Dell is the sixth-largest corporation in Texas, based on revenue, and has long been recognized as a Fortune 500 company. Dell has been recognized for its efforts to reduce greenhouse gas emissions that are part of the manufacturing process and has pledged to reduce the company's carbon footprint. Dell has also sought to reduce the toxins used in the manufacture of its machines.

Research Institute, and the Michael and Susan Dell Center for the Advancement of Healthy Living, all located on or near the university's campus. In recognition of this philanthropy, Dell received an honorary doctorate from Ireland's University of Limerick in 2002.

Dell has long had a love of automobiles and owns several, including a Porsche Boxter, a Porsche Carrera, and a Hummer H2. He also owns a Gulf Stream V jet airplane, which he uses for both business and personal travel. Although the CEO of a giant computer manufacturer, Dell continues to enjoy tinkering with and modifying PCs.

Stephen T. Schroth and Jamal A. Nelson

FURTHER READING

Dell, M., and C. Fredman. *Direct from Dell: Strategies That Revolutionized an Industry*. New York: HarperBusiness, 1999. Print. Dell shares his insights regarding processes and procedures he and his company used to turn it from a start-up into an industry leader.

Freiberger, P., and M. Swaine. *Fire in the Valley: The Making of the Personal Computer*. 2nd ed. New York: McGraw-Hill, 2000. Print. Recounts the struggles and successes of pioneer computer companies that worked to make the PC a common home appliance.

Holzner, S. *How Dell Does It: Using Speed and Innovation to Achieve Extraordinary Results*. New York: McGraw-Hill, 2006. Print. Examines how Dell uses innovations largely invented by others, improves upon them through strong implementation, and has been hugely successful in doing so.

Indovino, Shaina Carmel. *Michael Dell: From Child Entrepreneur to Computer Magnate*. Philadelphia: Mason Crest, 2012. Print. The inspirational story of Dell's rise to success.

Vecchio, P. D., V. Ndou, G. Passiante, and R. Laubacher. "Managing Corporate Reputation in the Blogosphere: The Case of Dell Computer." *Corporate Reputation Review* 14.2 (2011): 133–44. Print. Discusses challenges that corporations face in managing their reputations in the blogosphere, focusing on Dell.

Wallace, J., and J. Erickson. *Hard Drive: Bill Gates and the Making of the Microsoft Empire*. New York: Wiley, 1992. Print. Explores how the business practices of Microsoft benefited those companies, such as Dell, that were able to manufacture low-cost PC compatible machines.

E

J. PRESPER ECKERT

Cocreator of the ENIAC

Born: April 19, 1919; Philadelphia, Pennsylvania
Died: June 3, 1995; Bryn Mawr, Pennsylvania
Primary Field: Computer science
Specialty: Computer hardware
Primary Company/Organization: University of
    Pennsylvania

INTRODUCTION

*J. Presper Eckert with John William Mauchly invented
the first general-purpose digital electronic computer,
the Electronic Numerical Integrator and Computer,
or ENIAC. They also designed the Binary Automatic
Computer (BINAC). Their most notable contribution
to the early development of modern computing was the
Universal Automatic Computer (UNIVAC). Their business acumen was less than their technical inventiveness,
and their computer company was bought by Remington
Rand, which became Burroughs and eventually Unisys.*

EARLY LIFE

John Presper Eckert Jr., more familiarly Pres, was born
on April 9, 1919, in Philadelphia, Pennsylvania, to John
Presper Eckert and Ethel Hallowell Eckert. The family
was well off, part of the Philadelphia elite; John, Sr.,
was a self-made millionaire real estate developer. Pres
was an only child and spent much of his youth building
radios and other mechanical and electronic gadgets. He
traveled with his father frequently, meeting his father's
friends and associates. However, he preferred science
to celebrities. Pres liked to draw schematic diagrams
on loose scraps of paper, even restaurant checks. At
age twelve, he won his first science fair by building a
remote-controlled boat. Electromagnets under the boat

allowed him to steer it, and he developed a way of having the magnet release one boat and take on another.

Eckert was also highly skilled in mathematics,
scoring the second highest in the United States on the
mathematics section of the College Board examination
behind a classmate. He wanted to attend the Massachusetts Institute of Technology (MIT), but his mother did
not want him to move so far away. To keep his son close

J. Presper Eckert.

71

to home, John, Sr., claimed that he could not afford to pay MIT's steep tuition. Upon discovering his father's lie during his freshman year, Eckert became very angry, which may have had a negative effect on his grades at the Wharton School of Business; moreover, business bored Eckert, so he transferred to the University of Pennsylvania's Moore School of Electrical Engineering and earned his undergraduate degree in electrical engineering in 1941 and his master's degree in 1943.

Eckert remained at Moore after graduation, becoming an instructor. He was the top electronic engineer at the school. One of his summer school students was John Mauchly, chair of the physics department at Ursinus College ad twelve years his senior. When Mauchly became a professor at Moore, the two, already close friends, began discussing electronics and designing computers, seeking ever more speed. Eckert was twenty-four when he signed the contract to create the ENIAC. He had already spent time on electronics projects at Philo Farnsworth's television research laboratory in Philadelphia, and at Moore he had worked on ways to measure and time radar pulses.

LIFE'S WORK

The Moore School's computer was a mechanical combination of wheels, shafts, and gears run by an electrical motor. It could perform only one function at a time and took up to two days to set up. Faster models, electromechanical, used relays instead of gears, but they were still slow. Harvard had a computer that was simply a large-scale adding machine. MIT had a faster one, still mechanical. Eckert and Mauchly had abandoned the idea of moving parts, replacing them with vacuum tubes. The army was interested, invested, and thirty months later the army and Eckert/Mauchly had ENIAC.

The ENIAC debuted on February 14, 1946, and for many represented the first electronic computer. Its first purpose was to compute ballistics tables so artillery crews could compensate for gravity and wind. Before the first demonstration of Eckert's contribution to computing, fifty or so leading mathematicians and scientists dined on lobster bisque and filet mignon while listening to speeches. Then they walked three blocks to the Moore School of Electrical Engineering on the University of Pennsylvania campus. There they saw the first public demonstration of the room-sized ENIAC, which weighed 30 tons and included eighteen thousand vacuum tubes. Mauchly and Eckert showed the select attendees that ENIAC could compute a shell's trajectory before the shell could reach its target—a tangible

sign of its superiority over all previous calculators and an indication that computers had finally become useful rather than novelties.

Before ENIAC, a person with a pencil could add two ten-digit numbers in 10 seconds on average. A handheld calculator cut that time to 4 seconds. The Mark I, Harvard's electromechanical computer, took 0.3 second to add two ten-digit numbers. The ENIAC added the two numbers in 0.0002 second—fifty thousand times faster than a human, twenty times faster than a calculator, and fifteen hundred times faster than the Mark I. The ENIAC accepted additional data at any step of the process and could store data for future use. The ENIAC was even faster at specialized scientific calculations. Although some claim that the ENIAC was a four-function machine capable only of adding, subtracting, multiplying, and dividing, in fact it had the capability of performing three-dimensional second-order differential equations. Speed, memory, and versatility allowed scientists and engineers the option of computing rather than creating and testing scale models, as aircraft designers did to determine drag, something they could do in theory but not in practice because of the volume of calculation involved.

Eckert and Mauchly's decision to eliminate moving parts altogether in the ENIAC constituted one of its primary innovations. Mauchly had studied vacuum tubes, writing about his findings in 1942, and he and Eckert determined that tubes would count pulses. The idea was perceived as fanciful by those who had problems with electromechanical computing as a concept and was regarded as unworkable by those who realized that vacuum tubes were highly unreliable.

At the same time, the university had undertaken the project for developing the artillery tables, a task that was projected to last years because of the massive amount of calculations involved, performed by what was then called "computers" (in reference to the men and women who performed the calculations using mechanical calculators or pencil and paper). A single trajectory involved 750 multiplications, and each table had up to 3,000 trajectories, so the project amounted to a four-man-year exercise.

Seeking a faster way, the army commissioned the University of Pennsylvania to build an electronic computer. Mauchly the physicist and Eckert the electrical engineer built the machine. Then six women computers configured the three thousand switches and eighteen thousand vacuum tubes to solve equations they had previously worked out by hand or desktop calculator. There

---

Affiliation: Unisys

The Eckert-Mauchly Computer Corporation became part of a company whose history was filled with mergers and acquisitions. Remington began as a typewriter company in 1873. Burroughs made adding machines, and its first arithmometer debuted in 1885. Remington merged with Rand Kardex in 1927 to become Remington Rand. Sperry formed in 1933. Eckert and Mauchly invented the ENIAC in 1946, and Remington Rand produced the first business computer, the 409, in 1949. Eckert-Mauchly began in 1950. Sperry merged with Remington Rand to become Sperry Rand in 1955, while Burroughs shifted from adding machines to computers, absorbing Electro-Data in the mid-1950s. Burroughs and Sperry formed Unisys in 1986, and Unisys immediately in 1987 acquired workstation maker Convergent Technologies.

In 1991, Unisys settled a Department of Defense fraud and bribery case by paying $190 million in fines, damages, and penalties. Also, Unisys initially was inefficient because the merger did not consolidate all functions, leaving duplication and waste. The industry entered a slump, but in the early 1990s the company emerged by shifting from mainframe to networked systems and developing a services capability. The company slumped again, cutting its workforce and consolidating and selling nonperforming units, shifting to open systems software for proprietary hardware and shifting to Windows and Unix capabilities in the 1990s. By the turn of the century, Unisys was primarily a services company, and its future lay in overseas markets.

---

was no computer language, just manual adjustments of switches and wires. The women were integral, but they were classed as computer operators, the same as secretaries, and the hardware workers got the credit while the software workers were ignored in the back of the room.

The vacuum tubes were of ten different types and "off the shelf," and all the developers asked was that they be supplied in lots of them. Vacuum tubes blew out frequently, every few days. Some circuits were off the shelf but Eckert designed others: registers and integrated circuits. No modern computer still uses an Eckert circuit, but the concept of a subroutine that runs without human input persists (that was Mauchly's idea and eliminated the Mark I requirement to feed the same tape again and again for repeating the same computation). Programming was by wires and switches, with nothing hardwired and no software. Because mice liked to eat wires, Eckert and the ENIAC team caged mice, fed them samples of all the available insulated wires, and chose the one that the mice did not like to eat.

The ENIAC cost nearly $800,000 to build. Eckert and Mauchly's accomplishment—aside from proving wrong those experts who had said it was not feasible as well as those who had said that there would never be enough demand to justify even two of these huge and expensive machines—was putting together thousands of unstable components into a highly stable system. The resulting machine ushered in a new age of computing by demonstrating the practicality of all-electronic digital computing. After the debut of ENIAC, the Soviet Union (a U.S. ally during World War II but

its rival during the ensuing Cold War) wanted to order one. Moore declined because the machine was too great a breakthrough to share with America's Cold War enemy. The U.S. Army used the ENIAC for eight years to calculate ballistics tables, do computations for the H-bomb, and help in wind tunnel design before retiring it in 1955.

Eckert and Mauchly were the two most responsible for the design and creation of the ENIAC and later had commercial success with more sophisticated systems such as the Universal Automatic Computer (UNIVAC). The company they created was one of the concerns that merged into Unisys.

PERSONAL LIFE

On October 28, 1944, Eckert married Hester Caldwell. The couple had two sons, John Presper III and Christopher. Hester committed suicide in 1953. Eckert married Judith A. Rewalt on October 13, 1962, and with her had two more children, Laura and Gregory. After retirement Eckert remained involved in smaller electronics projects and advocated for personal computers. He died in 1995 of leukemia. Surviving him were Judith, his daughter Laura, and his sons John, Gregory, and Chris.

John H. Barnhill

FURTHER READING

Baranger, Walter R. J. "Presper Eckert, Coinventor of Early Computer, Dies at 76." *New York Times* 7 June 1995. Print. An obituary covering Eckert's major achievements.

DeAngelis, Gina, and David J. Bianco. *Computers: Processing the Data*. Minneapolis: Oliver, 2005. Print. Includes a chapter on Eckert and Mauchly.

Dyson, George. *Turing's Cathedral: The Origins of the Digital Universe*. New York: Pantheon, 2012. Print. A survey of the experimentation, mathematical insight, and creative endeavors leading to computers, digital television, genetics, and cosmological models based on computer code.

"ENIAC." *Time* 47.8 (1946): 92. *Academic Search Complete*. Web. 1 May 2012. The magazine article that introduced America's first general-purpose digital electronic computer to the public.

Flamm, Kenneth. *Creating the Computer: Government, Industry, and High Technology*. Washington, DC: Brookings Institution, 1988. Print. An older work but still useful for the development of the ENIAC.

Randall, Alexander V. "The Eckert Tapes: Computer Pioneer Says ENIAC Team Couldn't Afford to Fail—and Didn't." *Computerworld* 40.8 (2006): 18. *Academic Search Complete*. Web. 1 May 2012. Discusses interviews with Eckert, taped in 1989, in which he discusses ENIAC's technology and corrects some myths.

Sobel, Rachel K. "Faulty Memory." *U.S. News and World Report* 132.4 (2002): 70. *Academic Search Complete*. Web. 1 May 2012. Points to the historic omission of credit for the women "computers" who programmed the ENIAC.

Swedin, Eric G. and David L. Ferro. *Computers: The Life Story of a Technology*. Westport: Greenwood, 2005. Print. A history of computers from ancient beginnings to the time of publication, designed for a general audience.

"Unisys Corporation History." *International Directory of Company Histories*, Vol. 36. Detroit: St. James, 2001. Print. Profile that is dated but still useful on the history of Unisys, including mergers and restructurings well past the lifetime of Eckert.

BRENDAN EICH

Creator of the JavaScript programming language

Born: 1961; Pittsburgh, Pennsylvania
Died: -
Primary Field: Computer science
Specialty: Internet
Primary Company/Organization: Mozilla Corporation

INTRODUCTION

Perhaps Brendan Eich's most significant accomplishment was completing a specific assignment in about a week and a half. In that time, Eich, as a new employee at the Netscape Corporation, created a scripting language for presenting content that appeared on the Internet. Until then, everything that users saw on their web browsers was static, essentially pages they could open, read, or leave but with which they could not interact. Eich's invention, which came to be designated as JavaScript (now officially referred to as ECMA-262), allowed developers to create interactive web pages. Content was no longer merely passive but could be developed and presented to give an Internet user a wide range of options for interacting with and manipulating it. Since that time, Eich has been in the forefront of web browser development—leading the creation of the Firefox browser, for example—and the cause of open source software, supporting open and standardized development in order to allow anyone to bring content to the web and prevent single organizations from establishing monopolies.

EARLY LIFE

Brandon Eich was born in Pittsburgh, Pennsylvania, in 1961. His undergraduate studies were at Santa Clara University, where he earned a bachelor's degree in computer science and mathematics. He then attended the University of Illinois at Urbana-Champaign, where he earned a master's degree in computer science in 1986.

Eich's first job after graduating was at Silicon Graphics, a company that sold both hardware and software solutions. Eich was a programmer there for seven years. One of the significant factors surrounding Silicon Graphics (aside from its early commercial successes) was that it started the practice of making its code openly available to other developers. That practice seems to have informed much of Eich's development philosophy in subsequent years. Eich was part of the initial public offering (IPO) there in 1986, a circumstance that made him at least moderately wealthy.

Brendan Eich.

After leaving Silicon Graphics, Eich took a position as a programmer at MicroUnity Systems, an engineering company specializing in data-streaming processors to support video and audio transmission.

LIFE'S WORK

Eich began working at Netscape in April 1995. He described his first assignment as developing a language that could be used to create dynamic content. At that time, the Internet did not have the technical capabilities to support interactivity, as it does now. Every page was static; those who had not created the page could read the content—access the page, scroll up and down the page, and leave it—but could not interact with the content in any way. JavaScript would make such interactivity possible, including the ability to enter data into fields, make calculations, and thus participate in e-commerce. Eich wrote JavaScript to make such dynamic content possible, and did so in ten days.

How he was to go about creating the dynamic qualities required a certain degree of decision making, keeping in mind what might be done in the future and who would do it. One school of thought was that something could be done with the Java programming language, which had existed for a few years and which Netscape was licensed to use. Java was, like its "rival" language C++, an object-oriented programming language, a concept deriving from object orientation as developed initially by Kristen Nygaard, with his Simula programming language. Java is extremely complex, although powerful. Using it outright or adopting it would necessarily restrict the community that could develop interactive content on the web to a relatively small group of developers. Eich decided that the tool to be created would be better if it were a scripting language and thus less complex than a full programming language such as Java. With that decision made, Eich developed what would be known eventually as JavaScipt.

At first, his scripting language was known as Mocha, which was renamed LiveScript when it was released to the public as part of a Netscape release. It was finally christened JavaScript in a move that some thought was an effort to make the language more attractive by implying that it was part of, or derived from, the programming language Java. Eich has been clear that the name was determined by Netscape management.

JavaScript was successful and came to be adopted by everyone. Among those who used it for development was Netscape's main rival, Microsoft, for use in its Internet Explorer. JavaScript not only was widely accepted by developers but also was eventually standardized through Ecma International (a standards organization that has existed since 1961). The reason for moving the code to Ecma in 1996 was not only to guarantee standardization but also to prevent organizations such as Microsoft from taking the language over and creating a semiproprietary language that would defeat the open systems concept Netscape was embracing. JavaScript is still widely known by that name, but its technical nomenclature is ECMAScript or ECMA-262. JavaScript not only has been widely used in the past but also is the preferred development tool in the Cloud9 Development Environment maintained and run by Ajax.org (Eich is a Member of the Ajax Technical Board), a relatively new development initiative.

JavaScript has not been without its competitors, however. Google has developed a tool for its Chrome browser, named Dart, which it is claimed will eventually replace JavaScript. Eich has been extremely outspoken in his criticism of Dart. Both he and others have noted that major browsers Firefox, Internet Explorer, and Safari have no plans to adopt Dart. Unless and until that policy changes, it appears that JavaScript will remain the main tool for web development for anything developed for Google Chrome.

75

When the company offered its IPO (Eich's second) in 1995, Eich found himself well off. In an interview the following year with *The New York Times*, Eich was happy with the money he had made but was hinting of someday establishing his own company; however, that had not occurred as of 2012.

After its initial success, when it seemed that the browser on every computer connected to the Internet was Netscape Communicator, a dramatic switch occurred. Netscape became engaged in a battle with Microsoft that it would eventually lose in what came to be known as the first browser war. The result was the eventual disappearance of the Netscape browser. Through all of these developments, however, Eich remained at Netscape, continuing development projects. In 1998, he was named the lead architect for the Mozilla project.

As lead architect, Eich was involved in the open software approach that Netscape was taking. Open sourcing allowed any independent developer with a sufficient skill set to be able to develop products that would operate seamlessly with the host application (such as the Netscape browser). The open concept, which has gained in popularity, is based on more than making the base source code available. It also requires free distribution of software, providing source code with the program, allowing work to be derived from the code, technology neutrality, and a commitment to placing no restrictions on other software. The importance of this approach and the definition of open sourcing would be critical in the coming years, informing the technical and business approaches of the Mozilla Foundation and the Mozilla Corporation, both heavily influenced by Eich's vision.

In 2003, Eich, still with Netscape although it had been acquired by America Online, helped to found and become a board member for the Mozilla Foundation, a nonprofit organization that—although it possesses a full-time staff—relies on skilled unpaid volunteers to enhance its products, a merging of collaboration and the opportunities afforded by open systems.

Two years later, the foundation created the Mozilla Corporation, a for-profit organization that is a wholly owned subsidiary of the foundation. Eich was named as the company's chief technology officer (CTO).

PERSONAL LIFE

Eich is married and lives with his wife live and five children in California. Starting in the 1970s, Eich began studying the piano and is an accomplished musician at home, in the classical reportoire.

Affiliation: Mozilla

The name Mozilla has stood for different things at different times. It has been a code name for a browser development project, a brand with a logo, and the name given to two organizations: Mozilla Foundation and Mozilla Corporation.

Mozilla's most recent unbroken line as a series of organizations can be dated to 1998, when the Netscape Corporation gave that designation (known as the mozilla.org project) to its browser development initiative. In the following year, Netscape was acquired by America Online (AOL). By 2003, AOL had decided that it would not be developing browsers. Plans were made to spin off the Mozilla organization to become a nonprofit organization that would continue the browser's development. In July, the Mozilla Foundation was formed. Not only was Brendan Eich with that original organization but also the organization received support from Mitch Kapor, founder of Lotus Development Corporation and developer of Lotus 1-2-3.

Two years later (in 2005), Mozilla Corporation was formed. This for-profit entity supports the foundation and is responsible for the development of Mozilla's latest browser, Firefox. Firefox 1.0 was released in 2004 and has been successful as an alternative to Microsoft's Internet Explorer. Its innovations led to the Mozilla Foundation's selection as a Technology Pioneer in 2007. The claims of Firefox's advantages have been bolstered by its wide acceptance in the Internet community, at least in part because of its improved security. Mozilla claims that as of 2012, there have been more than a billion downloads of the Firefox browser, with more than three billion downloads of Firefox add-ons.

In 1998, Eich was named as Web Innovator of the Year (the first to receive the award) for his work with Netscape and his invention of JavaScript. In addition to his current activities as Mozilla Company's CTO, Eich is active in other areas. He joined the advisory board of Ajax.org (developers of a collaborative online development environment, Cloud9 IDE) in 2011.

In 2012, controversy followed Eich when the *Los Angeles Times* reported that he had donated $1,000 to support the passage of Proposition 8, an initiative to ban gay marriage in California, which passed in November 2008.

Robert N. Stacy

FURTHER READING

Booth, David R. *Peer Participation and Software: What Mozilla Has to Teach Government.* Cambridge: MIT, 2010. Print. Part of the John D. and Catherine T. MacArthur Foundation Reports series, this volume describes how Mozilla functions as a large organization staffed by paid professionals with extensive active participation by a large volunteer community and discusses how it can be a model for organizations wanting to produce something of value.

Clark, Jim. *Netscape Time: The Making of the Billion-Dollar Start-up That Took on Microsoft.* New York: St. Martin's, 1999. Print. A history of the Netscape corporation by its founder, discussing not only his business decisions (to avoid venture capitalists and concentrate on browser development) but also the reasons behind those decisions.

Eich, Brendan. "Part Artist, Part Hacker and a Full-Time Programmer." Interview by Steve Lohr. *New York Times* 9 Sept. 1996: n. pag. Print. Although this interview was conducted before Netscape's problems and eventual acquisition by AOL, it provides an interesting portrait of Eich as developer, who, at that stage, had aspirations to create his own start-up.

Lohr, Steve. "BITS: Mozilla Sets Its Sights on Aps." *New York Times* 27 Feb. 2012: n. pag. Print. Discusses Mozilla's strategy for combating what it considers to be the next threat to the open Internet: Apple and Google applications and web browsers. An interesting piece when taken together with Eich's technical arguments against Google's Dart scripting language.

Lohr, Steve, and John Markoff. "In the Battle of the Browsers '04, Firefox Aims at Microsoft." *New York Times* 15 Nov. 2004: n. pag. Print. An article about Eich and the development and release of Firefox 1.0, designed to compete for market share against Microsoft's Internet Explorer.

Seibel, Peter. *Coders at Work: Reflections on the Craft of Programming.* New York: Apress, 2009. Print. A collection of fifteen interbiews with influential programmers, one of them with Eich.

Severance, Charles. "JavaScript: Designing a Language in 10 Days." *Computer* 45.2 (2012): 7–8. *Academic Search Complete.* Web. 2 Aug. 2012. A short history of the development of JavaScript, which took a week and a half to be developed, and its influence since its 1995 release.

Spinello, R. A. "Competing Fairly in the New Economy: Lessons from the Browser Wars." *Journal of Business Ethics* 57.4 (2005): 343–61. Print. A detailed description of the battle between Netscape and Microsoft and its implications for conducting business. Microsoft was accused of creating a monopoly by bundling its browser with its operating system; eventually Netscape succumbed, and its market share dropped from 90 percent of Internet users to 1 percent.

LARRY ELLISON

Cofounder and CEO of Oracle

Born: August 17, 1944; New York, New York
Died: -
Primary Field: Business and commerce
Specialty: Management, executives, and investors
Primary Company/Organization: Oracle

INTRODUCTION

Larry Ellison is the cofounder and chief executive officer (CEO) of Oracle Corporation, one of the largest providers of enterprise software. Enterprise software is sold to businesses, government agencies, and other organizations and differs from that sold to individuals. Originally dominant in the database market, Oracle grew in a variety of other areas, including computer hardware systems, development software, collaboration tools, and middleware. Known for his aggressive business practices, Ellison is viewed by many as a visionary and a reliable ally. Steady growth at Oracle has permitted Ellison to become one of the most highly compensated business executives globally, and his luxurious lifestyle is not without its critics.

EARLY LIFE

Lawrence Joseph "Larry" Ellison was born on August 17, 1944, in the Bronx, New York, to a single mother, Florence Spellman, who was only nineteen years old at the time of his birth. His mother was of Jewish heritage and his father was an Italian American. His father

Larry Ellison.

was a U.S. Air Force pilot stationed abroad before Florence realized she was pregnant. When Ellison was nine months old, he caught pneumonia and his mother realized she was not able to take care of her child in the manner that would provide him with the best prospects. As a result, Florence arranged for Ellison to be adopted by his uncle and aunt, Louis and Lillian Spellman Ellison, in Chicago. Ellison's name was changed to Lawrence Joseph Ellison, and he was formally adopted by Louis and Lillian. Ellison would not meet his biological mother until he was forty-eight years old. Lillian, Louis's second wife, was considered a warm and loving caregiver. Louis, however, was remembered as cold, unsupportive, and often distant. He had immigrated in 1905 to the United States from Russia. Louis was a realtor who at one point owned his own real estate firm, although he lost this business during the Great Depression. Louis then became an auditor for the public housing authority.

Growing up, Ellison and his parents lived in a two-bedroom apartment on the south side of Chicago in a middle-class Jewish neighborhood. As a child, Ellison was considered independent and at times rebellious. Ellison's rebelliousness sometimes extended to the point where he would clash with his father. This unruly streak

has sometimes been attributed to Ellison's discovery at the age of twelve that he was adopted, but it might also have been an expression of his personality.

Ellison was raised in a Reform Jewish household and regularly attended synagogue with his parents. However, he considered himself a religious skeptic even as a child. Ellison has stated that, while he considers himself religious in one sense, the particular dogmas of Judaism are not those to which he would subscribe. Rather, Ellison has indicated he considers the faith of his parents to comprise interesting stories and mythology. While Ellison has stated that he respects those individuals who believe these stories and myths are literally true, he personally sees no evidence for such beliefs. In keeping with this perspective, when Ellison turned thirteen, he declined the opportunity to be bar mitzvahed.

As a child, Ellison also demonstrated talent at tasks involving mathematics and science. He attended Eugene Field Elementary School and then moved on to Sullivan High School before transferring to South Shore High School in 1959. After graduating from South Shore High School, Ellison was accepted into the University of Illinois at Urbana-Champaign. Ellison enjoyed initial success at Illinois and was named science student of the year at the completion of his first year at the university. Unfortunately, after Ellison's second year (but before he took his final examinations), his adoptive mother died, prompting his immediate departure for home. As a result of Lillian's death, Ellison decided to leave school and spent that summer in Northern California. While in California, Ellison lived with his friend Chuck Weiss, who was later to join Oracle as one of its first twenty-five employees. After the summer, Ellison enrolled in the University of Chicago for one term, after which he dropped out and returned to California. While at the University of Chicago, Ellison was first exposed to the then nascent field of computer programming. Although he was only twenty when he left Chicago, Ellison would never again live at home.

LIFE'S WORK

After his sudden move to California, Ellison's adoptive father expressed to him his belief that Ellison would never be successful and would ultimately end a failure. However, Ellison had learned enough computer programming in Chicago to believe that he would be successful in this new field. Moving first to Berkeley, California, Ellison had only enough money with him for a little food and a couple tanks of gasoline for his car. Despite his confidence that he could succeed as a computer programmer, Ellison bounced from job to job for the next several years, even working for a short time at Wells Fargo Bank. During the early 1970s, Ellison worked as a programmer at Amdahl Corporation, and while there he helped build the first mainframe systems compatible with those sold by the dominant supplier at the time, International Business Machines (IBM) Corporation. While at Amdahl, Ellison learned that although it was quite possible to develop hardware and software that were less expensive than those sold by IBM, customers were reluctant to deviate from the market leader unless the alternative was clearly superior. Ellison soon moved to the Ampex Corporation, which specialized in audio and video tape equipment and data storage solutions. While at Ampex, Ellison was assigned to develop a database for the Central Intelligence Agency (CIA), a client of Ampex. Although the development of the database was a relatively minor project, Ellison deeply enjoyed it, and he dubbed it Oracle.

Although as a student Ellison had been criticized for his impatience, this trait proved advantageous to him as an entrepreneur. In 1977, Ellison and two colleagues, Robert Miller and Ed Oates, started a company named Software Development Laboratories, Inc. (SDL). At about this time Ellison came across a paper, written by Edgar F. Codd, titled "A Relational Model of Data for Large Shared Data Banks." This became their basis of Oracle's primary product, the relational databases. Codd, who was employed by IBM, suggested that by using a series of formally defined tables, database programs could provide users with easy and quick access to data. Although Codd's employers saw no future in the concept of structured query language (SQL), Ellison did. As a result, Ellison invested $2,000 as start-up capital for SDL, which two years later was renamed Relational Software, Inc. (RSI). Using contacts he had made while working for Ampex, Ellison secured a two-year contract for RSI to make a database for the CIA, again code-named Oracle. Although Ellison wanted Oracle to be compatible with IBM's database, System R, IBM refused to share the code for that program, requiring Oracle to devise its own product based on Codd's theories.

In July 1979, RSI sold its initial release of Oracle 2 to the CIA for use at the Wright-Patterson Air Force Base, where it ran on Digital Equipment Corporation (DEC) PDP-11 computers. Although the first version of the product was named Oracle 2, there never was a version named Oracle 1. Ellison had decided to use Oracle 2 to suggest that the software was in its second release

and "bugs" present in the initial version had been eliminated. Early employees at RSI became accustomed to doing things "the Ellison way," which resulted in the initial release of Oracle a year early. This permitted RSI to spend the second year devising a commercial version of the software for sale to the public. The success of Oracle with both the CIA and the public led RSI to double its sales for the first several years it was in business. Competitor IBM even adopted the Oracle software for its own use. Based on the popularity of the company's signature product, Ellison in 1982 again changed the organization's name, this time to Oracle Systems Corporation. He helped lead Oracle in making its products available for Unix and Windows users, which would greatly boost sales. Throughout the 1980s, Oracle grew until it saw annual sales of nearly $600 million per year.

Despite this, Oracle nearly was forced to declare bankruptcy in 1990 as the result of accounting irregularities resulting from salespeople who booked sales when they were made rather than upon delivery; hence, if sales were later canceled, Oracle had to restate its sales and profit figures, downgrading them from the figures previously issued. The losses Oracle incurred forced it to lay off 10 percent of its workforce. To prevent such an incident from recurring, Ellison revamped Oracle's accounting procedures and brought in experienced executives as president and chief operating officer to help manage operations, although he remained as CEO.

With new management leadership in place, Ellison was able to focus his energy on the development side of the business. In 1992, Ellison announced the release of Oracle 7, which put Oracle at the forefront of database management software. During this period, Oracle's stock price recovered to surpass its 1990 height and profits reached record levels. Still, Oracle continued to face challenges from IBM, Informix, and Sybase, which all threatened to overtake Oracle in the database software market. Ellison managed Oracle's challenges from these rival database developers. For example, when Sybase, which briefly became the market leader, merged with Powersoft, many thought the resulting combination would become even more powerful. Instead, Sybase shifted its primary focus from core database technology. As a result, Sybase sold rights to its database, running under the Windows operating system, to Microsoft. As a result, Oracle once again rose to prominence in the database software industry. Similarly, when Informix was growing exponentially during the mid-1990s, Ellison remained calm and promoted the development of additional features in Oracle, which soared in market

Affiliation: Oracle

Oracle Corporation is a leader in both hardware and software solutions sold to businesses, government agencies, and other organizations. Long a leader in database software, Oracle has expanded its focus to include servers, storage, middleware, applications, and cloud services.

Oracle augments is products with customer service that is among the most highly ranked in the industry. Oracle's mix of products permit its customers to rely on Oracle's servers, cloud software, and applications to provide an integrated and reliable mix of products tailored to meet the customer's needs.

share when it became known that Informix had misstated its profit and loss.

In 2009, Oracle purchased Sun Microsystems, Inc., which gave Oracle control over the open source database MySQL. Oracle remains the market leader in database software, although it continues to face challenges from Microsoft and IBM.

PERSONAL LIFE

Ellison has been married and divorced four times. In 1967, Ellison married his girlfriend, Adda Quinn; the marriage lasted seven years and ended in divorce in 1974. In 1977, about the same time he founded SDL, Ellison married Nancy Wheeler Jenkins; this marriage also ended in divorce, a year after. Ellison was married to his third wife, Barbara Boothe, from 1983 to 1986, a union that resulted in two children. Finally, Ellison was married to romance novelist Melanie Craft from 2003 until 2010. Ellison was close friends with founder of Apple Steve Jobs, as well as other leaders in the technology field.

Ellison is well known for his love of the outdoors, a passion that has sometimes resulted in his sustaining bodily injuries. He owned the *Rising Sun*, the

eighth-largest yacht in the world, until he sold it to film producer David Geffen in 2010. Ellison has been involved with the America's Cup races as a challenger and, in 2010, as the sponsor of the winning BMW Oracle team. Ellison has also practiced aerobatics with private jets and fighter planes he owned. A lover of exotic automobiles, Ellison owns several, including an Audi R8 and a McLaren F1. An aficionado of Japanese culture, Ellison built his $110 million home in Woodside, California, to resemble a feudal Japanese encampment. In 2012, Ellison also spent more than $500 million to buy the Island of Lanai, the sixth-largest island of the Hawaiian chain. A billionaire, Ellison is one of the largest donors to charity in the United States.

Stephen T. Schroth and Melvin E. Taylor Jr.

FURTHER READING

"Island Shopping: Larry Ellison Recently Bought the Hawaiian Island of Lanai for a Reported $500 Million; He's Got Company." *Forbes* 190.1 (2012): 28. Print. Describes Ellison's purchase of the fiftieth state's sixth-largest island.

Stone, F. M. *The Oracle of Oracle: The Story of Volatile CEO Larry Ellison and the Strategies Behind His Company's Phenomenal Success.* New York: AMACON, 2002. Print. Explores the company's rise to become one of the leaders in database software sales and other technology products.

Symonds, M. *Softwar: An Intimate Portrait of Larry Ellison and Oracle.* New York: Simon, 2003. Print. Ellison participated in this book, which examines the risks, challenges, and successes Oracle faced in the process of becoming one of the globe's most important providers of enterprise software.

Wilson, M. *The Difference between God and Larry Ellison: *God Doesn't Think He's Larry Ellison."* New York: HarperBusiness, 2003. Print. Focuses on Ellison's mercurial personality and its effect on some of the many successes Oracle has enjoyed as well as a few of the challenges it presents.

DOUGLAS C. ENGELBART

Inventor of the computer mouse

Born: 1925; Portland, Oregon
Died: -
Primary Field: Computer science

Specialty: Computer software
Primary Company/Organization: Stanford Research Institute

INTRODUCTION

Douglas C. Engelbart is best known as the inventor of the computer mouse, but his life's work has focused on using computing systems to support organizations as "augmented knowledge workshops" using "online systems," the combination of tools such as e-mail, video conferencing, networking, and hypertext to advance organizations and cross-organizational efforts. He pioneered such tools to advance organizational transformation; his firsts include display editing, windows, cross-file editing, outline processing, hypermedia, and groupware. He is also the founder of the Bootstrap Institute, which is dedicated to deploying technology in service of collaboration.

EARLY LIFE

Born 1925 in Oregon, Douglas Carl Engelbart grew up on a small farm near Portland, Oregon, during the Great Depression. After high school graduation in 1942, he attended Oregon State College (now Oregon State University), majoring in electrical engineering. During World War II, he spent two years in the U.S. Navy in the Philippines as an electronic/radar technician. While in the Navy, he read Vannevar Bush's groundbreaking 1945 *Atlantic Monthly* article "As We May Think," in which Bush introduced the hypothetical information storage and retrieval machine known as the memex. After the war, Engelbart returned to school, earning his bachelor's degree in electrical engineering in 1948.

After his undergraduate work, Engelbart began working as an electrical engineer at Ames Laboratory in San Francisco for the National Advisory Committee for Aeronautics (NACA, the progenitor of the National Aeronautics and Space Administration, NASA). Engelbart left NACA in 1951, became engaged to be married, and began to assess and develop his life goals. He did not like the idea of spending 5.5 million seconds (his working life to age sixty) simply working at a job and supporting his family. Instead, he deliberately and consciously set himself the goal of contributing positively to the world and humankind, and he concluded that harnessing human potential could be greatly facilitated through the use of computers. At that time, he recognized the huge, untapped potential of computers to improve human effort and the human condition; he focused his interests on how computers and their human users interact. He began to visualize people in front of computer screens accessing cyberspace, developing and organizing ideas rapidly and easily. These dreams anticipate the Internet and the World Wide Web.

Douglas C. Engelbart.

After this epiphany about computing, Engelbart enrolled in the graduate school of electrical engineering at the University of California in Berkeley, from which he earned his Ph.D. in 1955. His graduate work would result in several patents. He then taught at Berkeley a year before moving to the Stanford Research Institute (SRI) in 1957.

LIFE'S WORK

By the 1960s, Engelbart was inventing significant computer products: groupware, hypertext, and onscreen windows with menus. In 1963 came his most significant invention, the computer mouse. The original mouse, developed with Bill English, was carved from wood and was so named because of the wire (tail) connecting it to the computer. SRI patented the mouse and (since Engelbart had developed it as an employee); as a result, Engelbart and English received no royalties for their invention.

It had two wheels perpendicular to each other, attached to an analog device that plotted location of the wheels on an x-y axis; the analog device was housed in the wooden shell and wired to a workstation. Engelbart also referred to the device as "peripheral": "If I were designing a car, the mouse was just a windshield wiper."

In fact, the mouse became the steering wheel. Although SRI owned the patent, it failed to recognize the value of the mouse, licensing it to Xerox Palo Alto Research Center and Apple for lifetime fees of merely $45,000 each. Other licenses earned even less. The patent lasted from 1970 to 1987, expiring just as the mouse became ubiquitous, so there were no royalties at all for the millions sold after 1987. For Engelbart, video teleconferencing and the early precursor to the Internet were more important.

Engelbart developed his ideas of human-computer interaction for raising collective organizational IQ until 1963, when he finally got the chance to establish the Augmentation Research Center at Stanford Research Institute. He created the mouse, help menus, and indeed many if not most of the basic interactive systems of modern computing. ARC funding ended in 1977, and Engelbart was unable to find funding from a private sector unable to understand what he was trying to accomplish. In 1996, he was able to partner with Sun Microsystems and Netscape Communications to realize his idea of bootstrapping: feeding back results to make the next iteration faster and easier. That reality involved organizations dialoguing and tracking the dialogue to build a cross-referenced knowledge base. Practical needs and abstract intellectual concepts alike belonged in the knowledge base. The effort was available to all who used Netscape's web browser and Sun's Java. Eventually, every PC would be able to access the data.

On December 9, 1968, Engelbart, still at the Stanford Research Institute, unveiled the SRI team's latest inventions at the Fall Joint Computer Conference in San Francisco in what has been dubbed the Mother of All Demos. With Bill English and the SRI team, Engelbart took an hour and a half to demonstrate the mouse, e-mail, word processing, cut-and-paste functions, hypertext, and video conferencing. For the first time, the world at large began to understand the potential of a computer network and the possibilities offered by human-computer interaction. Attendance at the demonstration was more than one thousand people, who at that time focused on Engelbart's now primitive black-and-white images on a 22-inch television screen.

Engelbart called his interactive functions the oN-Line System (NLS), which he envisioned to be an integrated system that would allow collaborating and bootstrapping for continual enhancement of human intellect and the human world. NLS was to provide a new way of thinking about how people learn, work, and live with one another. Engelbart and his team were at one of the first two Internet nodes. Before Engelbart, computers were stand-alone, giant machines, devoted mainly to mathematical and scientific calculations; some saw them mainly as glorified, efficient adding machines. Engelbart and the SRI team showed how computers could be much more: facilitating human communication, for example. However, Engelbart recognized and would persist in believing that the hardware and software were secondary to the potential of a galvanized human community acting together through the technology; he saw technology as serving, not dominating, human endeavor.

In November 1969, Engelbart received the first packets transmitted by Vinton Cerf and his team over the ARPANET (the precursor of the Internet) from at the University of California, Los Angeles (the first node of the later Internet) to SRI (the second node). Networked computing was old hat even then for Engelbart, who had been contemplating nets as early as 1951, when there were not even two dozen computers in existence.

On the fortieth anniversary of the NLS, Stanford and the Tech Museum of Innovation in San Jose held commemorations. Andries van Dam of Brown University said that he was overwhelmed at the time about the massive capacity for self-improvement in recurrent cycles that refined with each iteration, made the group smarter for the next iteration, and made the tools more useful the next time through. It was a continuous process. In the forty years since, the true integrated system had fallen by the wayside because of the need to dumb down links, the loss of WYSIWYG, and the loss of intellectual curiosity and knowledge of historical context. Rather than becoming smarter and better, computer geeks were locking themselves into smaller and smaller compartments, cut off from one another and from the broader world.

Engelbart, despite his prominence in the technological world, had higher priorities. His goal was to make humanity more adept at dealing with problems that may not have solutions. The computer is a tool for handling complexity, allowing people to use their brains more effectively. If it does that, it is more important than bronze or the printing press, according to Engelbart. In practice, Engelbart helps companies become more adept at coping with change, ever increasing and ever more complex change. Engelbart talks of a capability infrastructure: core competencies, workers, customers, facilities, whatever allows the business to function. This is where most managers spend their time and energies: developing organization, procedures, and human

Affiliation: Doug Engelbart Institute

Established in 1989, the Doug Engelbart Institute, original named the Bootstrap Institute for Engelbart's bootstrapping concept, is located in Fremont, California. Bootstrap occupies a small space in the headquarters of Logitech, the mouse manufacturer. Logitech provides the space free, perhaps the least it could do for the man who invented the product that made Logitech possible. Established in 1989, the organization has focused on combining small group knowledge nodes into larger and larger collectivities that can significantly enhance the ability of humanity to deal with urgent and complex problems. Dynamic knowledge repositories and networked improvement communities are still more of a vision than a reality, and civic and economic potential remain untapped. However, in December 2008, San Jose's forty-year-anniversary celebration of Engelbart's Mother of All Demos attested to the ongoing belief in that vision. The celebration included talks, a field trip to Stanford, and the first display of the interactive mural destined for a worldwide tour in the hope of attracting people to Engelbart's dream of using technology for human life enhancement. "Collective intelligence workshops" were conducted, attendees were invited to sign up for action committees for worldwide global intelligence issues, and the MIT Center for Collective Intelligence conducted a contest.

resources. More important to Engelbart is improvement of infrastructure, which gets neglected in times of rapid change (often the norm today). Engelbart also talks of *a*, *b*, and *c* activities, with *a* referring to the activities that directly apply to a business, *b* referring to activities to improve *a* activities, and *c* referring to activities that improve the improvement method. The *c* activities are the critical ones, yet they are the most likely to be forgotten.

C activities include more efficient knowledge transfer within the organization, better selection and operation of pilot programs, and so on. Tools for improving *c* activities include internal websites, databases, and data warehouses. Engelbart was working on intranets in the 1960s and at Tymshare (later owned by McDonnell Douglas) used intranet capability to integrate computing and communications. Technology makes people smarter by creating those lessons, databases, and collections of collective experience. However, technology alone does not solve the problem; Engelbart said that the neglected aspect is still the human. He was talking about basic quality circles in the 1990s. People had to be empowered to use the lessons learned, amplify them, act on them, and make decisions. Rather than project groups, task forces, and technology, businesses had to be communities.

PERSONAL LIFE

Although after 1976 Engelbart fell into relative obscurity, in 1997 he finally achieved recognition and succeeded financially when he won the Lemelson-MIT Prize for invention, which included an award of half a million dollars. The Lemelson-MIT, established by inventor Jerome H. Lemelson in 1994, is the largest cash award for American inventors. His goal remained to make human effort smarter by using technology to promote collaboration: computers, networks, and hypermedia. Upon receiving the award, Engelbart said that his greatest regret was that his inventions never accomplished what he sought: betterment of society. That goal remains the chief aim of the Bootstrap Institute, the think tank in Atherton, Calfornia, that Engelbart established in 1989. In fact, as of 1997 Engelbart was on record as saying that the problems of the past were small compared to those looming in the future.

After retirement, Engelbart remained in the Bay Area near his four children and nine grandchildren. His wife, Ballard, died in 1997 (the same year he won the Lemelson-MIT Prize) after forty-seven years of marriage. Three years afterward, Logitech supplied Engelbart with space, a free server, and tech support from Sun Microsystems. In 2000, he worked the lecture circuit for additional income. In 2007, Engelbart was diagnosed with Alzheimer's disease. In World War II he had served as a radar technician. His goal then was to get planes home safely. His goal remained to use technology in service of humanity.

John H. Barnhill

FURTHER READING

Bardini, Thierry. *Bootstrapping: Douglas Engelbart, Co-evolution, and the Origins of Personal Computing*. Stanford: Stanford UP, 2000. Print. An older but still useful perspective on Engelbart and his work.

Cockell, Moira. *Common Knowledge: The Challenge of Transdisciplinarity*. Lausanne: EPFL, 2011. Print. Includes a good chapter on collective intelligence and Engelbart.

Engelbart, Christina. "A Lifetime Pursuit." *Doug Engelbart Institute*. 2008. Web. 1 May 2012. Engelbart's daughter details her father's life and achievements. Includes photographs.

Frenkel, Karen A. "A Difficult, Unforgettable Idea." *Communications of the ACM* 52.3 (2009): 21. *Business Source Complete*. Web. 1 May 2012. Engelbart on how the revolution failed when the original NLS devolved forty years later into dumbing down of product and producers in the computer world.

Gallagher, Leigh. "Innovator's Dilemma." *Forbes* 166.5 (2000): 142. *Business Source Complete*. Web. 1 May 2012. The mouse as a bad business deal for Engelbart; he received virtually no royalties.

Hammond, Richard. "The Mouse Turns 40." *Information Today* 25.11 (2008): 1–48. *Academic Search Complete*. Web. 1 May 2012. From the Mother of All Demos to the Bootstrap Institute, in one short article. The emphasis is on the demo.

Holden, Constance. "Mouse Man Wins Big." *Science* 276.5312 (1997): 537. *Academic Search Complete*. Web. 1 May 2012. The Lemelson MIT award is defined, and Engelbart's Bootstrap Institute is mentioned.

Holwerda, Thom. "'The Mother of All Demos' Turns 40." 11 Dec. 2008. *OSNews*. Web. 31 July 2012.

Reviews the events of the fortieth anniversary of the Mother of All Demos, acknowledging Engelbart as "one of the greatest visionaries in the world of computing."

Markoff, John. *What the Dormouse Said*. New York: Penguin, 2009. Print. Examines the interconnectedness of the 1960s drug and computing subcultures, with particular emphasis on Engelbart and his vision.

Port, Otis. "The Man Behind the Mouse." *Businessweek* 3523 (1997): 48. *Business Source Complete*. Web. 2 May 2012. On the occasion of the Lemelson-MIT Prize, a retrospective on the mouse and a gloomy assessment of the future.

Ransdell, Eric. "The Man Who Sees the Future." *U.S. News and World Report* 120.20 (1996): 47. *Academic Search Complete*. Web. 1 May 2012. Another career overview, touching on the Navy and Engelbart's career decision and then discussing his accomplishments and bootstrapping.

Stewart, Thomas A. "Tools That Make Business Better and Better." *Fortune* 134.12 (1996): 237–40. *Business Source Complete*. Web. 1 May 2012. A brief overview of Bootstrap with reference to Engelbart's early career.

THELMA ESTRIN

Professor emerita, University of California, Los Angeles

Born: February 21, 1924; New York, New York
Died: -
Primary Field: Computer science
Specialty: Computer programming
Primary Company/Organization: University of California, Los Angeles

INTRODUCTION
Thelma Estrin, a pioneer in biomedical engineering, used computer technology and electrical engineering to solve problems in health care and medical research. She was one of the first women to earn a Ph.D. in engineering and designed the first system for analog-digital conversion of electrical activity from the nervous system. Throughout her career as a researcher and a professor, she served as a role model for other young women who would wish to pursue careers in science, technology, engineering, or medicine. She broke the barriers of gender and religious discrimination that existed in the corporate and research professions.

EARLY LIFE
Estrin was born Thelma Austern on February 21, 1924, to Jewish parents in Harlem in New York City. She was a premature twin at three pounds, and at birth her sibling died in the hospital. Thelma's mother, Mary Ginsburg Austern, was extremely focused on the care of her only daughter and would have no other children. Thelma's father, I. Billy Austern, was a traveling shoe salesman and often out of town, so Mary had a major influence on her daughter's development. Prior to marriage, Mary had managed an automobile parts store and even knew how to drive, unusual for women at that time. After marriage, Mary was active in the Democratic Party and the Freemasons in the Order of the Eastern Star. She also always helped the sick, elderly, and troubled while

still running a household and ensuring that Thelma had a hot lunch every day. Her mother's influence shaped Thelma's belief that one should be socially useful and independent.

From an early age, Thelma was a fast learner and always received good grades. Throughout elementary school, she had helped her apartment repairman's son with his homework. At the same time, Thelma was sloppy and absent-minded; she typically had ink stains on her hands and clothes, and she loved to play sports. It is possible that she had inherited this type of energy from her father, who also enjoyed sports and lively entertainment.

At Abraham Lincoln High School in Brighton Beach, a Brooklyn neighborhood where her family had moved during the Depression, Thelma developed an interest in politics and social justice. She joined the left-wing American Student Union, much to the dismay of her parents. Her mother had hoped that Thelma would become a lawyer, and the father of her best childhood friend had advised her to major in Spanish and become a commercial secretary. She had always been good in math, however, and took extra mathematics courses during her senior year; her first boyfriend, Richard Bellman, was head of the high school mathematics team

Thelma Estrin.

and later received a Medal of Honor from the Institute of Electrical and Electronics Engineers (IEEE) for his work in applied mathematics. Their political differences, however, led to their breakup.

Thelma enrolled in City College of New York (CCNY) in January 1941 to become an accountant. She chose CCNY because it accepted only seventy-five women per year; to be chosen was an honor. CCNY was also close to home, and her mother was dying of cancer. In June, Thelma met CCNY history major Gerald Estrin through the American Student Union; they were married in December, two weeks after Japan's attack on Pearl Harbor and the United States entry into World War II. During this period Thelma's parents both died.

In 1942, Gerald enlisted in the Army Signal Corps; he learned how to make electromagnetic relays at Kurman Electric Company before being called to active duty. At that point, Thelma took a three-month engineering assistant course at Stevens Institute of Technology. The course prepared her to work for two years at the Radio Receptor Company. She started in the tool and model shop but was transferred to the company laboratory, where she assembled test equipment and repaired radio transmitters. At this time, CCNY's the doors of its engineering school to women, and after work Thelma took classes there.

In 1945, the Army sent Gerald to San Bernardino, California, where Thelma joined him, working as a radio technician for the Army Air Force. When the European phase of the war ended, Gerald was transferred to Salt Lake City, Utah, and Thelma returned to New York City to resume her engineering classes. In December, Gerald was discharged from the Army; three months later, Thelma and Gerald moved to Madison, Wisconsin, to pursue undergraduate electrical engineering degrees at the University of Wisconsin. They supported themselves through the GI Bill, part-time work as teaching assistants, and the sale of Thelma's mother's diamond ring.

By working eighteen hours a day without vacations, Thelma earned her bachelor's, master's, and doctoral degrees in 1948, 1949, and 1951, respectively. As a graduate student, Gerald received research assistantships while Thelma received only teaching assistantships. It was assumed that a woman would lose interest in engineering once she had children. Thelma wished to balance her career and family obligations and concentrated on analytical rather than experimental electrical engineering. Her graduate research involved improved methods of calculation and problem solving.

LIFE'S WORK

After Thelma earned her Ph.D., Gerald received an offer to join John von Neumann's computer project at the Institute for Advanced Study (IAS); the Estrins moved to Princeton, New Jersey. Thelma had worked on this project for a few months, testing and documenting the arithmetic unit of the machine, but she wanted to work in a different place from her husband.

In 1951, Thelma finally found a position at the Electroencephalography (EEG) Department of the Neurological Institute of Columbia Presbyterian Hospital in New York. There she oversaw the maintenance of the clinical EEG equipment to ensure consistent performance. She also had the opportunity to collaborate with doctors on EEG and electromyography (EMG) studies. She made many improvements to existing systems, including the circuit design of a frequency analyzer for bioelectric potentials; she increased its stability and tunability. She also collaborated on a study of the action potential and refractory period of striated muscle. The Estrins would often go out to dinner with von Neumann and his wife, where she and von Neumann would discuss the electrical activity of the nervous system.

In 1952, Gerald had an opportunity to assist in the building of a computer at the Weizmann Institute of Science in Rehovot, Israel, near Tel Aviv. At that time, IAS planned to build versions of its computer at a dozen locations in the United States and Europe. Thelma accompanied Gerald with their three-month-old daughter, Margo, visiting computer groups in England, the Netherlands, France, and Italy before arriving in Israel. Upon arrival at the Weizmann Institute, Gerald was appointed director of the project, and Thelma was a principal member of the engineering group. After six months of redesigning the system, the WEIZAC computer performed its first calculation and became the first electronic computer in the Middle East. Thelma had her second daughter, Judith, while working in Israel.

After returning to Princeton in April 1955, Gerald resumed work at IAS and Thelma took a position as a mathematics instructor at Rutgers University in order to be closer to her two daughters. In 1956, the University of California, Los Angeles (UCLA), hired Gerald to develop a computer engineering program; the family moved again. UCLA policies would not allow Thelma to work at the School of Engineering with Gerald, so she found a half-time teaching position at Valley College, a community college in Los Angeles. She taught there for two years and also worked as a consultant.

In 1959, Professor H. W. Magoun of the UCLA Medical School developed an interdisciplinary neuroscience program there, leading to the establishment of the Brain Research Institute (BRI). After the birth of her third daughter, Deborah, Estrin was recognized by BRI for her work at Columbia on electroencephalography. In 1960, she was hired by BRI to organize a conference on computers in brain research. The conference made more biomedical researchers realize the potential of computers as research tools. After the conference, physiologist Mary A.B. Brazier, anatomy professor Ross Adey, M.D., and BRI director John D. French asked Thelma to draft a proposal to establish a data-processing laboratory at BRI. Estrin's proposal included funding for the design and implementation of an analog-to-digital conversion (ADC) system that would translate the electric "spikes" of neurons into numeric data. This system saved time and provided real-time analyses of neuron-firing patterns.

Estrin worked in various areas of BRI during her tenure at UCLA, focusing on improvements in the Data Processing Laboratory (DPL). In 1965, she designed a time-sharing system that would permit data processing in real time, while an experiment was conducted, at a number of BRI laboratories. In 1969, BRI director French asked Estrin to become acting director of DPL and to head a task force that would recommend improvements for lab organization; she became DPL director in 1970.

During the 1970s, Estrin pioneered the use of interactive graphics as a tool for neuroscientists and neurosurgeons, collaborating with multiple researchers, including Robert Sclabassi and Richard Buchness. In a 1974 paper, Estrin, Sclabassi, and Buchness described a computer system that combined diagnostic information from x-ray scans of a human head with general neuroanatomical brain atlas pictures to compute and graphically present a brain map. This work also made it possible to simulate and display the movement of an instrument while being used for an operation. The system could be used to plan an operation or monitor an existing one. During this time she also taught two courses, one on electronics for neuroscience and a graduate seminar on computer applications in health care delivery.

In 1980, Estrin was allowed to transfer to the UCLA Computer Science Department of the School of Engineering and Applied Science to pursue her research interests in biomedical computing. She retired in July 1991 at the age of sixty-seven.

Affiliation: Brain Research Institute

The Brain Research Institute (BRI), where Thelma Estrin headed the Data Processing Laboratory in the 1970s, was founded in 1959 by neuroscientists John French, Horace Magoun, Donald Lindsley and Charles Sawyer to establish neuroscience and brain research as a distinct research endeavor drawing on a range of scientific disciplines. Under the direction of Arnold Scheibel, professor of anatomy and of psychiatry, from 1987 to 1995, BRI established a system of working groups that meet regularly to discuss issues requiring interdisciplinary attention; one outgrowth was the Alzheimer's Disease Center. During the same period, the nueroscience Ph.D. program evolved to place more emphasis on molecular and cellular biology, led by Allan Tobin, who succeeded Scheibel as BRI director and served until 2003; according to an external review committee report, Tobin recaptured "the vision and scientific visibility that characterized this institute at its outset." Chris Evans, Professor of Psychiatry and Biobehavioral Science, succeeded him in 2004.

Today, the BRI encompasses nearly three hundred faculty members in twenty-seven departments across six schools. Its mission, according to the institute's website, is "to nurture the cross-pollination of ideas" and "to foster novel collaborations" in all aspects of neuroscience, "from molecules to the mind, from the laboratory bench to the patient's bedside." According to the website, BRI's multidisciplinary collaborations "have led to identification of pathogenic mechanisms and the formulation of new therapeutic approaches. Investigations span the genetic, molecular, cellular, systems, and behavioral levels. Members study the normal structure and workings of the nervous system, its development, its cognitive functions, its derangement by disease and injury, and the means of its repair and protection. BRI-associated researchers use advanced technologies ranging from genomics and proteomics to magnetic resonance imaging and positron emission tomography to biosensors and microelectromechanical systems. Many of these investigations are possible only through multidisciplinary collaborations among BRI members."

Estrin earned many honors for her work, including Outstanding Engineer of the Year Award from the California Institute for the Advancement of Engineering, the Achievement Award from the Society of Women Engineers, and the Superior Accomplishment Award from the National Science Foundation. She received the honorary degree of doctor of science from the University of Wisconsin–Madison in 1989 and was awarded a Fulbright fellowship at the Weizmann Institute in Israel to study EEG patterns in epileptics. She is also a founding Fellow of the American Institute for Medical and Biological Engineering and a 1977 IEEE Life Fellow "for contributions to the design and application of computer systems for neurophysical and brain research." She served as president of the IEEE Engineering in Medicine and Biology Society and on the Technical Activities Board. In 1982, she became IEEE's first female vice president and the first woman to be elected to the IEEE Board of Directors.

PERSONAL LIFE

Despite the long, hard hours of their careers, Thelma and Gerald Estrin had an active social life and enjoyed a marriage lasting more than seventy years. They enjoyed hosting dinner parties, walking on the beach, watching basketball, playing tennis, and attending the Metropolitan Opera. They had three daughters: Margo, a medical doctor; Judith, senior vice president of Cisco Systems; and Deborah, a computer science professor at the University of Southern California. Their time Thelma and Gerald spent in Israel made them identify more strongly with Judaism. Their daughters all speak Hebrew and maintain certain Jewish traditions, and the family members make annual visits to Israel. Gerald died on March 29, 2012.

Rachel Wexelbaum

FURTHER READING

Estrin, Judy. *Closing the Innovation Gap: Reigniting the Spark of Creativity in a Global Economy.* New York: McGraw-Hill, 2009. E-book. Daughter Judy includes interviews with her sister Deborah and cites her mother and father to address how to encourage and increase innovation.

Estrin, Thelma. "Oral-History: Thelma Estrin." Interview by Janet Abbate. *IEEE Global History Network.* 2002. Web. 28 June 2012. Interview that included Gerald as well as Thelma Estrin about their careers in science. Thelma addresses her experiences with gender and religious discrimination.

---. "Oral-History: Thelma Estrin." Interview by Frederick Nebeker. 1992. *IEEE Global History Network.* Web. 28 June 2012. Thelma discusses her early years and life's work.

Nebeker, Frederik, ed. "New Applications of the Computer: Thelma Estrin and Biomedical Engineering."

Sparks of Genius: Portraits of Engineering Excellence. New York: Institute of Electrical and Electronics Engineers, 1994. E-book. A detailed history of Estrin's life and professional accomplishments, with a scientific focus.

FEDERICO FAGGIN

Designer of the microchip

Born: December 1, 1941; Vicenza, Italy
Died: -
Primary Field: Applied science
Specialty: Physics and engineering
Primary Company/Organization: Foveon

INTRODUCTION

Federico Faggin is a physicist and electrical engineer whose most notable project to date is the design of the first commercial microprocessor, the Intel 4004, in 1971, as well as other influential chips behind the computer revolution: the 8008, the 8080, and the Z80. Faggin was the guiding force during the first five years of Intel's microprocessor effort. These chips were used for a variety of purposes, especially the first home computers, including the Altair 8800 kit and the TRS-80 from RadioShack. Forty years later, his innovations are still being used in the Pentium chips that power many computers. Starting in 1981, Faggin began a life as an entrepreneur and founded several successful companies. Among his many honors are a National Medal of Technology and Innovation, presented to him in 2010 by President Barack Obama.

EARLY LIFE

Federico Faggin was born December 1, 1941, in Vicenza, Italy, the son of Giuseppe Faggin, a teacher of the history of philosophy and general history, and Emma Faggin. Two years later, after the fall of fascism, his family moved to the countryside to escape Allied bombing during World War II and returned to Vicenza when Faggin was eight years old. It was his father's hope that Faggin would study the humanities, but Faggin was

fascinated by anything mechanical from an early age. He attended a technical high school, the A. Rossi Technical Institute in Vicenza, where he studied radio technology and electronics. In 1960, immediately after high school, he worked as an assistant engineer at business machine developer Olivetti Electronic R&D Laboratory near Milan. There, at the age of nineteen, he designed his first computer, using germanium transistors and

Federico Faggin.

magnetic core memory. It was 7 feet high and as wide as a door frame.

After this initial experience with computers, Faggin decided he needed to remedy his lack of advanced education and entered the University of Padua to study physics. He chose physics because he felt it would provide a better foundation for future endeavors than further study of engineering. He undertook a program of study that typically took five to seven years and completed it in four while working and tutoring. He received his doctorate in physics, summa cum laude, on December 1, 1965, his twenty-fourth birthday. After teaching briefly, he worked for CERES corporation, a small high-tech start-up begun by his former supervisor at Olivetti, and in 1967 he joined SGS Fairchild in Agrate Brianza, about twelve miles from Milan.

LIFE'S WORK

At SGS Fairchild, Faggin used metal oxide semiconductor (MOS) technology to design the company's first two MOS-integrated circuits. MOS circuits were smaller and easier to fabricate than those that used the then-prevalent bipolar technology; although MOS circuits were slower, they had the potential of carrying more logical gates with the same expenditure of power.

In 1968, Faggin visited Palo Alto, California, to study at SGS Fairchild's licensing company, Fairchild Semiconductor, and took classes that Stanford University was offering for employees. This research exchange program between the two companies was supposed to last six months, but Faggin stayed in the United States. At Fairchild, he worked on silicon gate technology, and his silicon gate integrated circuits were commercially available in 1968. This technology would be used for computer memory and the first microprocessor. While at Fairchild, Faggin also developed two ideas that would be important to microprocessors: the buried contact and the bootstrap load. These improved the speed and density of silicon gate technology, so that it would compete with chips made with metal gates. Within a few years, the entire industry had switched to silicon gates for its new designs, and the technology is still in use today.

In June 1968, Gordon E. Moore urged Faggin to give a paper at the International Electron Devices Meeting in October, and Faggin decided to remain at Fairchild rather than return to Italy. A month later, Moore and Robert Noyce, along with twenty other Fairchild employees, unexpectedly went to work at the newly formed Intel. Faggin expected that Intel would try to exploit his silicon gate technology, and this turned out

Affiliation: Foveon

Foveon, Inc., was founded in 1997, and one of the investing companies was Synaptics, Inc., founded by Federico Faggin. From 2003 to 2008, Faggin was Foveon's president and chief executive officer. The company was sold to Sigma in 2008.

Foveon released its X_3 color sensors in 2002. Each pixel of Foveon's X_3 image sensors uses silicon's color separation property to capture red, green, and blue light simultaneously. Three layers of silicon are used to capture these three primary colors; blue light is detected in the surface layer, green light in the middle, and red light in the deepest layer, so the sensor can detect a full-color image sharply. X_3 technology became available in cameras, personal digital assistants (PDAs), cell phones, and security cameras. The sensor is manufactured by the same CMOS process that makes the Pentium III processor.

Before X_3, a charge-coupled device (CCD) was used to create a digital image. In use since the early days of space exploration, CCDs can collect pixels of one color at a time because they use color filters. Missing information had to be interpolated by surrounding pixels, so CCD and related technologies can result in blurred images.

In 2011, Sigma released the professional-grade SD1, which employs a 46-megapixel X_3 sensor from Foveon. While a camera using a different process rated at 20 million pixels, half measure green light and a quarter measure red and blue, meaning that competitors lose some of the information coming from the source. The final image is recorded directly, without interpolation, and Foveon claims that images made this way look like they were taken with film. The claim is not spurious; film also uses three different layers to capture different colors of light.

to be true: Intel sought to replace magnetic core memory with semiconductor memory. Faggin later said that he was not initially invited to join the company because that would have tipped IBM's hand to Fairchild. Nevertheless, Faggin left Fairchild in 1970 to design a new chip for his former coworkers. While working on the Busicom Project, a design of seven chips for a calculator's integrated circuit, he took over work started by Ted Hoff and Stanley Mazor. Hoff had proposed to combine the three chips that would be used as the central processing unit (CPU), and Mazor had come up with the basic concept for the new proposal requiring only four chips, but no designs for the chips had been made; they were waiting for Faggin to complete the work on what came to called the 4000 family.

The combination of the three integrated circuits for the CPU, Faggin would remark later, was barely possible using existing processes, and no one had designed a chip of that complexity before. In fact, Intel had never designed a random-logic chip such as this, and there were few resources that it could provide to Faggin, given that its talent was busy designing computer memory. Although all four of the chips Faggin designed had novel features, the project is remembered for the design of the CPU: the Intel 4004, the first microprocessor. Faggin was so proud of his work that he signed his initials on the metal mask. The first 4004s arrived in the lab at the end of 1970, but they did not work; a technician had forgotten the buried contact. It took three weeks for new chips to be delivered, and these worked as expected. The 4004 was the first microprocessor, a sixteen-pin chip that held twenty-three hundred transistors and operated at 740 kilohertz, built nine years after Faggin had built his first computer with transistors. After negotiating with the Japanese company Busicom, which had commissioned the project, Intel advertised the arrival of the microprocessor in November 15, 1971, issue of *Electronic News*.

Faggin's methodology would be reused for other Intel microprocessors and microcontrollers. While the 4004 was still in the design phase, Mazor promised the Computer Terminal Corporation that Intel could design a CPU chip for it, not just the memory. Even though he was not a chip designer and the 4004 was not completed, he was able to get a contract for a new design, the 1201. Although work on the 1201 began at the same time that Faggin had joined Intel, its development stalled out. The project was put on hold until Faggin finished the 4004. Using what he had learned while working on the 4004, Faggin completed the work on the 1201 by the end of 1971; it was the first 8-bit microprocessor, and when sold by Intel starting in April 1972, it was referred to by the name 8008. It had thirty-five hundred transistors and used eighteen pins. In 1973, four computers for hobbyists were on the market, all using the 8008. This was the first of a successful line of x86 Intel microprocessors that are ubiquitous even today, given that it is the architecture behind the Pentium and Pentium Pro chips.

Faggin went on to propose an 8080 chip for Intel, but it took nine months to get permission to start work on it, and he designed the 4040 as well. The 8080 would be used by the successful personal computer kit, the Altair 8800, in 1975. Faggin was promoted to manager of the research and development department in 1974 at the age of thirty-two, but he felt unsupported and in the wrong place, given that Intel's core business was memory and Faggin wanted to design microprocessors. As a result, at the end of the year, with venture capital from Exxon Enterprises, Faggin founded Zilog Corporation, the first company devoted to microprocessors, where he helped to design the Z80 microprocessor. First available in 1976, this 8-bit processor was used for the RadioShack TRS-80 personal computer and other personal computers and is still in heavy production, at approximately 40 million units per year. This was the last engineering project Faggin directed. Exxon Enterprises acquired Zilog in 1981, and that year IBM selected Intel's chip over a Zilog chip for its personal computer. Freed from Zilog, Faggin began a career as an entrepreneur so that he could participate in start-ups, when the energy and passion of a company are at their highest.

After Zilog, Faggin founded companies that sought to improve the human-computer interface. The first was Cygnet Technologies, which would design intelligent voice and data devices that would accompany a personal computer. In 1986, Faggin cofounded Synaptics, Inc., with California Institute of Technology professor Carver A. Mead, hoping that they could devise a way to imprint the pattern of a neural net on a microchip. This ambitious goal was expected to result in a computer that recognized a user who sat in front of it and mechanisms that could perform dangerous tasks such as mining, but it is a difficult dream to implement. In order to maintain financing for this research project, Synaptics develops touch, sound, and sight computer interfaces. Synaptics made the touch sensors in T-Mobile's G1 phone, the first of the "Google phones" released in October 2008. From 2003 to 2008, Faggin was also the president and chief executive officer of Foveon, a developer of X_3, a three-layer image-sensor technology that captures color images without using color filters. In 2012, he was president of the nonprofit Federico and Elvia Faggin Foundation, dedicated to the study of consciousness.

PERSONAL LIFE

Faggin lives with his wife, Elvia, in Los Altos Hills, California. He became a naturalized American citizen in 1978 but continues to answer the phone with the Italian greeting "Pronto" and is likely to welcome guests with wine and antipasti.

In 1988, Faggin earned an International Marconi Fellowship Award as well as the Gold Medal for

Science and Technology, awarded by the president and government of Italy. In 1994, the Institute of Electrical and Electronics Engineers (IEEE) awarded him the W. Wallace-McDonald Award, and in 1996, the National Inventors Hall of Fame inducted Faggin for his invention of the microprocessor. In 1997, he was awarded the Kyoto Prize, Japan's highest honor for global achievement, by the Inamori Foundation. The AeA/Stanford Executive Institute Award for Outstanding Achievement by an alumnus was given to Faggin in 2003 (he had graduated from the AeA/Stanford Executive Institute in 1981). In 2006, he was honored with the Lifetime Achievement Award from the European Patent Organization. President Barack Obama awarded Faggin, along with Ted Hoff and Stanley Mazor, the United States' top honor for inventors, the National Medal of Technology and Innovation, in 2010.

Christopher Leslie

FURTHER READING

Aspray, William. "The Intel 4004 Microprocessor: What Constituted Invention?" *IEEE Annals of the History of Computing* 19.3 (1997): 4–14. Print. Aspray considers the context in which the Intel 4004 was developed, including contributions of Intel employees Hoff, Faggin, and others, such as Tadashi Sasaki and Masatoshi Shima, who have generally remained anonymous.

Faggin, Federico. "The Making of the First Microprocessor." *IEEE Solid-State Circuits Magazine* 1.1 (2009): 8–21. Print. Examines how the first microprocessor, the Intel 4004 CPU-on-a-chip, was created under the pressure of a very tight schedule.

Lee, Thomas H. "From Mechanism to Monolith: The Path to the Microprocessor." *IEEE Solid-State Circuits Magazine* 1.1 (2009): 69–75. Print. Relates the birth of the microprocessor, the Intel 4004, and its revolutionary influence.

Mazor, Stanley. "Intel 8080 CPU Chip Development." *IEEE Annals of the History of Computing* 29.2 (2007): 70–73. Print. Some crucial architectural decisions during the development of this early microprocessor are discussed by one of its creators.

DAVID FERRUCCI

Principal investigator for the Watson/DeepQA *Jeopardy!* project

Born: August 11, 1961; New York, New York
Died: -
Primary Field: Computer science
Specialty: Computer software
Primary Company/Organization: IBM

INTRODUCTION

Despite his early decision to become a physician, David Ferrucci's lot in life was destined to deal only indirectly with medicine. Instead, he became an expert in artificial intelligence, particularly in programming computers to understand natural human language. He led the team that designed Watson, the IBM supercomputer that managed to win against two top human competitors over three days of the television game show Jeopardy! *in February 2011. Watson provided a decisive victory for Ferrucci and his fellow programmers and for IBM, because it demonstrated that its ability to analyze data had implications in a variety of fields that went far beyond entertaining television audiences. Through Watson, Ferrucci was able to show that computers have the potential for improving—and possibly saving—the lives of humans as well as for improving proficiency and performance in academia and business.*

EARLY LIFE

David A. Ferrucci was born in the Bronx in New York on August 11, 1961. While few details of his personal life are known, it is public knowledge that he had planned to be a physician. However, at the age of seventeen, while taking a math course at New York's Iona College, he began working on a project in computer programming and became fascinated by the possibilities inherent in programming.

Ferrucci received a bachelor of science degree from Manhattan College in 1983, majoring in biology and minoring in computer science. He spent his spare time writing software code. Finally deciding that he preferred computers to medicine, he graduated two years later with a master's degree in computer science from Rensselaer Polytechnic Institute in Troy, New York.

David Ferrucci.

That year, Ferrucci began working as a research/software engineer at IBM in the Expert Systems in Manufacturing division. Two years later, he became the lead software engineer at his alma mater, Rensselaer, in the field of object-oriented computer-aided design.

By 1991, Ferrucci had returned to IBM as a researcher and predoctoral intern, assigned to work in the Automated Configuration Systems division. Specializing in knowledge representation and reasoning, he completed his Ph.D. in computer science at Rensselaer in 1994. The following year, he again returned to IBM, where he was a member of a research team conducting research on expert configuration systems, natural language processing, and architectures for natural language engineering.

LIFE'S WORK

As IBM's chief architect for unstructured information management applications (UIMA), Ferrucci works with interpreting natural language such as that of text, speech, videos, and images into language that can be understood by computers. UIMA has become the accepted OASIS standard and serves as an Apache open source standard. UIMA, which employs Java and C++ frameworks, is widely used in the business field as well as in academia.

Ferrucci's work on UIMA provided the foundation for what is likely to prove to be Ferrucci's defining project, the Watson/DeepQA *Jeopardy!* project, for which he serves as principal investigator. The project, which began in 2006 and continued for four years at a cost of some $30 million, gave Ferrucci and his team the ability to program Watson to communicate with humans in natural language.

Ironically, the idea for creating Watson was the result of a casual discussion about artificial conversation between Charles Lickel, an IBM executive, and a group of friends during a restaurant meal. The group witnessed fellow patrons becoming enthralled while watching Ken Jennings, the long-running *Jeopardy!* champion, on the restaurant's television. At the time, Ferrucci was already involved in the field of Deep Questioning Answering (Deep Q/A) at IBM, and he agreed to work on turning the concept of a computer that could win at *Jeopardy!* into reality. IBM was already working with a number of universities on projects designed to use DeepQA to test the ability of computers to interpret normal human communication methods. IBM had also been involved in a less ambitious project a few years earlier when it created the supercomputer Deep Blue to challenge world chess champion Garry Kasparov in 1996. The computer lost the original match, but a rematch in 1997 between Kasparov and a much-improved model of Deep Blue resulted in a victory for artificial intelligence.

The computer that came to be known popularly as Watson was named after the first president of IBM, Thomas J. Watson. The popular television quiz show *Jeopardy!*, which debuted in 1964, appeared to be the ideal venue for testing Watson's communicative and interpretive abilities and comparing them with those of human beings, because the show requires rapid access to information, analysis of possible responses at lightning speed, and the ability to remember to place respond in the required question format. Headed by Ferrucci, a team of approximately thirty researchers began programming Watson with Questioning Answering software to prepare Watson for the upcoming challenge. The team was composed of experts in natural language processing, software architecture, information retrieval, machine learning, and knowledge representation and reasoning. Initially, the process of programming Watson as a future *Jeopardy!* competitor was slow. It took approximately two hours for the computer to arrive at an answer, and it achieved only 15 percent accuracy. Thousands of language analysis algorithms were used to improve Watson's accuracy, and a correct response

Affiliation: IBM's Watson/DeepQA *Jeopardy!* Project

The computer known as Watson is composed of several floor units that combine ninetey IBM Power 750 servers, 2,880 processing cores, and fifteen terabytes of memory. Watson is named after IBM's first president, Thomas J. Watson. For Watson's appearance on *Jeopardy!*, the three days of the show were moved to IBM's T. J. Watson Research Center in Yorktown Heights, New York. During the show, Watson was presented as an avatar displaying colors that indicated communication processes. A mechanical device was used to activate a button when Watson was ready to answer. Watson's top three answer choices were displayed onscreen, and Watson was able to answer within an average time of three seconds, which is also average for human contestants.

A series of fifty practice rounds against previous *Jeopardy!* contestants were held before the final televised match, and David Ferrucci and his team from IBM were proud of the fact that Watson was able to identify "Who is [singer] Kenny Rogers?" as the correct question to the answer "A Texan who knew when to hold 'em and when to fold 'em." Watson was also able to understand typical *Jeopardy!* categories involving plays on words, such as "Etude Brute." However, Watson was unable to come up with answers on some subjects from popular culture, such as those dealing with King Kong, from the classic film of the same name, and APB (which stands for "all-points bulletin").

For the televised event, it was decided to pit Watson against two all-time *Jeopardy!* champions: Brad Rutter, who had amassed more total winnings than any champion in the history of the game, and Ken Jennings, who had the longest winning streak in the history of *Jeopardy!*, with seventy-four wins to his credit.

Watson's *Jeopardy!* appearance began on February 14, 2011, and continued for three days. On the second day of the competition, Watson upheld Ferrucci's claim that the computer was unable to think for itself by supplying "Toronto" as a response to an answer posed about airports in U.S. cities; the computer had failed to understand that "U.S." stood for the United States. On the final day, however, Watson successfully hedged its bet by risking only $947 of its $36,681 credit. Amassing a total of $77,147, Watson ultimately won the challenge, and its winnings were donated to two charities. Jennings won $24,000, and Rutter won $21,600. Both contestants also contributed a portion of their winnings to charity.

was based on agreement among at least half of those algorithms.

The result of the efforts of Ferrucci and his team was that Watson was eventually programmed to consider all possible answers to questions likely to appear on the game show and quickly determine the best answer, ultimately achieving 95 percent accuracy and answering questions, on average, within less than three seconds. In practice, Watson was not always able to understand acronyms and abbreviations and had some slight difficulty with concepts from popular culture. Also, Watson is a self-contained unit; it was not connected to the Internet during the game. Thus, its answers were derived only from information available in its own data banks, which consisted of 200 million pages of data that had been programmed into the machine. Unlike Deep Blue, which was dismantled after its rematch with Kasparov, IBM intended to continue to develop Watson's potential.

Even while applauding the success of the Ferrucci team and IBM's work with artificial intelligence, some critics were quick to point out that the Watson team had failed to produce a computer that could think for itself.

Ferrucci acknowledged that Watson was unable to think for itself, noting that it was simply a machine that had been programmed to complete particular tasks. He did not argue with the common conclusion that no computer had ever been invented that could match the flexibility of the human brain. However, he saw Watson's *Jeopardy!* win as a victory for the IBM team and stated that the feat could be considered a "pinnacle" in the field of artificial intelligence.

The implications of the Watson Project are far-reaching, with major potential for success in a variety of fields that include health care, finance, education, law, publishing, and customer service. The implications for the health care field may be the most significant, because Watson's abilities are already allowing medical professionals to identify the best health treatments for particular individuals, using existing medical knowledge and case histories of patients suffering from stipulated conditions and drawing on all available genomic and molecular data.

In September 2011, Watson was put to commercial use when WellPoint Health Insurance began using the supercomputer to determine the proper treatment for its client base of 34.2 million. WellPoint is basing treatment on analysis of charts, medical records, and treatment histories in conjunction with information derived from the database programmed into Watson. In the spring of 2012, IBM and Memorial Sloan-Kettering announced that they had formed a partnership involving Watson for facilitating cancer research. In March 2012, IBM announced that it had created the Watson Healthcare Advisory Board, a nine-member board composed of outstanding physicians, in order to use Watson to work with the medical community in the fields of primary patient care, oncology, biomedical informatics, and medical innovation.

PERSONAL LIFE

In 2011, IBM honored Ferrucci by designating him an IBM Fellow, the highest technical distinction awarded by the company. Only 238 other individuals have been awarded that honor since 1963, when it was created, and only 77 of those individuals were working for IBM at the time they were honored. Ferrucci also serves as an IBM researcher and vice president. In that context, he continues to work on the Watson Project and on semantic analysis and integration.

Elizabeth Rholetter Purdy

FURTHER READING

Arndt, Rachel Z. "Robo Force." *Fast Company* 154 (2011): 57–60. Print. Profile of the Watson computer.

Feldman, Susan. "IBM Watson: From Winning Games to Saving Lives." 26 Mar. 2012. *IDC Link*. Web. 2 Sept. 2012. An IBM white paper that details the Watson project and discuss its implications.

Ferrucci, David. "One Minute with … David Ferrucci." Interview by Justin Mullins. *New Scientist* 209.2799 (2011): n. pag. Print. Brief interview with Ferrucci that focuses on Watson's *Jeopardy!* appearance.

Kroeker, Kirk L. "Weighing Watson's Impact." *Communications of the ACM* 54.7 (2011): 13–15. Print. Detailed account of Watson's success on *Jeopardy!*

Livingstone, Paul. "Far More than Trivial." *R&D Magazine* 53.7 (2011): 12–14. Print. Traces the history of the Watson project.

Mack, Tim. "Watson: Pathfinder for Global Business." *World Future Review* 3.2 (2011): 26–36. Print. Indepth examination of Watson in the overall context of artificial intelligence and supercomputing.

Pieraccini, Robert. *The Voice in the Machine: Building Computers That Understand Speech*. Cambridge: MIT, 2012. Print. Illustrated. Overview of the field of designing computers that are able to communicate with humans beings using natural language.

CARLY FIORINA

Former CEO of Hewlett-Packard

Born: September 6, 1954; Austin, Texas
Died: -
Primary Field: Business and commerce
Specialty: Management, executives, and investors
Primary Company/Organization: Hewlett-Packard

INTRODUCTION

Carly Fiorina served in key leadership positions at Lucent Technologies and the Hewlett-Packard Company. While not all of her strategies proved successful, her aggressive and expansion-oriented management of both corporations kept these organizations, and Fiorina herself, in the headlines. After leaving corporate management, Fiorina served as an adviser to Republican presidential nominee John McCain in 2008 and later staged an unsuccessful run for the U.S. Senate as the 2010 Republican candidate for that office in California.

EARLY LIFE

On September 6, 1954, Fiorina was born Cara Carleton Sneed in Austin, Texas. Fiorina's parents were Joseph Tyree Sneed III and Madelon Montross Juergens. Joseph served as a professor at the University of Texas School of Law, Cornell University Law School, and Stanford Law School before becoming dean of the Duke University School of Law. Appointed in 1973 as a deputy U.S. attorney general, he was nominated in the same year by President Richard Nixon to serve as a judge on the U.S. Court of Appeals for the Ninth Circuit. Madelon, an artist of portraits and abstract works, was known for her use of bold strokes and vibrant colors. Fiorina moved frequently with her parents, as mandated by her father's profession, but the family, which included Fiorina's brother and sister, was close. Fiorina attended a variety of different schools, including the Channing

Carly Fiorina.

program funded by the Alfred P. Sloan Foundation and designed to permit mid-career professionals to obtain a master's degree in general management and leadership. With the aid of that fellowship, Fiorina earned a master's degree in leadership from the Sloan School of Management at the Massachusetts Institute of Technology (MIT) in 1989. While at AT&T, Fiorina rose from her management trainee position to become a senior vice president responsible for the company's hardware and systems division.

LIFE'S WORK

During the mid-1990s, AT&T began to realize that its equipment sales were impeded because rivals for the provision of telecommunications services were reluctant to purchase apparatus from their competitor. As a result, AT&T made the decision to spin off its equipment and technology divisions, which included the award-winning Bell Laboratories. Reporting to the chief executive officer (CEO) of what was to become Lucent Technologies, Fiorina helped to plan and implement Lucent's 1996 initial public offering (IPO). As a result of her success in this role, Fiorina was made president of Lucent's consumer products division, reporting directly to Rich McGinn, the company's president and chief operating officer. The following year, Fiorina was assigned the chairmanship of a consumer communications joint venture with Royal Philips Electronics (Philips). Also in 1997, Fiorina was made president of Lucent's global service provider group. With the technology boom experienced during the 1990s, Lucent's stock value soared; its equipment sales were seen as a vital part of the dot-com revolution.

During the late 1990s, a great deal of media attention was given to the increasing role played by women at large multinational corporations. Fiorina was the focus of much of this media attention, named "the most powerful woman in business" by *Fortune* magazine's inaugural listing of such leaders in 1998. While the concept of a metaphorical glass ceiling that hindered women's promotions within large organizations had been discussed for years, Fiorina was touted by many as the first woman to have broken through that barrier. When the Hewlett-Packard Company, a giant in computer hardware and software, went looking for a chairman and CEO to succeed Lewis E. Platt, Fiorina was hired in 1999 over a variety of other candidates, including Hewlett-Packard insider Ann Livermore. This move made Fiorina the first female CEO of a Dow-Jones 30 corporation.

School in London, before graduating from Charles E. Jordan High School in Durham, North Carolina. After high school, Fiorina entered Stanford University, where she studied medieval history and philosophy. During her college career, Fiorina worked a variety of summer jobs, including stints at a hair salon and as a secretary for Kelly Services. She graduated with a bachelor's degree from Stanford in 1976.

After graduating, Fiorina enrolled in the University of California, Los Angeles (UCLA) School of Law, but she dropped out during her first year. She then found employment working as a receptionist for a Los Angeles real estate firm, Marcus and Millichamp, eventually moving up to serve as a broker. In 1977 she and her first husband, Todd Bartlem, were married. Fiorina next moved to Italy, where she taught English, returning to the United States so that she could enter the University of Maryland's Robert H. Smith School of Business, from which she received a master's in business administration (MBA) with a concentration in marketing in 1980. Fiorina then joined American Telephone and Telegraph Company (AT&T) as a management trainee. After her marriage with Bartlem dissolved, Fiorina married her current husband, Frank Fiorina, in 1985. During the late 1980s, she was granted a Sloan fellowship, a

Fiorina was hired in part because it was perceived that she would take a more aggressive stance than Platt, whose low-key management style focused on promoting progressive values and long-term results. In contrast to Platt, who wore thick glasses, flew coach on business trips, and ate in the company cafeteria, Fiorina was initially embraced by investors and the media for her "rock star" approach to leadership. Fiorina was a highly visible CEO and immediately began to reorganize Hewlett-Packard upon taking over in mid-1999. In a spin-off of all Hewlett-Packard businesses that were not related to computers, imaging, or storage, these endeavors were grouped into a new company, Agilent Technologies. Agilent was offered to the public through an IPO, making it an $8 billion corporation with more than forty-five thousand. Although this move had been planned before she was made CEO, Fiorina was praised for executing what was at that time Silicon Valley's largest IPO.

Fiorina had the misfortune of presiding over Hewlett-Packard during the dot-com collapse of 2000–01, when many technology and Internet firms failed or lost much of their value. Despite this, in September 2001 Fiorina announced plans to merge Hewlett-Packard with smaller manufacturer Compaq Computer Corporation. The $25 billion proposed purchase, coming as it did on the heels of Dell, Inc.'s overtaking Compaq as the largest supplier of personal computer (PC) systems, was highly controversial. Many past and present Hewlett-Packard executives opposed the merger, which led to a proxy battle for control of the corporation. Those opposed to Hewlett-Packard's merger with Compaq included Walter Hewlett and David Packard (sons of the company's founders), the California Public Employees' Retirement System (CalPERS), and the Ontario Teachers Pension Plan (OTPP). Those opposed to the merger felt that Compaq and Hewlett-Packard had different and incongruent cultures, that the PC market was low-margin and risky, and that the value of Hewlett-Packard shares would be diluted. Despite this opposition, the merger was approved by shareholder vote in 2002.

During the three years after the Hewlett-Packard–Compaq merger, Fiorina laid off thousands of workers, the company's stock price declined, and profits were stagnant. Although the merger made the company the world's largest producer of PCs, it lost that title in 2003 because of declining sales (although it regained that position in 2006). Fiorina saw the transfer of some Hewlett-Packard jobs to overseas locations and was a strong backer of expanding the HB-1 visa program, which permits U.S. employers to hire foreign workers

Affiliation: Hewlett-Packard

Founded in 1939 by friends William Hewlett and David Packard, Hewlett-Packard grew from a start-up company begun in a garage to a multinational hardware and software company with headquarters in Palo Alto, California. Known for a multitude of products, Hewlett-Packard is an industry leader in printing and imaging technology, computer hardware, and consulting and information technology services.

Carly Fiorina became chair and CEO of Hewlett-Packard at a time when the company was reeling from the Asian financial crisis and was considered to have largely missed the Internet and dot-com boom of the late 1990s. Streamlining Hewlett-Packard's operations, Fiorina engineered a merger with Compaq Computer Corporation and spun off divisions not related to its core business interests.

During Fiorina's tenure at Hewlett-Packard, she maintained the company's long-lasting commitment to corporate giving and progressive action. For example, under Fiorina's leadership in 2004, Hewlett-Packard set the goal of recycling one billion pounds of ink cartridges, electronics, and related materials. This goal was met by 2008, after Fiorina had departed from Hewlett-Packard. Hewlett-Packard continues to receive recognition for its leadership in social responsibility.

in specialty occupations, such as programming. In early 2005, the Hewlett-Packard board of directors met with Fiorina to discuss ways of improving the company's operations. Chief among the board's suggestions was shifting some of Fiorina's responsibilities to various division leaders. Fiorina resisted these changes, and a month later the Hewlett-Packard board replaced Fiorina temporarily with Thomas Perkins, the former head of Hewlett-Packard's research division and past chairman of Tandem Computers. Patricia Dunn was later named Fiorina's permanent replacement. Fiorina received a severance package in excess of $20 million. Under Fiorina's leadership, Hewlett-Packard had doubled its annual revenues to $88 billion and had generated eleven patents per day.

After leaving Hewlett-Packard, Fiorina became a commentator on Fox Business Network, an American cable channel devoted to economic news. In 2008, she acted as an adviser to Senator John McCain's presidential campaign, providing counsel on matters related to business and technology. Fiorina became chair of a national Republican fund-raising campaign and spoke at the party's national convention in Saint Paul, Minnesota. After this experience, Fiorina announced in November 2009 that she would be seeking the Republican nomination for the U.S. Senate seat held by California's Barbara Boxer. Running what was often criticized as a very negative campaign, Fiorina defeated Republican rivals Tom Campbell and Chuck DeVore to win more than 50 percent of the vote, and her party's nomination, on June 8, 2010. During the campaign against Boxer, Fiorina took a conservative stance on many social issues—for example, opposing abortion and supporting California Proposition 8, which defined marriage as a union between a man and a woman. Despite her vigorous efforts, Boxer defeated Fiorina in the election, winning 52 percent of the vote to Fiorina's 42 percent.

PERSONAL LIFE
Shortly after graduating from Stanford, Fiorina (then Cara Sneed) married former classmate Todd Bartlem, a marriage that ended in divorce in 1984. The following year, Fiorina married fellow AT&T executive Frank Fiorina, who had also been married before. Although she became stepmother to Frank's two daughters, Fiorina and her husband were unable to have children together. Frank retired in 1998 to help his wife focus on her career. Diagnosed with breast cancer in 2009, Fiorina underwent a double mastectomy and, after radiation and chemotherapy, was declared cancer-free. Fiorina and her husband live in Los Altos Hills, California.

Fiorina has long been interested in education. While at Hewlett-Packard, she helped that company launch its Technology for Teaching program, which resulted in more than $10 million in grants annually being given to classrooms from kindergarten through the college level. A fan of popular music, while at Hewlett-Packard

Fiorina also engaged such celebrities as Sheryl Crow, Gwen Stefani, and U2's The Edge (David Howell Evans) to endorse Hewlett-Packard products.

Stephen T. Schroth and Jason A. Helfer

FURTHER READING
Anders, D. *Perfect Enough: Carly Fiorina and the Reinvention of Hewlett-Packard*. New York: Portfolio, 2003. Print. Explores Fiorina's experiences as chair and CEO of Hewlett-Packard, including her charisma, management style, encounters with sexism, and strategy in dealing with the "ghosts" of Hewlett-Packard's founders.

Burrows, P. *Backfire: Carly Fiorina's High-Stakes Battle for the Soul of Hewlett-Packard*. Hoboken: Wiley, 2003. Print. An examination of the underlying issues and concerns regarding the direction of Hewlett-Packard as a result of the Compaq merger.

Fiorina, C. *Tough Choices: A Memoir*. New York: Portfolio, 2006. Print. Fiorina addresses her experiences as the first woman to lead a multinational corporation, including her early career, the media spotlight, the fight over the Compaq merger, and dealing with the rumor mill.

House, C. H., and R. L. Price. *The HP Phenomenon: Innovation and Business Transformation*. Stanford: Stanford UP, 2009. Print. Explores how Hewlett-Packard's culture has allowed the company to transform itself numerous times while many of its rivals were unable to transform themselves even once, resulting in failure.

Malone, M. S. *Bill and Dave: How Hewlett and Packard Built the World's Greatest Company*. New York: Portfolio, 2007. Print. Concentrates on the formation of Hewlett-Packard and how the actions and leadership of its founders have continued to affect the company's culture to the present day.

TOMMY FLOWERS

Designer of the Colossus code-breaking computer

Born: December 22, 1905; London, England
Died: October 28, 1998; London, England
Primary Field: Computer science
Specialty: Computer hardware
Primary Company/Organization: Government Code and Cypher School (United Kingdom)

INTRODUCTION
Tommy Flowers was an English electronics engineer recruited by computer scientist Alan Turing to help with the code-breaking efforts of the British government during World War II, building on Turing's work breaking the German code known as Enigma. In response,

Flowers designed the Colossus code-breaking computer, which decrypted Nazi communiques critical to planning the 1944 D-day landings by the Allies on the beaches of Normandy. He later continued the work he had begun before the war on electronic telephone exchanges, publishing a book on the subject in 1976.

EARLY LIFE

Thomas Harold "Tommy" Flowers was born the son of a bricklayer's family on December 22, 1905, in the East End of London, England. As a young man, he worked as an apprentice mechanical engineer at the Royal Arsenal, Woolwich, in southeast London, which in the internecine period was constructing steam locomotives as well as armaments. By night he took courses in electrical engineering, and at age twenty-one he took a job with the General Post Office, working in telecommunications research. In the 1930s, he researched telephone exchanges and the use of electronics, planning a fully electronic telephone exchange system that was interrupted by World War II.

LIFE'S WORK

Computer scientist and mathematician Alan Turing had introduced several enduring concepts to computer

Tommy Flowers.

science and became one of the most prominent participants in Britain's code-breaking efforts in World War II, work he had begun in 1938. Although the Enigma machine produced the most famous of the German codes that were broken, its codes were neither the last nor the most difficult. After the primary work on Enigma was completed, Turing turned to recruiting more engineers and mathematicians for code-breaking work, among whom was Flowers.

Turing recruited Flowers to work on the bombe, a tool Turing had designed in 1939 at the Government Code and Cypher School at Bletchley Park, to help with the Enigma decryption efforts. Bletchley Park, now the home of the National Museum of Computing, is a Buckinghamshire estate that became the home to Ultra, the code name for the main Allied code-breaking efforts. The Government Code and Cypher School housed at Bletchley Park, wartime employer of both Turing and Flowers, had been formed in the internecine period to replace the separate signals intelligence agencies of Britain's army and navy. Although the German codes were the most famous that were deciphered, when Flowers was recruited codes and ciphers of twenty-six countries were being studied, in conjunction with the Far East Combined Bureau in Singapore.

Turing's bombe was the primary machine used in Enigma code breaking. Enigma was not a single code but a method for creating codes: The Germans used a rotor machine with a system of rotors, each of which had substitution characters on it. Each time a wheel turned to encrypt a letter, the rest of the rotors would turn, making for a complex polyalphabetical substitution cipher. Some of these codes were nearly impossible to decrypt using methods available at the time. The bombe, which had to be fed a crib (a fragment of possible decrypted text), generated likely rotor machine settings to assist in decryption efforts. The Lorenz machines, meanwhile, were based on a system similar to that used by the Enigma, but instead of the alphabet, Lorenz machines used the larger Baudot character set, which like today's ASCII included letters, numbers, and special characters. The Baudot character set was used in teletypewriters, and the Lorenz machines were used by the Germans to encrypt messages sent on such teletypewriters. It was these codes Flowers worked to decode, following in Turing's footsteps, on a team led by mathematician Max Newman.

What he proposed to do was build an electronic computer, the Colossus, in order to break the code. The government was unpersuaded; the Colossus design called for nearly two thousand vacuum tubes, more than ten times as many as had been used in a single device before. Flowers was accustomed to working with British telephone systems, which were just as complicated, and was convinced the computer would work. He staked some of his own money to begin the project, working at

Affiliation: Government Code and Cypher School

The Buckinghamshire estate of Bletchley Park served as the home for the Government Code and Cypher School (GC&CS), a British code-breaking agency formed after World War I to replace the separate signals intelligence agencies of the British Army and Navy. Bletchley Park has conventionally been used as the metonym to refer to the GC&CS, and sometimes the whole British code-breaking effort, although some of its teams were located in other facilities—much as the term *White House* in the United States refers to the executive branch of government and not just its domicile.

Bletchley Park is most famous for its work on the codes of the German electromechanical rotor machines, Enigma and Lorenz. Rotor machines used rotating disks with a series of letters on each disk, which rotate with each encrypted letter, producing a significantly more complex alphabetic substitution cipher. Properly used, they would have been unbreakable with the technology of the time; the computing power did not exist to solve these ciphers using brute force methods. The Bletchley Park code breakers took advantage of every slip-up of the Axis powers. Although people today speak of "the Enigma code," it was never one code; it was, rather, a type of machine (there were several variants and many individual models) used to generate a code, and it was not a single Enigma code that was broken but the system of Enigma code generation that was attacked by the code breakers. The Lorenz rotor machine was a later German invention, created during the war—the Enigma machine had been built in 1923, long before the war began—and was used to encrypt Baudot character-set teletypewriter messages. The Baudot character set, like ASCII today, consisted of a large number of characters beyond the alphabet; a separate machine using that character set was therefore necessary. At the same time, using a larger character set made for a more complex substitution cipher than a twenty-six-letter alphabetic or thirty-six-character alphanumeric set.

Commander Alastair Denniston was the head of operations at Bletchley Park from its formation until 1942. Recruitment through social networking was common; Bletchley Park workers were trusted to know which of their colleagues outside Bletchley Park might have the skills for the job and could be trusted. Individuals recruited were not always taken from careers connected to cryptography; they included linguists both professional and amateur, even crossword puzzle aficionados and chess players, on the strength of their analytical thinking. Part-time workers were also selected to contribute specific expertise, such as on the dialects of Germany and its allies and conquered peoples. This approach was a surprisingly strong one, although credit might also be given to the sheer size of the effort: At its peak, Bletchley Park employed nine thousand people, including both military personnel and civilians.

It was the mathematical work at Bletchley Park that was most famous, however, thanks to Alan Turing. The father of computer science and artificial intelligence, Turing was a computer scientist who was still in his twenties when the war began and had been only a teenager when Bletchley Park formed. After his graduate work at Princeton University in the United States, he worked, first part time, for GC&CS, on breaking German codes. He was instrumental in the efforts against Enigma and provided the specification for Bletchley Park's first bombe, a device used for code-breaking rotor machine ciphers. The bombe was the primary automated tool used against Enigma; after being programmed with a crib (a fragment of probable decrypted text), it would generate likely rotor machine parameter settings for the Enigma message from which the crib had originated. Within weeks of his work at Bletchley Park, Turing had made significant strides over previous efforts, and for a time he was placed in charge of naval code-breaking efforts.

When the Americans joined the war, resources were pooled and American cryptographers were added to the staff at Bletchley Park, joining efforts long in progress. The cooperation between the British and the Americans was very close; on the other hand, the Soviets (allies of the British and Americans during the war) were never officially told about Bletchley Park, although some decrypted intelligence was passed along to them. Winston Churchill never trusted the Communists and had allied with them only under duress.

the Post Office Research Station at Dollis Hill, London, with his own team. It took eleven months, from February to December 1943, to build the Colossus, and after a successful test it was sent to Bletchley Park for the code breakers to use, while Flowers and his team proceeded to design and build an improved model, the Colossus Mark 2, which was finished in 1944, used twenty-four hundred vacuum tubes, and was five times faster than the Mark 1. The original Colossus Mark 1 was later converted to a Mark 2 machine. By the end of the war, eleven Colossus computers had been built, greatly speeding cryptanalysis efforts, although parallel computing—in which two Colossus computers worked on different possibilities for solving the same problem—was used only occasionally.

The Colossus was the first programmable electronic digital computer. The first electronic digital computer, the Atanasoff-Berry Computer (ABC), had been built by John Vincent Atanasoff and Clifford E. Berry in the United States before the war, but few people were aware of it. The Colossus was programmable rather than being hardwired for a specific task, like the ABC. It emulated the Germans' rotor machines and generated possible key combinations for use in decrypting Lorenz messages, processing at a speed of five thousand characters per second—faster speeds risked destroying the punched paper tape the computer used. Flowers's telephone exchange experience was invaluable: The reason the government had been skeptical of an electronic device with so many vacuum tubes was that the risk of valve (vacuum tube) failure was higher the more tubes were used. Telephone exchanges were less subject to this problem because their circuits remained turned on all the time; the highest risk of failure was during the power surge that occurred when the computer was initially turned on. The Colossus computers were designed by Flowers to be operated the same way British telephone exchanges were, simply by remaining turned on. They were powered down only when repairs were needed following a malfunction—an expense that at the time only a government could afford.

The Colossus lacked stored programs. Operators adjusted plugs and switches in order to set new programs for an incoming task. It was also not a general-purpose computing machine; like the ABC it had been set up to perform specific kinds of mathematical operations—in this case, the Boolean operations and counting required of cryptanalysis. Like most early computers, it was thus not Turing-complete (computationally universal); the significance of Turing's definition of the computing machine had not yet been realized.

Flowers was never fully compensated for the money he spent on the Colossus, although he was granted £1,000 and made a member of the Order of the British Empire. Because the Colossus work was classified, he was not able to capitalize on it later in order to prove his credentials or the veracity of his ideas; he was denied a loan to build a computer, for instance, because the Bank of England believed he could not make it work, and he was unable to refer them to the near-dozen Colossus computers at Bletchley Park. He instead resumed his telephone exchange work at the Post Office Research Station, completing his all-electronic telephone exchange around 1950 despite the strained postwar British economy. He continued working as a telephone exchange engineer for the next few decades, and in the 1970s, after his role in the World War II code breaking had been declassified, he published *Introduction to Exchange Systems*, summarizing much of what he had learned.

PERSONAL LIFE

Flowers married Eileen Margaret Green in 1935, while conducting telephone exchange research for the General Post Office. They had two sons, John and Kenneth. He died in 1998 at the age of ninety-two. The access road at the housing development on the site of his old Post Office Research Station has been named Flowers Centre.

Bill Kte'pi

FURTHER READING

Copeland, B. Jack, ed. *Colossus: The Secrets of Bletchley Park's Codebreaking Computers*. Rpt. New York: Oxford UP, 2010. Print. Of all the histories of World War II code breaking, this one places the greatest focus on Flowers.

Flowers, Thomas Harold. *Introduction to Exchange Systems*. New York: Wiley, 1976. Print. Flowers's summary of what he learned and innovated working on the Colossus computers, long delayed by the classified nature of his work.

Hinsley, F. H., and Alan Stripp, eds. *Codebreakers: The Inside Story of Bletchley Park*. New York: Oxford UP, 2001. Print. A collection of essays by Bletchley Park code breakers.

McKay, Sinclair. *The Secret Life of Bletchley Park: The WWII Codebreaking Centre and the Men and Women Who Worked There*. London: Aurum, 2011. Print. A history of Britain's World War II code breakers.

Sebag-Montefiore, Hugh. *Enigma: The Battle for the Code*. New York: Wiley, 2004. Print. A broad history of the Allied effort to break the Enigma code.

G

BILL GATES

Cofounder, chairman, and former CEO of Microsoft

Born: October 28, 1955; Seattle, Washington
Died: -
Primary Field: Computer science
Specialty: Computer software
Primary Company/Organization: Microsoft

INTRODUCTION

Bill Gates, cofounder of Microsoft, helped to redefine the world of computing. By developing MS-DOS, which became the most widely used operating system in the 1980s, Gates and cofounder Paul Allen placed Microsoft in a position to become the world's leading software developer. Microsoft was at the forefront of the growth of home computing, which expanded from three hundred thousand users in 1980 to 2.9 million users in 1983. As the information superhighway, the Internet, emerged in the 1990s, Gates led Microsoft to release improved versions of Windows and related applications that allowed computer users to navigate cyberspace, communicate through e-mail, create and manage documents, calculate using spreadsheets, manage data relationally, and browse and shop online.

EARLY LIFE

William Henry Gates III, known to his family as Trey, was born into an affluent family on October 28, 1955, in Seattle, Washington. His father, William H. Gates, Sr., was a prominent attorney, and his mother, Mary Maxwell Gates, came from a wealthy banking family. Mary gave up a teaching career to devote herself to raising her family but remained active in civic work and served on a number of boards. Bill was the middle child, flanked by sisters Kristianne and Libby.

As a child, Gates was bookish and somewhat antisocial. Determined that he should widen his horizons, his parents sent him to Lakeside, a private preparatory school, at the age of eleven. At Lakeside, Gates discovered computers and became friends with Paul Allen. Two years older, Allen was also absorbed by computing. Very few schools in the country had computers at the time, and Gates, Allen, and their friends were

Bill Gates.

often left on their own to decipher their mysteries. Mathematically gifted, Gates was soon using the computer to create games such as Tic-Tac-Toe, and he programmed the computer to play Monopoly. At the age of thirteen, Gates crashed the system from which the school purchased time, and the Lakeside Programmers Group was subsequently given free computer time in exchange for finding bugs in the system.

In 1971, the group was hired to write a payroll program. By 1972, Gates and Allen were writing code for the 8008 processor. Their program was put to use in Traf-O-Data, a program they designed to help municipalities handle traffic counts. Before he finished at Lakeside, Gates was accepted at Harvard University. A decade later, Gates and Allen would donate $2.2 million to Lakeside for a science and mathematics center.

LIFE'S WORK

In 1975, living in the same dormitory at Harvard, Gates and Allen began working nonstop to develop the Beginner's All-purpose Symbolic Instruction Code (BASIC) for the Altair, the first personal computer available in the United States. Its microprocessor chip was designed by Micro Instrumentation and Telemetry Systems (MITS), a company that specialized in calculators. In 1976, Gates and Allen founded Microsoft. In May 1978, MITS was sold to Pertec, and the new owners announced that they would no longer allow Microsoft to license MS-DOS to other developers. Microsoft filed suit and ultimately won the right to sell the operating system without restrictions. MITS retained the right to use BASIC in its own computers. Microsoft issued a BASIC license to both Apple and RadioShack and opened a new market for BASIC in Japan. At the time, Microsoft had only five employees and annual sales of $500,000. In January 1977, Gates dropped out of Harvard to join Allen, who was working in Albuquerque. In 1978, Allen convinced Gates that Microsoft should move its headquarters to Seattle, home of both founders. At the end of the year, with thirteen employees, sales reached $1 million. By 1979, Microsoft was selling a million copies of BASIC and total sales had reached $2.5 million.

Microsoft's first big break came in 1981, when IBM needed a company to design an operating system for its line of personal computers (PCs). Together, Microsoft and Intel revolutionized the computer industry. In 1982, at the age of twenty-seven, Bill Gates appeared on the cover on *Money* magazine. The following year, Microsoft Word, the company's word-processing program, was released. It was too expensive for many

homes, selling for $475 with a mouse and $375 without. By that time, Microsoft was winning awards for Windows, its spreadsheet program Excel, its mouse, and its flight simulator. Gates was identified as one of the richest men in the world. The partnership with IBM dissolved in 1990, and Apple eventually became Microsoft's major rival. During the years of the Microsoft-Apple partnership, Gates and Apple's Steve Jobs had been close friends, even going out on double dates. As they became rivals, the friendship floundered. In March 1988, Apple filed suit against Microsoft, claiming copyright infringement of its graphical interface. The courts ultimately determined that the idea for the graphical interface could not be copyrighted.

Microsoft went public in 1986, selling at $25.75 per share. Gates held 11 million shares. *Money* stated in October 1987 that Gates had amassed more money than anyone else his age had ever made in any kind of business. That year, *Forbes* placed Gates twenty-ninth on its list of the world's richest people. By the time he was thirty-one years old, Gates's worth was estimated at more than $1 billion. Microsoft moved to Redmond, Washington, in 1985 to manage its growth. By that time, the company had grown to seven hundred employees and needed an entire campus for its operations.

The decade of the 1990s proved to be extremely profitable for Microsoft. The release of Windows 3.0 in May 1990 was an unmitigated success, and it became the only software program in history with more than $1 billion in sales. By that time, Microsoft had fifty-two hundred employees. Microsoft also began releasing software for the PC that had previously been available only on Apple computers running Microsoft software. By that time, Gates, who served as chair and chief executive officer (CEO) of the company, was being identified as an important force in the world of computing, and no other company came close to matching Microsoft's mastery of software for the personal computer.

In 1992, Gates was awarded the National Medal of Technology. By 1994, Microsoft was recording revenues of $4.65 billion. With Vice President Al Gore helping to spread the word about what was then being called the information superhighway, every home wanted a computer with Internet access. Microsoft adopted the slogan "information at your fingertips." By 1993, Windows was the top-selling application in history.

The debut of user-friendly Windows 95 in August 1995 changed home computing forever. Until that time, home computing had generally been cumbersome and difficult for the uninitiated. Gates turned the launch into

Affiliation: Microsoft

Bill Gates and Paul Allen founded Microsoft in August 1975 with Gates controlling 60 percent and Allen holding 40 percent. By the end of 1978, the Albuquerque-based company had surpassed the million-dollar mark in sales and had thirteen employees. Executive decisions were shared between Gates and Allen. Unlike most computer companies, Microsoft was owned in large part by its employees, with Gates and Allen maintaining control. The overriding philosophy in bringing in new people was to find employees who were willing to work hard and turn them loose to develop their own ideas. Small teams of developers were created to work on particular products. In July 1981, the name of the company was changed to Microsoft, Inc. Bill Gates served as Chairman of the Board, and both he and Paul Allen held the title of Executive Vice President. Over the next few years, the company became global.

By June 1984, Microsoft had become the first software company in history to record more than $100 million in annual sales. In 1986, Microsoft went public at $25.75 a share. By the end of the day, shares had risen to $27.75, and Microsoft's market value was estimated at $661 million. Gates was proclaimed as America's youngest billionaire. Microsoft continued to work hard at developing user-friendly software, which was instrumental in growing profits. By 2005, more than 400 million people were using Windows on their computers, Internet Explorer was well established as a web browser, and Netscape—the company that had helped engineer the 1998 antitrust suit against Microsoft—had virtually disappeared.

a major celebration, hosting a launch party on August 24. Emceed by Jay Leno, the party was attended by industry notables, celebrities, and twenty-five hundred journalists. The campaign reportedly cost a quarter of a billion dollars. Microsoft purchased the rights to use "Start Me Up," by the Rolling Stones, as its theme song. In New York City, the Empire State Building boasted the colors of the Microsoft logo. In Europe, Gates bought out a day's press of the London *Times* to promote the operating system. All Australian infants born on launch day received a free copy of the software. Many computer stores hosted midnight parties so that users could buy the program as soon as it went on sale.

Windows 95 sold 60 million copies around the world. *Forbes* identified Gates, who was thirty-nine at the time, as the richest man in the world. His net worth by then was $15 billion.

Although Allen left Microsoft in 1983 for health reasons, Gates remained with the company, leading it to new heights and spreading its reach with each new improvement of Windows and each update or new product introduced. Entering the browser wars with Internet Explorer gave Microsoft's operating system and other applications an advantage with consumers and led to the antitrust lawsuit *United States v. Microsoft*, filed in 1998 and settled in 2001, in which it was alleged that Microsoft's bundling of browser software (Internet Explorer) with its operating system (Windows) unfairly limited competition in the browser marketplace by taking advantage of the operating system's market dominance to make its browser automatically available to all Windows users. Under Gates's leadership, Microsoft survived the litigation, reaching a relatively favorable settlement in 2001.

The company continued to grow, constantly offering consumers new products and improved versions of existing products. In 2001, Microsoft expanded to video gaming with the introduction of the Xbox, added an online version the following year. Today, the Xbox 360 is the gaming console of choice for hardcore gamers, and families came on board in 2010 with the introduction of the Xbox Kinect, which turns the player's body into a game control device. In 2012, Microsoft signed a deal with Barnes and Noble that gave Microsoft access to that company's proprietary e-reader, the Nook, and its digital and educational assets, providing a ready market for Windows 8 tablet computers.

PERSONAL LIFE

In 1988, Bill Gates began dating Melinda French. They married on January 1, 1994, on the small, secluded island of Lanai, Hawaii, before 130 carefully selected guests, including Paul Allen, Berkshire-Hathaway founder Warren Buffett, and *Washington Post* publisher Katharine Graham. Gates's mother, Mary, succumbed to cancer on June 10 of that year. Five years later, Gates built a family compound on Puget Sound. Named Gateway, the compound covers more than three acres and contains four houses.

In 2005, the Gateses established the Bill and Melinda Gates Foundation, which by 2012 had donated some $26 billion to philanthropic causes including education, hunger prevention, disease eradication, and global development. In 2002, Gates joined investor and philanthropist Warren Buffet in creating the Giving Pledge, which encourages billionaires to pledge to give away at least half of their wealth to charitable causes. Individuals who have signed the pledge include media mogul Ted Turner, AOL's Steve Case, and Facebook's Mark Zuckerberg.

Elizabeth Rholetter Purdy

FURTHER READING

Aronson, Marc. *Up Close: Bill Gates, a Twentieth-Century Life*. New York: Penguin, 2009. Print. Written with young adults in mind, the book examines Gates's life and work and his impact on modern society. Illustrated.

Cusamano, Michael, and Richard W. Selby. *Microsoft Secrets: How the World's Most Powerful Software Company Creates Technology, Shapes Markets, and Manages People*. Print. New York: Free Press, 1995. In-depth study of Microsoft's rise to the top and explanations of why it has survived. Includes a chronology, description of Microsoft applications, list of related agreements, bibliography, and index.

Gillies, James, and Robert Cailliau. *How the Web Was Born: The Story of the World Wide Web*. Print. New York: Oxford UP, 2000. Extremely detailed examination of the development of the World Wide Web, tracing the roles played by key individuals. Includes a time line, bibliography, and index.

Ichbiah, Daniel, and Susan L. Knepper. *The Making of Microsoft: How Bill Gates and His Team Created the World's Most Successful Software Company*. Rocklin: Prima, 1991. Print. Examines the development of Microsoft in considerable detail. Includes key dates, a glossary, and an index.

Lesinski, Jeanne M. *Bill Gates: Entrepreneur and Philanthropist*. Minneapolis: Twenty-First Century, 2009. Print. Looks at Gates's life and work as a whole, emphasizing his impact on global issues as well as the computer industry. Includes a bibliography and an index.

Wainwright, Geoff. "Bill Gates: Perfect Vision." *Remembering the Future: Interviews from Personal Computer World*. Ed. Wendy M. Grossman. New York: Springer, 1997. 31–36. Print. Based on interviews from the 1990s as Microsoft continued its meteoric rise. Includes illustrations.

Wallace, James. *Overdrive: Bill Gates and the Race to Control Cyberspace*. New York: Wiley, 1997. Print. Written as an update to Wallace and Erickson's coauthored work *Hard Drive*, a chronicle of the rise of the Internet and important Microsoft milestones such as the launch of Windows 95. Includes illustrations and index.

Wallace, James, and Jim Erickson. *Hard Drive: Bill Gates and the Making of the Microsoft Software Empire*. New York: Wiley, 1992. Print. The authors use stories that previously appeared in the *Seattle Post-Intelligencer*, supplemented by interviews with current and former employees. Subsequently used against Microsoft in an antitrust suit. Includes illustrations and index.

CHARLES GESCHKE

Cofounder and cochairman of Adobe

Born: September 11, 1939; Cleveland, Ohio
Died: -
Primary Field: Computer science
Specialty: Computer software
Primary Company/Organization: Adobe

INTRODUCTION

Charles Geschke is cofounder of Adobe Systems. In 1982, he and John Warnock founded the company that became one of the world's largest software suppliers. He led the team that designed PostScript, the interpretive computer language that helped to start the desktop publishing revolution. Geschke made headlines in 1992, when he was kidnapped at gunpoint from the Adobe parking lot in Mountain View, California. He was rescued by agents of the Federal Bureau of Investigation (FBI) four days later. He retired as president of Adobe in 2000, but as of 2012 he still was serving as cochairman of the company's board of directors. In 2009, President Barack Obama presented Geschke with the National Medal of Technology and Innovation, the highest honor bestowed on scientists, engineers, and inventors by the U.S. government.

EARLY LIFE

Charles Geschke was born in Cleveland, Ohio, on September 11, 1939. His father was a letterpress photo engraver, as was his paternal grandfather, and his mother was a bankruptcy court paralegal. His parents viewed education as the means for their only child to enjoy a better life than theirs and encouraged him to pursue learning. He graduated from St. Ignatius High School in 1956 and continued his Jesuit education by enrolling at Xavier University in Cincinnati, Ohio.

He received an A.B. in classics from Xavier in 1962 and an M.S. in mathematics in 1963. He met his wife, Nan, at a religious conference on social action in the spring of 1961. The couple married in 1964. For the first years of their marriage, Geschke was employed as a mathematics professor at John Carroll University, a private, coeducational Jesuit Catholic university in University Heights, Ohio. In 1968, the Geschkes, who by this time were the parents of two children, moved to Pittsburgh, where Geschke enrolled as a graduate student in computer science at Carnegie Mellon University. He received his Ph.D. in 1972 and moved his family to Los Altos, California.

Geschke began work at the Xerox Palo Alto Research Center (PARC), where served as a principal scientist and researcher until 1980, when he formed the Imaging Sciences Laboratory at PARC. One of his responsibilities as head of the new laboratory was to hire a chief scientist. He knew John Warnock by reputation and contacted him about the position. The two men, both trained mathematicians and family men who coached soccer, were compatible. Geschke hired Warnock in 1978, and three decades later he described that move as the best business decision he had ever made. The two invented a page description language—a means of describing complex forms, such as typefaces, electronically—called Interpress, which became Xerox's internal standard. When Xerox refused to commercialize the language, Geschke and Warnock left PARC to start their own company.

LIFE'S WORK

Geschke and Warnock founded Adobe Systems in December 1982. They started the company in Warnock's garage and named the company after the creek that ran behind his house. They agreed that Warnock, who had briefly worked at a start-up, would be chief executive officer (CEO) and Geschke, who lacked business experience, would be president. Their salaries and stock options would be identical, and as a practical matter their

Charles Geschke.

titles made little difference; the two men were partners. Through Warnock's graduate adviser at the University of Utah, they met financier Bill Hambrecht, who invested $2.5 million in their company over two years. The original plan was that Adobe would build a complete publishing system, but potential customers persuaded them that what was needed was software that could interface computers, printers, and typesetting equipment.

Interpress evolved into PostScript, software that allows a printer to understand and reproduce a document created on a computer. Their first big break came in 1983, when Apple's Steve Jobs was so impressed with the software that he agreed to invest in Adobe and offered a licensing commitment of $1.5 million to include PostScript on the Apple LaserWriter. The launch of the LaserWriter in 1985 began the desktop publishing revolution and brought Adobe the recognition the company needed. By the end of 1986, Adobe reported sales of $16 million and income of $3.6 million. During this time, the company was taken public, and its expanding customer base included IBM and Digital Equipment Corporation (DEC).

PostScript's sophisticated technology for rendering digital typefaces moved the company into the retail software market. The business expanded even more

Affiliation: Adobe

Adobe is a diversified software company that operates internationally. The company was cofounded in 1982 by Charles Geschke and John Warnock. It offers a line of software and services that allow professionals and consumers to create, manage, and deliver content across multiple operating systems, devices, and media. The company's revenues for fiscal year 2011 were more than $4 million, with more than 40 percent of that amount generated by creative and interactive solutions.

Incorporated in California in 1983, the company, the same year, launched the Adobe PostScript technology that revolutionized the printing of text and images on paper. The company went public in 1986. The following year, it released Adobe Illustrator, a graphics software program used by artists and graphic designers to create scalable vector artwork. Photoshop, released in 1990, gave users the ability to edit photographs and other images. It was followed three years later by Acrobat, a desktop software suite that enabled users to create, edit, and deliver documents in portable document format (PDF) across different systems. The 1994 acquisition of Aldus, the inventor of PageMaker, gave the company the final element it needed to provide all the ingredients for electronic publishing.

The addition of Macromedia's Flash Player in 2005 positioned Adobe for a greater focus on web design and interactivity. In February 2008, the company introduced Adobe Integrated Runtime (AIR), a runtime environment that allows developers to build rich Internet applications (RIAs) across a variety of devices and platforms, including personal computers, smartphones, and televisions. The second quarter of 2010 saw Adobe launch digital viewer technology that enables print publishers to create digital versions of their magazines.

when, in 1987, the company introduced Adobe Illustrator, a design and illustration software program that allowed users to create high-quality line drawings. Illustrator quickly gained popularity among graphic designers, desktop publishers, and technical illustrators. The same year, an agreement with Canon of Japan allowed Adobe to expand into the international market. In 1988, Adobe licensed Photoshop, an imaging program for editing photographs and other bitmapped graphics created by Thomas and John Knoll. By the end of the decade, revenues had reached more than $121 million.

In June 1993, Adobe made available its Acrobat software for creating and viewing electronic documents using portable document format (PDF) files. Available in personal ($695) and professional ($2,495) versions,

with a $50 charge per user for the Acrobat Reader, sales were sluggish. However, when Adobe offered the Reader free a year later, sales increased. In 1995, Adobe partnered with Netscape to enable the Navigator browser to open PDF files on the web. Later PDF became available for the Internet Explorer browser as well. Print publishers found PDF files a convenient means of sending complex documents, and businesses discovered they could PDF files were an economical way to preserve format and graphics. By the time Acrobat 3.0 was introduced in 1996, the Internal Revenue Service had adopted the software, making it possible for tax preparers to use PDF tax forms. This was also the first version to support Japanese, and Acrobat expanded its range. By 2012, more than 600 million copies of the free Acrobat Reader had been downloaded, and PDF files had become standard worldwide.

With the acquisition of Aldus and its Page-Maker, a page layout application, in 1994, Adobe became even more successful. The world's first desktop-to-prepress document publishing system was widely available, and it cut publishing costs to a fraction of those of other available systems. However, the company faced its toughest challenge a few years later. Geschke, who had survived a kidnapping in 1992, was ready to consider retirement, but a successor needed to be groomed first. Adobe hired a handful of executives with this need in mind, but the competition and expense the new executives brought with them did not serve the company well. In January 1996, Adobe announced a loss of $11.8 million for the previous quarter, stock prices fell, and some questioned whether Adobe was prepared for the Internet age. By 1998, a major reorganization was under way. Dozens of employees were dismissed, most of them in middle management. In 1999, Adobe introduced InDesign, a professional publishing software package. Sales surpassed $1 billion for the first time. Both Geschke and Warnock retired in 2000, handing the reins to Bruce Chizen, who had been with the company since 1994.

The founders continued to serve as cochairmen of the board, playing an advisory role as Chizen almost doubled revenue to more than $2 billion by 2006. Geschke was involved in Adobe's acquisition of Macromedia, the maker of Flash (an Internet graphics application that provides the platform for sites such as YouTube), in 2005. Two months after Adobe's free Flash Player 10 was introduced in 2008, it had been downloaded to 55 percent of computers worldwide. PostScript, PDF, and Flash each revolutionized respectively typesetting and document printing, electronic document interchange, and web interactivity. In February 2008, the company introduced Adobe Integrated Runtime (AIR), a runtime environment that allows developers to build rich Internet applications (RIAs) across a variety of devices and platforms, including PCs, smartphones, and televisions. Thirty years after he cofounded Adobe, Geschke remains committed to seeing the company adapt to a changing market that focuses on mobile devices and to creating and distributing content across multiple devices and multiple operating systems.

PERSONAL LIFE

Geschke married Nancy McDonough in 1964. The Geschkes have three children—a daughter, Kathleen, born in 1968, and two sons, Peter, born in 1966, and John, born in 1970—and seven grandchildren.

Just before 9:00 A.M. on May 26, 1992, Geschke was kidnapped at gunpoint from the parking lot of Adobe Systems in Mountain View, California. He was held for four days before he was rescued by FBI agents. The incident drew the already close-knit Geschke family closer together, and more than two decades after the kidnapping, weekly family dinners and their shared Catholic faith keep the family close.

Both Charles and Nan Geschke are graduates of Catholic institutions, and parochial education is a major philanthropic interest of the couple. In 2012, they received the St. Elizabeth Ann Seton Award from the National Catholic Educational Association (NCEA) for their contributions to Catholic education.

In 2000, Geschke was ranked the seventh most influential graphics person of the last millennium by *Graphic Exchange* magazine. He received the Medal of Achievement from the American Electronics Association in 2006. In 2008, he was elected to the American Academy of Arts and Sciences, and in 2009 President Barack Obama awarded him the National Medal of Technology and Innovation. On October 15, 2010, the Marconi Society conferred on Geschke and his longtime friend and associate John Warnock the Marconi Prize, the equivalent of the Nobel Prize in the field of information technology.

Wylene Rholetter

FURTHER READING

Biancuzzi, Federico, and Shane Warden. "PostScript: Charles Geschke and John Warnock." *Masterminds of Programming*. Sebastopol: O'Reilly, 2009. 395–416. Print. The book consists of interviews with the creators of programming languages. Geschke and John Warnock, creators of PostScript, are among them. The interview includes details about design decisions, the goals the hoped to accomplish, and the effects of the language on programming.

Leibs, Scott. "Adobe Remolds Itself." *CFO* Mar. 2012: 44–46. Print. The article presents an interview with Adobe's chief financial officer, who discusses the three stages of the company's history: the PostScript period of the first decade, the period of focus on the Internet that followed, and the current stage, with its focus on mobile devices and social media.

Livingston, Jessica. "Charles Geschke: Adobe." *Founders at Work: Stories of Startups' Early Days*. Berkeley: Apress, 2008. 281–96. Print. The book is a collection of interviews with founders of well-known technology companies. Geschke, cofounder of Adobe Systems, recounts his early days with the company and what he learned from starting the business.

Teresko, John. "Can an Acrobat Tame the Paper Tiger?" *Industry Week* 4 Oct. 1993: 60–63. Print. The article is an early account of Geschke's vision for Adobe Acrobat and the changes he expects wider use of Acrobat to bring in the creation and storage of documents.

Verespe, Michael A. "Empire: Without Emperors." *Industry Week* 5 Feb. 1996: 13–16. Print. The article focuses on the corporate culture of Adobe Systems, cofounded by Geschke and John Warnock. It includes details on financial performance, number of employees, and acquisitions. Two photographs.

James Gosling

Creator of Java

Born: May 19, 1955; Calgary, Alberta, Canada
Died: -
Primary Field: Computer science
Specialty: Computer programming
Primary Company/Organization: Sun Microsystems

Introduction

The father of Java, James Gosling created the programming language while working at Sun Microsystems in the 1990s. Java became one of the most important programming languages of the Internet age, allowing the creation of programs that can run on a wide variety of vastly different computers without requiring separate versions to be coded for each computer setup.

Early Life

James Arthur Gosling was born on May 19, 1955, in a suburb of Calgary, Alberta, Canada. He attended the University of Calgary, earning a bachelor of science degree in computer science in 1977, and then attended Carnegie Mellon University, earning first a master's and then a doctoral degree in computer science. He worked under Bob Sproull, his thesis adviser, who later worked for Sun Microsystems (now Oracle). While at Carnegie Mellon in 1981, Gosling wrote an Emacs implementation called Gosling Emacs, or gosmacs. Emacs is an extensible text editor that became one of the two most popular editors in Unix systems. Gosmacs included a complicated algorithm to handle string-to-string correction; in the source code it is preceded by an ASCII skull and crossbones to warn programmers not to modify it. While Gosmacs was freely redistributed, it was used as part of the basis for GNU Emacs, which became the most popular implementation of Emacs. Gosling later sold gosmacs to UniPress. He also worked on an implementation of Unix and a mail system at Carnegie Mellon.

When he received his doctorate in 1983, Gosling accepted a job with IBM, something he later considered one of his top ten stupid career choices. He was living in Pittsburgh and his office was technically in New York, but he spent his time flying around the country to work on various projects. The day Andy Bechtolsheim, Scott McNealy, and Vinod Khosla formed Sun Microsystems, Gosling and Bechtolsheim had lunch. That was the beginning of their campaign to get Gosling to join Sun. In September 1984, Gosling became Sun's fourth or fifth employee.

Life's Work

At Sun, Gosling developed the Network-extensible Window System (NeWS) with David S. H. Rosenthal, based on PostScript. NeWS was a windowing system, implementing window managers and support for peripherals (like mice) for use in a desktop environment in Unix and Unix-like systems. (Microsoft Windows and later versions of Mac OS are operating systems with an windowing system built in, while a windowing system like NeWS adds windowing to an operating system that does not already incorporate it.) NeWS allowed for simple programs to be written for a graphical user interface (GUI); one of the programs used in demonstrations displayed a pair of eyes that "watched" the cursor as it moved around the screen. NeWS was developed through the early 1980s, and although it never became widespread, it was ported to the Macintosh and OS/2,

James Gosling.

Affiliation: Sun Microsystems

Stanford graduate students Scott McNealy, Andy Bechtolsheim, and Vinod Khosla founded Sun Microsystems on February 24, 1982, taking their name from the Stanford University Network (SUN) Unix workstation Bechtolsheim had designed. Bill Joy, who developed the Berkeley Software Distribution (BSD), joined in the first quarter and is today considered one of the original founders.

Sun posted profits from its first quarter and made an initial public offering in 1986. In the 1980s, Sun was principally a designer and manufacturer of professional workstations, offering low-cost workstations running Unix operating systems and later high-end servers and data storage centers. Its first workstation ran on UniSoft V7 Unix, but beginning in 1982 Sun developed SunOS, a customized version of Joy's BSD Unix. SunOS was succeeded by Solaris.

In 1987, Sun introduced SPARC (for "scalable processor architecture"), a central processing unit (CPU) architecture implemented in its workstation and server systems, originally for 32-bit and later 64-bit operation. It formed SPARC International in 1989 to promote SPARC architecture and encourage its adoption by other manufacturers, leading to some licensing to Texas Instruments, Fujitsu, and others. SPARC remains in development; it was implemented in Oracle's 2011 SPARC T4 multicore processor.

Originally known as a hardware company, Sun always had software in its DNA, thanks in part to Joy. Its most famous contribution to the computing industry is the Java programming language, released in 1995 as part of the Java platform. Java applications were designed to run on any computer regardless of the computer architecture, through the use of Java Virtual Machines, an isolated Java operating system environment installed within the host operating system. This freed programmers from having to port programs from one environment to another, which became a special advantage as the Internet became more popular. Java quickly became the most popular programming language for client-server web applications, and it remains so.

Sun also acquired a number of software companies and packages, including the OpenOffice suite (originally StarOffice), the MySQL database, and Netscape's nonbrowser software components. The company grew considerably during the dot-com bubble, but when the bubble burst in 2000, Sun suffered worse than many of the other survivors, with stock eventually falling below $10 per share, about a tenth of the value it had had immediately before the bubble. Layoffs and factory closures followed, and Sun narrowed its product focus. Another catastrophic fall came between 2007 and 2008, when Sun stock lost 80 percent of its value, forcing another round of layoffs and closures and eventually leading to the company's buyout.

Long an antagonist and critic of Microsoft, Sun resolved its differences with the company in 2004, taking a $1.95 billion payment to settle a series of legal disputes and supporting Microsoft Windows on its future x64 systems.

In 2009, Sun agreed to be acquired by Oracle, a deal that was completed in 2010, after another round of layoffs. Sun's Menlo Park, California, campus was sold off to become the headquarters of Facebook.

and several commercial products were released to run on it, including a version of SimCity.

The main reason for NeWS's failure in competition with the similar X Window system was that X Window was freely distributed by the Massachusetts Institute of Technology, whereas commercial products using NeWS had to be licensed by Sun, Adobe, and the Xerox Palo Alto Research Center (PARC). Although Adobe had an interest in NeWS because it was an extension of PostScript, it refused to port its flagship Photoshop and Illustrator products to Sun's operating systems because it perceived NeWS as a competitor to Display PostScript (DPS), which was much more limited and concerned mostly with drawing commands.

In the end, NeWS did not become a major product for Sun, but Gosling took lessons learned from it and applied them to the product with which he is most associated: the Java programming language. Java was developed in 1994, inspired by work Gosling had done as a graduate student with virtual machines. Virtual machines create an environment using one operating system within another host operating system, somewhat like the video game emulators available online to play old Atari games on modern computers. The use of a virtual machine allows a program written for one computing environment to run in another environment, without needing to be ported over (revised, rewritten, and adjusted—sometimes a more difficult task than writing the original program).

Java worked through the same principle. Development began in 1991 with Mike Sheridan and Patrick Naughton working with Gosling, who implemented the idea of virtual machines and introduced a C-like notation. It was originally intended for interactive television, which at the time was expected to be the next big development in television (and in entertainment in general). The software platform Gosling's team developed was too advanced to be affordably adapted to anything suitable for the twentieth century's digital cable technology. However, between the start of development and the first public implementation in 1995, the World Wide Web had arrived on the scene. Formally proposed in 1990, the World Wide Web became a publicly available service in the summer of 1991, adapting the concept of hypertext to an Internet application; in 1993, the first graphical browser, Mosaic, was released thanks to funding from a research grant initiate by Senator Al Gore. The blending of text and images gave the web the boost in appeal and popularity that it needed, just at the time that dial-up Internet access and commercial Internet service providers were becoming more common—leading many in the general public to conflate the concepts of "the net" and "the web."

Java allowed the web to do more. The portability of Java programs by means of "applets" allowed web browsers to run those programs within web pages. The programs were small, robust, architecture-neutral, and written with familiar programming languages and concepts, which meant experienced programmers learned Java with ease, which in turn encouraged its spread.

Java became so successful that in 2007, Sun Microsystems changed its stock symbol from SUNW to JAVA to boost the company's association with the product.

Sun Microsystems was acquired by Oracle in 2010. Gosling resigned shortly after. Initially remaining silent on his reasons for leaving in April, in September he became more open to discussing the situation in interviews. Among the problems he had with Oracle, he cited the low salary offers given to longtime employees by the new owners; his own salary offer, for instance, replicated his Sun salary but without any of the performance-based bonuses, which had accounted for a significant portion of his income. He was also demoted in rank in order to smooth out differences between the hierarchy of seniority at Sun and that at Oracle (and perhaps to privilege the authority and seniority of existing Oracle employees). Although he had initially accepted the salary offer, feeling that money alone was not reason enough to resign, he found that he had little of the decision-making ability he had previously enjoyed—even over Java, his own invention. Java design decisions were instead made by Oracle officers who had had no previous history with the product. Problems like this were felt across the board by former Sun senior officers. A day at an amusement park was planned to try to boost morale, but Oracle management canceled it because employee appreciation days were not part of Oracle's corporate culture. Some of these issues were foreseen by Sun, which nevertheless preferred to sell to Oracle rather than IBM, because IBM's track record indicated that it would eliminate a large number of jobs altogether.

In particular Gosling felt micromanaged by Oracle's Larry Ellison. While his criticism of Oracle was often general or diplomatic, about Ellison he minced no words, comparing him to a football team owner who hires a coach and then ignores him and manages the team himself.

From March to August 2011, Gosling worked for Google as a software engineer. He then took a job as chief software architect and member of the strategic advisory board of Liquid Robotics, an ocean data services provider based in Sunnyvale, California. Liquid Robotics operates the Wave Glider marine robot, which is propelled by wave energy and autonomously collects ocean data. Liquid Robotics has since expanded with the creation of Liquid Robotics Oil and Gas, developing oil and gas industry services using Wave Gliders. Wave Gliders can operate autonomously or by remote pilot, and are in use as part of British Petroleum's marine monitoring program in the Gulf of Mexico in the wake of the 2010 *Deepwater Horizon* accident. *Fast Company* named Liquid Robotics one of the 50 Most Innovative Companies in 2012. Gosling was awarded the Economist Innovation Award in 2002.

PERSONAL LIFE

Gosling and his wife, Judy, have two daughters, Kate and Kelsey, and live in Redwood City, California. Gosling enjoys cooking when he has time. He uses his MacBookPro for most of his work. In 2007, he was appointed an Officer of the Order of Canada, one of Canada's highest honors for civilians.

Bill Kte'pi

FURTHER READING

Ceruzzi, Paul E. *Computing: A Concise History*. Cambridge: MIT, 2012. Print. A broad history of computers, including Sun's role.

Hall, Mark, and John Barry. *Sunburst: The Ascent of Sun Microsystems*. New York: Contemporary, 1991. Print. More insightful than the Southwick, if dated.

Southwick, Karen. *High Noon: The Inside Story of Scott McNealy and the Rise of Sun Microsystems*. New York: Wiley, 1999. Print. Despite McNealy's name in the title, really a history of Sun's rise.

HELEN GREINER

Cofounder of iRobot

Born: December 6, 1967; London, England
Died: -
Primary Field: Applied science
Specialty: Physics and engineering
Primary Company/Organization: iRobot

INTRODUCTION

Helen Greiner, a renowned roboticist and pioneer in the robot industry, is a cofounder and former president of iRobot, the largest independent robotics company in the world. During her tenure at iRobot, the company moved from a Massachusetts Institute of Technology spin-off to an international leader in the industry. With a vision of designing robots that could be put to practical use in the consumer, industrial, academic, and military markets, Greiner developed robots that possessed greater mobility and intelligence than those previously in use. She brought the same imagination and ingenuity to CyPhyWorks, the company she founded in 2009, the year following her resignation from iRobot. As chief executive officer (CEO) of CyPhyWorks, Greiner leads the company in developing unmanned aerial vehicles.

EARLY LIFE

Helen Greiner was born December 6, 1967, in London, England. Her father, a refugee from Hungary, and her mother, a native of Yorkshire, met at the University of London. They moved to the United States when Greiner was five. Greiner and her older brother grew up on Long Island, New York. With a mother who taught mathematics and science and a businessman father who had been a chemistry major, Greiner's abilities in mathematics and science were not unexpected. She played chess with her father at five, and by middle school she was hacking the family computer in order to control her brother's radio-operated cars. A defining moment came in 1977, when she saw the movie *Star Wars*. R2-D2, the three-foot-tall android, captured her attention. Excited by a machine with intelligence, emotions, and gender, she was disillusioned

when her brother revealed that RS-D2 was really controlled by a man inside a plastic costume. Her goal from that day became to create the R2-D2 she had imagined.

That goal led her to enroll at the Massachusetts Institute of Technology (MIT). On her first day on campus, Greiner met Colin Angle, who shared her fascination with the science of robots. The two became friends, spending so much time together that friends thought there was a romance. However, Greiner and Angle were interested in the romance of making machines think like humans. The two worked in MIT's Artificial Intelligence Laboratory, headed by Rodney Brooks.

Greiner graduated with a bachelor's degree in mechanical engineering in 1989. She interned at the National

Helen Greiner.

Aeronautics and Space Administration's Jet Propulsion Laboratory in Pasadena, California, where she helped design robots that could make repairs in space. Her work there became part of her master's thesis. She received her master's in computer science from MIT in 1990 and returned to California, where she worked with California Cybernetics. Less than a year later, she returned to Massachusetts and joined Angle and Brooks to found iRobot Corporation.

LIFE'S WORK

In 1990, enthusiasm was high at the young company, which started in Angle's apartment. The partners adopted a motto: "Build cool stuff. Have fun. Change the world." Two-thirds of that mission was easily completed; the final third took more time. Within two months of starting, iRobot had built its first robot. It took twelve years to sell one at a profit. Early efforts were primitive prototypes with microprocessors that the company sold to universities for $3,000 apiece. Greiner and her partners bought components at RadioShack, hired interns from MIT at minimum wage, and carried $100,000 in bank debt in addition to maxing out their own credit cards. They worked eighteen-hour days, taking only $30,000 in annual salaries. Their first break came in 1992, when Japan hired the company to develop designs for nanorobots for medical application, but payments for the $500,000 deal were frequently late.

U.S. government research contracts saved the company. In 1993, the Advanced Research Projects Agency (DARPA) and the Office of Naval Research awarded iRobot a $50,000 contract to build an underwater minesweeper. Although the device was never employed, more government contracts followed. After the 1995 Oklahoma City bombing, Greiner and company won a $3 million Defense Department contract to build reconnaissance robots that could operate like minitanks to scope suspicious urban areas. Two years later, following the success Tamagotchi, the virtual pet, iRobot entered the toy market. In 1998, Hasbro agreed to a three-year exclusive contract and gave the company $1 million to develop My Real Baby, a robotic doll programmed to giggle, cried, and talked on cue. My Real Baby was on shelves in time for Christmas shoppers in 2000. On the high end of the doll market with a price tag of $96, My Real Baby sold 100,000 units.

With the company's success came recognition for its founders, particularly Greiner. She was named an Innovator for the Next Century by MIT's *Technology Review* in 2002. The next year, she was on *Fortune*'s list of Top 10 Innovators under 40 in the United States. Greiner led the company through its initial public offering (IPO) in 2005, a move that raised $70.6 million. When iRobot expanded in the consumer and military categories, Greiner secured $35 million in venture funding. She also initiated the company's Government and Industrial Robots Division. Government research funding in this area led to the first deployment of robots in

Affiliation: iRobot

In 1990, roboticists Helen Greiner, Colin Angle, and Rodney Brooks founded iRobot with the mission of developing robots that had practical applications. Their first robots were assembled in Angle's apartment with parts purchased from RadioShack. The company consisted of the three founders and five interns from the Massachusetts Institute of Technology (MIT) who worked for minimum wage. Little more than two decades later, the company, which went public in 2005, would have offices in five states and four countries outside the United States. In 2011, iRobot generated more than $465 million and employed more than six hundred professionals.

The firm's first success came through military robots created for the Department of Defense. Best known is the PackBot, a tanklike robot that can travel over rugged terrain and be used for such tasks as situational awareness, reconnaissance, and explosive ordnance disposal. After the terrorist attacks of September 11, 2001, PackBots were sent into the Manhattan disaster site to check the soundness of remaining structures. More than two thousand PackBots have been deployed for use in Afghanistan and Iraq. A second creation, the Bloodhound, has the capacity to find wounded soldiers on the battlefield, perform medical examinations, apply compounds to stop bleeding, and even inject medications.

More than eight million of iRobot's home robots have been sold worldwide. Chief among them is the Roomba vacuuming robot, first introduced in 2002. Both the Roomba and the Scooba, a floor-washing robot introduced in 2006, have earned the Good Housekeeping Seal of Approval. More recent innovations include the Verro, a pool-cleaning robot, and the Looj, a gutter-cleaning robot, both first marketed in 2007. In 2008, Greiner and Brooks left iRobot to found other companies. Angle remained as CEO and chairman of the board.

combat in Afghanistan and later in Iraq to search for enemy combatants and booby traps. PackBots, which carried a price tag of $45,000, proved well suited for use in the field because of their mobility and toughness; each weighed about 40 pounds and was capable of sustaining the equivalent of a 3-meter-drop onto concrete. Still in the developmental stage when they were first used in 2002, PackBots continued to be modified and improved based on feedback from soldiers: They were customized with modular payloads, cameras with night vision, and other features suited to specific missions. Greiner worked to win a $51.4 million development contract for small unmanned ground vehicles (SUGVs) from the U.S. Army's Future Combat Systems program.

Defense contracts may have provided the means for iRobot to hire more engineers and move into a building, but the creation of a home-cleaning robot that the 1960s cartoon family the Jetsons might have owned drew the greatest attention. Greiner led the design team responsible for the Roomba, a small, relatively inexpensive, disc-shaped vacuum that cruises around a room, using sensors to maneuver around furniture and avoid stairs. It was introduced in 2002, and successive generations of the domestic robot following in 2004, 2007, and 2011. It received the Good Housekeeping Seal of Approval in 2003, and Oprah Winfrey declared it a "favorite thing" in 2011.

Greiner's efforts on the defense and domestic fronts significantly contributed to public acceptance of robots as an important emerging technology. When Greiner and her colleagues founded iRobot, the public viewed robotics—if they thought of the field at all—with skepticism or trepidation. The rare robots that existed outside the imagination of science fiction writers were to be found in university research laboratories or manufacturing facilities, primarily in the automobile industry, where they were used for spray-painting and welding. With their specialized applications and costs in the tens of thousands of dollars, robots were still more experimental than practical. However, as the industry matured, with iRobot leading the way, Greiner's conviction that everyday application and commercial success were attainable proved valid.

On October 22, 2008, Greiner announced her resignation as iRobot's chairman of the board. CEO Angle replaced her, but Greiner continued to serve on the company's board of directors until 2011.

PERSONAL LIFE

An introvert with a fear of public speaking and flying, Greiner learned to overcome her reserve and her fears when her position as the head of a global company routinely required her to speak to crowds that sometimes numbered in the thousands and to travel by plane on a weekly basis. A woman in a field dominated by men, she networked with generals and secured government contracts. Petite and feminine in appearance, she enjoys kayaking, rock climbing, and paintballing, and her passion for snowboarding is second only to her passion for robotics.

After leaving iRobot, Greiner founded The Droid Works, later renamed CyPhyWorks, in 2009. In December of that year, the company received a $2.4 million grant from the National Institute of Standards and Technology to work with researchers at the Georgia Institute of Technology to develop small, hovering unmanned aerial vehicles (UAVs) equipped with video cameras and sensors.

Greiner was named one of America's Best Leaders by the Kennedy School at Harvard University in conjunction with *U.S. News and World Report* in 2005. She received the Pioneer Award from the Association for Unmanned Vehicle Systems International in 2006. Chair of the national Robotic Technology Consortium, the robotics advisory board of Worcester Polytechnic Institute, and the board of directors of the National Defense Industrial Association, she continues as CEO of CyPhyWorks.

Wylene Rholetter

FURTHER READING

Greiner, Helen. "Manufacturing the Future: An Interview with Helen Greiner." Interview by Deepa Kandaswamy. *Women in Business* 55.1 (2003): 35–37. Print. An interview with Greiner that focuses on her reasons for founding iRobot and provides details on the research projects and products of the company.

---. "Time for Robots to Get Real." *New Scientist* 213.2848 (2012): 20. Print. Greiner argues for the potential of robotics to change the world if innovators focus on the practical application of using robots to solve real problems.

Headden, Susan. "The Lady and Her Robots." *U.S. News and World Report* 139.23 (2005): 34–38. Print. A profile of Greiner that also takes a look at the development of iRobot and its $95 million in sales, particularly its success with Roomba and PackBots.

Howard, Courtney E. "Irobot Advances State of the Art In Military Robotics." *Military and Aerospace Electronics* 19.5 (2008): 3. Print. Focuses on iRobot's portable communications relay robot, developed for the U.S. Advanced Research Project Agency's LANdroids program in Burlington, Massachusetts.

Weir, Kirsten. "Robot Master." *Current Science* 88.13 (2003): 8–9. Print. A profile of Greiner that recounts her childhood fascination with a robot from the movie *Star Wars* and how it led to a successful career in robotics. Color photographs.

H

WENDY HALL

Professor of computer science, University of Southampton

Born: October 25, 1952; West London, England
Died: -
Primary Field: Computer science
Specialty: Internet
Primary Company/Organization: The Web Science Trust and Semantic Web

INTRODUCTION

Wendy Hall is one of the generation of computer innovators who are building on the work of the preceding generations to continue the spread of computing to as many people as possible around the world. Her focus is on making the Internet into a universal tool capable of delivering information in multimedia and hypermedia formats. She is a pioneer in digital libraries, the development of the Semantic Web, and the emerging discipline of web science.

EARLY LIFE

Born in West London, as a child Wendy Hall had a natural aptitude for mathematics and was the first in her family to attend university. At one time she considered a career in medicine. She earned her bachelor's degree with honors in mathematics from the University of Southampton in 1974. Her Ph.D. in pure mathematics from the same institution followed in 1977. In 1984, she became a lecturer in computer science at her alma mater. She then went on to earn a master's degree in computer science from City University of London in 1986.

LIFE'S WORK

Hall headed the team that in 1989 initiated the Microcosm Project, an open hypermedia system. Microcosm

provided users with cross-application dynamic hyperlinks and was touted as a tool for development of industrial information management because it stored original documents of all types in their original formats, allowing software to collect and arrange all media into a single document tied together through link bases while preserving the integrity of the originals. An associated development was the distributed link service

Wendy Hall.

Affiliation: The Web Science Trust and Semantic Web

Wendy Hall is cofounder of the Web Science Research Initiative (WSRI), later renamed the Web Science Trust (WST). The WSRI was designed to study the structure and sociology of the World Wide Web. Hall was among the first to study hypermedia and multimedia, and she has had a strong influence on the business world, an influence that was to grown with the implementation of the Institute of Web Science, funded by £30 million of UK government funding.

The WST/WSRI researched web development and promoted collaboration around the world by web science organizations. Web science in 2010 was a mere four years old but experiencing rapid growth as governments acknowledged the economic benefit to developed economies of the digital economy. Web science incorporates law, sociology, philosophy, and economics as well as the technology. The goal is to understand the impact of the web as it evolves into the Semantic Web: an extension of the World Wide Web that will allow people to share content beyond the limitations imposed by applications and will provide new services and businesses. The Semantic Web will make the Internet the world's primary database, social networking space, the repository of its documents. With the Semantic Web, machines can tie data together in ways not available at the moment. Such a tool has the backing of governments, notably in the United Kingdom at data.gov.uk and in the United States at data.gov, both Semantic Web elements.

that broadened Microcosm to allow multiple users in a distributed arrangement.

As an open hypermedia system, Microcosm was a forerunner of the World Wide Web. Hypermedia allow authors to create without concern for sequentiality any combination of text or visual elements that they can by using information space, browsing at will. There is no problem of cognitive overload or getting lost in hyperspace because of too many paths, too much information, or hyperdocuments with so many cross-references that the user becomes disoriented. "Open hypermedia" (OH) users define *hypermedia* as media that allow integration of process and information and interchangeability of author and reader. OH allows insertion of links without alteration of the original text. Hypermedia also allow the creation of an interactive manipulable archive that contains research documentation as it evolves from initial notes to final publication. Southampton designed and implemented such a system for orthopedic surgeons to access the ongoing research of their peers and maintain currency and training in the field.

In 1994, Microcosm was patented and spun off to a commercial venture through Hall's start-up company Multicosm, which later became Active Navigation. Microcosm won an award in 1995 from the International Test and Evaluation Association (ITEA) and a BCS IT award in 1996 from the British Computer Society. Today, Active Navigation focuses on Web-based link services.

Also in 1994, Hall was appointed professor of computer science at the University of Southampton. Two years later, she became a Senior Fellow at the Engineering and Physical Sciences Research Council (EPSRC), a distinction she held until 2002. In 1997, she also became a member of Council of EPSRC. In 2000, she was awarded the honor of Commander of the British Empire (CBE). She became a Fellow of the Royal Academy of Engineering (2000), president of the British Computer Society (2003–2004), a member of the Prime Minister's Council for Science and Technology (2004–2010), a member of the Scientific Council of the European Research Council (2005–2010), a senior vice president of the Royal Academy of Engineering (2005–2008), a recipient of the Anita Borg Award for Technical Leadership (2006), a founding director of the Web Science Research Initiative (2006), vice president (2006–2008) and then president (2008–2010) of the Association for Computing Machinery (ACM), a member of the British Library Board (2007), Dame Commander of the British Empire (2009), and a Fellow of the Royal Society (2009). She is also a founding member of the European Research Council's Scientific Council. She has published more than three hundred papers for journals and conferences.

Hall was head of the School of Electronics and Computer Science (ECS) at Southampton from 2002 to 2007. With Tim Berners-Lee (creator of the World Wide Web) and Nigel Shadbolt (professor of artificial intelligence at Southampton), Hall created the Web Science Research Initiative in 2006, which became the Web Science Trust in 2009. Although the Semantic Web—an extension of the World Wide Web designed to allow people to share content beyond the limitations imposed by applications and websites—is still in its early stages, one indicator of its promise is the ASBOrometer, which joins geographical information and data on antisocial behavior disorders (ASBOs) to show how many people in specific locations have such disorders. New data forms and new telecommunications devices have allowed projects such as the ASBOrometer and others yet unimagined. The Institute of Web Science is be a major trainer in the field, critical in the United Kingdom, where the shortages of digital and technological skills are glaring. The first developers of the web were the university-based scientists. The new move is led by governments and public sectors. As the first iteration of the web revolutionized business models in industries such as music and publishing, the new web is expected to overturn other business models, education, medicine, and academic disciplines as well.

In 2009, as president of ACM, Hall focused on doubling that group's membership and promoting better collaboration among international members of that organization. She sought to proliferate computer societies in Europe, China, and India. Her target of 100,000 for ACM's membership seemed within reach, given the millions of computer workers around the world. In fostering ACM collaborations with the media and the National Science Foundation and other organizations, she warned that there was a problem with the significant decline in interest in computing careers. She has worked with WGBH Boston on a program to encourage black and Hispanic girls to consider computer careers. She has explored options to get mainstream policy makers interested in computing and computer science issues. She has noted that her pride in her status as Dame Commander of the British Empire is not merely personal: It is good for the academic field, for the computing community, and for women in technology.

In line with these interests is Hall's concern for the decline in young girls' interest in computing and for what has become known as "dumbed down" computer science. As an inventor of the predecessor to the World Wide Web, Hall has suggested that perhaps girls should be taught how computers work rather than how to use computers for mundane tasks, such as creating spreadsheets or presentations or for learning secretarial competencies. In 2004, women in the United Kingdom accounted for only 19 percent of computer science majors, and by 2009 the percentage was down to 16 percent. Hall notes that it does not help that one of the early home computers in the United Kingdom, the ZX Spectrum, was commonly used to play war games. She has

also noted that her computer laboratory at Southampton is dominated by males, and there are few efforts to recruit women into the field. Some hopeful signs are that the British Computer Society has a program to recruit girls to computer science, the toy maker Mattel has marketed a Barbie doll who is a computer engineer.

PERSONAL LIFE

Hall is married to plasma physicist Peter Chandler, whom she met while she was working toward her Ph.D. Hall defines herself as a workaholic but works hard at enjoying holidays, too, particularly time on the beach and good meals and fine wine with her husband. She also defines herself as a shopper and "party animal."

Throughout her career, Hall, as a woman, has had to work harder and better than most men in her field. She was so ahead of her time that in early years her professors and colleagues failed to understand her work, regarding her as unlikely to succeed unless she followed a more conventional career path. She persisted in her belief that computers could provide access to a complete learning experience including video, audio, photographs, and other images—technology that is taken for granted today. Throughout her career, she has advocated for equality for women in information technology and as users and creators of Internet capabilities. The second female computer scientist to be named a Dame Commander of the British Empire (preceded only by technology entrepreneur Stephanie "Steve" Shirley), Hall has broken many glass ceilings.

Hall has continuously expressed her passion for computing and her sympathy for those stuck in work they do not enjoy. She notes that her career in computers has allowed her to travel the world, meet people, and exchange ideas—which a career in her original discipline, mathematics, would not have allowed, since mathematics is basically a solitary pursuit.

John H. Barnhill

FURTHER READING

"'Geek' Perception of Computer Science Putting Off Girls, Expert Warns, January 10, 2012." *The Guardian*. 10 Jan. 2012: n. pag. Web. 12 May 2012. Article on Hall's concerns about the difficulty in attracting girls and young women to computing.

Grange, Simon, et al. "The Dynamic Review Journal: A Scholarly Archive." *New Review of Hypermedia and Multimedia* 11.1 (2005): 69–89. *Academic Search Complete*. Web. 12 May 2012. Describes an extended digital library environment that the authors developed for orthopedic surgeons to help them collate and analyze patient data, as an example of the cycle of activity in which a digital archive resides.

Hall, Wendy."WOMEN: Computer Scientist but no Geek." Interview by Meera Murugesan. *New Straits Times* (Malaysia) 9 Apr. 2012: n. pag. Web. 12 May 2012. A newspaper reporter interviews Hall during a stopover in Kuala Lumpur about her career and her advocacy of women in computing.

Hoffmann, Leah. "Q&A: Our Dame Commander." *Communications of the ACM* 52.4 (2009): 112–11. *Business Source Complete*. Web. 30 Apr. 2012. Discusses Hall's philosophy and hopes for the future.

"Pioneer of Cyberspace Honoured." BBC. 31 Dec. 2008. Web. 1 May 2012. A news post announcing the award of Dame Commander of the British Empire to Hall as cocreator of the open hypermedia system Microcosm.

Schofield, Kevin M., et al. "Candidates for Members at Large." *Communications of the ACM* 47.5 (2004): 85–88. *Business Source Complete*. Web. 30 Apr. 2012. Biographical sketches and statements of candidates for offices in the 2004 ACM elections.

Thomson, Rebecca. "Trawling the Net for Digital Advances." *Computer Weekly* 20 Apr. 2010: 12. *Business Source Complete*. Web. 30 Apr. 2012. Technical article.

Wills, Gary B, et al. "Industrial Strength Hypermedia: Design, Implementation and Application." *International Journal of Computer Integrated Manufacturing* 13.3 (2000): 173–86. *Business Source Complete*. Web. 7 May 2012. Coauthored technical article about the potential for hypermedia in industry.

---. "An Inquiry-Led Personalised Navigation System (IPNS) Using Multi-dimensional Linkbases." *New Review of Hypermedia and Multimedia* 14.1 (2008): 33–55. *Academic Search Complete*. Web. 7 May 2012. A coauthored technical article.

MIKE HAMMOND

Cofounder of Gateway

Born: November 28, 1961; Des Moines, Iowa
Died: -
Primary Field: Business and commerce
Specialty: Management, executives, and investors
Primary Company/Organization: Gateway

INTRODUCTION

As the original cofounder of Gateway, Mike Hammond experienced business success at an early age. His expertise in manufacturing and distribution operations allowed the company to rise rapidly among the competition and become one of the dominant computer manufacturers during the 1990s.

EARLY LIFE

Mike Hammond was born in Des Moines, Iowa, on November 28, 1961. After dropping out of a Missouri College, he worked as a diesel mechanic, joined a band, and eventually became employed in a local Century Systems computer store. During this time, he befriended Ted Waitt from Sioux City, who eventually joined Century Systems as a retail associate. After nine months of intense exposure to sales work and the burgeoning computer industry, Hammond and Waitt left their positions and set out to begin their own computer business.

LIFE'S WORK

Upon securing a $10,000 loan, Waitt and Hammond founded the Texas Instruments Personal Computers (TIPC) Network. From a small office in Sioux City, Iowa, originally owned by Waitt's father, the two young entrepreneurs sold Texas Instruments computer parts over the phone. As their business venture moved forward, Hammond and Waitt began to build their own computers. By 1985, they had sold fifty computers and made $100,000 in revenue. Slowly, their small business venture gained momentum as customers were attracted to the economical prices they offered. The company's initial success allowed Hammond and Waitt to move their base of operations into the Sioux City Livestock Exchange Building.

In 1987, Hammond, Waitt, and Waitt's brother Norm officially founded Gateway 2000. One year later, an advertisement featuring the company was published in *Computer Shopper*, a popular monthly magazine that provided consumers with reviews and updates on computers. Gateway's advertisement offered a message asking, "Computers from Iowa?" Complementing the question was a picture of a herd of cows. This simple yet revealing advertisement focused on Gateway's friendly midwestern company dynamics. By the end of 1988, sales had risen dramatically: from $1.5 million to $12 million.

Gateway thrived on its direct sales approach, effective customer service, and youthful work culture. By 1989, sales had reached $70 million and the company moved into neighboring North Sioux City, South Dakota. In 1990, Gateway had more than fifteen hundred employees and had increased its revenue to $275 million. The company's distinctive midwestern brand was evident on each black-and-white cow-spotted box that it shipped to customers.

As the company continued to make incredible strides throughout the 1990s, Waitt, who became the company's chairman and chief executive officer (CEO), received the majority of publicity. However, behind the scenes, Hammond was just as important: He developed the company's highly organized manufacturing system and devoted attention and energy to the developing the company's commitment to customer satisfaction. By the end of the 1990s, Gateway was selling computers over the phone, online, and in company stores. Thirty-nine hundred telephone sales agents were in the company, along with sixty-six hundred service representatives. The company's commitment to its customers became one of its most important features.

As Gateway began to branch out and establish both domestic and foreign plants, Hammond was named the vice president of the Asia-Pacific organization. He assisted in the company's distribution network in Asia and the development of new plants in Malaysia, including centers of manufacturing in Malacca and Kuala Lumpur. By 1996, sales of Gateway computers had reached an astounding $5 billion. Three years later, sales topped $8.6 billion. Furthermore, by 1999, Gateway was composed of twenty-one thousand employees.

The run of success experienced by Gateway for nearly fifteen years, however, began to slow down by the end of the 1990s. In order to assist the company through a pending transformative period, Waitt decided in 1998 to add Jeffrey Weitzen, the former executive vice president of the business markets division at AT&T, to the upper management team. For two years, Weitzen served as the president and chief operating officer of Gateway. He brought a greater financial ethos to Gateway and helped guide the company into the new Internet age.

Under Weitzen's influence, Gateway also moved its headquarters to San Diego, California. The decision, made in order to attract talent to its leadership roles, rankled many within the company, including Hammond, who preferred the comfortable confines of South Dakota. Hammond, for his part, did not leave for California.

In 2000, Waitt stepped down as CEO of Gateway and assumed the role of chairman. He was replaced by Weitzen, who immediately faced struggles. His quiet and rigid philosophy contrasted greatly with that of Waitt. He also demoted many of the senior members, including Hammond, who was named the head of the Business Process Simplification Team. Hammond was expectedly not enamored of Weitzen's management skills. In an interview conducted one year later, he would publicly voice his displeasure.

By this time, Gateway was severely hindered by the troubles facing the entire information technology industry. At the end of the fiscal fourth quarter in 2000, the company suffered massive losses, upwards of $94.3 million. Its stock price also plummeted, by nearly 75 percent. The company appeared to be on the verge of collapse. Seeing his company decline, Waitt reassumed the role of CEO, and Weitzen resigned.

Waitt hoped to resurrect the failing company and immediately reinstated many of his previous staff. He named Hammond the senior vice president of operations. At this time, Hammond also agreed to move to the company's base in San Diego. The revitalization project was painfully slow, and Gateway was forced to close a number of its overseas operations. Many of the company's workers were laid off, and the company's plant in South Dakota was forced to shut down.

Amid the turmoil, Gateway attempted to regroup rapidly. At a time when the computer industry as a whole was at a crossroads, Gateway, under Waitt's leadership, began to place emphasis on consumer electronics, including digital televisions. In 2004, the company bought eMachines, a maker of low-cost computers. Once again, Waitt resigned from the CEO position and remained as chairman of the company. Wayne Inouye, CEO of eMachines, assumed the role of Gateway CEO. One year later, Waitt officially retired from Gateway. Hammond also left the company in order to pursue other interests.

PERSONAL LIFE

Since working as a diesel mechanic as a young man, Hammond has always had a deep fascination with cars.

Affiliation: Gateway

Gateway originated from the entrepreneurial ideas of Iowa natives Ted Waitt and Mike Hammond. After receiving a loan from Waitt's grandmother, the two entrepreneurs began selling computer parts for Texas Instruments Personal Computers (TIPC) Network out of Sioux City, Iowa. The business soon expanded to include full-sized computers, individually built by Waitt and Hammond. During the first year of business, they had made $300,000 in revenue.

In 1987, Gateway 2000 was established. Two years later, the base of operations moved to North Sioux City, South Dakota. The company promoted itself as a business that was distinctly personable and midwestern. The organization's commitment to provide sound and effective customer service along with inexpensive products attracted numerous customers. By 1988, Gateway's reputation had grown nationally in the information technology industry, evident with $12 million worth of sales. Two years later, Gateway amassed $275 million in revenue. The distinctive black-and-white cow spots that covered all its computer boxes provided an instant marketing tool and an attractive brand for this small company from the Midwest.

As the dot-com boom spread across the United States and international markets throughout the 1990s, Gateway witnessed immense success. At its peak in 1999, it achieved $8.6 billion in sales and twenty-one thousand people were employed by the company. Its centers of business had spread across the United States, Europe, Australia, and Asia. In 1999, Waitt, who had guided the company as the CEO for more than ten years, decided it was time to step back from day-to-day operations. He handed the position of CEO to Jeffrey Weitzen, a former executive vice president of the business markets division at AT&T. Under Weitzen's lead, Gateway struggled and in the fourth quarter of 2000 amassed losses of more than $94 million.

Waitt returned as Gateway's CEO at the end of 2001. He nevertheless could not revive the company and was forced to close a number of overseas centers. Gateway began to focus on consumer electronics, and in 2004 it acquired eMachines, a manufacturer of low-cost computers. Under the terms of the sale, eMachines CEO Wayne Inouye became the new head of Gateway. In 2007, Acer bought Gateway for $710 million.

During his years at Gateway, he built drag-racing cars. After retiring from Gateway in 2005, he returned to North Sioux City and opened Dakota Muscle Cars. Hammond's business restores, customizes, and repairs high-performance vehicles. The company is well regarded and widely known, both locally and nationally.

Gavin Wilk

FURTHER READING

Allan, Roy A. *A History of the Personal Computer: The People and the Technology*. London: Allan, 2001. Print. A broad historical discussion that examines the evolution of the computer and the information technology industry.

Brooker, Katrina. "I Built This Company, I Can Save It." *Fortune* 30 Apr. 2001. Web. 20 Aug. 2012. Article delves into how Ted Wait planned to resurrect Gateway after the company lost more than $94 million in the fiscal fourth quarter of 2000.

Dedrick, Jason, Kenneth L. Kraemer, and Bryan MacQuarrie. "Gateway Computer: Using E-commerce to Move Beyond the Box and to Move More Boxes." 1 Feb. 2001. *eScholarship, University of California*. Web. 20 Aug. 2012. Open access research article that describes how Gateway developed a highly efficient online sales and marketing campaign and was able to remain competitive.

Dreeszen, Dave. "Meet the Graduates of 'Gateway University.'" *Sioux City Journal* 17 Dec. 2007. Web. 20 Aug. 2012. Interesting piece that describes the lives of some of the former Gateway executives. The article covers Hammond and his new company, Dakota Muscle Cars.

Hyatt, J. "Betting the Farm." *Inc.* 13.36 (1991). *Business Source Complete*. Web. 20 Aug. 2012. Presents a glimpse at the transformation of Gateway from inception to the early 1990s.

Linck, Michelle. "Classic Cars Rev Their Way Back." *Sioux City Journal* 5 Mar. 2007. Web. 20 Aug. 2012. Reveals Hammond's deep passion for cars and provides interesting details about his current company, Dakota Muscle Cars.

Morgan, Adam. *Eating the Big Fish: How Challenger Brands Can Compete against Brand Leaders*. New York: Wiley, 1999. Print. Offers a brief look at Gateway's successful marketing strategies.

Walter, Russ. *The Secret Guide to Computers and Tricky Living*. 31st ed. Manchester: Russell Walter, 2012. Print. Offers full coverage and instructions on various computers and affiliated hardware and software components. Also provides extensive historical background about a number of computer companies, including Gateway.

JIM HARRIS

Cofounder of Compaq

Born: Date unknown; Texas
Died: -
Primary Field: Computer science
Specialty: Computer hardware
Primary Company/Organization: Compaq

INTRODUCTION

Jim Harris is best known for cofounding Compaq Computer Corporation with friends Rod Canion and Bill Murto in 1981. He was a key player in the company's operations during the 1980s and left the company with cofounder Canion in 1992 to form Insource Technology, where he works today.

EARLY LIFE

Jim Harris was born in Texas. He is a graduate of Texas A&M University and holds a bachelor of science degree in electrical engineering. He began his computing career in 1967 as an engineering project manager at Texas Instruments in Dallas, Texas.

LIFE'S WORK

Harris's career began in 1967, when, after college, he began working for Texas Instruments. He was a senior manager in the summer of 1981, when he and two colleagues, Joseph R. "Rod" Canion and William H. Murto, decided to start a company. Initially they were not certain what that company would produce, but they eventually decided to build portable personal computers that met IBM's industry standards. The name Compaq was an acronym for "compatibility and quality." Each man only had $1,000 to invest, so they sought financing from Ben Rosen, president of Sevin-Rosen Partners, a venture capital firm in Houston. Rosen offered $2.5 in funding and became Compaq's chairman. The company earned $111.1 million in its first year and enjoyed its first billion-dollar year in 1987.

During that time, Harris served as vice president of engineering, overseeing the development of new products such as the company's initial offering, the Compaq Portable Computer, and encouraging early adoption of technologies such as Intel's 286 and 386 processors.

Compaq Computer Corporation had made a long-standing commitment to in-house American production and to what cofounder Canion called "consensus management," which in part led to Canion's ouster from Compaq in 1991. When he left, Harris went with him. Harris and Canion founded a new company, Insource Technology, in 1992 using the same small office space they had first rented when founding Compaq. In his position as chairman of the board, Harris performs top-level executive functions and consults with midsize to large businesses to address their computing needs. He

Jim Harris.

Affiliation: Compaq

Founded on February 16, 1982, Compaq Computer corporation started humbly in Houston, Texas. The company founders, Jim Harris, Rod Canion, and Bill Murto, were hard-pressed to raise venture capital after leaving Texas Instruments in the previous year, and they have described their original office space as equipped with only a few card tables, folding chairs, and a cardboard box for a telephone stand.

In a quintessential American success story, the company enjoyed explosive growth in its first year of operation. Its debut product, the Compaq Portable Computer, sold more than fifty-three thousand units, grossing $111.1 million for the company in 1983.

The company enjoyed a long string of successes throughout the 1980s as Compaq's computers became more and more powerful. This innovation fueled demand, and Compaq, which garnered a reputation for producing solid-performing computers at a reasonable price, profited apace. Rather than go head to head with larger computer manufacturers IBM and Apple, Compaq focused its efforts on machines that were reliable (if unspectacular) in terms of performance, on low prices, and on public engagement through clever and aggressive media marketing.

The business model paid off. By the end of its first year of full production, Compaq was forced to construct a new headquarters building to accommodate the company's rapid growth in business and employee head count. Second- and third-year sales increased further, and in 1987 Compaq generated $1.2 billion.

The company continued to grow and flourish, opening an immensely profitable European division and continuing to hold a significant portion of the U.S. market share, until the very end of the 1980s. At that time, the company had grown too large for what cofounder Canion called a "consensus management" style, and consequently Compaq posted its first loss, $71 million, in 1991. By a unanimous vote by the board of directors, Canion was ousted from his position as chief executive officer in favor of Compaq Europe founder Eckhard Pfeiffer. When Canion left, several other key executives, including cofounder Harris, left with him.

Under Pfeiffer, Compaq took an even larger share of the world PC market and enjoyed even greater profits. During the 1990s, Compaq ventured into larger business solutions, such as servers, in order to undercut computing giant IBM. Meanwhile, Compaq was suffering from competition from companies like Gateway 2000 and Dell, which were introducing less expensive computers, made from standardized parts imported from Asia, into the U.S. PC market. Compaq took steps to streamline its operation and cut costs, but by the end of the 1990s these decisions began to affect quality, leading eventually to the forced resignation of Pfeiffer, who was replaced with Michael Capellas as chief executive officer.

By the time Capellas took over operations, Compaq had accrued significant debt and its stock prices had bottomed out. This made Compaq ripe for merger, and the company formed a partnership with (was essentially purchased by) Hewlett-Packard (HP) in 2002 for $24.2 billion. The merger was overwhelmingly supported by Compaq's shareholders, although HP board members were less agreeable. The two companies were merged and split much of their branding through the first decade of the 2000s. Ultimately, however, HP completely consumed Compaq to the point that the former partner company could no longer meaningfully be said to exist.

Although ultimately consumed by its former competitor, Compaq remains a symbol of entrepreneurship and innovation. The company left an indelible mark on the computing landscape and helped make computers affordable and accessible to personal users and small businesses.

also was instrumental in a number of start-up companies, namely, Ramteq and Echo Minerals, in Houston and San Antonio, Texas, respectively.

PERSONAL LIFE

Jim Harris lives in Houston, Texas. He has been a member of the board of the Stehlin Foundation for Cancer Research.

Vytautas Malesh

FURTHER READING

Burrows, Peter, and Andrew Park. "Compaq and HP: What's an Investor to Do?" *Businessweek* 18 Mar. 2002: 62–64. Print. This investment analysis article evaluates the earnings of both Compaq and Hewlett-Packard (HP) and makes soft predictions on the profitability of both following their merger.

Canion, Rod. "Consensus, Continuity, and Common Sense: An Interview with Compaq's Rod Canion."

Interview by Alan M. Webber. *Harvard Business Review*. July / August 1990. p. 114-123. Print. This lengthy interview briefly mentions the founding of Compaq computers and Harris's involvement as vice president of engineering. Focuses on Compaq's bottom-up business model and daily operational philosophy.

"The Compaq Story, Part 1 of 3: 1982 to 1983, the Beginning." 28 Sept. 2008. *YouTube.com* Web. 12 Aug. 2012. This video is the first in a three-part series detailing the dynamic rise of Compaq computers in the 1980s. This segment focuses on the foundations of the company and its first year of operation. Includes interview footage of Jim Harris and other Compaq cofounders.

"The Compaq Story, Part 2 of 3: 1983 to 1984, Early Success." 2 Oct. 2008. *YouTube.com*. Web. 12 Aug. 2012. This video is the second in a three-part series detailing the dynamic rise of Compaq computers in the 1980s. This segment focuses on moves taken by the company after its first year of operation, including the foundation of a new headquarters building. Includes interview footage of Jim Harris and other Compaq cofounders.

"The Compaq Story, Part 3 of 3: 1984 to 1988, Record Growth." *YouTube.com*. 2 Oct. 2008. *YouTube.com*. Web. 12 Aug. 2012. The third in the three-part series detailing the dynamic rise of Compaq computers in the 1980s. This segment focuses on Compaq's meteoric rise toward its first billion-dollar year in 1987. Includes interview footage of Jim Harris and other Compaq cofounders.

Dawley, Heidi, Steve Hamm, and Cathy Yang. "Compaq's Rockin' Boss." *Businessweek* 4 Sept. 2000.

Print. This lengthy interview and article discusses the introduction of Compaq's final chief executive officer, Michael Capellas, and his strategies for Compaq's operation.

"Insource Technology." n.d. *Linkedin.com*. Web. 12 Aug. 2012. The official company profile for Harris's consulting company, Insource Technology, found at LinkedIn. There is no biographical or professional discussion of Harris, though his name is mentioned.

Insource Technology Corporation. "About Us: Management Team." n.d. *Insource.com*. Web. 12 Aug. 2012. Official short biographies for Insource senior executives and management, including a profile of cofounder Jim Harris.

"Jim Harris." n.d. *Spoke.com*. Web. 12 Aug. 2012. An unofficial personal biography of Harris; contains some outdated information but is a useful personal and career summary.

"Joseph R. 'Rod' Canion." 10 Oct. 2008. *Entrepeneur.com*. Web. 12 Aug. 2012. Delves into the rise and fall of Compaq and the foundation of Insource Technology. Focuses largely on Canion, but does mention Harris and their business partnership.

"Rod Canion Announces the Formation of Insource Technology Corporation." 15 Nov. 1994. *Thefreelibrary.com*. Web. 12 Aug. 2012. Canion and Harris left Compaq in 1991 and shortly after formed Insource Technology. This press release covers some of their offerings.

Nee, Eric. "Compaq Computer Corp." *Forbes* 12 Jan. 1998: 90–94. Print. Nee's article details Compaq's forays into the NT server market and its efforts to remain competitive in the face of industry rivals such as Hewlett-Packard and IBM.

BILL HEWLETT

Cofounder and former CEO of Hewlett-Packard

Born: May 20, 1913; Ann Arbor, Michigan
Died: January 12, 2001; Palo Alto, California
Primary Field: Business and commerce
Specialty: Management, executives, and investors
Primary Company/Organization: Hewlett-Packard

INTRODUCTION
Together with his longtime friend and business partner, David Packard, Bill Hewlett helped create the modern technological industry. Although quiet and self-effacing, Hewlett was known for his leadership abilities and served as president, chief executive officer (CEO), and chairman of the Hewlett-Packard Company, which he cofounded with Packard. A model for many other high-tech companies, Hewlett-Packard combined cutting-edge technology, creativity, and a progressive working environment. It has served as a model for generations of technology entrepreneurs.

EARLY LIFE

On May 20, 1913, William Redington "Bill" Hewlett was born in Ann Arbor, Michigan. His father was a professor at the University of Michigan's medical school. In 1916, Hewlett and his family moved to San Francisco, California, his father's home state, so that he could join the faculty of the Stanford Medical School, which was located in that city at the time. There, Hewlett's father introduced his son to the culture, science, and literature of the San Francisco Bay area. After entering school, Hewlett learned that he was dyslexic. Throughout his life, he would experience challenges in his academic career as a result of his difficulties with reading. However, his talent for engineering allowed him to adapt, and he memorized subject matter by repeating it to himself. His dyslexia thus instilled in him a belief that life's obstacles required unusual and innovative solutions, and he became known at a very young age as adept at solving problems that stemmed from a variety of sources.

Hewlett indicated a preference for an engineering career at an early age. This preference manifested itself in a desire to cause a variety of objects and substances to explode. Hewlett's method involved stuffing doorknobs full of explosive and then igniting them in a variety of ways. He preferred doorknobs because they were

Bill Hewlett.

hollow and compact; they could be used as bomb shells with little modification. Despite this hobby, young Hewlett was a good-natured and well-behaved child. Although pleasant, he was considered introverted by many, a trait that persisted throughout his life. Hewlett's dyslexia caused him to spend a great deal of energy trying to grow out of his disability. To do so, he developed a deep passion for mountain climbing and camping, two activities that he was firmly convinced helped him to overcome his condition. When Hewlett turned twelve years old, his father died of a brain tumor, a situation that was difficult for the boy. Hewlett used his school's science laboratory and the mountains to distract him from this tragedy. In part to deal with this stress of his loss, he and his sister Louise were moved to France for a year. His grandparents mentored him there.

Upon his family's return to San Francisco, Hewlett enrolled at Lowell High School, a well-regarded preparatory academy. Hewlett's goal was to graduate and attend Stanford University, where his father had taught. Despite his keen intelligence, Hewlett's abilities did not translate to high school success, given his challenging dyslexia. However, Hewlett loved to learn how things worked, which he called "tinkering," and he always worked hard at that endeavor. When he graduated from high school and requested a letter of recommendation from Lowell's principal, she initially refused, believing Hewlett unlikely to succeed at Stanford. However, she learned that Bill's father was Albion Hewlett, one of the best students she had previously taught. This information, coupled with Hewlett's persistence and tenacity, won her admiration and prompted her to write the recommendation letter, which opened the way for enrollment at Stanford in 1930. Hewlett became a cadet in the Reserve Officers' Training Corps (ROTC) at Stanford, serving after graduation as a reserve officer in the Army, specializing in ordnance. He received his bachelor's degree from Stanford in 1934 and two years later a master's degree in electrical engineering from the Massachusetts Institute of Technology (MIT). In 1939, Hewlett received the degree of electrical engineer from Stanford.

LIFE'S WORK

During his time as an undergraduate, Hewlett studied under and was mentored by professor of electrical engineering Frederick Terman, who mentored to many aspiring electrical engineers and is considered by many to have been largely responsible for the development of the culture that evolved into the Bay Area's so-called

Silicon Valley. While Hewlett was enrolled in Terman's classes, he became acquainted with a classmate named David Packard. The two young men had much in common, although their personalities were different: While Packard was social and outgoing, Hewlett was neither. Soon, however, Hewlett discovered that Packard shared his love for blowing things up, as well as hunting, fishing, skiing, and mountain climbing. Both had a passion to discover and invent.

Hewlett and Packard first considered forming a company together in August 1937. After discussing the matter with Terman, who endorsed the idea, the duo formed the Hewlett-Packard Company on January 1, 1939. The order of the two men's names in the company name was based on a coin flip. Short on funds, Hewlett-Packard's initial corporate office and laboratories were situated in Packard's garage at his home in Palo Alto. In the beginning, the two young entrepreneurs had a total of $538 to invest in their company. With the Great Depression still in full force, the company's start was not easy.

The pressures Hewlett and Packard faced, however, motivated them to perform at a high level. The two devised a series of unique and seemingly unrelated products in an attempt to generate revenue and turn a profit. The company developed a foul line indicator for bowling lanes, a device that would make a urinal flush automatically as soon as a user stepped in front of it, and a shock machine that was intended to help people lose weight. The contrasting personalities of the two founders led each to assume a role that best fit his strengths. Packard became the administrative specialist, while Hewlett devised the technical innovations.

The first successful invention to gain the company attention as an innovator was the audio frequency oscillator, which allowed motion-picture studios to test the advanced sound equipment used on sound stages and in television studios. Hewlett-Packard gave the audio frequency oscillator the stock number 200A, because the duo believed naming it the 1A would betray their inexperience and alienate potential customers. The device proved to be an inexpensive, reliable instrument that filmmakers could use to ensure that sound equipment was in working order before filming began, thus curtailing the need for expensive reshoots. Walt Disney heard of the invention and purchased eight of the oscillators for $71.50 each for his studio's upcoming film *Fantasia*. After this film was widely praised for its animation, special effects, and sound, many competitor studios also purchased audio frequency oscillators to assure that they remained competitive with the Disney studio.

With the popularity of this and other products, Hewlett-Packard enjoyed increasing success. Hewlett discovered a market for devices that could test and correct equipment manufactured by others. This range of products utilized technology already in existence and fit the needs of an existing market. Hewlett-Packard also found that a product created for one market could often be sold to other groups. The audio frequency oscillator, for example, was created and marketed initially to the movie industry, but it also proved useful to clinics and hospitals, geologists, engineers, oil and mining companies, and even the military. As Hewlett-Packard learned to market its products differently to different clients, it learned the importance of continuing to think about products even after they had generated sales. From the 1930s through the 1990s, Hewlett-Packard developed and sold a range of electronic test equipment, including frequency counters, oscilloscopes, thermometers, time standards, voltmeters, and wave analyzers. During these early years, Hewlett-Packard's products developed a reputation for being carefully engineered, sensitive, and well made.

In 1941, Hewlett was drafted to serve in the armed forces during World War II. He initially feared that this would prove difficult for him, but he transitioned well into military life and found its rigors to be fairly easy for him. Hewlett began serving in the Aviation Ordnance Department (AOD). While he was not able to apply his many technical skills in this assignment, he was able to exercise his ROTC training. Packard, who remained in charge of the company, transitioning it into a useful cog in the defense industry, was able to forge connections that allowed him to trumpet Hewlett's technical skills to those in high places. Packard was able to persuade Colonel Roger Colton of the Army Signal Corps to transfer Hewlett in order to put his electrical and technical skills to use in the American war effort. In 1941, Hewlett-Packard changed its legal status from a partnership to a corporation, which allowed Hewlett to be identified as a "key employee" and permitted him to return to Palo Alto briefly to assist in the company's operations. After the December 7 attack on Pearl Harbor, however, Hewlett was transferred to New Jersey's Fort Monmouth, where he would serve until 1947.

When Hewlett returned, he found out that the company had become a thriving concern. It had more than two hundred employees and was growing quickly. Hewlett was named vice president. The 1950s saw the company develop a wide range of electronic devices for industrial and agricultural use. During the 1960s,

Affiliation: Hewlett-Packard Company

The Hewlett-Packard Company was famously begun in a garage in Palo Alto, California, by two college chums with a total initial capitalization of $538. Initially known for developing a series of electronic devices used as test equipment, the company later developed a successful line of business equipment and calculators. Today the company concentrates on computers, storage, and imaging products and has annual revenues in excess of $125 billion.

Hewlett-Packard has long been an innovator in both hardware and software and is considered one of the more progressive employers globally. Although its products are sometimes seen as less innovative than those of its rivals, it has developed an outstanding reputation for sturdy, well-built, usable goods.

Hewlett-Packard began developing semiconductors for use in a variety of calculators and other business devices. At this time, the company also entered into a partnership with Sony Corporation and Yokogawa Electric Corporation to license production of some of Hewlett-Packard's products in Japan. In 1968, Hewlett-Packard introduced the 9100A, a programmable calculator that has since been referred to as the first personal computer (PC). During the 1970s, the company introduced the first handheld scientific electronic calculator and the first symbolic and graphing calculator. These products had a reputation as sturdy and usable and were highly popular with corporate users.

Hewlett served as president of Hewlett-Packard from 1964 to 1977 and as CEO from 1968 to 1978. He continued as chairman of the company's executive committee until 1983 and as vice chairman of the board until 1987. He once received a telephone call from a ninth-grader requesting a part for a frequency counter. The ninth-grader, Steve Jobs, so impressed Hewlett that he offered Jobs summer employment at Hewlett-Packard. The company later employed Jobs's future Apple Computer cofounder, Steve Wozniak, who designed the prototype for the Apple I computer while working at Hewlett-Packard. In 1985, President Ronald Reagan awarded Hewlett the National Medal of Science, the nation's highest honor for scientific accomplishment.

Hewlett died of heart failure in Palo Alto, California, on January 12, 2001, and was buried in Los Gatos Memorial Park in San Jose, California.

PERSONAL LIFE

While at Stanford, Hewlett was a member of the social fraternity Kappa Sigma. In 1939, he married his fiancée, Flora Lamson. Their marriage eventually resulted in five children and twelve grandchildren. The couple remained together until Flora died in 1977. One year later, in 1978, Hewlett married Rosemary Bradford.

Hewlett was a tireless advocate for education and medicine throughout his life. He was a longtime director of the Palo Alto/Stanford Hospital Center, serving a term as that organization's president. He was also a member of the board of directors of the Kaiser Foundation Hospital and Health Plan and served on the U.S. Drug Abuse Council. His William and Flora Hewlett Foundation, with assets exceeding $7 billion, supports a variety of causes, including education, the performing arts, global development, and sustainability. Hewlett loved the outdoors: He worked as a botanist and rancher in his spare time and enjoyed mountain climbing, skiing, and fishing.

Stephen T. Schroth and Melvin E. Taylor, Jr.

FURTHER READING

House, C. H., and R. L. Price. *The HP Phenomenon: Innovation and Business Transformation.* Stanford: Stanford UP, 2009. Print. Explores how Hewlett-Packard's culture has allowed the company to transform itself numerous times while many of its rivals were unable to adapt to changing times, resulting in their failure.

Malone, M. S. *Bill and Dave: How Hewlett and Packard Built the World's Greatest Company.* New York: Portfolio, 2007. Print. Concentrates on the formation of Hewlett-Packard and how the actions and leadership of its founders have continued to affect the company's culture to the present day.

Packard, D. *The HP Way: How Bill Hewlett and I Built Our Company.* New York: HarperBusiness, 1995. Print. Packard's memoir, in which he explores how two young friends used vision, innovation, and hard work to build Hewlett-Packard into a global corporation.

KAZUO HIRAI

President and CEO of Sony Corporation and chairman of Sony Computer Entertainment

Born: December 22, 1960; Tokyo, Japan
Died: -
Primary Field: Internet
Specialty: Management, executives, and investors
Primary Company/Organization: Sony

INTRODUCTION

In 2004, Vanity Fair *named Kazuo Hirai to its New Establishment List, labeling him a "mogul in the running."* Entertainment Weekly *has named him as one of the world's most powerful business executives. Hirai began with Sony as a young man and has spent his entire career breaking new ground in the video gaming and networked entertainment venues. He is credited with making Sony's PlayStation 2 a must-have entertainment system for homes throughout the industrialized world and for turning video gaming into a popular activity no longer limited to young adult males. By 2006, the PlayStation Network, which connects the PlayStation 3 to the PlayStation Store and to the computers of "friends" around the world, boasted more than 20 million subscribers. When Sony appeared headed for financial disaster in 2011, Hirai was chosen as the individual most likely to turn the company around.*

EARLY LIFE

Kazuo "Kaz" Hirai was born in Tokyo on December 22, 1960 (his birth year has incorrectly been reported as 1964 by many sources). Hirai's father was a wealthy banker with Mitsui Bank (later SMBC) who frequently had his family accompany him when he traveled to the United States and Canada. Hirai therefore grew up fluent in both Japanese and English. His interest in video gaming developed as gaming technologies constantly improved and the industry was becoming more sophisticated. Growing up, Hirai loved board games such as Life, Monopoly, Battleship, and Scrabble.

Hirai earned a bachelor's degree in 1984 from International Christian University in Tokyo, Japan. He Kazuo Hirai began his career with CBS/Sony, which became Sony Music Entertainment, in 1984. As a junior marketing executive, he was responsible for marketing the music of Sony's international artists within Japan. He was also assigned the task of translating for groups such as the Beastie Boys and Journey when they came to Japan.

LIFE'S WORK

Hirai was so successful that he was soon heading the international business affairs department. Hirai's fluency in English led to a transfer to New York, where he began marketing Japanese music to an American audience. By August 1995, Hirai had been assigned to the video gaming division of Sony. Within two years, he had finished his first video game.

The PlayStation 1 was introduced in the United States in 1995, selling approximately 125 million units and becoming the best-selling console in history to that time. As the protégé of Ken Kutaragi, Hirai had been involved in marketing the PlayStation since its early days. However, it was the introduction of the PlayStation 2 in 2000 that propelled Sony to the top of the video gaming industry. The PS2 sold 100,000 units per minute on the Sony website, making it necessary for Sony to shut the site down temporarily. Hirai became instrumental in PS2's success by securing popular games such as *Grand Theft Auto* for the system and widening its appeal by placing Sony ads at popular sporting events.

Kazuo Hirai.

Affiliation: Sony

Kaz Hirai found his life's work at Sony, the Japanese company that built an international reputation in selling music, films, video gaming consoles, video games, telephones, cameras, telephones, and medical equipment. Sony was founded by Masaru Ibuka and Akio Morita in post-World War II Japan as the country shifted its focus from building its military might to becoming an industrial power.

When Sony introduced its Sony Walkman in Tokyo in June 1979, the product was considered revolutionary. The small device, which included earphones, soon replaced the massive boom boxes that had been popular throughout the decade. The Walkman was much easier to carry around during a walk, run, or bike ride. The earphones allowed users to listen to music privately, both diminishing external noises and without bothering others. In 2002, however, Sony's Walkman became virtually obsolete with the release of Apple's iPod, which came to control almost three-fourths of the market over the course of the next decade. Sony lost $10 billion as a result of declining Walkman sales coupled with the release of Apple's iPhone and Samsung's smart phone, which drastically cut into the sales of Sony's mobile phones. At the same time, imported televisions from South Korea and Taiwan were causing the sales of Sony televisions to continue a downward slide that had begun in 2004.

Critics have suggested that Sony should remove itself from the business of manufacturing televisions, but Hirai has announced plans to develop a three-dimensional television that will double the resolution of televisions currently on the market.

Between 2000 and 2005, the PlayStation and PS-related products accounted for 58 to 60 percent of Sony's sales, and Sony stock rose to more than $300 per share.

By July 2006, Hirai had been promoted to vice president of Sony's Executive Group. Four months later, Sony launched the PlayStation 3, which, unlike Microsoft's already released Xbox 360, contained its own Blu-ray player and had a price tag of between $240 and $307, depending on the capacity of the internal hard drive. By 2008, the PS3 had helped to raise Sony profits to $3.3 billion. However, both Microsoft's Xbox 360 and Nintendo's Wii were outselling the PlayStation 3. Because of a major reorganization launched in April 2009, Sony's electronic and games division became Consumer Products and Devices Group and Networked Products and Services Group (NPSG), and Hirai was designated as corporate executive officer and executive vice president of Sony Corporation while continuing to serve as president of NPSG.

In April 2011, Sony reorganized again, merging electronics, games, and networked services into the Consumer Products and Services Group, and Hirai became representative corporate executive officer and executive deputy president of the entire organization. By September 2011, Hirai had been named chair of Sony Computer Entertainment.

Sony suffered substantial losses as a result of the tsunami that hit northeast Japan after the earthquake of March 11, 2011. Immediately after the tsunami, Sony workers in Sendai, which suffered massive damage, used shipping containers as boats to float in supplies to stranded victims. The tsunami created economic problems throughout Japan, and Sony was forced to shut down ten of its plants temporarily, which delayed the shipment of products outside the country as well as within Japan.

Sony received another major blow when computer hackers attacked the PlayStation Network on April 19, 2011, gaining access to credit card numbers and passwords. The following day, Sony was forced to shut down the entire system, which meant that the company steadily lost sales because 24.6 million subscribers could not access the PlayStation Store from their PlayStation 3 consoles. Total losses were estimated at $173 million. Facing the real threat of gamers deserting the PlayStation 3 for Microsoft's Xbox 360 and Nintendo's Wii, Sony enticed subscribers to the system when it was restored in early June with free games, free music, and a free membership in PlayStation Plus. Trust in Sony's security capabilities suffered additional damage, however, when hackers subsequently attacked ten thousand Sony websites around the world. In July, Sony component plants were shut down as a result of major floods in Thailand; in August, Sony warehouses were burned down during riots in London.

In 2011, Sony was reporting losses of $5.8 billion. Insiders suggested that some of Sony's losses were on paper only, resulting from the decision to move away from the practice of carrying tax losses as an asset. On February 1, 2012, Sony announced that Hirai, who was then fifty-one years old, would succeed Sir Howard Stringer as the head of the company, effective April 1. Stringer, the first non-Japanese head of Sony, had been grooming Hirai as his replacement for years and agreed that it was time for Hirai to take over the company.

Sony placed considerable confidence in the ability of Hirai to turn the company around. Almost immediately, he cut ten thousand jobs, despite the Japanese tradition of employing staff for life. Like other heads of Sony, Hirai was forced to deal with the fact that because Japanese culture promotes consensus building, the company has not always been comfortable with the cut-throat competition that thrives among international corporations. On June 5, 2012, Sony announced that Hirai and six other top executives had returned all performance-based pay received for 2011 to the company and promised that all seven would forgo bonuses in 2012. Outside observers suggested that many of Sony's woes were due to the fact that it sells more than two thousand different products. As part of a downsizing initiative, Hirai announced that Sony would shift its focus away from poorly performing products and toward top-performing products such as video games, mobile phones, cameras, and image-sensing microchips. Because Hirai was with Sony as it developed its interactive entertainment capabilities, his actions indicated that he understood that Sony's future success depended on its ability to deliver interactive content for televisions, smart phones, tablets, and computers.

Hirai has been steering Sony through the introduction of new products and has heightened promotion of existing products. The company has high hopes for the PlayStation Vita, which was released on December 17, 2011, and had already sold 1.2 million units by March 2012. The Vita is the successor to the PlayStation Portable, released in 2004 and updated as the PSP Go in 2009. With its five-inch OLED screen, Wi-Fi capability, dual cameras, motion sensors, touch panels, and dual analog sticks, the Vita combines many features of a portable system with those of a regular game console, even allowing users to transfer games in progress from the PS3 to the Vita. Its price tag of approximately $250, plus the cost of a memory card (which ranges from $20 to $99), has turned away some would-be purchasers. However, the Vita continues to gain attention for its extraordinary graphic capabilities, and new applications are constantly being added to enhance its appeal. Sony is also developing the next-generation PlayStation console, the PS4. In 2012, Sony projected a profit of $381 million.

When Microsoft announced that it had signed an exclusive deal with J. K. Rowling, author of the Harry Potter series of stories about a boy wizard that became a global merchandising phenomenon, to create a new Harry Potter game exclusive to the Xbox 360 format, it appeared to be devastating news for Sony's PlayStation 3, which has carried all Harry Potter games released since 2006. However, Sony followed Microsoft's announcement with one of its own, stating that Sony had signed a deal with Rowling to create the *Harry Potter Wonderbook*, exclusive to the PlayStation 3, allowing gamers to use the PlayStation 3 Move as a wand when performing spells.

Despite its financial woes internationally, Sony continues to be the biggest brand within Japan, and the Japanese people have retained their loyalty to the PlayStation despite the dominance of Microsoft's Xbox 360 in much of the world.

PERSONAL LIFE

Hirai's responsibilities as the head of Sony require him to travel frequently between California and Tokyo, but his family remains at their home in California during most of his trips. In his time away from Sony, Hirai spends time with his family and on his hobbies, which include cycling, photography, and driving. He is also an avid collector of cameras, watches, model railroads, and telescopes.

Elizabeth Rholetter Purdy

FURTHER READING

"Back in Japanese Hands." *The Economist* 402.8780 (2012): 74. Print. Examines Sony's financial troubles.

Dominic, Jeff. "Sony Sales After Tsunami." *The Scotsman*, 11 May 2010. Print. Report on how a series of unforeseen events added to Sony's financial woes in 2011.

Gruley, Brian, and Cliff Edward. "Sony: All Chewed." *Management Today*, Feb. 2012: 50–56. Print. Traces Hirai's career in relation to the rise of Sony. Illustrated.

Warman, Matt. "Kaz Hirai, There's a Lot to Fix at Sony." *London Telegraph* 31 Mar. 2012. Print. Profiles Hirai and deals with the problems he was expected to handle at Sony.

Westlake, Adam. "Sony Cuts Executives' Pay to Make Up for Years of Losses." *Japan Daily Press* 6 June 2012. Print. Report on Sony's ongoing efforts to turn the company around.

BETTY HOLBERTON

Programmer of the ENIAC

Born: March 7, 1917; Philadelphia, Pennsylvania
Died: December 8, 2001; Rockville, Maryland
Primary Field: Computer science
Specialty: Computer programming
Primary Company/Organization: Remington Rand

INTRODUCTION

Betty Holberton was an early computer programmer and pioneer in the fields of computer science and information technology. During World War II, the U.S. Army chose Holberton and five other women to program the Electronic Numerical Integrator and Computer (ENIAC), the first general-purpose electronic digital computer. The ENIAC programmers worked at the University of Pennsylvania. Although best known for her work on the ENIAC, Holberton also had several notable postwar career achievements, including the design of the control console and instruction code for the Universal Automatic Computer (UNIVAC), one of the earliest commercial computers produced by J. Presper Eckert and John W. Mauchly at Remington Rand. She is also renowned for her development of the SORT/MERGE data-sorting program and her role in the development of the COBOL and Fortran computer programming languages. The latter two programs are still in use.

EARLY LIFE

Frances Elizabeth "Betty" Snyder was born on March 7, 1917, in Philadelphia, Pennsylvania. She expressed an early aptitude for mathematics, a field difficult for women to enter at that time. She endured taunts at school for being left-handed and cross-eyed. She attended the University of Pennsylvania, where she initially decided to pursue her early love of mathematics. She quickly became discouraged, however, when on her first day of classes one of her mathematics professors suggested that she return home, get married, and start a family, because mathematics was a traditionally male field. She was determined to complete her higher education but switched to the field of journalism, one of the few majors women were allowed to pursue. She was also intrigued by the field's opportunities for travel.

LIFE'S WORK

Holberton finally had a chance to use her mathematical skills professionally after the United States entered World War II in 1941. She became one of the many women employed by the military because of a wartime shortages of male labor; she was assigned to calculate ballistics trajectories manually, a long and laborious mathematical task. Women assigned to this task were called computers. Although the government and military viewed these women as primarily clerical workers, Holberton and the others quickly demonstrated the value of their mathematical abilities, and the role allowed her to enter the developing field of computer programming.

Betty began her career at the Moore School of Electrical Engineering at the University of Pennsylvania, working on the development of the Electronic Numerical Integrator and Computer, commonly known as the ENIAC. When the Army expressed interest in the ENIAC's potential to perform the mathematical calculation of ballistics firing trajectories, primarily artillery

Betty Holberton.

shells, at a higher rate of speed than could be accomplished manually, she worked at the Army's Ballistics Research Laboratory in Aberdeen Proving Ground, Maryland. The Army selected Betty and five others to be the original ENIAC programmers. The five other original ENIAC programmers were Jean (Jennings) Bartik, Kay (McNulty) Antonelli, Marlyn (Wescoff) Meltzer, Ruth (Lichterman) Teitelbaum, and Frances (Bilas) Spence. The women were chosen based on their mathematical abilities and superior job performance. They are now widely considered to be the world's first computer programmers. The group began its training on old punch card equipment provided by International Business Machines (IBM) company; these were similar to what would be used with the ENIAC.

The ENIAC was a large machine weighing 30 tons that had to be housed in a room measuring 30 by 50 feet. The programmers were largely self-taught, initially generating their programs from electrical wiring blueprints in a separate room from the ENIAC because the project was classified. Later, the group gained access to the ENIAC itself in order to implement and test the programs that they had developed. The hard-wired programming required the group to set the machine's multitude of linked switches and dials manually, as well as manipulate the heavy black cables in a variety of configurations depending on the calculation to be performed.

ENIAC was functional by 1945 and was successfully demonstrated in February 1946, debuting too late to help the U.S. war effort in World War II. However, ENIAC reduced the time needed to calculate ballistics flight trajectories from approximately twenty hours to less than a minute. The military also utilized the ENIAC for the top-secret Manhattan Project, which developed the world's first atomic bomb. The ENIAC's vacuum-tube-based technology could support high-speed digital computing. The machine came to be recognized as the first general-purpose electronic digital computer.

The programming team went their separate ways after their work on ENIAC, but their work proved to be a pioneering achievement in the development of modern computer programming. The women had faced discrimination in their work, which was considered clerical and nonprofessional, and stories often circulated that they had to clean up after their male colleagues at the end of the workday. They also received little recognition for their work, both at the time and for decades afterward, although they ultimately would be celebrated as computer programming pioneers.

Holberton would remain in the field of computer programming for the rest of her life. After World War II, she found employment with renowned typewriter manufacturer Remington Rand, whose 1950 acquisition of the Eckert-Mauchly Computer Corporation—where Holberton worked with owners and fellow ENIAC programmers J. Presper Eckert and John W. Mauchly—marked its entry into the computer industry. Eckert, Mauchly, and Holberton had begun the development of the Universal Automatic Computer (UNIVAC) for the U.S. Census Bureau but found government funding inadequate for completion. Remington Rand's completed UNIVAC was one of the first mainframe computers sold on the commercial market after its 1951 introduction. Holberton was involved in the development of UNIVAC hardware and software, designing both its control console and its instruction code. UNIVAC could calculate additions in 120 microseconds, multiplications in 1,800 microseconds, and divisions in 3,600 microseconds. It received widespread public attention for its prediction of the 1952 presidential election results, calling the victory for Dwight Eisenhower before the polls had closed.

Holberton also assisted Mauchly with the development of the C-10 programming instructions used for the Binary Automatic Computer (BINAC), which is considered a forerunner of modern programming languages. During this time, Holberton also developed the first generative programming system known as SORT/MERGE. The program simplified the laborious process of sorting and merging large data files that at the time were stored on reels of magnetic tape, making the use of such files more practical. The U.S. Census Bureau used its first statistical analysis program, designed by Holberton, for the 1950 U.S. Census data.

Holberton next worked at the U.S. Navy's Applied Mathematics Laboratory at the David Taylor Model Basin in Maryland from 1953 to 1966. She was supervisor of advanced programming and was promoted to chief of the Programming Research Branch in 1959. There, she worked with fellow computer programming pioneer Admiral Grace Murray Hopper in the development and standardization of both Common Business Oriented Language (COBOL) and Fortran, groundbreaking computer programming languages. In 1959, Holberton chaired the committee that developed the, which was introduced in 1960. COBOL was designed to bring computer programming into the business world by allowing computers to describe business data visually. Despite criticisms of its hasty development and inadequacies, which Holberton readily acknowledged,

Affiliation: Remington Rand

Remington Rand began life as E. Remington and Sons in the nineteenth century. The corporation achieved its highest recognition for its production of typewriters. The first commercially viable typewriter appeared in 1873 and the first American electric typewriter appeared in 1925. Remington Rand was formed in 1927 through the merger of Remington Typewriter and Rand Kardex.

The corporation entered the computer industry with its 1950 acquisition of the Eckert-Mauchly Computer Corporation, which had received federal funding to develop a computer for the U.S. Census Bureau. The creation of the UNIVAC division, which produced the Universal Automatic Computer (UNIVAC), brought the company early success. Dr. John Presper Eckert and Dr. John Mauchly, former members of the team that had developed the ENIAC computer, also led the development of the UNIVAC. Betty Holberton joined Eckert and Mauchly in their new business venture and at Remington Rand, developing the UNIVAC instruction code and control console. UNIVAC was one of the first electronic digital computers to appear on the commercial market. It initially competed successfully with IBM for market share.

Remington Rand merged with the Sperry Corporation in 1955, becoming known as Sperry Rand. It lost its market lead in the rapidly developing computer and information technology field to other corporations, notably IBM, in the 1960s. A later merger with Burroughs led to the corporation's latest incarnation as Unisys.

Although Holberton and the other female programmers received little recognition at the debut of ENIAC, they have come to be recognized pioneers both as women in traditionally male fields and as computer programmers. The six original female ENIAC programmers were inducted into the Women in Technology International Hall of Fame on June 5, 1997. Both the ENIAC and the UNIVAC computers are housed at the Smithsonian museum in Washington, D.C. Holberton received the 1997 Augusta Ada Lovelace Award from the U.S. National Association for Women in Computing, the organization's highest award, at a ceremony in Arlington, Virginia. She also received the 1997 Computer Pioneer Award from the Institute of Electrical and Electronics Engineers (IEEE) for her SORT/MERGE data-sorting program and its influence on later developments in the area of data compilation.

PERSONAL LIFE

Betty Snyder married husband John Vaughn Holberton in 1950. The couple had two daughters, Priscilla and Pamela. She spent her last years in a Rockville, Maryland, nursing home and died at age eighty-four on December 8, 2001, of complications from heart disease, diabetes, and an earlier stroke. She was survived by her children, two sisters, and a brother.

Marcella Bush Trevino

FURTHER READING

Ensmenger, Nathan. *The Computer Boys Take Over: Computers, Programmers, and the Politics of Technical Expertise.* Cambridge: MIT, 2010. Print. Discusses the historical development of computer programming in its sociological and political contexts. Also covers the ENIAC and examines gender issues in the field, the latter especially relevant to Holberton.

Hally, Mike. *Electronic Brains: Stories from the Dawn of the Computer Age.* Washington, D.C.: Joseph Henry, 2005. Print. Covers the global development of the earliest modern electronic, multipurpose computers, including both the ENIAC and UNIVAC as well as Holberton's data-sorting program, used by the U.S. Census Bureau. Includes interviews with computer pioneers.

Layne, Margaret E. *Women in Engineering: Pioneers and Trailblazers.* Reston: American Society of Civil Engineers, 2009. Print. Provides biographical and career overviews of Holberton and other women who broke ground in the field.

updated versions of COBOL have remained in use since its inception. Hopper credited Holberton for both her computer programming abilities and her influence on Hopper's development of an early compiler, which translated human programming commands into instruction codes that computers could interpret and subsequently perform.

Holberton spent her last several decades of employment working at the U.S. National Bureau of Standards after joining the agency in 1966. There she contributed to the ability of various computers to communicate globally regardless of their manufacturer or brand specifications, a key to later development of the Internet.

McCartney, Scott. *ENIAC: The Triumphs and Tragedies of the World's First Computer*. New York: Walker, 1999. Print. Critically examines the development and use of the ENIAC, including its successful demonstration and applications as well as its failures.

Stern, Nancy B. *From ENIAC to UNIVAC: An Appraisal of the Eckert-Mauchly Computers*. Bedford: Digital, 1981. Print. Provides an overview and analysis of the computers developed under J. Presper Eckert and John W. Mauchly, with whom Holberton worked on both the ENIAC and UNIVAC projects.

GRACE HOPPER

Computer programmer and U.S. Navy rear admiral

Born: December 9, 1906; New York, New York
Died: January 1, 1992; Arlington, Virginia
Primary Field: Computer science
Specialty: Computer programming
Primary Company/Organization: U.S. Navy

INTRODUCTION

At a time when women in the field of mathematics and science were anomalies, Grace Hooper was instrumental in the development of computer languages that allowed individuals without a thorough understanding of mathematics to use computers as they evolved over the course of the twentieth century. She is considered the major force in the development of the computer system used by the U.S. Navy and across-the-board military computing technologies. She foresaw that data would be stored in computers, eliminating the need for reams of paper. Her work on COBOL was a necessary precursor to the development of BASIC, which was used in the operating systems of early computers such as IBM and Apple and in the development of Microsoft Windows. For her contributions to computer programming, Hopper earned the nicknames the Grand Lady of Software, the Grandmother of COBOL, and Amazing Grace.

EARLY LIFE

Grace Brewster Murray Hopper was born into a wealthy family. Her father, Walter Fletcher Murray, was in the family's insurance brokerage business. Because he had health problems that led to a double amputation, Hopper's mother, Mary Campbell Van Horne Murray, who had always loved mathematics, assumed responsibility for handling financial tasks within the household. As a child, Grace shared her mother's love of mathematics and developed an abiding interest in taking things apart to see what made them work. She and her siblings, Mary

and Roger, were encouraged to excel in their classes at the private schools they attended. While growing up in New York City, Hopper spent her summers visiting her grandparents on Lake Wentworth in Wolfeboro, New Hampshire, developing a lasting love for the ocean. Her maternal grandfather, John Van Horne, was a surveyor in New York City, and young Grace sometimes helped him with his work. Her great-grandfather Alexander Russell had been a rear admiral in the U.S. Navy.

Grace attended Hartridge, a girl's boarding school in Plainfield, New Jersey, before enrolling at Vassar in Poughkeepsie, New York, in 1924. Since women at that

Grace Hopper.

Affiliation: U.S. Navy

When Grace Hopper began working on Harvard's Mark I computer for the U.S. Navy, the computer was 8 feet high and needed an entire room to house it. Weighing 5 tons and containing more than parts, the Mark I had been designed by Howard Aiken of Harvard and built by IBM. Known originally as the Automatic Sequence Controlled Calculator, it was the first digital calculator built in the United States. Computations that had taken six months for individuals to complete could be done in a day by the Mark I.

During World War II, Hopper worked on calculations that were used in guns, rockets, mines, and shortwaves. She was involved in developing the computer calculations that were used in the development of the atomic bombs that brought World War II to a close. The entry of the Mark II and Mark III brought additional speed and more compact computers, but it not until the 1960s did computers begin to approach modern standards. At that time, transistors replaced vacuum tubes.

In 1966, Hopper attained the rank of commander, and she was ordered to retire. Her unique knowledge of computing led the top naval brass to reconsider, however, and she was called back to work on the computing language that became known as USA Standard COBOL. In her office at the Pentagon, Hopper placed a clock that ran backward to illustrate that nothing had to operate as it had in the past. She left the clock for her successor when she retired.

career challenging norms. That desire for innovation and change affected her academic studies, her chosen professions, and the way she lived her life. Throughout her career, she would be known for her combative personality and high energy level. By 1931, she was teaching algebra, trigonometry, calculus, probability theory, and statistics at Vassar. As a teacher, she proved unique, using cards and dice to teach probability and having her students simulate the building and operation of cities.

When the United States entered World War II in 1941 after the bombing of Pearl Harbor, Hopper was anxious to enlist in the newly created Women Accepted for Voluntary Emergency Service (WAVES), a division of the Navy. Her brother was in the Army Air Forces, her father was on the Selective Service Board, her mother served on the ration board, and Grace had a cousin who was a nurse. However, she was told that, at age thirty-six, she was too old to enlist. Weighing only 105 pounds, she also failed to meet the weight requirement. Instead, she spent the summer of 1943 teaching mathematics to women who worked in military laboratories.

Hopper was persistent; and after taking temporary leave from Vassar, she persuaded the Navy to allow her to enlist. She finished at the top of her midshipmen's class, which included many former students, in June 1944. In a move that forever changed the direction of her life, Lieutenant (JG) Grace Hopper was assigned to work on the Mark I computer at Harvard University in the Navy's Bureau of Ordnance Computation Project, writing computer programs for military use. Hopper remained in the Navy after the war as a reservist and turned down a full professorship at Vassar to continue her work on computer programming at Harvard.

As Hopper's interest in computers expanded, she developed the unprecedented notion that programs could be written so that even those who were not mathematically minded could work on computers. She understood the drawbacks in the common practice of writing languages specific to particular computers. Such ideas led her to write standard codes in plain language that could be translated into binary code. She eventually called her computer language FLOW-MATIC.

In 1949, Hopper accepted a position as senior programmer at the newly created Eckert-Mauchly Computer

time were discouraged from becoming engineers, she majored in mathematics and physics. According to the customs of the day, she was allowed to audit classes in botany, physiology, geology, business, and economics in addition to courses for credit. After receiving a B.A. with honors from Vassar in 1928, she was awarded two fellowships to continue her studies elsewhere and began working on a master's degree in mathematics at Yale University. At Lake Wentworth, she met Vincent Hopper, who taught mathematics at New York University. The couple married in 1930, and she graduated from Yale with a Ph.D. in mathematics in 1934. Between 1934 and 1937, Yale had awarded only seven doctorates in mathematics. Hopper, whose dissertation was titled "The Irreducibility of Algebraic Equations," was the first woman to receive a Ph.D. in mathematics from Yale and the only woman in that group of seven to receive one. After living apart for several years, the Hoppers divorced in 1945.

LIFE'S WORK

Known as Amazing Grace by the media and her colleagues in the Navy, Hopper spent her sixty-five-year

Corporation in Philadelphia while continuing as a Navy reservist. She worked on the Universal Automatic Computer (UNIVAC) 1, the first computer built in the United States for commercial use. At 14 feet long and 8 feet high, the UNIVAC I was at that time the smallest computer ever built. It was able to process three thousand operations per second. Since it had internal memory, it was not dependent on the punch cards or tape that characterized most computers of the time. Hopper recruited other women to work with her.

By the time UNIVAC I was operating, in 1951, Remington Rand had purchased Eckert-Mauchly and Hopper was working on developing computer programs for business use, tailoring many of them to specific businesses. In 1952, she was promoted to lieutenant colonel. By 1955, she was continuing to develop her own codes while providing technical advice to a team working on COBOL. She therefore became known as the grandmother of COBOL (an acronym for Common Business-Oriented Language). Also in 1952, Remington Rand merged with the Sperry Corporation; the company would later become today's Unisys. By 1962, the computer giant IBM was using COBOL in its computer programs, and computers had developed the capability of processing three million instructions per second. Hopper left Sperry Rand in 1967. After a brief forced retirement, in 1967, at the age of sixty-one, Hopper was named the director of the Navy Programming Languages Group in the Navy's Office of Information Systems Planning and Development. She remained there for the rest of her naval career.

In 1983, at the age of seventy-six, Hopper was promoted to the rank of commodore by special presidential appointment. Two years later, the title was changed to rear admiral. On August 14, 1986, she retired as the oldest commissioned naval officer still on active duty. At her request, the ceremony was held in Boston Harbor aboard the USS *Constitution* (*Old Ironsides*), the oldest ship in the American fleet. Not content to rest on her laurels, Hopper continued working as a consultant for Digital Equipment Corporation. Over the following years, her health declined, and she died on January 1, 1992, and was buried with full military honors at Arlington National Cemetery.

PERSONAL LIFE

Later in life, Hopper received attention as a public figure. She enjoyed giving interviews and appeared on both radio and television programs, such as *60 Minutes*. She also promoted some of the myths that had grown up around her life. One myth was that she had coined the phrase "computer bug" when she discovered a moth in a naval computer that was interfering with its operation. It was also falsely reported that her husband had died in World War II and that she was the creator of COBOL. Before her death, she destroyed most of her personal correspondence.

Hopper remains one of the most celebrated women in the history of the American military. She was awarded forty honorary doctorates. In 1969, the Data Processing Management Association named her its "man" of the year. In 1973, she became the only American ever to be designated as a distinguished Fellow of the British Computer Society. In 1980, Hopper was awarded the Navy's Meritorious Service Medal for her work on the tactical data systems used by the Navy's fleet of nuclear submarines. In 1987, the Navy honored Hopper's overall contributions to the computer industry by naming its San Diego computer center after her. In 1991, she became the first woman to be awarded the National Medal of Technology. In 1994, she was inducted into the National Women's Hall of Fame. In 1996, a guided missile destroyer, the USS *Hopper*, was christened in her honor.

Elizabeth Rholetter Purdy

FURTHER READING

Beyer, Kurt. *Grace Hopper and the Invention of the Information Age*. Cambridge: MIT, 2009. Print. Focuses on Hopper's role in the development of computers using material gathered from interviews with Hopper's colleagues. Includes illustrations, a notes section, and an index.

Billings, Charlene W. *Grace Hopper: Navy Admiral and Computer Pioneer*. Hillside: Enslow, 1989. Print. Derived from extensive interviews with members of Hopper's family. Includes bibliography, index, and list of professional achievements.

Reynolds, Moira Davison. "Grace Hopper: Pioneer Computer Programmer and Naval Officer." In *American Women Scientists: 23 Inspiring Biographies, 1900-2000*. Jefferson: McFarland, 1999. 88–94. Print. Contains multiple biographies of women who made great contributions to their fields. Includes separate illustrations and bibliographies and an overall index.

Thomas, Petty. *Grace Hopper*. Parsippany: Pearson Learning Group, 2008. Print. Designed for a juvenile audience, and introduction to Hopper and her achievements especially inspirational to girls interested in science and technology.

Whitelaw, Nancy. *Grace Hopper: Programming Pioneer*. New York: Freeman, 1995. Print. Geared for young adult audience, this biography traces Hopper from her childhood through her long career with the U.S. Navy. Includes illustrations, index, and glossary.

Williams, Kathleen Broome. *Grace Hopper: Admiral of the Cyber Sea*. Annapolis: Naval Institute, 2005.

Print. The focus is on Hopper's naval career. Includes an extensive bibliography and an index.

---. "Grace Murray Hopper: Computer Scientist." *Improbable Warriors: Women Scientists and the U.S. Navy in World War II*. Annapolis: Naval Institute, 2001. 113–53. Print. Traces Hopper's personal life and naval career. Includes bibliography and index.

FENG-HSIUNG HSU

Cocreator of the Deep Blue computer

Born: 1959; Keelung, Taiwan (Republic of China)
Died: -
Primary Field: Computer science
Specialty: Computer programming
Primary Company/Organization: IBM

INTRODUCTION

Feng-hsiung Hsu is a pioneer in computer science, focusing most of his work on developing a computer that could play chess well enough to defeat a human grandmaster. Hsu and his team from IBM succeeded on May 11, 1997, when their Deep Blue computer defeated reigning world chess champion Garry Kasparov in a series of six matches, by a score of 3½ to 2½. Hsu went on to become the research manager of the Hardware Computing Group for Microsoft's Asia Research Center.

EARLY LIFE

Feng-hsiung Hsu was born in Keelung, a major seaport of about 200,000 people, in Taiwan. As a child, he learned to play Chinese chess (xiangqi), Western chess, and Go, and he has stated that Go was the most influential in teaching him strategy. Hsu received his bachelor's degree in electrical engineering from National Taiwan University in 1985; while a sophomore, he became interested in the problem of building a machine that could beat a human grandmaster in chess after reading Peter Frey's 1977 book *Chess Skill in Man and Machine*. While at National Taiwan University, Hsu became involved with a microprocessor research project, and after hearing a lecture by a representative of Taiwan's Electronics Research and Services Organization, he decided he wanted to study the design of computer chips. After graduation, Hsu spent two years doing his mandatory military service, then came to the United States to study computer science at Carnegie Mellon

University. At Carnegie Mellon, he found an active community of people interested in computer chess and was particularly influenced by a talk given by Kenneth Thompson of Bell Laboratories about Belle, a chess-playing computer developed at Bell Labs. Hsu continued his interest in developing a chess-playing computer, and he earned his Ph.D. in 1989; his dissertation was titled "Large Scale Parallelization of Alpha-Beta Search: An Algorithmic and Architectural Study with Computer Chess." While a student at Carnegie Mellon, Hsu won the Friedkin Intermediate Prize for his work on

Feng-hsiung Hsu.

Affiliation: IBM

Feng-hsiung Hsu began working at IBM in 1989, joining an ongoing effort to build a computer that could defeat a human grandmaster at chess. This effort was not merely an exercise in creating a computer that could play a game well; the team wanted to solve basic problems in the design of computer architecture and to enable artificial intelligence approaches that could be applied to real-world problems, including designing novel drugs, performing complex financial modeling, and enabling large-scale and efficient database searches.

The problem of creating a chess-playing machine had interested computer scientists since at least the nineteenth century, when Charles Babbage discussed the possibility; Babbage became interested after hearing of the eighteenth century Mechanical Turk, a purported chess-playing machine that was in fact operated by a midget concealed within it. In 1949, Claude Shannon, one of the creators of the field of information science, delivered a lecture that laid the foundation for modern chess computers, and many believed that within a few years it would be possible to build a computer that could be the best human player in the world. However, this problem (known as the computer chess problem) proved more intractable. IBM scientists began working on the problem of constructing a chess-playing computer in the 1950s, but by the early 1980s the computer chess problem was far from being solved—in fact, the best computer chess players could play only at the level of a national master.

When Hsu arrived at IBM in 1989, he joined an active research group. His Carnegie Mellon classmate Murray Campbell joined the IBM team at the same time. Their computer, Deep Blue, was defeated by world chess champion Garry Kasparov in 1996, but in 1997 the improved Deep Blue defeated Kasparov over a series of six matches, marking the first time a computer had defeated the best human chess player in the world. The matches received a great deal of publicity, and Deep Blue's success inspired other efforts, including the IBM-built computer Watson that in 2011 demonstrated its ability to beat human champions in *Jeopardy!*, a game that required processing natural language and searching for responses from a massive store of information. After the historic matches in which Deep Blue defeated Kasparov, the computer was returned to IBM, where it was used for research.

Chiptest, a computer that achieved grandmaster performance in chess, and also won the Mephisto Award in 1990 for his doctoral dissertation.

LIFE'S WORK

Hsu began working at IBM in 1989, joining the team that was working on IBM's Deep Thought chess-playing computer. Hsu became the principal designer for the team that developed Deep Blue, the succeessor to Deep Thought; other members of the Deep Blue team included Chung-Jen Tan, Murray Campbell, Joseph Hoane Jr., Jerry Brody, and Joel Benjamin. Deep Blue (technically, the IBM RS/6000 SP supercomuter) achieved its success not by trying to mimic human thought—which relies on recognizing patterns and solving problems thorugh efficient, heuristic-based searches—but instead by capitalizing on the processing speed and vast storage available in a modern supercomputer. This approach, often characterized as "brute force," uses the computer's capability to consider all possible moves and the positions they would create and evaluate the strength of each, using the rules programmed into it. The Deep Blue machine that beat Kasparov was able to evaluate 200 million positions per second, double the amount that the previous Deep Blue, which Kasparov defeated, was able to achieve; the improved Deep Blue had a superior central processing unit (CPU).

The first six chess games between Kasparov and Deep Blue had been played in Philadelphia, Pennsylvania, and ended with Kasparov winning 4–2: he won three games, drew two, and lost one. The rematch, which made history as the first occasion in which a computer defeated the best human player in the world, was played in New York City; Deep Blue won 3½–2½, claiming the victory in two games, drawing three, and losing only one. Kasparov accused the Deep Blue team of cheating by using human chess players during the games (by the rules of the challenge, human intervention was allowed only between games, by way of the programmers' further adapting the computer to Kasparov's game) and claimed that the matches were unfair because he had not had access to Deep Blue's recent games. Another, more general criticism of Deep Blue's success was that it required a team of programmers and chess experts to create a computer capable of defeating a single human player, while in a tournament a player would have to defeat multiple opponents with different playing styles.

Although Deep Blue succeeded in defeating the best human chess player in the world, a task once considered impossible, this accomplishment was possible only because of the humans who had programmed it and who had made adjustments between matches, calibrating the computer specifically to defeat Kasparov. Hsu has stated that the true match was not between a man and a machine but between two men (or teams of men): those creating and programming Deep Blue, and Kasparov and his support team. Hsu has also noted that the process of creating a computer to play chess at the highest level demonstrates the usefulness of supercomputers to amplify human intelligence, rather than to replace it—none of the computer scientists working with Deep Blue could play chess at anything like Kasparov's level, but working as a group and with the capabilities of the supercomputer, they were able to defeat him. Hsu also noted that the brute-force approach to computer problem solving is a good complement to human capabilities, such as pattern recognition and concept formation, and that it makes sense to design computers not to imitate human thought but to perform the tasks (for example, extremely rapid calculation) that a computer can do better than a person.

After Deep Blue's success, Hsu continued to work on creating a better chess chip. When it became clear that there would be no rematch between Deep Blue (or any other computer) and Kasparov, Hsu shifted his interest away from chess-playing computers and left IBM in October 1999. Hsu became the research manager of the Hardware Computing Group for Microsoft's Asia Research Center in Beijing. His group is focused on creating innovative computer hardware that can achieve tasks faster and more efficiently through improvements in fundamental functions of computing through the design of computer architecture and memory hierarchies.

Hsu won the Grace Murray Hopper Award in 1991 from the Association for Computing Machinery (ACM) for his work on Deep Blue. In 1997, Hsu, Hoane, and Campbell received the $100,000 Friedkin Prize from the Association for the Advancement of Artificial Intelligence for creating a chess machine that defeated the human chess world champion.

PERSONAL LIFE

Hsu received the nickname Crazy Bird while in junior high school, referring both to his eccentric personality and to the fact that *feng* is a homonym in Mandarin for "crazy." He continued to use this nickname and the associated initials, C.B., as an adult.

Sarah Boslaugh

FURTHER READING

Christian, Brian. *The Most Human Human: What Talking with Computers Teaches Us about What It Means to Be Alive*. New York: Doubleday, 2011. Print. A popular book about the differences between human and artificial intelligence, focusing on the 2009 Turing Test (a competition in which programmers strove to build computers that could interact with a user so well that the user could not tell if he or she was interacting with a human being or a computer), but with consideration also of what Deep Blue meant to the debate surrounding human versus artificial intelligence.

Hsu, Feng-hsiung. *Behind Deep Blue: Building the Computer that Defeated the World Chess Champion*. Princeton, NJ: Princeton UP, 2004. Print. The story of the team of IBM researchers who built Deep Blue, the first computer able to defeat a human grandmaster in chess, written for a popular audience but with clear presentation of the technical ideas behind the construction of Deep Blue.

Hsu, Feng-hsiung. "Cracking Go: Brute-Force Computation Has Eclipsed Humans in Chess, and It Could Soon Do the Same in This Ancient Asian Game." *IEEE Spectrum* 44.10 (2007): 51–55. Print. Popular article on the process of developing the Deep Blue computer and current efforts to develop a computer that can beat a human being at Go. Hsu compares the two games and discusses different approaches to programming a computer to play Go.

Hsu, Feng-hsiung. "Oral History of Feng-hsiung Hsu." Interview by Dag Spicer. 14 Feb. 2005. *Computer History Museum*. Web. 4 Sept. 2012. In this interview for the Computer History Museum, Hsu discusses his love of chess and his philosophy of the use of computing to complement rather than replace human intelligence.

Newborn, Monty. *Beyond Deep Blue: Chess in the Stratosphere*. London: Springer, 2011. Print. A history of computer chess beginning with Deep Blue's series of games with chess world champion Garry Kasparov in 1996 and 1997. A total of 118 computer chess games are analyzed in this volume, from 1996 to 2010, including games from the Internet Chess Club tournaments and from ten World

Computer Chess Championships, as well as three matches played between two computers. The author is a retired computer science professor from McGill University.

Rasskin-Gutman, Diego. *Chess Metaphors: Artificial Intelligence and the Human Mind*. Cambridge: MIT, 2009. Print. Written by a theoretical biologist, this book discusses the cognitive task of problem solving, using the tasks presented by a chess game as a jumping-off point to examine other types of cognition. Rasskin-Gutman presents both human and artificial intelligence approaches to cognitive tasks, including the creation of a computer (Deep Blue) that could beat a human grandmaster at chess.

J

FREDERICK JELINEK

Developer of speech recognition technology

Born: November 18, 1932; Kladno, Czechoslovakia
(now Czech Republic)
Died: September 14, 2010; Baltimore, Maryland
Primary Field: Applied science
Specialty: Mathematics and logic
Primary Company/Organization: IBM

INTRODUCTION

Frederick Jelinek was a pioneer of information theory whose work created the foundation of modern computer language translation and speech recognition technology. Jelinek and colleagues at IBM took a novel approach to computer language processing, based on the specific strengths of the computer rather than trying to imitate human thought; the statistical methods they developed proved crucial to enabling computers to transcribe, understand, and translate natural human speech.

EARLY LIFE

Frederick Jelinek was born Bedřich Jelínek in 1932 to a Jewish family in Kladno, Czechoslovakia, a city near Prague; his father was a dentist. Jelinek's early education was sporadic and unconventional: Because of his Jewish heritage, he was barred from attending local public schools and instead attended makeshift classes organized by Jewish members of the community. Jelinek recalls the classes having an ever-changing roster of teachers, as members of the Jewish community were sent off to concentration camps. Even that formal education ceased in 1942, when the Nazis forbade any instruction for Jews. Jelinek's father, who was Jewish, died in the Terezin concentration camp, but his mother, a convert to Judaism, was allowed to remain free, as

were her children, who were considered to be half Jewish. This allowed them to survive the Holocaust, and Jelinek resumed his education in Czechoslovakia. However, because of his lack of formal education, he did poorly in the gymnasium (the equivalent of a college preparatory high school).

In 1949, Jelinek immigrated with his mother and sister to New York City, where he found the opportunity to

Frederick Jeliner.

141

demonstrate his academic abilities. Although his original goal was to be a lawyer, after graduating from high school he took courses in electrical engineering at City College, then attended the Massachusetts Institute of Technology (MIT) with financial assistance from the National Committee for a Free Europe. He received his doctorate in engineering from MIT in 1962 and joined the faculty of Cornell University.

LIFE'S WORK

Although Jelinek has said that he entered the field of engineering out of expediency rather than aptitude or personal interest, his studies in that field allowed him to begin his work in information theory and gave him the mathematical background for his pioneering work in computer translation and speech recognition. He studied at MIT in the years 1954–62, a period in which MIT was also a center of research into information theory. Among the faculty members at MIT during this time were Claude Shannon, who essentially created the field of information theory; Robert Fano, who developed the Shannon-Fano coding system in collaboration with Shannon; and Peter Elias, who developed convolutional codes, a type of code used in data transfer. Jelinek was also exposed to the ideas of some of the most important linguists of the day while at MIT, including the Russian linguist and literary theorist Roman Jakobson, who pioneered the structural access of language, and Noam Chomsky, who developed the theory of transformational grammar. Jelinek became so interested in linguistics and information theory that he considered leaving the field of engineering, but he was convinced by his thesis adviser, Fano, that he should finish his Ph.D. studies in electrical engineering and could shift his focus afterward.

Jelinek's first faculty position, which he accepted in 1962, was at Cornell University; he was attracted to the university in part by the opportunity to work with the linguist Charles F. Hockett in applying information theory methods to linguistics. Although that collaboration did not work out, Jelinek remained at Cornell for ten years, working in the field of information theory. In 1972 he applied for a summer position at the Thomas J. Watson Research Center at IBM, where research on speech recognition was just beginning.

With this position, Jelinek began his first work in computer speech recognition. When the group's leader, Joe Raviv, accepted a job in Israel, Jelinek was promoted to the head of the Continuous Speech Recognition Group at IBM; he remained with the company for twenty-one years, until his retirement in 1993. Jelinek's group at IBM consisted primarily of Ph.D.'s in fields such as physics and information theory rather than linguistics or another speech-related subject; this allowed them to take a completely novel approach to speech recognition. The current approach was based on teaching the computer to process speech in a manner similar to that used by human beings. To allow a computer to follow this approach, it was necessary to break speech down into its smallest identifiable units, called *phones*, compare the sequence of phones with known word pronunciations, and accept as correct a transcription of the speech that best matched recognized sequences of phones. Jelinek's group took a different approach, one that capitalized on the specific capabilities of computers, that is, the ability to store large amounts of data and perform rapid computations. They decided that it would be impossible to specify an adequate series of rules for this process to succeed and instead applied mathematical and statistical methods that form the basis of modern speech recognition and transcription programs.

After retirement, Jelinek became the director of the Center for Language and Speech Processing at Johns Hopkins University, where he also held the position of Julian S. Smith Professor of Electrical Engineering; he worked at Johns Hopkins for nearly two decades, until his death in 2010. At Johns Hopkins, Jelinek continued to work closely with students and faculty, leading a series of summer workshops that brought together students and professionals from a variety of fields and professions to work on speech and language-processing problems.

Jelinek continued to visit Czechoslovakia as an adult, and after the fall of communism in that country in 1989, he initiated relationships with Czech researchers working in speech science and linguistics. He was instrumental in persuading IBM to set up a computer center at Charles University in Prague, taught in Czechoslovakia, and brought Czech scientists to work with his group at IBM. In this action he was fulfilling a promise made when he accepted funding from the Committee for a Free Europe, that he would help rebuild Czechoslovakia once it was no longer a Communist country.

Jelinek received an honorary doctorate from Charles University in 2001. He also received many other honors, including election to the National Academy of Engineering, being named one of the first twelve Fellows of the International Speech Communication Association, being named a Fellow of the Institute of Electrical and Electronics Engineers, and induction into the National Academy of Engineering in 2006.

Affiliation: IBM

Frederick Jelinek began working at IBM in 1972, just as the company was starting to become involved in research on computer speech recognition and translation. One reason for this research program was to create more demand for computers manufactured by IBM; at the time it was feared that computers were becoming so efficient that there would soon be no market for them, because everyone would already have all the computing power needed. At the time, the dominant approach to computer linguistics problems was based on studying how humans perceive and process speech and trying to replicate that process with the computer.

Jelinek and his group took a different approach, largely emerging from the fact that they all had scientific or engineering backgrounds and hence began from a different intellectual vantage points from those educated in linguistics or other language-oriented fields. Jelinek's approached problems of machine speech recognition and translation based on what a computer could do well—store huge amounts of information, access it quickly, and perform computations quickly—rather than trying to make the computer model the way the human mind processes speech. At first this approach was controversial, but it proved to be a more useful approach than trying to get a computer to work as an imitation of the human mind, and the probabilistic methods Jelinek and his colleagues developed at IBM have become standard in the field.

PERSONAL LIFE

Jelinek died of a heart attack while conducting research on the Johns Hopkins campus. He had been married since 1961 to Milena Jelinek, a Czech filmmaker, screenwriter, and professor of film studies whom he had met in 1957 on a visit to Czechoslovakia; they applied for a marriage license several times but were denied by the Czech government, and they could not be married until Milena was granted permission to visit the United States. The marriage produced a daughter, Hannah Sarbin, and a son, William. Jelinek was also survived by his sister, Susan Abramowitz; his half sister, Hirina Hlavac; and his grandchildren, Alex Sarbin, Sophie Jelinek, and Benjamin Jelinek.

Jelinek once commented that his career was largely a result of luck and circumstances and that he originally intended to be a physician, then a lawyer, rather than an engineer. He chose engineering in part because the course of study was only four years and in part because he felt his accent would be less of a hindrance in engineering than in law.

Sarah Boslaugh

FURTHER READING

Geller, Tom. "Talking to Machines." *Communications of the ACM* 55.4 (2012): 14–16. Print. A nontechnical article about computer voice recognition programs, using Apple Computer's Siri program as an example. Geller reviews the various tasks that must be performed and integrated by the program, including voice recognition, artificial intelligence, user interface, and task fulfillment, that must be solved rapidly in order for the program to respond correctly to human voice commands.

Jelinek, Frederick. "The Dawn of Statistical ASR and MT." *Computational Linguistics* 35.4 (2009): 483–94. Print. Transcript of a speech Jelinek delivered at Johns Hopkins University on the occasion of his winning the Lifetime Achievement Award from the Association for Computational Linguistics. The speech covers the growth of his interest in applying information theory to natural language processing as well as some of the techniques used in the process.

Jelinek, Frederick. "Some of My Best Friends Are Linguists." *Language Resources and Evaluation* 39.1 (2005): 25–34. Print. Jelinek discusses his work at IBM in natural language processing and automatic speech recognition, including its relationship to linguistics. He contrasts his approach with that of Noam Chomsky, whose method was based on rules; Jelinek's approach, in contrast, was based on intuition and statistical methods for parameter estimation.

Jelinek, Frederick. *Statistical Methods for Speech Recognition.* Cambridge: Massachusetts Institute of Technology, 1997. Print. Jelinek's textbook on speech recognition, intended for those with a serious interest in the subject. However, understanding the book does not require advanced mathematics; Jelinek presents information in a way that makes intuitive sense.

Lohr, Steve. "Frederick Jelinek, Who Gave Machines the Key to Human Speech, Dies at 77." *New York Times* 24 Sept. 2010: 10. Print. Obituary focusing on Jelinek's accomplishments in computer speech recognition and his probabilistic approach to the problem, as well as his life in Czechoslovakia and the United States.

STEVE JOBS

Cofounder and former chairman and CEO of Apple

Born: February 24, 1955; San Francisco, California
Died: October 5, 2011; Palo Alto, California
Primary Field: Computer science
Specialty: Computer hardware
Primary Company/Organization: Apple

INTRODUCTION

Steve Jobs was one of the leading innovators of the information age. Throughout his career as chief executive officer (CEO) of both Apple and Pixar Animation Studios, he consistently raised the bar on industry standards in computing and digital media. Jobs's quest for innovation was coupled with his desire to create rather than follow trends, a tendency that earned him the respect of competitors and consumers alike. Jobs's charisma and ability to convince others of the importance of his ideas were a key part of his success.

EARLY LIFE

Steven Paul Jobs was born to an American mother and a Lebanese college professor on February 24, 1955, in

Steve Jobs.

San Francisco, California. At the time of his birth, his parents were not married, and he was given up for adoption a week later. Jobs learned later that his biological parents did eventually marry, and as an adult he learned that he had a younger sister, novelist Mona Simpson.

Jobs was adopted as an infant by Paul and Clara Jobs. He proved to be a strong-willed, energetic, and curious child, and he was often in trouble. Highly intelligent, Jobs learned to read before he entered school, where he was frequently bored. His misbehavior during one year of grade school led him to be expelled.

Jobs showed an interest in machines very early in his life, and as a high school student he attended lectures at Hewlett-Packard, then a small company in Silicon Valley. There, he met Steve Wozniak, a computer technology expert who became his friend and longtime business partner. Following high school, Jobs attended one year of classes at Reed College in Oregon but dropped out and returned to Silicon Valley in 1976 to take a job at the video game company Atari, where Wozniak was employed. At Atari, Jobs and Wozniak designed video games and other products.

LIFE'S WORK

Jobs and Wozniak were part of a group of technology enthusiasts whose focus was building homemade computers and computer chips. Where Wozniak focused on building hardware, Jobs foresaw the marketing potential and appeal of the group's inventions. He and Wozniak managed to sell one hundred homemade computers to a local computer store. Apple Computer was born.

Apple Computer was run out of the Jobs family basement until the company made enough money to move to an office in Silicon Valley. The Apple I computer, which sold for less than $700, proved successful, but the Apple II computer, released in 1979, launched the company to national status. The Apple II was widely praised for its user-friendliness.

Apple Computer became a publicly traded company in 1980. Jobs hired former PepsiCo executive John Sculley to run business operations and oversee the company's expansion. With Sculley's help, Apple established its reputation as a unique innovator, unveiling the Macintosh line of computers in 1984 after nearly four years of development.

Apple's Macintosh line represented a major step forward in the evolution of personal computing. It used a fast processor, the Motorola 68000, and its operating system was fully integrated with the hardware, making it easy to use. The creation of this operating system was a triumph of computer programing, relegating complex tasks to "behind the scenes" software codes that the user did not see.

The Macintosh was also the first computer to use a graphical user interface (GUI), which allowed users to use a mouse to click on pictures to navigate the computer, rather than type instructions into a command line. Coupled with an attractive shell (one of Jobs's primary contributions), Macintosh computers earned a reputation as reliable, powerful, and well-designed machines.

Nonetheless, Jobs became involved in conflicts with Sculley and was eventually forced to leave the company. Jobs's ouster from Apple is attributed to the company's change in focus—moving from home computing to the small business market. Jobs was also obsessed with perfecting hardware technology, which made the computers he designed expensive compared to other companies, particularly that of IBM, Apple's primary competitor at the time.

Both the Apple II and early Macintoshes were built to be affordable, and Jobs's insistence on building cutting-edge home computers ran against the company's vision. In 1986, Jobs founded the NeXT computer company to further his ideas about hardware. However, both NeXT and Apple struggled to make a profit because of increasing competition from companies such as Microsoft, IBM, and Sun Microsystems.

Jobs also purchased the computer graphics division of LucasFilm in 1986, renaming it Pixar Animation Studios. The studio generated funds by creating small computer-animated cartoon shorts, then began to produce commercials for major companies in 1989. After several successful smaller films, Pixar produced the megahit *Toy Story* (1995), the world's first fully computer-animated feature length film. That year, Pixar became a publicly traded company, selling nearly 7 million shares at $22 per share.

Although it was nearly bankrupt, Apple Computer bought NeXT in 1996. Jobs was reappointed CEO of Apple in 1997. He immediately restructured the company's focus, scrapping a number of projects, including the Newton line, which included personal digital assistants (PDAs) and mini-keyboards intended to be used in education. Wozniak, although he had long before been removed from executive decisions in the company, officially left Apple after this restructuring.

Affiliation: Apple

Steve Jobs met Steve Wozniak in the mid-1970s, when they began attending meetings of the Homebrew Computer Club, a group for computer professionals and hobbyists. In 1976, Jobs and Wozniak founded Apple Computer with the release of the Apple I. In 1977, Jobs and Wozniak created the Apple II, which set off a revolution in the industry. It was the first fully assembled programmable desktop computer for beginners and general users. The Macintosh was released in 1984. The Mac offered a unique operating system with a graphical user interface (GUI). With the GUI, the new Mac became the first home computer, usable and accessible to the average user.

These early Apple computers helped convince the world that there was a market for computers for the average person, and the company developed a strong market presence, known for its loyal customers. With these computers, Apple is credited with establishing the personal computer industry. Since its inception, Apple has extended its user-friendly, customer-based mission by developing other consumer products such as iPods and iPads.

After Jobs's return to Apple in 1997, the release of iTunes in 2001 revolutionized the music industry. The subsequent iPod, iPhone, and iPad secured Apple's quest to stay ahead of the competition and have made the company a leader in consumer electronics and personal computing.

Apple suffered significant financial losses in 1997 and 1998, and many predicted that it would go out of business. The company released several poorly received computer designs in the late 1990s. With Apple in serious trouble, it became clear to Jobs that he needed to make radical changes in the company and consider new technologies to market. Turning away from its focus on perfecting personal computing hardware, Apple introduced its first and most famous software release in January 2001: iTunes, a digital music converter and player. This was followed in October of that year by the iPod, a handheld digital music player that revolutionized portable music technology and the music business.

The iPod, when first released, was compatible only with the Macintosh computer, which helped to revive public interest in the Apple brand. Apple released a PC-compatible version of iTunes and the iPod in 2002, which resulted in skyrocketing sales. Apple went on to control more than 90 percent of the market share for digital music players.

In 2003, the iTunes Music Store was introduced, selling more than one million songs over the Internet for about a dollar each. Subsequent generations of iPods, including the iPod Touch, the iPod Nano, and the iPod Shuffle, boosted Apple's reputation as a digital media giant. The success of Apple's digital media division in turn led to more vigorous sales of Apple computers. The company's retail franchise, the Apple Store, was founded in 2001 to distribute the company's digital media hardware, as well as computers and peripherals.

In January 2006, Jobs sold Pixar to the Walt Disney Company for $4.7 billion, earning a seat on Disney's board as a major shareholder. A number of business analysts were surprised by the turn of events, given Pixar's commercial success in comparison to Disney's in computer animation.

In 2007, Apple introduced the iPhone. The handheld camera, cellphone, video camera, and media player with a built-in web browser also runs countless software applications, or "apps," that are made available on iTunes. A global success, the iPhone revolutionized the concept of the smart phone. Subsequent products, including the ultra-thin MacBook Air laptop computer and the iPad tablet, solidified Apple's reputation as a manufacturer of revolutionary and beautifully designed technological products.

Throughout his career, Jobs's fiery personality and extreme self-confidence often left employees and colleagues fearful, as well as awestruck. At times he seemed to implement his ambitious visions by sheer force of will. Some said that Jobs's approach to business was based on his sense of personal mission more than a desire to be a major financial player in the technology sector or a powerful business. As CEO of Apple, he famously accepted an annual salary of only one dollar.

PERSONAL LIFE

In 1978, Jobs and girlfriend Chrisann Brennan had a child, Lisa. At first, Jobs denied paternity, but after a paternity test confirmed that he was the father, he acknowledged his daughter and helped in her support. In 1991, he married Laurene Powell. The couple had three children.

Jobs was diagnosed with a rare form of pancreatic cancer in 2004. Because he had a less aggressive type of cancer, his condition was treated rather quickly. During his absence, Apple executive Tim Cook, the company's chief operating officer, temporarily replaced Jobs as CEO. In 2009, Jobs had a liver transplant after suffering for several years with a hormone imbalance. He took another leave of absence from the company in January 2011, citing unspecified concerns regarding his health. It was reported, however, that Jobs was continuing to suffer from complications related to pancreatic cancer. Cook was again named as Jobs's replacement during his leave of absence.

On August 25, 2011, Jobs officially stepped down from his post as Apple's CEO, citing health concerns. Cook was named as Jobs's successor. Jobs remained chairman of Apple's board of directors.

Jobs died on October 5, 2011, at the age of fifty-six. Upon news of his death, U.S. president Barack Obama, along with countless others and media reports, hailed Jobs as a visionary and one of the greatest American inventors.

Pilar Quezzaire

FURTHER READING

Carlton, Jim. *Apple: The Inside Story of Intrigue, Egomania, and Business Blunders*. New York: Random House, 1997. Print. Corporate history of Apple, from its foundation by Jobs and Wozniak to Jobs's return.

Imbibo, Anthony. *Steve Jobs: The Brilliant Mind behind Apple*. Pleasantville: Gareth Stevens, 2009. Print. Presents significant coverage of Jobs's adolescence. Contains photographs, a time line, and a bibliography.

Isaacson, Walter. *Steve Jobs*. New York: Simon, 2011. Print. Isaacson gleans information from more than forty interviews of Jobs, friends, relatives, and competitors.

Levy, Steven. *The Perfect Thing: How the iPod Shuffles Commerce, Culture, and Coolness*. New York: Simon, 2006. Print. A discussion of the iPod within the context of both Apple's innovative history and twenty-first-century world culture.

Malone, Michael S. *Infinite Loop: How Apple, the World's Most Insanely Great Computer Company, Went Insane*. New York: Doubleday, 1999. Print. Company history, including a great deal of information on the corporate politics that surrounded Jobs during the time shortly before he was pushed out of the company, as well as his return.

Stross, Randall E. *Steve Jobs and the NeXT Big Thing*. New York: Atheneum, 1993. Print. Focuses on Jobs's early years and his work with NeXT.

Wilson, Suzan. *Steve Jobs: Wizard of Apple Computer*. Berkeley Heights: Enslow, 2001. Print. Aimed at younger readers, this book gives a basic overview of Jobs's life up to 2000.

Young, Jeffrey S., and William L. Simon. *iCon: Steve Jobs—The Greatest Second Act in the History of Business*. Hoboken: Wiley, 2005. Print. "Warts-and-all" biography of Jobs that is sharply critical of his more outrageous exploits and was subsequently banned from Apple stores.

BILL JOY

Cofounder of Sun Microsystems

Born: November 8, 1954; Farmington Hills, Michigan
Died: -
Primary Field: Computer science
Specialty: Computer software
Primary Company/Organization: Sun Microsystems

INTRODUCTION

Second only to Bill Gates in influence was William Joy at his peak. Gates made money; Joy made technology. The day after he announced his retirement, Joy indicated that he believed he had been working the same problems for more than two decades and needed something new. In the 1970s, he moved Internet technology into the Unix operating system. His brainchild, which came later, was Java, and he pushed Sun Microsystems into developing the technology that made e-business common. However, he was not satisfied to sit on that accomplishment but instead pushed for tiny embedded computers that allowed devices to speak directly to each other, eliminating human intervention.

EARLY LIFE

William "Bill" Joy was born to William and Ruth Joy in Farmington Hills, Michigan, in 1954. His father was a schoolteacher who eventually became a stockbroker and business professor.

The eldest of three, Bill Joy was a reader at age three, in kindergarten at four, working advanced mathematics at five, and inevitably began skipping grades, being younger than his classmates and raising worries about his social development. At thirteen, he memorized the periodic table of the elements in a single night. He graduated from high school at fifteen and (to use his own term) was a "no-date nerd."

He moved to the University of Michigan, where he became interested in computing, working after class for a professor studying parallel supercomputing, arraying microprocessors in a tight network. Joy was courted to do graduate work at Stanford University, the California Institute of Technology, and the University of California

at Berkeley. He chose Berkeley in 1975 because it had the worst computer facilities of the three and Joy wanted the challenge that would pose to his ingenuity.

Shortly after he arrived at Berkeley, Joy and some computer science colleagues began debugging the Unix operating system of the department's Digital Equipment Corporation (DEC) computer. They put the fixes onto a tape and sold the tapes to other universities with comparable machines for $50 per copy, enough to recoup their costs. This was the time before the personal computer, when computer geeks begged for time on university and business minicomputers and mainframes. When the university bought a DEC model called a VAX, Joy and his friends wrote their own Unix version, selling it for $300. The VAX was a hot seller at $200,000 or more;

Bill Joy.

147

cost-conscious laboratories and universities bought theirs without software or disk drives and added third-party versions. Joy wrote and circulated a memo, "How to Buy a VAX," that explained just how much less expensive that approach was. The Berkeley Unix became a hot item, with hundreds of orders.

In the late 1970s, as a graduate student, Joy made Unix an operating system that was strong enough to compete with Microsoft Windows. He also incorporated network capacities that would eventually make the Internet viable. He designed the circuits on the chips that made Sun's SPARC (for "scalable processor architecture") microprocessors smart enough to drive Sun's $10 billion-per-year business in workstations and servers.

Affiliation: Sun Microsystems

As Sun Microsystems grew through the late 1980s, Joy took on more responsibility, becoming chief scientist and director of technology and thus involved with killing projects, hitting budget targets, hiring and firing, settling turf wars, and attending endless meetings. He was still contributing to Sun innovation, but he needed space. In the early 1990s, he relinquished his clout in the company, including his access to the boss and potentially his relevance to the firm, and headed for Aspen, Colorado. In 2003, after twenty-one years with Sun, Joy for unannounced reasons decided to retire.

Called the Internet Edison, the "other Bill" (in reference to Bill Gates), Joy left Sun when the computer company was in disarray. However, he had effectively left years before, when he moved to Aspen. His contributions included the Unix code that made Sun possible, his work on Java and other open source technology, and keeping Sun's reputation strong as a leading-edge company. When asked why he was leaving at that time, he said the real question was why he had stayed so long. His first inclination to leave had come in 1987, and thirty years was more than enough.

At that point, Sun was beginning to use the SPARC processor architecture that would be at the core of its business for the next two decades. The company would sell servers and workstations built on SPARC as well as AMD and Intel processors, storage systems, and software such as the Solaris operating system, developer tools, Web infrastructure software, identity management applications, the Java platform, MySQL, and NFS. The company supported and advanced the concept of open systems (especially Unix). In 2010, Oracle acquired Sun, ending that company's nearly three-decade independent run, to form Oracle America. Further development of machines based on the SPARC architecture would be done by Oracle's hardware division.

Life's Work

As early as the 1970s, Joy was confident that computing could be much simpler than it was. Microsoft's Windows 2000 did much of what Unix had done and went a step further. It required up to 30 million lines of code. On that scale, debugging was impossible and crashes were inevitable. Joy was obsessed with maximizing simplicity—or at least hiding the complexity within the network and letting the user see only the ease of getting and using data.

In 1978, Joy and his team beat some DEC programmers for a Defense Advanced Research Projects Agency (DARPA) contract to write the software to connect VAX machines to something called an internet. Joy took the opportunity to learn about networking protocols and add them to Unix.

In 1982, Joy was visited by Vinod Khosla, Scott McNealy, and Andreas Bechtolsheim. Bechtolsheim had created a desktop computer, a Stanford University Network (SUN), and Khosla wanted to market it. He needed a Unix expert, and the consensus in the industry was that Joy fit the bill. After six years, Joy was stalled on his Ph.D. and ready to move on.

The SUN desktop was what Joy had wanted for years. It was a networkable station. Joy joined the group, which became Sun Microsystems, and the business took off because the computers, if somewhat slow, were reliable and inexpensive. It took only six years for Sun to exceed $1 billion a year, largely due to Joy's Unix version, later renamed Solaris. When Sun went public in 1986, Joy was suddenly worth more than $10 million. Unlike McNealy, whose stock holdings mushroomed to the billion-dollar mark, Joy was relatively poor because he sold his shares within a couple of years, not wanting to risk the vagaries of the market.

Rather than Silicon Valley, Joy worked with his four-person team in Aspen, Colorado, close to ski slopes. Joy at Sun provided the work for a technological shift to an era when businesses did not need to own computers but instead could farm them out but people would be more tied to nets than ever.

In 1988, John Gage defined Joy's idea in a slogan: "The network is the computer." Networked companies did not need farms full of mainframes and servers but instead subscribed to utilities via the net. Their hardware needs were for PCs or pocket-sized computers. Joy also anticipated the personal network, wherein the individual would have network access regardless of where he or she was and for whatever purpose: work, play, shopping, household management, and connection to friends and family. Joy even envisioned the impact of wireless technologies. He foresaw the evolution of wireless devices being transparent to the user, like telephones and televisions, whereby the user did not have to be a technician.

Java in 1994 was languishing in Sun's labs before Joy made it a standard for a million or more users, made the Internet exciting, and slowed Microsoft's plan to dominate the Internet. His workspace was Aspen Smallworks, a think tank for Joy and creative associates to develop new ideas away from the noise, meetings, and McNealy, all of which disrupted Joy's thinking. At Aspen, Joy made Java (originally named Oak in the mid-1980s) viable. When the web began to grow in 1994, Joy thought back to the failed Oak effort and recognized that it was ideal for enhancing web interactivity because it could write small and efficient just-in-time programs for virtually any type of computer. Java was so hot that Sun established a subsidiary for it; Microsoft adopted it; Kleiner, Perkins, Caulfield and Byers put up $100 million to finance start-ups willing to write applications for it; student demand forced universities to offer programming classes in it; and Joy hit the conference circuit because of it.

Joy pushed Sun to the forefront of the computer industry and made the Internet not only a means of communication but also a rapidly growing tool for business and social applications. Joy in 1999 was involved in at least half of the hot technology trends of the day; Sun chief executive officer (CEO) McNealy noted that Joy was as productive as the legendary Bell Laboratories and more cost-effective.

Sun also invented Jini, which made game systems and other home entertainment formats networkable and transparent to users. Jini came five years after Sun had established the Java subsidiary. It was supposed to link not only home entertainment but also any electronic device, including cameras, phones, and the then popular personal data assistants (PDAs), appliances with embedded Java chips. With Jini, every networked device told the network what it could do and helped the other devices to use its capabilities. Jini was the technology that most simplified the network for ordinary users.

PERSONAL LIFE

Joy was noted for his broad interests, the range of his reading, and his ability to retain and link diverse subject matter, from Meso-American art to cattle ranching to Jungian theory to G. I. Gurdjieff's mysticism and stock market theories. Innovation requires freedom from structure; according to Joy, overly planned, overly organized companies rarely innovate.

Joy is tall, a stereotypical geek in appearance, with tousled hair and the ability for intense focus and concentration. He can take the essential nugget from a stream of chatter and move a conversation toward a new and vital idea. He has been described as eccentric, a polymath, a whiz, and a tinkerer. He has owned a San Francisco gallery featuring primitive art, has worked as Bill Clinton's technology adviser, taught himself to speak Spanish, and is an occasional cattle rancher. A passionate reader, he sometimes starts a book in the middle to see if he can figure out what happened in earlier chapters.

In 2000, Joy wrote an article in *Wired* magazine, "Why the Future Doesn't Need Us," in which he discussed his concern that biotech and nanotechnology were progressing too rapidly and had the potential to run amok. He nevertheless remains an optimist about both Sun and the technological future, believing that the Internet will become virus and spam resistant.

A report of his retirement from Sun Microsystems in 2003 indicated that he was no longer interested in information technology but was moving into bioengineering and nanotechnology. Future plans included a book on the dangers of nanotechnology and biotech and other emerging technologies. He hinted at possibly starting a new company. In 1999, he two colleagues, Andreas Bechtolsheim and Roy Thiele-Sardiña, had founded the venture capital firm HighBAR Ventures, and in 2005 Joy became a partner in venture capital firm Kleiner, Perkins, Caulfield and Byers, investing in green technologies.

In 2006, at age fifty-two, Joy was building an eco-friendly 190-foot, $50 million sailboat that would use wind power not only for propulsion but also to generate electricity. The *Ethereal* was going to be a self-contained community, not just a yacht, and it had to have capacity to deal with waste as well as comfort. Joy used a world-class designer, to whom he taught integrative design process. He was inducted as a Fellow of the Computer History Museum in 2011.

John H. Barnhill

FURTHER READING

Burrows, Peter. "Out of Sun's Orbit." *Businessweek* 3850 (2003): 42. *Business Source Complete*. Web. 1 May 2012. An article on Joy's retirement announcement and future plans.

---. "William Joy." *Businessweek* 3648 (1999): EB44. *Business Source Complete*. Web. 1 May 2012. A short profile of Joy, defining him as a visionary who sees a decade into the future.

Ceruzzi, Paul E. *A History of Modern Computing*. Cambridge: MIT, 2012. Print. Provides an overview that contains semitechnical material on Joy, Sun, and Unix.

"Co-founder Bill Joy Departing from Sun." *Eweek* 20.37 (2003): 22. *Academic Search Complete*. Web. 1 May 2012. The article briefly notes Joy's legacy at Sun and his future interests.

Joy, Bill. "Why the Future Doesn't Need Us." *Wired* 8.04 (2000): n. pag. Web. 1 May 2012. Joy's Cassandra article, in which he posits that technology is making human beings obsolete.

Redman, Christopher. "The Green Sailor." *Fortune* 154.5 (2006): 82–88. *Business Source Complete*. Web. 1 May 2012. Aside from describing the *Ethereal*, this article deals with the superyacht industry.

Schlender, Brent. "The Edison of the Internet." *Fortune* 139.3 (1999): 84–90. *Business Source Complete*. Web. 1 May 2012. A six-page biography covering Joy's work and life up to 1999, with emphasis on Java and some coverage of Jini.

---. "An Ode to Joy." *Fortune* 148.6 (2003): 36. *Business Source Complete*. Web. 1 May 2012. Another profile, this as Joy prepared to leave Sun, covering some of his philosophy and character quirks.

Southwick, Karen. *High Noon: The Inside Story of Scott McNealy and the Rise of Sun Microsystems*. New York: Wiley, 1999. Print. A history of the company from its founding in 1982 to the late 1990s.

Teich, Albert H., ed. *Technology and the Future*. Boston: Wadsworth Cengage Learning, 2009. Print. A collection of more than two dozen seminal articles on the future of technology in the twenty-first century, including Joy's "Why the Future Doesn't Need Us."

K

PETER KARMANOS JR.

Cofounder, executive chairman, and former CEO of Compuware

Born: March 11, 1943; Detroit, Michigan
Died: -
Primary Field: Business and commerce
Specialty: Management, executives, and investors
Primary Company/Organization: Compuware

INTRODUCTION

Peter Karmanos Jr., is one of the founders of Compuware, which he has called a "blue-collar computer company." As head of Compuware, Karmanos has been involved in every aspect of the business, working as a hands-on manager and building a company that consistently generated industry-leading profits through the 1990s. After a period of complacency, the company successfully rebuilt itself in the 2000s. Karmanos also owns the Carolina Hurricanes, the Plymouth Whalers, and the Florida Everblades hockey franchises.

EARLY LIFE

Born March 11, 1943, to Greek immigrants, Peter Karmanos Jr., first started speaking English when he was in elementary school. His first work experience was waiting tables and operating the cash register at the family diner, and there he learned the necessity of satisfying customer expectations. He also learned to go to work and accomplish something every day. After graduation from Henry Ford High School, where he met his first wife, Barbara Ann, he attended Wayne State University. He and Barbara married in 1965.

LIFE'S WORK

In 1973, with Thomas Thewes and Allen Cutting, Karmanos founded Compuware. Each man put up $3,000

of his tax return money. Their ambition was to have between twenty and twenty-five skilled workers creating software to help programmers. From the beginning Karmanos was involved in all aspects of the software and services business.

Compuware began by offering software services for mainframe users, then moved into mainframe software development and quality assurance, and later to

Peter Karmanos Jr.

Affiliation: Compuware

Compuware started by selling consulting services to mainframe users, helping them use use their computer systems more efficiently. It grew into a major provider of software for information technology (IT) professionals, helping them build and maintain data networks.

Today, most of Compuware's original competitors are gone or absorbed into other companies. Compuware broadened into distributed computing and other more current areas, but it still kept the mainframe attitude, attempting to market mainframe solutions in competition with companies like IBM, BMC Software, and CA. In 2008, in the quarterly earnings statement before the introduction of Compuware 2.0, mainframes in the fourth quarter were still growing 40 percent over the earlier quarter and 80 percent year over the previous year. However, although the mainframe business was viable and still profitable, many mainframe clients were unaware that Compuware also handled distributed computing needs, and distributed users did not know it did mainframe support. Customers agreed that Compuware provided good tools for quality assurance, development, and other services that made their IT better, but Compuware did not "rock."

A new approach was to sell problem-solving rather than specific products and services. The company implemented a five-hundred-person development team for distributed computing alone. The IT service management software Vantage and Changepoint were given new interest and investment for development and integration into the other packages the company offered. The Product Related Service Group became the Solution Delivery Group, with local level management and virtual teams by specific expertise. The company was committing to using its own products but also to using open source software where desirable. Compuware 2.0 incorporated best practices and technology from Java and open source, web aspects, collaboration, and software as a service, but the main thrust was to maintain the core mainframe IT customer service values.

By 2011, the company was earning more than $1 billion a year, renewals were at 92 percent, and profits were solid again. At the end of July 2012, the company announced the general availability of Changepoint 2012, the latest edition of its professional services automation (PSA) and project portfolio management (PPM) software, touted as offering "more flexibility to support global organizations."

application life-cycle management and other tools and services for distributed systems. Compuware would build the tools that enable businesses to create better and more error free software. For nearly thirty years, annual revenue growth met or exceeded 30 percent annually under Karmanos. In 1999, the company rose to sixth in the *Businessweek*'s list of top fifty performers. In 2000, the company had an annual income of $1.2 billion.

In 1999, Karmanos announced that he would relocate Compuware's headquarters and its then sixty-five hundred high-skill, high-paying jobs from Farmington Hills, Michigan, to downtown Detroit. The company got the land for its building from the city for a mere dollar; building on a vacant lot was cheaper than relocating to another suburb, so in 2002 the company moved downtown. Karmanos wanted to give back to the city and to demonstrate to his employees, who had been suburbanites for generations, that city life was not all bad.

Karmanos put a charter school, the University Preparatory Academy Science and Math Middle School,

into his headquarters building temporarily while the permanent site was being prepared. Compuware personnel provided job-shadowing, mentoring, and educational opportunities to the students. The headquarters building stood fifteen stories high and boasted amenities suited to a five-star hotel, including a Hard Rock Café, a Ben and Jerry's ice cream shop, and an optical company as tenants. Karmanos takes provided his employees with a gourmet cafeteria, day care, and a modern gym, making a position in his company among the most desired jobs in Detroit.

Compuware began 2000 with high hopes for its move to e-commerce, but the effort was unsuccessful. Retraining of employees took longer than anticipated, profit margins thinned, and longtime customers, faced with major price increases from Compuware, moved to rivals who offered lower prices. Compuware's stock plummeted 40 percent in one day to $1.00, the lowest price in two years. For the quarter ending March 31, 2000, Compuware indicated software sales between $193 and $198 million, down from the $300 million

analysts expected. The company had fourteen major contracts worth $140 million that should have been signed but were still pending because of missing paperwork or customers being unavailable.

Compuware remained a leader in troubleshooting software for mainframe problems, but once the vaunted risks of Y2K (the year 2000 and its anticipated software problems) passed and companies were no longer afraid to change vendors or otherwise disrupt their networks, it appeared that Compuware was arrogant, refusing to negotiate and hiking prices for a captive customer base. Rivals began taking Compuware customers. Compuware denied that it was losing business, but two top executives in the professional services unit were let go. The real problem, according to analysts, was a software division in disarray, and software accounted for 60 percent of Compuware's business. At the same time, Karmanos was facing two sexual harassment charges and double bypass surgery in January 2000. Even so, revenue growth was anticipated to be 25 percent, disappointing by Compuware standards but excellent for most businesses.

Compuware was in downtown Detroit when it decided to launch Compuware 2.0 in an attempt to rebrand the thirty-five-year-old company. Despite the outdated labeling of the change as 2.0, Compuware was doing the right thing in improving its performance with the customers. The quality of its products had never been in question, but its performance in selling them was troubling. Rebranding, refocusing, shaking up the leadership, and a new logo (a three-dimensional guitar pick to represent Compuware's determination to "rock" the information technology industry) were put to work to revitalize the business. Karmanos hired Jason Vines from Detroit's automobile industry as chief of communications; Vines had been responsible for the initial success of the Chrysler 300.

In 2011, Karmanos stepped down as chief executive officer (CEO) and became executive chair.

PERSONAL LIFE

Karmanos's wife, Barbara, was diagnosed with cancer in 1981. Karmanos offered to sell the business to be with her. She died in 1989, and in 1995 Karmanos donated $15 million to a Detroit research facility that renamed itself in Barbara's name.

In the spring of 1998, Karmanos was fifty-five years old and head of Compuware. Earnings were strong, sales were elevated, and stock stood high on Wall Street. Karmanos held 12 percent of the company, a $656 million

asset. On May 20, at the quarterly meeting, Karmanos announced to the board that Sheila McKinnon, senior vice president for human resources, had accused him of sexual harassment, alleging to other company officials that he had propositioned her and touched her, turning abusive when she rebuffed him. McKinnon also asserted that Karmanos had harassed former secretary Troy Strong. Within days, McKinnon sued Karmanos and Compuware for harassment and retaliation. Strong also sued. Karmanos and Compuware countersued McKinnon before dropping the case later and coming to an out-of-court settlement in April. Strong continued her suit.

Karmanos belongs to the high-IQ group Mensa. At the same time, he has been described as loud and profane. He established a recognition program within Compuware, the Eagles (exceptionally good, exceptionally enthusiastic workers among his developers). Karmanos is recognized as a hero to the people of his hometown of Detroit for his philanthropy and involvement with the community. He has donated millions of dollars to cancer research.

Karmanos also owns at least part of three hockey teams: the Carolina Hurricanes and two minor league franchises. In 1974, Compuware started sponsoring Detroit youth hockey teams in a league dominated by teams sponsored by pizza chain Little Caesars, owned by Mike Ilitch. The two businessmen were sports-mad rivals. Compuware recruited coaches and players heavily and challenged Ilitch's Little Caesers teams. The rivalry became bitter, intensifying when Karmanos bought the Hartford Whalers in 1994, giving him a rival National Hockey League team to Ilitch's Detroit Redwings. In 1995, Ilitch evicted Karmanos's Ontario Hockey League champion Junior Red Wings out of the Joe Louis Arena, where the Junior Wings had played for five years. In 1998, Karmanos tendered a Wings star $38 million over six years with a $12 bonus for making the conference finals with the last-place Carolina team. Ilitch had to match the offer to keep the player, and winning the Stanley Cup that year cost $28 million over four months.

Karmanos loaned large amounts of money to Detroit's mayor Kwame Kilpatrick, who was indicted for lying under oath about a relationship with a former aide. Karmanos remained loyal to the mayor as he headed off to jail in 2008. A Texas subsidiary of Compuware employed Kilpatrick but let him go in 2010 after he was sentenced to prison.

In 2005, more than fifteen years after Barbara's death, Karmanos married his second wife, Danialle.

They would have three children. At that time, Karmanos was sixty-two. By 2011, he had eight grandchildren.

John H. Barnhill

FURTHER READING

"Barbara Ann Karmanos, 1943–1989." *Karmanos.org.* Web. 1 May 2012. Describes the cancer center and Karmanos's first wife.

Greene, Jamal. "Suit vs. Suit." *Sports Illustrated* 96.25 (2002): 21. *Academic Search Complete.* Web. 1 May 2012. The rivalry between Karmanos and Ilitch of Little Caesars in hockey.

Karmanos, Peter. "Q&A with Compuware's Peter Karmanos." *Bloomberg Businessweek* 12 Mar. 1999: n. pag. Web. 12 May 2012. An interview with Karmanos in which he discusses the success of Compuware and its strategies for growth.

Kovelle, Kim. "Good 'Karma,' Danialle Karmanos" Balance is Key for This Oakland County Mom, from her Quest to Conquer Childhood Obesity with Yoga, to Raising Three Small Kids of Her Own." *Metro Parent* July 2011: n. pag. Web. 1 May 2012. Profile of Danialle with some coverage of husband Karmanos.

Muller, Joann. "Compuware's Y2k Bug." *Businessweek* 3680 (2000): 91–92. *Business Source Complete.* Web. 1 May 2012. Describe's Compuware's doldrums, with business losses, ineptitude, and Karmanos's harassment charges hanging over it all.

---. "How Compuware Mishandled Its Explosive Sexual-Harassment Case." *Businessweek* 3636 (1999): 74–81. *Business Source Complete.* Web. 1 May 2012. Slogs through the details of the harassment case but also provides a brief profile of Karmanos.

Taft, Darryl K. "In the House That Pete Built." *Eweek* 25.18 (2008): D4–D5. *Academic Search Complete.* Web. 1 May 2012. An overview history of Compuware with information on Karmanos's personal life.

---. "Reworking Compuware." *Eweek* 25.16 (2008): 17–18. *Business Source Complete.* Web. 16 May 2012. The new and improved Compuware of 2008. The story of how Compuware got into a bind, then rebranded to catch up with changes in the computer business.

Walsh, Tom. "Compuware CEO Peter Karmanos Plans for Exit by Early 2013." *Detroit Free Press* 18 Jan. 2011: n. pag. Print. Profiles Karmanos's outside interests and personal life along with his career and impending departure from Compuware.

JOHN G. KEMENY

Codesigner of the BASIC programming language

Born: May 31, 1926; Budapest, Hungary
Died: December 26, 1992; Lebanon, New Hampshire
Primary Field: Computer science
Specialty: Computer programming
Primary Company/Organization: Dartmouth College

INTRODUCTION

John G. Kemeny, who spent his career as a mathematician, computer programming educator, and president of Dartmouth College, was coauthor of the BASIC programming language, which he and colleague Thomas Kurtz wrote and later made more powerful with True BASIC. Their invention of the first computer time-sharing system, Dartmouth Time-Sharing System (DTSS), was equally important, adapted by universities and government agencies and foreshadowing the networked environment in which we live today.

EARLY LIFE

John George Kemeny was born in Budapest on May 31, 1926. His father left in 1938, fearing the Nazi regime of Adolf Hitler, and his wife, daughter, and son followed in 1940. Kemeny arrived in New York City in 1940, attended George Washington High School, and graduated in 1943 at the top of his class. He entered Princeton University, studying mathematics, but one year later he was drafted and sent to Los Alamos, Mexico, to work on the Manhattan Project as a human "computer." The computer center where Kemeny worked had nothing more advanced than IBM bookkeeping calculators that were fed punch cards. Simple computations could take a week.

At Los Alamos, Kemeny heard John von Neumann speak. Von Neumann outlined his vision for a fully electronic computer using a binary number system, with internal memory for data processing and storage. For

John G. Kemeny.

the human computers and others attending his lecture, the speed and accuracy of calculations that would result were exciting yet, for Kemeny, seemed like a dream he might not see realized in his lifetime.

In 1947, Kemeny earned his bachelor's degree from Princeton with the highest grade point average that institution in twenty years. By the age of twenty-three, he had earned his Ph.D, despite the year he had spent at Los Alamos. He was chief assistant to Albert Einstein at the Institute for Advanced Study in 1948–1949, where von Neumann was also working. In the summer of 1953, during a consulting job at the Rand Corporation, Kemeny had a chance to work with and write program language for a copy of von Neumann's computer, the JONIAC.

LIFE'S WORK

In 1953, at age twenty-seven, Kemeny took a position at Dartmouth College as a professor of mathematics. He would make his career at Dartmouth, becoming department chair at twenty-nine and president of the college at forty-three. Dartmouth had no computer when Kemeny joined the faculty, so he would drive more than one hundred miles each way to use a computer at the Massachusetts Institute of Technology (MIT), where he

saw the advent of Fortran and could see the possibilities of programming languages that made it easier for all humans to access the power of these machines.

In 1959, the Alfred P. Sloan Foundation granted half a million dollars to Dartmouth to pay for the mathematics half of the building that the mathematics department was to share with the psychology department. The grant was awarded because of the work of thirty-two-year-old Kemeny. Kemeny revitalized the Dartmouth mathematics department; in 1959, many of the department's faculty were his appointees, and he changed the curriculum to incorporate abstract algebra, probability, topology, and other fields that, at the time, were new. He changed created two programs, one designed for mathematics majors and the other liberal arts majors. As a teacher, he was demanding, challenging, and effective, with a "cornball" sense of humor and no patience with professors who looked down on freshman classes or refused to do research.

Also in 1959, Dartmouth got its first computer, an LGP-30. Computer science was expanding beyond wartime decoding machines and punch-card-fed calculators. By the 1960s, expectations were greater, based on the insights of visionaries such as von Neumann, Alan Turing, and Kemeny himself. In an article published in *Scientific American*, "Man Viewed as a Machine," Kemeny described the eventual design of a universal machine that, "given enough time he can learn to do anything." Assembler languages had been written, but they were difficult to learn. Fortran was for scientists, COBOL was for business people, and both were intimidatingly technical. Kemeny and fellow faculty member Thomas Kurtz at Dartmouth understood computers and shared the dedication of MIT's John McCarthy to time sharing, wanting to give all the students and faculty access to computers. This led Kemeny and Kurtz to develop a system to give multiple users access to the central computer from remote terminals; up and running by 1964, the system was dubbed the Dartmouth Time-Sharing System (DTSS).

Kemeny and Kurtz realized, however, that time sharing needed to be joined by another tool: a high-level language for nonprogrammers. Kemeny broached the idea to Kurtz, worried that they would be teaching a language that nobody could use outside Dartmouth, since Fortran was the standard in the world. In 1962, Kemeny and a student assistant, Sidney Marshall, had created DOPE, the Dartmouth Oversimplified Programming Experiment, but DOPE had flopped. Kemeny and Kurtz then developed Beginners All-Purpose Symbolic

Instruction Code, BASIC. The language used commands based on plain English and high school algebra, requiring only minimal learning of syntax. It was interactive, with real-time error messages that the programmer could correct on the spot. No longer was it necessary for users to labor endlessly on code, get a few minutes of "run time" (access to the computer), watch the program fail, then trudge back to try to locate the programming error again and again. BASIC also had a built-in random number generator, making it easy to create games. Kemeny also tied the university computing center to faculty offices and areas where students could use the computer through telephone-linked terminals.

When Kemeny became Dartmouth's president in 1970, he replaced John Sloan Dickey, who during his quarter century as president was a major transformer of Dartmouth's infrastructure and endowments. In contrast to the Waspish, traditional headmaster figure cut by Dickey, Kemeny was a Jewish intellectual immigrant, former assistant to Einstein, and computer hobbiest who was expected to speed change for the college's thirty-

eight hundred students during a time of social change, perhaps even to bring Dartmouth into line with other Ivy League schools in offering undergraduate education to women. Kemeny committed to increasing enrollment of Native Americans and also saw the admission of women to the college, in 1972.

Kemeny's tenure as Dartmouth president lasted eleven years. He converted Dartmouth to a trimester system that allowed students time for off-campus projects and provided more efficient use of dormitories and teaching centers. He recruited minorities, abandoned the school's American Indian mascot (despite alumni protests), saw the college transition to a coeducational institution, and rejected the rise of conservatism on the campus in the final years of his presidency, criticizing the conservative *Dartmouth Review* and warning students in 1981 against intolerance.

Jimmy Carter appointed Kemeny as head of the commission that investigated the Three Mile Island nuclear plant accident of 1979. Kemeny's commission found that federal regulators and industry were both

Affiliation: True BASIC, Inc.

John Kemeny was the coinventor, with fellow Dartmouth mathematics professor Thomas Kurtz, of Beginner's All-purpose Symbolic Instruction Code, BASIC, a programming language that made it possible for nonspecialists in machine language to program computers. The first BASIC program ran in 1964.

BASIC became nearly universal, and virtually every small computer had at least one version. However, that was the problem: Hundreds of different implementations, hundreds of BASIC dialects, not all of which were compatible with the others. The American National Standards Institute (ANSI) in 1974 began working on a voluntary standard for BASIC, with a minimal standard was released in 1978 with the full standard due in 1984. As chair of the ANSI subcommittee on the BASIC standard, Kurtz saw an opportunity. He and Kemeny reworked their language and built a version that complied with the new standard. Driving their effort was the bad reputation that BASIC had acquired because some of the implementations were exceedingly poor. Original BASIC, which they had copyrighted, was still provided free of charge to anyone who wanted it. Given the second chance and the 1984 deadline, Kurtz and Kemeny wanted to beat the bad versions to the punch. In 1983, they founded the company True BASIC, Inc.,

headquartered at Hanover, near the Dartmouth campus. What had been BASIC 7 was issued as True BASIC in versions that were compatible with both the PC (IBM) and Mac (Apple) operating systems.

True BASIC added structured programming, allowing programmers to write subroutines as building blocks for larger programs. It added a graphics module so people could draw on their monitors. It was much larger and more complex than original BASIC, but it was still accessible to beginners. The first version of True BASIC was aimed for the IBM PC, with implementation for other brands occurring every three months thereafter. It had graphics and other attractive features that Kemeny and Kurtz hoped would lure BASIC users away from the nonstandard mess, and it complied with the ANSI standard. They also sought to replace the PASCAL programming language as the standard. Kemeny and Kurtz copyrighted True BASIC to keep variations at bay but provided copies generously at $150.00 apiece. Their intent was to hold prices down and therefore maximize distribution and use. True BASIC, Inc. also issued an instructional mathematics package for high school and college students, and True BASIC became standard on Commodore's Amiga computer.

responsible for lax safety standards. The commission's October 1979 report sought basic change in reactor construction and operation. Three Mile Island culminated an antinuclear-power movement that had been growing for several decades. Coming just after the coincidental release of the movie *The China Syndrome*, about an accident at a nuclear power plant, the accident at Three Mile Island was met by an antinuclear backlash that placed the future of nuclear energy in doubt. To calm fears, Carter chose his commission, surprising even Kemeny, who had had no expertise in nuclear energy, when selecting him as chair. The commission found that the technology was not at fault and was in fact quite good. It also learned that an operator error had transformed a minor incident into a major accident and that the operators had never received training on how to deal with the small failure. Kemeny's commission recommended that engineers not be allowed to do training (Kemeny believed that engineers are incomprehensible at best). The commission also recommended that the Nuclear Regulatory Commission and the nuclear industry change their attitudes and practices or expect another near meltdown. Carter took the commission's advice, the industry stabilized, and no other major accident occurred at any of the more than one hundred reactors in the United States. However, no new reactors were built for thirty years afterward.

In 1981, Kemeny resigned as president of Dartmouth to resume teaching in the mathematics department until 1990. After returning to teaching, Kemeny took stock of the use of computers especially in education. However, his focus remained on making computers available to all users, and the slow pace of progress in computer education frustrated him. Moreover, over time, versions of BASIC had proliferated, and some were not particularly good, giving BASIC a bad reputation. When the American National Standards Institute (ANSI) decided to set a standard, the two saw an opportunity to revitalize their creation. Between 1983 and 1985, Kemeny and Kurtz went back to work and produced a more powerful version of their original BASIC, True BASIC.

PERSONAL LIFE

In 1950, Kemeny married Jean Alexander, and the couple had two children: a son, Robert, and a daughter, Jennifer. He died in 1992 following a heart attack at the Dartmouth-Hitchcock Medical Center in Lebanon, New Hampshire. He was sixty-six years old. Speaking after her husband's death, Jean, the author of both fiction and nonfiction, described John's personality and interests as follows: "He liked science fiction, football games, shrimp, all kinds of puzzles, Agatha Christie, and solitude (for two). He did not enjoy socializing. Before he retired, John recognized only two flowers, the tulip and the rose, and two pieces of music, the 1812 Overture and 'Poor Little Buttercup.' These last years he had time to enjoy Mozart, wildflowers, pileated woodpeckers, eclipses. Sometimes he liked just to sit still and think."

Above all, computers and programming were Kemeny's greatest hobbies. He spent a career at Dartmouth during which he witnessed and contributed significantly not only to the computer revolution but also to profound social changes, including the expansion of Dartmouth's education to a diverse population of students through both liberalized admissions policies and the extension of computing to users who would otherwise have had little opportunity for access. Over the course of his career, Kemeny was the recipient of twenty honorary degrees and many awards, including election to the American Academy of Arts and Sciences (1967), the New York Academy of Sciences Award (1984), the Computer Pioneer Award from the Computer Society of the Institute of Electrical and Electronics Engineers (1986), and the Louis Robinson Award (1990).

John H. Barnhill

FURTHER READING

Hauben, Jay Robert. "John G. Kemeny: BASIC and DTSS; Everyone a Programmer." *Computer Pioneers*. Ed. John A. N. Lee. Los Alamitos: IEEE Computer Society Press, 1995. N. pag. Print. Rehearses Kemeny's career with emphasis on the evolution of his thinking and contributions to human-computer interactions.

"High Math at Hanover." *Time* 73.8 (1959): 83. *Academic Search Complete*. Web. 1 May 2012. Early article about the grant of half a million dollars for a mathematics and psychology building at Dartmouth, covering the early career of Kemeny as chair of the mathematics department.

Kemeny, Jean. *It's Different at Dartmouth*. Brattleboro: Greene, 1979. Print. Jean Kemeny's autobiography and narrative of her life as Dartmouth College's "first lady." Provides insight into Dartmouth College and her husband's tenure as president.

---. *Man and the Computer*. New York: Scribner, 1972. Print. The history of computing and human interactions with computers from one of the pioneers of that evolution, the coauthor of BASIC.

---. "Man Viewed as a Machine." *Scientific American* 192 (1955): 58–67. Print. A seminal article in which he summarized von Neumann's thought and answered his own question, "What can a computer do better than a man?"

Mahoney, Matt. "Notes on a Meltdown." *Technology Review* 112.6 (2009): 88. *Academic Search Com-* plete. Web. 1 May 2012. Discusses Kemeny's role in the Three Mile Island investigation.

Slater, Robert. *Portraits in Silicon*. Cambridge: MIT, 1989. Print. Chapters deal with computing pioneers, the founders and movers as of the late 1980s. Although dated, contains informative material on Kemeny, Kurtz, and both BASIC and True BASIC.

TOM KILBURN

Cocreator of the Manchester Mark I computer

Born: August 11, 1921; Dewsbury, England
Died: January 17, 2001; Manchester, England
Primary Field: Computer science
Specialty: Computer hardware
Primary Company/Organization: Victoria University of Manchester

INTRODUCTION

Tom Kilburn was instrumental in developing the English computing industry after World War II. His even more lasting legacy lies in the development of computer science at the Victoria University of Manchester, to which he devoted the bulk of his career.

EARLY LIFE

Tom Kilburn was born in the West Yorkshire town of Dewsbury to a moderately successful company man, John William Kilburn. Tom attended Wheelwright Grammar School, concentrating almost entirely on mathematics from age fourteen because that was the headmaster's choice. In 1940, he went to Cambridge as a scholarship student, finishing a compressed course of study in 1942 with first-class honors in the first part of the three-part mathematics program and in the preliminary examination for the second part. Although many of the Cambridge mathematicians were at Bletchley Park and otherwise serving in World War II, Cambridge still had a solid department, and Kilburn contributed his share. He was in the New Pythagoreans subset of the university mathematical society, and other men of future importance to the development of computing were also there, including Geoff Tootill and Gordon Welchman. The students also heard speakers from several who would be prominent at Bletchley Park (although mathematician Alan Turing had departed for Bletchley in 1939). Kilburn earned his bachelor's and master's degrees in mathematics at Cambridge by 1944 and his Ph.D. (1948) and D.Sc. (1953) degrees from Manchester University.

LIFE'S WORK

Kilburn's first employment was at Telecommunications Research Establishment (TRE) in Malvern, from 1942 to 1947. Thereafter, he was at Victoria University of Manchester as lecturer, professor, department head, dean, and pro vice chancellor, retiring in 1981.

Kilburn chose not to be in the Royal Air Force because he could not be a pilot, taking short electronics

Tom Kilburn.

courses before being called up to TRE Malvern. At TRE, Kilburn, who wore glasses, worked on radar. His initial reception was cool because the group wanted an experienced electronics person, not a twenty-one-year-old recent graduate. The mission of TRE Malvern was to design and debug circuits and solve problems that other groups encountered. Kilburn had no experience and no great interest in electronics. He made strong progress, however, and rose through the ranks. When his boss left for Manchester in 1946, he wanted to bring Kilburn along to work on cathode-ray tubes (CRTs).

The group worked to solve to the problem of electronic storage, without which digital electronic computing would never happen. The head of the Mark I team was Frederic C. Williams. Williams and Kilburn in 1946 created the first high-speed random access memory device. The two worked on information storage in CRTs. This research culminated in creation of the Williams tube, which more appropriately is called the Williams-Kilburn tube. The tube used persisting images of dots on the phosphor screen of the tube to store data. A dot drawn on a CRT remains for a length of time that depends on the type of phosphor used, on average around 0.2 second. Additionally, the electrical charge around the dot changes slightly, so researchers could measure the change and create a primitive form of memory that lasted for a specified length of time, depending on the phosphor type. The charge gradually left, so periodically a scan and rewrite were required, similar to the refresh cycles in modern computer systems.

Williams stored a bit on a CRT in late 1946. In 1947, Kilburn heard Turing lecture on the design of the National Physics Laboratory's computer using mercury acoustic delay lines for storage. Kilburn rejected the Turing approach. In early 1947, Kilburn moved the whole apparatus to Manchester and by March had a better method of storing bits sufficient that by the end of the year they could store 2,048 bits on the Williams tube, and they built a computer around it. American and Russian organizations would copy the Williams tube. By the end of 1947, they had a CRT that stored patterns over extended stretches of time. Kilburn and Williams, with the aid of Geoff Tootill, in 1948 built the Manchester "Baby" around the prototype CRT storage device. The Baby showed the workability of the tube and used a stored program, a seventeen-line program to calculate the highest factor of a number. The program first ran on June 21, 1948. It was the first stored-program digital electronic computer (a prototype; Cambridge's Early Delay Storage Automatic Calculator, or EDSAC, built

by Maurice Wilkes and his team, would become the first in-service digital stored-program computer). The Baby was the basis for the development of Manchester as a leader in the new field of computer science.

After completion of the Manchester Baby, Kilburn planned to return to TRE, but the Ministry of Supply contracted with the company Ferranti to design a full-scale computer to Williams's specifications. The university prototype was the Manchester Mark I, and Kilburn remained on staff, receiving appointment as university lecturer. By autumn 1949 the Manchester Mark I, including a backup drum storage capability, was finished and ran continuously for nearly a year. Nine Ferranti Mark I computers were sold between 1951 and 1957. During the three years after development of the Baby, the computing function moved to engineering, and Kilburn took over from Williams. In 1951, Kilburn began working on the Mark II, the megacycle machine that used solid-state diodes and increased clock rate tenfold while being more reliable and adding a floating point operation. To keep serial CRT memory from being a bottleneck, Kilburn designed a 10-bit parallel memory for the Mark II. Meg, as the Mark II was nicknamed, debuted in the summer of 1954, and Ferranti produced a commercial version called Mercury; nineteen were sold, including six overseas.

While Kilburn and two others worked on Meg, two more members of the team began work to shrink computers using transistors, and by November 1953 they had created the 48-bit first operational transistor computer. STC manufactured this one, and a larger one appeared in April 1955, commercialized in a modified form as the Metrovick 950. Kilburn's interest was that the machines provided experience in creating transistor circuits.

Kilburn's big venture was the MUSE (microsecond) computer. When the machine was finished, it incorporated techniques such as multiprogramming, spooling, virtual storage, and others that were not yet developed when he started in 1956. MUSE was on a level with the UNIVAC LARC and the IBM Stretch, beyond the resources of Manchester. After failing to attract support from the government or Ferranti, Kilburn shrank the original plan. When Ferranti came aboard in 1959 along with a £300,000 grant from the National Research Development Corporation, the now-named Atlas was under way. It included a capacity to deal with core and drum interchangeably as well as a precursor to virtual memory. Kilburn was manager and designer of some circuits. The three Atlas systems went to the

Universities of London and Manchester and the Rutherford Laboratory.

In 1960, Kilburn became professor of computer engineering, and in 1963 he began a multiyear creation of the United Kingdom's first computer science department. In 1964, he became head, with twelve members in the department. The department, originating from engineering, was more oriented toward hardware than many departments elsewhere, which tended to arise from mathematics.

In 1966, Kilburn began the MU5, his last major project. MU5 was to consist of three machines capable of running high-level language programs: a small and low-priced computer, a scientific computer with twenty times the throughput of Atlas, and a multiprocessor. Only the scientific computer actually materialized. The design proposal was resented in 1968. The university and International Computers and Tabulators (ICT) worked together, and the Science Research Council provided £630,000 because of the economic potential. ICT was bought by a company that did not acknowledge the contributions of Kilburn and the university, and a dispute ensued that lasted until Kilburn retired in 1981.

PERSONAL LIFE

Kilburn was not impressed with the research into "thinking machines, talking machines, and all that sort of claptrap," according to his secretary, Joan Hart. On first impression he was self-contained and cautious, speaking carefully and choosing exactly the right words. He was, however, a powerful figure, a natural leader with a strong and at times dominating personality, and those who worked with or under him were loyal, devoted to him and even fond of him.

Over the course of his career, Kilburn received many honors: He became a Fellow of the Royal Society in 1965; won the W. Wallace McDowell Award, awarded by the Institute of Electrical and Electronics Engineers (IEEE), in 1971; became a Commander of the British Empire in 1973; won the British Computer Society IT Award in 1973; was named a Distinguished Fellow of the British Computer Society in 1974; won the Royal Medal of the Royal Society in 1978; received an honorary doctorate of science from the University of Bath in 1979; and became a Fellow of the Computer History Museum in 2000. He won the IEEE Computer Society Computer Pioneer Award (1982), the Eckert-Mauchly Award (1983), and the Mountbatten Medal (1997). At the University of Manchester, the building that houses the computer science school is named after him.

> ### Affiliation: Victoria University of Manchester
>
> After being seconded from radar work at Telecommunications Research Establishment (TRE), Tom Kilburn remained at Manchester University for the remainder of his professional career. There he and Frederic C. Williams developed the first high-speed random access memory, the CRT storage device that provided the basis for the Manchester Baby and later digital stored-program computers. Kilburn and his associates also developed commercial computers into the mid-1960s. Meanwhile, he was rising through the ranks, creating the first British computer science department and eventually becoming chancellor of the university. He retired in 1981.

In 1943, he had married Irene Marsden, and together they raised a son and a daughter. He gardened, played piano, and followed the Manchester United football team. When the Mercury was finished in 1958, the department was having a celebration party when a phone call to an engineer notified them about the Manchester United tragedy at Munich, with the loss of most of the team and eight journalists. The party ended abruptly. Kilburn was thrilled when Manchester United won the European Cup in 1968; he went to Wembley for the match, and he was in the crowd that welcomed the team home in Manchester. He was equally excited with the team's triple success in 1999, when it won the Union of European Football Associations (UEFA) Super Cup.

Kilburn retired in 1981, at age sixty, to spend more time with Irene; she died, however, two weeks before his retirement. He spent one day per month in the department, but most of his time he spent with his son and daughter. He died in 2001 following pneumonia contracted after abdominal surgery.

John H. Barnhill

FURTHER READING

Anderson, David P. "Tom Kilburn: A Pioneer of Computer Design." *Annals of the History of Computing* 31.2 (2009): 82–86. Print. A well-documented brief overview of the life and career of Tom Kilburn that includes abundant sources suitable for additional research.

Copeland, B. Jack, ed. *Alan Turing's Automatic Computing Engine: The Master Codebreaker's Struggle to Build the Modern Computer*. New York: Oxford UP, 2005. Print. Emphasizes that credit for the Kilburn-Williams computer should be shared with Alan Turing and John von Newman, that Kilburn and Williams had no knowledge of computers when they arrived at Manchester.

—, ed. *Colossus: The Secrets of Bletchley Park's Codebreaking Computers.* Rpt. New York: Oxford UP, 2010. Print. A collection of essays about the successful British code breaking effort in World War II. Includes information on Kilburn.

Hart, Joan. "Personal Memories of the Late Professor Tom Kilburn CBE FRS." 1 May 2001. School of Computer Science, University of Manchester. Web. 1 May 2012. Recollections by Kilburn's longtime secretary from a personal perspective.

Napper, Brian. "Tom Kilburn (1921–2001)." Jan. 2001. School of Computer Science, University of Manchester. Web. 1 May 2012. A detailed chronological overview of Kilburn's professional career.

"Thanks for the Memory." *Computerworld* 39.43 (2005): 27. *Academic Search Complete.* Web. 25 May 2012. A brief and straightforward sidebar discusses how the Williams-Kilburn tube worked and why it mattered.

JACK KILBY

Cocreator of the integrated circuit

Born: November 8, 1923; Jefferson City, Missouri
Died: June 20, 2005; Dallas, Texas
Primary Field: Computer science
Specialty: Computer hardware
Primary Company/Organization: Texas Instruments

INTRODUCTION

Integrated circuits are the foundation for modern electronics. Jack Kilby was coinventor of the integrated circuit. Kilby also patented the portable electronic calculator and a thermal printer among his sixty patents. The Australian Computer Society's Information Age *magazine listed Kilby as number one in its list of top fifty innovators, ranking ahead of Steve Jobs, Bill Gates, Tim Berners-Lee, Douglas Engelbart, Gordon E. Moore, and others. According to the chairman of Texas Instruments, Tom Engibous, Kilby ranks with Henry Ford, Thomas Edison, and the Wright brothers for the significance of his contributions to the way the world's people now live.*

EARLY LIFE

Jack St. Clair Kilby grew up n Great Bend, Kansas, where his father ran the local power company. When Kilby was in high school, an ice storm knocked out power lines. Kilby used amateur radio to let his audience know what was happening. That was Kilby's first exposure to the ability of electronics to bring people closer and reduce the fears generated by being isolated. Kilby became fascinated by electronics, which he studied at the University of Illinois. He spent two years at Illinois; then, during World War II, he enlisted in the Army, where he went through radio operator school in the Signal Corps and then served in the Office of Strategic Services (predecessor to the Central Intelligence Agency) in communications. He completed his undergraduate work after the war ended, taking electrical engineering courses at the University of Illinois in 1946.

Jack Kilby.

Anticipating his career after college, Kilby sent letters to more than two dozen electronics companies inquiring about work, and in 1948 he took a position at Centralab (a subsidiary of Globe-Union), located in Milwaukee, which produced switches, volume controls, ceramic capacitors, and other devices for consumer electronics. At the same time, he earned a master's in electrical engineering from the University of Wisconsin Extension in Milwaukee, awarded in 1950. Kilby's first job at Centralab was to work on silk screen circuits to make resistor-capacitor combinations for the burgeoning manufacture of television sets. This work involved integrating vacuum tubes into larger circuits and standardizing connections to make not only televisions but also hearing aids and other electronic devices. Like all the best engineers of the time, Kilby faced a reality that the technology available was inadequate to allow them to create the electrical products they could envision. The technology required assembling and connecting by hand hundreds, perhaps thousands, of components, soldering them, and then connecting them to vacuum tubes.

LIFE'S WORK

Throughout the 1950s, vacuum tube technology had defined the limits of progress in electronics. The transistor had been developed by William Shockley, Walter Brattain, and John Bardeen at Bell Laboratories. However, the technology was not yet commercially disseminated. In 1952, however, Bell licensed the technology to more than two dozen companies, among them Centralab, and Kilby was among approximately one hundred engineers sent to attend lectures at Bell Labs' headquarters in Murray Hill, New Jersey, to learn about the technology. Kilby then returned to Centralab to work on making transistors for use in Centralab's hearing aids.

In May 1958, Kilby moved to Dallas and joined Texas Instruments to work in microminiaturization. His job was to figure out how to shrink electronics, to make the components as small as possible. The Signal Corps Micro-Module program was working with the idea that the components could be put onto small square ceramic wafers and connected to each other by three riser wires along the edges. RCA had the prime contract. Kilby did not like the idea. He wanted to make all the components in one operation with the same material. Kilby was thinking about capacitors and resistors and transistors, about how to array them, how to make them most efficient. On July 24, 1958, he had an idea. If capacitors, resistors, and transistors were all made of the same material instead of being made of different material as the

Affiliation: Texas Instruments

Texas Instruments debuted the integrated circuit on March 24, 1959, as the "solid circuit" at the Institute of Radio Engineers' convention in New York's Waldorf-Astoria Hotel. The demonstration model was a multivibrator. The first major release was the Series 51 of October 1961, which sold for $95 in small amounts, $65 in lots of one hundred. The Series 52 came out in late 1962, the Series 54 that swept the transistor market in 1964. While Texas Instruments fiddled, Intel took over the personal computer microchip market. Then Texas Instruments reorganized and tripled market value from 1996 to $35 billion, bringing in $1.35 billion per year in free cash flow. It recovered by taking the market for the microprocessors that made cell phones into multifeatured handheld camera-jukebox devices. It also dominated the market for big-screen television technology, making it brighter, bigger, and cheaper but also highly profitable. Texas Instruments beat not only Intel but also Qualcomm. In the early 1990s, the company was in oil and gas exploration, radar and missiles, educational toys; it was bloated and losing semiconductors as Intel took the PC microprocessor market and the memory chip, Texas Instrument's long-standing bread and butter, became dirt cheap. Texas Instruments then lost CEO Jerry Junkins to a heart attack in 1996 as he was trying to turn the company around. The semiconductor chief had figured out that chips that were previously used only for speak and spell were a natural for the cell phone. Then the big screen chip market came alive, and so did Texas Instruments.

conventional wisdom dictated, then the same chip could be resistor, capacitor, or transistor, and he could connect without restriction to form a circuit. He said that he used the bulk effect in the silicon for resistors and p-n junctions for capacitors. Left alone while the others vacationed, he created the prototype of the integrated circuit with resistors diffused in silicon or using the bulk effect and capacitors using p-n junctions.

Kilby's invention was based on a transistor only a decade old. His working model was the basis for the smart device revolution. He recognized, like all smart engineers, that the massive wiring jobs, the tyranny of numbers, was going to kill electronics. He used the semiconductor germanium, transistors, and wires, and built the prototype, which management did not recognize as significant until he later put it into a working pocket calculator. By September 12, 1958, his idea was to use a sliver of germanium on a piece of glass, half the size of a paper clip, connected to an oscilloscope by a few wires. Kilby threw a switch and his colleagues saw a working circuit. The same idea came to Robert Noyce on the West Coast four months later. Kilby showed his sketches to his bosses and began building the circuit he had demonstrated on September 12. Work continued, and on March 6, 1959, Texas Instruments announced the breakthrough. In 1960, the company sent out chips to customers for evaluation.

Integrated circuits were not an overnight success. They had only tens of components rather than the hundreds or thousands of vacuum tubes. The first major contract was for the Minuteman missile, a contract to design and build twenty-two special circuits, and after that the chip began finding uses in consumer products. In 1966, Kilby found a commercial application when he created the first handheld calculator. By the end of his career, Kilby had more than sixty patents.

The floodgates opened, and engineers' imaginations ran wild. Smaller and smaller chips held more and more components, with a Pentium 4 chip holding 169 million transistors. The microchip made personal computing possible and ever faster. Kilby never ceased to be amazed and delighted at the way his invention spread into unimagined tools, which dropped precipitously in cost.

Kilby shared the Nobel Prize in Physics with Zhores I. Alferov and Herbert Kroemer. The latter two received the award, in the words of the Nobel Foundation, "for developing semiconductor heterostructures used in high-speed- and opto-electronics"; the other half of the award went to Kilby's foundational work "for his part in the invention of the integrated circuit." Noyce of Fairchild Semiconductor, now acknowledged as coinventor of the microchip with Kilby, had died in 1990; he was also a cofounder of Intel. Noyce had used silicon rather than germanium. The legal battle between Texas Instruments and Fairchild was resolved on appeal in Noyce's favor, but before that, in 1966, both sides agreed that Kilby was the originator of the integrated circuit.

Although Kilby's invention became ubiquitous—in computers and mobile phones and elsewhere—he was content to work without notice, just like his integrated circuit. His Nobel lecture incorporated a quote from laser-inventor Charles Townes: "It's like the beaver told the rabbit as they stared at the Hoover Dam. 'No,

I didn't build it myself. However, it's based on an idea of mine!'"

PERSONAL LIFE

While overseeing developments at Texas Instruments, Kilby worked as an independent consultant during leave time. He also held the title of distinguished professor of electrical engineering from 1978 to 1984 or 1985 at Texas A&M University. He loved big band music and considered himself lucky if he could locate a radio station that played it.

After retirement from Texas Instruments in 1983, Kilby continued to consult for the firm and remained in a "significant" relationship with the company. He was awarded the David Sarnoff Award (1966), the Medal of Honor from the Institute of Electrical and Electronics Engineers (1986), the National Medal of Science and National Medal of Technology (one of only thirteen to receive the highest technical recognition given by the U.S. government), and the Nobel Prize in Physics (2000). He died from cancer at age eighty-one.

John H. Barnhill

FURTHER READING

Agarwal, Arun. *Nobel Prize Winners in Physics*. New Delhi: APH, 2008. Print. Aside from a history of the awards, the work features brief biographies as well as information on the laureates' contributions.

DeAngelis, Gina, and David J. Bianco. *Computers: Processing the Data*. Minneapolis: Oliver, 2005. Print. Includes a chapter on Noyce and Kilby and the integrated circuit debate.

Gawel, Richard. "Jack Kilby, Inventor of the Integrated Circuit." *Electronic Design*. 53.16 (2005): 25. Web. 1 May 2012. A brief overview of Kilby's accomplishment, with a focus on his breakthrough during his first summer Texas Instruments.

Huff, Howard R. *Into the Nano Era: Moore's Law Beyond Planar Silicon CMOS*. Berlin: Springer, 2009. Print. On the fiftieth anniversary of the creation of the integrated circuit, the question is whether Moore's law and increasing capacity/decreasing cost remain valid.

"Jack Kilby." *The Economist*, 9 July 2005: 75. *Academic Search Complete*. Web. 1 May 2012. A biographical sketch, from Kilby's early life in Kansas to the end of his career.

Kilby, Jack. "Autobiography." 8 Dec. 2000. *Nobelprize. org*. Web. 12 Aug. 2012. Kilby's thousand-word sketch of his life, written upon the occasion of his winning the Nobel Prize in Physics.

---. "An Interview with Jack S. Kilby." Interview by Arthur L. Norberg. 21 June 1984. Charles Babbage Institute. Web. 12 Aug. 2012. Detailed first-hand coverage of Kilby's entire career to 1984.

---. "Turning Potential into Reality: The Invention of the Integrated Circuit." 8 Dec. 2000. *Nobelprize.org.* Web. 12 Aug. 2012. Kilby's Nobel lecture upon his becoming a Nobel laureate in physics "for his part in the invention of the integrated circuit." Recount-

ing the developments that laid the foundation for microcomputing.

Rostky, George. "The IC's Surprising Birth." *Mechanical Engineering* 122.6 (2000): 68. *Academic Search Complete.* Web. 29 May 2012. Overview of the development of the integrated circuit.

Ulanoff, Lance."Thank You, Jack Kilby." *PC Magazine* 27.13 (2008): 8. *Academic Search Complete.* Web. 29 May 2012. Short sidebar about the significance of Kilby's invention.

Thomas Kurtz

Codesigner of the BASIC programming language

Born: February 22, 1928; Oak Park, Illinois
Died: -
Primary Field: Computer science
Specialty: Computer software
Primary Company/Organization: Dartmouth College

Introduction

Thomas Kurtz taught computer science and mathematics at Dartmouth for thirty-seven years. With John G. Kemeny, Kurtz collaborated on projects including the design and development of the Dartmouth Time-Sharing System (DTSS) and the Beginner's All-purpose Symbolic Instruction Code (BASIC). In 1974, they received the American Federation of Information Processing Societies' first Pioneer's Day award, and in 1983 they founded True BASIC, Inc., to market and promote their standardized version of BASIC.

Early Life

Thomas Eugene Kurtz was born in the Chicago suburb of Oak Park, to Oscar Christ Kurtz, who was employed at the headquarters of the International Lion's Club, and Helen Bell Kurtz. Kurtz attended Knox College in Galesburg, Illinois, planning to major in physics. After taking all available mathematics courses, he switched to statistics, accepting his adviser's suggestion that the field would allow him to use his mathematical background in many different scientific areas. Kurtz graduated with a bachelor's degree in mathematics in 1950.

Kurtz went to graduate school at Princeton University. Forman Acton of the electrical engineering department triggered his interest in computing. Acton got Kurtz a summer position at the Institute of Numerical

Analysis, National Bureau of Standards, on the University of California, Los Angeles, campus. Kurtz spent the summer attending lectures on computing and getting acquainted with many of the early computer pioneers.

Kurtz spent 1952 through 1956 as research assistant in the Analytical Research Group at Princeton, writing programs to solve classified problems, including those dealing with effectiveness of air-to-air rocket

Thomas Kurtz.

salvoes. He used an IBM card-programmed calculator. Sometimes he transferred cards from the output bin to the input hopper on the night shift. In 1956, he received his Ph.D. in mathematical statistics from Princeton.

LIFE'S WORK

John Kemeny recruited Kurtz to the Dartmouth mathematics department, which Kemeny chaired. Kemeny had taught at Princeton until 1953, even living a short distance from Kurtz for a time, but the two did not meet before the recruitment. Kurtz was assigned to liaise with the New England Regional Computer Center at the Massachusetts Institute of Technology (MIT). The IBM-funded center gave access to northeastern educational institutions. At MIT, Kurtz learned assembly language programming for the IBM 704, the first commercial machine with a magnetic core memory. When Dartmouth bought an LGP-30 in 1959, Kurtz became director of computing. The machine at first attracted only a handful of faculty and student users; Kurtz wanted to give access to the entire student body. Because users could not reserve time but had to give their programs to staff for batch processing, it could take a day to deliver results to users. Kurtz and Kemeny began working on a primitive time-sharing computer, to allow many users to access the computer simultaneously, with the computer running each user's program for short stretches of time. Their first true time-sharing computer, developed with General Electric, went into operation in 1964, and the Dartmouth Time-Sharing System (DTSS) was born. Kurtz and Kemeny also developed the DTSS to resolve the problem of long delays between runs of a debugging process.

The DTTS was the prototype for university and other organizations' time-sharing systems, quickly adopted across the country. It used the GE-235 as a central processor and a GE Datanet-30 for communications with terminals across the campus. Functions could be as simple as checking out a library book. All Dartmouth students and students from area colleges had unlimited access. Small jobs, more commonly associated with students, had priority over large ones, more typically faculty jobs. Over time, Kurtz and Kemeny simplified the interface so an average student could learn enough in an hour to use the system.

Their work on the DTSS reflected Kurtz and Kemeny's goal of providing a friendly computing experience for all users, especially undergraduates—including those who were not scientifically or mathematically inclined. The first simplified language was the Dartmouth Simplified code (Darsimco), followed by the Dartmouth Oversimplified Programming Experiment (DOPE). Beginning in 1963, after seven years, BASIC began to emerge. In 1964, it debuted, gaining rapid acceptance among not only students but also faculty and staff. BASIC, a descendant of the more difficult languages Fortran and ALGOL, was much easier to use. Kurtz and Kemeny relied heavily on undergraduate programmers for support. They included BASIC in the two introductory courses that most undergraduates took, and they required that all students write a program as part of the course. BASIC commands are based in English and thus intuitive and transparent: SAVE, RUN, END, PRINT, and so on. BASIC spread through a grassroots movement to high schools, colleges, and businesses—and new varieties of BASIC began to emerge and spread as well.

The original BASIC, although copyrighted, was free to all. Because hundreds of iterations developed, there was incompatibility and chaos. Kurtz and Kemeny wanted to remove the bad reputation that some of the poor versions were giving BASIC. In 1974, the American National Standards Institute (ANSI) began seeking a voluntary standard; the minimal standard would appear in 1978 and the full standard in 1984. Kurtz chaired the subcommittee on standardization and took the opportunity to improve BASIC while meeting the new specifications.

Kemeny and Kurtz had written the original version of BASIC from scratch. Their BASIC offered matrix manipulation, local variables, advanced graphics, and features that other BASIC versions lacked. They were naturally embarrassed by the simplistic imitators of the early versions, the ones they had long surpassed, especially when the dumbed-down clones became standard on virtually every computer, from PC to mainframe. BASIC became passé as critics defined it, based on the impostors, as out of date. To keep really bad versions of BASIC from entering the standardization competition, Kurtz and Kemeny put together True BASIC. In 1983, Kurtz, Kemeny, and others established True BASIC, Inc., to sell True BASIC to schools and colleges. The price was to be low enough to allow widespread use. Testing began at Dartmouth, with the first version intended for an IBM PC and versions for other brands to be issued each quarter thereafter. True BASIC included the capacity for structured programming, which allows the writing of small and clear segments (subroutines) and use of those segments to build larger programs. True BASIC also has a graphics module that makes

Affiliation: True BASIC, Inc.

In the wee hours of May 1, 1964, about 4:00 A.M., two Dartmouth undergraduates, pulling an all-nighter while the professors slept, successfully ran BASIC programs on two separate teletype terminals in the basement of Dartmouth's College Hall. Thus began BASIC, which ran on the Dartmouth Time-Sharing System (DTSS), the network of simple terminals tied to a large computer, an idea five years in the making. DTSS was the prototype for larger and more sophisticated time-sharing networks and in conjunction with BASIC became the basis for many modern applications. Microsoft founders Paul Allen and Bill Gates would take BASIC to the personal computer in 1975, and it continued after the turn of the century to be a popular introductory language for would-be programmers.

True BASIC was John Kemeny and Thomas Kurtz's reaction to the proliferating versions of BASIC. True BASIC was a trim version compliant with the standards of both the American National Standards Institute (ANSI) and the International Standards Organization (ISO). True BASIC met the ANSI standard, while QuickBASIC, GWBASIC, and others did not. However, QBASIC and QuickBASIC ran on tens to hundreds of thousands of PCs, making them, not True BASIC, the de facto (if not the approved) standard. Nevertheless, with an ANSI standard (and only True BASIC qualified), all the Macintoshes, Sun workstations, Amigas, and other machines would be using the same language. Thus, Kurtz and Kemeny founded True BASIC, Inc., to promote the standard BASIC for all the different machines. The company headquarters were in West Lebanon, New Hampshire.

picture drawing on a monitor easier. True BASIC was powerful but simple enough for a beginner, thus holding the same value as the original.

First on the market with the only ANSI standard, Kurtz and Kemeny sold a sampler edition. This $14.95 version was available for any PC-compatible or Macintosh machine, and it included a full version of the language, capability to create files up to 150 lines, and a paperback book by Kurtz and Kemeny that explained BASIC in 208 pages. The handbook ignored Microsoft, making conversion difficult but not giving publicity to a competitor. True BASIC differed from other BASICS: It had a background program compiler capability

like QuickBASIC, so it was fast and convenient. It was strong in mathematics and string handling. However, it had a clunky environment, not up to the quality of more sophisticated menu-driven alternatives.

Aside from his Dartmouth duties, Kurtz was director of Dartmouth's Kiewit Computation Center from 1966 to 1975 and director of the Office of Academic Computing from 1975 to 1978. Between 1974 and 1984, he chaired the American National Standards Institute committee to develop a standard BASIC; this was the period during which he and Kemeny formed True BASIC, Inc. and promoted it for standardization of BASIC. Kurtz was also the director of the Computer and Information Systems program at Dartmouth from 1980 to 1988. He worked as principal investigator for a variety of National Science Foundation programs that promoted computing in education, and he was active in other bodies devoted to using computing in teaching, including the Pierce Panel of the President's Scientific Advisory Committee. From 1987 to 1994, he was with the International Standards Organization's working group on an international BASIC standard.

PERSONAL LIFE

Kurtz regarded his work as his life. There is little evidence that he had a life outside the department and his association with Kemeny. The two coauthored *Basic Statistics* (published in 1963) and *BASIC Programming* (published in 1967).

Kurtz held an honorary degree from Knox College (1985) and was named a Computer Pioneer by the Institute of Electrical and Electronics Engineers (IEEE) in 1991. He became a Fellow of the Association for Computing Machinery in 1994.

John H. Barnhill

FURTHER READING

Alfred, Randy. "May 1, 1964: First Basic Program Runs." 1 May 2008. Dartmouth College. Web. 15 May 2012. A brief entry appearing on the Dartmouth alumni website on the notable first success of BASIC.

Campbell, Tom. "Basically, a True Bargain." *Compute!* 15.8 (1993): 56. *Academic Search Complete*. Web. 15 May 2012. A 1993 article evaluating True BASIC.

Hauben, Jay Robert. "John G. Kemeny: BASIC and DTSS; Everyone a Programmer." *Computer Pioneers*. Ed. John A. N. Lee. Los Alamitos: IEEE Computer Society Press, 1995. N. pag. Print. Rehearses Kemeny's career and the development, with Kurtz, of BASIC and the DTSS.

Kemeny, John. *Man and the Computer*. New York: Scribner, 1972. Print. The history of computing and human interactions with computers from one of the pioneers of that evolution, the coauthor of BASIC.

Knapp, Susan. "Back to BASICs 40 Years Later." *Vox*. 3 May 2004. Web. 15 May 2012. A retrospective in the online version of the Dartmouth magazine, *Vox*.

Lohr, Steve. *Go To: The Story of the Math Majors, Bridge Players, Engineers, Chess Wizards, Maverick Scientists and Iconoclasts*. New York: Basic, 2001. Print. Includes some interesting pages on the content of the Dartmouth Time-Sharing System and the liberal arts BASIC course.

Peterson, I. "A BASIC Standard for Digital Dialects." *Science News* 124.26/27 (1983): 404. Print. *Academic Search Complete*. Web. 15 May 2012. The spread of BASIC led to the need for a national standard, explained in this 1983 article.

Slater, Robert. *Portraits in Silicon*. Cambridge: MIT, 1989. Print. Chapters deal with computing pioneers, the founders and movers as of the late 1980s. Although dated, contains informative material on Kurtz, Kemeny, and both BASIC and True BASIC.

SANDRA L. KURTZIG

Founder of ASK Computer Systems

Born: October 21, 1947; Chicago, Illinois
Died: -
Primary Field: Computer science
Specialty: Computer software
Primary Company/Organization: ASK

INTRODUCTION

The first multimillion-dollar software entrepreneur was not Bill Gates of Microsoft, Marc Andreessen of Netscape, or Larry Ellison of Oracle. Rather, it was Sandra L. Kurtzig of ASK, a company she founded in 1972 to provide inventory-tracking software to manufacturing companies, which at its peak had annual sales of $450 million. Kurtzig was a key player in establishing the business-to-business software industry. She began what is now common in the industry, the creation of easy-to-use business management software for manufacturing companies.

EARLY LIFE

Sandra L. Kurtzig was born in Chicago in 1946. Her father, Barney Brody, the son of Russian immigrants, developed real estate, and her mother, Marian, wrote as a police reporter for a newspaper before taking on the job of decorator for the father's real estate ventures. The family relocated to Los Angeles when Sandra was eleven.

In high school, Kurtzig took advanced courses graduated with an A average. She sold towels at the Bullocks department store in high school. At the University of California, Los Angeles (UCLA), she majored in mathematics with minored in chemistry. Her summer job at the computer center showed her that she did not know much about computers, so her next summer job was as a mathematics aide at TRW, the aircraft systems company. She learned the computer language BASIC instead of the more difficult assembler language

Sandra L. Kurtzig.

that had stumped her at the computer center. She graduated from UCLA at age twenty and then earned her master's in aeronautical engineering at Stanford University. She then accepted a sales job at IBM, was dissatisfied there, went to Europe for the summer, then married Arie Kurtzig on December 1, 1968. In New Jersey she had a few short-term sales jobs before taking a position at General Electric (GE) selling computer time-sharing services.

LIFE'S WORK

In 1972, Kurtzig left her job at GE to start a family. Because she wanted additional income and something to keep her mind occupied, she started a part-time software programming business at home. Her initial capital investment was $2,000. Her first client asked her to write a program for tracking inventory and giving timely manufacturing information. She hired several computer and engineering graduates to write standardized applications that would suit not only the first customer but also manufacturers in the local area. She took her technical background and awareness of customer needs and through her staff worked to produce the software.

In 1972, the business was based in her apartment; Kurtzig had wanted a part-time job that she could manage while the children were sleeping. Soon, however, she was working eighteen-hour days. In 1974, she incorporated her company as ASK Computer Systems, Inc.

Because she could not attract venture capital in Silicon Valley, she reinvested earnings into the company. She persuaded the local Hewlett-Packard (HP) management to let her crews use the one of the plant's 3000 series minicomputers at night, working from 6:00 P.M. to 6:00 A.M. By 1976, ASK was in its own building. By 1978, the company had its first salable product, MaMa, later called ManMan, a package of programs in manufacturing management. ManMan was one of the first enterprise product management (ERP) and inventory control programs. Next Kurtzig convinced HP to preload her software on its minicomputers, allowing her to market a turnkey system to managers leery of computers in the precomputer era.

The company grew, despite being unable to afford a marketing staff and brochures. It emphasized ideas, hard work, and commitment, selling systems to large corporate clients such as HP and Hughes Electronics. Having the HP tie gave ASK entré into other corporations and markets. ASK sales rose from $2.8 million in 1979 to $39 million in 1983, making it the eleventh

fastest-growing American company between 1978 and 1982. Kurtzig took the company public in 1981, and in two years a small equity offering and a two-for-one split meant that earnings per share doubled.

ManMan tracked inventory and customer orders on the floor. Kurtzig had created versions for use on Digital Equipment Corporation (DEC) and Hewlett-Packard minicomputers at $40,000 to $200,000 per package. That worked during the 1970s, but by the late 1980s customers wanted portability, which meant rewriting ManMan to be compatible with the nearly universal Unix operating system. Kurtzig acknowledged that ASK was coasting, living off past successes, and living reasonably well with decent earnings and revenues. That opportunities passed ASK by did not seem to be an urgent problem. Kurtzig tried to light a fire under the board, and when that failed she quit in February 1989.

Kurtzig left the company in the hands of fifty-one-year-old Ronald Braniff, a division chief at Tymshare and an ASK board member since 1980. He seemed a good fit, and Kurtzig blessed the choice. For four years the company did well, with profits rising. However, in 1989 sales flattened at $79 million. The product line was still ManMan, last updated contemporaneously with Kurtzig's decision to step down.

Flat sales and the prospect of ongoing stagnation led the board to ask Kurtzig to return. Braniff resigned shortly thereafter. Kurtzig revitalized the company by ignoring the hierarchy, finding the person she needed when she needed that person, heedless of the managers and supervisors in between. Morale was elevated. Kurtzig put in twelve-hour days and bought back 1.3 million shares of ASK, bringing her stake to nearly 10 percent. The stock was at $8 per share, down from its 1985 peak of $25.

ASK developed software for HP, DEC, and Sun using Unix. Marketing, which was fragmented after the 1989 purchase of Data 3 Systems (a maker of manufacturing software for IBM minicomputers), reorganized into a single department. Kurtzig went on the road to reassure investors and customers that ASK was repenting past sins and moving in a new direction. At that point the largest customer was Seagate Technologies, maker of disk drives, and Oracle was threatening to suck ASK's customers into its database software. "Kiss your ASK goodbye" was the slogan, according to Julie Pitta in *Forbes*. Kurtzig, however, was accustomed to competition. ASK remained the leading independent supplier of manufacturing planning software despite the

Affiliation: ASK

The ASK Group produces business software, known as enterprise resource planning software, that meets the needs of manufacturing companies. Working out of her apartment's spare bedroom, Sandra Kurtzig initially developed business applications. In 1974, ASK was incorporated, but not until 1978 did the flagship product, ManMan, a minicomputer application that allowed small businesses to control operations in an entire factory, take off. ManMan, short for manufacturing management, was sold at a six-figure price point and was targeted to small or medium-sized manufacturers. For smaller users, time sharing was available for a small monthly fee. Kurtzig got rich, retired, and let the company fend for itself.

ASK prospered after Kurtzig left, with profits at $13.5 million in fiscal year 1989. However, sales flattened out at $79 million, and the product line had not been upgraded since Kurtzig left. In late 1989 the board asked Kurtzig to resume a more active role. She brought in new entrepreneurial talent, had employees rate the managers, then gave awards to the highly rated ones and pink slips to the others. She discontinued the practice of allowing senior managers to set their own bonuses and raises. She made the software compatible with multiple platforms. New products aided communication between different systems and programs. ManMan/X, introduced in 1992, was an update of the original, and it had twenty-seven nodules.

Restructuring in 1992 into the ASK Group with three businesses—ASK Computer Systems, Data 3, and Ingres—the company also underwent a management shakeup. By 1992, ASK was again soaring, and sales of $400 million made it the largest public company founded and run by a woman. Kurtzig retired again to the chairmanship, let the professionals manage her company, and left permanently in 1993. Charles Wang's Computer Associates bought ASK in 1994.

best efforts of rivals Cullinet (absorbed by Computer Associates), IBM, and HP.

Kurtzig rejected the then-standard argument that a woman in a man's world had to think like a man. She refused to manage through the male-dictated hierarchical arrangement. Rather, she was honest and open, sharing information with workers, leaving her door open most of the time. She also walked the floor, provided strokes such as hugs and compliments to staff in front of their peers, allowing natural empathy and emotion to come through, something that men tended to avoid, if they even had the capacity. She was among the first to establish the softer approach to management—and negotiation, being willing to give instead of regarding a victory as winner-take-all.

In 1990, ASK purchased the Ingres Corporation. To acquire the revenues to do so, it had to sell 30 percent of the company to HP and Electronic Data Systems (EDS), and many shareholders were not pleased by the financing move. However, ASK was already using Ingres software to link its clients' accounting and manufacturing departments to the ASK database, and HP made the hardware that ran ASK's software, in return for which ASK resold HP products. Along with HP, EDS had a history of alliances with manufacturing companies that could offer business to ASK. The deal made sense, therefore, on several levels. ASK became ASK Group (consisting of ASK Computer Systems, Data 3, and Ingres) in 1992, a global company with annual revenues of $400 million, and launched an update of its main product as ManMan/X.

Nonetheless, ASK declined. Kurtzig left the company in 1993, and by 1994, it was purchased by Computer Associates. Kurtzig became a managing partner of SLK Investment Partners and mentored investors in entrepreneurial technology companies. She also taught a business for engineering course at Stanford University.

In 2008, Kurtzig was chairman of the board of E-Benefits, a human resources and insurance provider she had founded with her son Andrew in 1996. In 2011, she decided to come out of retirement after talking with Salesforce.com chief executive officer (CEO) Marc Benjoff, her Hawaiian neighbor, about how the world of manufacturing management software had changed since the 1970s. Benjoff wanted software to handle the worldwide scope of the business of the twenty-first century, and she agreed to start up a new company, albeit reluctantly. Her ManMan software was still in use and had a solid reputation. In 2012, she started Kenandy, Inc., to transform the world of enterprise management software, this time designed to work in the cloud to support the community of global manufacturing companies. Her capitalization was $10.5 million. The company is named after sons Ken and Andy.

PERSONAL LIFE

Kurtzig and her husband Arie had two sons, Ken and Andy. In 1982, the couple divorced; the boys were nine and six. By 1983, Kurtzig had a net worth of $65 million. In 1985, tired of the pace, she resigned all but her chairmanship of ASK and turned her attention to her family. She achieved her goals of spending more time with her two sons, traveling, and writing her autobiography before returning to ASK in 1989.

For four years, Kurtzig did other things, including a stint with ABC's *Good Morning America*. She and her family built a home in Hawaii, and she wrote her autobiography. Although she returned to ASK in 1989 and stayed for only four years, during that time she set the company on a stable footing before its declining performance led to its acquisition by Computer Associates.

Kurtzig has received many awards. As the first woman to take a technology company public, she has appeared in *Business Week*'s list of the top fifty corporate leaders. She has served on the boards of Harvard Business School, the Hoover Institution, Stanford's School of Engineering, Stanford Engineering Strategic Council, UCLA's Anderson Graduate School of Management, and the University of California, Berkeley's Haas School of Management.

John H. Barnhill

FURTHER READING

Gage, Deborah. "Silicon Valley Pioneer Sandra Kurtzig Back in Start-Up Game with Kenandy." *Wall Street Journal* 29 Aug. 2011. Web. 4 May 2012. A brief discussion of how Kurtzig came out of retirement, this time with venture capital, to create a new cloud-based software company. Lighthearted and positive.

Hyatt, J. "Should You Start a Business?" *Inc.* 14.2 (1992): 48. *Academic Search Complete*. Web. 4 May 2012. Discusses the experiences of women entrepreneurs in general, with elements of Kurtzig's experience.

Kurtzig, Sandra L., with Tom Parker. *CEO: Building a $400 Million Company from the Ground Up*. New York: Norton, 1991. Print. The autobiography Kurtzig wrote after she left her company the first time. Covers the early years of ASK, up to the company's period of peak performance.

Pitta, Julie. "Mommy Track, Revised." *Forbes* 145.6 (1990): 158–59. *Business Source Complete*. Web. 4 May 2012. Tells the story of Kurtzig's founding, leaving, and returning to ASK, with details of her reasons for doing so.

"Sandra Kurtzig: The First Lady of Computers." *Entrepreneur* 10 Oct. 2008. Web. 4 May 2012. An overview of Kurtzig's career, particularly her role at ASK, with some discussion of her managerial style.

KEN KUTARAGI

Former executive at Sony Computer Entertainment

Born: August 8, 1950; Tokyo, Japan
Died: -
Primary Field: Computer science
Specialty: Computer hardware
Primary Company/Organization: Sony Computer Entertainment

INTRODUCTION

Ken Kutaragi was in large part responsible for the home game console phenomenon, almost singlehandedly forcing Sony out of its complacency and into the PlayStation era. Known as the father of the PlayStation and the Gutenberg of Gaming, Kutaragi was an iconoclast who did not fit the Sony mold. When he began, video games were a relatively small market with a nerdy image; he drove the PlayStation video game system to become a major money maker for Sony.

EARLY LIFE

Ken Kutaragi was born in Tokyo, Japan. His father had a small printing plant, and Kutaragi helped his father after school. Kutaragi always had the desire to tinker, often taking apart toys as a child to see how they worked. This curiosity continued through his teenage years. He learned the intricacies of electronics at Denki Tsushin University, where he acquired a degree in electronics engineering.

LIFE'S WORK

Immediately after graduation, in 1975, Kutaragi began working for Sony in its digital research labs. Sony at that time was a high-energy, creative company, and Kutaragi felt that Sony was on the "fast track." He quickly gained a reputation as an excellent problem solver and a forward-thinking engineer. In the 1970s, as

Ken Kutaragi.

a researcher for Sony, Kutaragi created a liquid crystal display (LCD) projector that Sony rejected; the company thereby failed to capitalize on the new LCD market. Kutaragi's disk-storage camera was years ahead of its time. His sound-processing chip, inspired by a desire to improve on the inferior sound of the Nintendo system his daughter was playing, was produced in secret for Nintendo while he was working for Sony, which had no interest; however, the higher-ups were enraged when they discovered Kutaragi's activities on behalf of a rival firm; he avoided being fired, however, with the support of chief executive officer (CEO) Norio Ohga.

Kutaragi was vindicated in 1990, however, after building the PlayStation, which quickly surpassed the Super Nintendeo Entertainment System as the leading home gaming system. In 1990, when Nintendo backed away from a partnership with Sony to build a game platform, most in Sony wanted to give up on game machines. Kutaragi and a small cadre of in-house dissidents built their own game console from the ground up, and it debuted in 1994. Even then, PlayStation was regarded as undeserving of respect because it was just a game machine. By the end of the 1990s, however, the PlayStation was bringing in 40 percent of the company's profits. PlayStation proved Kutaragi's business model—the use

of low-margin hardware to sell high-margin software—and the rest of Sony began copying him.

In 2000, Kutaragi got the parent company to commit $2.5 billion to the PlayStation 2 (PS2), a departure from the historical game console pattern of combining off-the-shelf components in that it was a completely dedicated game machine. To make the PS2 viable, Kutaragi made sure that developers created ample and original software. In the first thirty months after its introduction PS2 sold 40 million units, double the sales of the original PlayStation in the same number of months. The PS2 as of 2003 was the number-one seller in the global market.

Game players around the world regarded the father of the PlayStation as an object of adoration, but his peers at Sony regarded the PlayStation as a fluke, a lucky guess. Slowly they became aware that it was not all that easy to bring a business to $8 billion from zero. Kutaragi's company provided $1 billion to the parent company in the fiscal year ending March 2003, 60 percent of Sony's operating profits.

When Kutaragi was preparing to debut the PS2 in Japan, his online order site developed a glitch. He was up all night. That was but one of his worries. Kutaragi could be fretful. He also worried about delayed deliveries, a sluggish market, and machines collecting dust in the warehouses. The PS2 was a 128-bit machine that could also play DVD movies and CD music. The PS2 retailed for $370 and provided high-speed, clear graphics offering shadow and a level of detail never before seen in a video game. There was a plan for U.S. owners the next year to tie their PS2s to cable television for downloading and multiplayer online games. The PS2 took $2.5 billion to start but took 75 percent of the market by 2003. Both PS and PS2 exceeded 100 million units sold. Even massive start-up losses were recouped by the sales of the machines and software royalties.

Kutaragi had plans to make PlayStation a separate brand, free of the Sony network. He figured that only an open platform, not one tied to Sony, would attract the game developers. Kutaragi was not sure how such a product would bring in money, but he noted that PS was really boosting Sony stock. The company gave him quite a bit of leeway, because his division was so profitable; in fact, the PS would prove to be Sony's most profitable product. Kutaragi's games division was a $10 billion sales activity, bringing in 58 percent of the company's operating profits.

However, Kutaragi was moving beyond games, assigned the mission of reestablishing the ailing

Affiliation: Sony Computer Entertainment

Founded in the aftermath of World War II and building its early success on transistor radios, Sony is now a $35 billion multinational conglomerate specializing in consumer electronics and ranking seventy-third in the Fortune 500. Sony Computer Entertainment dates to the 1990s, when Ken Kutaragi failed to get a deal with Nintendo to create a CD-ROM-based Nintendo and convinced Sony management to let him create his own, the PlayStation. When Kutaragi prepared to leave in 2007, he left behind a PS3 trailing both Nintendo's and Microsoft's offerings. Cost overruns and problems with the technology cost the company profits and made CEO Howard Stringer's job harder, even as he was two years into selling assets and reforming the company, particularly electronics. In fiscal year 2005, games accounted for 10 percent of Sony's $60 billion in sales but 38 percent of the $560 million operating profit.

Stringer reshuffled games management in November 2006 because of the larger than anticipated losses of $2 billion for the fiscal year. Operating profits were just $635 million. When Kazuo Hirai became chair upon Akira Sato's August 31 retirement, the new president and CEO of Sony Computer Entertainment, the division that produces the PlayStation, was Andrew House. In April 2007, Kutaragi had retired from the ceremonial position as honorary chair of the division. He had given up active management when he moved down from the group CEO position in 2006. In 2011, Sony Computer Entertainment had its first fiscal year profit in five years—$429 million on $19 billion in revenue—mostly by lowering PS3 production costs. Sony planned to release the portable Vita in 2011 as well as to continue growing PS3 and expanding nongaming components.

Kutaragi was Japan-centric. His replacement, Hirai, was Americanized, able to deal with Walmart and software developers on better terms than Kutaragi had done. PS3 stabilized and profits were restored, but Kutaragi was gone from the division he had built from nothing to $9 billion.

electronics firm and steering it toward a brighter future. The rest of Sony was slumping, especially consumer electronics. Kutaragi became a member of the executive board in 2003 and was rumored to be next in line as chairman and CEO, to replace Nobuyuki Idei, age sixty-six. His promotion to the board was intended to revitalize the company, and he did partner Sony with Samsung in the LCD screen business, where Sony had previously failed. He also was working on a simple-to-understand interface for the various Sony digital products—his effort to combine PS2 and the PSX digital video recorder did not fare well in the Japanese market. Kutaragi is an impatient micromanager, and he criticized those who blocked his attempts to revitalize consumer electronics, those who kept the company from working with other companies—both in public and in private. While running the consumer electronics part of the business, he also had to get onto the market the PS Portable, Sony's first handheld (released in 2004), and the PS3.

Kutaragi's move to head consumer electronics in 2003 did not work. Idei handpicked Howard Stringer to run the $60 billion company, removed Kutaragi from the board, and sent him back to being a full-time division chief. After the demotion, Kutaragi took a low-profile stance and let Stringer be the voice of Sony. Kutaragi said he that, although he had liked being in the inner circle, he was back at home in the entertainment division with his team and his PlayStation and was happy to have Stringer and the management team taking care of day-to-day matters so Kutaragi could develop the PS, which represented 120 percent of his life.

Six years earlier, Kutaragi had timed the PS3 to release at the same time as Blu-ray DVD and the Cell multimedia chip. The PS3 was to be the home control center, and Hollywood committed strongly to Sony's Blu-ray format, one of two formats competing to control the high-definition DVD market. The Cell chip was extremely fast, allowing lifelike graphics and realistic game play.

In November 2006, as Kutaragi prepared to put the PS3 into the hands of gamers, he ran into serious problems and had to delay its debut by six months. He acknowledged that incorporating Blu-ray, Cell, and Sixaxis as well as other state-of-the-art technology, set back the PS3 and led to manufacturing delays that kept the PS3 out of players' hands longer than desirable. Analysts said that Kutaragi had mismanaged the product. Subsequent problems slipped the European release into March 2007, halving the number of machines available in Japan and the United States, forcing the company to revise its earnings to reflect larger-than-planned losses in the games division. Once the PS3 was available, users learned that it did not run older games. Three weeks after the debut, the games division reorganized. Kutaragi stepped down in April 2007.

PS and PS2 were smash record breakers, but the PS3 and Station.com (the online service) were not competitive with Xbox Live, the favorite of online gamers. The PS3 with Blu-ray DVD and the Cell microprocessor, was technologically superior to the Wii, but Wii had motion-sensing remote controllers that PS3 lacked. PS3 was still a game machine not a home entertainment hub. U.S. sales of the PS3 as of March 2007 were 1.2 million units. Wii sold 2.1 million, and Xbox 360 sold 5.3 million.

PERSONAL LIFE

Kutaragi is married with children and neither drinks nor smokes. His first dream was to retire at age fifty. Kutaragi is an engineer with marketing savvy and a vision. He was not the typical Sony company man; he was blunt, outspoken, and critical of his colleagues rather than conforming to the Sony style of working by consensus. Kutaragi was in some views cocky, hands-on, and not good at delegating, a lover of the limelight but a visionary who could see ten years in the future and bring his vision to fruition technically.

John H. Barnhill

FURTHER READING

"The Best Managers." *Businessweek* 3815 (2003): 60–69. *Business Source Complete*. Web. 4 May 2012. Discusses Kutaragi's innovative non-Japanese approach in building games into a potential launching pad for Sony's top leadership position. In 2003, he was still a hot property.

"Can Sony's Kutaragi Score Big?" *Businessweek Online* 9 Feb. 2006: 12. *Business Source Complete*. Web. 4 May 2012. The PS3 had problems, and Kutaragi got bumped down, his star diminished. Reportedly he was chastened and quieter, becoming more of a team player.

Frederick, Jim. "Playing His Way to the Next Level." *Time* 162.22 (2003): 84. *Academic Search Complete*. Web. 4 May 2012. The article notes that Kutaragi was hot, with the PS and PS2, and rumored to be in line for the chair's chair. Kutaragi's money comment was that Sony was built on innovation, not gimmicky marketing and sexy design.

Grossman, Lev. "Ken Kutaragi: Gutenberg of Video Games." *Time* 163.17 (2004): 93. *Academic Search Complete*. Web. 4 May 2012. Discusses the way Kutaragi defied the experts and built his reputation and Sony's profits with the PlayStations.

Hall, Kenji. "Game On for Sony PlayStation's New Chief." Businessweek Online 30 Apr. 2007. Business Source Complete. Web. 4 May 2012. Covers Kutaragi's retirement as PS lost market share to Wii and Xbox in 2007.

---. "New Leader for Sony's PlayStation Unit." *Businessweek Online* 13 Dec. 2006: 23. *Business Source Complete*. Web. 4 May 2012. Examines the problems with PS3 that tarnished the Kutaragi mystique.

Kunii, Irene M. "Sony's Indispensable Samurai." *Businessweek* 3673 (2000): 58. *Business Source Complete*. Web. 4 Mar 2012. Covers early PS2 problems with PS3 already in the works.

Lee, Tyler. "PlayStation's Ken Kutaragi Working on Something 'Totally Cool.'" *Ubergizmo.com*. 2 Dec. 2011. Web. 4 May 2012. Kutaragi in 2012 was still the subject of rumors about another breakthrough, a PS4, even as he left the business.

Levy, Steven. "The Father of PlayStation." *Newsweek* 148.21 (2006): 74. *Academic Search Complete*. Web. 4 May 2012. The PS3 was supposed to be the culmination of the Kutaragi's career, the realization of his dream after he had been moved back to design and engineering by Stringer.

Levy, Steven, and Kay Itoi. "Now He's Playing Sony's Game." *Newsweek* 144.17 (2004): 82. Print. Discusses the chastened Kutaragi, with a touch on his early life in his father's shop.

Pham, Alex. "Sony Promotes Andrew House; PlayStation 'Father' Ken Kutaragi Retires." *Los Angeles Times* 29 June 2011. Web. 4 May 2012. Kutaragi officially retired after his term in the position of honorary chair of the entertainment division.

Swearingen, Jake. "Great Intrapreneurs in Business History." 10 Apr. 2008. Web. 4 May 2012. Short sketches of significant computer entrepreneurs.

L

DUY-LOAN LE

First woman named Texas Instruments Senior Fellow

Born: July 17, 1962; Saigon, Vietnam
Died: -
Primary Field: Computer science
Specialty: Computer hardware
Primary Company/Organization: Texas Instruments

INTRODUCTION

Duy-Loan Le came to the United States as a junior high student with limited English proficiency. She worked hard and graduated as her high school valedictorian at age sixteen, graduating from the University of Texas at nineteen. As an engineer at Texas Instruments, she rose through the ranks to become a manager of wireless communications projects and the first Asian American and first woman to be elected a Senior Fellow at that company. She is also known for her dedication to family, community service, and philanthropy.

EARLY LIFE

In 1975, Duy-Loan T. Le came to the United States without her father but with a nine-member family: She is the seventh child in a family of six daughters and three sons. Her father is Thanh Thien Le and her mother, Huong Thi Tang.

Vietnam in the 1970s had only a single engineering school, and her father wanted her to be an engineer. Her father valued education for girls and boys alike, and she graduated second from Nguyen Binh Khiem elementary school in 1973. First in her family to enter junior high school, she seemed headed for an exceptional career.

Then South Vietnam fell to North Vietnam in 1975. Because a sister had married and left for the United States in 1972, Le's mother and eight other siblings left for Houston, Texas, with less than $100—but by luckily airplane rather than among the "boat people." They left Vietnam on April 22, 1975, when Le was only twelve years old; her father and eldest brother stayed behind. The country collapsed, surrendering to North Vietnam, eight days later. Remaining in Vietnam for four years after the family left, Le's father attempted to save some

Duy-Loan Le.

Affiliation: Texas Instruments

Based in Dallas, Texas Instruments is a pioneer in silicon transistors, integrated circuits, semiconductor microprocessors, and pocket calculators. It began, however, in Tulsa, Oklahoma, in 1924, when physicists John Clarence Karcher and Eugene B. McDermott, working in oil exploration, formed Geophysical Research Corporation, a subsidiary of Amerada Petroleum. Relocated to Dallas in 1930, the two formed Geophysical Service, Incorporated, which built military electronics during World War II. In 1951, still focused on military electronics, the company became Texas Instruments (TI).

Shortly thereafter, TI became the first commercial producer of transistors. It created the first portable transistor radio, the first silicon transistors, and the first integrated circuit. In 1959, TI merged with Metals and Controls Corporation of Attleboro, Massachusetts, and during those years it broadened its line of products. The next major step came in 1967, when TI introduced the handheld electronic calculator. This and other consumer electronics were made possible by the microprocessor, or "computer on a chip." In the 1980s, TI sought to produce larger consumer items, such as microcomputers, but indifferent success led to layoffs. Military contracts remained a major contributor to the company's profit margin and, as the company had ups and downs in the 1990s, it attempted to restore profitability through acquisition.

In 2010, TI had revenues nearing $14 billion and approximately 35,000 employees worldwide—down from more than 42,000 employees a decade earlier; in 2001, the semiconductor industry worldwide had experienced a precipitous drop near 40 percent, and so did TI's profitability. In 2011 TI acquired National Semiconductor, and today the revitalized company is a recognized producer of analog electronics, calculators, digital signal processors, digital light processors, integrated circuits, and radio-frequency identification.

---

of the family's assets but failed, and he finally walked out through Thailand, whence the family brought him to the United States.

In Houston, Le was sent back to the sixth grade (in Vietnam she would have been in the eighth grade) because of the language barrier. Initially, she struggled with all but mathematics and art. Baseball helped her to get along with classmates, and her painting drew the attention of the school principal. To overcome the setback, Le worked hard to learn English, carrying a dictionary with her and studying it every day; with help from the school principal and her teachers, she succeeded in getting moved to junior high school, where she belonged, then entering Alief Hastings High School. She cooked for the family, cleaned, worked in a restaurant in the evenings between 5:00 P.M. and 2:00 A.M., and still managed to finish in 1979 as a sixteen-year-old valedictorian in a class of 335 students.

At the University of Texas at Austin, Le took between nineteen and twenty-one hours of course work per semester, in a hurry to get done because she was breaching tradition that said a woman did not leave home until she married. She earned a bachelor of science degree in electrical engineering in 1982, magna cum laude, and her master's degree in business administration while she was working full time. With the income she earned, she bought her parents a house and then bought one of her own. She also became engaged. In 1981, Le was feature in a *Houston Chronicle* article as a "scholastic wonder," and she also received a commendation from the Netherlands' ambassador for her scholastic performance and fund raising on behalf of Vietnamese refugees.

LIFE'S WORK

In 1982, at age nineteen, Le began working at Texas Instruments as a memory design engineer. Between 1985 and 1989, she worked as a liaison between the Texas design team and a Japanese engineering team. The Japanese were accustomed to women serving tea and cleaning the restrooms, not engineering. They got over it and professional respect built a relationship that spanned decades. In 1989, Le became design manager and in 1994 a program manager. Her worldwide projects involved the multibillion-dollar Texas Instruments memory device line in joint ventures with partners on three continents.

In 1998, TI decided to sell the memory division, and Le decided to look for a new job rather than move to the new company. She interviewed with Compaq, but Texas Instruments wanted to keep her, so it put her into digital signal processing; in 2000, she became Digital Signal Processor Advanced Technology Ramp Manager. Texas Instruments also made her a TI Fellow along with another woman, one of the originators of the digital signal processing group. In 2002, Le was elected Senior

Fellow: the first Asian American and the first woman to achieve that honor at Texas Instruments; only four other people, all men, held the title.

Also in 2002, Le founded Sunflower and became the first woman on the National Instruments Corporation board of directors. National Instruments is a NASDAQ company in Austin, and she was the sole woman on its board. It ranked 183rd on *Forbes'* list of 200 Best Small Companies in 2009 and fifty-first on the list of 100 Best Midcaps in 2008.

Le holds more than two dozen patents, with more applications pending. Aside from her patents, she developed a six-month technical training program in use in seven plants in five countries. She was one of the Top 20 Houston Women in Technology in 2000. Her work as advanced technology ramp manager involves digital signal processors, including one that holds a 2004 Guinness record as the fastest single-core digital signal processor in the world. She has been inducted into the Women in Technology International Hall of Fame, has been named a Women of Color National Technologist of the Year and Asian American Engineer of the Year, and is a recipient of the Vietnamese American Golden Torch and the Anita Borg Institute's Women of Vision leadership award.

PERSONAL LIFE

Le married Tuan N. Dao on December 18, 1982, in a Vietnamese traditional wedding. Her husband graduated from the University of Texas the year she started. He is about seven years older, from a family of a dozen children, and a 1975 immigrant from Vietnam. Dao is a senior executive consultant with an oil and gas delivery systems project management company. They decided to wait a decade before having children, allowing time for career development. They then had their first son, Dan Quy-Le Dao, on August 30, 1993. Their second son, Don Quy-Le Dao, was born February 22, 1997.

Le has worked at Texas Instruments on behalf of career advancement for women and minorities, including but not restricted to Vietnamese Americans. In the community, she participates in United Way, Junior Achievement, and fund raising for orphanages, colleges, and foundations, particularly those focused on educating Third World children with an emphasis on Asian Pacific Islanders. She was cofounder of the Science National Honor Society, whose purpose is to promote and improve education in mathematics and science at the high school level.

Le is a founding member and her husband is chair of the Sunflower Mission, a 501(c)3 organization providing educational assistance to Vietnamese. She also serves as director of the Mona Foundation, which works toward education and gender equality to end poverty, conflict, and disease.

Le holds a black belt in taekwondo and has won state-level medals and trophies. She enjoys travel, has spent extensive time overseas, and relaxes through deep-sea fishing, classical music, painting, watching movies, reading, playing poker, or enjoying a Wii game or Frisbee with her boys. She is also a motivational speaker. However, she says that all accomplishments do not matter if she cannot maintain family and friends as well as her career. Her boys have to grow up in both American and Vietnamese cultures. Unlike many career women, she takes her boys on her travels whenever she can and involves them in her work, professional and community alike.

John H. Barnhill

FURTHER READING

"Ambitious, and Proud of It: Duy-Loan Le, 'Be Inspired by Family.'" *Working Mother* Mar. 2005. Print. Another profile of Le, illustrating her focus on family in this feature covering several accomplished mothers.

Anita Borg Institute for Women and Technology. "Who We Are: Duy-Loan T. Le." 2008 Anita Borg Institute for Women and Technology. Web. 12 May 2012. A profile of Le.

Castaneda, Katiana. "Faces in the Crowd: Duy-Loan Le." *Houston Chronicle* 21 Apr. 2005. Print. Profile of Le and her rise to the top through hard work and determination.

"Duy-Loan Le: Profile." *Forbes*. Web. 16 Aug. 2012. Profile of Le with "at a glance" data points and statistics.

"Duy-Loan Le, Senior Fellow, Texas Instruments." 2001. Women in Technology International Hall of Fame. Web. 12 May 2012. Profile of Le at the time of her induction.

Oltersdorf, Cora. "Saigon to Silicon: Duy-Loan Le, BS '82, Is Technologist of the Year." *The Alcalde* Nov. 2002. Web. Google Books. 12 May 2012. The University of Texas alumni publication profiles a Longhorn success.

Ongaro, Laura. "Successful Professional Puts Focus on Her Family." *Houston Chronicle* 29 Nov. 2001. Print. Emphasizes the Vietnamese cultural elements in Le's thinking, including her focus on family—the other side of the driven professional.

"Texas Instruments, Inc. History." Fundinguniverse.com. Web. 16 Aug. 2012. A company history in time line form that ends at 2001.

RASMUS LERDORF

Creator of the PHP scripting language

Born: November 22, 1968; Qeqertarsuaq, Greenland
Died: -
Primary Field: Computer science
Specialty: Computer programming
Primary Company/Organization: PHP Group

INTRODUCTION

Danish programmer Rasmus Lerdorf developed the PHP scripting language in the mid-1990s. Originally developed as a set of tools to help him maintain his own web page, PHP quickly grew to become one of the most popular scripting languages, used in millions of websites and incorporated into popular platforms such as Wordpress. His later work included contributions to the MySQL database management program and the Apache HTTP Server.

EARLY LIFE

Rasmus Lerdorf was born on November 22, 1968, in Qeqertarsuaq, Greenland, an autonomous country within Denmark. As a child, he immigrated with his family

Rasmus Lerdorf.

to Canada. He attended King City Secondary School in Ontario, graduating in 1988 and enrolling in Ontario's University of Waterloo, where he earned a bachelor's degree in applied science (with a focus on systems design engineering) in 1993.

LIFE'S WORK

In 1994, a year after he had left college, when graphical web browsers were still new—Mosaic had been introduced the previous year, and Internet Explorer was still a year from release—Lerdorf developed a series of scripts in the dynamic programming language Perl to help him maintain his web page. After a year of tinkering, he released these scripts to the public as PHP (which stood for "personal home page" tools). His original scripts had been written to automate tasks on his website such as displaying his résumé (without having to reenter information to the web page manually after updating his resume) and monitoring visitor traffic. Generalizing from these tasks, he developed a scripting language with more flexible options, written in the programming language C as Common Gateway Interface (CGI) binaries, with Perl-like syntax and the ability to build basic dynamic web applications. He announced the availability of PHP on the Usenet group comp.infosystems.www.authoring.cgi on June 8, 1995.

The first implementation was PHP/FI: Personal Home Page/Forms Interpreter, which included variables similar to Perl's and the ability to embed HTML and handle forms. His hope was to build small, simple web applications in order to create more interesting, useful, and interactive web pages rather than pages that were little more than formatted text arranged with images. It is worth noting that PHP was developed in the same year as the earliest version of Flash (then called FutureSplash Animator) and the public release of Java. The combination of the three has much to do with the significant differences between the look and feel of even the most basic web page in 2012 compared to 1995.

At the time that he developed PHP, Lerdorf was working as an information technology consultant in Toronto, which he continued to do through 1999. After the development of PHP, Lerdorf worked in various jobs related to Internet infrastructure, including a long stint at Yahoo! (2002–09) as an infrastructure architecture engineer. He worked for IBM (1999–2000), developing

Affiliation: PHP Group

The PHP Group is responsible for producing and implementing PHP, a server-side scripting language developed by Rasmus Lerdorf in 1995 to be embedded in HTML files to produce dynamic web pages. Most web servers are compatible with PHP, and it can operate as a stand-alone shell in almost any operating system. PHP today is installed on more than 1 million web servers and is used by prominent software packages such as Wordpress, an open source blogging tool and dynamic content management system which is used by more than 15 percent of websites; MediaWiki, the web-based wiki software that runs Wikipedia and its offshoots and is free to use for others; Joomla, a content management framework for web- and intranet-publishing, used by Linux.com; concrete5, an open source content management system for web and intranet publishing, with wikilike version management; Facebook, the predominant social network; Digg, the major social news site; MyBB, an open source forum software package used to power many online message boards and forums; and Drupal, an open source content management system and content management framework that provides the back end to about 2 percent of the Internet's websites, including whitehouse.gov. PHP is distributed for free, under the PHP License. Under the terms of that license, the PHP License copyright statement must be included.

PHP is a recursive initialism for "PHP: Hypertext Preprocessor," although it originally meant "personal home page," when Rasmus Lerdorf developed it as a package of Perl scripts to maintain his home page. The PHP Group formed in 1997, three years after Lerdorf developed the scripts and two years after he released PHP to the public. New developers, notably Andi Gutmans and Zeev Suraski at the Technion Israeli Institute of Technology, rewrote the original PHP parser and gave it its new name. Gutmans and Suraski later formed Zend Technologies (a portmanteau of Zeev and Andy), based in Israel, to support their products as well as their rewrite of PHP. Zend released PHP 3, 4, and 5. PHP 4 is based on the Zend Engine, an open source scripting engine for interpreting PHP. It was originally written in C as a modular back-end, and the extensibility of the engine contributed to PHP's popularity, which really grew after the 1999 release. The Zend Engine is still in active development; the current version is Zend Engine II, around which PHP 5 is built. Like PHP, it is freely available under the PHP License.

Zend also offers a number of other products related to PHP. Zend Server is a PHP application server introduced in 2009, under Windows or various versions of Linux. Zend Framework is a web application framework using PHP 5 and licensed under the New BSD License, another open source license. Other developers who have been part of the group include Jim Winstead, Stig Bakken, and Shane Caraveo.

PHP takes the instructions contained in its scripts and produces output usually in the form of an HTML file. Originally written to generate dynamic web pages, it is now used principally for server-side scripting, providing some of the foundation on which web pages using software platforms like Wordpress are built. PHP scripting often leads to security vulnerabilities; about a third of the vulnerabilities tallied by the National Vulnerability Database are PHP-related, though this is the result in most cases of programmers being sloppy and failing to follow best practices. In other words, the prevalence of PHP vulnerabilities attests more to the popularity of the scripting language than to vulnerabilities inherent in the language and its core libraries, which accounts for only a small number of the problems.

PHP is essentially a filter, producing output that is usually coded as HTML. When one logs into Facebook and is presented with one's news feed, which is unique both in the sense that no other user has the same news feed (one has different friends and has liked different pages) and in the sense that the news feed is constantly in flux as friends and pages make updates, so that this morning's news feed is not the same as last night's; the web page one is looking at was created with a web content management system written in PHP. A PHP script took instructions as a result of opening the page and translated a stream of data into a web page formatted according to Facebook's specifications. That is the essence of how PHP is used today, albeit not what it was originally designed for.

The current version of PHP is PHP 5, released in 2004. The PHP 5 release was built around the Zend Engine II, developed by Zend Technologies, and supported object-oriented programming through the PDO (PHP data objects) extension. When PHP 4 support was discontinued in 2008, PHP 5 became the only

---

Affiliation: PHP Group (Continued)

supported version. A new version has been under development alongside PHP 5, with full Unicode support, but has taken longer than expected. Some of its intended features were incorporated into PHP 5 in releases 5.3 and 5.4.

PHP is a free software package, licensed with the requirement that no software derived from it include "PHP" in the name, though developers "may indicate that [their] software works in conjunction with PHP by saying Foo For PHP instead of calling it PHP FOO." This restriction on use of the PHP name conflicts with the GNU General Public License, the most widely used free software license, and is the only respect in which the PHP License significantly differs from it.

---

internal IBM products and Apache 2.0 architecture, and Linuxcare (2000–01), handling large-scale application architecture. He has made contributions both to the Apache HTTP server and to the MySQL database management program. He has advised sites such as Etsy, Room77, WePay (an online payment platform), and MySQL and is on the Apache Software Foundation board of directors. Since 2011, he has worked as a freelance consultant. He has also published books on PHP for O'Reilly.

PERSONAL LIFE

Lerdorf is active on the Internet, maintaining accounts on both Twitter and Etsy, as well as a personal blog. He is noted for not having a cell phone. He is also an avid soccer fan and open source advocate. He has pointed out on numerous occasions that he does not think of himself as a programmer, nor does he believe that he should be considered a good one; rather, he is a problem solver, and on occasion programming has been the tool he has used to solve problems.

Bill Kte'pi

FURTHER READING

Lerdorf, Rasmus, Kevin Tatroe, and Peter MacIntyre. *Programming PHP*. Sebastopol: O'Reilly, 2006. Print. A guide to the PHP scripting language.

MacIntyre, Peter. *PHP: The Good Parts*. Sebastopol: O'Reilly, 2010. Print. An overview of the language by a prominent member of the PHP community.

Meggs, Philip B., and Alston W. Purvis. *Meggs' History of Graphic Design*. New York: Wiley, 2011. Print. A comprehensive and visually rich history of graphic design, including modern web design.

BARBARA LISKOV

Institute Professor, Massachusetts Institute of Technology

Born: November 7, 1939; Los Angeles, California
Died: -
Primary Field: Computer science
Specialty: Computer programming
Primary Company/Organization: Massachusetts Institute of Technology

INTRODUCTION

Barbara Liskov was the first woman to earn a Ph.D. from a computer science department at a U.S. university. She did not allow gender discrimination in mathematics and science to discourage her from pursuing her academic and professional goals. Liskov developed computer languages that are still used in modern software and system applications, and she attributes her success to the assistance of her many graduate students. In her esteemed position as an Institute Professor at the Massachusetts Institute of Technology (MIT), Liskov has hired women in the computer science department and mentors a new generation of women pursuing careers in science and technology.

EARLY LIFE

Barbara Jane Huberman Liskov was born on November 7, 1939, to a lawyer and a homemaker in Los Angeles, California. She was the oldest of four children. While Liskov's parents valued education, they were indifferent toward her love of mathematics and science. While in high school, Liskov took all of the mathematics and science courses that were available but had to keep

Barbara Liskov.

her interest a secret from her friends. During Liskov's youth, mathematics and science were not considered suitable interests for a girl, and she kept a low profile in her classes. Liskov's father suggested that she take a typing course so she could support herself as a secretary, and she took his advice. She discovered that typing was one of the most useful skills she ever learned; the ability to work quickly on QWERTY keyboards would become essential to her work with computers.

Although Liskov's parents expected that she would go to college, they did not expect her to pursue a career. She enrolled at the University of California at Berkeley, originally as a physics major and then switching to mathematics. Liskov remembers being only one of two women in her classes, and she was too intimidated to say anything in class. She received her bachelor's degree in mathematics in 1961. She applied to graduate mathematics programs at Berkeley and Princeton. Princeton returned her application with a letter informing her that the institution did not accept women. Berkeley accepted her, but Liskov had tired of taking classes and decided to look for a job as a mathematician. She was also eager to live elsewhere in the United States, and decided to move to Boston, her father's home town.

LIFE'S WORK

Although Liskov did not find a satisfying job as a mathematician, she accepted a position as a computer programmer at the Mitre Corporation. At Mitre, Liskov discovered her aptitude for computers and programming and decided to pursue a career as a computer scientist. While she found the work rewarding, she had witnessed cases of gender discrimination at the company. She stayed at Mitre for a year, then took on a difficult programming project at Harvard, where she was expected to translate natural language. The project made Liskov realize that she needed to go back to school to learn the fundamentals of programming. She reapplied ot the mathematics program at the University of California at Berkeley, as well as the computer science programs at Harvard and Stanford. She was admitted to both Harvard and Stanford and chose Stanford because she wanted to return to California.

During her first semester at Stanford, Liskov met former mathematician and MIT professor John McCarthy. McCarthy had worked with cognitive scientist Marvin Minsky to establish the field of artificial intelligence (AI). Because Liskov received no financial support from Stanford, she asked McCarthy if he would provide funding for her doctoral studies. After McCarthy heard about her work at Harvard on language translation, he said yes. There were so few people of either gender doing this work that Liskov's experience made her an expert in McCarthy's eyes. Under McCarthy's mentorship, Liskov published her dissertation on chess and games, a work that is still cited. By the time that Liskov graduated in 1968, Stanford had formed a computer science department; she became the first woman in the United States to receive a doctorate from an official computer science department.

After graduation, Liskov returned to Boston to look for work. During her second trip to Boston, she met MIT electrical engineering graduate Nate Liskov; in 1970, they were married. Gender discrimination in employment was still rampant; Barbara ended up returning to Mitre for a staff research position. There she designed computer architecture and implemented it using microcode. She also invented Venus, a new operating system, which she designed and deployed to make better use of the computer architecture. She wrote a paper describing Venus and presented it at the Symposium on Operating System Principles, where it won an award for best paper. MIT faculty member Jerry Saltzer, chair of the session where Barbara had made her presentation, was impressed by her work and urged her to apply for

Affiliation: Massachusetts Institute of Technology

Barbara Liskov began her career at the Massachusetts Institute of Technology (MIT) in 1972 as the first female faculty member in the university's computer science department. Because women on the faculty at MIT were so rare, faculty often introduced themselves to Liskov's husband Nathan at social events, believing that he was the new computer science faculty member. Although Liskov had to teach herself electrical engineering in order to teach the computer architecture curriculum to her students, she thrived in the research environment and enjoyed working with graduate students on developing computer languages and solving software problems.

Liskov's accomplishments at MIT include the development and implementation of data abstraction, distributed computing, and advancing programming methodology as an academic discipline. As of 2012, Liskov was an Institute Professor and head of the Programming Methodology Group in the Electrical Engineering and Computer Science Department of MIT. Her research interests include programming methodology, programming languages and systems, and distributed computing. She is also working on cloud security, Byzantine-fault-tolerant storage systems, peer-to-peer computing, and support for automatic deployment of software upgrades in large-scale distributed systems. Liskov has served on the graduate admissions committee for her department and on increasing the number of female graduate students in the program, and as associate department head she has helped increase the number of women on MIT's computer science faculty.

a faculty position at MIT. At the time there were very few women on the MIT faculty, and the university president was strongly encouraging departments to hire more women. Liskov was hired to work in the Computer Science Department in 1972; she was MIT's first female faculty member in computer science. Because female MIT faculty were so rare, MIT faculty often introduced themselves to Barbara's husband Nathan at social events, believing that he was the new faculty member.

Barbara had a challenging first year at MIT. Although she had the practical experience from Mitre to teach a computer architecture course, the curriculum covered a great deal of electrical engineering, which

she had to learn for the first time. She also began thinking of how to improve the organization and structure of computer programs. Software programmers need to divide their code into smaller pieces, called modules, that could conduct some independent reasoning. Just a year after the microprocessor was invented, Liskov thought of and tested a way to modularize software code. This method, called data abstraction, appears in all major programming languages today. It makes the programs reliable, secure, and easy to use. Liskov did much of her initial work on data abstraction with Steve Zilles, her first graduate student. By her second year at MIT, Barbara had attracted a few other students to her research group. They began to work on CLU, a programming language designed to support use of data abstraction in computer programs. Every major programming language since 1975 has borrowed concepts from CLU.

In the 1980s, Liskov started working on distributed computing: computing carried out by many computers connected by a communications network. She developed a programming language called Argus that allowed a programmer to write distributed applications for networked computers. She would continue to work on distributed programs for networked computers throughout her career.

Liskov earned tenure and promotion for her work at MIT, serving as associate department head for computer science from 2001 to 2004, again the first woman to hold that position. Under her supervision, the computer science department added five female faculty members. She has also run the MIT computer science graduate admissions committee, working hard at increasing the number of women accepted into the doctoral program.

In 1996, Liskov received the Society of Women Engineers Achievement Award. In 2002, she was named by *Discover* magazine as one of the fifty most important women in science. In 2004, she received the John von Neumann Medal from the Institute of Electrical and Electronics Engineers (IEEE), and in 2005 she was awarded the title of ETH Honorary Doctor by the Swiss Federal Institute of Technology Zurich (ETH). In 2008, Liskov was named by MIT as an Institute Professor, the highest honor awarded to an MIT faculty member. In the same year, she earned the Turing Award of the Association for Computing Machinery (ACM), known as the Nobel Prize of computing—the second woman to have received this honor. She also received the ACM SIGPLAN Programming Languages Achievement Award.

Liskov is a member of the National Academy of Engineering, a Fellow of ACM and of the American

Academy of Arts and Sciences. She has served on the National Science Foundation's Computer and Information Science (CISE) Advisory Committee, as well as the Computer Science and Telecommunications Board (CTSB) of the National Research Council. She has written three books, including *Abstraction and Specification in Program Development* (1986) with John Guttag, which has served as a classic textbook on how to write good software. In 2012, Liskov was inducted into the National Inventors Hall of Fame for her innovations in computer programming languages.

As of 2012, Liskov continued her work at MIT as Institute Professor and head of the Programming Methodology Group in the Computer Science Department. Her research interests include programming methodology, programming languages and systems, and distributed computing. She is also working on cloud security, Byzantine-fault-tolerant storage systems, peer-to-peer computing, and support for automatic deployment of software upgrades in large-scale distributed systems.

PERSONAL LIFE

Liskov is a both a people person and a problem solver. She likes making things work and finding practical, elegant solutions to problems. In these endeavors, she enjoys collaborating with others, especially her students, who she says keep her young with their questions and fresh perspectives. Liskov provides advice and support for female graduate students at MIT and has also said that developing software is a hobby.

Liskov credits her success in academia to a work-life balance. When she is not at work, she enjoys reading, gardening, cooking, travel, and birdwatching with her husband Nathan. In 1975, she had a son, Moses, who earned a Ph.D. in computer science from MIT in 2004.

Rachel Wexelbaum

FURTHER READING

Frenkel, K. A. "Liskov's Creative Joy: Barbara Liskov Muses about the Creative Process of Problem Solving, Finding the Perfect Design Point, and Pursuing a Research Path." *Communications—ACM* 52.7 (2009): 20–22. Print. Liskov considers what it is that makes her love her work.

Guttag, John V. "Barbara Liskov." *The Electron and the Bit—EECS at MIT: 1902–2002*. 2003: n. pag. Department of Electrical Engineering and Computer Science, Massachusetts Institute of Technology. Web. 1 May 2012. A biography of Barbara Liskov by her coauthor of *Abstraction and Specification in Program Development*. Examines Liskov's attitudes toward academia, work, research, and women in the sciences.

Liskov, Barbara."An Interview with Barbara Liskov." Interview by Stephen Ibaraki. 2008. Web. Association for Computing Machinery. 1 May 2012. Liskov describes her career. The web page includes additional links to Liskov's MIT web page as well as ACM's feature page on Liskov in recognition of her ACM Turing Award.

LIU CHUANZHI

Founder of Lenovo

Born: April 29, 1944; Shanghai, China
Died: -
Primary Field: Computer science
Specialty: Computer hardware
Primary Company/Organization: Lenovo

INTRODUCTION

Chinese business tycoon Liu Chuanzhi is the founder of Lenovo, which by 2012 was the world's second-largest computer manufacturer. Having taken advantage of Chinese market reforms, he continues to be a pioneer of Chinese capitalism, and his management style is widely studied.

EARLY LIFE

Liu Chuanzhi was born on April 29, 1944, in Shanghai, China. His paternal grandfather was the head of a Chinese bank in Zhenjiang, and his father was a senior executive with the Bank of China. His maternal grandfather was the finance minister for Sun Chuanfang, a warlord who was the leader of the League of Five Provinces. The Liu family moved to China's capital, Beijing, after the Communist revolution in 1949, and Liu's father joined the Communist Party.

After high school, Liu intended to become a military pilot, but he was rejected because of the political affiliation of a family member. He attended the People's

Liberation Army Institute of Telecommunication Engineering, studying engineering and radar science. He had intended to study nuclear weapons, but again the political connection held him back, and he was barred from certain classes. It was during his education that he was first exposed to computers. Upon graduation in 1966, Liu took a job as a researcher at the Chinese Academy of Sciences.

During the Cultural Revolution, Mao Zedong closed all schools and universities, and many young people were sent to work on farms. In 1966, Liu was sent by the state to a Macanese rice farm. After working on the rice farm, he was sent to another farm in Hunan Province, which specialized in the reeducation of political criminals.

In 1970, he returned to Beijing and took a job as an engineer at the Computer Institute. He worked there for fourteen years, developing mainframe computers, before leaving in 1984. He briefly worked at the Chinese Academy of Sciences before cofounding Lianxiang, the company known in the West as Legend Holdings.

LIFE'S WORK

A few years after economic reforms began in China, with foreign investment now permitted and some entrepreneurial activity encouraged, Liu founded Lianxiang with ten other engineers in Beijing, working together in a small office. The word *lianxiang* is translated as *legend* (thus Legend Holdings). Lianxiang is a holding company that owns numerous smaller companies, and Lenovo is used when referring to the computer company that was Legend Holdings' first business. In part because of China's socialist heritage, two generations old when the company was founded, it was difficult to transition from science to business, because business was seen as a less serious endeavor and beneath the dignity of a skilled scientist.

Lianxiang struggled as a result and attempted various ventures, including television imports and digital watch manufacturing. Liu has spoken openly about the way his management team learned from their failures. They did not know the business world and did not know how to apply their engineering knowledge to making money and running a company. The pressure of starting the business in a country that was not friendly to entrepreneurs exacerbated Liu's chronic insomnia, but he never considered giving up. The first real success the company had was in developing the Han-Card, a circuit board that would process Chinese characters for personal computers. Following that lead, the company began to manufacture computers.

Liu Chuanzhi.

Liu's management style was severe in the early days. Again, he has spoken and written openly about the lessons he learned and the major differences between the Lenovo of the 1980s and 1990s and the Lenovo of the twenty-first century. In the twentieth century, he was an authoritarian, even a tyrant. Those who were late for meetings were expected to shame themselves by standing in silence. Those who did not deliver the results Liu wanted could expect to be verbally dressed down in front of their coworkers. However, over time, Liu learned to run a business, just as Lenovo was learning to be a business, and it began to attract increasingly higher-quality employees.

In 1988, Lenovo was one of the first postreform Chinese companies to place an advertisement looking for employees, resulting in five hundred applicants for sixteen slots. Liu was instrumental in the decision to hire fifty-eight people instead of sixteen, in order to capitalize on the influx of talented interest. One of the fifty-eight was Yang Yuanqing, who would later succeed Liu as Lenovo's chief executive officer.

Liu's ties to the Academy of Sciences helped secure early working capital and contracts. Lenovo took advantage of government incentives to expand to Hong Kong, where the company formed a partnership with a government-run business headed by Liu's father.

Affiliation: Lenovo

Lenovo is owned by Legend Holdings, Ltd., which owns companies in the investment, real estate, agricultural, coal, and information technology (IT) sectors. Legend Holdings also controls several venture capital firms and provides early-stage venture capital investments to IT developers and service providers, infrastructure suppliers, and health care, in addition to selected growth-stage capital to companies in the clean technology and consumer goods sectors. Its private equity service focuses on construction, consumer goods, entertainment, energy industries, pharmaceuticals, and financial services. In addition to Lenovo, Legend owns Digital China, Hony Investment, Legend Capital, and Raycom Real Estate Development. It was founded in 1984 by eleven scientific researchers.

Economic reforms began in the People's Republic of China in late 1978. The result is sometimes called a socialist market economy, or socialism with Chinese characteristics. China's capitalism is neither Soviet-style socialism nor Western-style capitalism, nor should it be thought of as a simple combination of elements of each, although in many ways it is very similar to state capitalism, in which commercial, profit-making activity is undertaken by the state, which controls the forces of production. China's capitalist reforms began in rural areas of the country, as agriculture was decollectivized. Foreign investments were permitted, and entrepreneurs were allowed to begin businesses. Later stages of reform, in the 1990s, privatized some of the state-controlled industries and lifted protectionist policies in order to allow a greater degree of international trade between China and Western partners.

It was in this environment of reform that Lianxiang—translated as both "Legend" and "Lenovo"—was founded in 1984, and it is one of the biggest success stories of the reforms, as the company has gone on to dominate a global industry. Today, Legend is used in the West to refer to the holding company, while Lenovo refers to its IT business.

Lenovo developed several different ventures before settling on the computer industry as the one in which it had had the most success. It pursued this course for nearly twenty years before buying IBM's line of personal computers in 2005, becoming overnight the second-largest computer manufacturer in the world. This was followed by a joint venture with Japanese computer manufacturer NEC and internal development of new consumer-friendly premium personal computers: the IdeaPad and the IdeaCentre, the names deliberately playing off the more business-oriented ThinkPad and ThinkCentre (the latter a desktop line that IBM had introduced shortly before the sale). Lenovo also offers ThinkStation workstations, ThinkServer servers, ThinkVision projectors, and Lenovo 3000 desktops. It has recently developed tablets and smart phones as well.

In 2011, a new service was announced: Lenovo Cloud, a cloud computing service with 200 gigabytes of online storage in order to sync multiple devices and stream content to numerous multiple devices at once. Lenovo Cloud is expected to increase the appeal and functionality of Lenovo's recently introduced mobile devices and its smart television, LeTV. LeTV runs on Android and has been released only in China so far. It incorporates face-recognition technology to allow parents to ration their children's television viewing time and can be controlled by voice or remotely by smart phone or tablet. It includes 1 gigabyte of RAM, 8 gigabytes of flash storage (in addition to the eventual cloud storage), and game controllers, and models range in size from 42 to 55 inches. All but the 42-inch LeTV are also 3-D-compatible. Approximately one thousand apps have been developed for the LeTV, and social media tools seem to play heavily in the inventory. A streaming service is available with several hundred thousand hours of streaming on-demand television shows and movies, through a joint venture with BesTV.

In 2011, Liu Chuanzhi went into "honorary retirement" from Lenovo, having selected a successor in Yang Yuanqing. He continued to run Legend Holdings, the parent company that owns Lenovo.

As successful as it was in China, Lenovo was unknown to many Americans until 2005, when it acquired IBM's personal computer business, including the famous ThinkPad line of notebook computers named for IBM's nearly century-old slogan. Developing the PC portfolio and forming a joint venture with Japanese company NEC made Lenovo the world's second-largest computer manufacturer. It continues to develop the ThinkPad line and has introduced the IdeaPad, the result of internal research and development. While the

ThinkPad was designed for business customers, the IdeaPad—not coincidentally bright white like Apple's products, in contrast to the ThinkPad's black design—is intended as a consumer product. Similarly, Lenovo continues to sell the ThinkCenter line of desktop computers introduced by IBM shortly before the sale, while developing IdeaCentre desktops. Unlike most desktops, IdeaCentres are all-in-one systems, incorporating both the processor and the monitor into a one case. Each IdeaCentre model has a distinctly different design and incorporates Veriface facial recognition technology. Other products include the IdeaPad tablets, the LePhone smart phone, and the LeTV smart television, released in 2012.

In 2011, Liu went into "honorary retirement" but remained the chairman of Legend Holdings, Lenovo's parent company, and continues to control multiple information technology (IT) companies and venture capital groups. He is considered one of the most powerful businesspersons not only in China but also in the world. In his so-called retirement he seems to have focused on diversifying Legend Holdings and enhancing its non-IT assets, including real estate, coal, and agricultural business. Liu is expected to take the company public by 2016. In May 2012, Legend Holdings engaged a number of banks to arrange a $200 million three-year bullet loan, partly to refinance debt.

PERSONAL LIFE
Liu is married and has three children. He lives in Beijing.

Bill Kte'pi

FURTHER READING
Huang, Yasheng. *Capitalism with Chinese Characteristics*. Cambridge: Cambridge UP, 2008. Print. A contrast between rural China and state-controlled urban China, including an examination of the effects of Chinese culture on China's new approach to capitalism.

Kynge, James. *China Shakes the World*. Boston: Mariner, 2007. Print. Coverage of China's twenty-first-century economic rise by the former Asian bureau chief of the *Financial Times*.

Zhijun, Ling. *The Lenovo Affair: The Growth of China's Computer Giant and Its Takeover of IBM-PC*. New York: Wiley, 2006. Print. An extremely detailed account of Lenovo's impressive success by a well-known Chinese journalist, translated by Martha Avery.

ADA LOVELACE

Mathematician and author of a program for Babbage's analytical engine

Born: December 10, 1815; London, England
Died: November 27, 1852; London, England
Primary Field: Computer science
Specialty: Computer programming
Primary Company/Organization: Babbage analytical engine

INTRODUCTION
Augusta Ada King (née Byron), the Countess of Lovelace, was an English noblewoman whose work on Charles Babbage's analytical engine constituted some of the first work in computer programming, and she is often called the first computer programmer. She was also the first to envision uses for computers beyond mathematics, which even Babbage did not do.

EARLY LIFE
Augusta Ada King was born Augusta Ada Byron, the only legitimate child of George Gordon, Lord Byron (the Romantic poet who was the sixth Baron Byron). Her mother was Anne Isabella Milbanke, the only child of Sir Ralph Milbanke, the sixth baronet. Her father died when Ada was nine, and she had no relationship with him (nor did she meet her half sister, Allegra Byron). When Ada was still an infant, her parents separated, and her mother returned to her parents' home. Her mother was gifted intellectually, and her parents engaged a Cambridge tutor to further Ada's education; she was especially intrigued by mathematics.

Frequently ill as a child, Lovelace pursued her education from her sickbed and was taught mathematics in the hope that it would prevent the insanity her mother suspected had plagued her father. She was tutored by truly skilled mathematicians and logicians, including Augustus de Morgan, and by her late teens her genius for mathematics was evident. She was acquainted, especially as she became an adult, with many of the luminaries of British life of the day, although never as well with her late father's friends and associates, principally by her own choice—her mother had inculcated in her a distrust of Lord Byron's social circle, and she took an immediate dislike to many of them when she did meet them, even many years after Byron's death.

LIFE'S WORK

The famous scientist Mary Somerville was a friend of Lovelace and introduced her to Charles Babbage in 1833, when Lovelace was still a teenager. Babbage, now considered the father of computing, was a well-educated mathematician who worked throughout much of his adult life on mechanical computers. None of the machines he designed were actually built in full, because of the expense, although he did oversee the construction of similar steam-powered machines. Babbage called many of his machines "engines"; the term *computer* at the time still referred to "one who computes," that is, a person who did performed computations, or calculations, generally arithmetical. Babbage's basic computer design was fundamentally similar to modern computers, with instruction-based operations, but purely mechanical in its workings rather than the electronic (digital) computers of today. He received funding from the government to pursue his projects, but it was never sufficient.

Lovelace corresponded with Babbage on a number of occasions, particularly in the period from 1842 to 1843, when she was his sounding board for many of his ideas on his difference engine and analytical engine, the two designs for which he became famous. He called her the Enchantress of Numbers, while she translated mathematician Luigi Menabrea's work on Babbage's analytical engine, including a set of notes of her own work. Menabrea was a young engineer who would later become the prime minister of Italy; he had written about the analytical engine following Babbage's lecture at the University of Turin. Lovelace translated the work at Babbage's request. The notes included an appendix detailing instructions for calculating a Bernoulli number sequence on the analytical engine and is recognized as the first computer program.

The analytical engine was proposed as the successor to Babbage's difference engine. The difference engine handled polynomial functions—such as divided differences, the polynomial function that gave its name to the engine. Polynomials can be used to approximate both logarithmic and trigonometric functions, which gave the difference engine great flexibility. Babbage had proposed the difference engine in 1822 and received funding from the British government the following year. After nineteen years, however, the government defunded the project, in part because it had gone enormously over budget—ten times beyond the initial allocation—without producing results, and in part because Babbage had begun developing his analytical engine and the government officials making the decisions did not understand enough about the technology to understand why they should continue to fund the difference engine if he had developed something better. The government's real interest was in astronomical and mathematical tables; Babbage had promised that with a difference engine, such tables could be produced cheaply.

The analytical engine was first described in 1837, when the difference engine project was still in progress. While the difference engine was designed for a specific class of mathematical operations, the analytical engine was a general-purpose computer that, if it had been built, would have been what later was termed Turing-complete (after mathematician and modern computer pioneer Alan M. Turing). Turing completeness, in reference to computers, means that any Turing-computable function can be computed by the system. (Turing-computable functions, in turn, are those functions that can be computed by the hypothetical Turing machine, which represents both the benchmark against which a possible computer must be compared to determine if it is indeed a computer and the limit of mechanical computing power.)

Although the British government's decision to defund Babbage has been bemoaned by computer history buffs, it must be admitted that it was not entirely wrong. For one thing, it was clear that it was not possible for Babbage to provide the government with an economical means of producing mathematical tables: Even if the tables were free after the machine was built, the cost of construction was so high that there were really no practical tasks it could be expected to accomplish that would make the project profitable, let alone break-even. Despite being built to meet a specific need, the difference and analytical engines were really exercises in pure research, in the modern sense of a scientific endeavor undertaken to advance science and understanding rather than accomplish a practical end, as applied research does. It was in the former area that Babbage and Lovelace were really revolutionaries, because it would be a long time before people thought of computing as a science in that sense. It would not have been immediately apparent to many, even the learned, how building a machine—no matter how complicated—advanced

Affiliation: Babbage Analytical Engine

The story of what many believe to be the first computer program is tied inexorably to the story of Charles Babbage and the first computer. Ada Lovelace met Babbage in 1833, and the two struck up a lively and productive correspondence. Babbage was so impressed with Lovelace's mathematical ability that he dubbed her the "Enchantress of Numbers."

One of the many topics Lovelace took an interest in and worked with Babbage on was his analytical engine. The engine, though never actually built, was the first complete design for a general-purpose computer. (Babbage's previous project had been the difference engine, which was essentially a mechanical calculator.)

The birth of the first computer program occurred in a rather roundabout fashion. In early 1842, an article was published in French that recounted a symposium Babbage had given describing his analytical engine. Lovelace translated the article for a British science journal, and at Babbage's request, she included with the translation an extensive set of detailed notes. The notes were lettered A through G and showed how Babbage's analytical engine would work. Note G provided a set of sequential instructions for the machine, which amounted to an algorithm for using the engine to calculate a sequence of Bernoulli numbers (rational numbers important to number theory).

In addition to creating the first computer program, Lovelace was also the first to foresee the potential for computers outside the realm of mathematics; her notes predict that machines such as the analytical engine would someday compose original and complex music, be able to produce graphic illustrations, and be used for both scientific and practical purposes. In 1953, Lovelace's notes on the analytical engine were republished, and the engine was acknowledged as a model for a computer, while Lovelace's notes were recognized as a description not only of a computer but of the accompanying software as well.

In 1998, the London Science Museum constructed an analytical engine following Babbage's specifications. The machine was built using only the materials and the design and engineering knowledge that would have been available in Babbage's time. Once completed, it successfully ran the program devised by Lovelace.

Lovelace's immediate appreciation of his work helped to validate his convictions.

Furthermore, the analytical engine was the better machine. Both engines were revolutionary, but even once the computing age truly began in the middle of the twentieth century, the first computers would not be general-purpose computers, as the analytical engine was intended to be. It is not that no one thought of one, only that it seemed too ambitious—one hundred years later, it seemed too ambitious to do what Babbage hoped to do in the 1830s.

Babbage asked Lovelace to expand her notes for publication on their own—they were longer than Menabrea's article—and they were published under the name "AAL" in two magazines, *Taylor's Scientific Memoirs* and *The Ladies' Diary*. It was the republication of these notes in 1953, as the modern computer age was getting under way, that led to a surge of interest in Lovelace and her work. In particular, her notes have since been found to be an accurate program for the analytical engine.

Since the rediscovery of Lovelace, there has been argument over the extent of her contribution to Babbage's work. Some claim Babbage was responsible for most of the substantive content in her analytical engine article. Historian Bruce Collier, writing in 1990, even claimed that Lovelace had no mathematical skill to speak of—that she did, in fact, suffer from the "insanity" of her father (what Collier calls manic depression and professionals would now term bipolar disorder), and that well-meaning friends and family encouraged her delusions of genius as a comfort to her.

PERSONAL LIFE

On July 8, 1835, at the age of nineteen, Lovelace married William King, the Baron King, later the first Earl of Lovelace. For most of her married life, she was addressed as the Right Honorable the Countess of Lovelace, and she has been known to history as Ada Lovelace. The Lovelaces had three children: Byron (born May 12, 1836), Anne "Annabella" Isabella (born September 22, 1837), later the Lady Anne Blunt), and Ralph Gordon (born July 2, 1839). In 1841, Ada was told that the daughter of Byron's half sister Augusta

scientific understanding of anything, except perhaps certain mechanical principles in physics. Babbage understood the value, even if he was not able to convey it to government officials—and perhaps was not even able to clearly see that they needed it conveyed to them.

Leigh, Medora Leigh, was Byron's daughter. Ada responded that she had always suspected this but considered it improper to have had it confirmed; furthermore, despite her mother's influence on her, she blamed not her father but Augusta Leigh, assuming her father had been incestuously seduced.

Like her father, Ada Lovelace died young. She passed away at age thirty-six, on November 27, 1852, of uterine cancer. She is buried at the Church of St. Mary Magdalene in Hucknall, Nottingham, England.

The computer language Ada is named for her; an extension of Pascal, it is a high-level object-oriented language released in 1980 and developed for the Department of Defense by French American computer scientist Jean Ichbiah.

Bill Kte'pi

FURTHER READING

Babbage, Charles. *The Writings of Charles Babbage.* New York: Halcyon Classics, 2009. Print. Reprints Babbage's work on his attempt at building the first computer.

Stein, Dorothy. *Ada: A Life and a Legacy.* Cambridge: MIT, 1985. Print. One of the strongest biographies of Lovelace, by an author who understands the science.

Tool, Betty Alexandra. *A Selection from the Letters of Ada Lovelace and Her Description of the First Computer.* Mount Prospect: Critical Connection, 1992. Print. Reprints much of the relevant work of Lovelace.

Woolley, Benjamin. *The Bride of Science: Romance, Reason, and Byron's Daughter.* New York: McGraw-Hill, 2000. Print. A more recent biography than Stein's.

M

MIKE MARKKULA

Former CEO of Apple

Born: February 11, 1942; Los Angeles, California
Died: -
Primary Field: Business and commerce
Specialty: Management, executives, and investors
Primary Company/Organization: Apple

INTRODUCTION

Mike Markkula is best known as the second chief executive officer (CEO) of Apple, a position he held for only two years, between 1981 and 1983. He served the company for twenty years, working as vice president of marketing and as a company director. He was chairman of Apple's board from 1985 to 1997, but his most important contribution to the company was the financing he provided during the formation of Apple in 1977, a total of $250,000 in equity investment and loans. A dozen years older than Steve Jobs and seven years senior to Steve Wozniak, Markkula, who became Apple's third employee, is often described as having provided the adult supervision the young visionaries required in the company's early years. Wozniak credits Markkula with much of Apple's success. In 1986, Markkula and his wife provided $3.5 million as a seed grant for Santa Clara University's Markkula Center for Applied Ethics.

EARLY LIFE

Mike Markkula was born February 11, 1942, in Los Angeles, California. Christened Armas Clifford Markkula, he grew up in southern California. He received both B.S. and M.S. degrees in electrical engineering from the University of Southern California. His first job was as a member of the technical staff in the research and development laboratory at Hughes Aircraft Company. He left Hughes for Fairchild Semiconductor, where he became marketing director for integrated circuits.

When Robert Noyce and Gordon E. Moore left Fairchild to found Intel Corporation in 1968, Markkula followed them. He worked at Intel from 1970 to 1974. At Intel, he guided the development of the computer system for processing customer orders and eventually became product marketing manager for memory chips.

Mike Markkula.

189

He was considered a steady and reliable employee, but he lacked the genius and charisma that marked the stars of the industry. However, he developed a reputation for hating both his given names (and hence came to be known as Mike) and for his skills at the marketing.

Markkula set a goal of becoming a millionaire by the age of thirty, and Intel made it possible for him to achieve that goal. He bought Intel stock before it went public in 1971. When a colleague was promoted over him as vice president of marketing, he retired. At thirty-two, he was a "small multimillionaire" who could live comfortably and never work again. A dedicated family man, he seemed content to spend time at his home in Cupertino, California, building cabinets for his stereo system and strumming a guitar. His life changed dramatically in 1976, however, when Don Valentine, an investor at Atari, urged him to talk with two young men building computers in a garage a few miles from his house.

LIFE'S WORK

Markkula may have met with Jobs and Wozniak originally at the request of Valentine, but he was soon captivated by the possibilities of the business the two were building. He began meeting with them regularly, helping them to draw up a business plan that predicted Apple would be a Fortune 500 company within five years. After talking the situation over with his wife, Markkula agreed to give Apple four years. He also agreed to invest a quarter of a million dollars. He offered $91,000 of his own money and underwrote a bank loan for the remainder. His investment was crucial in launching Apple.

As important as Markkula's financial contribution was, his business experience may have been more valuable. He brought organizational skills, marketing strategies, and a stabilizing influence on the mercurial Jobs. He also seems to have understood the vital roles of both Jobs and Wozniak. Markkula made Wozniak's quitting his job at Hewlett-Packard and committing to Apple full-time a condition of his investment. Wozniak was reluctant, since he was skeptical of Markkula's optimistic view of what Apple could achieve, but once assured that he could remain an engineer, he agreed to the stipulation. Markkula's appreciation for the genius of Jobs did not blind him to the weaknesses of the man. Acting as mentor in the early years, Markkula penned the famous Apple marketing philosophy in a memo to Jobs. His use of the terms *empathy*, *focus*, and the awkward *impute*—which stressed the importance of how a product looked to the consumer—served the company well long after Markkula left.

Affiliation: Apple

Steve Wozniak and Steve Jobs introduced the first Apple I computer, created by Wozniak, in 1976. The following year, with an investment of $250,000 from Mike Markkula, Apple was incorporated. Apple II was launched in 1980. By 1981, sales reached $600 million, and the company went public. Two years later, Apple was a Fortune 500 company, the first to achieve this rank in such a brief a period. Internal conflict led to the firing of the company's first CEO, Michael Scott. Mike Markkula reluctantly accepted the job until a successor for Scott could be found. He served as CEO for two years.

The Macintosh, introduced in 1984, with its mouse and graphical user interface, made personal computers easier to use. The introduction of the LaserWriter printer and Aldus PageMaker the following year boosted sales, but both founders left the company that year. Wozniak chose to leave, but Jobs lost in a power struggle with John Sculley, the CEO he had courted assiduously a few years earlier. The next decade brought the launch of Microsoft Windows 95 and a flurry of inexpensive personal computers. Apple lost $68 million in 1995–96. Jobs returned in 1997, first as an adviser and then as CEO. The next ten years were marked by innovations that transformed entire industries and made communications mobile. Jobs led the company in the introduction of iTunes and the iPod MP3 player. By June 2008, the music arm accounted for 50 percent of the company's revenues. Apple first sold the iPhone in June 2007; a year later, 11.6 million iPhones were in the hands of consumers. In 2010, the company introduced the iPad, a device for reading print, viewing film and web content, playing music and games, and employing a wide assortment of other applications.

Jobs resigned in August 2011, less than two months before his death on October 5, 2011. Tim Cook, his successor at Apple, had filled in on three occasions when Jobs took leaves of absence for health reasons. Although the change in CEOs caused Apple's stock to fall briefly, by the end of Cook's first year in charge, the company's stock was up 44 percent. Based on market capitalization, Apple had become the most valuable company in the world.

On January 3, 1977, Apple Computer was officially formed. Markkula was given one-third of the company for his investment and became the third employee of the new company. Knowing his dislike of conflict, he decided that his strengths at diplomacy, business planning, and market strategy could be utilized more effectively if someone else were responsible for the day-to-day workings of the company. He suggested Michael Scott, a friend since their days at Fairchild, for the position of president. With Scott running the company, Markkula could turn his attention to other matters.

The first priority was investors. In the fall of 1977, a crisis brought on by problems with the plastic cases that housed the computers left the company's cash reserves so low that Markkula and Scott underwrote loans of $200,000 to meet immediate needs. It was clear that Apple needed venture capitalists, but Markkula was determined that investment would come from those respected and influential enough to catch the attention of Wall Street while at the same time minimizing the control that the company's executives would lose.

With these goals in mind, he contacted Hank Smith, an acquaintance from his days at Fairchild and Intel, who was a general partner at Venrock, the venture capital wing of the Rockefeller family. The firm had a reputation for making smart investments. Moreover, Venrock had yet to invest in a personal computer company. The round of investments completed in January 1978 totaled more than $500,000; Venrock invested $288,000. Smith later admitted that had he not known Markkula, he probably would never have looked at Apple. Markkula was only partially successful with another contact. He wanted the highly respected Andy Grove, president of Intel, on Apple's board. Grove bought fifteen thousand shares of Apple, but he refused a seat on the board. However, Markkula's demonstration of the Apple II for Grove and Intel's board yielded an unexpected dividend. One of the Intel directors, Arthur Rock, who had backed both Fairchild and Intel when they started, contacted Apple to express his interest in investing. By the end of its first year as an incorporated company, Apple was valued at $3 million.

With the company flourishing, Markkula began looking toward the time he could be less engaged at Apple. He had promised his wife to limit his term of service to four years, and, as the end fo that period drew near, he was eager to enjoy a second retirement. When Scott, overwhelmed by his responsibilities as president and CEO, asked Markkula to split those responsibilities with him, Markkula refused. A few months later, in April 1981, the beleaguered Scott was forced out.

Markkula handed his position as chairman of the board over to Jobs and took over as president and CEO, a position he held until April 8, 1983, when John Sculley was named CEO. During Markkula's tenure, Apple went public and became the first personal computer company whose sales reached $1 billion. Markkula's own share in the company was valued at $239 million.

With Sculley in charge, Markkula withdrew from the day-to-day operations of Apple, but he was pulled back as conflict escalated between Sculley and Jobs. Markkula had been mentor and even father figure to Jobs, but he acquiesced as the Apple board removed Jobs as head of the Macintosh division, as he had acquiesced when Jobs pushed Jef Raskin out of the Macintosh project earlier. When the showdown came on September 16, 1985, and Jobs looked to his old mentor for assistance in retaining control of Apple, Markkula, whose net worth had dropped $200 million during the company's internecine wars, sided with Sculley. Jobs felt betrayed and the relationship between the two men was never the same.

Markkula returned as chairman of the board when Sculley resigned under pressure in 1993 and continued in that position through the brief tenure of Michael Spindler (1993–96) and the even briefer one of Gil Amelio (1996–97). Jobs had returned as special adviser to Amelio shortly before the board demanded Amelio's resignation, and he was named interim CEO in the wake of the resignation. On August 6, 1997, Jobs announced the reorganization of Apple's board. Only two members retained their seats. Markkula was not one of them. After twenty years as a power functioning largely out of the spotlight, Markkula no longer had a place at Apple. Years later, Wozniak commented that, although Markkula rarely received credit, without his contributions Apple would never have achieved its success.

PERSONAL LIFE

Markkula, with entrepreneur Ken Oshman, founded Echelon, a company that develops smart chips that can automate devices for homes and offices, in 1988 and served as vice chairman of the board of directors beginning in 1989. A certified pilot, he owned the ACM jet center in San Jose for a time. His contributions to technology were recognized by his alma mater in 1983, when the University of Southern California (USC) School of Engineering named him Outstanding Alumnus. USC awarded him an honorary doctorate in 2012.

Markkula has been associated with Santa Clara University since 1984. The university awarded him an honorary doctorate in 1992. He served as chairman of the board of trustees from 2003 through 2009. He and his wife, Linda, provided initial funding for the university's Center for Applied Ethics in 1986 and launched the center's endowment with a $5 million contribution in the mid-1990s. The Markkulas are the parents of two children.

Wylene Rholetter

FURTHER READING

Isaacson, Walter. *Steve Jobs*. New York: Simon, 2011. Print. This best-selling biography of Jobs, published just weeks after his death in October 2011, is a comprehensive examination of his life and achievements. His relationship with Markkula is among the many subjects recounted.

Malone, Michael S. *Infinite Loop: How the World's Most Insanely Great Computer Company Went Insane*. New York: Doubleday, 1999. Print. The book, by a writer who knew Steve Jobs and Steve Wozniak in high school and who has written extensively about Apple for periodicals, takes a critical look at the company's history, its successes, and its mistakes.

Markoff, John. "The Apple World According to Markkula: An 'Unknown' Cofounder Leaves After 20 Years Of Glory and Turmoil." 1 Sept. 1997. *New York Times*. Web. 2 Sept. 2012. Looks at Markkula's twenty-year career at Apple, his role in the company's success, and his relationship with Steve Jobs.

O'Grady, Jason D. *Apple, Inc. Corporations That Changed the World*. Westport: Greenwood, 2009. Print. This book, by an author who has written frequently about Apple, examines the history of Apple and its creators. Markkula's role is analyzed.

MICH MATHEWS

Former senior vice president of Microsoft's Central Marketing Group

Born: 1968; United Kingdom
Died: -
Primary Field: Computer science
Specialty: Computer software
Primary Company/Organization: Microsoft

INTRODUCTION

Hired in 1989, when Microsoft was well known in the computer industry but far from the household name it would become outside it, Mich Mathews rose through the ranks of marketing positions at Microsoft and became principally responsible for its public image in the 1990s and 2000s. She handled the transformation of founder Bill Gates's public image and focused strongly on creating subbrand identities for Microsoft properties such as Windows, Office, MSN, Bing, and the Xbox, rather than trying to create a consistent cross-brand identity.

EARLY LIFE

Michelle "Mich" Mathews was born in 1968 in the United Kingdom, and after graduating from high school at sixteen, she worked in an apprenticeship program with General Motors. This was followed by work with a British consulting firm, Text 100 Public Relations Consultancy, which led to her hiring by Microsoft.

Mich Mathews.

LIFE'S WORK

Mathews joined Microsoft 1993, after four years of working as its UK consultant. She was placed at the head of Microsoft's Corporate Public Relations and became an officer in 1999. She continued to move up the ladder of Microsoft's marketing positions.

Mathews built numerous partnerships between the marketing and engineering teams at Microsoft, partnering with engineers to create measurement analytic and RM systems. Marketing insights were incorporated into the product development cycle. Public relations research events furthered relationship marketing, and Mathews oversaw integrated marketing endeavors in more than seventy countries.

Mathews was responsible for public relations during the Windows 95 launch, the most successful marketing campaign in Microsoft history. The launch centered on commercials using the Rolling Stones' hit "Start Me Up," in reference to the program's Start button, which played a prominent, interface-defining role in the operating system. The rumor that Microsoft paid more than $10 million for the rights to use the song in the ad was in fact started by Mathews's people in order to increase the brand's premium image.

Mathews's work included the "I'm a PC" campaign, created by the Crispin Porter + Bogusky ad agency, which was a response to Apple's "I'm a Mac, I'm a PC" campaign. While Apple's campaign portrayed PCs as boring and stodgy, the I'm a PC campaign showed showed real-life PC users in interesting jobs, including celebrities such as Eva Longoria.

Mathews was also responsible for the makeover of Bill Gates's public image. Over time, Gates began to dress better and use personal stylists, assisting in his transition from a scruffy geek to a powerful businessman. Part of the inspiration for the transition was Gates's arrogant defiance during a Justice Department antitrust deposition leading up to the *United States v. Microsoft* suit; it was exactly that arrogance that Mathews needed to keep out of the public eye, and the new Gates was more humble and plainspoken. Mathews was also responsible for the ads featuring Gates and Jerry Seinfeld together, which were widely criticized because of Gates's lack of television charisma and somewhat stilted presence. The ads ran for only a brief period, despite the cost of Seinfeld's involvement.

Mathews was featured in a number of articles and lists on women in powerful corporate or computer industry positions, including *Newsweek*'s 10 Power Women Getting Ahead, *Ad Age*'s 2009 list of Power Players, and *Business Pundit*'s 25 Hottest Women in Business.

As senior vice president of Microsoft's Central Marketing Group, Mathews oversaw $1 billion in marketing expenditures annually, including marketing for the Xbox, Bing, and Windows. Key colleagues working with Mathews included Gayle Troberman, the general manager of Consumer Engagement and Advertising; Michael Delman, the corporate vice president of Global Marketing of the Interactive Entertainment Business (the Xbox); and David Webster, general manager of Brand Marketing.

When Kevin Turner joined Microsoft from Walmart in 2005 as its chief operating officer—wielding more influence than anyone but chief executive officer Steve Ballmer—Mathews lost her officer position. Mathews announced her retirement in 2011, the same week as Microsoft's online marketing leadership summit Imagine 2011, amid a number of other resignations, including chief software architect Ray Ozzie, Server and Tools president Bob Muglia, Entertainment and Devices president Robbie Bach, chief financial officer Chris Liddell, Microsoft Business Division president Stephen Elop, global ad sales head Carolyn Everson, and Windows marketing chief Brad Brooks. Mathews's was one of the most surprising resignations; although Ozzie's was surprising given how much authority he had at the company, he had only been there for a few years. Mathews, on the other hand, was a fixture in Microsoft corporate culture, one of the few 1980s hires still working for the software giant. Mathews was replaced by Chris Capossela, formerly a senior vice president in charge of marketing in the Microsoft Office division, where he oversaw the launches of Office 2007 and Office 2010. Some have speculated that Mathews's resignation may have been related to a stagnation of the Microsoft brand under the leadership of CEO Ballmer, who many feel has failed to innovate the way Gates did.

Before retiring, Mathews managed the transition as Microsoft reorganized its media replationships. Starcom Mediavest, part of the Publicis Groupe, was put in charge of global planning and strategy, as well as U.S. buying for the company. Universal McCann, part of the Interpublic Group of Companies, handles buying duties outside the United States, having previously handled much of the company's North American spending. These new relationships were part of Mathews's ongoing effort to change Microsoft's agency model and marketing mix.

Just before her resignation, Mathews praised the launch of the Xbox Kinect, an accessory sensor that opened up new possibilities for game play. The sensors were promoted four months before their global launch, in a tour that let fans play with the Kinect before it was

Affiliation: Microsoft

One of the world's foremost computer companies and the largest software maker, Microsoft was founded in 1975 by Bill Gates and Paul Allen, who designed a BASIC compiler for the new Altair 8800 system, without even having an Altair to test it, and won Microsoft's first contract when they successfully demonstrated it to the company. It moved on to other implementations of BASIC, the dominant home computer programming language of the era, as well as Xenix, a Unix variant released in 1980. Xenix was the first operating system they released to the public and was the platform on which the first release of Microsoft Word (then called Multi-Tool Word) ran.

Microsoft Word made a big splash, thanks in part to the free demonstration copies of the MS-DOS version that were bundled with the November 1983 issue of *PC World*—the first software distributed on diskette bundled with a magazine, which became a standard and useful way of distributing demo software and shareware until Internet access became common enough and fast enough for downloads to be more practical. In Word's case, the free sample boosted sales and interest because the program significantly moved word processing forward: It was one of the few programs to allow use of a mouse and could display bold and italicized characters.

DOS (including MS-DOS and PC-DOS) was the operating system with which Microsoft was most associated during the early 1980s. PC-DOS was developed for IBM, with one-third of Microsoft's employees devoted to the project, so that when the IBM PC launched, Microsoft was the only company offering a full range of software for it—an operating system, programming language, and various applications, as well as Microsoft Mouse. This was followed by MS-DOS for PC-compatible computers.

The first version of Windows was released in 1985. It was originally a graphical user interface extension of MS-DOS, although early versions of Windows did assume some operating system functions and allowed multitasking, which DOS alone would not.

The most significant Windows releases were Windows NT, the first professional operating system (later redesigned and released for home computers as Windows XP), in 1993; and Windows 95, which replaced rather than riding atop of MS-DOS, as subsequent versions of Windows have done. These releases helped Microsoft dominate both the corporate and the home market in the 1990s.

The 1990s also saw the rise of the Internet, and Microsoft introduced Internet Explorer to compete with other web browsers, assisted by the fact that it was automatically installed along with Windows. Internet Explorer, along with the Microsoft Network (MSN), were aggressively marketed in order to make up for Microsoft's early failure to account for the popularity of the Internet and exploit its rapid spread.

The early 2000s were marked by the company's troubles in court, as the U.S. Justice Department targeted Microsoft for anticompetitive practices. The Supreme Court's ruling in *United States v. Microsoft* called the company "an abusive monopoly." Despite originally being ordered to split into separate units, Microsoft appealed the case and was able to settle in 2001.

Although principally a software company, Microsoft has periodically entered the hardware market, with varying degrees of success. Its Zune MP3 player failed to put a dent in iPod's market share and was widely considered a failure. The Xbox, its video game console, was expected to fail similarly, but in time—after a launch that was probably mishandled—it managed to overtake the Nintendo Gamecube, although the PlayStation 2 outsold both of its competitors put together, by a wide margin. The Xbox 360, the next-generation release, successfully competed with Sony's Playstation 3. While the Nintendo Wii outsells them both, the Wii offers a different gaming experience and does not exactly compete directly with the Xbox and PS3, both of which focus on games for teenagers and adults and multiplayer online experiences; Wii, by contrast, has a much lower price point and focuses on family and party games.

Microsoft has also entered the lucrative tablet market with its planned Surface, designed to compete with Apple's iPad—an aspiration which has been met with no small amount of skepticism.

Founder Bill Gates has gradually scaled down his involvement with Microsoft, although he remains the strongest voice in its direction. He stepped down as CEO in 2000, handing the reins to Steve Ballmer, who had been with the company since 1980, and retired as chief software architect in 2008, succeeded by Lotus Notes developer Ray Ozzie.

released and upload video of themselves doing so. By the time the Kinect appeared on the market, it had more than 4 million Facebook fans; 8 million units sold in the first two months.

PERSONAL LIFE

After resigning from Microsoft, Mathews relocated from Seattle to Los Angeles's Holmby Hills neighborhood, paying $11.5 million for the 12,000-square-foot home formerly owned by Condé Nast president Dawn Ostroff. She is a fan of the animated television comedy *The Simpsons*, Justin Bieber, the movie *The Hunger Games*, the *Angry Birds* video game, the television series *Game of Thrones* and *Downton Abbey*, and soccer.

Bill Kte'pi

FURTHER READING

Auletta, Ken. *The Highwaymen: Warriors of the Information Superhighway*. San Diego: Harcourt Brace, 1998. Print. Includes coverage of Microsoft in the 1980s and 1990s.

Edstrom, Jennifer. *Barbarians Led by Bill Gates: Microsoft from the Inside: How the World's Richest Corporation Wields Its Power*. New York: Henry Holt, 1998. Print. Covers Microsoft in the 1990s.

Eichenwald, Kurt. "Microsoft's Lost Decade." *Vanity Fair* Aug. 2012: n. pag. Print. A critical account of Microsoft under Steve Ballmer. The perception that the company has largely coasted on its reputation since Gates stepped down as chief executive officer may have played a role in Mathews's resignation.

JOHN MAUCHLY

Cocreator of the ENIAC

Born: August 30, 1907; Cincinnati, Ohio
Died: January 8, 1980; Ambler, Pennsylvania
Primary Field: Computer science
Specialty: Computer hardware
Primary Company/Organization: Unisys

INTRODUCTION

With J. Presper Eckert, John Mauchly designed the first general-purpose electronic digital computer, the Electronic Numerical Integrator and Computer (ENIAC). The team also designed the Electronic Discrete Variable Automatic Computer (EDVAC), the Binary Automatic Computer (BINAC), and the Universal Automatic Computer (UNIVAC) I, the latter the first commercial computer in the United States. Eckert-Mauchly Computer Corporation was the first computer company. The team also originated basic concepts such as programming languages, stored programs, and subroutines. Their work was vital to the development and spread of computers in the late 1940s and after.

EARLY LIFE

John William Mauchly was born to Sebastian J. and Rachel Scheidemantel Mauchly. He grew up in Chevy Chase, Maryland, and attended schools in Washington, D.C. The Mauchly family was solidly middle class. They lived in a four-bedroom, one-bath frame house

John Mauchly.

in Chevy Chase. Rachel was active in the Women's Club, nagged John about his penmanship, arranged his piano lessons, and made sure the family could afford summer vacations on the Jersey shore. Sebastian was a high school science teacher who received a Ph.D. in physics from the University of Cincinnati and, when John was eight years old, became chief physicist at the Carnegie Institution's newly created Department of Terrestrial Magnetism. Sebastian became prominent after his discovery of diurnal variation in the Earth's magnetic field.

Mauchly attended McKinley Technical High School after showing his engineering potential in elementary school, when he built and installed electric doorbells to replace mechanical bells for the neighbors and also troubleshot the neighbors' electrical problems. His high school performance was stellar, with exceptional achievement in mathematics and physics, editorship of the school paper in 1925 (his senior year), tennis, and walks through the woods with his friends, where they read the works of Edgar Allan Poe. Mauchly received a Maryland state scholarship in 1925 and he

used it to attend Johns Hopkins University in Baltimore. His initial major was in electrical engineering. Sebastian developed a chronic illness and between 1925 and 1928 worked from the Jersey shore, where he was convalescing. He died in 1928.

Mauchly decided to switch his focus to physics and used a special rule that allowed exceptional students to move directly to the Ph.D. program without an undergraduate degree. He received a series of scholarships, continued his education after his father died, and earned a Ph.D. in 1932. His dissertation was titled "The Third Positive Group of Carbon Monoxide Bands."

LIFE'S WORK

Mauchly taught introductory physics at Ursinus College from 1933 to 1941. There he first became interested in creating electronic computers, a project that combined physics and his original background in electronic engineering. The school was too small to afford the laboratory equipment a research physicist required in the 1930s, so he attempted to develop his own instruments.

Mauchly also researched weather analysis at the Carnegie Institution, concluding that there was a need for a mechanical device of some sort to process the massive volume of data involved in weather research: He found a massive volume of weather information but lacked the capability of performing calculations on the tabular data. He bought a used Marchant calculator to perform calculations of molecular energy levels extracted from the weather data.

In the summer of 1936, Mauchly became a temporary assistant physicist in his father's former department at Carnegie, the Department of Terrestrial Magnetism, working as a human computer for his father's old boss. (At that time the term *computer* referred to a human who performed calculations using pencil and paper or, at best, a mechanical calculating machine.) After three summers, he submitted an article to the *Journal of Terrestrial Magnetism and Atmospheric Electricity*, but the article was rejected because the period of data analysis was too brief. Mauchly sought a method of computing larger volumes of data.

Computers of the day were the product of large engineering projects, particularly electrical engineering. Mauchly used the National

Affiliation: Unisys

The Eckert-Mauchly Computer Corporation became part of a company whose history was filled with mergers and acquisitions. Remington began as a typewriter company in 1873. Burroughs made adding machines, and its first arithmometer debuted in 1885. Remington merged with Rand Kardex in 1927 to become Remington Rand. Sperry formed in 1933. Eckert and Mauchly invented ENIAC in 1946, and Remington Rand produced the first business computer, the 409, in 1949. Eckert-Mauchly began in 1950. Sperry merged with Remington Rand to become Sperry Rand in 1955, while Burroughs shifted from adding machines to computers while absorbing ElectroData in the mid-1950s. Burroughs and Sperry formed Unisys in 1986, and in 1987 Unisys acquired workstation maker Convergent Technologies.

In 1991, the company settled a Department of Defense fraud and bribery case by paying $190 million in fines, damages, and penalties. Also, Unisys initially was inefficient because the merger did not consolidate all functions, leaving duplication and waste. The industry entered a slump, but in the early 1990s the company emerged by shifting from mainframe to networked systems and developing a services capability. The company slumped again, cutting its workforce and consolidating and selling nonperforming units, shifting to open systems software for proprietary hardware, and shifting to Windows and Unix capabilities in the 1990s. By the turn of the century, Unisys was primarily a services company, and its future lay in overseas markets.

Youth Administration to hire students as computers and began looking into tabulating machines. Mauchly focused on finding methods of creating electrical circuits suitable for computing. He and some of his students visited establishments where work was taking place on creating circuits to perform arithmetic computations. He began attempting to build circuits for counting. His new focus and an encounter with John Vincent Atanasoff led him in 1941 to the University of Pennsylvania's Moore School of Electrical Engineering, the heart of a regional electrical industry in radio, telephones, and other electronic technologies.

At the time, the United States was entering World War II, and the war pushed academics into military-related research. Mauchly was no exception. Moore had a contract with the U.S. Army to teach a ten-week course in electrical engineering for defense industries, a course aimed at mathematics and physics graduates because the Army needed engineers to operate electronic communications and weapons systems. Mauchly completed a course in electronics for defense purposes and afterward became instructor at Moore. He had an opportunity to take a better-paying job in defense training at another university, but Moore had greater appeal. Moore was a center of computer-based research, with the centerpiece Vannevar Bush's differential analyzer, designed to integrate systems of differential equations. The machine required a great deal of manual effort to configure, and it consisted of replaceable shafts, wheels, handles, gears, electric motors, and disks. For small problems, engineers used mathematics rather than wasting the days required to set up the machine, but it was worthwhile for projects lasting weeks. Moore already had the differential analyzer, a mechanical analog computer that used wheels and disks to solve differential equations, and Mauchly and J. Presper Eckert, one of Mauchly's instructors in the defense electronics course, both worked heavily on the contract to create trajectory tables.

Mauchly tried to get other staffers at the school interested in his ideas for a better computer, but most ignored him. The exception was Eckert; developing a close friendship, the two took every opportunity to exchange and expand on their ideas about electronic computers, and Mauchly wrote a report on the design of an electronic computer that would be easier and faster than the Bush analyzer.

A new director of the Ballistic Research Laboratory, a joint project of the Aberdeen Proving Ground and the Moore School, read Mauchly's report, handed it out for evaluation, and approved funding in April 1943.

Then came ENIAC, the Eckert-Mauchly Computer Corporation (with Mauchly on the business end while Eckert handled engineering), and the sale of the company and patents to Remington Rand, later bought by Sperry. Mauchly worked for both Remington and Sperry before leaving in 1959 to form his consulting company. Dynatrend was also a consultancy.

Mauchly and Eckert then built the Electronic Integrator and Computer (ENIAC), a general-purpose computer with a specific function, creating tables for the trajectories of bombs and shells. The computer, when finished in February 1946 (too late for use in the war), was 2.5 meters tall and 24 meters long. It contained eighteen thousand vacuum tubes and was one thousand times faster than the best electromechanical processor, performed up to five thousand additions per second. Control was through manipulation of wires on plugboards on the outside of the machine. ENIAC was the most complex and influential computer of its day.

Although World War II was over, government secrecy did not dissolve as the Cold War got under way. The ENIAC proved valuable in handling top-secret problems concerning development of nuclear weapons. Mathematician John von Neumann was involved with the nuclear project and used the ENIAC to handle partial differential equations essential to the development of atomic weapons at Los Alamos, New Mexico.

In October 1946, Mauchly and Eckert left Moore to form their Electronic Control Company. Their big order was from Northrop Aircraft, for whom they built the Binary Automatic Computer (BINAC). In use starting in August 1950, BINAC featured data storage on magnetic tape rather than punched cards. Electronic Control became Eckert-Mauchly Computer Corporation, which received an order from the National Bureau of Standards for what became the Universal Automatic Computer (UNIVAC), the first commercial computer in the United States. In all, there were forty-six UNIVACs. The UNIVAC was the first computer able to handle both alphabetical and numeric data equally well.

Eckert and Mauchly were not good businessmen, and it was nearly impossible to estimate costs of what was a totally new business, so their company struggled financially. It became the UNIVAC division of Remington Rand in 1950. Mauchly left Remington Rand to form Mauchly Associates, serving as president from 1959 to 1965, at which point he became chairman of the board. Between 1968 and his death in 1980, he was president of Dynatrend, Inc., and from 1970 until his death he was president of Marketrend, Inc.

Mauchly and Eckert's enterprise also suffered from the impact of patent litigation: ENIAC's patent was held by the Sperry Rand Corporation, which in 1967 sued the Honeywell Corporation for infringing that patent. At the same time, Honeywell countersued for fraud and antitrust violations, claiming that the ENIAC patent was invalid because the work was not unique: Mauchly had earlier examined the John Vincent Atanasoff and Clifford Berry's Atanasoff-Berry Computer (ABC). Eventually ENIAC's patent was ruled invalid, although mainly for technical reasons rather than the originality of Mauchly and Eckert's design. Moreover, in 1973 the U.S. District Court ruled that the ABC had been the first electronic digital computer and the electronic digital computer was in the public domain. This conclusion had the long-term salutary impact on the computer industry but of course a negative impact on Eckert and Mauchly's business.

Mauchly became a Fellow of the Institute of Radio Engineers (the IRE, which later became the Institute of Electrical and Electronics Engineers, or IEEE) in 1957, a Fellow of the American Statistical Association, and a lifetime member of the Franklin Institute, the National Academy of Engineering, and the Society for the Advancement of Management. He received the Computer Society's Harry M. Goode Memorial Award in 1966 as a pioneer in the field of computing, particularly the application of electronic computers to business and scientific problems and the creation of ENIAC, BINAC, and UNIVAC. He also received the Potts Medal (awarded by the Franklin Institute) in 1949, the John Scott Award in 1961, and the Philadelphia Award, the Emanuel R. Piore Award, and honorary degrees from Ursinus College and the University of Pennsylvania.

PERSONAL LIFE

Mauchly was handsome, with brown hair and hazel eyes. He was about six feet tall and weighed 180 pounds. Well read, soft-spoken, whimsical, and long-limbed, he conveyed the personality and aura of a scientist. His wife, Mary Augusta Walzl, was a mathematician. They married in 1930 and had two sons

Tragically, Mary was swept out to sea while she and John were swimming in the Atlantic Ocean in 1946. Mauchly later married Kathleen R. McNulty, a former ENIAC programmer, on February 7, 1948, and they had four daughters and a son. Mauchly suffered all his life from a hereditary genetic disease, hemorrhagic telangiectasia, which involved anemia, internal bleeding,

bloody noses, and other symptoms. Late in life, he required oxygen to breathe normally.

Although his career was hampered by litigation and tragedy touched his personal life, Mauchly succeeded in developing what is widely regarded as the first large-scale general-purpose electronic computer, built a start-up that he sold at a profit to the subsequent manufacturer of his machine, and headed a successful string of consulting businesses. He retired to the Philadelphia suburb of Ambler, dying there in 1980 of complications from an infection during heart surgery.

John H. Barnhill

FURTHER READING

DeAngelis, Gina, and David J. Bianco. *Computers: Processing the Data*. Minneapolis: Oliver, 2005. Print. Includes a chapter on Eckert and Mauchly.

Dyson, George. *Turing's Cathedral: The Origins of the Digital Universe*. New York: Pantheon, 2012. Print. A survey of the experimentation, mathematical insight, and creative endeavors leading to computers, digital television, genetics, and cosmological models based on computer code.

"ENIAC." *Time* 47.8 (1946): 92. *Academic Search Complete*. Web. 1 May 2012. The magazine article that introduced America's first general-purpose digital electronic computer to the public.

Flamm, Kenneth. *Creating the Computer: Government, Industry, and High Technology*. Washington, DC: Brookings Institution, 1988. Print. An older work but still useful for the development of the ENIAC.

McCartney, Scott. *ENIAC: The Triumphs and Tragedies of the World's First Computer*. New York: Walker, 1999. Print. A balanced treatment of the development of ENIAC.

Miller, Frederic P., Agnes F. Vandome, and John McBrewster *John Mauchly*. Beau-Bassin: Alphascript, 2010. Print. A concise biography at only 84 pages; a good overview and starting point.

Randall, Alexander V. "The Eckert Tapes: Computer Pioneer Says ENIAC Team Couldn't Afford to Fail—and Didn't." *Computerworld* 40.8 (2006): 18. *Academic Search Complete*. Web. 1 May 2012. Discusses interviews with Eckert, taped in 1989, in which he discusses ENIAC's technology and corrects some myths.

Sobel, Rachel K. "Faulty Memory." *U.S. News and World Report* 132.4 (2002): 70. *Academic Search Complete*. Web. 1 May 2012. Points to the historic omission of credit for the women "computers" who programmed the ENIAC.

Swedin, Eric G., and David L. Ferro. *Computers: The Life Story of a Technology*. Westport: Greenwood, 2005. Print. A history of computers from ancient beginnings to the time of publication, designed for a general audience.

"Unisys Corporation History." *International Directory of Company Histories*, Vol. 36. Detroit: St. James, 2001. Print. Profile that is dated but still useful on the history of Unisys, including mergers and restructurings well past the lifetime of Eckert.

JOHN MCCARTHY

Creator of the Lisp programming language

Born: September 4, 1927; Boston, Massachusetts
Died: October 24, 2011; Stanford, California
Primary Field: Computer science
Specialty: Computer programming
Primary Company/Organization: Stanford Artificial Intelligence Laboratory

INTRODUCTION

John McCarthy's research into artificial intelligence focused on formalizing commonsense knowledge and reasoning. His career spanned several important developments in the computer era. Like many early computer scientists, he was trained as a mathematician. By initiating experimentation into time sharing, he represented a shift into a new paradigm for computing, where researchers interacted with their own computer resources. His Stanford Artificial Intelligence Laboratory (SAIL) was funded in part by the Defense Advanced Research Projects Agency (DARPA) and was one of the first sites connected to the ARPANET. McCarthy's dedication to the field of artificial intelligence earned him the A. M. Turing Award in 1971, but equally impressive is the fact that sixteen researchers affiliated with SAIL have also been honored.

EARLY LIFE

John McCarthy has been called a red-diaper baby by historian John Markoff because his parents were members of the American Communist Party and his father, John Patrick McCarthy, was the business manager of the *Daily Worker*, the national newspaper of the Communist Party. (McCarthy was a member of the Communist Party for a short time in 1949.) John Patrick immigrated to the United States from Ireland. His wife, Ida Glatt, immigrated from Lithuania. They had son John in Boston but lost their house shortly thereafter, during the Great Depression, and moved to Los Angeles, where John Patrick organized members of the Amalgamated

Clothing Workers union. Son John graduated from Belmont High School, Los Angeles, in 1943.

At the age of fifteen, McCarthy bought a textbook being used at the California Institute of Technology (Caltech) and taught himself calculus. By the time he entered Caltech at the age of sixteen, he had learned too much calculus for undergraduate courses and so took a graduate class. He failed physical education because he refused to attend class, left the school, and was drafted into the Army. After being stationed in Texas, McCarthy was allowed to reenter Caltech; he graduated with a bachelor of science degree in mathematics in 1948. The next year, he continued his study of mathematics

John McCarthy.

at the graduate level at Princeton University, where he presented his research to John von Neumann and became friends with Marvin Minsky; he graduated two years later. In the summer of 1952, McCarthy worked at Bell Laboratories, where he met Claude Shannon and with him edited a volume of essays on intelligent machines, *Automata Studies* (1956). McCarthy was an instructor of mathematics at Princeton from 1951 to 1953 and at Stanford University from September 1953 to January 1955. His background as a mathematician was not unusual. In the 1950s, computer programmers were largely industry experts who learned from practical projects, such as IBM's involvement with the SAGE missile defense system. Computer programming had not yet advanced to an academic discipline, but it was beginning to be taught at the university level in mathematics departments, where it naturally fit.

LIFE'S WORK

In the spring of 1955, McCarthy was named assistant professor of mathematics at Dartmouth College. At Dartmouth, based on his acquaintance with Shannon and their shared interest in intelligent machines, McCarthy is credited for coining the term *artificial intelligence* in a research proposal he wrote with colleagues to the Rockefeller Foundation. The proposal resulted in the 1956 Dartmouth Conference, a two-month, ten-person symposium that marked the start of research into artificial intelligence.

Through the auspices of the Sloan Foundation, McCarthy went to the Computation Center at the Massachusetts Institute of Technology (MIT) for a one-year fellowship in 1957; he did not return to Dartmouth. From 1958 to 1961, he was an assistant professor of communication science at MIT. At MIT, he initiated research into time sharing with a memo he wrote, "A Time Sharing Operator Program for Our Projected IBM 709." The computers at the time were used by means of "batch-processing" systems. The "batch" referred to a set of punch cards, and the implication was that only one user could work with a computer at a time. For each computer program to be run, programmers waited for the card reader to process the punch cards, the results to be calculated, and the output to be printed. It became clear that the processor was active for only a small part of that time, and given that the machines were very expensive, that idle time represented wasted money. An early form of time sharing was available for the SAGE system, where multiple users had access to the same information, but McCarthy took this idea further in

his memo. He hypothesized that a user could be given the illusion of full access to a machine if the computer quickly cycled among all requests, and users could debug their programs simultaneously.

McCarthy was not comfortable proposing hardware modifications, given that his specialty was not in electronics, and so he proposed what he called minimal changes to computer circuits. His demonstration of the concept of "time stealing" (as they called it then) involved McCarthy in a computer room and the audience in a lecture hall, connected by closed-circuit television. While an ordinary batch job was running on the computer, it also collected input from a teletype machine and processed that input when the other job was completed. This inspired Fernando Corbato and his colleagues to build a prototype time-sharing operating system called Computer Time-Sharing System (CTSS) in November 1961; when this system was operational in 1963, it initiated the Project on Mathematics and Computation (Project MAC). With Ed Fredkin, McCarthy put together a time-sharing system on a Digital Electronics Corporation (DEC) PDP-1 computer at Bolt, Beranek, and Newman, which was operational in 1962. McCarthy declined to take this work further; he wanted to return to research on artificial intelligence. Instead, Alan Kotok, one of McCarthy's students, designed the first commercial time-sharing system, the DEC PDP-6. Time sharing would become a research priority for DARPA under J. C. R. Licklider, who funded several projects in that field beginning in 1963. The importance of time sharing cannot be underestimated, as indicated by the fact that what would become the ARPANET was imagined as a cooperative network of time-sharing computers.

Time sharing, however, was not McCarthy's primary interest; it was merely a tool to aid research on artificial intelligence (AI). When Minsky joined McCarthy at MIT, they founded the MIT Artificial Intelligence Laboratory. His Teddington Symposium paper presented his early thinking on how to incorporate commonsense reasoning into AI and was published in 1959 as "Programs with Common Sense." In it, McCarthy described how a program could use sentences in a logical language, acquire new knowledge, and then draw inferences from the stored information. He and his students created a computer program to play chess, later known as Kotok-McCarthy, soon after teaching what Markoff says was the first undergraduate course in computer science. In 1958, McCarthy invented the programming language Lisp, the second-oldest programming

Affiliation: Stanford Artificial Intelligence Laboratory

John McCarthy created the Stanford Artificial Intelligence Laboratory (SAIL) in 1963. In 1966, the lab moved to the half-finished facility built as the Donald C. Power Laboratory on a plot of land close to the main campus. The lab had been started but abandoned by General Telephone and Electronics. Les Earnest, an engineer from the MITRE Corporation, was hired as an executive officer, and McCarthy acted as director from 1965 to 1980.

The lab acquired a PDP-6 computer from a DARPA contract and was known for its loosely organized group of eclectic researchers. Although it established an innovative set of time-sharing terminals, because it was officially an artificial intelligence laboratory the achievement of a terminal on every desk was largely unrecognized. SAIL was one of the first ARPANET nodes, connected in 1970 during the network's first year of operation. In October 1972, as part of the International Conference on Computer Communication in Washington, D.C., which helped present the capabilities of ARPANET to a wider public, SAIL participated in a unique way. In response to the Doctor simulation of a psychotherapist, written at the Massachusetts Institute of Technology, researchers at SAIL had invented Parry, a program that simulated a paranoid patient. Researchers from the University of California at Los Angeles established a connection between the Doctor and Parry over the ARPANET, putting the two programs into a humorous conversation with each other.

SAIL was a leader in artificial intelligence research, and sixteen Turing Awards have been given to affiliated researchers. When Xerox's Palo Alto Research Center (PARC) opened in the 1970s, several researchers (including Alan Kay and Larry Tesler), brought the SAIL culture with them, while others moved to Lucasfilm to develop the technology needed to support the first film in the *Star Wars* series. Cisco Systems also used technology developed in the lab, and John Chowning invented the technology behind music synthesizers there. Steve Jobs and Steve Wozniak were visitors to SAIL when they were in high school. Les Earnest created Finger there in the early 1970s; Earnest claims that the "pieces-of-glass" created for the SAIL time-sharing system were the precursors to the "windows" invented at Xerox PARC. McCarthy and his researchers also developed the first speech recognition system, the forerunner to vocal interfaces such as that behind Apple's Siri.

language (the first being Fortran), which would be used for symbolic processing needed for artificial intelligence research. The first paper describing Lisp was published in the *Communications of the ACM* in 1960, and its examples would be widely used in Lisp textbooks. McCarthy's 1959 "advice taker" paper, "Programs with Common Sense," proposed that reasoning for everyday problems was just as worthy of study as abstract programs, and both could be represented in mathematical logic.

After six years at MIT, McCarthy returned to Stanford's mathematics department in 1962, where he remained until he retired in 2000. He created the Stanford University AI Project in 1963, which after 1971 was known as the Stanford Artificial Intelligence Laboratory (SAIL), and served as its director from 1965 to 1980. From the start, SAIL was an innovative place. In a symposium honoring his achievements, McCarthy's students and colleagues praised his flexible, inquiry-based mentoring style and his willingness to secure research positions for them.

Starting in 1965, McCarthy made several visits to the Soviet Union. In 1965, he brought the chess-playing program written by MIT undergraduates, and a computer chess match against the program, written by researchers at the Institute for Theoretical and Experimental Physics in Moscow, was the result. Moves were transmitted via telegraphy from 1966 to 1967. In 1968, McCarthy taught in Akademgorodok in Novosibirsk, and in 1975, he helped persuade the Soviet Union to allow cybernetics researcher Alexander Lerner to speak at the International Joint Conference on Artificial Intelligence. McCarthy is said to have smuggled a fax machine and copier to the Soviet linguist Larisa Bogoraz.

Although student researchers at SAIL had access to a time-sharing system, undergraduates at Stanford had to use a batch-processing system with punch cards until 1976. In order to justify the cost of a time-sharing system for them, McCarthy set up a research project that would provide a time-sharing system for undergraduates, calling it the Low Overhead Time-Sharing System (LOTSS). By 1979, years before personal computers were widely available, undergraduates had access to a computing system, helping to create a community of undergraduate computer scientists.

As an established leader in the field, McCarthy continued to do research, published papers, mentor graduate students, and participate in professional conferences. At the turn of the century, he was working on a new programming language, Elephant. He hoped it would be a natural language interface between computers and humans, useful for commercial transactions but also research. Although it was based on other popular AI languages, the Elephant proposal indicates he was hoping to integrate past knowledge more directly into the processing of information. Also, in 2004, he wrote a sardonic science-fiction story, "The Robot and the Baby," that gives credibility to reports of McCarthy's irreverent attitude and demonstrates his awareness of the interactions among government, science, and industry bureaucracies that shaped the development of computer science. The story features the commonsense reasoning of R781, a household robot who finds itself at the center of a child-care controversy.

McCarthy has many times been honored for his work. In 1971, the Association for Computing Machinery honored him with its A. M. Turing Award. He was elected to National Academy of Engineering in 1987. He won the Kyoto Prize from the Inamori Foundation in November 1988. He was elected to the National Academy of Sciences in 1989 and was awarded a National Medal of Science in 1990. The California Institute of Technology has named him a distinguished alumnus.

PERSONAL LIFE

McCarthy retired from his full-time position at Stanford in 2001 and was named professor emeritus. He was married three times: to Martha Coyote, Vera Watson, and Carolyn Talcott. His second wife was an IBM programmer who died in a 1978 climbing accident in Nepal. He had three children, two from his first wife and one from his third. He died in his Palo Alto home at the age of eighty-four from complications related to heart disease.

Christopher Leslie

FURTHER READING

Lifschitz, Vladimir. "John McCarthy (1927–2011)." *Nature* 480 (2011): 40. Print. An obituary by a well-known professor of computer science and artificial intelligence at the Univesity of Texas at Austin.

Markoff, John. *What the Dormouse Said: How the 60s Counterculture Shaped the Personal Computer Industry*. New York: Penguin, 2005. Print. Examines the interconnectedness of the 1960s drug and computing subcultures, including McCarthy and his accomplishments.

Morgenstern, Leora, and Sheila A. McIlraith. "John McCarthy's Legacy." *Artificial Intelligence* 175 (2011): 1–24. Print. A detailed overview of what McCarthy contributed to the AI field.

Patrick, J. Hayes and Leora Morgenstern. "On John McCarthy's 80th Birthday, in Honor of His Contributions." *AI Magazine* 28.4 (2012): 93–102. Print. A tribute that looks back on McCarthy's career and achievements.

SCOTT MCNEALY

Cofounder and former CEO of Sun Microsystems

Born: November 13, 1954; Columbus, Indiana
Died: -
Primary Field: Computer science
Specialty: Computer hardware
Primary Company/Organization: Sun Microsystems

INTRODUCTION

In 1982, Scott McNealy cofounded Sun Microsystems with Andy Bechtolsheim, Vinod Khosla, and Bill Joy, as part of the high-tech boom of Silicon Valley during the 1980s. Unlike most senior executives in Silicon Valley *then and now, McNealy had a business background and little experience in computers or engineering; he had been recruited by fellow Stanford alumnus Khosla for exactly that reason.*

EARLY LIFE

Scott McNealy was born on November 13, 1954, in Columbus, Indiana, and moved as a child to Bloomfield Hills, Michigan. His father was a factory worker in the automobile industry. McNealy attended Cranbrook, an elite preparatory school, and has praised the experience,

Scott McNealy.

especially that of being treated as a more responsible young adult than he had been acknowledged to be in public school. Although not a diligent student, he found that prep school eased his way into the Ivy League. McNealy attended Harvard University, earning a bachelor's degree in economics. He applied to the Stanford Graduate School of Business but did not get in on his first try, so he spent two years working as a plant foreman overseeing the manufacture of tractor body panels in a Rockwell factory. On his third attempt, he was accepted at Stanford, becoming one of the few students at the school working toward his master's in business administration with a focus on manufacturing.

After graduate school, McNealy took a job with the FMC Corporation, which built Bradley tanks, and after a year he moved on to Onyx Systems, in Cupertino, California, a Unix-based microprocessor manufacturer. He had been recruited for the job by his former economics professor at Harvard, William Raduchel. Raduchel had been the reason McNealy majored in economics—he had entered Harvard as a declared premedical student, but Raduchel had inspired an interest in economics. McNealy had not been a hacker or amateur programmer and had no contact with what is now called geek

culture; unlike many of those involved in Silicon Valley start-ups, his background was strictly in business, and it was as much happenstance as anything else that brought him into the computer industry.

In 1982, when McNealy was working at Onyx Systems as director of manufacturing, Stanford classmate Vinod Khosla got in touch with him, looking for someone with business experience to join Andy Bechtolsheim's start-up, Sun Microsystems.

LIFE'S WORK

McNealy not only joined Sun (as vice president of operations); he assumed the chief executive officer (CEO) role in 1984. A year later, Khosla left the company. McNealy served as CEO for twenty-two years before stepping down. While at Sun, he hired Raduchel as chief information officer.

Although the term "Silicon Valley" had first been coined in 1971 in reference to the number of silicon chips manufactured in the region, it did not become popular until the high-tech boom of the 1980s. Sun was a large part of this boom, along with Oracle, 3Com, Silicon Graphics, and Apple.

McNealy has long advocated network solutions, and Sun's motto at one time was "The Network Is the Computer." He has expressed skepticism of technologies that focus on client-side resources over network resources—the iPod is his common example, as he believes it represents a transitional technology, like the answering machine, that will soon be rendered obsolete by a replacement that streams music stored on a network. In this respect he has much in common with cloud computing advocates such as Ray Ozzie.

Although rarely in the spotlight to the extent of many other Silicon Valley CEOs, McNealy did not censor himself either; he once referred to Microsoft's Bill Gates as "a convicted monopolist." McNealy has occasionally been the focus of controversy because of his libertarian yet defeatist attitudes toward privacy in an age of increasing privacy concerns. He is on the record as saying that the age of privacy has come to an end, a common concern of both libertarians and others; rather than seek remedy for this, though, or protections for what privacy is left, he seems to think this loss should simply be accepted as inevitable.

In 2006, McNealy retired from the CEO position. He and his successor as CEO, Jonathan Schwartz, both testified in 2012 in a trial concerning Google's use of Java in its Android operating system. McNealy testified that while Sun had typically allowed other companies to

Affiliation: Sun Microsystems

Stanford graduate students Scott McNealy, Andy Bechtolsheim, and Vinod Khosla founded Sun Microsystems on February 24, 1982, taking their name from the Stanford University Network Unix workstation that Bechtolsheim had designed. Bill Joy, who developed the Berkeley Software Distribution (BSD), joined in the first quarter and is today considered one of the original founders.

Sun posted profits from its first quarter and made an initial public offering in 1986. In the 1980s, Sun was principally a designer and manufacturer of professional workstations, offering low-cost workstations running Unix operating systems and later high-end servers and data storage centers. Its first workstation ran on UniSoft V7 Unix, but beginning in 1982 Sun developed SunOS, a customized version of Joy's BSD Unix. SunOS was succeeded by Solaris.

In 1987, Sun introduced SPARC (for "scalable processor architecture"), a central processing unit (CPU) architecture implemented in its workstation and server systems, originally for 32-bit and later 64-bit operation. It formed SPARC International in 1989 to promote SPARC architecture and encourage its adoption by other manufacturers, leading to some licensing to Texas Instruments, Fujitsu, and others. SPARC remains in development; it was implemented in Oracle's 2011 SPARC T4 multicore processor.

Originally known as a hardware company, Sun always had software in its DNA, thanks in part to Joy. Its most famous contribution to the computing industry is the Java programming language, released in 1995 as part of the Java platform. Java applications were designed to run on any computer regardless of the computer architecture, through the use of Java Virtual Machines, an isolated Java operating system environment installed within the host operating system. This freed programmers from having to port programs from one environment to another, which became a special advantage as the Internet became more popular. Java quickly became the most popular programming language for client-server web applications, and it remains so.

Sun also acquired a number of software companies and packages, including the OpenOffice suite (originally StarOffice), the MySQL database, and Netscape's nonbrowser software components. The company grew considerably during the dot-com bubble, but when the bubble burst in 2000, Sun suffered worse than many of the other survivors, with stock eventually falling below $10 per share, about a tenth of the value it had had immediately before the bubble. Layoffs and factory closures followed, and Sun narrowed its product focus. Another catastrophic fall came between 2007 and 2008, when Sun stock lost 80 percent of its value, forcing another round of layoffs and closures and eventually leading to the company's buyout.

Long an antagonist and critic of Microsoft, Sun resolved its differences with the company in 2004, taking a $1.95 billion payment to settle a series of legal disputes and supporting Microsoft Windows on its future x64 systems.

In 2009, Sun agreed to be acquired by Oracle, a deal that was completed in 2010, after another round of layoffs. Sun's Menlo Park, California, campus was sold off to become the headquarters of Facebook.

use Java, it had required that the company obtain a commercial license and that it retain Java's compatibility. Schwartz testified that he had hoped Google would take out a commercial license but had opted not to sue Google.

McNealy continued to serve as chairman of Sun's board of directors until 2010, when the company was bought by Oracle. In 2011, he began seeking funding for WayIn, a social media start-up based in Denver. WayIn launched quietly, offering a service focused on opinion polls users can both create and vote in, while connecting to other users and linking polls to other social networks. The service launched with apps for the iPhone, iPad, and Android devices, as well as a website. As with other social networks, the revenue generation comes from selling consumer preference data to marketers; WayIn's focus on polls promises significant depth of such information if the service becomes widely used.

McNealy has also served as an adviser to Hardcore Computer (based in Rochester, Minnesota), a designer of custom computer systems using liquid submersion cooling; Crucial Point, a national security technology firm offering consulting, research, and due diligence; Nyoombl ("nimble"), a Palo Alto–based video website that makes video conversations between two parties public in order to post debates and interviews; and Greenplum Software, a data-warehousing company that develops database software and a customer and partner portal for instant downloads of database products.

PERSONAL LIFE

McNealy married Susan Ingemanson in 1994. The couple have four sons: Maverick, Dakota, Colt, and Scout. Politically, McNealy is a libertarian. A devoted and skilled golfer, he is the commissioner of the Alternative Golf Association; *Golf Digest* named him the top golfer among CEOs in 2002. He is also an amateur ice hockey player.

Bill Kte'pi

FURTHER READING

Ceruzzi, Paul E. *Computing: A Concise History*. Cambridge: MIT, 2012. Print. A broad history of computers, including Sun's role.

Hall, Mark, and John Barry. *Sunburst: The Ascent of Sun Microsystems*. New York: Contemporary, 1991. Print. Although an older account, this is more insightful than the book by Southwick and good on the company's early years.

Southwick, Karen. *High Noon: The Inside Story of Scott McNealy and the Rise of Sun Microsystems*. New York: Wiley, 1999. Print. Focuses more on Sun than on McNealy, but one of the few book-length treatments.

BOB MINER

Cofounder of Oracle

Born: December 23, 1941; Cicero, Illinois
Died: November 11, 1994; San Francisco, California
Primary Field: Computer science
Specialty: Computer software
Primary Company/Organization: Oracle

INTRODUCTION

The cofounder of Oracle Corporation, which popularized and dominated the market for relational database management systems, Bob Miner met cofounder Larry Ellison while supervising him at Ampex in the 1970s. At Oracle, Miner was in charge of product development from 1977 to 1992. He retired a year later after receiving a diagnosis of cancer.

EARLY LIFE

Robert Nimrod Miner was born on December 23, 1941, in Cicero, Illinois, a suburb of Chicago. His parents were both Assyrian immigrants from northwest Iran. He majored in mathematics at the University of Illinois at Urbana-Champaign, graduating in 1963. He took a job at Ampex, an electronics company that principally manufactured professional tape recorders (and introduced instant replay and electronic video editing) but also developed customized database programs. At Ampex, Miner met Larry Ellison, whom he supervised. Together with fellow Ampex employee Ed Oates, Miner and Ellison founded Software Development Laboratories (SDL), which eventually became Oracle Systems, named for its Oracle Database product.

LIFE'S WORK

Software Development Laboratories was incorporated on June 16, 1977, in Santa Clara, California, and the first version of Oracle was released in 1978. Named for a project for the Central Intelligence Agency (CIA) on

Bob Miner.

Affiliation: Oracle

In 2001, the dawn of the twenty-first century, ninety-eight of the Fortune 100 companies used Oracle software to manage their business files. Customer interactions ranging from paying a phone bill to buying a plane ticket, making a hotel reservation, withdrawing cash from an automated teller, paying for a purchase with a credit card, and conducting a search on Google—all involved the use of an Oracle software package somewhere behind the scenes. Oracle never became a household name, and what mainstream fame it did have was largely because of CEO Larry Ellison's outsized personality, but business owners knew the name as well as their employees recognized brands like Starbucks.

Oracle was founded in 1977 by Ellison, his former supervisor Bob Miner, their colleague at Ampex Ed Oates, and Bruce Scott, the company's first hire. Originally called Software Development Laboratories (SDL), it renamed itself Relational Software, Inc. (RSI) in 1979 but eventually took the name Oracle in honor of its flagship software package. The Oracle software was a relational database management system, inspired by a paper circulated at IBM and applied by SDL to smaller computers than conventional wisdom in the 1970s said was possible.

Relational database management systems (RDBMS's) such as the one Oracle pioneered have become a standard tool in business operations—ironic for a company that had so little business savvy when it began, particularly when it came to bookkeeping. The company's first chief financial officer began as a pizza delivery boy—SDL was on his route, and no one at the company had any idea how to approach accounting (nor did anyone formally keep the books for a full two years), so the founders hired him when they discovered that he had majored in accounting. The rest of the practicalities of business, Ellison taught himself.

In 1983, RSI introduced the first commercial portable RDBMS, which could be run on the wide range of hardware and operating systems that had become available during the explosive growth of the computing industry. The product was instrumental in the company's doubling its revenues that year, and RSI was renamed Oracle Corporation, capitalizing on the fame of its flagship product (and the cancellation of a CIA project for which the company had won a contract). New versions released in 1985 allowed a single database to be accessed by multiple applications, making the Oracle system more flexible and customizable. The following year, structured query language (SQL), developed by IBM in the 1970s, was adopted as the standard language of the database industry, which boosted Oracle's prominence, as it was the best-known and longest-established SQL-compatible RDBMS.

On March 15, 1986, Oracle went public with an initial public offering of 2.1 million shares and a market value of $270 million. It had grown over a little less than ten years from four partners to 450 employees, with a customer base of more than two thousand firms and government organizations. Twenty years later, it had grown from 450 employees to 65,000, revenues five hundred times higher than 1986's $20 million. In 1989, the company was added to the Standard and Poor's 500, only three years after going public.

Oracle expanded into applications, principally for use with databases, while Ellison delegated most of his CEO responsibilities to others in order to focus on expanding product diversity. A suite of accounting and bookkeeping programs followed, as well as a transaction process subsystem (TPS) package for use with financial transactions. New backup programs were developed in order to generate data archives for businesses. A subsidiary, Oracle Data Publishing, was formed in 1989 to sell reference material in digital form.

Some minor troubles developed in 1990, when shareholders filed a lawsuit alleging that Oracle's earnings forecasts had been deliberately misleading; In 1990's first quarter, net earnings had been nearly flat, and the day after this was announced, Oracle's stock fell from $25.38 to $17.50 per share. Oracle conducted an internal audit and formed a separate subsidiary, Oracle US, to solve its management problems. Ellison's over-the-top personality had too often been coupled with a short attention span: He would work hard on a project for weeks, burn himself out, and leave for a European vacation before coming back to bear down hard on another project. His own self-evaluation of his behavior varied considerably: Sometimes he took pride

Affiliation: Oracle (Continued)

in his reputation as a wildcard because he believed it reflected the company's innovativeness; other times he admitted that he might be holding the company back.

In 1992, major changes took place throughout the company. Cofounder Miner—who had balanced Ellison's managerial style in the early days—first left his post as head of product development, which he had held since the company began, and then left the company altogether because of a cancer diagnosis. New executives were brought in to shore up the corporation's weak areas. Oracle7, the last product Miner oversaw, was released after six years of development and testing and was exceptionally well received, particularly its compatibility with networks and the implication of Internet compatibility in the future. By the end of the year, the balance sheet had improved and bank debt had been cleared from the books.

Oracle, especially Ellison, butted heads with Microsoft and Bill Gates in the 1990s over the Internet, with Oracle fighting to popularize cheap network computers that would run Internet applications as a substitute for more expensive Intel machines running Windows products that would require expensive software upgrades. Suites of Internet business applications fol-lowed in the late 1990s, with Oracle E-Business Suite Release 11i, which Ellison marketed with a $300 million campaign, the cornerstone of which was the implementation of 11i at the Oracle Corporation and the demonstration that doing so saved Oracle $1 billion a year.

Key to Oracle's twenty-first century development has been flexibility and scalability in its products, which are suitable for concerns ranging from small businesses with a single point of sale to multinational corporations and government agencies. Oracle also succeeded in a hostile takeover of competitor PeopleSoft, conducted in 2003–04, and acquired Sun Microsystems—its ally in the fight against Microsoft—in January 2010, interested primarily in its Java programming language and the Solaris operating system.

In 2010, Oracle was indicted by the federal government for fraud, for presenting misleading information about the bulk discounts given to federal buyers. A month later, Oracle brought suit against Google for patent violation and copyright infringement, alleging the use of material protected by Java patents in Google's Android system. In 2012, a jury found in favor of Google.

---

which the SDL founders had worked at Ampex, Oracle was designed to be a relational database to sell to that project. Bruce Scott joined as the fourth partner, and the cofounders pooled together $2,000 in start-up funding and rented an office in Belmont, California. Miner and Ellison had contacts at the CIA and were able to persuade the CIA to give them the $50,000 contract to develop the database.

The idea of a relational database had been introduced by Ted Codd, a mathematical programmer at IBM, in "A Relational Model of Data for Large Shared Data Banks." The paper was published in 1970 after an earlier draft circulated internally at IBM. Seven years had passed, and IBM had yet to release, or apparently even develop, a relational database; it seemed the commercial possibilities had eluded them, and SDL moved forward to capitalize on their neglect. Miner and Ellison had read and discussed the paper and predicted that if IBM did move forward in developing relational databases, IBM would incorporate them—and the structured query language (SQL) that it had

developed—into future mainframes but not minicomputers (which were smaller than mainframes but still huge compared to the personal computers that would eventually dominate). As opposed to a flat database (in which all fields are located in a single text file with fields delineated by character strings, thus requiring awkward and time-consuming searches to find related data), a relational database makes it possible to sort multiple types of data by any field, compiling multiple fields on the basis of queries that create tailored tables. Relational databases thus allow users to match data stored in the database according to specified common characteristics, or relations. While there are many business applications, the appeal to the CIA was the ability to automate the process of searching through their numerous files looking for patterns that might be relevant to the work at hand.

While Ellison was business-minded and developed a distinctive culture at Oracle, Miner took charge of developing the company's database products. The two frequently clashed over issues of workplace culture,

Miner objecting to Ellison's insistence on keeping the programmers working late. While Ellison aggressively courted clients, Miner oversaw the advances in software development and code.

The CIA project never went anywhere, although it did generate anecdotes the partners would tell at various gatherings when they later became famous for their private sector work. The first release of Oracle was called version 2, which was Ellison's innovation—he was afraid people would not take a chance on the software if they knew it was the first release. Miner did much of the work on version 2, and the subsequent release, version 3, was almost entirely his work.

Miner continued to head product development of Oracle's database systems from the inception of the company until shortly before his retirement. When Oracle faced financial troubles in 1990 following a lawsuit filed by shareholders over possible accounting errors, the company was shaken up internally, with many on the board calling for the eccentric Ellison's resignation and a domestic subsidiary formed to address management concerns. Miner, who never enjoyed those kinds of conflicts, wanted to sell his shares and cash out, but he was persuaded to remain. Instead, shortly after in 1992, Miner began an advanced technology group in Oracle, handing over the product development reins. He retired the following year because of illness.

PERSONAL LIFE

Miner and his wife Mary had three children, Nicola, Justine, and Luke. He purchased Oakville Ranch Vineyards in 1989, which is now managed by his nephew Dave, who produces Miner Family Vineyards wine. One of their red wines is called The Oracle.

Miner was diagnosed in 1993 with lung cancer as the result of exposure to asbestos and resigned from Oracle's board of directors. He died on November 11, 1994, in San Francisco, at the age of fifty-two.

Bill Kte'pi

FURTHER READING

Codd, E. F. "A Relational Model of Data for Large Shared Data Banks." *Communications of the ACM* 13.6 (1970): n. pag. Print. Ted Codd's original paper introducing the concept of the relational database, on which Oracle was based.

Cringely, Robert X. *Accidental Empires: How the Boys of Silicon Valley Make Their Millions, Battle Foreign Competition, and Still Can't Get a Date*. New York: HarperBusiness, 1996. Print. A history of Silicon valley from before the dot-com bubble burst.

Kenney, Martin. *Understanding Silicon Valley: The Anatomy of an Entrepreneurial Region*. Stanford: Stanford UP, 2000. Print. An overview of Silicon Valley, the culture from which Oracle emerged.

Rao, Arun, and Piero Scarulfi. *A History of Silicon Valley*. San Francisco: Omniware, 2011. Print. An overview of the Silicon Valley tech company culture.

Symonds, Matthew. *Softwar: An Intimate Portrait of Larry Ellison and Oracle*. New York: Simon, 2003. Print. As the title indicates, the focus is on Ellison's distinctive managerial style and personality, but Miner and Oates also are heavily featured.

Wilson, Mike. *The Difference between God and Larry Ellison (God Doesn't Think He's Larry Ellison): Inside Oracle Corporation*. New York: William Morrow, 1997. Print. Ellison-centric, but the other partners at Oracle also receive significant coverage.

CHARLES H. MOORE

Creator of the Forth programming language

Born: 1938; McKeesport, Pennsylvania
Died: -
Primary Field: Computer science
Specialty: Computer programming
Primary Company/Organization: FOURTH, Inc.

INTRODUCTION

Charles H. Moore is best known as the creator of Forth, a programming language for process control, instrumentation, and peripherals that is still in use by the National Aeronautics and Space Administration (NASA). The name originally was Fourth, but the

IBM 1130 minicomputer for which Moore originally wrote the language allowed only five-character names. Moore also founded FORTH, Inc. and created color-Forth when the American National Standards Institute (ANSI) codified megaForth (which Moore found to be cumbersome and unwieldy) as the standard version of Forth. Moore is an advocate of the KISS concept (keep it simple, stupid) and improved on the original Forth to make the simpler, faster, and more versatile colorForth. He is also a follower of John McCarthy, primarily involved in artificial intelligence, in contradistinction to the other school of computing, led by Doug Engelbart, which focused on how computers could enhance the human mind.

EARLY LIFE

Charles H. "Chuck" Moore was born in McKeesport, Pennsylvania, in 1938, and was reared in Flint, Michigan. He was valedictorian of Central High School in 1956 and was awarded a National Merit Scholarship to the Massachusetts Institute of Technology (MIT), where he joined the Kappa Sigma fraternity. In 1960, Moore earned a degree in physics with a thesis on data reduction for the Explorer 11 gamma-ray satellite, which was launched in June 1961. From 1961 to 1963, he studied mathematics at Stanford University.

LIFE'S WORK

Moore mastered several computer languages. He learned Lisp from McCarthy at Stanford and then moved to the Smithsonian Astrophysical Observatory (SAO) in Cambridge, Massachusetts, in 1958 learning Fortran II for an IBM 704 to predict Moonwatch satellite orbits. The job at SAO was part time.

In 1962, Moore started learning ALGOL for the Burroughs B5500 at the Stanford Linear Accelerator Center. Founding Charles Moore and Associates in 1964, he wrote a Fortran-ALGOL translator for his time-sharing service.

In 1968, Moore moved to suburban Amsterdam, New York, where he took a job with a carpet and furniture manufacturer, Mohasco Industries. He also mastered COBOL for the IBM 1130 in use at Mohasco, with the goal of using computer graphics to design carpets. Moore had to deal with a new IBM 1130, whose programming in Fortran required multiple card decks, and Fortran could not use the disk and graphics display. Moore created Forth, which used both disk and graphics display, making it interactive and its programming easier and faster.

In 1971, George Conant offered Moore a position at the U.S. National Radio Astronomy Observatory (NRAO). At NRAO, Moore's job involved controlling several telescopes and data collection/reduction systems. While working at NRAO, Moore adapted Forth to the Honeywell 316 to control radio telescopes and data collection and reduction systems. Conant did not like Moore's using Forth to control the telescope when all the other work at NRAO was in Fortran. However, he agreed when Moore demonstrated that he could finish projects with better capabilities in weeks rather than years. At NRAO, Moore, met Elizabeth Rather, who was hired to provide support, which involving learning and documenting Forth. They worked to reprogram computers at NRAO and completed Forth. As Moore put it on his website, www.colorforth.com: "NRAO appreciated what I had wrought. They had an arrangement with a consulting firm to identify spin-off technology. The issue of patenting Forth was discussed at length. But since software patents were controversial and might involve the Supreme Court, NRAO declined to pursue the matter. Whereupon, rights reverted to me. I don't think ideas should be patentable. Hindsight agrees that Forth's only chance lay in the public domain. Where it has flourished." In 1971, Moore and Rather founded FORTH, Inc.

Charles H. Moore.

209

Moore next decided to build a Forth chip to realize the architecture intrinsic to Forth. He was a founder of Novix, Inc., and implemented the NC4000 (1983) as a gate array. He developed and sold kits to promote the chip. A derivative was eventually sold to Harris Semiconductor, which marketed it as the RTX2000 for space applications (1988).

Founding Computer Cowboys, Moore designed the Sh-Boom microprocessor in 1985. In 1990, he developed his own design tools for the MuP21, with multiple specialized processors; in 1993, the F21, featuring a network interface; and in 1996, the i21 for his new enterprise iTv Corp., with a similar architecture with enhanced performance designed for Internet applications. In 2001, he designed the c18 microcomputer, a simple core that can be replicated many times on a single chip. Each of his chips has emphasized high performance and low power.

When the American National Standards Institute (ANSI) designated megaForth, which Moore considered unwieldy, as the standard version of Forth, Moore, refuting the decision, developed colorForth. Moore defines colorForth as a dialect of Forth, a simpler Forth, and a return with enhancements to the original idea. It is faster and more efficient in using compile time rather than run time, although it has been mostly ignored by the Forth community.

In the early 2000s, early patents for reduced instruction set computing (RISC) processors began expiring, among them the set covered by the Moore microprocessor patent awarded in 1989 and good through 2012. The patents were in dispute between IntellaSys and its parent company Technology Properties Limited (TPL), in Cupertino, California (where Moore served as chief technology officer), and Patriotic Scientific of Carlsbad, California.

Moore had hoped to achieve his long-standing goal of creating high-performance, low-dissipation Forth chips. He planned a "sea of processors platform" to maximize per-watt performance for embedded applications. The initial publicity in October 2005 was light on details and strong on hope, with a planned beta version by early 2006. The company was just ramping up, interviewing people for engineering and manufacturing jobs. Intellasys was the result of a settlement in 2006 of the long-standing intellectual property dispute with Patriotic Scientific CPU developers over several patents covering the Moore microprocessor package. After the two firms agreed to cooperate, TPL began selling the technology through Alliacense, and buyers included

Affiliation: FORTH, Inc.

Having created the Forth language, Moore founded FORTH, Inc. in 1971 with cofounder Elizabeth Rather (who at that time was a colleague at the National Radio Astronomy Observatory and the only other Forth programmer) with $5,000 from an angel investor. Moore had written the first iteration of Forth using Fortran when he was at NRAO, but the second Forth was written in COBOL at the carpet manufacturer Mohasco. Until he wrote the compiler and made it a language, Forth was an interpreter (through its third iteration). The compiler was for speed; Forth was already fast, but projects got more complex and Moore needed interactivity rather than following the edit-compile-link-load sequence that was standard. With Forth the sequence was edit-load.

For the next ten years, Moore ported Forth to numerous mini-, micro-, and mainframe computers, programming numerous applications from databases to robotics. The Forth standard approved by the American National Standards Institute (ANSI), megaForth, does not express Moore's vision of Forth. Moore believes the ANSI standard is far too large and complex, and he does not see much value in any standard, since people should write their own Forth. It is fair to say that most of the Forth community disagrees. Moore left the mainstream of Forth several years ago, and has since worked mainly on chips that directly run Forth as their instruction set. In 2012 he continued to work on the next generation of Forth language, colorForth. He maintains a blog and site at www.colorforth.com.

Intel, AMD, Casio, Hewlett Packard, and Sony. The Sony license was a big step, Sony being a major player. Alliacense also had negotiations under way with dozens of other companies. However, others were unimpressed with the tools. More important, TPL was moving beyond licensing to production, including the Intellasys component; Moore was working on a $10 chip running Forth natively without a clock. Intellasys intended to use a 24-core Forth microcontroller initially with a 40-core seaForth 40C18 in 2008. Early in 2009, Intellasys folded, and Moore formed GreenArray, hired the core Intellasys team, and began producing a chip with 144 Forth cores. In 2010, Moore sued TPL and Alliacense for fraud and breach of contract.

Moore's software remained in common use in 2009. In 2009, Forth was still the National Aeronautics and Space Administration's language of choice because it was still the best for instrumentation, peripherals, and process control. Ahead of his time, Moore waited for the programming world to catch up with his belief that simplicity promotes effective software development. Forth was the forebear of PostScript and STOIC.

PERSONAL LIFE

Moore married Winifred Bellis in 1967. Their son Eric was born in 1969. With her he traveled around the world, moved often in his career, and spent time hiking and exploring from the Appalachian to the San Gabriel Mountains. When finances forced Moore and the family to move to Sierra City, California, from San Francisco, they continued hiking, she led a library knitting group, he became a fire commissioner. In 2005, she died suddenly of heart failure in Phoenix on one of his business trips, just before he became prosperous. As Moore put it, "I lost half of my memory and life will never be the same without her."

Developing a new language is a daunting prospect because it requires vast expenditure of creative man-years. Moore originally intended to keep Forth simple, to get it done quickly. He continued using Forth for quick programs after the turn of the century and as mental stimulation; as he put it, writing Forth programs was more fun and better for his brain than crossword puzzles or Sudoku.

John H. Barnhill

FURTHER READING

Biancuzzi, Federico, and Shane Warden. *Masterminds of Programming: Conversations with the Creators of Major Programming Languages*. Sebastopol: O'Reilly, 2009. Print. Includes a chapter on Forth and Moore.

Brodie, Leo. *Thinking Forth: A Language and Philosophy for Solving Problems*. Englewood Cliffs: Prentice-Hall, 1984. Print. Deals with Forth as a case study in the philosophy and practice of programming rather than a technical discussion of Forth, using interviews with Moore and other Forth users.

Catsoulis, John. *Designing Embedded Hardware*. Sebastopol: O'Reilly, 2005. Print. The focus is on hardware, but the book includes an explanation of what Forth is and how it works, arguing that hardware design has to accommodate the software that the hardware runs.

"Charles Moore: Carpet Patterns, Telescopes and Forth." InfoWorld 4.40 (1982): 17+. Print. Profile of Moore and Forth, but good for the early years. This issue of InfoWorld focused on Forth.

Clarke, Peter. "Microprocessor Pioneer Sues Patent Pool Firms." *Electronic Engineering Times* 11 Oct. 2010: 20. *Academic Search Complete*. Web. 8 May 2012. Moore had difficulties with TPL, leading to litigation in 2010.

Flaherty, Nick. "Untitled." *Electronics Weekly* 2250 (2006): 21. *Business Source Complete*. Web. 8 May 2012. Fairly detailed article about patents and potential infringement as early RISC patents expire but others remain in force; includes coverage of Moore's patents.

Moore, Charles H. "The A–Z of Programming Languages: Forth." Interview by Naomi Hamilton. 27 June 2008. *Computerworld*. Web. 16 Aug. 2012. Moore discusses why he invented Forth and why he still uses it.

---. "Chuck Moore: Geek of the Week." Interview bny Richard Moore. 5 August 2009. Web. *Simple-Talk*. 12 May 2012. Moore looks back on his career and discusses Forth.

Rather, Elizabeth, Donald R. Coburn, and Charles H. Moore. *The Evolution of Forth*. Mar. 1993. *Forth.com*. Web. 16 Aug. 2012. A detailed history of Forth from its original creation by Moore through its development beyond Moore.

"Startup Intelasys Targets Multicore Processors." *Electronic News* 51.44 (2005): n. pag. *Academic Search Complete*. Web. 15 May 2012. Describes Intelasys, with background on Moore and his partner Chester Brown.

Williams, Greg. "Threads of a Forth Tapestry." *Byte* 5.8 (1980): n. pag. Web. 15 May 2012. This editorial by Williams focuses on the inner workings of the Moore Forth operation; the editorial appears in a special issue of *Byte* on the Forth language.

GORDON E. MOORE

Cofounder and CEO of Intel

Born: January 3, 1929; San Francisco, California
Died: -
Primary Field: Computer science
Specialty: Computer hardware
Primary Company/Organization: Intel

INTRODUCTION

Chemist, entrepreneur, and philanthropist Gordon Moore was a founding father of the Silicon Valley culture. One of the so-called Traitorous Eight who left the company of Nobel laureate William Shockley to found Fairchild Semiconductor, he predicted in 1965 that the power and complexity of silicon chips would double every year for ten years, accompanied by decreases in cost. Three years after he made his famous postulation, which came to be known as Moore's law, he cofounded Intel Corporation, the world's leading manufacturer of silicon chips. After twenty-seven years at Intel, he retired and with his wife established the Gordon E. and Betty Moore Foundation, which has contributed billions of dollars to education, scientific research, and the environment.

EARLY LIFE

Gordon Earle Moore was born on January 3, 1929, in San Francisco, California. He spent the first decade of his life in Pescadero, a small farming community south of the city, where his father, Walter Harold Moore, was deputy sheriff, and the family of his mother, Florence Williamson Moore, owned a general store. A promotion for his father required the family to move to Redwood City, California, in 1939.

Thanks to a neighbor's chemistry set, Moore developed an interest in chemistry when he was just a boy and by the time he was twelve had decided to become a chemist. In high school, however, athletics had become more important to him than academics. Although mathematics and science came easily to him, he was a disinterested student. He lettered in four sports, and it was not until his senior year that he became a serious student. After graduation from Sequoia High School, he entered San Jose State University, becoming the first member of his family to attend college. He spent two years at San Jose State and then transferred to the University of California at Berkeley, where he received a B.S. degree in chemistry in 1950. He and his college sweetheart, Betty Whittaker, were married in 1950, shortly before he entered graduate school at the California Institute of Technology. In 1954, he received a Ph.D. in chemistry and physics.

Moore accepted a position with the Applied Physics Laboratory at the Johns Hopkins University in Baltimore, Maryland. He spent two and a half years at Johns Hopkins, but Moore was more interested in practical applications than in research. He was ready for a change, and both he and his wife were eager to return to California. By this time the Moores had a son, Kenneth. A second son, Steven, was born in 1959.

LIFE'S WORK

Moore was still at Johns Hopkins when he received a phone call from William Shockley, coinventor of the transistor and one of three recipients of the Nobel Prize in Physics in 1956. Shockley was looking for a chemist to join the newly established Shockley Semiconductor Laboratory, a division of Beckman Instruments. In 1956, Moore became the eighteenth person Shockley

Gordon E. Moore.

hired for the new company. While Shockley's brilliance in his field was undeniable, he was less talented in dealing with people. Many of the young men Shockley hired found working for him increasingly difficult. When he decided to table the work on a silicon transistor that had attracted them to his company, their dissatisfaction increased. Eight of the engineers, all between the ages of twenty-eight and thirty-four, wanted to continue to work together. Their idea was to find a company that would hire all eight of them. A young Harvard M.B.A., Arthur Rock, suggested they start their own company instead. On September 18, 1957, Moore along with C. Sheldon Roberts, Eugene Kleiner, Robert N. Noyce, Victor H. Grinich, Julius Blank, Jay T. Last, and Jean A. Hoerni left Shockley to do just that; they were termed the Traitorous Eight or, less pejoratively, the Fairchild Eight by the media. Rock, after forty-one rejections, found an investor in Sherman M. Fairchild, a pioneer in the fields of photography and aviation and the founder of the Fairchild Camera and Instrument Corporation and the Fairchild Engine and Airplane Corporation. With $1.5 million from Fairchild and $500 from each of the eight men, the group founded Fairchild Semiconductor. The company developed the manufacturing process for the earliest silicon chips and invented the first commercially produced integrated circuit. Because not many start-up companies could be found in California's Santa Clara Valley in the late 1950s, the eight are also credited with sparking the creation of what later was called Silicon Valley. By some estimates, as many as four hundred companies trace their beginnings to these eight men. Moore served as manager of engineering from 1957 to 1959 and as director of research and development at Fairchild Camera and Instrument Corporation from 1959 to 1968.

On April 19, 1965, Moore published an article in *Electronics* in which he predicted that the integrated circuit would annually, over the next ten years, double the number of transistors implanted on a computer chip. Based on Noyce's discovery in 1959 that an entire circuit could be created on a single chip, Moore's prediction also included proportionate decreases in costs. Four years earlier, the U.S. Patent Office had awarded the first patent for an integrated chip to Fairchild, inaugurating the age of the microchip. Moore's prediction, which came to be known as Moore's law, with some revision proved accurate over the next thirty years.

Despite the success of Fairchild, Moore was growing frustrated with the pace of production. When the board of directors passed over Noyce and hired an outsider as chief executive officer (CEO) in 1968, Noyce decided to leave. Moore agreed that the time was right for departure. With a one-page proposal in hand, the two approached venture capitalist Rock. He was intrigued and within two days had secured twenty-five investors for the new company. By July 1968, Intel had been launched. From the beginning, the company was known for its innovation. Its first product, a bipolar microchip manufactured in 1969, was used in the automation of chicken houses, in electronic marijuana sniffers, and in blood analysis. In 1970, the company invented dynamic random access memory (DRAM), used for data-storage chips in computers, and a year later they created the first microprocessor for Busicom, a Japanese manufacturer of calculators. The one chip Intel proposed to replace the thirteen complex circuits Busicom thought they needed became the Intel 4004. When Intel bought the rights back from Busicom for Busicom's initial $65,000 development investment, Intel was free to use the microprocessor in other applications, and Intel's place as the leader of the computer industry was secure.

It was Moore who argued for selling IBM a piece of Intel to provide the capital to develop the processors, and it was Moore who saw the company's future in microprocessors. Intel became the world's largest and wealthiest maker of semiconductor chips, and Moore himself became one of America's wealthiest citizens. Moore served as president and CEO of Intel from 1975 to 1979 and as chairman and CEO from 1979 to 1987. He turned over the CEO's job to Andrew Grove in 1987 but remained as chairman for another decade. He was part of the company's leadership in 1993, when Intel released its Pentium processor with 3.1 million transistors. A mandatory retirement-age policy he himself had helped implement forced him to yield the chairmanship to Grove in 1997. Moore served as chairman emeritus from 1997 until 2001.

In 1965, when Moore wrote the essay in which he articulated the premise that became Moore's law, mainframe computers required wings of buildings to house them and cost more than a million dollars. Moore's recognition that the silicon microchip would revolutionize the computer industry to the degree that computers would become as common in offices and homes as typewriters was visionary. An idea man, known as much for his humility as for his achievements, Moore was a key player in the personal computer revolution.

PERSONAL LIFE

By the time his role at Intel was decreasing, Moore was involved in other activities. An avid fisherman and

Affiliation: Intel

When Gordon Moore and Robert Noyce, two pioneers of the early semiconductor industry, founded their company in Santa Clara, California, in 1968, a hotel chain had already trademarked the name Moore Noyce, so the two agreed to name their new company Intel for "integrated electronics." Arthur Rock, the venture capitalist who raised $2.5 million in two days to give the company its initial investment, became the first chairman of Intel. Although the young company found success within its first year of operation, the company would claim its first major victory in 1981, when IBM, best known at the time for its mainframe computers and other office machinery, chose Intel to supply the processor for the first IBM personal computer.

Competition from Japanese semiconductor companies in 1985 posed a serious threat to Intel's market share, but a loan from IBM allowed Intel to develop the Intel 386, with 275,000 transistors on one chip, making it one of the most advanced microprocessors at that time. The first Pentium processor, in 1997, had 3.1 million transistors. Intel eventually supplied about 80 percent of the microprocessor chips in personal computers worldwide. When recession bit sharply into computer sales in 2008, Intel expanded into other markets. The company entered security technology with the purchase in 2010 of McAfee, a maker of antivirus software, and pushed aggressively to put chips in smart phones, televisions, and other electronic devices.

outdoorsman, in 1990 he became a director of Conservation International (CI), an environmental organization that works through corporations and governments to protect and preserve wilderness areas and biodiversity. He had donated $35 million to CI by 1998. In 2000, he and his wife created the Gordon and Betty Moore Foundation, and in 2001 he announced the he and his wife planned to donate $261 million to CI over the next ten years. The foundation now awards approximately $200 million annually to environmental, educational, and research causes and became the largest donor to the Thirty Meter Telescope (TMT), contributing $50 million for its design and pledging an additional $200 million toward its construction. TMT, which will be the largest and most advanced land-based telescope in the world, is being built on Mauna Kea, Hawaii. The Moores are part-time residents of Hawaii.

Moore has received many honors over his long career. Among the most prestigious are the Computer Pioneer Award from the Institute of Electrical and Electronics Engineers (IEEE), in 1984; the National Medal of Technology, which honors the country's greatest technical innovators, in 1990; and the Presidential Medal of Freedom, the nation's highest civilian honor, in 2002.

Wylene Rholetter

FURTHER READING

Homans, Charles. "Moore's Flaw." *Foreign Policy* 182 (2010):31–32. Print. An analysis of the faults in Moore's law and an explanation of why its peculiarly American promise of an unlimited future had such wide appeal.

Lécuyer, Christophe, and David C. Brock. *Makers of the Microchip: A Documentary History of Fairchild Semiconductor*. Cambridge: MIT, 2010. Print. An account of the development of the silicon integrated circuit at Fairchild Semiconductor Corporation in the company's first four years of business and the role of the device in the digital world.

Moore, Gordon. "Laying Down the Law." Interview by Robert Buderi. *Technology Review* 104.4 (2001): 64. Print. A conversation with Moore, conducted at his home in Hawaii, in which he discusses Moore's Law and the creation of the Gordon and Betty Moore Foundation.

---. "Moore Looks Beyond the Law." Interview by Jermey N. A. Matthews. *Physics Today* 61.3 (2008): 20. Print. An interview with Moore in which he discusses developments in the semiconductor industry and his philanthropic work.

Riordan, Michael, and Lillian Hoddeson. *Crystal Fire: The Birth of the Information Age*. New York: Norton, 1997. Print. The story of William Shockley and the transistor team that formed the first semiconductor company in the world. Looks at the beginning of Silicon Valley and how Shockley's company spawned countless other businesses.

NATHAN P. MYHRVOLD

Former Microsoft CTO and founder of Intellectual Ventures

Born: August 3, 1959; Seattle, Washington
Died: -
Primary Field: Computer science
Specialty: Computer software
Primary Company/Organization: Microsoft

INTRODUCTION

Nathan P. Myhrvold worked for Microsoft for thirteen years as its chief technology officer, founding Microsoft Research, the first major industrial research laboratory in more than a generation. Microsoft Research was instrumental in transforming Microsoft from a software producer with a narrow focus in the 1980s to the giant it has become in the twenty-first century, despite some notable hardware product failures. The single laboratory has since expanded to research initiatives throughout the world. After Microsoft, the former child prodigy started Intellectual Ventures and wrote the Modernist Cuisine *cookbook, which has helped to revolutionize twenty-first-century cuisine.*

Nathan P. Myhrvold.

EARLY LIFE

Nathan Paul Myhrvold was born in Seattle, Washington, on August 3, 1959. A child prodigy, he attended the then recently formed Mirman School for Gifted Children before enrolling in college at age fourteen. He earned his bachelor of science and master's degrees from the University of California, Los Angeles, in mathematics and physics before accepting a Hertz Foundation fellowship for graduate study, enrolling at Princeton University for another master's program (in mathematical economics), followed by his Ph.D. in theoretical and mathematical physics. He was twenty-three when he finished his work at Princeton in 1973. He then spent a year at the University of Cambridge working on physicist Stephen Hawking's team on quantum field theory and gravitation.

After Cambridge, Myhrvold founded Dynamical Systems Research, Inc., a software company producing a multitasking environment for the DOS operating system. When Microsoft bought out the company in 1986, Myhrvold accepted a job with the software giant.

LIFE'S WORK

At Microsoft, Myhrvold was chief technology officer and founded Microsoft Research, the company's research division, to explore and develop new ideas in computer science and their applications in Microsoft products. The original Microsoft Research campus was opened in Redmond, Washington, in 1991. In later years, laboratories opened in Cambridge, England (1997), with a close association with the University of Cambridge; Beijing, China (1998); Mountain View, California (2001), which later merged with Microsoft's Bay Area Research Center in San Francisco; Bangalore, India (2005); Cairo, Egypt (2006); Cambridge, Massachusetts (2008); and New York City (2012). Microsoft also started a research and development program in Israel in 1991, which became Microsoft Israel Innovation Labs in 2006. In 2003, the Advanced Technology Center, an independent research and development group, spun off from Microsoft Research Asia.

Microsoft Research was the first major industrial research lab opened in more than a generation. Myhrvold intended it to be comparable to Xerox's Palo Alto Research Center (PARC) and Bell Laboratories, both of which have accomplished legendary feats in science and technology. Microsoft Research grew from a

Affiliation: Microsoft

In 1991, Nathan Myhrvold founded Microsoft Research, the research and development arm of computer giant Microsoft. Microsoft Research is devoted to computer science research in a number of core areas and develops ideas that can be turned into marketable Microsoft products. It categorizes such research into the following groups:

- *Communication and collaboration*, including a family archiving system, an audio processing project, 3G asynchronous network architecture, a distributed meetings teleconferencing tool, and tools to assist with collaborative work;
- *Computational linguistics*, including language learning tools and a contact search engine;
- *Computational sciences*, including a programming language for DNA and an environmental science search engine;
- *Computer systems and networking*, including improvements to online advertising;
- *Economics*, including e-commerce;
- *Education*, including an academic search engine and a time line tool for history studies;
- *Gaming*, including audio processing algorithms, a Go game, and computer opponents for driving games;
- *Graphics and multimedia*, including three-dimensional video, video acceleration, and a digital exhibition of the AIDS quilt;
- *Hardware and devices*, including three-dimensional surface computing and an emotional prosthetic system;
- *Health and well-being*, including Domestic 2.0, research into constructing and partitioning family space;
- *Human-computer interaction*, including grammar-learning systems for speech recognition software;
- *Information retrieval and management*, including information retrieval toolkits;
- *Machine learning*, including acoustic modeling and visual summaries for search results pages;
- *Other*, a miscellaneous category that has included the Argo online image advertising system, the Blews news aggregation and real-time analysis tool, and add-ins for Word;
- *Security and privacy*, including anonymous data aggregation and anonymous credentials;
- *Social science*, including mood-based detection software for Twitter;
- *Software development*, including Ajax, a program enabling the developer to control the behavior of web applications on the user's desktop; and
- *Theory*, including cryptography and cloud computing.

Microsoft Research products have included Avalanche, a peer-to-peer network that sought to improve scalability and efficiency compared to BitTorrent, and which was released to the public in 2007 under the name Microsoft Secure Content Downloader; the experimental operating system Barrelfish, for multi-core processors, the first version of which was released in 2009; the Bartok optimizing compiler for authoring operating systems; BitVault, a distributed storage platform using peer-to-peer networking; Conference XP, a distance learning videoconferencing program developed in 2001 and supported by the Center for Collaborative Technologies at the University of Washington; C (pronounced "see omega"), an extension to the C# programming language, released in 2003; the F-Sharp programming language for the .NET framework; the Gazelle web browser, released in 2009; HomeOS, an announced home automation operating system; the Microsoft Research Image Composite Editor, released in 2011; the Kodu Game Lab, a development environment that runs on both Windows and the Xbox 360; Microsoft Comic Chat, a discontinued graphical IRC client released in 1996; Microsoft Courier, a developed but not released booklet PC; Microsoft Research Maps, an online repository of public domain aerial imagery and topographic maps, launched in 1997; the Midori operating system, still under development and likely related to the Singularity operating system that had been developed in 2003; So.cl, a social network similar to Google+ and launched in December 2011; the TouchLight touch screen gesture interaction system; the Wallop social network; and the World Wide Telescope program, released in 2008.

A long-term Microsoft Research project is MyLifeBits, currently tested by (or on) computer scientist Gordon Bell. MyLifeBits is a life-logging project inspired by computer scientist Vannevar Bush's hypothetical memex, a computer system that would automatically store the experiences of one's lifetime, for later search and retrieval. Bell digitizes all documents he reads, as well as other media he ingests. He records

Affiliation: Microsoft (Continued)

conversations and e-mails, and wears a Microsoft Sense-Cam, a wearable camera equipped with sensors that trigger automatic photographs in response to movement or temperature changes.

Other Microsoft Research innovations have been incorporated into releases of Microsoft Office, Windows XP, Windows XP Tablet PC Edition, Windows Server, Windows Live, MSN, Windows Vista, and the Xbox.

In 2005, Microsoft Research began a joint venture with Italy's University of Trento: COSBI, the Centre for Computational Systems Biology, developing algorithmic systems biology research applications. Microsoft Research also briefly sponsored the Microsoft Award, given by the United Kingdom's Royal Society and France's Académie des Sciences, from 2006 to 2009.

software company whose major successes were in operating systems and a small number of applications to a giant in the gaming industry as well as other areas.

Myhrvold left Microsoft in 2000 to found Intellectual Ventures, a patent portfolio developer formed as a private partnership by Myhrvold, Intel's Peter Detkin, Microsoft's Edward Jung, and attorney Gregory Gorder. In the next ten years it became one of the top five owners of U.S. patents. The partnership has purchased more than thirty thousanad patents or patent applications while developing another several thousand internally. Although not as ambitious as Microsoft Research, the Intellectual Ventures lab, opened in 2009, works on prototypes and developing patents in Intellectual Ventures' portfolio. One of the ideas developed by Intellectual Ventures, promoted on talk show appearances and in the book *SuperFreakonomics*, is a geoengineering method for reducing the effects of climate change by simulating the effects of a volcanic eruption. A less widely reported but potentially groundbreaking patent, developed internally, is a nuclear reactor that uses uranium waste as fuel.

Intellectual Ventures has faced significant criticism for its balance of purchased patents to internally developed innovations. Because it is a private partnership, it is not clear how much of its revenue comes from developing its patents and how much derives from patent infringement lawsuits, though it has been accused of profiting from litigation and patenting ideas it has no intention of developing in order to sue other companies for infringement later. A December 2010 lawsuit against Check Point, Symantec, Trend Micro, Altera, Lattice, Elpida, Hynix, Microsemi, and McAfee was described by a critic on a radio program as a "shakedown." Others have characterized Intellectual Ventures' activities as "patent trolling."

PERSONAL LIFE

Myhrvold is a prizewinning amateur photographer, barbecue champion, scientist, and chef. His scientific

articles have appeared in *Nature*, *Science*, and *Paleobiology*, and he has gone on paleontological expeditions with the Museum of the Rockies. He has donated money both to the Search for Extraterrestrial Intelligence (SETI) project and to the reconstruction of Charles Babbage's difference engine (including a second reconstruction of the difference engine for himself).

Myhrvold's "amateur" work in cuisine could be as significant as his founding of Microsoft Research. A longtime amateur cook, he has participated in championship-winning barbecue teams, studied French cooking, and apprenticed at Seattle restaurant Rover's before turning to molecular gastronomy, or what is increasingly called Modernist Cuisine, which is also the title of his groundbreaking 2011 book. Molecular gastronomy (a term no chef embraced) began in Spain with the work of Ferran Adrià, who used food ingredients such as xanthan gum and methylcellulose, commonly used in the packaged foods industry, in high-end cooking. Characteristic techniques included constructing "caviar" of drops of liquid surrounded by thin membranes, manipulating textures through gels and other additives, and combining ingredients in unexpected ways, such as Adrià's sour cherry surrounded by what appears to be fondant or white chocolate but is actually Iberico ham fat. New equipment was put to use as well: sous-vide water baths were used to transform the texture of meat, PacoJet high-speed blenders allowed any ingredient to be frozen and blended into a sorbet, and vacuum-sealing was used to compress high-water ingredients such as cucumbers and melons to change their textures without cooking them. At the same time, Adrià's cooking was solidly grounded in traditional Spanish cuisine and ingredients, and many of the most successful chefs to follow in his footsteps in the early twenty-first century likewise maintained a proximity to traditional flavors.

Although Adrià had published an exhaustive text on his work at his restaurant El Bulli, English translations were rare, expensive, and increasingly out of date. Myhrvold's book, cowritten with Chris Young and Maxime Bilet from the London restaurant The Fat Duck, serves as an examination of the field, collecting knowledge from disparate sources and presenting it in a six-volume tour de force of more than twenty-four hundred pages. Wayt Gibbs, an Intellectual Ventures employee, served as editor in chief.

Bill Kte'pi

FURTHER READING

Auletta, Ken. *The Highwaymen: Warriors of the Information Superhighway*. San Diego: Harcourt Brace, 1998. Print. Devotes a chapter to Myhrvold's time at Microsoft.

Edstrom, Jennifer. *Barbarians Led by Bill Gates: Microsoft from the Inside; How the World's Richest Corporation Wields Its Power*. New York: Henry Holt, 1998. Print. Covers Microsoft during the Myhrvold era.

Myhrvold, Nathan, and Maxime Bilet. *Modernist Cuisine at Home*. Seattle: The Cooking Lab, 2012. Print. The first major book on adapting the new modernist cuisine to home kitchens.

Myhrvold, Nathan, Chris Young, and Maxime Bilet. *Modernist Cuisine: The Art and Science of Cooking*. 6 vols. Seattle: The Cooking Lab, 2011. Print. Myhrvold's revolutionary work on the new cooking science.

N

NICHOLAS P. NEGROPONTE

Founder of the MIT Media Lab and One Laptop Per Child

Born: December 1, 1943; New York, New York
Died: -
Primary Field: Computer science
Specialty: Computer hardware
Primary Company/Organization: Massachusetts Institute of Technology

INTRODUCTION

In 1985, Nicholas P. Negroponte founded the Media Lab at the Massachusetts Institute of Technology, pioneering research on human-computer interfaces. He is also a prominent futurist, one of the founders of Wired *magazine, and the founder of the One Laptop Per Child Association (OLPC). Since stepping down as chair of the Media Lab, he has been involved in angel investing and running OLPC.*

EARLY LIFE

Nicholas P. Negroponte was born on December 1, 1943, in New York City. His father, Dimitri John Negroponte, was a Greek shipping tycoon, and his older brother is American diplomat John Negroponte, former ambassador to the United Nations and former director of National Intelligence. Like his brother, Nicholas attended all the best schools—the Buckley School in New York City, Le Rosey in Switzerland, and Choate in Connecticut. When he graduated in 1961, he enrolled in college at MIT, earning first and second professional degrees in architecture, in 1966. Upon graduation, he joined the MIT faculty, although during part of the 1960s he also taught at Yale and the University of California, Berkeley, as a visiting professor.

LIFE'S WORK

Negroponte's graduate research was on computer-aided design (CAD). In his second year as an MIT professor, he founded the Architecture Machine Group, a think tank studying human-computer interaction. This was followed in 1985 by the founding of the MIT Media Lab, also devoted to the human-computer interface,

Nicholas P. Negroponte.

Affiliation: MIT Media Lab

The Massachusetts Institute of Technology's Media Lab was founded in 1985 by MIT professor and noted futurist Nicholas Negroponte and former MIT President Jerome Wiesner. The lab is headquartered in the I. M. Pei–designed Wiesner Building. It is formally part of the MIT School of Architecture and Planning, growing out of the Architecture Machine Group Negroponte founded in the late 1960s. Negroponte served as the lab's first director, succeeded by Walter Bender in 2000, Frank Moss in 2006, and Joichi Ito in 2011.

The Media Lab is a think tank and working laboratory for research related to human-computer interactions, and while some of that research takes a traditional interpretation of that topic—the Media Lab hosted a 2007 symposium on neural-digital interfaces for the disabled—the lab is especially noted for research groups that interpret the topic broadly. In 2012, two of the lab's prominent areas of research were intelligent objects and smart toys. The former are equipped with sensors that allow them to respond to their environment and take action predictively; the latter blur the line between play activities and learning activities, with applications such as programmable Lego bricks. Another area of considerable interest is the intersection between art and engineering. Many Media Lab groups develop new musical instruments or approaches to music, new expressions or art through media, and new tools for artists. Typical of MIT, work at the Media Lab is usually very hands-on.

As part of the School of Architecture and Planning, the Media Lab offers an alternative freshman year, undergraduate courses, a master of science program, and a Ph.D. program, all through the Media Arts and Sciences program, which functions as the classroom extension of the Media Lab. All affiliated graduate students are given free tuition and a stipend, working as research assistants. Occasionally graduate students in other master's programs, especially engineering students, conduct their research in the Media Lab.

The Media Lab is funded almost entirely by corporate sponsorship. Sponsors do not fund specific projects or groups, but rather themes of research. This approach allows the Media Lab to retain considerable flexibility and spontaneity. Companies contributing at a high enough level share in intellectual property benefits without paying licensing fees, and there is a two-year embargo on licensing to nonsponsors after the disclosure of a completed project is made to the college. Since 2001, about twenty patents per year have come out of the Media Lab, although this is arguably an understated measure of the Media Lab's output. A small number of project- or researcher-specific grants are provided by federal institutions such as the Defense Advanced Research Projects Agency (DARPA) and the National Science Foundation.

Joint ventures include the Observatory of Economic Complexity (OEC), with Harvard's Center for International Development, which develops tools for macroeconomic decision making. The concept of economic complexity as a measure of production characteristics of an economy was proposed as a predictive tool for economic growth, and the work at the OEC furthers that concept.

which became the leading computer science laboratory studying new media. Negroponte opened the lab with Jerome Wiesner, a former president of MIT who was one of the twenty academicians on President Richard Nixon's "enemies list." Negroponte served as the Media Lab's Director from 1985 to 2000, and remained as chairman until 2006.

Negroponte is a well-known futurist who has advocated technologies such as customized digital news feeds, which he discussed in his 1995 book *Being Digital*, popularizing the term *daily me*. His work on the human-computer interface in the 1970s led directly to his belief, as the Internet became more widespread and sophisticated in the 1990s, in using intelligent agents to customize the experience of using the Internet. Rather than flipping through a physical newspaper, much of which consists of content sourced from beyond the newspaper's staff (articles from wire services such as Reuters and the Associated Press and syndicated content such as opinion columns and comic strips), users of customized digital news feeds would be given daily content tailored to their preference profile, which would be generated by some initial preferences modified by reading habits and other behavior. The Internet has indeed taken that direction: Amazon and Netflix depend heavily on the use of recommendation engines, and Google has begun tailoring its displayed search results according to the behavior of the logged-in user looking at them. Critics have pointed out that this sort of customization has a number of pitfalls: It requires some kind of static identity, which may not be anonymous or, worse, may appear to be anonymous while actually constituting a profile from which one's identity could easily be derived (for example, there can be only so many independent scholars working as freelance writers of reference books in the 03063 ZIP code). Another criticism is that recommendation engines may give people what they want but not what they need (similar to letting a six-year-old pick what he wants for dinner), whereas physical interaction with an unfiltered newspaper introduces passive exposure to headlines that one may not read but still inform one's understanding of current events. Finally, customization contributes, especially for some users, in the "echo chamber" phenomenon, whereby spaces are carved out on the Internet in which nothing can be heard except people who already agree with the user and augment their existing biases.

The "Negroponte switch" refers to an idea Negroponte introduced, since picked up by other futurists, that traditionally wireless technologies become wired (for example, broadcast television is in the process of being displaced by cable and streaming video) while traditionally wired technologies become wireless (as cell phones become more common, the popularity of ground-line telephones has declined). In *Being Digital*, Negroponte discussed both ideas and collected several of the columns he had written for *Wired*. That magazine had been founded by journalist Louis Rossetto in 1992 and first published the following January. It was financially supported by Negroponte and software entrepreneur Charlie Jackson. It billed itself as "the *Rolling Stone* of technology" and was a more serious, less pretty, and cheaper companion magazine to *Mondo 2000*, the cyberculture magazine that had begun publication in 1984. William Gibson, a writer regularly featured in *Mondo 2000*, posed for the cover of the fourth issue of *Wired*. As anarchic as *Mondo 2000* despite a plainer look, *Boing Boing*, a zine started in 1988, eventually shared many of the same contributors as *Mondo 2000*. Somewhere between the two—more professional-looking than *Boing Boing* and dryer than either—was *Wired*, which proved the survivor of the three. *Mondo 2000* ceased publication in 1996; that year, *Boing Boing* ended its print magazine, althoug it maintains its web presence. *Wired*, meanwhile, has expanded to four international editions, garnering several national magazine awards and a new owner in magazine publishing giant Condé Nast. It introduced terms central to the twenty-first century's discussion of itself, such as the *long tail* and *crowdsourcing*. Negroponte continued to write a monthly column for *Wired* until 1998.

After leaving the Media Lab, Negroponte devoted more of his time to the One Laptop Per Child project, which grew out of research at the Media Lab. The project is supported by two nonprofit associations, the Cambridge-based OLPC Foundation and the Miami-based One Laptop Per Child Association. Intel briefly manufactured computers for the project, which creates and provides affordable educational computers in the developing world, but ended its association over a dispute with Negroponte.

Negroponte named $100 as the target price of a laptop in 2006, with a target date of 2008. In 2012, the price point of the most affordable laptops remains above $200, and the project has developed more slowly than expected, in part because of the financial crisis that began in 2008. The project has promoted the OLPC XO-1 laptop, also known as the Children's Machine, a low-power flash-memory computer with a rugged construction that can survive drops and rough transit. Its mobile ad hoc networking is based on 802.11s wireless network protocol, allowing users to share an Internet connection. Theft is discouraged with an optional cryptographic lease, which locks the computer if the correct code is not entered. In 2012, an updated XO-3, a tablet, was expected to be released that year or in early 2013 with a price point of $100.

XO laptops are sold to governments, whose education departments distribute them, with the goal of giving each child in the education system a laptop. Countries participating in OLPC have included Ethiopia, Gaza, Ghana, Rwanda, Sierra Leone, Canada's First Nations communities, Mexico, the United States (Birmingham, Alabama), Argentina, Colombia, Haiti, Peru, Uruguay (the most significant participant, by the numbers), Afghanistan, Cambodia, Mongolia, Australia, Kiribati, Nauru, New Caledonia, Niue, Papua New Guinea, the Solomon Islands, Tuvalu, and Vanuatu. Some funding has been raised through "give one get one" programs, in which for a donation of $399 a consumer receives one XO laptop while another is donated to the program. The promotion was last offered in 2008, and it is not certain if the project will continue to offer GOGO programs for future XO models.

PERSONAL LIFE

Negroponte is married to Deborah Porter, the book critic who founded the Boston Book Festival and Boston's One City, One Story project. The couple has one child, Dmitri Negroponte.

Bill Kte'pi

FURTHER READING

Brand, Stewart. *The Media Lab: Inventing the Future at MIT*. New York: Penguin, 1988. Print. An early look at MIT's Media Lab.

Carr, Nicholas G. *Does IT Matter?* Cambridge: Harvard Business Review, 2004. Print. An analysis of the role of information technology.

Kaiser, David. *Becoming MIT: Moments of Decision*. Cambridge: MIT, 2010. Print. A history of MIT emphasizing the developing of its pedagogic philosophies.

Moss, Frank. *The Sorcerers and Their Apprentices: How the Digital Magicians of the MIT Media Lab*

Are Creating the Innovative Technologies That Will Transform Their Lives. New York: Crown Business, 2011. Print. An in-depth look at the work of the MIT Media Lab.

Negroponte, Nicholas. *Being Digital*. New York: Vintage, 2006. Print. Negroponte's popular book collecting some of his essays for *Wired*.

White, Pepper. *The Idea Factory: Learning to Think at MIT*. Cambridge: MIT, 2001. Print. A memoir of the unique experience of being educated at MIT.

ALLEN NEWELL

Developer of the Soar artificial intelligence system

Born: March 19, 1927; San Francisco, California
Died: July 19, 1992; Pittsburgh, Pennsylvania
Primary Field: Computer science
Specialty: Computer programming
Primary Company/Organization: RAND Corporation

INTRODUCTION

Allen Newell is best known for his research and work in developing artificial intelligence (AI) systems from both practical and theoretical perspectives. He developed the Soar problem-solving architecture, which survives today. Newell was instrumental in developing programs that would solve problems effectively, work that was informed by his keen awareness of not only technical issues but also the psychological factors influencing users and their methods in seeking solutions. Newell believed that whatever the scope and extent of technical advances, if they do not operate in harmony with and do not effectively extend human capabilities, they will serve no great purpose.

EARLY LIFE

Allen Newell was born in San Francisco, California, on March 19, 1927, the younger of two children. His parents were Jeanette and Robert R. Newell, a professor of radiology at Stanford's school of medicine.

After working briefly in a shipyard for a summer during World War II, Newell enlisted in the U.S. Navy. He was discharged from the service and returned to being a student in 1945. The following year, he was in the Pacific as an assistant to his father, who worked on

measuring radiation patterns following the atomic bomb tests on the Bikini Atoll. Newell said later that despite the fact that his father and father's colleagues were scientists, he never had an interest in science as a career until the tests at Bikini. In the same way that the development of atomic weapons horrified physicist and

Allen Newell.

222

director of the Manhattan Project Robert Oppenheimer, it created in Newell a sense of the possibilities that could arise from scientific research.

Back home after the tests, Newell in 1947 married Noel McKenna, his high school sweetheart. He graduated from Stanford in 1949 with a bachelor's degree in physics. While he was an undergraduate, he had taken mathematics courses under the direction of Hungarian mathematician George Pólya. Pólya, both in his classes and in his books (notably *How to Solve It*), was extremely influential in championing the study of heuristics (the use of simplified rules to solve problems). The heuristic method would have a major effect on Newell's research and study in artificial intelligence and methods of problem solving.

In the same year that Newell graduated from Stanford, he went to Princeton University to begin graduate study in mathematics. After a year at Princeton, Newell went to work for the RAND Corporation, where he would stay until 1961. In 1955, he began work toward a doctorate at the Carnegie Institute of Technology (CIT), which he received in 1957 while working at RAND. In 1961, he accepted an appointment as a professor of computer science and psychology at CIT.

LIFE'S WORK

When Newell first joined RAND, he was assigned to projects that required the use of game theory, with which he had become acquainted at Princeton. This work led to further projects in decision-making experiments at RAND's System Research Center. This organization would eventually become a separate entity, Systems Development Corporation, later to become SDC Burroughs and still later part of the Unisys Corporation. In these experiments on decision making (usually as part of studies to determine how operators at Air Force tracking stations performed), Newell became interested in working out how people actually processed information prior to making decisions.

After he had been at RAND for two years, Newell met Herbert Simon, with whom he would collaborate on enhancing human intelligence and how it might be supported and enhanced by computers. A little more than twenty years after they met, the two would together receive the Alan M. Turing Award from the Association for Computing Machinery.

In the mid-1950s, Newell began working toward his doctorate at what would eventually become Carnegie Mellon University while continuing to work at RAND. Simon was his adviser, and together they

developed what has been recognized as the first artificial intelligence program. Their work expanded to include list processing (essentially the techniques that can be employed to reorder and manipulate data contained in lists to get a result). In 1958, they developed another program that could perform some problem-solving tasks, which they named The General Problem Solver.

In the 1960s and the 1970s, Newell became interested in topics such as computer architectures and human-machine interfaces. He not only continued to pursue his research but also was an active and effective administrator and manager who made significant contributions to developing the Computer Center at Carnegie Mellon into a world-class facility.

By the 1970s, he had begun a new project, which would occupy him until his death in 1992 and became his most significant achievement: the development and enhancement of Soar, in collaboration with John Laird and Paul Rosenbloom. The goal of the project, which Newell said he hoped would outlive him, was to create a way to construct an intelligence that would function in the same fashion as human intelligence but with greater speed and efficiency. This last consideration was always important to Newell, who believed that the goal was to develop systems that would operate along the same general path that human minds worked, albeit in a more efficient fashion. His idea was that a system that solved problems should be able to do so in the same way humans did. If and when it failed, it should fail in the same way the human mind would fail.

As Newell envisioned Soar (which originally stood for "state, operator, and result"), it would be an architecture that could be used to develop intelligent systems. In a very simple sense, this architecture is the combination of different types of software that can be joined together (much like objects in the object-oriented programming developed by Kristen Nygaard) to solve a particular problem.

In this concept there may be several blocks that can basically perform the same function, but the developers looking for the solution will have a choice of capabilities that differ from block to block. Some may have functionality that others do not have, and several may have the same general abilities but perform some aspects better than others. The solution seekers can choose what goes best together to form a total problem-solving architecture. The resulting constructed architecture would then be applied to solving the problem. In the minds of Newell and his collaborators, this architecture would make a clear distinction between the tools (the

Affiliation: RAND Corporation

The RAND (originally Research and Development) Corporation was created in 1946 as an Air Force Research project. Although World War II had just ended, new tensions between the Western allies and the Soviet Union presaged the Cold War and meant that military research and development, while not required and funded to its previous extent, would need to continue.

The initial work was contracted to Douglas Aircraft and the initial task was to perform technical research concerning the performance and potential uses of aviation technology. Two years after the creation of RAND and two years before Allen Newell joined it, the organization became a separate, nonprofit organization. The initial stated objective of RAND was to "further promote scientific, educational, and charitable purposes, all for the public welfare and security of the United States of America."

Funding at this early stage was provided by the Ford Foundation, with some government funding coming principally from defense contracts. During the 1960s, one of its more prominent defense researchers was Herman Kahn, who hypothesized that nuclear wars could be "winnable." He was a cousin of Robert Kahn, the coinventor of the TCP/IP protocols.

As of 2012, RAND had seventeen hundred employees located worldwide. RAND is most often associated with the Department of Defense, advising on strategy and technical issues; in fact, more than half of RAND's yearly income is derived from the DoD. However, RAND also performs research and analysis for private and public companies and foundations as well as for governments of UN member nations other than the United States. Research issues include scientific and technical projects, public policy, and public health. RAND's publications range from defense studies to reports on whether characters in children's movies will influence their audiences to take up smoking at a later date.

blocks that made up the architecture) and the problem (the "content"). The problem-solving process also includes rules (for example, "if … then" contingencies). It also includes the assumption that certain actions can be deconstructed into smaller tasks (another similarity with object-oriented programming).

Soar was obviously the product of a highly integrated and multidisciplinary approach in which psychology was as important as computer science. The resulting architecture is still the subject of ongoing development at the University of Michigan. As of April 2012, it existed in its 9.3.2 version.

PERSONAL LIFE

During the course of his career, Newell wrote (alone or with collaborators) ten books and 250 articles. He received honorary degrees and was a leading member of many technical organizations, including the National Academy of Sciences, the National Academy of Engineering, and the American Academy of Arts and Sciences.

Newell received many awards for his work conducted at both RAND and Carnegie Mellon. These included the Association for Computing Machinery's A. M. Turing Award, which he received in 1975 with his colleague Herbert Simon for their work in artificial intelligence; the Alexander C. Williams Jr. Award, from the Human Factors and Ergonomics Society, in 1979; the first Institute of Electrical and Electronics Engineers (IEEE) Computer Society Computer Pioneer Award in 1981; the Distinguished Scientific Contribution Award from the American Psychological Association in 1985; and in June 1992, the month before his death, the National Medal of Science from President George H. W. Bush.

Newell died on July 19, 1992, of cancer in Pittsburgh, Pennsylvania. He left his wife, Noel, and one son. His papers are available online at Carnegie Mellon's website. The Alan Newell Award is now awarded annually by the Association for Computing Machinery and the American Association for Artificial Intelligence "for career contributions that had breadth within computer science, or that bridge computer science and other disciplines."

Robert N. Stacy

FURTHER READING

Abella, Alex. *Soldiers of Reason: The Rand Corporation and the Rise of the American Empire*. Orlando: Harcourt, 2008. Print. A general history of the RAND corporation with special emphasis on its ties to and contract work for the U.S. government, especially the Department of Defense. The extent of RAND's influence on government decision making in the areas of international policy and the military is covered.

Boden, Margaret. *Mind as Machine: A History of Cognitive Science*. New York: Oxford UP, 2006. Print. A comprehensive, perhaps definitive, history of the development and achievements of cognitive science, with Newell's work discussed in the larger context of the discipline as a whole.

Laird, John E., and Paul S. Rosenbloom. "The Research of Allen Newell." *AI Magazine* 13.4 (1992): 17–45. Print. A summary of Newell's work by his two major SOAR collaborators.

Michon, John, and Aladin Akyurek, eds. *Soar: A Cognitive Architecture in Perspective*. Norwell: Kluwer Academic, 1992. Print. A thorough description of the SOAR project, from its beginnings to its state of development at the time of Newell's death.

Newell, Allen, and Herbert A. Simon. *Human Problem Solving*. Englewood Cliffs: Prentice-Hall, 1972. Print. Simon was a professor at Carnegie when he and Newell met in 1952 at RAND. Their meeting began a long collaboration between the two on projects in cognitive science, heuristics, and the use of symbols in thought.

Pólya, George. *How to Solve It: A New Aspect of Mathematical Method*. Princeton: Princeton UP, 2004. Print. A reprint of an extremely influential book by Newell's professor at Stanford. The discussion has its basis in mathematics but also has relevance to general problem solving.

Steier, David, and Tom M. Mitchell, eds. *Mind Matters: A Tribute to Allen Newell*. Mahwah: Erlbaum, 1996. Print. A collection of essays from a Conference honoring the work of Newell. Covers a wide variety of topics, including the evolution and use of SOAR, software architectures, and patterns of learning, discussed by a panel of experts in the field.

WILLIAM C. NORRIS

Cofounder and CEO of Control Data Corporation

Born: July 14, 1911; Red Cloud, Nebraska
Died: August 21, 2006; Bloomington, Minnesota
Primary Field: Business and commerce
Specialty: Management, executives, and investors
Primary Company/Organization: Control Data Corporation

INTRODUCTION
William C. Norris was a pioneering computer executive, serving as president of Control Data Corporation (CDC) during the period when it was one of the nine largest computer companies in the United States. CDC was well known both for the speed of its computers and for its commitment to social justice. CDC under Norris's leadership came to define supercomputing and also developed a highly profitable line of peripherals and services. During the 1980s, as users turned to personal computers (PCs) rather than the mainframes for which CDC was known, the company struggled. Eventually CDC left the computer industry, unable to compete in the changing marketplace.

EARLY LIFE
William Charles Norris was born with his twin sister Willa on July 14, 1911, near Red Cloud, Nebraska. On their farm, which had been homesteaded by his grandfather in 1872, his parents raised cattle and hogs and grew corn. Norris and Willa had an older sister, and the three attended a one-room country schoolhouse where physics quickly became Norris's favorite subject. Even as a child, he was fascinated by electronics, becoming a ham radio operator after building a mail-order radio set. Always a strong student, Norris enrolled at the University of Nebraska, where he studied electrical engineering, graduating in 1932.

LIFE'S WORK
After graduating from the university, Norris joined Westinghouse Electric Company, then a major manufacturer of electronics, broadcasting equipment, weapons, and other products. Norris served in the U.S. Navy for five years during World War II, working as a cryptographer in the Communications Supplementary Activity-Washington (CSAW) division. Norris worked on code breaking and developing electronic devices that would assist in this process. Upon his honorable discharge from the Navy, Norris joined a group of fellow veterans to form Engineering Research Associates (ERA), a pioneering firm devoted to building scientific computers.

William C. Norris.

Norris and his colleagues Joseph Wenger and Howard Engstrom began searching for investors to assist in supporting ERA, but initially they were unsuccessful because most investment firms were doubtful about the future of computers. In 1946, Norris, Wenger, and Engstrom met with John Parker, an investment banker who during the war had run Northwest Aeronautical Corporation (NAC), a division of Chase Aircraft Company. NAC was in the process of closing its operations in Saint Paul, Minnesota, and Parker wanted to keep the factory running. Although he knew nothing about ERA's products, Parker backed the new company, and under Norris's leadership ERA moved into the former NAC factory in 1946.

During its early years, ERA devoted a great deal of its time devising code-breaking machines for the Navy. Among the machines ERA completed were the Goldberg machine, which used a magnetic drum memory system, created by physically gluing magnetic tape to the surface of a metal cylinder. ERA next completed Demon machines, which used paper tape to feed data into the mechanism. Finally, ERA created the first device with stored memory, the ERA 1101, with drum memory using magnetic data storage. In 1952, after a controversy instigated by newspaper columnist Drew

Pearson, who suggested that ERA, through its officers Norris and Engstrom, had ignored conflicts of interest to profit from their wartime service, ERA was sold to the Remington Rand Corporation. Three years later, Remington Rand was acquired by Sperry Corporation, creating the Sperry Rand Corporation. Sperry Rand discontinued much of ERA's work, causing displeasure among Norris, Engstrom, and others who remained with the company. Especially troubling to the ERA veterans was the use of their magnetic drums in the Sperry Rand UNIVAC 1103, a successor to the ERA 1101. A group of these disgruntled ERA employees left Sperry Rand in 1957 to form CDC, moving to a new research facility in Minneapolis at 501 Park Avenue, directly across the Mississippi River from Sperry Rand's laboratories.

Once established in Minneapolis, Norris began CDC's operations by developing business, initially focused mainly on selling subsystems, such as drum memory systems, to other manufacturers of computers and business machines. Using the concept initially realized for the UNIVAC 1103, in 1959 a team of CDC engineers under the leadership of Seymour Cray developed a 46-bit transistorized computer, the CDC 1604, the first such machine to be commercially successful. Legend has it the number 1604 was devised by adding the 1103 from the UNIVAC model to the 501 from CDC's Minneapolis street address. CDC delivered the first 1604 to the U.S. Navy for use with fleet operations control centers, and by 1964 CDC had built more than fifty such systems. During the mid-1960s, the CDC 3000 succeeded the 1604 and was highly successful with the business community. By the time the CDC 3000 was introduced, CDC was one of the nine major computer manufacturers in the United States, along with Burroughs Corporation, Digital Equipment Corporation (DEC), General Electric Company (GE), Honeywell, Inc., International Business Machines Corporation (IBM), the National Cash Register Company (NCR), the Radio Corporation of America (RCA), and Sperry Rand. CDC also created a smaller, 12-bit version of the computer, the CDC 160A, which it introduced in 1960 and which was one of the first minicomputers.

Cray continued working to devise more powerful computers, vowing that his next machine would be fifty times faster than the CDC 1604. Although the project took longer than expected, when CDC management demanded more accountability from Cray he insisted that CDC build him his own laboratory in his hometown of Chippewa Falls, Wisconsin. Cray's influence was such that CDC built the laboratory for him, which no one, including Norris, was permitted to visit. During this period, CDC also built its peripheral business, focusing on tape transport, card readers, card punches, tape drives, drum printers, and other such devices. CDC developed its peripheral business in part because Norris believed that in order to compete with industry leader IBM, the company needed to offer a full line of products. Norris also instituted a series of money-losing "service bureaus," designed to provide computing expertise to smaller companies unable to afford their own machines.

By 1964, Cray had unveiled the CDC 6600, a machine ten times faster than its closest competitor. The rollout of the CDC 6600 caused IBM to develop a team of more than two hundred to develop a computer that was faster than CDC's machine. IBM's Advanced Computing System worked on a prototype supercomputer, the ACS-1, for most of the 1960s, although the machine was never produced commercially. Disappointment in the program's cancellation in 1969 led many of IBM's top engineers to leave the company. Ultimately, IBM announced that it had developed a version of its popular 360 system that was faster than the CDC 6600; although this was untrue, sales of the CDC 6600 declined dramatically. CDC ultimately sued IBM for unfair trade practices and won an $80 million settlement.

CDC continued to develop faster computers, unveiling the CDC 7600 in 1969. The CDC 7600 was four times faster than the CDC 6600 and remained the fastest computer available worldwide until approximately 1975. Although fast, the CDC 7600 was incompatible with the 6600 and had the reputation for being unreliable, damaging CDC's reputation as a result. Cray left CDC in 1972 to form his own company but continued to receive strong support from Norris. CDC remained committed to producing supercomputers through the 1980s. After several Japanese companies entered the supercomputer field during the early to mid-1980s, however, Norris decided it was in CDC's best interests to focus instead on other markets, such as hard drives. Although its technology was often superior to that of the competition, CDC found it difficult to compete in many markets, often losing market share to other companies. Norris was forced to retire in 1986, and CDC began the process of winding down as a going concern. As a result, CDC sold off many divisions during the 1980s as it attempted to reorganize. By 1992, all that remained of CDC was its services business, which was renamed Ceridian Corporation, which continued as a successful information services company.

Affiliation: Control Data Corporation

Control Data Corporation (CDC) was a major player in the United States' computer industry during the 1960s and 1970s. Known for the speed of its supercomputers, CDC created large computer systems that were used by universities, research centers, government agencies, and corporations to perform calculations that had been impossible just a few years before.

Although CDC was known for the technological sophistication of many of its products, the company struggled to find a niche as competition from the Japanese harmed its supercomputer markets and low-cost providers captured the majority of peripheral product sales. Known for its many progressive policies, CDC invested heavily in the Programmed Logic for Automated Teaching Operations (PLATO) system, a computer-assisted means of providing educational services. Under Norris's leadership, CDC also made attempts to provide job training and other opportunities for the economically disadvantaged and members of ethnic minority groups.

Norris's leadership of CDC saw efforts that established the sale of what are today well-known products and expertise, such as large-scale scientific computers, computer services, and applications of technology in education. Norris also stressed the creation of a supportive and nurturing workplace. While chief executive officer (CEO) of CDC, Norris frequently engaged in activities that pursued new business opportunities for the underserved through cooperation with the public and nonprofit sectors. Under Norris's leadership, CDC often supported small-business incubators, which are estimated to have led to more than one thousand start-up businesses and more than thirteen thousand jobs.

PERSONAL LIFE

Norris and his wife, Jane Malley Norris, had eight children—William, George, Daniel, Brian, Roger, David, Constance, and Mary Keck. A devoted family man, Norris was deeply committed throughout his life to corporate sponsorship of community projects, charitable giving, and making business decisions that would have a positive impact on the community. In 1967, for example, Norris attended a seminar hosted by the National Urban League, where he spoke with civil rights leader Whitney Young regarding the social injustices facing many African Americans. Moved to respond, Norris transferred some CDC manufacturing capacity to inner-city factories, provided training to a host of new employees, and vigorously attempted to recruit minority workers. Norris also served as an advocate for an educational system developed at the University of Illinois, Programmed Logic for Automated Teaching Operations (PLATO). The PLATO system was devised during the early 1960s as a means to provide educational opportunity to students who otherwise did not have access to good teachers. After funding from the National Science Foundation (NSF) expired in the early 1970s, Norris had CDC support the program in an effort to continue what he saw as a means of ensuring social justice.

After leaving CDC, in 1988 Norris founded the William C. Norris Institute, a nonprofit organization for which he served as chair until 2000. The Norris Institute supported a variety of projects, including attempts to improve education through the use of technology, providing technical training in Russia, and supporting small business incubators in low-income neighborhoods in Saint Paul, Minnesota. In 2001, Norris merged the Institute with St. Thomas University, where it has sought to assist with the development of commercial uses of Minnesota entrepreneurs' innovative and socially beneficial technologies.

After a long struggle with Parkinson's disease, Norris died on August 21, 2006, in a nursing home in Bloomington, Minnesota, survived by his wife, children, twenty-one grandchildren, and six great-grandchildren.

Stephen T. Schroth and Jason A. Helfer

FURTHER READING

DiConti, M. A. *Entrepreneurship in Training: The Multinational Corporation in Mexico and Canada.* Columbia: U of South Carolina P, 1992. Print. Examines efforts by a variety of multinational corporations, including CDC, to improve living conditions in the communities where they establish branches and manufacturing facilities.

Hart, D. M. "From 'Ward of the State' to 'Revolutionary Without a Movement': The Political Development of William C. Norris and Control Data Corporation, 1957–1986." *Enterprise and Society* 6.2 (2005): 197–223. Print. A history of the company and its founder.

Johnson, T. *Time to Take Control: The Impact of Change on Corporate Computer Systems.* Newton: Butterworth-Heinemann, 1997. Print. Examines some of the pressures facing corporations and their leaders when implementing changes to computer systems.

Worthy, J. C. *William C. Norris: Portrait of a Maverick.* New York: Ballinger, 1987. Print. Explores the life of Norris, taking account of both his many corporate successes and his efforts to promote social justice through CDC's actions.

ROBERT NOYCE

Coinventor of the microchip and cofounder of Intel

Born: December 12, 1927; Burlington, Iowa
Died: June 3, 1990; Austin, Texas
Primary Field: Computer science
Specialty: Computer hardware
Primary Company/Organization: Intel

INTRODUCTION

Robert Noyce began his career with Philco and Shockley Semiconductor Laboratory in the 1950s. He left Shockley to cofound Fairchild Semiconductor in 1957 at the age of twenty-nine. Noyce's 1959 coinvention of the integrated computer chip, also known as the microchip, was a vital technological step in the later development of microprocessors, helping to launch a consumer revolution in the computer industry. He

would receive sixteen patents related to semiconductors over the course of his career and was noted for his insight and leadership abilities. In 1968, he and Gordon Moore left Fairchild and cofounded Intel, which would eventually dominate the market for semiconductor microchip processors. He also served as an industry spokesman, cofounding of the Semiconductor Industry Association, beoming the first chief executive officer (CEO) of the nonprofit consortium of semiconductor chip manufacturers SEMATECH, and earning the nickname Mayor of Silicon Valley.

EARLY LIFE

Robert Norton Noyce was born on December 12, 1927, in Burlington, Iowa, and spent his childhood and

Robert Noyce.

adolescence in nearby Grinnell, Iowa. He was the third of four sons born to Ralph and Harriet (Norton) Noyce. Noyce's father was a preacher for the Iowa Conference of Congregational Churches. He excelled at his studies, notably mathematics and science. He took Grinnell College's freshman course in physics as a high school senior. His other childhood interests included sports, music, and theater. Noyce attended Grinnell College, majoring in physics. While there, he led a notorious prank, stealing a local farmer's pig for a luau. He later paid for the lost pig. He received his bachelor's degree in physics in 1949, graduating Phi Beta Kappa. His professor and mentor, physics department head Gale Grant, had introduced Noyce to early model transistors acquired from Bell Laboratories.

Noyce pursued his interest in transistors at the Massachusetts Institute of Technology (MIT), where he found that his knowledge of the new field was greater than that of his professors. He believed that transistors had the potential to replace the inefficient vacuum tubes used in computers of the time. He received his Ph.D. from MIT in 1954 but expressed no interest in academic research.

Noyce worked briefly in Philadelphia, Pennsylvania, making semiconductors for electronics manufactur-

er Philco at the outset of his career, but he left in 1956 to move to what became the Silicon Valley area of California and seek work at Shockley Semiconductor Laboratory. Nobel laureate and transistor coinventor William Shockley was the founder and Noyce's boss. Even during his education and early career, Noyce was noted for his confident demeanor and leadership abilities.

LIFE'S WORK
Noyce entered the entrepreneurial ranks at a young age. At twenty-nine, he was the leader of a group of eight engineers who decided to leave Shockley in 1957 over their disappointment regarding differences in the company's scientific direction and management. The former Shockley employees founded Fairchild Semiconductor that year with financing from Fairchild Camera and Instrument Corporation. Semiconductors were made of materials that allowed the conductivity of electrical currents at a rate lower than that of conductors but higher than that of insulators. Noyce served as the new company's general manager. Fairchild became a computer industry pioneer with the invention of what became known as the microchip.

Noyce was the coinventor of the silicon integrated circuit (microchip) in 1959, receiving a patent in 1961. This electronic component consisted of a chip coated with silicon oxide and etched with various transistors, eliminating the need for separate transistors connected by wires. Jack Kilby of Texas Instruments is credited as the microchip's coinventor. Its successful introduction was a milestone in both the semiconductor and modern electronics industries and is widely considered among the century's most critical technological developments.

A competitive microchip industry quickly grew and the microchip became Fairchild's leading product, making Noyce a millionaire by the end of the decade. Noyce was becoming increasingly dissatisfied at Fairchild, however, because of what he believed was a lack of control. Noyce and fellow entrepreneur and scientist Gordon E. Moore left Fairchild in 1968 to found a new company in Mountain View, California. Its headquarters later became established in Santa Clara, California. Venture capitalist Arthur Rock provided most of the start-up capital.

The company was first incorporated as NM Electronics and later rechristened INTEL, an abbreviation of "integrated electronics." The eventually lowercased Intel specialized in the development and manufacture of large-scale integrated (LSI) semiconductor memory (data storage). Its founders believed that such

Affiliation: Intel Corporation

U.S.-based transnational semiconductor chip manufacturer Intel Corporation is headquartered in Santa Clara, California. Fellow scientists, inventors, and entrepreneurs Robert Noyce and Gordon E. Moore founded Intel as NM Electronics in 1968, changing the name to Intel (short for "integrated electronics") the following year. Venture capitalist Arthur Rock was the initial investor and chairman of the board. Engineer Andrew Grove soon joined Noyce and Moore as the company's first employees, rising to become one of the company's most widely recognized CEOs in the 1980s and 1990s.

Intel first manufactured semiconductors. Its first product was the Schottky TTL bipolar 64-bit static random access memory (SRAM) chip, which debuted in 1969. The company rapidly expanded its product line in the 1970s, remaining focused on dynamic random access memory (DRAM) chips. Intel was also instrumental in the fight for intellectual property rights and the passage of the Semiconductor Chip Protection Act of 1984 as well as a number of related property rights and antitrust lawsuits brought by and against the company.

International competition and the rise to prominence of the IBM personal computer (PC) in the 1980s led then-CEO Grove to switch the company's focus from semiconductors to microprocessors. Intel had introduced its first commercial microprocessor, the Intel 4004, in 1971. During the 1980s, Intel emerged as the leading microprocessor and hardware supplier to the lucrative PC industry.

Intel continued its market dominance into the 1990s with its line of Pentium processors, raising its global brand recognition through its "Intel Inside" marketing campaign. The company was hurt by increased competition, slowed market demand for microprocessors, and failed attempts at diversification in the early twenty-first century. However, Intel continued to be a major market presence, despite these setbacks, adapting its corporate mission to reflect the growth of the Internet.

of state-of-the-art research and development and top-quality manufacturing capacity.

Intel scientists developed the world's first microprocessor, in 1971. The company offered its first public stock in that year. The Intel 8008, the first 8-bit microprocessor, debuted in 1972, followed by the even faster Intel 8080 processor in 1974. Microprocessors revolutionized computing by allowing for the development of the microcomputer (or personal computers) as well as a variety of handheld electronic devices such as calculators. The microprocessor quickly moved Intel to the forefront of the computer industry, fueled in part by IBM's decision to incorporate the Intel 8008 microprocessor in its first personal computer (PC), which made its commercial debut in 1981.

Intel moved into computer design and debuted its highly successful Pentium chip line in the 1990s. The company has also benefited from an ongoing alliance with Bill Gates's Microsoft Corporation and its Windows products, an alliance commonly referred to by the nickname Wintel. Intel emerged as the leading global semiconductor manufacturer by the end of the twentieth century and expanded its facilities to include Europe and Asia. The company achieved $1 billion in revenues by 1983 and $1 billion in net income by 1992. It also began to focus on the rise of the Internet and the Internet economy.

During his career at Fairchild and Intel, Noyce was known for his vision, natural leadership abilities, and laid-back management style. His personal business philosophy centered on optimism, risk taking, and allowing employees the freedom he felt necessary for innovation. The work environment was loosely structured, and executives were expected to forgo executive perqs such as fancy offices, as Noyce did himself. His management style would become generally associated with the California-based computer and information technology industries.

Even after his retirement from daily operations at Intel at age fifty-eight, Noyce remained connected to the semiconductor industry for the remainder of his life. He had secured sixteen patents in the semiconductor field throughout his career. One of his chief concerns was the future competitiveness of U.S.-based companies in the face of increasing competition from international

technology would soon supplant magnetic cores through improved speed and efficiency and lowered costs. Under Noyce's leadership, the company advanced the consumer electronics revolution. Noyce would become Intel's chairman of the board in 1974.

The company's first competitive products debuted in the 1970s and featured a variety of devices, including integrated circuits featuring shift register memory, static random access memory (SRAM), and high-speed dynamic random access memory (DRAM). Even in its early years, the company became known for its combination

entrants into the marketplace, such as the Japanese. Noyce became president and CEO of SEMATECH, a semiconductor manufacturers' consortium working in partnership with the U.S. government to increase national competitiveness in the international market. He would also be chosen as a member of the President's Commission on Industrial Competitiveness.

Noyce was also widely recognized as a leading industry spokesman, cofounding and chairing the Semiconductor Industry Association (SIA). He was an investor and adviser with several other companies as well. His work outside the industry included serving as a regent for the University of California. As one of the original computer entrepreneurs and a dominant force in the industry, he came to be known as the Mayor of Silicon Valley.

PERSONAL LIFE

Noyce spent most of his adult life in California. He married Elizabeth Bottomley in 1953, and the couple had four children before divorcing. He later married second wife Ann Bowers. His hobbies and interests reflected his risk-taking personality and included piloting airplanes, hang gliding, scuba diving, and daredevil skiing as well as more cerebral pursuits, such as reading the works of Ernest Hemingway and singing madrigals. Recognition for his work included the Medal of Honor from the Institute of Electrical and Electronics Engineers (1978), the National Medal of Science (1980), the National Medal of Technology (1987), and induction into the Consumer Electronics Association Hall of Fame (2000); he was also inducted into the National Inventors Hall of Fame.

Noyce died unexpectedly of heart failure while in his home in Austin, Texas, on June 3, 1990. He was sixty-two years of age. Intel recognized his long-term contributions to the company's success through the dedication of its Robert Noyce Building in Santa Clara, California, which houses the corporate Intel Museum. The museum features a permanent exhibition titled

Robert Noyce: A Life Celebrated. The Noyce family established the Robert Noyce Foundation in honor of his legacy. The foundation promotes education in the areas of science, mathematics, and literacy and is involved in educational policy advocacy.

Marcella Bush Trevino

FURTHER READING

Berlin, Leslie. *The Man Behind the Microchip: Robert Noyce and the Invention of Silicon Valley*. New York: Oxford UP, 2005. Print. Biographical account that examines Noyce's inventiveness and entrepreneurship, focusing on his invention of the integrated chip and its impact on the later development of the microchip. Also explores his risk-taking lifestyle.

Lecuyer, Christophe, David C. Brock, and Jay Last. *Makers of the Microchip: A Documentary History of Fairchild Semiconductor*. Cambridge: MIT, 2010. Print. Covers Noyce's role in cofounding the company, the development of the microchip, the rise of Silicon Valley, and the role of venture capitalism in the industry.

Orton, John W. *The Story of Semiconductors*. New York: Oxford UP, 2009. Print. Details the history of semiconductors and explains the science and technology behind them.

Reid, T. R. *The Chip: How Two Americans Invented the Microchip and Launched a Revolution*. New York: Random House, 2001. Print. Updated version of the 1985 work. Explores Noyce's career alongside that of fellow inventor Jack Kilby, including the impact of their work on later technological developments and inventions.

Riordan, Michael, and Lillian Hoddeson. *Crystal Fire: The Birth of the Information Age*. Norton, 1998. Print. Technological examination of the history of the invention and development of the transistor. Also covers the people involved and the growth of the associated lucrative industry.

KRISTEN NYGAARD

Coinventor of Simula and object-oriented programming

Born: August 27, 1926; Oslo, Norway
Died: August 10, 2002; Oslo, Norway
Primary Field: Computer science

Specialty: Computer programming
Primary Company/Organization: Norwegian Computing Center

INTRODUCTION

In the 1960s, the Norwegian computer scientist Kristen Nygaard, in collaboration with Ole-John Dahl, developed a new programming language, Simula, and a new methodology for programming, object-oriented programming, that would result in computer programs that would more closely follow the way people work. This system, based on chunks of code (objects) that could be assembled and modified in almost limitless fashion, made it possible to create programs with greater power and to reduce the time required to devise code. In the first part of the twenty-first century, object-oriented programming is used in countless business applications and is the basis for developing applications on the Internet. In addition to his technical contributions, Nygaard was an active and articulate participant in his nation's political process, seeking to keep Norway's social and economic foundations intact.

EARLY LIFE

Kristen Nygaard was born in Oslo, Norway, on August 27, 1926. His life, like that of all his fellow Norwegians, was profoundly affected by the 1940 German invasion at the beginning of World War II. The invasion and subsequent occupation by the Germans disrupted the

Kristen Nygaard.

country's educational system: Initially, classes were canceled; eventually, the Nazi occupiers imposed mass arrests of teachers. Nygaard nonetheless managed to complete school, graduating from high school in 1945, the year the war ended.

In that year, Nygaard enrolled at the University of Oslo, where he earned a bachelor's degree in mathematics. Nygaard, like all young men in postwar Norway, was obliged to perform national service. Unlike others, however, who might have served as soldiers or sailors, Nygaard worked at the Norwegian Defense Ministry's Defense Research Establishment. From 1948 until the early 1950s, Nygaard performed general mathematical support for defense projects. Continuing his education while working, he received a master's degree in mathematics from the University of Oslo in 1956. His specialty was Monte Carlo simulations (large-scale algorithmic computations based on large random samples to see not only all possible outcomes of a decision but also the probable outcomes).

Starting in 1952, at the Defense Research Establishment, Nygaard became involved in operations research (OR) the process whereby practitioners search for quantitative solutions to support the decision-making process. He would remain in the OR section, eventually heading it in 1957, until he departed in 1960. In that year he moved to the Norwegian Computing Center (Norsk Regnesentral), eventually becoming its head in 1962.

LIFE'S WORK

Computer programming in the early 1960s had neither the variety of languages (allowing a choice for developers) nor the power that languages existing in the twenty-first century have. Programming languages were based on the premise that a task to be performed would be broken into a string of procedures. In other words, a program was a set of instructions in linear form that would prescribe the entire process from beginning to end.

What struck Nygaard and his collaborator, Dahl, was that this style of programming did not necessarily capture how people work to accomplish a specific set of objectives (their workflows). Nygaard and Dahl began to think of creating programs that would respond to a way of modeling the set of instructions that better reflect how people work. Their response was to begin to create their own programming language. What they developed was released in 1962 as Simula I. Simula I was not an entirely new language; it was built on an already existing language, Algorithmic Language 1960 (ALGOL 60, designated as 60 because it was officially released in

1960). ALGOL 60 was the latest version of a language that contained a new feature, "nested functions." Nested functions meant that a procedure could contain subprocedures within it as part of its structure. That ability would prove to be an important point of departure for what Nygaard and Dahl would eventually do. They would build on properties contained in that language as well as ideas about organizing code that had started to be developed by others in the late 1950s. Building a language on the capacities of another language was the method by which Niklaus Wirth would develop his own language, Pascal, also based on ALGOL 60.

Simula I and, more specifically, its successor, Simula 67, put into place a new model for how problems would be examined by analysts and how the analysis would be put into a working program by coders. The process would be known as object-oriented programming (OOP). OOP has been often referred to as code that is similar to Lego blocks. Just as Lego blocks can be assembled in different ways to make many different structures, OOP is based on chunks (blocks) of code that can be assembled together. These chunksm or objects, can contain both the data and the processes that operate inside them. They can then be assembled in various ways (in other words, determining the relationships or instructions or communications among the blocks) to create the program needed to solve the real-world problem. What is most valuable about these objects is that after one has been created (called an "instance"), it can be stored, copied, and modified for use in other programs to solve other problems.

By the late 1960s, the basic premise of OOP was in place, although developments in the coming years would increase OOP's sophistication (too much so, according to Nygaard) and power. OOP was becoming the basis for new languages that were developed in the 1970s and 1980s and that became widely adopted in the 1990s. Apple's computer developers began to use it. The Xerox Palo Alto Research Center (PARC, where Nygaard worked while on sabbatical) developed the object-oriented language SmallTalk. Bell Laboratories would develop C++, another object-oriented language, using the already existing language C as it base, similar to the way Nygaard and Dahl had subsumed ALGOL 60 as the base for Simula. Java, which is widely used to develop Internet applications, is another object-oriented language.

Although he took a degree of satisfaction in his accomplishment, Nygaard was not entirely happy with how things had developed by the end of the 1990s. First, he thought OOP languages had become too complex.

Affiliation: Norwegian Computing Center

Norsk Regnesentral (NR)—in English, the Norwegian Computing Center—was established in 1952. Functioning in a manner similar to the American RAND corporation, NR describes itself as an independent, nonprofit private foundation. Some funding comes from the Norwegian government. NR conducts research for business organizations, the government at all levels, and private organizations both in Norway and abroad.

NR is headquartered in the Nygaard House on the campus of the University of Oslo. As one might expect of an organization where Kristen Nygaard worked, in its early years (until 1970) the emphasis was on mathematics, statistics, and mathematical modeling. Today, NR performs research in a large number of business and technological areas, such as the energy industry, environmental issues, finance, and information systems. Some of NR's ongoing projects in 2012 included e-health and studies to find better ways to serve disabled voters. Projects are staffed by full-time employees of NR, but several academics and graduate students, from the University of Oslo and other organizations, support NR's efforts on a part-time basis as well.

Second, he believed that the manner in which analysts and programmers were taught OOP was not satisfactory. In order to remedy that problem, he started to develop comprehensive object-oriented learning (COOL) to provide the basis for effective use of object-oriented languages. He had started on this project at the time of his death and it has been continued by others since his death.

PERSONAL LIFE

Nygaard's life encompassed a great deal more than developing solutions to technical problems; he seems never to have thought of technology as a self-contained entity without social implications. The effects of science and technology on society informed much of his thought; he was keenly aware of economic, social, and economic developments in Norway. His activities included technical work to support and assist workers as well as actively participating in the Norwegian political system.

In the late 1960s, Nygaard performed work for the Norwegian Iron and Metal Miners so they could better evaluate computer technologies as they might affect how miners performed their jobs and use them most effectively. As part of this effort, Nygaard developed training materials for miners so they could better understand the impact of new technologies.

At the same time that he was providing technical assistance to the labor union, Nygaard became involved in national politics. He would remain visible, active, and successful until shortly before his death. In the 1960s, Nygaard was a member of the Norwegian Liberal Party, changing his affiliation in 1971, when he became an active member of the Norwegian Labor Party. A strong believer in Norway's welfare state, Nygaard throughout the 1990s strongly opposed Norway's entry into the Eurozone. His opposition was based primarily on what he saw as the fiscal restrictions that would be placed on Norway's management of its finances (particularly social welfare programs) if it were to join. The forced austerity measures on some Eurozone members in 2012 have proven him to be correct, at least from Norway's perspective. The proposal was defeated and Norway never joined.

Nygaard received several major awards. These included the Association for Computing Machinery's A. M. Turing Award and the Institute of Electrical and Electronics Engineers' John von Neumann Medal. He also won the Norbert Wiener Prize from the American Association of Computer Professionals for Social Responsibility and the Order of Saint Olav from the king of Norway.

Nygaard was married, with three children. He and his wife, Johanna Ur, were married in Oslo on January 27, 1951. Their first children, a set of twins, were born in May of that year. He died of a heart attack in Oslo on August 10, 2002, a few weeks after the death of his collaborator, Ole-John Dahl, whose obituary he had written.

Robert N. Stacy

FURTHER READING

Atkinson, J. B. "Object Orientation, Discrete Simulation and Simula." *Journal of the Operational Research Society* 46.12 (1995): 1510–13. Print. A general history of Nygaard's efforts and their results in the areas of the Simula programming language, as well as the importance of object-oriented programming.

Berntsen, Drude, Knut Elgsaas, and Håvard Hegna. "The Many Dimensions of Kristen Nygaard, Creator of Object-Oriented Programming and the Scandinavian School of System Development." *History of Computing: Learning from the Past*. Ed. Arthur Tatnall. IFIP Advances in Information and Communication Technology, Vol. 325. Boston: Springer, 2010. 38–49. Print. An account of Nygaard, his developmental work as well as his political activities.

Holmevik, Jan Rune. *Educating the Machine: A Study in the History of Computing and the Construction of the Simula Programming Language*. Dragvoll: University of Trondheim, Center for Technology and Society, 1994. Print. A historical account of Nygaard and Dahl's development of Simula and the further development of the object-oriented paradigm.

Waldrop, M. Mitchell. "Frustrated with Fortran? Bored by Basic? Try OOP!" *Science*, new series, 261.5123 (1993): 849–50. Print. In the early 1990s, when several early programming languages were still being used, OOP was beginning to be considered the next big thing in programming. This article describes OOP's perceived advantages.

ED OATES

Cofounder of Oracle

Born: 1946; Los Angeles, California
Died: -
Primary Field: Computer science
Specialty: Computer software
Primary Company/Organization: Oracle

INTRODUCTION

Ed Oates was one of the three founders (soon joined by a fourth employee) who left Ampex Corporation to form Software Development Laboratories, a relational database and services company that was eventually renamed the Oracle Corporation in honor of its flagship product, the world's leading relational database management system.

EARLY LIFE

Edward Albert "Ed" Oates was born in 1946 in Los Angeles, California, and grew up in Campbell. He majored in mathematics at San Jose State University and received his bachelor's degree in 1968. He was drafted into the U.S. Army, where he was assigned to the Personnel Information Systems Command (PERSIN-SCOM). After completing his obligation, he worked for Singer, Memorex, and Ampex, an electronics company known mainly for professional tape recorders (having introduced instant replay), which also developed customized database software for government agencies. While working at Ampex, he happened to pass by Bob Miner's office, when Miner was talking to his supervisee, Larry Ellison. Ellison mentioned his wife, whose name Oates recognized, having gone to high school with her. The resulting conversation led to Oates joining Ellison and Miner when they left Ampex to form Software

Development Laboratories—the company that would become the Oracle Corporation—in August 1977.

LIFE'S WORK

Together the partners pooled $2,000 to rent an office in Belmont, California, and Ellison and Miner persuaded their contacts at the Central Intelligence Agency (CIA) to award them a $50,000 contract to develop a relational

Ed Oates.

235

Affiliation: Oracle

In 2001, the dawn of the twenty-first century, ninety-eight of the Fortune 100 companies used Oracle software to manage their business files. Customer interactions ranging from paying a phone bill to buying a plane ticket, making a hotel reservation, withdrawing cash from an automated teller, paying for a purchase with a credit card, and conducting a search on Google—all involved the use of an Oracle software package somewhere behind the scenes. Oracle never became a household name, and what mainstream fame it did have was largely because of CEO Larry Ellison's outsized personality, but business owners knew the name as well as their employees recognized brands like Starbucks.

Oracle was founded in 1977 by Ellison, his former supervisor Bob Miner, their colleague at Ampex Ed Oates, and Bruce Scott, the company's first hire. Originally called Software Development Laboratories (SDL), it renamed itself Relational Software, Inc. (RSI) in 1979 but eventually took the name Oracle in honor of its flagship software package. The Oracle software was a relational database management system, inspired by a paper circulated at IBM and applied by SDL to smaller computers than conventional wisdom in the 1970s said was possible.

Relational database management systems (RDBMS's) such as the one Oracle pioneered have become a standard tool in business operations—ironic for a company that had so little business savvy when it began, particularly when it came to bookkeeping. The company's first chief financial officer began as a pizza delivery boy—SDL was on his route, and no one at the company had any idea how to approach accounting (nor did anyone formally keep the books for a full two years), so the founders hired him when they discovered that he had majored in accounting. The rest of the practicalities of business, Ellison taught himself.

In 1983, RSI introduced the first commercial portable RDBMS, which could be run on the wide range of hardware and operating systems that had become available during the explosive growth of the computing industry. The product was instrumental in the company's doubling its revenues that year, and RSI was renamed Oracle Corporation, capitalizing on the fame of its flagship product (and the cancellation of a CIA project for which the company had won a contract). New versions released in 1985 allowed a single database to be accessed by multiple applications, making the Oracle system more flexible and customizable. The following year, structured query language (SQL), developed by IBM in the 1970s, was adopted as the standard language of the database industry, which boosted Oracle's prominence, as it was the best-known and longest-established SQL-compatible RDBMS.

On March 15, 1986, Oracle went public with an initial public offering of 2.1 million shares and a market value of $270 million. It had grown over a little less than ten years from four partners to 450 employees, with a customer base of more than two thousand firms and government organizations. Twenty years later, it had grown from 450 employees to 65,000, revenues five hundred times higher than 1986's $20 million. In 1989, the company was added to the Standard and Poor's 500, only three years after going public.

Oracle expanded into applications, principally for use with databases, while Ellison delegated most of his CEO responsibilities to others in order to focus on expanding product diversity. A suite of accounting and bookkeeping programs followed, as well as a transaction process subsystem (TPS) package for use with financial transactions. New backup programs were developed in order to generate data archives for businesses. A subsidiary, Oracle Data Publishing, was formed in 1989 to sell reference material in digital form.

Some minor troubles developed in 1990, when shareholders filed a lawsuit alleging that Oracle's earnings forecasts had been deliberately misleading; In 1990's first quarter, net earnings had been nearly flat, and the day after this was announced, Oracle's stock fell from $25.38 to $17.50 per share. Oracle conducted an internal audit and formed a separate subsidiary, Oracle US, to solve its management problems. Ellison's over-the-top personality had too often been coupled with a short attention span: He would work hard on a project for weeks, burn himself out, and leave for a European vacation before coming back to bear down hard on another project. His own self-evaluation of his behavior varied considerably: Sometimes he took pride in his reputation as a wildcard because he believed it

Affiliation: Oracle (Continued)

reflected the company's innovativeness; other times he admitted that he might be holding the company back.

In 1992, major changes took place throughout the company. Cofounder Miner—who had balanced Ellison's managerial style in the early days—first left his post as head of product development, which he had held since the company began, and then left the company altogether because of a cancer diagnosis. New executives were brought in to shore up the corporation's weak areas. Oracle7, the last product Miner oversaw, was released after six years of development and testing and was exceptionally well received, particularly its compatibility with networks and the implication of Internet compatibility in the future. By the end of the year, the balance sheet had improved and bank debt had been cleared from the books.

Oracle, especially Ellison, butted heads with Microsoft and Bill Gates in the 1990s over the Internet, with Oracle fighting to popularize cheap network computers that would run Internet applications as a substitute for more expensive Intel machines running Windows products that would require expensive software upgrades. Suites of Internet business applications followed in the late 1990s, with Oracle E-Business Suite Release 11i, which Ellison marketed with a $300 million campaign, the cornerstone of which was the implementation of 11i at the Oracle Corporation and the demonstration that doing so saved Oracle $1 billion a year.

Key to Oracle's twenty-first century development has been flexibility and scalability in its products, which are suitable for concerns ranging from small businesses with a single point of sale to multinational corporations and government agencies. Oracle also succeeded in a hostile takeover of competitor PeopleSoft, conducted in 2003–04, and acquired Sun Microsystems—its ally in the fight against Microsoft—in January 2010, interested primarily in its Java programming language and the Solaris operating system.

In 2010, Oracle was indicted by the federal government for fraud, for presenting misleading information about the bulk discounts given to federal buyers. A month later, Oracle brought suit against Google for patent violation and copyright infringement, alleging the use of material protected by Java patents in Google's Android system. In 2012, a jury found in favor of Google.

---

database. Ellison was in charge of business management, and his management style was at times erratic, as he was given to grand gestures. At Ampex, they had all been unhappy with their compensation model, so Ellison made a point of rewarding hard work and good results at Oracle, even paying bonuses with gold coins. He was also demanding and often abrasive. Miner, who took charge of product development from the company's start until shortly before his retirement in 1993, kept Ellison in check, protesting when employees were kept at work too late.

The company—which was soon renamed Relational Software, Inc. (RSI) in 1979, a name it kept until becoming Oracle Systems Corporation in 1982 in honor of its flagship product—was devoted to relational database management systems, which had been introduced in a 1970 paper and were being developed by IBM, but only for mainframes, and even then at a slow pace. Relational databases allowed users to search for data based on common characteristics, or relations. Oates, Ellison, and Miner realized there was an opportunity to develop commercial and government applications for relational databases, especially on smaller computers, which the industry had dismissed as an impractical application. (In time, Oracle would become associated with great flexibility and scalability, producing software that could be used by multinational corporations or small mom-and-pop businesses.) While Miner developed product and wrote the code with Bruce Scott (the company's first hire), Oates had hands-on general computer knowledge that came into play in determining how to adapt Miner's products to different implementations.

Unlike the founders of most successful start-ups now, the founders of Oracle have freely admitted that in their early days they had no idea what they were doing with regard to their business administration. They badly misjudged the bids they made on contracts, struggled with determining what to charge for their work, and essentially made things up as they went along, with each partner having a clearly defined role and area of control: Oates was the consultant, working with the customers whom Ellison cultivated to sell, adapt, and implement the products that Miner developed. They hired people on impulse, often with little idea of how to evaluate a candidate's suitability for a job; famously, the chief financial officer had begun as their pizza boy. Early customers were mainly government agencies and the intelligence community, fields in which large amounts of data were in use and in need of analysis.

In 1996, Oates, who was never interested in running a large company, retired from Oracle. He had been made wealthy by his stock shares, after the company went public in 1986—though not as wealthy as he could have been, having sold some of his shares back to Oracle in order to meet the terms of a divorce settlement. He sits on the boards of the San Francisco Zoological Society and the Tower Foundation of San Jose State University. He also bought a home theater store, Audible Difference, which he ran from 1996 to 1999.

PERSONAL LIFE

Oates is an avid skier and scale-model railroad aficionado. A limited partner in Rock and Roll Fantasy Camp, he has attended the camp several times and plays in the amateur rock band Choc'd.

Bill Kte'pi

FURTHER READING

Codd, E. F. "A Relational Model of Data for Large Shared Data Banks." *Communications of the ACM* 13.6 (1970): n. pag. Print. Ted Codd's original paper introducing the concept of the relational database, the application on which Oracle was based.

Cringely, Robert X. *Accidental Empires: How the Boys of Silicon Valley Make Their Millions, Battle Foreign Competition, and Still Can't Get a Date.* New York: HarperBusiness, 1996. Print. A history of Silicon valley from before the dot-com bubble burst.

Kenney, Martin. *Understanding Silicon Valley: The Anatomy of an Entrepreneurial Region.* Stanford: Stanford UP, 2000. Print. An overview of Silicon Valley, the culture from which Oracle emerged.

Rao, Arun, and Piero Scarulfi. *A History of Silicon Valley.* San Francisco: Omniware, 2011. Print. Overview of the Silicon Valley tech company culture.

KENNETH H. OLSEN

Cofounder of Digital Equipment Corporation

Born: February 20, 1926; Bridgeport, Connecticut
Died: February 6, 2011; Indianapolis, Indiana
Primary Field: Business and commerce
Specialty: Management, executives, and investors
Primary Company/Organization: Digital Equipment Corporation

INTRODUCTION

Kenneth H. Olsen is cofounder of Digital Equipment Corporation (DEC, or Digital). His love for engineering and his philosophy of getting the job done and giving the customer value made his company a leading competitor against IBM in computer sales in the 1980s. He developed a management style unheard of in the 1960s, placing faith in and giving latitude to his employees. In 1992, Olsen resigned as president and chief executive officer (CEO) of the DEC, which was bought by Compaq in 1998 for $9.6 billion.

EARLY LIFE

Kenneth Harry Olsen was born to Oswald and Elizabeth Olsen, whose families were of Swedish and Norwegian descent, in Bridgeport, Connecticut. Oswald was a fundamentalist Christian and believed in discipline, but his son, who like his father was quiet and determined, needed little supervision. Oswald was an engineer by trade and an exceptional machine tool designer. He instilled in his sons a love for mechanical and electrical things, allowing them to tinker with the tools in his basement. Olsen helped fix neighbors' radios and once set up a radio transmitter with assistance from his brother Stan. Olsen and his brother broke into a local radio station with their transmitter to broadcast a jingle that Stan had written, "Murphy's Meatballs." In high school, Olsen played center for the Stanford High School football team.

Just as World War II was coming to a close, Olsen joined the U.S. Navy. He never saw combat, but he received useful technical training. In one year, he completed the electronics technician training course and ran his ship's radio shack. This served as a springboard to his study of engineering after he returned to civilian life. Thanks to the G.I. Bill, Olsen was able to enter the Massachusetts Institute of Technology (MIT) in February 1947. Instead of studying electronics, as he had initially planned, he studied electrical engineering at the

Kenneth H. Olsen.

encouragement of his professors. In 1950, he was given the chance to work on the Whirlwind, a computer built to power a cockpit flight simulator for the Navy. MIT also created Lincoln Laboratory in Lexington, Massachusetts, to conduct further research in defense systems. Olsen was chosen as one of four hundred highly skilled engineers to work on the Semi-Automatic Ground Environment (SAGE) defense system, for which Whirlwind had been the base. Olsen helped produce a test computer for SAGE within nine months, establishing a reputation as an efficient, determined, and skilled worker.

In 1953, Olsen became the liaison for Lincoln Laboratory and the International Business Machines Corporation (IBM), which had established a subcontract with the laboratory. However, Olsen was stifled and frustrated at IBM. MIT had exposed Olsen to a certain degree of working freedom that could not exist in the business world of IBM. Olsen became fed up with the bureaucracy of IBM and described his work there as akin to "going to a communist state." He believed that he could do what IBM was doing, only better. He was ready to start his own company.

LIFE'S WORK

To start this new computer company, Olsen enlisted Harlan Anderson, with whom he had worked on the Whirlwind. They went to American Research and Development Corporation (ARD), a venture capital company, for investment backing. They got the support of George Doriot, the French founder of the company. Doriot, impressed by Olsen's demonstration of playing Bach on his computer, took a liking to Olsen. Doriot's disbelief in making quick profit and selling out enabled the two engineers to get their start-up funding. ARD invested $100,000, expecting $70,000 in shares in exchange. As a result, ARD would own more than 70 percent of the company. Believing the term *computer* to be ahead of their time, Doriot suggested the company of Digital Equipment Corporation (DEC). In 1957, DEC was born.

Because of their extremely tight budget, Olsen and Anderson cut corners wherever possible. They rented out space in an old woolen mill (the Mill) that dated back to the Civil War, in Maynard, Massachusetts, not far from Lincoln Lab. They used whatever desks and chairs came with the space instead of refurnishing, and they even refused to buy doors, considering them too expensive to purchase and install. Instead of buying insulators, they used bottle caps. "Spend as little as possible," was DEC's motto. If they could do something themselves they would, even if they had to build a machine to do it. Olsen's wife even came to the Mill from time to time to sweep floors. An advertisement was placed in newspapers seeking employees, and engineers from MIT were recruited. Although Olsen had founded a new company, he wanted to keep some of the work ideals he had learned at MIT, chiefly openness and honesty, and to create an environment that fostered new ideas and tolerated mistakes. DEC progressed quickly, and by the end of its first year it had twelve employees and had made $94,000 selling its digital laboratory modules and digital systems modules. Doriot was impressed yet saddened, because companies with such early successes usually failed quickly. Little did he know what staying power DEC would have.

DEC served as an inspiration for both students and professional engineers. They saw DEC as the environment in which they could work creatively and well, given DEC's casual yet intense atmosphere. In June 1960, Chester Gordon Bell left MIT to work for DEC. He became DEC's second computer engineer. Olsen had set out to build computers, so in 1959, two years after starting the company, he and Bell started designing DEC's first one. Olsen thought that computers should be accessible to the individual, without the need of a programmer to run it. The result was the PDP-1, a breakthrough in computer technology, revolutionary for its small size (about the size of a refrigerator, which was very small compared to MIT's room-sized computers) and its accessibility: It did not need a sterile environment, nor did it need a professional programmer to tell it what to do. The machine was called a programmed data processor because Doriot remained cautious about attracting the attention and competition of IBM. By avoiding the term *computer*, DEC was able to enter the market without much fanfare. The PDP-1 did not have the same power as a giant mainframe, but for the relatively low price of $120,000 it had more computing power than customers expected. Olsen donated a PDP-1 to MIT to allow students to work with a real computer. He strongly supported the academic aspect of engineering, not just the commercial, and employed interns from MIT as well.

As DEC grew, new machines were planned. The PDP-2 was supposed to be a 24-bit machine, while the PDP-3 was going to be a 36-bit machine. DEC built neither of these machines, but it did create the PDP-4. The Canadian engineers who bought the first PDP-4, however, complained that it was too complex. The PDP-5 was built in response, serving as the precursor to the minicomputers DEC would build. At this time, Bell was developing the PDP-6, a 36-bit machine that was ultimately a failure. In 1965, however, the PDP-8 brought DEC into its own. The small computer was 12-bit machine and the size of a cabinet, allowing it to be placed on laboratory countertops. The PDP-8 was very powerful, especially in relation to its extremely low price of $18,000. Another benefit was that DEC neither produced software nor bought it from third-party software designers. Rather, DEC's customers could use whatever software they wanted on their machines, be it third-party or self-designed, making DEC's machines much more flexible than hardware with preloaded software from other companies. DEC gained a monopoly in the market of minicomputers, and imitations from other companies, such as IBM could not compete with DEC computers' size, speed, or power.

Olsen had a management style unusual for his time. He did not want to impose the system of hierarchy that he had experienced at IBM and that was common in most businesses. Olsen saw titles as meaningless if nothing got done and new ideas were not being created. To prevent this problem, Olsen established a management system that would later be known as "matrix management." Every employee reported to two or three managers, which spreading the responsibility across managers. Although the matrix created a sort of organized chaos,

Olsen was a strong believer in responsibility. Once an idea was pitched and approved, the person in charge was responsible for its completion, and if things went wrong, he or she had no excuses. Olsen had a reputation for criticizing employees for their mistakes, getting loud and aggressive. Nevertheless, he had a way of making people want to please him and to get back in his good graces. He also insisted on avoiding nepotism. After asking his brother Stan to help him start the company, Olsen refused jobs to other family members. This was his business, not his family's.

Despite some harsh principles, Olsen looked out for his employees. There existed at DEC an unspoken no-firing policy. If someone did not work out in a department, they were sent into a new one, until the right fit was found. This led to a strong bond between employees and Olsen. He even had his managers attend retreats to his lakeside cabin, where many problems could be solved while groups of managers took walks. Olsen fostered "group discovery," leading conversations and discussions whereby the group

Affiliation: Digital Equipment Corporation

Digital Equipment Corporation (DEC) was a leading supplier of computer systems for much of the latter half of the twentieth century, well known for its PDP and VAX systems. With its headquarters located in Maynard, Massachusetts, DEC was at one point during the 1980s the second-largest employer in the state, trailing only the Massachusetts state government.

In addition to the mainframes and minicomputers for which it was known, DEC was a pioneer in the microcomputer market. The company's early desktop model, the DEC Professional, debuted in 1982 and was technically superior to the IBM PC, which had been released one year earlier. The DEC Professional was more expensive than, and incompatible with, the IBM PC, however, causing DEC to struggle to compete in thd PC market. At one point during the late 1980s, DEC employed more than 100,000 and seemed poised to dethrone IBM as the industry's leader. Growing competition from personal computers, however, caused the company to struggle in the early 1990s, and DEC was ultimately acquired by Hewlett-Packard through its acquisition of Compaq Computer Corporation, which had merged with DEC in 1998.

would generally come to a consensus. He believed that this took much of the responsibility of decision making off his shoulders, as well as allowing his team to come up with the best solutions possible. Sometimes the organized chaos got Olsen in trouble, however. In the mid-1980s, management problems led to losses in revenue. The press said that Olsen had lost his touch and called for his resignation. Olsen was not ready to let go of his company, however, and he fought through this period, emerging strong on the other end.

In 1975, DEC came out with the VAX line of computers. They were based on the PDP-11, which had become outdated, allowing potential customers to be familiar with the machine's structure. However, the VAX helped move DEC into the new era of computers. During this period, the press started comparing DEC to IBM. IBM came out with a minicomputer of its own, the Series-1, to rival DEC's computers. DEC had had a monopoly on the minicomputer market for such a long time, however, that IBM could not compete in this area. It was the personal computer (PC), or microcomputer (as opposed to the larger minicomputers), that became IBM's signature product and eventually outcompeted DEC. Olsen failed to recognize the potential and appeal of the PC, and at first he dismissed the thought of DEC creating one of its own. It was not until IBM had successfully developed a line of PCs that DEC made one. Olsen took apart an IBM PC and laughed at how it had been slapped together. One year later, DEC came out with its own personal computer. By this time, however, IBM had monopolized the market. As a result, Olsen began to retreat from the PC market. In 1986, however, he returned strong, and *Fortune* magazine called him the most successful entrepreneur of all time, taking a company from nothing and creating a $7.6 billion corporation.

In the early 1990s, Olsen's company again struggled, this time as a result of an industrywide recession. DEC's low-priced microprocessors were not catching on and some of its other product lines were struggling as well. In 1993, after thirty-five years with DEC, Olsen left the company he had founded. Six years later, DEC was sold to Compaq for $9.6 billion. Although the company eventually lost ground, DEC had led in innovation for most of its life, creating machines that were often the first used by many of today's leading computer engineers.

PERSONAL LIFE

Olsen met his wife, Eeva-Liisa Aulikki Valve, a Finnish exchange student, through his roommate in college.

She decided not to finish college in the United States, so Olsen took a break from his work at MIT and followed her to Europe. Taking a job at a ball-bearing factory in Sweden, Olsen was able to reunite with Aulikki, and they soon became engaged. As the Cold War intensified, Olsen needed special permission to marry and bring his foreign bride back into the United States. Family connections with a friend in the U.S. State Department helped cut through the red tape, and Aulikki's father married the couple in December of 1950. Olsen brought her back home, and they soon had the first of three sons.

Olsen was always a religious man, never swearing, drinking, or smoking. He treated his employees more like family than people on a payroll, and almost everybody called him Ken. He was also a modest man: Even after his company's successes, he refused to move into a bigger house and continued to drive his trusty Ford. One day, a coworker noticed that he had been seen driving a Mercedes, and Olsen, embarrassed, admitted that he had borrowed his wife's car.

Olsen received many honors for his work, including induction into the National Inventors Hall of Fame, a seat on the Computer Science and Engineering Board of the National Academy of Sciences in Washington, D.C., and the Vermilye Medal in 1980. Olsen died February 6, 2011, in Indianapolis while in hospice care. He was eighty-four years old.

Stephen T. Schroth and Lena Brandis

FURTHER READING

Earls, A. R. *Digital Equipment Corporation: Images of America*. Portsmouth: Arcadia, 2004. Print. Tells the full story of DEC and its contributions to the advent of the personal computer, the first computer games, computer networks, the Internet revolution. Includes photographs of people, events, and machines.

Kilbane, Doris. "Ken Olsen: Faith, Work, and Charity Support a Computing Career." *Electronic Design* 59.16 (2011): 66–68. Web. 1 May 2012. An obituary focusing on the Olsen's innovative management style, philosophy, and philanthropy.

Rifkin, G., and G. Harrar. *The Ultimate Entrepreneur: The Story of Ken Olsen and Digital Equipment Corporation*. New York: Prima, 1994. Print. The story of how DEC launched the minicomputer revolution but botched the transition to the personal computer, in which IBM and Apple eventually triumphed, despite the company's innovative foray into computer-networking software. Suited for the technically initiated.

Rosenberger, Jack. "Ken Olsen, DEC President and CEO, 1926-2011." *Communications of the ACM* 54.4 (2011): 20. Print. Obituary of Olsen.

Schein, E. H., P. S. DeLisi, P. J. Kampas, and M. M. Sonduck. *DEC Is Dead, Long Live DEC: The Lasting Legacy of Digital Equipment Corporation*. San Francisco: Berrett-Koehler, 2003. Print. The author, a consultant at DEC, provides an inside view of the key developments across the company's history, including insight into the influence of its founder and CEO, Olsen.

Scientific American, ed. *Understanding Supercomputing*. New York: Byron Preiss Visual, 2002. Print. A collection of fifteen articles published in *Scientific American* between 1995 and 2001 that together provide basic grounding in the technology of supercomputers.

Slater, R. "The Hermit of Chippewa Falls and His 'Simple, Dumb Things.'" *Portraits in Silicon*. Cambridge: MIT, 1989. 195–206. Print. A brief biography of Olsen in this collection of sketches on pioneers in computer science.

RAY OZZIE

Chief software architect at Microsoft and creator of Lotus Notes

Born: November 20, 1955; Chicago, Illinois
Died: -
Primary Field: Computer science
Specialty: Computer software
Primary Company/Organization: Microsoft

INTRODUCTION

Ray Ozzie developed the groundbreaking collaboration software Lotus Notes after developing the integrated suite Lotus Symphony. He joined Microsoft in the twenty-first century, first as its chief technical officer and then taking over the chief software architect position from Bill Gates. He left the company dissatisfied with its progress in cloud computing.

EARLY LIFE

Raymond Ozzie was born on November 20, 1955, in Chicago, Illinois, and grew up in the prosperous suburb of Park Ridge. He attended Park Ridge's Maine South High School, which is known for its extensive Applied Arts and Technology department, and began his computer programming education on a GE-400 time-sharing computer. In his senior year of high school, he worked as a systems programmer at Protection Mutual Insurance Company. He graduated in 1973 and enrolled in the University of Illinois at Urbana-Champaign, majoring in computer science. While at the University of Illinois, he worked on their Programmed Logic for Automated Teaching Operations (PLATO) project as a systems programmer.

PLATO had been developed in an attempt to automate elements of the teaching experience, in order to deal with the explosive and steady growth of higher education enrollment since the end of World War II. It was a software platform, first developed in 1960, that ran on the LILIAC computer with a television set for displaying computer graphics, which were an integral part of the system. Multiple programs could be run at once, piped to different terminals. PLATO III, the system in use when Ozzie began college, accepted new lesson modules written in the TUTOR programming

Ray Ozzie.

language designed for use especially with the system and with some hope that nonprogrammers could pick it up. PLATO IV, which included a terminal with a plasma display and vector line drawing capability, was introduced in 1972 while Ozzie was working on the project. It incorporated a revolutionary 16-by-16-inch infrared touch screen that students could use to answer questions and a standard keyboard substantially similar to today's desktop keyboards (although it lacked a numeric pad).

Although designed for educational purposes, PLATO project influenced both the Xerox Palo Alto Research Center (PARC) and Apple, pioneering communications technology. It was an early home to multiplayer online games, which became popular enough that a program called the Enforcer was written in order to shut down or limit game play in order to free computing resources for their designed purpose. PLATO was the first exposure Ozzie—and many others—had to e-mail, instant messaging, chat rooms, and online collaboration. One of the first online message boards was introduced on PLATO was well: PLATO Notes, released in 1973, which inspired Ozzie's own Lotus Notes.

LIFE'S WORK

Ozzie graduated from the University of Illinois at Urbana-Champaign in 1979 with a bachelor's degree in computer science and was hired by Data General to write an operating system for a local-area-network-based system using MicroNOVA workstations and file and print servers. Data General was one of the first minicomputer firms, founded in 1968 by former Digital employees. After Data General and a failed attempt to obtain funding for a workstation start-up, Ozzie took a job at Software Arts, the software company that had been founded to develop VisiCalc, the first personal computer spreadsheet program. More than any other product—hardware or software—VisiCalc was instrumental in popularizing microcomputers (personal computers) in business environments, where computers previously had been recreational; functions like word processing simply did not offer enough practical benefit to justify the cost.

In 1982, after reading Ted Nelson's work on the future of computers, Ozzie attempted to obtain funding to start a software company to develop the program that would become known as Lotus Notes. His experience using a prerelease IBM PC at Software Arts and the 3Com Ethernet card persuaded him that a revolution in personal computers and networking was in the immediate future. He failed to obtain funding, but he took a job at Lotus Development Corporation in 1983. Lotus was a

software company in Westford, Massachusetts, known for the Lotus 1-2-3 spreadsheet program (packaged with a graphics package and database manager—hence the name), which was released that year. While VisiCalc ushered in the age of the spreadsheet, Lotus 1-2-3 is widely acknowledged as the superior product, and Lotus later sued various developers for infringing on its copyright in attempting to produce cheap clones of the software. Ozzie was hired to develop the follow-up software package, Lotus Symphony, an integrated suite for MS-DOS systems, including a word processor, spreadsheet, communications program, database management system, and charting program. Microsoft Works was a similar successor product; Symphony was one of the first to take advantage of assigning commands to all eighty-four of the keys on IBM's PC keyboard.

Software Arts had created VisiCalc, while another company, Personal Software, developed it. That arrangement inspired Ozzie, after proving himself to Lotus founder Mitch Kapor with the Symphony product, to propose the same. He formed Iris Associates, which developed his Lotus Notes idea. Iris was in charge of product development; Lotus Development would handle sales and marketing. Kapor agreed, and Iris Associates was founded at the end of 1984 in Littleton, Massachusetts. Ozzie hired Tim Halvorsen and Len Kawell, with whom he had worked on the PLATO project.

Building on the online message board concept of PLATO Notes, Lotus Notes integrated collaboration functionality in one place, including—in eventual versions—voice and video conferencing, online meetings, blogging, file sharing, discussion forums, contacts management, calendaring, e-mail, and instant messaging, as well as collaborative document creation.

Iris was bought by Lotus Development in 1994 for $84 million, which in turn was acquired by IBM in 1995 for $3.5 billion, of which $3 billion of the purchase price was attributed to the value of Notes. Ozzie continued his Iris work until 1997, when he founded Groove Networks with his brother Jack, Ken Moore, and Eric Patey. Groove originated with Ozzie's belief that the collaboration requirements of decentralized business environments needed to be met with decentralized desktop software, not server-based architecture. Groove Networks was acquired by Microsoft in 2005, and the Groove software became Microsoft Office Groove, succeeded by Microsoft SharePoint Workspace, which has been replaced in Office 2013 with Skydrive Pro.

With the purchase of Groove by Microsoft, Ozzie became Microsoft's chief technical officer (CTO). In

Affiliation: Microsoft

One of the world's foremost computer companies and the largest software maker, Microsoft was founded in 1975 by Bill Gates and Paul Allen, who designed a BASIC compiler for the new Altair 8800 system, without even having an Altair to test it, and won Microsoft's first contract when they successfully demonstrated it to the company. It moved on to other implementations of BASIC, the dominant home computer programming language of the era, as well as Xenix, a Unix variant released in 1980. Xenix was the first operating system they released to the public and was the platform on which the first release of Microsoft Word (then called Multi-Tool Word) ran.

Microsoft Word made a big splash, thanks in part to the free demonstration copies of the MS-DOS version that were bundled with the November 1983 issue of *PC World*—the first software distributed on diskette bundled with a magazine, which became a standard and useful way of distributing demo software and shareware until Internet access became common enough and fast enough for downloads to be more practical. In Word's case, the free sample boosted sales and interest because the program significantly moved word processing forward: It was one of the few programs to allow use of a mouse and could display bold and italicized characters.

DOS (including MS-DOS and PC-DOS) was the operating system with which Microsoft was most associated during the early 1980s. PC-DOS was developed for IBM, with one-third of Microsoft's employees devoted to the project, so that when the IBM PC launched, Microsoft was the only company offering a full range of software for it—an operating system, programming language, and various applications, as well as Microsoft Mouse. This was followed by MS-DOS for PC-compatible computers.

The first version of Windows was released in 1985. It was originally a graphical user interface extension of MS-DOS, although early versions of Windows did assume some operating system functions and allowed multitasking, which DOS alone would not.

The most significant Windows releases were Windows NT, the first professional operating system (later redesigned and released for home computers as Windows XP), in 1993; and Windows 95, which replaced rather than riding atop of MS-DOS, as subsequent versions of Windows have done. These releases helped Microsoft dominate both the corporate and the home market in the 1990s.

The 1990s also saw the rise of the Internet, and Microsoft introduced Internet Explorer to compete with other web browsers, assisted by the fact that it was automatically installed along with Windows. Internet Explorer, along with the Microsoft Network (MSN), were aggressively marketed in order to make up for Microsoft's early failure to account for the popularity of the Internet and exploit its rapid spread.

The early 2000s were marked by the company's troubles in court, as the U.S. Justice Department targeted Microsoft for anticompetitive practices. The Supreme Court's ruling in *United States v. Microsoft* called the company "an abusive monopoly." Despite originally being ordered to split into separate units, Microsoft appealed the case and was able to settle in 2001.

Although principally a software company, Microsoft has periodically entered the hardware market, with varying degrees of success. Its Zune MP3 player failed to put a dent in iPod's market share and was widely considered a failure. The Xbox, its video game console, was expected to fail similarly, but in time—after a launch that was probably mishandled—it managed to overtake the Nintendo Gamecube, although the PlayStation 2 outsold both of its competitors put together, by a wide margin. The Xbox 360, the next-generation release, successfully competed with Sony's Playstation 3. While the Nintendo Wii outsells them both, the Wii offers a different gaming experience and does not exactly compete directly with the Xbox and PS3, both of which focus on games for teenagers and adults and multiplayer online experiences; Wii, by contrast, has a much lower price point and focuses on family and party games.

Microsoft has also entered the lucrative tablet market with its planned Surface, designed to compete with Apple's iPad—an aspiration which has been met with no small amount of skepticism.

Founder Bill Gates has gradually scaled down his involvement with Microsoft, although he remains the strongest voice in its direction. He stepped down as CEO in 2000, handing the reins to Steve Ballmer, who had been with the company since 1980, and retired as chief software architect in 2008, succeeded by Lotus Notes developer Ray Ozzie.

2006, he succeeded Microsoft founder Bill Gates as Microsoft's chief software architect (CSA). Unexpectedly, he resigned from the position in 2010. While Ozzie, as both CTO and CSA, had been the driving force behind Microsoft's progress in cloud computing, he was unhappy with how slowly it was progressing. He considered cloud computing the future of computing—the "post-PC age." Azure, the cloud computing operating system for which he oversaw the development, was not pursued enthusiastically at Microsoft and was reassigned to another team at the end of 2009 during a corporate reorganization.

In 2011, Ozzie formed Cocomo, which his website describes as "working on a new class of mobile-centric software and services."

PERSONAL LIFE

Ozzie is married to Dawna Bousquet, and they have two children, Neil and Jill.

Bill Kte'pi

FURTHER READING

Eichenwald, Kurt. "Microsoft's Lost Decade." Aug. 2012. *Vanity Fair*. Web. 14 Sept. 2012. Lengthy article on Microsoft's travails and decreasing relevance under chief executive officer Steve Ballmer, during the era when Ozzie worked for the company.

Jones, William. *Keeping Found Things Found: The Study and Practice of Personal Information Management*. Burlington: Morgan Kaufmann, 2008. Print. Includes coverage of Lotus Notes.

Livingston, Jessica. *Founders at Work: Stories of Startups' Early Days*. New York: Apress, 2008. Print. Devotes a chapter to Ozzie's Iris Associates and Groove Networks.

Rosenberg, Josty, and Arthur Mateos. *The Cloud at Your Service*. Greenwich, CT: Manning, 2010. Print. An introduction to cloud computing, of which Ozzie is an advocate.

DAVID PACKARD

Cofounder and former CEO of Hewlett-Packard

Born: September 7, 1912; Pueblo, Colorado
Died: March 26, 1996; Stanford, California
Primary Field: Business and commerce
Specialty: Management, executives, and investors
Primary Company/Organization: Hewlett-Packard

INTRODUCTION

David Packard worked with his longtime friend and associate William Redington "Bill" Hewlett to create the Hewlett-Packard Company. As outgoing and gregarious as his partner was quiet and self-effacing, Packard was known for his administrative and sales abilities and served as president, chief executive officer (CEO), and chairman. Packard also took a break from Hewlett-Packard to serve as the U.S. Deputy Secretary of Defense, afterward returning to the company he helped create. Well known for his deep commitment to a variety of philanthropic activities, he was awarded the Presidential Medal of Freedom in 1988.

EARLY LIFE

David "Dave" Packard was born on September 7, 1912, in Pueblo, Colorado, to a family that respected and valued education. Packard's father was a lawyer and his mother a schoolteacher, and they encouraged their son in his academic endeavors. Packard excelled in science courses as a high school student, and he was well known for his athletic prowess. Fascinated by radios from an early age, Packard applied to Stanford University to study electrical engineering and was enrolled in 1930. Once at Stanford, Packard became a strong presence on campus, winning varsity letters from both the football and basketball teams and being inducted into the

national honor society, Phi Beta Kappa. He was also a member of the literary society Alpha Delta Phi. Successful in his studies, Packard earned his bachelor's degree from Stanford in 1934.

As prodigious as his accomplishments were in the classroom and on the playing fields, Packard considered his most important accomplishment at Stanford to have been his introduction to two fellow students: Hewlett,

David Packard.

who would become his friend and business partner, and Lucile Salter, who became his wife. Upon graduation from Stanford, Packard returned home, where he briefly enrolled at the University of Colorado and then accepted a job offer from the General Electric Company at a facility in Schenectady, New York. Keeping in touch with Hewlett during this time, he met with him in California in 1937, where they discussed going into business together and decided the company should concentrate on manufacturing medical equipment, high-frequency receivers, and components for televisions. At that point, the two young entrepreneurs determined that they would name their endeavor the Engineering Service Company. In 1938, Packard returned to Stanford to earn a master's degree in electrical engineering.

LIFE'S WORK

Hewlett and Packard formed the Hewlett-Packard Company on January 1, 1939. The order of the two men's names in the company was based on the results of a coin flipped to decide the matter. Had Packard not lost, the company would have been named the Packard-Hewlett Company. Friends since they had been undergraduates, Packard and Hewlett made a good team. While Packard was social and outgoing, Hewlett was quiet and withdrawn. Both men, however, shared a love for blowing things up, as well as hunting, fishing, skiing, and mountain climbing. Both men also had a passion to discover and invent. The company began inauspiciously, in a garage behind Packard's home in Palo Alto. In the beginning, Packard and Hewlett pooled their belongings to provide the new company with a start, Hewlett contributing the $538 he had invested in a savings account and Packard contributing some tools and equipment that he had brought back with him from Schenectady.

The talents each man brought to the company soon became apparent. Hewlett proved adept at making technical adjustments to existing products and innovations that resulted in new products, while Packard proved to be an exemplary administrator. The company's first product, an audio frequency oscillator, stemmed from work Hewlett had done for his master's thesis at Stanford. The oscillator was given the model number 200A so that potential customers would not know that it was their first offering. The 200A had a variety of uses; it represented the first low-cost, practical means of ensuring high-quality audio frequencies. As high-quality audio frequencies were needed by communications companies, the defense industry, geophysicists, and medicine,

the 200A proved to have a waiting market. The duo decided to price the 200A at $54.40, mainly because they liked the sound of the amount. Since the 200A cost more to produce, however, the new company actually lost money on its first sale. Fortunately, its nearest competitor charged more than $400 for its machine, so Packard was able to raise the price to $71.50 each. The initial 200A units were handmade by Packard and Hewlett, who sawed lumber, nailed together cabinets, and spray-painted the panels. The Hewlett-Packard Company famously sold eight 200A machines to the Walt Disney Company, which used them to make the film *Fantasia*. Because this film received a great deal of attention for its technical proficiency, Hewlett-Packard soon made more sales to movie studios and record companies.

By the end of 1940, Hewlett-Packard was doing well: It had moved to a new building, had engaged a secretary, and expanded to ten employees to meet growing sales. In 1941, however, Hewlett was drafted to serve in the armed forces during World War II, while Packard remained at home to run their company. As many of Hewlett-Packard's products were needed for the war effort, the company grew quickly. When Hewlett returned, he found that the company had grown to more than two hundred employees and was generating revenues of almost $1 million per year. Hewlett also discovered that in his absence, no employee, including Packard, had made more than his officer's salary; Packard had felt that Hewlett's service to his country should be recognized as more valuable than his own. Soon after his return, Hewlett was named vice president of the company. In order to recognize the efforts of their employees, Packard and Hewlett soon instituted an incentive program that offered bonuses when the company met incentives. It is a testament to Packard's administrative skills that the company never ran an annual deficit during his tenure.

The 1950s saw the company develop a wide range of electronic devices for industrial and agricultural use. During the 1960s, Hewlett-Packard began developing semiconductors for use in a variety of calculators and other business devices. At this time the company also entered into a partnership with Sony Corporation and Yokogawa Electric Corporation to license production of some of Hewlett-Packard's products in Japan. In 1968, Hewlett-Packard introduced the 9100A, a programmable calculator that has since been referred to as the first personal computer (PC). During the 1970s, the company introduced the first handheld scientific electronic calculator and the first symbolic and graphing calculator.

Affiliation: Hewlett-Packard Company

The Hewlett-Packard Company was famously begun in a garage in Palo Alto, California, by two college chums with a total initial capitalization of $538. Originally known for developing a series of electronic devices used as test equipment, the company later developed a successful line of business equipment and calculators. Today the company concentrates on computers, storage, and imaging products and has annual revenues in excess of $125 billion.

Hewlett-Packard has long been an innovator in both hardware and software and is considered one of the more progressive employers globally. Although its products are sometimes seen as less innovative than those of its rivals, it has developed an outstanding reputation for sturdy, well-built, usable goods.

These products had a reputation as sturdy and usable, and they were popular with corporate users.

Packard and Hewlett feared having their company accrue debt, so research and development initiatives were funded by reinvested profits, not long-term borrowing. This approach permitted Hewlett-Packard to weather economic downturns. Financially, the 1950s were a boom era for the company and saw sales revenue double in most years. During this period, Hewlett-Packard also instituted a program that paid employee full wages and tuition while they were enrolled in graduate programs at Stanford provided that they agreed to return to the company upon graduation. This program allowed the company access to some of the best engineering talent in the United States. By 1957, Hewlett-Packard had grown to more than twelve hundred employees and made an initial public offering (IPO) of its stock. The late 1950s also saw the company open its first international sales office and become increasingly involved in the development of microwave technology. The company funded a consistent research and development program, which provided it with a steady stream of new products.

Until 1980, Hewlett-Packard had little experience with consumer markets, which changed when it introduced its laser-jet printer in 1984. The company was able to do very well in the printer market, and subsequent models of the laser-jet printer contained more features for less money. Under Packard's leadership, Hewlett-Packard was one of the first companies to offer

employees and their families health insurance, and it also was a leader in providing wellness services to its workers. This sense of social responsibility extended to the communities in which Hewlett-Packard was present, since the company made efforts to behave in environmentally and socially responsible ways.

Packard served as Hewlett-Packard's president from 1947 until 1964, at which point he was elected CEO and chairman of the board of directors, posts in which he served until 1968. In 1969, President Richard Nixon appointed Packard deputy secretary of defense. Serving under Secretary of Defense Melvin Laird, Packard continued in this role until the end of 1971. Although he continued to serve in various advisory positions to the Defense Department throughout the 1980s, Packard returned to Hewlett-Packard in 1972 as chairman of the board, where he served until 1993. Packard died on March 26, 1996, and was buried in Alta Mesa Memorial Park in Palo Alto, California.

PERSONAL LIFE

Packard was keenly interested in athletics his entire life, and he was a fan of baseball, football, and basketball, all of which he had played at a competitive level in high school or college. Packard and his wife, Lucile, who predeceased him in 1987, had four children. The couple were committed to a broad array of charitable activities, to which they devoted time and money. For example, the Packard family gave $55 million to assist in the establishment of the Monterey Bay Aquarium, and Packard served as vice chairman of the California Nature Conservancy. A supporter of the arts, Packard also served as a director for the Wolf Trap Foundation, a national organization located in Vienna, Virginia, devoted to music and other performing arts.

Packard and his wife founded the David and Lucile Packard Foundation in 1964, which has provided support to colleges and universities, community groups, hospitals and health centers, national organizations, and youth groups. The couple funded the construction of the Lucile Packard Children's Hospital, located on the Stanford campus, which is one of the United States' most highly regarded children's hospitals. Packard was honored by a variety of organizations and received the National Medal of Technology, the Institute of Electrical and Electronics Engineers (IEEE) Founders Medal, the Presidential Medal of Freedom, and the Lemelson-MIT Prize. Several colleges and universities conferred honorary doctorates on Packard, including Colorado College, Catholic University, and the University of Notre Dame. Upon his death,

Packard left the David and Lucile Packard Foundation an amount in excess of $4 billion.

Stephen T. Schroth and Lloyd L. Scott Jr.

FURTHER READING

House, C. H., and R. L. Price. *The HP Phenomenon: Innovation and Business Transformation*. Stanford: Stanford UP, 2009. Print. Explores how Hewlett-Packard's culture has allowed the company to transform itself numerous times while many of its rivals were unable to adapt to changing times, resulting in their failure.

Malone, M. S. *Bill and Dave: How Hewlett and Packard Built the World's Greatest Company*. New York: Portfolio, 2007. Print. Concentrates on the formation of Hewlett-Packard and how the actions and leadership of its founders have continued to affect the company's culture to the present day.

Packard, D. *The HP Way: How Bill Hewlett and I Built Our Company*. New York: HarperBusiness, 1995. Print. Packard's memoir, in which he explores how two young friends used vision, innovation, and hard work to build Hewlett-Packard into a global corporation.

SEYMOUR PAPERT

Cocreator of the Logo programming language and theorist in artificial intelligence

Born: March 1, 1928; Pretoria, South Africa
Died: -
Primary Field: Computer science
Specialty: Computer programming
Primary Company/Organization: Massachusetts Institute of Technology

INTRODUCTION

Mathematician Seymour Papert developed the Logo programming language, a dialect of Lisp, which is used mainly to teach programming concepts. He is also a prominent theorist in the field of artificial intelligence, serving as a faculty member in of the Artificial Intelligence Laboratory at the Massachusetts Institute of Technology (MIT) from 1967 to 1981. His work has long been concerned with theories of learning and with child development, and he was instrumental in the One Laptop Per Child project, which seeks to provide low-cost educational computers to children in developing nations.

EARLY LIFE

Seymour Papert was born in Pretoria, South Africa, on February 29, 1928 (a leap year). He attended university in Johannesburg, earning a B.A. and Ph.D. in mathematics in 1949 and 1952, respectively, before leaving the country to work and study abroad. While in London studying at Cambridge University (from which he was awarded another Ph.D. in mathematics in 1959), he was a prominent member of the socialist group that published the *Socialist Review*, which began publication in 1950.

LIFE'S WORK

From 1959 to 1963, Papert worked as a researcher at a wide variety of institutions: the National Physical Laboratory (London), St. John's College (Cambridge), the University of Geneva, and the Henri Poincaré Institute (Paris). In 1963, he relocated to Cambridge, Massachusetts, to take a job as a research associate at MIT. He became part of the Artificial Intelligence Laboratory, which formed at MIT in 1970.

Papert worked closely with Marvin Minsky, who had joined MIT's faculty in 1958 and became the first director of the Artificial Intelligence Laboratory when it formed in 1970 as a separate entity spun off from the computer science lab's Project on Mathematics and Computation (Project MAC). Minsky worked with Papert and Wally Feurzeig on the creation of the Logo programming language. Based on Lisp, Logo was intended to allow users to write programs that would perform simple tasks and to produce helpful error messages when a program was written or executed incorrectly. Although associated now with "virtual" turtles (cursors that move on the screen according to the Logo program's instructions and were originally meant for debugging), actual physical "turtles," robots designed for use with Logo, were built in 1969, originally tethered to the floor by a cord, but later controlled wirelessly. The turtle has a "pen" that can draw a line using commands such as PENUP, PENDOWN, and PENERASE.

Papert's work on Logo was influenced by the theories of Jean Piaget on the psychology of child development. Papert had worked with Piaget at Geneva, and

Seymour Papert.

Piaget called him the best of his protégés. Logo is an educational programming language that teaches basic programming concepts while allowing students to create programs with demonstrable, tangible results and understandable errors. Beginning in 1970 at Bridge School in Lexington, Massachusetts, Logo software and turtle robots were provided to classrooms. Since then, classrooms have more commonly used only the virtual turtles of the display screen, and Logo has been a popular part of public school curricula. In many states, a unit on the Logo language was part of the state-mandated computer literacy requirement, chosen in favor of similar novitiate languages such as BASIC and the later VisualBasic. Minsky's contribution was to collaborate on the construction of the turtle robot itself. The language was the work of Papert and Feurzeig.

Papert has continued to promote Logo (and the Logo Foundation research group), not only as a tool for introducing programming concepts to children but also as a means of strengthening their cognitive capacities and learning skills. Papert is also a proponent of constructing programming languages that can be used simultaneously to teach novices and offer more complicated functionality in order to be a practical language choice for real programming—rather than expect novice programmers to learn new languages as they progress.

Papert and other members of the Logo development team at MIT formed Logo Computer Systems, Inc., with Papert serving as chairman of the board of directors until 2002. There is no single Logo language definition, and there are many differences among the 197 different Logo variants and implementations. Furthermore, some programs inaccurately refer to themselves as Logo variants because they deal with turtle graphics. Recent variants of Logo support multiple turtles, Lego brick interfaces (though Logo is not the language used in the commercial Lego Mindstorms product), and the ability to create animated GIF image files. The StarLogo implementation, developed at MIT, supports thousands of turtles for the purpose of studying emergent phenomena.

Papert and Minsky also developed the theory of natural intelligence, which Minsky dubbed as "the society of mind" in a book of the same name. The model developed out of Minsky's work using a computer with a video camera and a robotic arm to manipulate Legos, and it describes human intelligence as the congregation of mindless parts called agents. The interactions among these agents creates the mind. The theory is purely conceptual, talking about the *mind* rather than the *brain*: Minsky is famous for his formulation that "the mind is what the brain does."

In 1969, Minsky and Papert collaborated on *Perceptrons: An Introduction to Computational Geometry*, which was significantly expanded for a 1987 release. The perceptron of the title is an artificial neural network developed in the 1950s. The book made fairly pessimistic predictions about the success of artificial intelligence, and as the field failed to achieve many of the accomplishments it set out for itself, the book was subsequently blamed for changing the direction of research. However, two of the major setbacks in artificial intelligence research—the failure of machine translation and the field's abandonment of connectionism—occurred in the 1960s, well before the book was widely distributed. The twenty-first century has seen a significant increase in interest in artificial intelligence, albeit in very different directions from what was pursued in the 1960s and 1970s in the wake of developments since then in neuroscience and theories of cognition.

Papert's work often talks about a hypothetical device called the Knowledge Machine. The Knowledge Machine is a device or environment that allows children to engage actively with the learning experience and

Affiliation: MIT Computer Science and Artificial Intelligence Laboratory

The Massachusetts Institute of Technology's Computer Science and Artificial Intelligence Laboratory (CSAIL) was formed in 2003 by a merger of two older laboratories, the Artificial Intelligence Laboratory and the Laboratory for Computer Science. Although the MIT Media Lab is better known, CSAIL is today the school's largest laboratory by membership. CSAIL hosts W3C, the World Wide Web Consortium, founded in 1994 by MIT professor Tim Berners-Lee. W3C is the international standards organization for the World Wide Web.

Computer research has a long history at MIT, where Claude Shannon developed Boolean algebra in the 1930s and the Defense Department's Advanced Research Projects Agency (DARPA) grant money funding numerous projects during the Cold War period. The Project on Mathematics and Computation (Project MAC) was formed in 1963 with one such DARPA grant and conducted important research in artificial intelligence (AI) and the theory of computation. Major AI researchers attached to the project included Marvin Minsky and John McCarthy, inventor of the Lisp programming language. The AI group within Project MAC worked out of a computer room for which they developed the information technology services time-sharing operating system. When it sought more space, it became easier to form a new entity; a new laboratory was, because of university practices, more likely to be granted space than an existing entity was to be given extra space. The AI specialists split off from Project MAC to form the Artificial Intelligence Laboratory in 1970. Minsky, the first director, was succeeded by Patrick Winston in 1972 and Rodney Brooks in 1997.

Meanwhile, the remains of Project MAC formed the Laboratory for Computer Science, focusing on programming languages, distributed systems, the theory of computation, and operating systems. (Project MAC technically continued in the form of MIT professors of electrical engineering and computer science Hal Abelson and Gerald Jay Sussman, the only two who joined neither new group and whose research group was generally referred to as Switzerland.) In 2003, the Laboratory for Computer Science rejoined the Artificial Intelligence Laboratory to create the current entity.

explore any situation. The idea is often invoked when discussing the educational potential of virtual reality and immersive simulations.

Also at MIT, Papert worked with the MIT Architecture Machine Group (AMG), the precursor to the Media Lab, which was created in 1985. Within the AMG, Papert created and led the Epistemology and Learning Research Group, developing the theory of constructionism, a theory of learning based on Piaget's work and his own theory of constructivism. In Papert's words, constructionism says that learning is most effective "when part of an activity the learner experiences is constructing a meaningful product." This is the underlying goal of Logo, after all: to teach programming not through simple drills but by designing a language simple enough that children can be expected to write programs that have results they can witness and understand.

In his later life, Papert became involved with the One Laptop Per Child project, which spun out of work at the MIT Media Lab and was spearheaded by Nicholas P. Negroponte. The project seeks to develop low-cost (under $100), durable, low-power educational laptops (and perhaps tablets) for use by children in developing countries. The use of computers in education is among Papert's passions, one he has pursued his entire professional life.

PERSONAL LIFE

Papert has been married four times. As of 2012, he was married to Suzanne Massie Papert, the American author whose histories of Russia led to her informal participation in U.S.-Soviet diplomacy during the presidency of Ronald Reagan. Papert's third wife, Sherry Turkle, is an MIT professor who has written extensively on the social studies of science and human-computer interactions.

While attending a conference in Hanoi, Vietnam, in 2006, the then seventy-eight-year-old Papert was hit by a motorcycle and hospitalized. Brain surgery removed a dangerous blood clot that had formed, and after many strings were pulled, Papert was transferred by a specialized Swiss Air Ambulance (complete with an on-board intensive care unit) from Vietnam to Boston, Massachusetts, where he was processed through customs immediately thanks to the intervention of Massachusetts senator John Kerry. After a month at Massachusetts General Hospital, Papert was transferred to a hospital in his home state of Maine, where he continued to receive treatment. His initial injuries led to further complications: septicemia and the need for a heart valve operation. Two years later, he had recovered most of his faculties, but he has continued to work with a rehabilitation team on a lingering speech difficulty. Minsky has called Papert the greatest living mathematics educator.

Bill Kte'pi

FURTHER READING

Kaiser, David. *Becoming MIT: Moments of Decision.* Cambridge: MIT, 2010. Print. A history of MIT emphasizing the developing of its pedagogical philosophies.

Moss, Frank. *The Sorcerers and Their Apprentices: How the Digital Magicians of the MIT Media Lab Are Creating the Innovative Technologies that Will Transform Their Lives.* New York: Crown, 2011. Print. An in-depth look at the work of the MIT Media Lab.

Papert, Seymour. *The Children's Machine: Rethinking School in the Age of the Computer.* New York: Basic, 1993. Print. Out of date in some respects, but surprisingly current in others.

BLAISE PASCAL

Mathematician, physicist, and inventor of the mechanical calculator

Born: June 19, 1623; Clermont-Ferrand, France
Died: August 19, 1662; Paris, France
Primary Field: Applied science
Specialty: Mathematics and logic
Primary Company/Organization: Jansenites

INTRODUCTION

Blaise Pascal was a French philosopher, inventor, writer, mathematician, and physicist. He created the first mechanical calculating machine and was also an important mathematician. Although he explored projective geometry, his work on probability theory still resonates with economists and computer scientists today. Pascal's name was given to a programming language as a means of honoring his many accomplishments related to computer science.

EARLY LIFE

Blaise Pascal was born on June 19, 1623, in Clermont-Ferrand, a city located in central France. Pascal's father, Étienne, was a local judge who also dabbled in mathematics and science. Étienne was a member of the Noblesse de Robe, which indicates that he was of high birth and most likely had inherited his position. Pascal's mother, Antoinette Begon, died when he was three years old, leaving him and his two sisters, Jacqueline and Gilberte, in the care of their father. Pascal, who was a child prodigy, was educated primarily by Étienne and demonstrated an aptitude for mathematics and scientific work.

In 1631, Étienne, hoping to ensure a stable stream of income for his family, sold his judgeship, as was permitted under the French system, and purchased a government bond. After Cardinal Richelieu stopped

payments on government bonds in order to finance the Thirty Years' War in 1638, however, Étienne saw his net worth drop by 90 percent. After expressing opposition to Richelieu's policies, Étienne was forced to flee Paris as part of a general uprising of 1638. The following year, however, Étienne regained the favor of the cardinal and was appointed as the king's commissioner of taxes for the city of Rouen. Pascal and his sisters moved with their father to Rouen in 1639 so that Étienne could assume his position.

LIFE'S WORK

As part of his new position in Rouen, Étienne nightly had to perform calculations related to tax revenues generated during the day. To alleviate his father's work calculating taxes owed and collected, Pascal invented a mechanical calculator that was capable of performing addition and subtraction. Although accurate, Pascal's calculator (the Pascaline) proved too expensive for any but the wealthy, who used it as a toy. Despite this, the Pascaline was a forerunner to modern calculators and was fully functional. Pascal continued to make refinements to his design of the Pascaline, and he sold about twenty machines during his life.

Soon thereafter, Pascal produced a short treatise related to projective geometry. Pascal was interested in conic sections, the curves formed by the intersection of a cone with a plane. Intrigued by the work of Gérard Desargues, the then sixteen-year-old Pascal produced a proof for what was called the Mystic Hexagram. Pascal's monograph, *Essai pour les coniques* (essay on conics), was sent to Marin Mersenne in Paris. Mersenne, sometimes referred to as the father of acoustics

Blaise Pascal.

and a Catholic priest, was the foremost mathematician in France and responded warmly to Pascal's treatise. This work, known today as Pascal's theorem, states that when a hexagon is inscribed in a conic section, the three intersection points of opposite sides lie on a line known as the "Pascal line." Although the treatise was instantly recognized as significant, not all observers believed that it was the product of a sixteen-year-old child. René Descartes, often considered the founder of analytical geometry, was convinced that the monograph must have been composed by Étienne, although Mersenne assured him it was the boy's work.

Pascal continued to make important contributions to mathematics over the next few years. In 1653, Pascal wrote the monograph *Traité du triangle arithmétique* (treatise on the arithmetical triangle), although it was not published until 1665, three years after his death. Pascal's triangle, as it is commonly known, shows that binomial coefficients can be arranged in a manner that produces certain results. Pascal's triangle has proven significant in probability theory, a topic Pascal explored further in a series of letters exchanged with Pierre de Fermat, an amateur mathematician whose work influenced the development of infinitesimal calculus. Pascal wrote Fermat after a friend, Antoine Gombaud, had asked a question regarding a hypothetical card game between two players wherein one player wanted to end the game early. Gombaud wanted to know whether, if two players had agreed to play seven games but needed to stop after four and one player had won three games to his counterpart's one, there was a way to predict the outcome of the remaining three games. The correspondence between Pascal and Fermat is considered the foundation of the modern theory of probability, which later advanced early work on computers that were used for cryptanalysis.

Pascal stopped most of his work in mathematics after a religious conversion that occurred in 1646, but he also made contributions to the physical sciences. Fascinated by hydraulics, he invented the hydraulic press and the syringe, both predicated on the understanding that hydrostatic pressure depends on elevation difference, not the difference in weight. In 1647, Pascal published some findings related to his experiments with vacuums, work that contradicted some declarations by Aristotle that vacuums could not exist. Pascal was able to demonstrate that vacuums existed above the liquid in a barometer tube and that various liquids could be supported by air pressure to varying degrees.

Pascal also found time for more lighthearted inventions. During the seventeenth century it was popular for inventors to attempt to create a perpetual motion machine, a hypothetical device that would run forever once set in motion. When Pascal attempted to build such a machine, his device became a rudimentary form of a roulette wheel.

PERSONAL LIFE

Pascal and his family held fairly conventional religious beliefs through 1646. Nominally Roman Catholic, they adhered to Church dogma and rules, although they often focused on outward compliance with these rather than maintaining any deep sense of religious commitment. In 1646, however, Étienne suffered a broken hip and demanded that his son return to his side to assist him during his convalescence. Once Blaise had returned to his father's house, he was exposed to advocates of a more profound expression of religious belief through members of a religious order at Port-Royal-des-Champs, an abbey of Cistercian nuns. From these sources, Pascal and his sister Jacqueline were exposed to, and became advocates of, the moral and theological belief system known as Jansenism.

Jansenism was a form of Augustinianism that became popular within the Roman Catholic Church during the seventeenth century. Jansenism involved a repudiation of free will, an acceptance of predestination, and a belief that divine grace, rather than good works, was the key to eternal salvation. Port-Royal and its inhabitants formed one of the centers from which Jansenism was disseminated, and Pascal became a firm adherent of the belief system. As a result of this conversion, Pascal began to turn away from the world and instead focus his attention on God and prayer. He was a strong advocate for Jansenism and was able to win his family over to this form of spiritual life in short order. Pascal was his family's informal spiritual adviser, although he still struggled with the conflicting goals of worldly success and the ascetic life. After his conversion and until his father's death in 1651, Pascal continued with his scientific work, publishing at a prodigious rate.

At about the time of Étienne's death, Pascal suffered a breakdown from overwork, exacerbated by Jacqueline's decision to go to Port-Royal as a postulate. Pascal opposed her decision but not on religious grounds; he desired her assistance during his period of ill health. In addition, Jacqueline's presence by his side made a significant monetary difference to Pascal: Gilberte had taken one-third of Étienne's estate with her when she married in the form of a dowry, and payment of an equal sum to Port-Royal would leave Pascal in near poverty. Despite his concerns, Pascal eventually acceded to Jacqueline's wishes and deposited the whole of Jacqueline's inheritance with the sisters of Port-Royal in 1653.

In November 1654, Pascal experienced what is sometimes referred to as his second conversion. During the night, he experienced a vision that he recorded on a sheet of paper. Pascal believed that his vision indicated that he should abandon worldly concerns in favor of the spiritual. To that end, Pascal went on a two-week retreat to Port-Royal in early 1655. After this retreat, he would devote most of his energies over the next four years to religious writings. During this period he composed his *Lettres provinciales* (the provincial letters, of which there were eighteen), in which he denounced moral laxity and a variety of sins. This work incurred the wrath of the authorities and was ordered burned by King Louis XIV. Pascal's *Lettres provinciales* were influential in religious circles and have enjoyed a considerable reputation as literary exemplars of the use of satire, variety, humor, brevity, and mockery. The *Lettres provinciales* influenced subsequent generations of French writers, including Jean-Jacques Rousseau and Voltaire.

Louis XIV formally suppressed Jansenism and in 1661 shut down the abbey at Port-Royal that supported it. Later that year, Pascal's sister Jacqueline died, whcih caused him great sorrow. Although Pascal through his writings urged the adherents of Jansenism not to succumb to the monarch's pressure, his health continued to decline. By 1662 Pascal was in great pain, and he died in August of that year. His remains were buried in the graveyard of St.-Étienne-du-Mond. After his death, Pascal's uncompleted *Pensées* (thoughts) were published. The *Pensées* are considered to be Pascal's greatest theological work, examining the conflict between skepticism and stoicism in an attempt to bring unbelievers to the point that they will embrace God. Highly valued for its elegant and polished prose, *Pensées* remains a landmark in French literature.

Pascal has been greatly honored since his death. His name was used for a computer programming language, for the standard Système Internationale (SI) unit of pressure, and a theorem of hydrostatics. In France, academic chairs in Pascal's name have been awarded to

Affiliation: Probability Theory

The development of probability theory was perhaps Blaise Pascal's most significant contribution to mathematics. While Pascal and Pierre de Fermat originally applied probability theory to gambling, it has grown in importance over the following four centuries to become an extremely important component of economics, actuarial science, and computer programming.

Probability theory examines random phenomena and uses mathematics to attempt to determine likely outcomes. As such, probability theory uses random variables, random processes, and events to make predictions regarding future events. Although Pascal and Fermat only began to address some of the issues related to probability theory, their contributions were significant. For example, their insistence that the likelihood of future events was governed more by possible outcomes than by history was groundbreaking. Although Christiaan Huygens would later write the first book on probability theory, he based much of his work on the theories of Pascal and Fermat. Although Pascal stopped writing about mathematics under his own name, it is likely that he continued his work, as is suggested by a book on logic published by the Port-Royal abbey in 1662.

influential foreign scientists to conduct research in Paris, and the Université Blaise Pascal is named in his honor. His works are seen as models of French prose and continue to be read today.

Stephen T. Schroth and Jason A. Helfer

FURTHER READING

Adamson, Donald. *Blaise Pascal: Mathematician, Physicist, and Thinker about God*. New York: St. Martin's, 1995. Print. A chronological survey of Pascal's work in mathematics, physics, religion, and philosophy.

Coleman, Francis X. J. *Neither Angel nor Beast: The Life and Work of Blaise Pascal*. New York: Routledge, 1986. Print. A somewhat poorly organized but still-insightful overview of Pascal's life and work. Good at placing Pascal in the context of seventeenth century thought.

Connor, J. A. *Pascal's Wager: The Man Who Played Dice with God*. New York: HarperOne, 2006. Print. Biography of Pascal that looks at his brilliant mathematical background and how his religious beliefs affected some of his explorations later in life.

Gowers, Timothy, June Barrow-Green, and Imre Leader, eds. *The Princeton Companion to Mathematics*. Princeton: Princeton UP, 2008. Print. This hefty reference work, winner of the 2011 Mathematical Association of America's Euler Book Prize, includes articles on Pascal, Fermat, and probability distributions.

Groothius, Douglas. *On Pascal*. Belmont: Thomson/Wadsworth, 2003. Print. Concise introduction to Pascal's most important ideas, placing these concepts in historical context.

Hammond, Nicholas, ed. *The Cambridge Companion to Pascal*. New York: Cambridge UP, 2003. Print. A variety of scholars explore Pascal's many achievements and provide context for his work by presenting some of the intellectual background behind it.

Krailsheimer, Alban. *Pascal*. New York: Hill & Wang, 1980. Print. An examination of the life of Pascal with special emphasis on his writings and the contemporary reception of his work.

Moriarty, Michael. *Early Modern French Thought: The Age of Suspicion*. New York: Oxford UP, 2003. Print. Examines the philosophy of Pascal, René Descartes, and Nicolas Malebranche.

Nelson, Robert J. *Pascal: Adversary and Advocate*. Cambridge: Harvard UP, 1981. Print. One of the more comprehensive and ambitious studies of Pascal. Takes a psychological approach to Pascal's biography and work, with extensive critical study of individual works.

Paciaroni, M. "Visual Experiences of Blaise Pascal." *Neurological Disorders in Famous Artists*. Vol. 3. Ed. Julien Bogousslavsky et al. London: Karger, 2010. N. pag. Print. A neuroscientist provides a fascinating take on Pascal from evidence that he suffered from migraines and accompanying visual hallucinations that may well have inspired him, influencing his philosophy and spirituality.

Pascal, Blaise. *Pensées*. London: Penguin Classics, 1995. Print. Pascal's unfinished apologia for the Christian faith, upon which much of his literary reputation rests.

ROSALIND PICARD

Founder of MIT's Affective Computing Research Group and cofounder of Affectiva

Born: May 17, 1962; Boston, Massachusetts
Died: -
Primary Field: Computer science
Specialty: Applications
Primary Company/Organization: Massachusetts Institute of Technology

INTRODUCTION

Rosalind Picard, founder and director of the Affective Computing Group at the Massachusetts Institute of Technology (MIT) Media Lab, wrote Affective Computing *(1997), the seminal textbook in the field she helped establish. Affective computing is computing that relates to or influences emotion and other affective phenomena. Picard, professor of media arts and sciences at MIT, is also codirector of the Things That Think Consortium, an association, begun in 1995, of more than fifty companies and research groups with an interest in embedding computation into the environment and everyday objects. She also cofounded Affectiva, Inc., in 2009 to provide emotion-measurement technologies to companies, corporations, agencies, and universities. An inventor in addition to her other roles, Picard holds patents on several sensors, algorithms, and systems related to affective computing.*

EARLY LIFE

Rosalind Wright Picard was born on May 17, 1962, in Boston, Massachusetts. She was adopted as an infant and grew up in Boston; Monterey, California; Key West, Florida; Keflavik, Iceland; and Atlanta, Georgia. She has one brother, Rob Wright. Her father, an engineer, fostered her interest in mathematics and gave her confidence that a girl was capable of mastering not only mathematics but also practical skills often identified with males, such as how to tune up a car. Her mother, a teacher, helped her earn Girl Scout badges and trained her in the domestic arts appropriate for a southern belle. Picard credits both her parents with giving her a sense of security and self-worth and with instilling in her a love of learning and a belief in her ability to tackle tough projects.

Picard received a bachelor's degree in electrical engineering with highest honors from the Georgia Institute of Technology in 1984. She earned a master of science degree in electrical engineering and computing in 1986 and a doctor of science degree in electrical

Rosalind Picard.

engineering and computing in 1991, both from MIT. From 1984 to 1987, she worked at AT&T Bell Laboratories, where she designed very-large-scale integration (VLSI) chips for digital signal processing and developed new methods of image compression and analysis.

LIFE'S WORK

Picard joined the faculty of MIT in July 1991 as assistant professor of media technology. Her early work in MIT's Media Lab involved content-based retrieval of images and video. She codeveloped the Photobook system, a set of interactive tools for browsing and searching images and image sequences that allows flexible, intuitive searches of large databases. Her work in this area was described as pioneering, and she was amassing an impressive string of publications and proving her worth as a fund-raiser, bringing in more than a million dollars in research funds. In the mid-1990s, her research focused on signal-processing technology and how it could be used to improve computer cognition. Later, she became interested in the connections between reason and emotion. The more she discovered, the more convinced she became that the intelligent machines engineers dreamed of creating were possible only if designers understood the importance of emotions. In 1997, she wrote *Affective Computing*, laying the groundwork for a new field of research that uses technology to understand and directly influence emotion and other affective phenomena.

The new field was not without its detractors. Experts in artificial intelligence generally preferred systems that relied solely on rules to those that involved emotions, which most considered nonessential to intelligence. Picard's argument was that computers should be designed to consider, express, and influence users' emotions. Artificial intelligence, she believed, had placed a disproportionate emphasis on verbal and mathematical intelligences while for the most part ignoring the significant role of social-emotional intelligence. In 1995, Picard renamed her research group in MIT's Media Lab the Affective Computing Group.

Other scientists found her ideas provocative, and by 1999 MIT's Media Lab had become the center of affective computing. Picard led the first development of technology that interpreted and responded empathetically to affect in such things as posture, face, gesture, physiology, and task behavior. The products that she and her colleagues developed held the promise of applications in fields as far ranging as autism studies and customer service. Among these is a glovelike device that can measure emotions via skin conductance. Picard and one of her graduate students also used software linked to an ordinary webcam to measure heart rate, blood pressure, and skin temperature without surface contact with the body. Dr. Rana el Kaliouby, a visiting scientist with the Affective Computing Group, and Picard have worked together to create glasses that enable the wearer to analyze the facial expressions of a conversation partner. Employing a camera the size of a grain of rice and software developed by Picard, the glasses record twenty-four "feature points" and analyze them. The device has been used effectively with autistic people and others who often find reading emotional cues from others extremely difficult. Picard is quick to point out that these devices serve only to amplify cues that are voluntarily given and do not extract information from unwilling participants.

Picard also serves as cofounder and director of the Autism and Communication Technology Initiative at the MIT Media Lab. Researchers in this group are engaged in the development of innovative technologies that contribute to autism research and therapy. They are particularly interested in creating technologies that improve communication and promote independent living in autistic people. Often technologies developed to help those on the autism spectrum prove to have applications for other groups as well. Wireless wristbands, for example, which were developed to show levels of emotional stress in the autistic, have also been used successfully to signal early signs of seizures in epileptics and to monitor sleep patterns of those with sleep disorders, a problem common among autistic children but not limited to them.

In April 2009, Picard and el Kaliouby founded Affectiva, Inc. The company was a natural extension of the collaborations with sponsors in the research conducted in the MIT laboratory. Picard has said that she and her cofounder were approached by people interested in using their technology in applications in clinical research for a variety of problems other than autism, including obesity, substance abuse, stress and anxiety disorders, and epilepsy. Research also made clear that the technologies held applications for distance learning, market research, professional training, and other fields. Once a product proved its effectiveness and adaptability, commercial markets were viable. Affectiva, based in Waltham, Massachusetts, began by marketing the Q Sensor, a device worn on the wrist to measure emotional arousal using skin conductance, temperature, and activity, and Affdex, glasses that use a webcam to read facial expressions. Q Sensors have

Affiliation: Affective Computing Group

The Affective Computing Group at the Massachusetts Institute of Technology (MIT) was founded in 1995 by Rosalind Picard, who continues as director of the group. The cross-disciplinary group combines engineering and computer science with psychology, cognitive science, neuroscience, sociology, education, ethics, and other fields. Basing their work the idea that emotion influences cognition, perception, learning, communication, and rationality, researchers in the Affective Computing Group develop new technologies and theories that advance understanding of affect and its role in human experience. Computers can be used to measure affect by obtaining physiological and psychological signals through the use of sensors, cameras, microphones, and other devices. Research by the group has led to such inventions as an emotional-social intelligence prosthesis that helps people on the autism spectrum to read social cues more effectively and a wristband that monitors epilepsy patients as accurately as, and less intrusively than, electroencephalograms.

In 2009, Picard and Rana el Kaliouby, a colleague from the Affective Computing Group, founded Affectiva, a spin-off company that markets technology developed through their research at MIT. Many of the products originated from their work with the autistic. Products already being sold include the Q Sensor, a wearable, wireless biosensor that measures emotional arousal via skin conductance; and Affdex, facial expression recognition technology that provides feedback on consumer responses to advertisements and media products. Customers include Disney Media, Millward Brown, and 150 universities and nonprofit organizations.

been successfully used to help caregivers and educators working with autistic children, with veterans suffering from post-traumatic stress disorder, and with drug addicts. They are expected to have commercial applications in a wide range of areas, including therapy, education, and market research. Affdex promises to give marketers useful, accurate insights into consumer responses to advertising and media and to deliver the insights more quickly than other means. The products are being used by Fortune 500 companies, advertising agencies, and academic researchers at Stanford, Harvard, and Notre Dame. Picard serves the company as chair and chief scientist.

Picard was granted tenure at MIT in 1998. She was named a full professor in 2005. She is the author of nearly two hundred scientific articles and chapters in books. She holds multiple patents for sensors, algorithms, and systems for sensing, recognizing, and responding to human affective information. She is recognized as an international leader in innovative technology in her field and is a popular keynote speaker for professional conferences and public forums.

Personal Life

Picard married Len Picard in 1988. They are the parents of three sons, Michael, Chris, and Luc. The family lives in Newton, Massachusetts. Formerly a self-described "staunch atheist," Picard converted to Christianity and has been vocal about her faith, her dislike of religiosity, and her belief that it is possible to be both a hard-core scientist and a committed Christian.

Picard was named a Fellow of the Institute of Electrical and Electronics Engineers for contributions to image and video analysis and affective computing in 2005. She has served on the Advisory Committee for the National Science Foundation's (NSF's) division of Computers in Science and Engineering (CISE), the Advisory Board for the Georgia Tech College of Computing, and the editorial board of *User Modeling and User-Adapted Interaction: The Journal of Personalization Research*. She has frequently been engaged as a consultant by such companies as Apple, AT&T, Hewlett-Packard, iRobot, and Motorola. The Social-Cue Reader developed by Picard and el Kaliouby was among the *New York Times Magazine*'s Best Ideas of 2006, and a mirror that monitors vital signs was on *Popular Science*'s Top Ten Inventions of 2011.

Wylene Rholetter

Further Reading

Adee, Sally. "Your Seventh Sense." *New Scientist* 2 July 2011: 32–36. Print. The article considers glasses, designed by Picard and el Kaliouby of the University of Cambridge, used with people on the autism spectrum. Mention is made of Picard and el Kaliouby's company, Affectiva.

Daviss, Bennett. "Tell Laura I Love Her." *New Scientist* 3 Dec. 2005: 42–46. Print. The article focuses on the development of Laura, emotionally intelligent software developed by Timothy Bickmore, a graduate student in Picard's laboratory at MIT in 2003. Picard's pioneering role in affective computing is recognized.

Durham, Tony. "A HAL of a Way to Take the Chip off Marvin's Cold Shoulder." *Times Higher Education Supplement* 1323 (1998): III. Print. The article looks at the early work of Picard and her students in teaching computers to recognize smiles and frowns and considers the argument for affective computing.

Ming-Zher, Poh, Nicholas C. Swenson, and Rosalind W. Picard. "A Wearable Sensor for Unobtrusive, Long-Term Assessment of Electrodermal Activity." *IEEE Transactions on Biomedical Engineering* 57.5 (2010): 1243–52. Print. This technical article describes the development of the wrist-worn integrated sensor by Picard and her associates and reports their findings on the first time long-term, continuous assessment of electrodermal activity (EDA) outside a laboratory setting. The authors also consider opportunities for further, related research.

Picard, Rosalind W. *Affective Computing*. Cambridge: MIT, 1997. Print. The book consists of two parts. Part I is an overview of the general conception of emotion and a review of the research on emotion. Part II considers the ways computers could represent emotions and recognize them. It also surveys the efforts of others to integrate emotion into computer systems and examines methods of implementing affect recognition and expression into the new technology of wearable computers.

Hasso Plattner

Cofounder of SAP AG

Born: January 21, 1944; Berlin, Germany
Died: -
Primary Field: Computer science
Specialty: Computer software
Primary Company/Organization: SAP AG

Introduction

Known for his many hobbies and pragmatic nature, Hasso Plattner is a German entrpreneur with a global perspective. He cofounded the world's largest software development company, SAP AG, and has more than forty years' experience in the technology industry, making him a founding member of the digital revolution. Plattner's analytical approach to business and consensus management theory are two of the main contributors to SAP's success. By providing corporate customers with real-time solutions to their business-reporting needs, Plattner and SAP have changed the way people do business.

EARLY LIFE

Hasso Plattner was born in Berlin, Germany, on January 21, 1944. World War II was drawing to a close, and Plattner's father, Horst Plattner, an eye surgeon, had managed to keep the family out of the war. Plattner's mother's name was Inge. Plattner graduated with a master's degree in communications engineering from the University of Karlsruhe. After leaving school, he began working at IBM in Mannheim, Germany, where he and four of his colleagues were assigned a task that was taken away from them; they were told their job was to sell computer products, not develop software. Plattner and his coworkers saw the gap in the emerging technology market and decided IBM was wrong. They resigned from IBM to establish their own company.

LIFE'S WORK

Plattner, along with former IBM colleagues Hans Werner Hector, Dietmar Hopp, Klaus Tschira, and Claus Wellenreuther, decided to form a company that would provide real-time data-processing software for corporate clients. The year was 1972. They name the company SAP, which originally stood for "systems analysis and program development" but later came to mean "systems, applications, and products in data processing."

SAP started as a weekend and evening project in Mannheim, where Plattner and the four cofounders used borrowed computers and equipment to write their code and programs. Once they had a couple of clients (they were unable to get their start-up funded with venture capital), they began to build momentum, and the new company moved down the road to Walldorf, Germany.

During the 1970s, revenue and the number of employees continued to climb. By 1980, SAP was developing software in both OS and DOS formats and attending trade shows to promote the brand. In 1981, SAP had two hundred corporate customers. The software specialized in digitally tracking the day-to-day operations of a business and was proving popular. More and more German companies began to invest in SAP software.

Hasso Plattner.

As the 1980s flew by, SAP hired more people to meet the ever-growing demand of their increasing customer base. The decade saw a string of construction projects and foreign subsidiaries for SAP. The company went public in October 1988. By this time, SAP had more than a thousand corporate customers, the majority of which were German companies. Slowly utility companies and government entities began to recognize the need for real-time business-tracking software as the world turned digital. Still working in a competition vacuum, Plattner and his colleagues took advantage of their market share and kept growing the business as fast as they could. Platter recognized that the technology world was fast-paced and constantly changing, even in those early years.

After the company was up and running, Plattner's main role at SAP was to develop software. He realized how important it was to stay one step ahead of the competition and the evolving technology market. SAP AG uses a consensus-based management system to develop ideas and keep the company on track. This management style, coupled with Plattner's love of debating, may account for the relatively long time it took to make decisions in the company's early years; however, this approach also ensured that the five cofounders knew they were all on the same page when their decisions were reached.

Plattner realized that the American market was a good place to expand SAP's global presence, and he began to seek out American companies to bolster SAP and improve revenue. For Plattner and his fellow founders, the 1990s are marked by their effort to increase the quality and usefulness of their real-time analytic software R/2 and the newer R/3. In 1993, SAP worked with Microsoft to make the new R/3 software compatible with Windows NT. In 1996, soft drinks maker Coca-Cola joined its customer ranks, and as a result SAP was named Company of the Year by the European Business Association. In four years, between 1997 and 2001, SAP's sales went from $660 million to $3.5 billion. In 1998, SAP employed nineteen thousand people.

In 1999, when the Internet was experiencing some dramatic transformations, it became clear to the folks at SAP that the company was losing its place at the top of the accessible software market. Plattner devised a new brand image for the company, known as MySap.com. The new website would provide the same software

SAP had always provided and act as a vehicle for larger corporations to funnel their online activity. Plattner remarked in a *Business Week* interview that the new website was "like AOL for corporations." Unfortunately, the remarketing did not work, and Plattner returned to the drawing board to redesign his company to make it successful in a fast-paced, Internet-focused computing world. SAP began to outsource some tasks. By partnering with established marketing and technology firms, Plattner was able to rebound from the failed MySap.com and move the company forward, increasing revenue almost 30 percent after the first year of change. At the dawn of the new millennium, SAP was the number-one corporate software developer on the planet.

Between 2000 and 2009, things were going well for SAP. Plattner's project, the R/3 management system, had more than 2 million users in 2004. The software provides business owners and operators the means by which to track sales and orders, inventory and accounting in a single software package. In 2004, SAP's software integration product, called NetWeaver, was a hit.

During the 2000s, SAP received numerous accolades and awards, proving to be a good place to work and a good provider for the business technology world.

All was well with SAP until 2009. Established customers became unhappy with the direction the company was taking and the services they were receiving. A price hike proved offputting to the point that SAP had to lay off several employees to rise above the revenue issues. By this time, Plattner had stepped down from the board but remained active at the company. He, like many others, realized that a major change was once again necessary.

On February 7, 2010, Bill McDermott and Jim Hagemann Snabe become CEOs of SAP. They changed the branded message and the focus of the corporate software giant. Instead of continuing to focus on business management software, SAP moved toward more consumer-friendly applications for smart phones as well as cloud technology development. The idea was to show SAP's customers that they were still relevant and still the provider to turn to in the fast-paced technology arena.

The new approach appears to have worked. For fiscal year 2011, SAP reported $19.8 billion in revenue. Of the Fortune 500 companies, 80

Affiliation: SAP AG

SAP AG came into being when five disgruntled IBM workers in Mannheim, Germany, decided to quit their jobs and start their own business software development company. SAP stands for "systems, applications and products in data processing." Software development was a new niche in the infant world of computer technology, and SAP quickly cornered the market. As computers penetrated every aspect of modern business, SAP developed business management software that assisted companies in developing their technology infrastructures. SAP was unable to secure funding for its ideas, so the company began slowly, with the cofounders working at night and on the weekends using other people's computers as they tried to build a customer base. They did, however, manage to produce revenue the first year. More and more companies began to utilize SAP's products to streamline their business operations. It was not long before rapid yet fairly sustainable growth took the company from a five-man part-time operation to the technology giant it is today.

SAP's most popular product, its R/3 software, provides businesses with a single software hub for all their digital reporting needs. By 2011, SAP was valued at $85 billion and was expanding into the mobile technology and cloud platform arenas. Plattner stepped down as co-CEO in 2003, the last of the original founders to leave the board of directors. Despite that, SAP continues to rise annually to new levels of success.

percent use SAP software in their daily business management. A few smart acquisitions since 2012 have provided SAP with the people and the knowhow to develop cloud-friendly products. Stock value has increased almost 40 percent since McDermott and Snabe took the reins of SAP. The company was valued at $85 billion at the beginning of 2012.

Today Plattner serves as the chairman of SAP's advisory council. As he explained in a 2012 interview, he thought rapid growth was the key to success in the ever fickle software industry, as his own story with SAP proves. He thought it important to start focusing on the individual user when developing future product and marketing strategies. From the time he was cochairman of the SAP board, Plattner believed in meeting with clients face to face, focusing on the customer and trying new ways to collaborate in order to succeed in the tech business world. Plattner is the ultimate executive team player, building a brand with the aid of his experts and colleagues to become the leader in business management software and development. His business philosophy of trying to find a balance between emerging technology and the needs of the corporate customer has served SAP well for several decades.

PERSONAL LIFE

Plattner retired from the board of SAP on May 9, 2003, moving from a leadership to an advisory capacity. The change was as good as a rest, and since taking a seat on the SAP sidelines, Plattner has become a business philanthropist, start-up adviser, and college benefactor. He invested in several education projects such as the Hasso Plattner Institute in Pottsdam and California; the Hasso Plattner Institute of Design, based at Stanford University; and the refurbishing of a German college library.

Plattner is well known for his love of competitive sailboat racing and can often be found aboard his own vessel, *The Morning Glory*. He enjoys a wide variety of other sports as well, including golf, tennis, surfing, and snowboarding. In 2001, *Time* magazine ranked Plattner first among technology personalities.

Trish Popovitch

FURTHER READING

Baker, Stephen, and Steve Hamm. "Less Ego, More Success." *Business Week* 23 Jul. 2001. Web. 8 Aug. 2012. Chronicles a downturn for SAP in 1999, when it lost market share. Discusses the success and failures of MySap.com. Provides a comparison for the success of Plattner's other big idea, the R/3.

Bartholomew, Doug. "Hasso Plattner: Growing Software's Quiet Giant." *Industry Week Magazine* 21 Dec. 2004. Web. 8 Aug. 2012. Includes ample details on how SAP AG operates and the focus of its business. Explains the benefits of Plattner's business management software, R/3.

"Corporate History." *SAP.com*. 2012. Web. 8 Aug. 2012. Company history from SAP AG's corporate website. Provides year-by-year details of SAP's corporate life and path, including software development, executive changes, and corporate structure and management.

Lev-Ram, Michal. "Inside SAP's Radical Makeover." *Fortune* 29 Mar. 2012. Web. 7 Aug. 2012. Discusses the appointment of Bill McDermott and Jim Hagemann Snabe to the positions of joint chief executive officer of SAP. Mentions new marketing directions and possible future projects.

Nussbaum, Bruce. "To Innovate, Collaborate." *Business Week* 17 Oct. 2005. Web. 8 Aug. 2012. Discusses the donation by Plattner of $35 million to begin a design school at Stanford University to encourage students to enter engineering. School to be called the Plattner Design Institute.

"Sap Co Founder Hasso Plattner." *Der Spiegel* 3 Mar. 2012. Web. 7 Aug. 2012. Provides a frank interview with Plattner that questions his view of the German business world. Plattner explains differences between business attitudes in different countries and addresses the customer in the SAP strategy.

KIM POLESE

Cofounder of Marimba and CEO of SpikeSource

Born: November 13, 1961; place unknown
Died: -
Primary Field: Computer science

Specialty: Computer software
Primary Company/Organization: Marimba

INTRODUCTION

Kim Polese was product manager for one of the most influential languages in computing, Java. She co-founded Marimba, a company specializing in "push" technology, and served as chief executive officer of SpikeSource, a company specializing in supporting open source software. She has been one of the most visible women working in Silicon Valley since the 1990s and a champion for encouraging more young women to consider careers in computing, information technology, and entrepreneurship.

EARLY LIFE

Kim Karin Polese earned her bachelor's degree at the University of California, Berkeley, in 1984, with a concentration in biophysics. She also studied computer science at the University of Washington in Seattle.

LIFE'S WORK

Polese began working as an applications engineer IntelliCorp in 1985. She held several marketing positions at Sun Microsystems from 1989 to 1996; she was the project manager for the object-oriented language C++, and in 1993 she became project manager for Oak, a programming language better known under the name

Kim Polese.

Polese suggested for it: Java. Polese founded Marimba, Inc., in 1996 with Arthur van Hoff, Jonathan Payne, and Sami Shaio. All four had been colleagues at Sun Microsystems, and all had worked on Java: Polese as the product manager, and Shaio, Payne, and van Hoff as developers. Polese served as president and CEO of Marimba until July 2006. The company began without a specific product in mind and first tried developing an Internet user interface; they abandoned that plan after a similar product was acquired by Netscape. They decided to focus on software distribution and developed the concept of "push" technology, a method of distributing software and performing maintenance tasks over the Internet. This technology ws particularly focused on businesses, allowing them to keep many computers identically configured and upgraded with a minimum of effort; with push technology, rather than requiring each user to visit a website and download and install files in order to upgrade the software he or she used, the company could subscribe to a "channel" and the upgrades would be delivered automatically.

In 2000, Polese articulated her vision for the Internet as a way to provide everyone with universally accessible information and services, and she cites this vision as an important motivation for her work on Java, a language designed to be used on any computer and that Polese says she convinced Sun to distribute over the Internet for free. She also predicted that the Internet would increasingly facilitate commercial transactions (such as selling recorded music as MP3 files distributed over the Internet, rather than CDs purchased in a store) and that other software distributors would develop ways to provide their services (for example, accounting) over the Internet.

In 2005, Polese became CEO of SpikeSource, a company founded in 2003 by Murugan Pal. Originally the company provided maintenance and support for open source software to businesses, and in 2005 it began collaborating with Intel and Carnegie Mellon University on a rating system, called Business Readiness Ratings, to evaluate the reliability of open source software products. This system rated products in twelve categories, including technical support, documentation, security, usability, and functionality, using a scale from 1 to 5 for each category. In 2008 the company shifted its focus to providing automated testing and support services, including an automated system for patching security problems; the same year, Intel invested $10 million in the company. Polese resigned as CEO of SpikeSource in May 2010, and in November the company's assets were acquired by Black Duck Software, a company specializing in application development using open source software. Polese next took the chairmanship at Clear-Street, a company that helps individuals manage their money.

In September 2011, Polese became a member of the board of directors for the Public Policy Institute of California, a think tank dedicated to improving public policy in California through nonpartisan research. She is also a member of the Executive Council of Technet, an organization of leaders in technology industries that seeks to shape public policy in ways favorable to innovation. In 2010, Polese received the National Center for Women and Information Technology (NCWIT) Symons Innovator Award for her achievements with SpikeSource; the award is given annually to a woman who has built and funded an information technology company. The award noted that it was particularly

---

Affiliation: Marimba

Kim Polese founded Marimba in 1996 with three colleagues from Sun Microsystems; the name was chosen, Polese said, because it suggested vibrancy and dynamism. Cofounder Arthur van Hoff recalls that when he, Polese, Sami Shaio, and Jonathan Payne founded Marimba, they did not have a particular product or goal in mind, and began working out of a modest office financed by initial investments of $25,000 from each of the founders.

The company's first product was Bongo, a Java tool, but their breakthrough product was Castanet, a technology facilitating rapid software transfer over the Internet. The concept behind the company was that businesses would subscribe to a service that would provide them with software and updates to the software. The technology of Castanet functioned like a radio transmitter and tuner: The Castanet server was the transmitter, sending software and information on channels; subscribers received a tuner that allowed them to receive the "broadcast" from their chosen channel. Marimba proved popular with businesses because it provided them with a way to keep all their software updated and to be sure all employees were using the same version of a given product. Marimba grew rapidly in its early years and had more than three hundred employees at the time of its initial public offering in 1999. In 2004, BMC Software acquired Marimba for $239 million.

---

unusual for women to work in open source technology—only about 1.5 percent of those who work in open source technology are female, much lower than the percentage of all information technology workers who are female (about 25 percent). Also in 2011, Polese received an honorary doctorate in business and economics from California State University. In 2012, Polese was honored by the National Italian American Foundation with the NIAF Special Achievement Award in Technology.

Polese has attracted media attention because of her relatively unusual position as a female CEO in Silicon Valley and because of her beauty and charisma; for instance, she was featured in 1997 as one of America's 25 Most Influential People by *Time* magazine (other "most influentials" included Harvard professor Henry Louis Gates and U.S. secretary of state Madeleine Albright) at a time when the company she founded, Marimba, had fewer than thirty employees. In 1998, Anne Klein photographed Polese for an advertisement that appeared in high-circulation magazines such as *Harper's Bazaar* and *Vogue*. The media attention was at least partially the product of a public relations campaign for Marimba that focused on the company's founders rather than its product. Although this strategy garnered media attention and positive reporting, it also fostered backlash when Marimba was not as successful as expected. However, the cycle of products receiving extreme amounts of publicity only to prove less successful than predicted is not unique to Marimba; in fact, the phenomenon of high expectations and dramatic pronouncements followed by a disappointing reality is well known in Silicon Valley. Moreover, the news media's focus on stories that will attract readers (including stories about attractive and successful young women)—even if they are not particularly newsworthy—is also nothing new. One could interpret Marimba's strategy as savvy manipulation of existing tendencies in the media.

Marimba cofounder van Hoff recalled being surprised at the amount of publicity Marimba got almost from its founding, long before it had a product to sell, but also recalls that the publicity was partially helpful to the young company, because it facilitated connections with other companies and with venture capitalists. On the other hand, he also noted that the extreme focus on Polese might have detracted from the company's credibility, although he understood that it was easier to write and sell a story about a personality than it was to focus on the software itself.

PERSONAL LIFE

Polese is a jazz dancer, and her interest in music is reflected in the name of the company most associated with her, Marimba (Salsa and Tango were also considered as names for the company, but they were not available), as well as its principal product, Castanet.

Sarah Boslaugh

FURTHER READING

Book, Esther Wachs. *Why the Best Man for the Job Is a Woman: The Unique Female Qualities of Leadership.* New York: HarperBusiness, 2001. Print. Profiles of fourteen leading female executives, written by a business journalist, identifying ways that female leaders are changing the rules of management and power in corporations. Polese is cited several times in support of the author's argument.

Livingston, Jessica. *Founders at Work: Stories of Startups' Early Days.* New York: Apress, 2008. Print. Interviews with many of the leading entrepreneurs of Silicon Valley, including Max Levchin (PayPal), Steve Wozniak (Apple), Sabeer Bhatia (Hotmail), and Arthur van Hoff (Marimba). Van Hoff, who left Marimba in 2002 to found Strangeberry, recalls the early days at Marimba, including his views of the publicity accorded the company and Polese, and offers advice for people who want to start their own companies.

Rezvani, Selena. *The Next Generation of Women Leaders: What You Need to Lead but Won't Learn in Business School.* Santa Barbara: ABC-CLIO, 2009. Print. An analysis of the requirements for women to succeed as business and organizational leaders, including practical advice on how to achieve those goals, based on interviews with successful women in a variety of businesses, nonprofit organizations, and government agencies.

Tapscott, Don, and Anthony D. Williams. *Wikinomics: How Mass Collaboration Changes Everything.* Expanded edition. New York: Portfolio Trade, 2008. Print. A business-oriented examination of the usefulness of global collaboration, with examples including Wikipedia, Linux, BMW, and Procter & Gamble. Polese is cited with regard to the usefulness of open source software for businesses.

Warner, Melanie. "The Beauty of Hype." *Fortune* 139.4 (1999): 140–48. Print. A feature story about Marimba and its choice to feature Polese at the center of its marketing campaign. Warner argues that, because of her beauty, Polese received publicity far in excess of her accomplishments and that focusing on her rather than the product ultimately hurt Marimba.

R

DENNIS RITCHIE

Creator of the C programming language and cocreator of the Unix operating system

Born: September 9, 1941; Bronxville, New York
Died: October 12, 2011; Berkeley Heights, New Jersey
Primary Field: Computer science
Specialty: Computer software
Primary Company/Organization: Bell Laboratories

INTRODUCTION

Dennis Ritchie was a codeveloper of the Unix operating system at Bell Laboratories and created the programming language C. Both remain widely used today, as do their descendants, including the object-oriented language C++ and the open source version of Unix, Linux.

EARLY LIFE

Dennis Ritchie was born in Bronxville, a suburb of New York City, and grew up in Summit, New Jersey. His father, Alistair Ritchie, was an engineer for Bell Laboratories and an expert in switching theory, while his mother, Jean McGee Ritchie, was a homemaker. Ritchie received his bachelor's degree in physics from Harvard University in Cambridge, Massachusetts, in 1963; he would later remark that this experience as an undergraduate persuaded him that he was not smart enough to be a physicist. Ritchie began his Ph.D. studies in mathematics at Harvard as well, although he did not complete that degree. A lecture on the Univac I sparked his interest in computer science, and he worked on the computers at the Massachusetts Institute of Technology (MIT), also located in Cambridge. Besides the programming experience, an important aspect of Ritchie's time at MIT was his exposure to the cooperative methods of solving programming problems favored by the university's students, which influenced his interest in distributed computing. Ritchie was recruited by Sandia National Laboratories while in graduate school but chose instead to join the Computer Science Department at Bell Laboratories; he began working for Bell Labs in 1967, where he met his frequent collaborator Kenneth Thompson.

Dennis Ritchie.

LIFE'S WORK

Ritchie spent his career at Bell Laboratories in New Jersey, first as a computer scientist and later as a manager. He initially worked on the Multics (multiplexed information and computing service) project at Bell Labs, a collaboration of Bell Labs, MIT, and General Electric to develop an operating system that would allow multiple users to work simultaneously on a computer; early mainframes could accommodate only batch processing, meaning that only one person could use the computer at a time. This was an ambitious project (the goal was to allow time sharing among three hundred users simultaneously) but was ultimately abandoned by Bell Labs in 1969. After the end of the Multics project, Thompson, Ritchie, and colleagues began working on a new project, which ultimately led to the development of the Unix operating system as well as the C programming language. Bell Labs was not originally in favor of devoting resources to developing another operating system so soon after the failure of Multics, but Ritchie and Thompson persisted, wanting to create a new type of operating system that would facilitate interaction and information sharing among programmers.

Ritchie and his colleagues began their work on the new operating system using an out-of-date minicomputer, the PDP-7, manufactured by the Digital Equipment Corporation (DEC); the limitations of this computer (it had only 8 kilobytes of memory) forced them to be efficient, and they chose the name Unix for their new system to emphasize that they were creating a simpler version of the failed system, Multics. Unix incorporated many capabilities that are now taken for granted in modern operating systems, including utility programs to perform tasks such as copying and editing files, moving files from one location to another, and printing files. Bell adopted Unix for internal use and began licensing it to outside users as well. Ritchie and Thompson published a paper on the operating system in 1974, attracting the interest of other institutions. Because Unix could run on different computer systems (as opposed to older, machine-specific operating systems), a community of Unix users grew and began to develop and share utilities. This teamwork echoed the cooperative programming culture Ritchie had experienced at MIT and was a forerunner of later open source approaches to software championed by Richard Stallman and others.

In the process of developing Unix, Ritchie developed the C programming language; Unix was written in C, a fact that contributed to its portability. Although based on earlier languages (one of which was named B,

explaining the origins of the name C), C was innovative because it combined features of both machine languages and high-level languages, thus providing the programmer with both the specificity and control of a machine language and the ease of use of a high-level language. Like Unix, C was portable, so that code could be shared among different computers. It was also more efficient than competing high-level languages and allowed programs to be run more quickly, a key consideration when computer time was at a premium. In addition, the popularity of C led to the development of the object-oriented languages C++ and Java.

The world of computing was changing rapidly in the early 1970s, and features of C and Unix were well adapted to these changes. Most important, computing was moving away from the centralized use of large mainframes and toward the use of multiple smaller computers to do the same work. Computer prices were also dropping, and the increased use of computers in all kinds of business applications meant that there was an increased call for people trained to use computers and to write code for them. University programs in computer science expanded, and C became a common language of instruction and use in higher education. Multiple factors influenced this development: the inherent properties of C (its logical nature, efficiency, and portability), its use

---

Affiliation: Bell Laboratories

Dennis Ritchie worked his entire adult life at Bell Laboratories in New Jersey, and his most important professional relationship was with a Bell Labs colleague, Kenneth Thompson. Ritchie's work exemplifies one aspect of the type of work funded by Bell: While working to solve concrete problems in communications (the need for interactive, distributed, and portable computing), he created two lasting innovations—the C language and the Unix operating system—whose influence is felt throughout computing and has facilitated many innovations we take for granted in modern life. Earlier examples of practical innovations developed at Bell Labs that had widespread societal effects include the transistor (developed by John Bardeen, William Shockley, and Walter Brattain in 1947), the laser (prompted in part by a 1958 article published by Bell Labs scientists Charles Hard Townes and Arthur Leonard Schawlow), and the communications satellite (Telstar I was built by a Bell Labs team, and launched in 1962).

in the popular Unix operating system, and the fact it was not protected by copyright (because of federal antitrust regulations) after the parent owner of Bell Labs, AT&T, was broken up into many smaller corporations. The result was that C became one of the most popular computer languages of the 1970s and 1980s; the popularity of the Unix operating system during this period also helped spread the use of C. Finally, Ritchie and Brian Kernighan wrote an important textbook, *C Programming Language*, which broadened the language's popularity and is still in use today; many instructional manuals for other languages have adapted elements of Ritchie and Kernighan's approach, most famously the "Hello, world" assignment in which the programmer writes code to make the phrase "Hello, world" appear on the computer screen.

Ritchie became head of the Computing Techniques Research Department at Bell Labs in 1990. In 1995, he and his colleagues released an experimental operating system, Plan 9 (named after the 1959 Ed Wood movie *Plan 9 from Outer Space*), which expands on the concepts of networking and decentralization. The Inferno operating system expands on the concepts behind Plan 9, was described in a 1997 article by Ritchie and colleagues, and remains available as free software from the British company Vita Nuova.

Ritchie retired from Bell Labs in 2007. He received many honors during his career, perhaps most notably a National Medal of Technology (shared with Thompson) in 1998. In 1974, he won an award from the Association for Computing Machinery (ACM) for a paper on systems and language. In 1982, the Computer Society of the Institute of Electrical and Electronics Engineers (IEEE) awarded him the Emmanuel Piore Award for his contributions to information-processing systems, and in 1983 he and Thompson were jointly awarded ACM's coveted Turing Award for their lasting technical innovations in the computer science field. Ritchie was made a Fellow of Bell Laboratories in the same year, and in 1988 he became a member of the U.S. National Academy of Engineering. In 1989 he received the Lifetime Achievement Award for Technical Excellence from *PC Magazine*, in 1990 he won IEEE's Richard W. Hamming Medal for his contributions to information science and technology, and in 1994 the IEEE gave him its Computer Pioneer Award.

PERSONAL LIFE

As an adult, Ritchie led a work-centered life, and despite having many outside interests (including reading and travel), he continued to work after retirement. Toward the end of his life, he fell into ill health, suffering from prostate cancer and heart disease; he was found dead in his home on October 12, 2011. He was survived by two brothers, Bill and John, and a sister, Lynn.

Colleagues remember Ritchie as a modest and unassuming person who never sought public recognition for his work, in contrast to such better-known figures as Steve Jobs or Bill Gates, who had become household names. Ritchie was noted for the clarity and precision of both his computer code and his writing.

He was also known as a practical joker: The most famous of his pranks, known as labscam, was accomplished with the help of his colleague Rob Pike and the magicians Penn and Teller (Penn Jillette and Raymond Joseph Teller). This prank was pulled on Arno Allan Penzias, the Nobel Prize–winning physicist and Ritchie's boss at the time; it made Penzias think he was taking part in an experiment to test a computer program that could understand natural speech (Penzias's) and select and combine fragments of video footage of Penn and Teller to form sensible answers to Penzias's questions, while in fact the real Penn and Teller were in the next room and were being videotaped giving the answers.

Sarah Boslaugh

FURTHER READING

Hyman, Paul. "Dennis Ritchie, 1941–2011." *Communications of the ACM* 54.12 (2011): 21. Print. Obituary of Ritchie, focusing on his technical accomplishments and role in creating C and Unix and emphasizing that the accomplishments of more famous computer pioneers, such as Steve Jobs, were possible in part because of the groundwork laid by Ritchie and his colleagues.

Lohr, Steve. "Dennis Ritchie, Trailblazer in Digital Era, Dies at 70." *New York Times* 13 Oct. 2011: 22. Print. Obituary of Ritchie by the technology correspondent for the *New York Times*, reviewing his accomplishments, working style, and influence on the field of computer science.

---. *Go To: The Story of the Math Majors, Bridge Players, Engineers, Chess Wizards, Maverick Scientists and Iconoclasts—the Programmers Who Created the Software Revolution*. New York: Basic, 2001. Print. A narrative of the early days of software programming, with an emphasis on the personalities of the individuals involved and their varied working styles, as well as their technical accomplishments.

O'Regan, Gerard. *A Brief History of Computing*. Berlin: Springer, 2008. Print. A history of computing, written for the general reader and beginning students in computer science, including the accomplishments of Ritchie and his colleagues in creating C and Unix.

Slater, Robert. *Portraits in Silicon*. Cambridge: MIT, 1987. Print. Aimed at a general audience (Slater at the time of writing was a journalist for *Time* magazine), this book consists of brief sketches of thirty-one people involved in the early computer industry, as well as precursors such as Charles Babbage, and covers Ritchie and Kenneth Thompson.

VIRGINIA ROMETTY

Former president and CEO of IBM

Born: 1958; Chicago, Illinois
Died: -
Primary Field: Internet
Specialty: Management, executives, and investors
Primary Company/Organization: IBM

INTRODUCTION

Virginia Rometty, a computer scientist and electrical engineer, became president and chief executive officer (CEO) of IBM on January 1, 2012, the first woman named to lead the company in its one hundred years in business. Rometty joined IBM as a systems engineer in 1981 and spent the next three decades rising through the ranks. She held a variety of positions, establishing a reputation for technological expertise and people skills that had insiders speculating about her as a possible CEO at least a decade before the historic announcement that she would lead the company. Immediately prior to being named IBM's top executive, she served as senior vice president and group executive for IBM Sales, Marketing and Strategy. She was a key player in IBM's transformation from a seller of goods into provider of technological solutions to problems in finance, insurance, health care, and transportation.

EARLY LIFE

Virginia Marie "Ginni" Nicosia was born in Chicago, Illinois, in 1958. Her parents divorced when she was young, and she and her three younger siblings were brought up by their mother, a strong woman who fostered an expectation of high achievement in her children. Rometty's brother rose from being a commodities trader to CEO of the Allenberg Cotton Company, a major international cotton-trading firm. One sister, Annette Ripper, a computer scientist, was a partner with the management-consultant company Accenture for

eighteen years. Another sister, Darlene Nicosia, became director of Europe procurement for Coca-Cola.

Rometty majored in computer science and electrical engineering at the Northwestern University's McCormick School of Engineering and Applied Science in Evanston, Illinois, at a time when few women were training as engineers. In 1979, she graduated with highest honors with a B.S. degree. Rometty credits her years at Northwestern with honing her problem-solving skills, an education more valuable than the specific knowledge she acquired. After graduation, she began an internship

Virginia Rometty.

with the General Motors Institute (now Kettering University). General Motors used the institute, which became a degree-granting college known for its commitment to co-operative education in 1945, as a training ground for its own engineers and managers. Rometty met and married her husband, Mark Rometty, while they were both students at the institute. The training she received gave her an edge in 1981, when she accepted a job as a systems engineer with IBM in Detroit, Michigan.

LIFE'S WORK

During her early years at IBM, Rometty held several positions, quickly moving through a series of management jobs, developing her abilities to work well with people, and gaining experience in working with clients in a variety of industries. She worked as a business and information-technology consultant and as a general manager in IBM's global insurance and financial services sector. In the latter position, she established a consulting service for the insurance sector. She also served a term as general manager for IBM's global services in the Americas. She played a role in transitioning IBM from its dependence on petroleum-based fuels to using sources of green energy.

In 2002, Rometty was IBM's general manager for Sales, Marketing and Strategy. In IBM's Global Services division, she was one of the key players in finalizing the deal between IBM and American Express whereby IBM became sole manager of American Express's website, network servers, data storage, and support services. The $4 billion, seven-year transaction was the largest such deal ever negotiated by IBM Global Services. At the same time the American Express deal was being negotiated, Rometty was part of the IBM team engaged in acquiring Price Waterhouse Coopers Consulting (PwC). The technology industry was in the middle of its biggest slump since the mid-1980s, and many pundits viewed the $3.5 billion PwC deal as foolishly risky. Rometty was one of the executives charged with promoting and explaining the deal in the media. She proved her value to IBM further when she oversaw the integration of PwC's thirty thousand consulting professionals, who had been working in 160 countries, into the consulting arm of the more structured IBM.

Rometty was promoted to senior vice president of IBM Global Business Services in 2005. She boosted profit at the unit 42 percent in her first two years on the job. Another of her achievements in this office was the development of IBM's cloud-computing capacity. In 2009, then CEO Samuel Palmisano placed her

at the head of IBM's sales force. A primary focus for her in this position was investment in emerging markets in China, Russia, and Brazil. On October 25, 2011, IBM announced that its board of directors had chosen Rometty to succeed Palmisano as president and CEO. On January 1, 2012, Rometty became the ninth person and first woman to head the venerable company. She also earned a seat on the board. Palmisano continued as chairman.

The experience in sales, service, and acquisitions that Rometty brought to her new role, coupled with her part in developing the strategies Palmisano had in place, suggested that she would follow the five-year plan she had helped construct. Steady profit growth saw IBM shares reach their highest level since 1915, when the company went public. Rometty's record attests to her belief in analytics and emerging markets. Both expanded under her watch. Goals for 2015 include continuing expansions in markets such as cloud computing and analytics; spending $20 billion to buy companies (more money than IBM used for this purpose in the previous decade); ramping up growth in China, India, and other emerging markets; and doubling the company's earnings per share by that year. New appointments and changes in in-house communications demonstrated that Rometty would put her own mark on the office; her focus seemed steady and her goals ambitious.

Palmisano stressed that Rometty's new office came through her merits and that her gender was irrelevant. The spring after Rometty took office, she was showcased in newspaper and magazine stories and in both in-person and virtual conversations across the country in an incident that suggested her gender could prove to be an issue. The Augusta National Golf Club, where the Masters Golf Tournament has been played since 1933, has traditionally extended membership to the CEOs of its corporate sponsors: IBM, Exxon Mobil, and AT&T. With Rometty as IBM's CEO, Augusta was forced to choose between amending its men-only policy and snubbing a sponsor. Membership was granted to four of Rometty's male predecessors. Augusta's chairman, Billy Payne, dodged media questions by refusing to comment on the board's private deliberations while everyone from local residents to President Obama expressed an opinion. Local opinion was divided; the president favored admitting women. Feminists called for boycotting IBM if the company accepted the insult. Rometty and IBM remained silent. Rometty attended the Masters Tournament and saw clients there, but she wore pink; there was no sign of a green jacket, the traditional color

Affiliation: IBM

In 2011, International Business Machines Corporation (IBM) celebrated the one hundredth anniversary of the company's founding on June 16, 1911. Over a century, the company has marked such milestones as investing in a research laboratory during a time when the United States was facing the greatest economic crisis in its history; aiding the U.S. government in creating the Social Security System; inventing the IBM personal computer, which began the PC revolution; developing the first hard disk drive and creating the data storage industry; and developing Watson, the computer that conquered the human champions of the television game show *Jeopardy!*

The CEO during IBM's centennial year was Samuel Palmisano, who took office in 2002 and over the next nine years transformed what was once the largest computer company into essentially a services and software firm. Palsimano's heir apparent, Robert Moffat, senior vice president and general manager of IBM's Systems and Technology Group, was arrested and charged with involvement in a $20 million insider trader scheme. In September 2010, he was sentenced to six months in jail. Just over a year later, IBM's board of directors announced that Virginia Rometty, a thirty-year veteran of the company, would succeed Palmisano on January 1, 2012, the first woman in the company's history to hold the top job.

The appointment of Rometty, who has a background in technology, signaled the company's future as a firm focused on business services. After a near-death experience in the 1980s and early 1990s, IBM resurrected itself as a technology company boasting annual revenues of $100 billion by the end of the first decade of the twenty-first century.

change, IBM's acquisition of Price Waterhouse Coopers Consulting in 2002, that provided the opportunity for Rometty to earn the attention of Palmisano and others. Challenge and change would continue to be hallmarks of Rometty's career.

PERSONAL LIFE

Rometty has been married to Mark Rometty for more than three decades. The couple maintain homes in White Plains, New York, and Bonita Springs, Florida, where Mark works as manager, treasurer, and principal investor in the Bam Oil Company. Friends say that he is an intensely private man who has pursued a career that allowed him the flexibility to support his wife's ascension to the leadership of an international corporation. The Romettys enjoy Broadway plays and scuba diving in their leisure time.

As a participant in IBM's Women in Technology Council and Women's Leadership Council, Rometty has actively promoted diversity within IBM. Beyond her responsibilities at IBM, she is a member of the Council on Foreign Relations, an independent, nonpartisan think tank committed to the study of U.S. foreign policy and international affairs. She also serves on the board of overseers and board of managers of the Memorial Sloan-Kettering Cancer Center, the board of directors of American Productivity and Quality Center, and the board of trustees of Northwestern University. In 2006, the Association of Management Consulting Firms honored her with the Carl S. Sloane Award for Excellence in Management Consulting. In 2010, Northwestern University Alumni Association recognized her with the Alumni Merit Award. She was named to *Fortune* magazine's 50 Most Powerful Women in Business for seven consecutive years through 2011.

Wylene Rholetter

associated with the club. (The issue gradually faded from public debate until August 2012, when the club finally opened its doors to women members, inviting former secretary of state Condoleezza Rice and financier Darla Moore to join.)

Rometty made clear that as leader of IBM she expected to be a risk taker willing to embrace change. She remembered the $16 billion in losses the company suffered between 1991 and 1993, and she was instrumental in the transformation of the company from a maker of hardware into a technology services company with $100 billion in sales in 2010. It was a major and risky

FURTHER READING

Crosman, Penny. "IBM Appoints Virginia Rometty First Female CEO." *American Banker* 176.165 (2011): n. pag. Print. This article announces Rometty's appointment as CEO and provides a brief overview of her career at IBM, quoting both her and her predecessor, Samuel Palmisano.

Hymowitz, Carol, and Sarah Frier. "Can This IBMer Keep Big Blue's Edge?" *Bloomberg Businessweek* 31 Oct. 2011: 31–32. Print. The article focuses on the challenges Rometty faces as CEO of IBM and provides information about her plans to continue the company's transition to a competitive technology company.

Lohr, Steve. "I.B.M. Names a New Chief." *New York Times* 25 Oct. 2011: B1. Print. The article announces Rometty's ascension to CEO at IBM and provides limited biographical data and an extended overview of her career.

Mayer, Marissa. "Virginia Rometty." *Time* 30 Apr. 2012: 115. Print. The article, by the woman appointed CEO of Yahoo! a few months after writing it, considers Rometty as one of the magazine's choices for the 100 Most Influential People of 2012. Mayer examines Rometty's background as a computer scientist and electrical engineer and her contributions to IBM's global success.

Stewart, James B. "Top Aide to a C.E.O.: Her Husband." *New York Times* 4 Nov. 2011: B1. Print. The article looks at the role husbands of female CEOs play in the success of their wives. Mark Rometty is examined as representative of the group.

GUIDO VAN ROSSUM

Creator of the Python programming language

Born: January 31, 1956; Haarlem, North Holland, Netherlands
Died: -
Primary Field: Computer science
Specialty: Computer programming
Primary Company/Organization: Google

INTRODUCTION

Guido van Rossum is the creator of Python, one of the most popular scripting languages for the Internet. Originally released in 1991, Python takes its name from the comedy group Monty Python and began as a hobby. Although Python has become one of the most widely used languages in Internet applications (Google relies heavily on it), van Rossum gave no thought to its practical ends when designing it; he was more interested in principles of programming language design than in the purposes to which that language was put. He continues to develop Python today while working for Google.

EARLY LIFE

Guido van Rossum was born on January 31, 1956, in Haarlem, the Netherlands. His brother Just, ten years his junior, is a computer programmer and typeface designer. Although Guido did not know what a computer was until he went to college, he tinkered with electronics as a boy and hoped to learn how to build his own calculator in school.

He attended the University of Amsterdam, where he earned a master's degree in mathematics and computer science in 1982. While at the university, he was introduced to computers and learned to use punch cards: the IBM 80-column format, which originated in 1928. The first language he learned to program in was ALGOL 60, after which he began to study Pascal. As much as programming, he was interested in studying different programming languages and the different concepts they used, and he began to learn Fortran, Lisp, BASIC, and COBOL. Practical ends of programming interested him much less than the languages themselves, although he did write a program for John Horton Conway's *Game of Life*.

Van Rossum has worked for a number of research institutes in the Netherlands and the United States,

Guido van Rossumv.

Affiliation: Google

Google was founded in 1998 by Stanford University students Larry Page and Sergey Brin. Initially, the company was concerned with building a better search engine, using the technology PageRank, which calculated the value of potential search results according to their perceived relevance and presented them accordingly. This was a step forward from raw results, especially as the Internet grew so quickly, and required less work than curated categories such as those offered by rival search engine Yahoo! on its front page. Google's search engine was originally nicknamed BackRub, because it checked backlinks in estimating relevance, but was eventually named Google in reference to the number googol (1 {multi} 10^{100}, or 1 followed by 100 zeros).

Funding for Google came from Andy Bechtolsheim, a Sun Microsystems cofounder (and fellow Stanford alumnus). An initial public offering eventually came in 2004, with many Google employees becoming overnight millionaires, thanks to their stock options.

Since 2001, Google has acquired numerous other companies and has long since ceased to be only a search engine company. Many of the sites Google has purchased have been rebranded or folded into Google services. The GrandCentral voice-mail service became Google Voice, for instance. Major Google products beyond the search page include Google's e-mail service GMail, the Facebook competitor Google+, Google Earth, Blogger and Feedburner, the Google Drive backup service, YouTube, and specialized search engines such as Google Scholar, Google Books, Google Patent Search, Google Image Search, and Google Shopping. Google has also introduced Google Chrome, its web browser for Windows, Linux, and Mac OS X, as well as Android, a mobile device operating system used for smart phones, some tablets, and Amazon's Kindle products. The Google Chrome OS is a Linux-based operating system using web applications, which is used to power the Chromebook and Chromebox computers, both of which are designed to power up and connect to the Internet in mere seconds.

Google is one of several Internet companies to be investigated by the Federal Trade Commission (FTC) over privacy violations. In 2011, following an investigation of the disastrous launch of the Google Buzz product—which lacked a reasonable standard of transparency and broadcast many people's contacts without their permission—the FTC put the company on a twenty-year probation program, requiring the company to take extra steps to preserve consumer privacy during that time or face stiffer than average penalties. It was the first time the FTC had used such a measure, which it soon applied to Facebook in response to a similar violation. Former CEO and current executive chairman Eric Schmidt has publicly downplayed privacy concerns, famously saying, "If you have nothing to hide, you have nothing to fear." Most, 99 percent, of Google's revenue comes from advertising.

---

including Centrum Wiskunde and Informatica, the Corporation for National Research Initiatives, and the U.S. National Institute of Standards and Technology (as a guest researcher on mobile agents in distributed systems). He wrote a glob() routine (a pattern-matching routine) for BSD Unix in 1986 and was involved in the development of the ABC programming language.

ABC is a general-purpose programming environment like Pascal or BASIC, with support for top-down programming. Mainly used as a teaching or tutorial language, it does not have direct access to the file system or operating system and is not a systems-programming language. It consists of only five data types: numbers, texts (strings), compounds (records without field names), lists, and tables. The programs are much smaller than those of Pascal, and defined functions, procedures, and global variables remain in the programming environment after logging out, so that there is no need to create files. The environment also suggests command completions while the user types, even user-defined commands. Van Rossum's work on ABC led directly to his creation of Python in 1991.

Life's Work

Python originated with van Rossum's brainstorming while he was looking for a project to occupy him during his Christmas vacation in 1989. He decided to write an interpreter for a language similar to ABC and appealing to Unix and C hackers. The result was Python, a general-purpose high-level programming language with clear, easy-to-understand syntax. Python is one of the best-known multiparadigm programming languages, meaning that it can work with several different styles of programming, including structured or object-oriented programming. Some paradigms require extensions for support, but the language is intended to be extremely extensible—the opposite of ABC, which had frustrated van Rossum for that reason. Python has a small core and a large standard library. Where ABC protected users by limiting some of their access, Python encourages innovation.

Today, Python is typically used as a scripting language for the Internet or is embedded in software packages (including imaging programs such as GIMP and PaintShop Pro). Artificial intelligence researchers sometimes rely on it, and it has a following in the natural language processing community, as well as the information security industry. Python ships with most flavors of Linux. Google has relied heavily on Python (the Google App Engine, the platform for web app development and hosting, uses Python as its scripting language), and the original BitTorrent client was written in it, as is Spotify. The widespread use of Python is ironic, given that van Rossum never had specific practical uses in mind for it and in fact has said that he considered it a language with a narrow niche. The extensibility has something to do with that, making Python a language easy to put to uses that were not envisioned at the time of its design.

Van Rossum's funding proposal for further work on Python, submitted to the Advanced Research Projects Agency (ARPA) in 1999, was called "Computer Programming for Everybody" and identified Python as a language that would be open source, with code in plain English, which was useful for everyday tasks and easy to learn.

Python has influenced a number of other languages, including Ruby, Cobra, Go, Pyrex and Cython, Boo, and Groovy, which applied the Python philosophy to Java. That design philosophy—ease of use and extensibility—is an important part of Python, and Python developers bring a sense of fun to their work. That sensibility is reflected, for instance, in van Rossum's title in the Python community (as the language's lead developer): Benevolent Dictator for Life. Code is considered "pythonic" when it flows naturally and fits well with Python idioms and "unpythonic" when it acts too much like code from another language ported into Python. By extension, the Py prefix is often attached to products that are Python-related. Monty Python references make their way into the community as well: The traditional variables "foo" and "bar" are replaced in Python with "spam" and "eggs."

Python enhancement proposals, or PEPs, are part of the official process for enacting changes in future versions of Python. PEPs were adopted in order to better frame development discussions, by giving them the goal of drafting a PEP that could then be considered and weighed against its alternatives and ramifications—a process that focused Python development.

In 2005, van Rossum was hired by Google, to spend half his work hours developing Python. His first Google project, Mondrian, was unveiled in November 2006. Mondrian is a web-based code review system with a Python-powered front end, which Google adopted companywide, replacing the previous e-mail-based code review method. The web-based system made sense for Google's shared development environment, in which every developer works on code in a workspace readable by anyone in the company (automated processes record snapshots for archiving). Shifting the code review process to the web incorporated the strengths of web-based collaboration, which Google has promoted through services like Google Documents. Rather than just exchanging e-mails back and forth, Mondrian allows programmers features such as in-line commenting, statistics tracking, and task-specific dashboards. Reviewers are invited from within the Mondrian interface, and files can be quickly compared to previous versions. Moreover, there is no danger of losing or deleting e-mails, since everything related to the workflow is captured and relevant data are distilled. In the talk presenting the first Mondrian demonstration, van Rossum estimated that developing Mondrian had occupied about a quarter of his time since joining Google and that the process of working on it had given him a crash course on Google technologies and the Google work environment. The name Mondrian, of course, refers to Piet Mondrian, one of the most famous Dutch painters.

Van Rossum also worked on the Google Compute Engine release in the summer of 2012, an "infrastructure as a service" product offering scalable virtual machine computing capabilities through the cloud. Google Compute Engine allows users to launch Linux virtual machines and to run their workloads on Google's infrastructure. Data are encrypted, and the service promises strong security and data privacy. Because Google's infrastructure is so efficient, it promises up to 50 percent more computing power for the money than other cloud providers do.

Van Rossum received the Award for the Advancement of Free Software in 2001 from the Free Software Foundation. He was named a Distinguished Engineer by the Association for Computing Machinery in 2006. As of 2012, Python is the third most popular language on the social coding site Github, after JavaScript and Ruby. Python 3.3 was released in August 2012.

PERSONAL LIFE

Van Rossum moved to the United States in 1995 and today lives in California with his wife, Kim Knapp. They were married in 2000 and have a son, Orlijn, born in 2001. Until 2003, the van Rossums lived in the Washington, D.C., area. He is a big Monty Python fan, having named his programming language after the troupe. He also is a fan of the film *Pulp Fiction* and has referred to Winston Wolf (portrayed by Harvey Keitel) as his favorite film character. Van Rossum is unusual among programmers in that, beyond Monty Python and Douglas Adams's *Hitchhiker's Guide to the Galaxy*, he has no interest in typical "geek culture," such as science fiction and role-playing games, and he is steadfastly uninterested in video games.

Bill Kte'pi

FURTHER READING

Biancuzzi, Federico. *Masterminds of Programming: Conversations with the Creators of Major Programming Languages*. Sebastopol: O'Reilly, 2009. Print. Includes an interview with van Rossum, but the other interviews provide good context as well, and programmers are often surprisingly frank in their assessments of other people's languages.

Downey, Allen B. *Think Python: How to Think Like a Computer Scientist*. Cambridge: Cambridge UP, 2012. Print. An in-depth guide to programming with Python.

van Rossum, Guido. *An Introduction to Python*. New York: Network Theory, 2003. Print. Van Rossum's guide to his programming language.

S

JEAN SAMMET

Developer of FORMAC

Born: March 23, 1928; New York, New York
Died: -
Primary Field: Computer science
Specialty: Computer programming
Primary Company/Organization: IBM

INTRODUCTION

Jean Sammet is an influential programmer who assisted in the creation of COBOL, developed FORMAC, oversaw the development of Ada, and wrote a 1969 book on the history and fundamentals of programming that is considered a classic. She was active in the computer industry in the 1960s and 1970s, holding a number of key positions in industry groups and organizing the first conference on the history of programming languages of the Association for Computing Machinery (ACM) and its Special Interest Group on Symbolic and Algebraic Manipulation. She was also the ACM's first woman president.

EARLY LIFE

Jean E. Sammet was born on March 23, 1928, in New York City to lawyers Harry and Ruth Sammet. Her father's practice focused on wills and estates; her mother stopped practicing law when she married. Both Jean and her younger sister, Helen, attended local public schools. Although she had displayed an apptitude for mathematics at an early age, Sammet could not attend the all-boys Bronx High School of Science. Instead, she attended the all-girls Julia Richman High School and enrolled in every mathematics course it offered. After high school, she attended Mount Holyoke College in South Hadley, Massachusetts. She had looked

through the course catalogs from several women's colleges before choosing Mount Holyoke because of the strength of its math program. In 1948, she received a bachelor's degree in mathematics (minoring in political science and taking enough education courses to be certified for teaching). Sammet continued her studies at the University of Illinois at Urbana-Champaign, earning her master's degree in mathematics in 1949. She began

Jean Sammet.

275

Affiliation: IBM

Today a multinational technology and consulting company (and one of the largest corporations in America), and once the driving force behind the personal computer revolution of the 1970s and 1980s, IBM began as the Computing Tabulating Recording Company (CTR). CTR was created in 1911 through the merger of three late Industrial Revolution business machine companies: the Computing Scale Company, the International Time Recording Company, and the Tabulating Machine Company. Each company had built devices for specific niches in the growing world of business: machines for precise measurements, machines for employees to punch their time cards on, and machines for tabulating figures for accounting. This area—making machines that measured or calculated rather than machines that assembled or refined (as had dominated most of the Industrial Revolution)—was as much a growth industry as digital computers would become later and was critical to the growth and development of the economy, especially in the United States. More and more Americans were moving to the city, and more and more young Americans were taking business jobs rather than farm, factory, or service jobs: The white-collar sector was booming.

IBM's corporate identity was formed by Thomas J. Watson Sr., who was hired in 1914. He doubled revenues in four years and expanded the company to four other continents, but he also changed the way the company worked. It now focused on large-scale business solutions, especially custom-built ones for wealthy business customers. In this area it had little competition. Watson introduced the slogan "Think," which has been associated with IBM ever since: THINK signs were posted all around work areas at IBM, and the twenty-first century ThinkPad notebook computer would named for the slogan.

CTR was renamed International Business Machines in 1924. Watson continued to run the company until 1952, when his son succeeded him as president. By the time Thomas J. Watson Jr., took the reins, IBM had already entered the computer industry—large tabulating machines had been built for the government in the New Deal era—but the 1950s saw a rapid increase in IBM's commitment to the field. An IBM laboratory demonstrated the first self-learning program, a check-

ers program that got better the more it played. More practically, IBM developed Fortran under John Backus. A high-level programming language, Fortran was easier to write than assembly language, and it used an optimizing compiler so that its programs would be just as efficient. The shift to Fortran—and later to other programming languages—made the task of programming easier and more efficient, accelerating the development of the industry.

IBM built the computers used by the Mercury, Gemini, and Saturn space programs, as well as the Apollo mission that landed Neil Armstrong and Buzz Aldrin on the Moon. IBM had also accepted the economic practicality of offering smaller-scale solutions as well, and the IBM Selectric (an electric typewriter), introduced in 1961, was an enormous success, becoming ubiquitous in offices for the next two decades. Another success was the development of the Universal Product Code in 1973—the bar code that now appears on every product sold, to be scanned at cash registers.

After offering business computers for years, IBM introduced the IBM PC (for "personal computer") in 1981. Thanks in part to a collaboration with Microsoft, which developed the operating system for the PC and its successors, along with high-quality application software for it, the PC gradually became the industry standard, and other companies began manufacturing PC-compatible computers instead of their own designs (Apple being the obvious major exception). However, IBM PCs remained more expensive than PC-compatibles, and over time the PC's universality actually hurt IBM's sales: More and more people were using PCs, but fewer and fewer of them were buying them from IBM when there were so many alternatives. IBM returned its focus to business solutions and consulting, and in 2005 it sold its personal computer business to the Chinese company Lenovo.

Today, research continues to be an intense concern at IBM. The company's employees have been awarded six Turing Awards, nine National Medals of Technology, five National Medals of Science, and five Nobel Prizes. It operates nine research laboratories, holds more patents than any other American company, and in 2011 demonstrated Watson, an artificial intelligence program, on the game show *Jeopardy!*

work on her Ph.D. in mathematics 1948 while working as a teaching assistant in the mathematics department. Although she did not complete the degree, Mount Holyoke conferred an honorary doctorate of science on Sammet in 1978.

In 1951, Sammet tried to find a position teaching mathematics in New York City, but the city was not hiring new teachers at the high school level. She tried New Jersey, but it would not hire her because she had not taken two prerequisite courses for teachers: a course on the history of New Jersey and an education course. Sammet argued that the courses were irrelevant to the teaching of mathematics, but she lost that argument. She wound up working for the Metropolitan Life Insurance Company and became part of an in-house training program in punch-card accounting machines. She enjoyed it but was not offered a job using the machines, so she returned to school to work on her doctorate at Columbia University while teaching at Barnard College. The academic life did not interest her, however, and she sought out work with computers.

LIFE'S WORK

From 1955 to 1958, Sammet was in charge of the first scientific computer programming group; she was programming computers for use by scientists at Sperry Rand. Sperry Rand had been created that year when Sperry Gyroscope, an aviation equipment manufacturer that had expanded into electronics and computing, acquired Remington Rand, the company that built the UNIVAC I (the Universal Automatic Computer) in 1951. (Divisions of Sperry Rand exist today as Unisys and Honeywell.)

After leaving Sperry Rand, Sammet worked for Sylvania, an electric products company that merged in 1959 with General Telephone and expanded into electronics. She was hired to develop software for MOBID-IC, a computing machine Sylvania was building for the U.S. Army Signal Corps. She worked as a consultant in programming research for Sylvania from 1958 to 1961 as part of the original COBOL group, which developed the Common Business-Oriented Language (COBOL), a programming language for use in business and administration. COBOL was built on the FLOW-MATIC language of Grace Hopper and was developed as a joint effort by Sylvania, Sperry Rand, RCA, Honeywell, IBM, the Burroughs Corporation, and the federal government (specifically the Air Force, the National Bureau of Standards, and the David Taylor Model Basin). An initial series of meetings held at the Pentagon to set up the administrative and working bodies that would develop

COBOL called for an executive committee to perform oversight and separate committees to make recommendations for a business-oriented programming language on short-range, intermediate, and long-range bases. The long-range committee was never formed, and the intermediate committee never began operations, so the whole of the project in practice fell to the short-range committee. Sammet was one of six members of the subcommittee of the short-range committee that developed the language's specifications. The other members were Vernon Reeves of Sylvania Electric Products, William Selden and Gertrude Tierney of IBM, and Howard Bromberg and Howard Discount of RCA.

At the end of 1960, COBOL compilers were successfully demonstrated, including the running of a COBOL program on computers from two different manufacturers (including UNIVAC), to demonstrate compatibility. This first version of COBOL was approved by the executive committee and defined as COBOL 60; later versions would be similarly named after their year of specification. One of the unique features of COBOL—even compared to later languages—was that it explicitly supported self-modifying code, one of the few high-level languages to do so; the "Alter X to proceed to Y" statement would modify X statements after the Alter statement to read as Y statements instead. COBOL also introduced copybooks, sections of code that can be copied from a master program and inserted into other programs in order to ensure consistency. Many of the languages that followed did likewise. Today, COBOL is still in wide use by business and government systems.

After the release of COBOL, Sammet joined IBM to manage the Boston Advanced Programming Center. At IBM, she proposed and developed FORMAC: the Formula Manipulation Compiler, an extension of Fortran that allowed for advanced mathematics beyond what Fortran could do. Fortran, the IBM Mathematical Formula Translating System, was a scientific programming language developed by IBM in the 1950s under John Backus as an alternative to assembly language. Fortran had introduced the first optimizing compiler in order to keep the execution time-efficient.

Sammet's programming work continued at IBM, and she became one of the most prominent programmers, writing a groundbreaking history and overview of programming languages in 1969. She pioneered work in natural language (language speakers have natural facility with, as opposed to the highly symbolic language of a mathematical formula) in mathematics programming, and she was made the programming technology planning manager for IBM's Federal Systems Division in 1968, serving until 1974. In 1979, IBM made her software technology manager, and she oversaw work on IBM's Ada. Ada is an object-oriented high-level computer programming language, largely extended from Pascal, named for Ada Lovelace, who assited Charles Babbage in the nineteenth century and is considered the first computer programmer.

Sammet was a member of the Association for Computing Machinery (ACM), the largest and most prestigious computing society, which is organized into a number of special interest groups (SIGs), where most of its activity transpires. Many of the SIGs have become famous or influential in themselves, in their respective subfields. Sammet chaired SIGPLAN, the ACM Special Interest Group for Programming Languages, which today holds numerous programming conferences. She also founded SIGSAM, the Special Interest Group on Symbolic and Algebraic Manipulation. From 1974 to 1976, she was ACM's first woman president. At other times held the positions of vice president, editor in chief of *ACM Computing Reviews* and *The ACM Guide to Computing Literature*, and, in 1978, chair of the first SIGPLAN History of Programming Languages Conference.

In 1994, Sammet was made a Fellow of the ACM. She also was made a Fellow of the Computer History Museum in 2001. SIGPLAN awarded her its Distinguished Service Award in 1997. The Computer Society of the Institute of Electrical and Electronics Engineers (IEEE) bestowed the Computer Pioneer Award on her in 2009.

PERSONAL LIFE

In 1956–58, at Adelphi College, she taught one of the first graduate programming courses in the United States. Today she is retired.

Bill Kte'pi

FURTHER READING

Ensmerger, Nathan L. *The Computer Boys Take Over: Computers, Programmers, and the Politics of Technical Expertise.* Cambridge: MIT, 2010. Print. A history of software development from a sociological and political context.

Lohr, Steve. *Go To: The Story of the Math Majors, Bridge Players, Engineers, Chess Wizards, Maverick Scientists, and Iconoclasts; The Programmers Who Created the Software Revolution.* New York: Basic, 2001. Print. A behind-the-scenes history of the computer industry, focusing on advances in software and programming in Sammet's era.

Sammet, Jean. *Programming Languages: History and Fundamentals.* Englewood Cliffs: Prentice-Hall, 1969. Print. Sammet's nontechnical introduction to programming languages in the early days of computer programming.

Stanley, Autumn. *Mothers and Daughters of Invention: Notes for a Revised History of Technology.* Newark: Rutgers UP, 1995. Print. A major work on the role of women in the history of technology and the overlooked contributions of Sammet and others.

L<small>UCY</small> S<small>ANDERS</small>

Cofounder and CEO of the National Center for Women and Information Technology and Bell Laboratories Fellow

Born: April 4, 1954; Indianapolis, Indiana
Died: -
Primary Field: Internet
Specialty: Ethics and policy
Primary Company/Organization: National Center for Women and Information Technology

INTRODUCTION

Lucy Sanders is cofounder and chief executive officer (CEO) of the National Center for Women and Information Technology, a consortium of more than three hundred corporations, universities, and nonprofits that work to increase the participation of girls and women in computing and information technology. Sanders also serves as executive in residence for the Alliance for Technology, Learning, and Society at the University of Colorado at Boulder, a campuswide interdisciplinary initiative. She worked at AT&T Bell Laboratories (Bell Labs), Lucent Bell Labs, and Avaya Labs for two decades and is a Bell Labs Fellow, the highest technical accomplishment bestowed by that prestigious organization. Sanders holds several patents in the area of communications technology.

EARLY LIFE

Born Lucinda McWilliams in Indianapolis, Indiana, on April 4, 1954, Sanders is the youngest of the three daughters of Bill and Doris McWilliams. Her father was a department chief at Western Electric; her mother, a politician, served on the Caddo Parish Police Jury and was president of the Louisiana League of Women Voters. The McWilliams family moved to New Jersey when Sanders was six. A few years later they moved to Shreveport, Louisiana, where Sanders grew up. It was while she was a student at Captain Shreve High School that Sanders was introduced to computer programming by her advanced math teacher, Sandra McCalla. Sanders learned how to program in the Fortran and BASIC computing languages, knowledge that provided a base for her focus in college and beyond.

After graduating from high school, Sanders attended Colorado State University for one year before transferring to Louisiana State University. Majoring in computer science, she was one of only a few women to enter this field at the time. A diligent student, Sanders graduated summa cum laude and won the President's Medal and Distinguished Achievement Award. She was also a member of the Kappa Alpha Theta sorority. Degree in hand, she and the man she would later marry, Bruce

Lucy Sanders.

Sanders, moved to Boulder, Colorado. She enrolled at the University of Colorado as a graduate student in computer science, earning a master of science degree in 1978. While still a graduate student, she also worked at AT&T Bell Labs as a member of the technical staff. Her oldest sister, Mary, is also a computer scientist; her other sister, Marjorie, is a lawyer.

LIFE'S WORK

Sanders remained at Bell Labs for seventeen years. She became research and development manager in 1982 and served as research and development director from January 1995 to August 1996 when she assumed the position of chief technology officer (CTO). As CTO, she was in charge of more than six hundred engineers and managed an annual budget of $110 million. In 1996, her work on leading-edge software architectures for telecommunications—including an operating system called Oryx/Pecos that helped pave the way for the use of Voice over Internet Protocol (VoIP) in enterprise telephony systems—earned her a Bell Labs Fellow Award, the highest recognition for technical achievement within the company. Sanders holds several communications technology patents.

In May 1999, when the communications and call center businesses left Lucent to form Avaya, Inc., Sanders left Lucent Bell Labs to become vice president of research and development and CTO for Avaya, CRM Solutions, and Avaya Labs, where she continued to work in systems-level software and solutions. She remained in this position until August 2001. She accepted the position of executive in residence at the Alliance for Technology, Learning, and Society (ATLAS) at the University of Colorado at Boulder in September 2001. ATLAS is an interdisciplinary program that combines liberal arts and technology to prepare students for careers in the networked information age.

Concerned by the underrepresentation of women among computer science graduates and in the professional fields of information technology and computing, Sanders agreed to cofound and serve as founding CEO of the National Center for Women and Information Technology (NCWIT). In May 2004, the National Science Foundation (NSF) announced that it had awarded $3.25 to establish NCWIT, a collaborative effort among universities, industry, government, and nonprofits led by the University of Colorado at Boulder and the Anita Borg Institute for Women and Technology. The award, spread over a four-year period, was the largest education and workforce award ever made by NSF's

Affiliation: National Center for Women and Information Technology

The National Center for Women and Information Technology (NCWIT) was created in 2004 in response to the shrinking numbers of women in information technology. Founded by Lucy Sanders, a Bell Labs Fellow, with funding by the National Science Foundation and several corporations—including Microsoft, Bank of America, and Avaya—NCWIT has the ultimate goal of achieving parity for women in the professional information technology workforce, in both academia and industry, within twenty years.

NCWIT consists of a broad national consortium of academic institutions, government agencies, corporations, and nonprofits. It is led by the University of Colorado at Boulder and the Anita Borg Institute for Women and Technology and is organized into alliances. The K–12 Alliance works to improve the image of computing and the teaching of foundational computing skills at the primary, elementary, and secondary levels. The Academic Alliance brings together colleges and universities to implement change in higher education. The Workforce Alliance leads NCWIT's efforts in corporate organizational reform. The Entrepreneurial Alliance works with young companies to establish diversity at the start. The Affinity Group Alliance unites and communicates with women in technology through professional groups. The Social Science Advisory Board provides NCWIT alliances with evaluation and research foundations.

In the years since its founding, NCWIT has become a trusted source of statistical information concerning women entering and advancing in information technology, from the attitudes and skills of schoolgirls to the research centers and boardrooms of academia and corporate America. NCWIT also has an increasing presence in Washington, D.C.

Computer and Information Science and Engineering (CISE) directorate. Additional start-up funds were provided by Avaya, Microsoft, Pfizer, Bank of America, Intel, Hewlett-Packard, the Kauffman Foundation, and Qualcomm.

On May 18, 2004, with Sanders at the helm, NCWIT was launched. The center committed to identifying the research and interventions that could best attract and retain women in information technology, increase the effectiveness of existing efforts, and build a united, national platform for progress. The goal was to achieve parity for women in the professional information technology (IT) workforce, in both academia and industry, with measurable, tangible progress achieved within twenty years. Sanders declared that the NCWIT would "build a national movement for change." Over the next six years, she led the fund-raising that resulted in corporate contributions of $24 million.

By 2012, the consortium collaborating to achieve the twenty-year goal of NCWIT included almost three hundred academic institutions, government agencies, corporations, and nonprofits. The consortium, organized into alliances, allows the center to serve as a learning community that works toward reform across the full education and career spectrum. The K–12 Alliance strives to improve the image of computing and the teaching of foundational computing skills. The Academic Alliance brings together a diverse range of colleges and universities to implement institutional change in higher education. Founding members of the Academic Alliance include Brown University, Carnegie Mellon University, Columbia University, Florida State University, Indiana University, Smith College, Spelman College, Stanford University, Texas A&M University, the University of California at San Diego, the University of Maryland–Baltimore County, the University of Texas–El Paso, the University of Washington, and the University of Wisconsin. The Workforce Alliance leads NCWIT's efforts in corporate organizational reform. Industry Alliance founding members include Avaya, Bank of America, Hewlett-Packard, IBM, Intel, Microsoft, and Sun. The Entrepreneurial Alliance works with young companies to establish diversity at the start. The Affinity Group Alliance unites and communicates with technical women through professional groups. The Social Science Advisory Board provides NCWIT alliances with evaluation and research foundations.

Sanders announced in April 2011 that the NCWIT Entrepreneurial Alliance was joining President Barack Obama's Startup America Initiative. The center pledged to help high-tech start-ups capitalize on the increased innovation and business benefits of gender diversity in addition to promoting the achievements of women entrepreneurs. In her statement announcing NCWIT's participation, Sanders promised that the center would work with Startup America at the national level to ensure that technical start-ups received the resources they need to recruit, retain, and advance women in technology.

PERSONAL LIFE

Sanders lives in Boulder, Colorado, with her husband, Bruce, an emeritus faculty member in computer science at the University of Colorado. The couple have two children. Zack is an Internet security specialist with his own company and a poker guru. Casey graduated from the University of Colorado with a degree in marketing in 2012; he has worked in sports information. When she is not working, Sanders enjoys tending to her vegetable garden and traveling the world. She is also an enthusiastic runner with a particular fondness for Boulder's numerous walking trails.

Sanders has served on several high-tech start-up and nonprofit boards, and she frequently advises young technology companies. She has served on the board of trustees of the Mathematical Sciences Research Institute at the University of California, Berkeley, as well as on the Information Technology Research and Development Ecosystem Commission for the National Academies. In 2004, Sanders received the Distinguished Alumni Award from the Department of Engineering at the University of Colorado. In 2007, she was inducted into the Women in Technology International Hall of Fame. In 2011, the U.S. secretary of commerce appointed her to serve on the Department of Commerce's Innovation Advisory Board. In 2012, the Computing Research Association awarded the 2012 A. Nico Habermann Award to Sanders, along with Robert Schnabel (dean at the School of Informatics, Indiana University) and Telle Whitney (CEO and president of the Anita Borg Institute for Women and Technology), for their joint efforts to establish and sustain the NCWIT and its dedication to encouraging greater participation of women in the development of computing technology.

Wylene Rholetter

FURTHER READING

"Computer Science Awards." *Communications of the ACM* May 2012: 16. Print. Announces the 2012 inductees into the National Investors Hall of Fame and the winners of the 2012 Computing Research Association A. Nico Habermann Award: Sanders, Robert Schnabel, and Telle Whitney.

"Improving Gender Composition in Computing." *Communications of the ACM* 55.4 (2012): 29–31. Print. The article looks at the Pacesetters program of National Center for Women and Information Technology. The purpose of the program is to increase the number of women in computing careers in the United States by one thousand "Net New Women" by 2012.

"Lucy Sanders." *Computerworld* 27 Feb. 2006: 45. Print. The article provides information about collaboration between the National Center for Women and Information Technology and Cisco, Systems to increase awareness of education and career opportunities for girls and women in science, technology, math, and engineering through a comprehensive digital library. One color photograph.

Margolis, Jane, et al. *Stuck in the Shallow End: Education, Race, and Computing.* Cambridge: MIT, 2008. Print. Includes a description of a 2006 conference in Washington, D.C., sponsored by the National Center for Women and Information Technology, which brought together representatives from government, all levels of computer science education, the computer industry, and national organizations that share a commitment to broadening participation in computing.

Sanders, Lucy. "A Grand Challenge: Inspiring Women to Embrace IT Careers." *ColoradoBiz* Sept. 2007: 13. Print. Refers to the NCWIT's interview with Donna Auguste, an entrepreneur who earned four patents for her work on the Apple Newton, as an example of what a woman inspired to enter information technology can accomplish. The article also cites NCWIT research that found that mixed-gender teams produced the most frequently cited patents; citation rates were 26 percent to 42 percent higher than the norm. Argues for the need to inspire more women to choose computing careers.

LINDA S. SANFORD

Senior vice president, Enterprise Transformation, IBM

Born: 1953; Laurel, New York
Died: -
Primary Field: Business and commerce

Specialty: Management, executives, and investors
Primary Company/Organization: IBM

INTRODUCTION

Linda Szabat Sanford is a senior vice president at IBM, making her one of the highest-ranking women in the company. She has spent her entire professional career at IBM and led the company's internal transformation to becoming a globally integrated enterprise organized around the on-demand principle. As an extremely visible and successful woman achieving success at the highest levels of technology and business management, she has received many honors and serves on numerous boards, including the board of directors of the Partnership for New York City, a membership organization of top corporate leadership dedicated to enhancing the city's position as a center of finance, commerce, and innovation.

EARLY LIFE

Linda Sanford grew up the oldest of five girls on her family's potato farm on New York's Long Island. She credits her early experience growing and marketing produce with fostering her interest in math and science, as well as her taste for hard work. Sanford has said that her daily chores and the example set by her parents helped her acquire the self-discipline and problem-solving skills on which she has relied throughout her career. All five girls did well in science and mathematics and later chose to pursue those fields; Sanford says that her parents encouraged their children to pursue higher education. Initially she intended to teach mathematics after obtaining her degree, but after reading a book on the application of operations research in the business world, she knew that field would be a great fit for her background. Sanford earned her bachelor's degree in mathematics from St. John's University in Queens, New York City, and in 1975 a master's in operations research from Rensselaer Polytechnic Institute.

LIFE'S WORK

Linda S. Sanford began working for IBM in 1975 as an engineer in the typewriter division. The job was in Lexington, Kentucky, where she did simulation modeling of the work performed by typists and used that information to develop new features for IBM typewriters. After about one year, she moved on to her next position, working in development for copiers and printers, at the company branch in Boulder, Colorado. She remained in Boulder for ten years before moving to New York, where she became an executive assistant to company chairman John Akers.

In 1998, Sanford became chief of IBM's sales force, a change from her previous work in product development, and also a groundbreaking role because sales was then considered primarily a male domain. The sales force at that time generated about 70 percent of IBM's annual revenue and included about seventeen thousand employees. In 2000, she became a Senior vice president of "enterprise transformation," and in January 2003 became senior vice president of "enterprise on-demand transformation"; in the latter position, she led the effort to change the way the company was organized, moving from a vertical structure to one connected horizontally and to a customer-driven company that can respond quickly to changes in consumer demand. In 2006, Sanford, along with entrepreneur Dave Taylor, coauthored *Let Go to Grow: Escaping the Commodity Trap*, a book detailing IBM's transformation to an on-demand culture with suggestions for how other businesses could help their companies adjust to the modern world of commerce.

Sanford described IBM's transition to an on-demand organization as a gradual process involving all aspects of the company's functioning; the transformation was estimated to require ten years and cost about $10 billion. She noted that the transformation would

Linda S. Sanford.

Affiliation: IBM

International Business Machines, or IBM, is a multinational computer manufacturer and technology company with more than 350,000 employees and revenues of $91.4 billion in 2008. IBM has been a pioneer in the development and manufacture of computers, beginning with simpler tabulating machines; in fact, the origins of IBM lie in the merger of several companies that performed various types of tabulation activities. The company that became IBM was incorporated in 1911 in New York State as the Computing Tabulating Recording (CTR) company. One of the companies merged to form CTR was the Tabulating Machine Company, which specialized in data-processing equipment using punched cardboard cards, a process that remained in use into the middle of the twentieth century; one of its initial breakthroughs was the use of punched-card technology during the tabulation of the 1890 U.S. census. In 1944, IBM developed its first computer, the Mark I, and in 1948 it introduced a digital calculating machine, the IBM 604 Electronic Calculating Punch. In 1952, IBM introduced the first large computer using vacuum tubes, the IBM 701, and by the end of the decade IBM was producing computers based on transistors, then a new technology developed at Bell Laboratories after World War II. IBM produced other types of office equipment as well; in 1961, for instance, it introduced the Selectric typewriter and its ball-shaped, replaceable "element" on which embossed metal type fonts were inscribed and which spun to produce the correct letter or symbol; Selectrics became popular because they allowed users to produce text with different alphabets (such as Hebrew) and fonts using the same typewriter by switching out the type elements. In 1964, an improved model, the IBM Magnetic Tape Selectric Typewriter, was introduced; it recorded and stored the text typed, allowing a typist to go back later and make changes or corrections, and was the forerunner of modern word-processing systems. In the late 1960s and 1970s, similar "word processors" (enhanced typewriters, essentially) at different price points would hit the market and prime it for the oncoming personal computer (PC) revolution.

In 1964, IBM 360 series computers were introduced, and soon their 8-bit "byte" became standard in the industry. In 1981, IBM introduced the PC; it had a floppy disk drive and 16 kilobytes of memory, and it used an Intel processor chip and the DOS operating system, the latter developed by Microsoft. In 1986, IBM demonstrated an experimental computer system, intended for office use, to transcribe human speech. In the 1980s and the 1990s, IBM had to adapt to several changes in the computer market, including the widespread use of personal computers linked into networks (rather than mainframes accessed through terminals), and the shift from integrated systems to piece-part technologies. The company faced serious financial losses in these years, with a $8 billion in net losses in 1993 alone. Sanford played a key role in restructuring the company to adapt to the new realities of the marketplace.

The success of the IBM computer Deep Blue, which defeated then-world champion Garry Kasparov in a series of six chess matches, helped reestablish the company's image, particularly given the practical applications for the breakthroughs in processing speed offered by the new computer. In 2000, IBM introduced the IBM eServer series, Unix servers using open standards to meet the expanding needs of e-businesses. Also in 2000, IBM was awarded the U.S. National Medal of Technology for its work in storage technology. In 2003, IBM sold the 20 millionth ThinkPad, a laptop computer introduced in 1992, and in 2004 introduced a ThinkPad with a fingerprint reader (for security purposes, to identify a user). In 2005, IBM sold its personal computer division to Lenovo and returned its focus to business solutions.

save IBM money in terms of greater productivity and efficiency and said that the company saved about $5.6 billion in one year alone (2002) through implementation of an integrated supply chain system. She also noted that the on-demand structure was intended to serve IBM's customers better, in particular that increased collaboration within the company would help to produce a more integrated line of products that could deliver the service a customer required without the customer's having to be particularly knowledgeable about computer and technology or even about the specific IBM products—customers wanted solutions, and they wanted IBM to provide them with a system so the customer could concentrate on their core business.

While at IBM, Sanford proved that she could function in both technical and sales environments. She was also an active participant in IBM's extensive mentoring program and notes that her career benefited from her work with powerful mentors when she was coming up in the company. Sanford was an executive assistant for former IBM president Jack Kuehler early in her career and credits him with encouraging her to develop her skills. She also worked with senior vice president Nick Donofrio and former chief executive officer Louis V. Gerstner Jr., both of whom she credits with helping develop her career. She also served as a mentor to younger employees within the company, including Martha Morris, Charles Lickel, and Joan Buzzallino. Sanford has been a strong proponent of encouraging girls and women to study mathematics and pursue technical professions.

Sanford has received many honors for her work at IBM. She is a member of the National Academy of Engineering and a member of the Women in Technology International Hall of Fame. *Fortune* magazine named her one of the 50 Most Influential Women in Business, *Working Woman* magazine named her one of the 10 Most Influential Women in Technology, *Pink* magazine named her one of the Top 15 Women in Business, and *Information Week* magazine named her one of the Top Ten Iinovators in the technology industry. Sanford serves on the board of trustees for the State University of New York and the boards of directors for Rensselaer Polytechnic Institute, St. John's University, and the Partnership for New York City. She was named a nonexecutive member of the supervisory board of Reed Elsevier NV in July 2012.

PERSONAL LIFE

Sanford lives in Chappaqua, New York. She is divorced from James L. Sanford, a retired IBM engineer; they have two adult children, Cathi and William. When her children were younger, Sanford coached basketball and organized games. Today she mentors young women who seek careers in science and mathematics.

Sarah Boslaugh

FURTHER READING

Ensher, Ellen A., and Susan Elaine Murphy. *Power Mentoring: How Successful Mentors and Protégés Get the Most Out of Their Relationships*. Hoboken: Jossey-Bass, 2005. Print. A practical guide to forming successful mentoring relationships, based on interviews with fifty U.S. business and industry leaders, primarily in the fields of technology, government, and entertainment; Sanford is included both as a protégé and as a mentor. Includes a summary of prior research on mentoring, detailed descriptions of how the information was gathered, and analyzed for this book, and charts showing the relationships among the mentors and mentees.

Mohr, Jakki J., Sanjit Sengupta, and Stanley Slater. *Marketing of High-Technology Products and Innovations*. 2nd ed. Upper Saddle River: Pearson Education, 2009. Print. A handbook to marketing high-tech products and to creative solutions to problems such as soaring fuel costs, climate change, the impact of manufacturing on the local and global ecology, and the political situation in different parts of the world. Sanford is cited as an example of a business leader who fosters a culture of innovation.

Sanford, Linda S., and Dave Taylor. *Let Go to Grow: Escaping the Commodity Trap*. Upper Saddle River: Pearson, 2006. Print. Written for business executives interested in learning about IBM's on-demand strategy and ways they can transform their own business operations to meet the expectations of the contemporary marketplace. Sanford's coauthor is an entrepreneur who has created and sold four Internet start-ups.

Schermerhorn, John R. Jr. *Exploring Management*. 2nd ed. Hoboken: Wiley, 2010. Print. A textbook for university students of business, covering managers and the management process, techniques of planning and control, different types of organization, leadership styles, and issues of diversity, globalization, and entrepreneurship. Sanford's experiences with IBM are used as an example of a management style based on control and measurement.

Taft, Darryl K. "Reinventing a Company." *eWeek* 21.13 (2004): 20. Print. Interview with Sanford, then a senior vice president of enterprise on-demand transformation and information technology at IBM, concerning IBM's efforts to adjust to the on-demand approach to business. In the interview, Sanford stresses the broad changes then taking place in IBM's internal culture, as well as her belief that ultimately the company will be stronger and will better serve their customers through the on-demand structure.

MICHAEL SAYLOR

Cofounder of MicroStrategy

Born: February 4, 1965; Lincoln, Nebraska
Died: -
Primary Field: Computer science
Specialty: Computer software
Primary Company/Organization: MicroStrategy

INTRODUCTION

Michael Saylor was one of the key innovators who developed the system of establishing relational databases through decision support systems (DSS). This allowed him to combine information from a large number of separate databases, often held by the same company, and trace connections among them, which, in turn, could be used by executives at that company to monitor existing sales, identify successes or failures related to promotions and advertising campaigns, and then predict the possibility of improving sales through the use of the same or different strategies.

EARLY LIFE

Michael J. Saylor was born on February 4, 1965, in Lincoln, Nebraska. His father was a noncommissioned officer in the U.S. Air Force, rising to the rank of sergeant. Much of Saylor's childhood was spent moving with his family when father was transferred from one base to another. Saylor therefore grew up in several locations in the United States, as well as Japan and New Zealand. He went to high school at Fairborn, Ohio, when his father was posted to the Wright-Patterson Air Force Base in Dayton.

The influence of his father was very important to Saylor, who once told an interviewer that he could not remember a single time when his father spoke an untruth or even a half truth. He attributes his moral character to his father and his charisma to his mother. As a young boy, he also was influenced by the space race between the Soviet Union and the United States, which the latter was winning. His favorite book was Robert Heinlein's *Have Space Suit—Will Travel* (1958), which was about a high school student, Kip, who wins a space suit in a writing competition and is then abducted and taken to the Moon. He escapes but is recaptured and taken to Pluto and must then travel out of the solar system in order to find a way of saving the Earth from a monster called Wormface. The boy in the story manages to return to the Earth, where he is rewarded with a full scholarship to the Massachusetts Institute of Technology (MIT).

The teenage Saylor had already set his sights on attending MIT with his tuition fees paid entirely by a scholarship from the Air Force Reserve Officers' Training Corps (ROTC). He went to MIT's Sloan School of Management and completed his thesis on creating a mathematical model for Niccolò Machiavelli's *Discourses*, in which he argued that war, famine, and natural disasters have different effects on the various systems of government that have operated in the world. He completed a double degree in aeronautics and astronautics, graduating with honors.

Although he had planned to go into the U.S. Air Force, and had been accepted to a jet-pilot program, a routine medical examination revealed that he had a benign heart murmur, so he was not allowed to train. Placed in the reserves, he no longer had a career in the Air Force.

LIFE'S WORK

Always interested in computing, Saylor became a systems engineer and went to work for Federal Group, a

Michael Saylor.

management consulting firm. In New York he helped to design computer simulation models. Because his employer wanted him to sign an agreement not to work for competing companies, he left and started working for the chemical division of E. I. du Pont de Nemours and Company in Wilmington, Delaware. He offered to build a global computer model for the titanium sector of Du Pont's business, and he predicted the decline in demand for some of Du Pont's products. He was paid $250,000 and used the money to establish the company MicroStrategy, which started operations in 1989.

Initially, as with many new companies, the first years involved the owner and a small number of employees working for long hours on their initial contracts. The first major one was with McDonald's, which wanted to have a system by which they would monitor the successes or failures of their promotional campaigns. This project earned MicroStrategy some $10 million. The McDonald's contract led Saylor to devise a system called relational online analytical processing (ROLAP), which allowed for the integration of information drawn from a large number of separate databases, and by merging them, allow the answering of specific questions easily. This was later developed into what became known as decision support system (DSS), whereby company executives could locate data on particular products, marketing campaigns, sales offers, and advertising.

As the company grew, Saylor had two main business partners, both of whom he had met at MIT. Sanjeev "Sanju" Bansal, who had cofounded MicroStrategy, had a master's degree in computer science and lived in Burke, Virginia; Thomas Spahr had been a consultant with Booz Allen and Hamilton in Bethesda, Maryland. They decided to move from Wilmington to Tyson's Corner, Virginia. Work was so intense that for the first three months Saylor slept on a couch at a friend's house. He then managed to buy a house but again was working so hard with MicroStrategy that it was three years before he furnished it.

In 1995, MicroStrategy was the ninth-largest creator of DSS software in the United States. In the following year, Saylor was named the KPMG Washington High-Tech Entrepreneur of the Year. The company expanded and moved again, this time to Vienna, Virginia. Two years later, in June 1998, MicroStrategy was transformed into a public company. It was a difficult process and Saylor worked hard, apparently going through as many as five hundred drafts of prospectuses. What he wanted to do was to raise capital for the company and ensure that he and the ten other founding executives of MicroStrategy kept control of the company after it went

Affiliation: MicroStrategy

Established in 1989 by three friends who met at the Massachusetts Institute of Technology (MIT), MicroStrategy found its driving force in Michael Saylor, who, along with Sanju Bansal, devised a system of relating business information from different parts of the same business to provide companies with the details they need to make more effective strategic business decisions.

The company has expanded into all forms of business intelligence, delivering this information via the Internet and a wide variety of mobile devices. The first major customer of MicroStrategy was McDonald's, and its current and past customers include eBay, Facebook, and LinkedIn.

public. The method eventually settled upon was to have a voting system whereby the eleven executives had ten votes for every share they owned and new stockholders would get only one vote per share.

When MicroStrategy made its debut as a public company, Saylor went from being in debt by about $11 million to becoming very wealthy. The shares' value soared in a year from $7 per share to $333 (although they later fell to $248). With Saylor initially owning some 44 million shares, it was not long before he was a billionaire.

The company continued to flourish. A growing number of large corporations began to see the importance of DSS software, which enabled many of them to save large sums of money and provide a better focus for their advertising budgets. Department stores were able to analyze which items were selling more than others and were able to compare sales by city, time of year, and particular advertising or promotional campaigns.

In addition to marketing his software to private companies, Saylor was keen to get the government to use his technology. He knew that it would enable local authorities to predict the use of new roads and identify crime "hot spots," for example. Although some saw the software as somewhat Orwellian, providing the government a Big Brother ability to observe what people are doing through the use of telescreens, MicroStrategy saw their relational databases as allowing authorities to predict places when and where crimes were most likely to occur, thus allowing police and other law enforcement authorities to be more alert at specific times and places. Other innovations by Saylor and MicroStrategy have been in the area of business intelligence, computer and wireless security, and speech automation. Altogether Saylor has registered thirty patents.

MicroStrategy also boasted a strong company ethic. The annual turnover of staff was about 10 percent, much lower than in many other computer companies. Saylor ensured that all staff were treated well, and indeed during the winter, the company's employees joined him on a Caribbean cruise.

In 2000, the company faced problems in the wake of an investigation by the U.S. Securities and Exchange Commission (SEC). The SEC was looking into charges that company earnings were not as high as had been claimed and that MicroStrategy had actually suffered a loss in 1999. The company stock fell from $226 to $86 and then reached $4 before recovering. By August 2012, MicroStrategy's per-share value was $127.

Saylor remains the chairman of MicroStrategy's board of directors, its chief executive officer, and its president. He has written a book, *The Mobile Wave: How Mobile Intelligence Will Change Everything*, which was published in 2012 and reached seventh place on *The New York Times* nonfiction best-sellers list.

PERSONAL LIFE

Saylor was single as of 2012. Bansal famously told *Washington Post* correspondent Jeff Glasser that Saylor had decided that "women are an incredible time sink.… Work is more enjoyable for him in that it is a growing experience. Dating's a fluff experience for him."

Having been influenced not only by his parents, whom he continues to credit for inspiring him, but also by science-fiction writer Robert Heinlein as a teenager, Saylor remains interested in U.S. history and has long been fascinated by the career of Abraham Lincoln as well as the British wartime prime minister Sir Winston Churchill. Other interests include the lives of Thomas Edison and Julius Caesar. He enjoys architecture and remains a voracious reader of military history, the

Romans, and a range of other subjects. He has long credited his broad interests in general knowledge for helping him in his business work by often providing answers to some of the problems he has faced. In his speeches to new employees, he is reported to have spoken on one occasion for eight hours.

Saylor has established the Saylor Foundation and has contributed to a number of charities, including the Georgetown University Medical Center's Lombardi Comprehensive Cancer Center; Courage for Kids; and Fight for Children. In 2000, he pledged $100 million to establish a free Internet university.

Justin Corfield

FURTHER READING

Bonner, William, Addison Wiggin, and Kate Incontrera. *Financial Reckoning Day Fallout: Surviving Today's Global Depression*. Hoboken: Wiley, 2008. Print. A critical coverage of Saylor and MicroStrategy.

Hiraoka, Leslie S. *Underwriting the Internet: How Technical Advances, Financial Engineering and Entrepreneurial Genius Are Building the Information Highway*. Armonk: M. E. Sharpe, 2005. Print. A critical approach of MicroStrategy published at a time when the company was facing major problems.

"Michael Saylor." *Current Biography Yearbook, 2000.* New York: H. W. Wilson, 2000. 493–96. Print. A detailed biographical article from a well-regarded reference source.

Saylor, Michael. *The Mobile Wave: How Mobile Intelligence Will Change Everything*. New York: Perseus, 2012. Print. Saylor's account of his belief that mobile technology will change the lives of everybody in the world.

"Technology Billionaire Pledges 100 Million for Free Internet University." *CNN Tech* 22 Mar. 2000: n. pag. Web. 20 Aug. 2012. An overview of Saylor's Internet university plan.

ERIC SCHMIDT

Former executive chairman and CEO of Google

Born: April 27, 1955; Washington, D.C.
Died: -
Primary Field: Computer science
Specialty: Computer software
Primary Company/Organization: Google

INTRODUCTION

Former chief executive of Google from 2001 to 2011, Eric Schmidt continues to serve as its executive chairman. He has a long history in the computer industry, including work at think tanks Bell Laboratories and

Xerox Palo Alto Research Center (PARC) and a long stint at Sun Microsystems, where he was its first software manager.

Early Life

Eric Emerson Schmidt was born on April 27, 1955, in Washington, D.C. He attended Yorktown High School in Arlington, Virginia, before earning his bachelor of science degree in electrical engineering from Princeton University (1976) and his master of science degree at the University of California, Berkeley (1979). His thesis work was on the design and implementation of a campus computer network. He completed his education with a Ph.D., also from Berkeley, in electrical engineering and computer science.

While at Princeton, Schmidt developed the Lex program with Mike Lesk of Bell Labs. A Unix program that generates lexical analyzers, or lexers, Lex became the standard Unix lexical analyzer. Open source versions are now distributed as part of open source Unix variants such as Bell Labs' Plan 9 from Bell Labs. Lex is usually used with a parser generator; Yacc (which stands for "yet another compiler compiler") was the one commonly in use on Unix systems when Schmidt and Lesk developed Lex.

Eric Schmidt.

Life's Work

Schmidt worked for PARC's Computer Science Lab, as well as taking a research position with Bell Labs, before being hired by Sun Microsystems, a Silicon Valley computer start-up focused mainly on workstations at the time, in 1983. He was its first software manager and eventually became the president of Sun Technology Enterprises. One of the products developed at Sun during Schmidt's time was the Java platform and programming language, originally intended to run web applets but later used mainly server-side. Java has had an enormous impact on the internet, but one of the reasons for Sun's eventual fall and buyout by Oracle (after Schmidt had left) was its failure to monetize the product.

After leaving Sun in 1997, Schmidt became chief executive officer (CEO) of the software company Novell. Based in Provo, Utah, Novell had been founded as a hardware manufacturer in 1979 and in the 1980s had become prosperous selling its network operating system, ShareNet, the popularity of which was boosted by Novell's selling its Ethernet cards as a loss leader. In the 1990s, Novell had transitioned into software products that worked with the Internet as well as local-area networks (office LANs), and Schmidt oversaw much of that transition. The last major product introduced during Schmidt's time was DirXML, which synchronized data across various systems. It later became the core of Novell's product line. Schmidt left Novell in 2001 after it acquired Cambridge Technology Partners (CTP), an acquisition engineered by Jack Messman, founding board member of Novell and CTP's CEO.

Schmidt was recruited by Google and hired in 2001. He became the chairman of the board of directors in March and the CEO in August. Schmidt ran the company jointly with founders Larry Page and Sergey Brin, focusing mainly on the management of vice presidents and subdivisions. During the ten years Schmidt served as Google's CEO, the company saw vast expansion from one still largely focused on the search engine to one that seemed to offer a service or product for every method of interacting with the Internet (including services, such as Google Docs, that involved the Internet in applications that had previously been offline)—while still offering nearly everything for free and depending on advertising for 99 percent of the company's revenue. Along the way, the company acquired many start-ups and products that either rivaled its own or could be rebranded as part of the Google line.

From 2004 to 2010, Schmidt and the Google founders Brin and Page were paid a base annual salary of $1.

Affiliation: Google

The search engine and Internet services company Google was founded in 1998 by Stanford University students Larry Page and Sergey Brin. Initially, the company was concerned with building a better search engine, using the technology PageRank, which calculated the value of potential search results according to their perceived relevance and presented them accordingly. This was a step forward from raw results, especially as the Internet grew so quickly, and required less work than curated categories such as those offered by rival search engine Yahoo! on its front page. Google's search engine was originally nicknamed BackRub, because it checked backlinks in estimating relevance, but was eventually named Google in reference to the number googol (1 {multi} 10^{100}, or 1 followed by 100 zeros).

Funding for Google came from Andy Bechtolsheim, a Sun Microsystems cofounder (and fellow Stanford alumnus). An initial public offering eventually came in 2004, with many Google employees becoming overnight millionaires, thanks to their stock options.

Since 2001, Google has acquired numerous other companies and has long since ceased to be only a search engine company. Many of the sites Google has purchased have been rebranded or folded into Google services. The GrandCentral voice-mail service became Google Voice, for instance. Major Google products beyond the search page include Google's e-mail service GMail, the Facebook competitor Google+, Google Earth, Blogger and Feedburner, the Google Drive backup service, You-Tube, and specialized search engines such as Google Scholar, Google Books, Google Patent Search, Google Image Search, and Google Shopping. Google has also introduced Google Chrome, its web browser for Windows, Linux, and Mac OS X, as well as Android, a mobile device operating system used for smart phones, some tablets, and Amazon's Kindle products. The Google Chrome OS is a Linux-based operating system using web applications, which is used to power the Chromebook and Chromebox computers, both of which are designed to power up and connect to the Internet in mere seconds.

Google is one of several Internet companies to be investigated by the Federal Trade Commission (FTC) over privacy violations. In 2011, following an investigation of the disastrous launch of the Google Buzz product—which lacked a reasonable standard of transparency and broadcast many people's contacts without their permission—the FTC put the company on a twenty-year probation program, requiring the company to take extra steps to preserve consumer privacy during that time or face stiffer than average penalties. It was the first time the FTC had used such a measure, which it soon applied to Facebook in response to a similar violation. Former CEO and current executive chairman Eric Schmidt has publicly downplayed privacy concerns, famously saying, "If you have nothing to hide, you have nothing to fear." Most, 99 percent, of Google's revenue comes from advertising.

Most of Schmidt's wealth—in 2011, *Fortune* listed him as the 136th richest person in the world—comes from his stock options, while his Google compensation was principally for airplane charters and security. In 2011, he stepped down as CEO (with a departing bonus of $100 million) but continued to serve as executive chairman.

Since 2008, Schmidt has been the chairman of the board of directors of the New America Foundation, a nonpartisan public policy think tank based in New York City. New America is home to the National Security Studies Program and several specific-issue programs, as well as the Open Technology Institute, which has worked on developing distributed communications networks and other initiatives.

In 2010, Schmidt cofounded Innovation Endeavors in Palo Alto, California, with Dror Berman. A venture capital company, Innovation Endeavors has funded several dozen businesses, seeking game-changing ventures while supporting a pre-idea search fund. Schmidt is also the founder of TomorrowVentures, founded in 2009, an early-stage venture capital fund with similar goals. TomorrowVentures has invested in a variety of enterprises, including wind power; the for-profit Gifts That Give e-commerce company, which generates revenue for nonprofit companies; mobile social games; and BondFactor, a municipal bond insurance company. Schmidt has also personally invested in companies such as the people-to-people lending marketplace Prosper.com; high-end art buying company Art.sy; online ad company Spongecell; ICON Aircraft; data management start-up WibiData; and DailyWorth, an online personal finance community for women.

Schmidt served on the board of directors of Apple from 2006 to 2009 but resigned because of potential conflicts of interest. He has sat on the board of trustees for Carnegie Mellon University and his alma mater, Princeton.

PERSONAL LIFE

Schmidt has been married once, to Wendy Schmidt. The couple founded the Eric Schmidt Family Foundation, a charitable foundation concerned with sustainability, especially on the island of Nantucket. After the 2010 *Deepwater Horizon* disaster, when a BP oil right exploded and dumped thousands of gallons of oil into the Gulf of Mexico, Wendy donated the prize purse ($1.4 million total, in three prizes) for the Wendy Schmidt Oil Cleanup X Challenge, offered through the X Prize Foundation, for the best solutions for cleaning up crude oil from ocean water. Schmidt was a campaign adviser for Barack Obama in the 2008 presidential campaign and was considered as a candidate for secretary of commerce in Obama's cabinet. He served on Obama's transition advisory board after the election was won and promoted the prioritizing of renewable energy investments in the proposed economic stimulus plan.

Bill Kte'pi

FURTHER READING

Edwards, Douglas. *I'm Feeling Lucky: The Confessions of Google Employee Number 59*. Boston: Mariner, 2012. Print. A memoir about working at the company.

Girard, Bernard. *The Google Way: How One Company Is Revolutionizing Management as We Know It*. San Francisco: No Starch, 2009. Print. Focuses on Google's unique management practices.

Levy, Steven. *In the Plex: How Google Thinks, Works, and Shapes Our Lives*. New York: Simon, 2011. Print. *Wired* writer Levy considers the effects of Google and its corporate culture.

Poundstone, William. *Are You Smart Enough to Work at Google?* New York: Little, Brown, 2012. Print. Uses Google as an example of a powerful company in the new economy.

CLAUDE SHANNON

Developer of information theory

Born: April 30, 1916; Petoskey, Michigan
Died: February 24, 2001; Medford, Massachusetts
Primary Field: Computer science
Specialty: Computer hardware
Primary Company/Organization: Bell Laboratories

INTRODUCTION

Claude Shannon has been called the father of information theory. Information theory quantifies information and originated in the context of signal processing and the compression, storage, and communication of data; it has since been applied to areas as diverse as quantum computing, natural language processing, and the evolution of molecular codes. A cryptographer, mathematician, and engineer, Shannon laid much of the groundwork for digital computers and circuitry while still a graduate student at the Massachusetts Institute of Technology (MIT), and he later contributed to the code-breaking efforts of the Allies during World War II.

EARLY LIFE

Claude Elwood Shannon was born on April 30, 1916, in Petroskey, Michigan. His father, who died when Claude was a teenager, was a local businessman. His mother, a second-generation German American, was a teacher who later became principal of Gaylord High School, which Claude attended. Shannon's grandfather had been a farmer and inventor who had invented a type of washing machine and numerous pieces of farm machinery. As a boy, Claude idolized Thomas Edison, who had been lionized as the Platonic ideal of the great American inventor. Young Claude was the sort of child who tinkers with everything for fun; he built a wireless telegraph system and model airplanes. He had an after-school job with Western Union, delivering messages. After graduating in 1932, he attended the University of Michigan, graduating four years later with two bachelor's degrees, in mathematics and electrical engineering.

LIFE'S WORK

After graduation, Shannon was accepted as a graduate student at MIT in Cambridge, Massachusetts. For his thesis, he combined the Boolean algebra to which he had been introduced as an undergraduate with what he had learned of circuitry at MIT by studying an analog computer designed by Vannevar Bush. In that thesis, he

Claude Shannon.

showed the electrical applications of Boolean algebra, which could be used to simplify electromechanical relays—and that electromechanical relays, in turn, could be used to solve Boolean algebraic problems. A paper distilled from his thesis was published in 1938, "A Symbolic Analysis of Relay and Switching Circuits," and he won the Alfred Nobel American Institute of American Engineers award. The thesis has been called the most important master's thesis in history: It ushered in the age of the digital computer by demonstrating that electrical switches could be made to do mathematics, the fundamental operation of all computers. This not only inspired the birth of digital computers—which had been spurred by government funding at the beginning of World War II—but also transformed the field of digital circuitry.

Bush suggested that Shannon study at the Cold Spring Harbor Laboratory, which was funded by the Carnegie Institution (of which Bush was head), and Shannon did so, completing a 1940 doctoral dissertation, through MIT, titled *An Algebra for Theoretical Genetics*. The same year, he was made a National Research Fellow at the Institute for Advanced Study in Princeton, New Jersey (home of his father's family) and worked alongside mathematician and computer scientist John von Neumann.

During the war, Shannon worked for the think tank Bell Laboratories on cryptography and fire-control systems. In the course of his cryptography work, he had several conversations with the British mathematician Alan Turing, who was also instrumental in ushering in the computer age. In September 1945, Shannon prepared a classified memorandum titled "A Mathematical Theory of Cryptography," which was declassified and published in 1949 as "Communication Theory of Secrecy Systems" in the *Bell System Technical Journal*. Cryptography had led him to communication theory, the study of the transmission of information, on which he would continue to focus throughout his career. Another critical contribution to cryptography was Shannon's proof that the one-time pad (OTP) system—a type of encryption—is unbreakable and, more significant, that any unbreakable system must share basic characteristics with the OTP system, which assigns a truly random key to each character (or bit) of plaintext; when the key is never reused for another character and the randomization is kept strictly secret, the resulting cyphertext is impossible to break. This work was published after the war, in 1949.

Fire-control systems, meanwhile, prefigured his information theory work. With Ralph Beebe Blackman and Hendrik Wade Bode, Shannon coauthored a paper presented at the close of the war, "Data Smoothing and Prediction in Fire-Control Systems," which used the analogy of "separating a signal from interfering noise" to the problem of data smoothing in fire control and provided the groundwork for work on signal processing.

In 1948, Shannon published "A Mathematical Theory of Communication," a work to which he had alluded in the work he wrote during the war but did not have time to develop. Perhaps the founding document of information theory, this paper divided communication problems into the technical, semantic, and influential, defining the basic components of communication as the information source, the transmitter, the channel, the receiver, and the destination. The article was further expanded with Warren Weaver for publication as a book the following year, with a minor change: In the intervening time, Shannon had realized the broad applicability of his work and called the book *The Mathematical Theory of Communication*. The book introduced the Shannon-Weaver model of communication, which embodies in one model most of the elements of information theory. The model has become especially popular in the social sciences.

The 1948 article introduced the data compression technique now known as Shannon-Fano coding, named

Affiliation: Bell Laboratories

Bell Laboratories (often called Bell Labs) was, in its most famous period, a research laboratory and think tank operated by AT&T and home to some of the most remarkable accomplishments in the United States in the twentieth century. Although Alexander Graham Bell had previously run laboratories that were the spiritual ancestors of Bell Labs, Bell Labs was officially created as Bell Telephone Laboratories, Inc., a separate entity from AT&T, in 1925 as a joint venture between AT&T and Western Electric Research Laboratories.

It was intended to research and develop technology related to Bell System operations, especially the equipment Western Electric built for AT&T. However, Frank B. Jewett, president of research from Bell Labs' inception until 1940, also allocated a few researchers for pure research, which proved fruitful. Bell Labs researcher Clinton J. Davisson in 1937 became the first Bell Labs researcher to receive a Nobel Prize for work done at the Labs. He was awarded a share of the Nobel Prize in Physics for demonstrating matter's wave nature.

The innovations developed at Bell Labs are numerous. Television signals were transmitted in 1927. The one-time pad (OTP) cipher was developed in the 1920s, with employee Claude Shannon proving during World War II that OTP was not only unbreakable but also a model for the characteristics any unbreakable system must possess. Shannon also pioneered information theory when working at Bell Labs on behalf of the war effort. The groundwork for radio astronomy and solid-state electronics was done in the 1930s, and the vocoder was invented in 1937. One of the most famous Nobel Prizes awarded for work done at Bell Labs was awarded in 1956 to John Bardeen, Walter H. Brattain, and William Shockley for inventing the first transistors in 1947.

Information theory, particularly binary code systems, was further developed in the 1950s. The first solar cell was invented in 1954, the first transatlantic telephone cable was laid in 1956, the first computer program playing music was written in 1957, and the laser was invented (on paper) in 1958. The first continuous-light laser followed at Bell Labs only two years later, and the carbon dioxide laser in 1964.

Bell Labs scientists Arno Penzias and Robert Wilson discovered the cosmic microwave background radiation in 1965, receiving the Nobel Prize in Physics for this work in 1978. The Unix operating system was introduced in 1969, and computing became a major Bell Labs concern in the following decades: Dennis Ritchie developed the C programming language in 1970, the first fiber optics systems were introduced in 1976, and the first single-chip 32-bit microprocessor was introduced in 1980. An extension of C, the C++ programming language, was developed at Bell in 1983.

The following year, the federal government forced the breakup of AT&T after years of discussion of antitrust complaints. Bell Telephone Laboratories, Inc., became a wholly owned subsidiary of AT&T Technologies (formerly Western Electric), and Bellcore was split off as a separate entity, now known as Telcordia Technologies. Bell Telephone Laboratories was spun off in 1996 to become Lucent Technologies, which became Alcatel-Lucent after being acquired by Alcatel SA, a French corporation.

for Shannon and Robert Fano, to whom Shannon attributed it. It also introduced the word *bit* to mean a piece of information.

The Shannon-Hartley theorem is also named for Shannon, with electronics researcher Ralph Hartley. The theorem determines the maximum rate of information transmission over a noisy communications channel of a given bandwidth. The resulting maximum rate is known as the Shannon limit. Shannon was expanding on ideas introduced by Hartley in the study of the telegraph in the 1920s.

Shannon also worked on game theory, writing a 1950 paper, "Programming a Computer for Playing Chess," that introduced the still-vibrant field of computer chess. Even in this first paper, he made a significant discovery: The Shannon number, which others named for him, is the estimated lower bound on the game-tree complexity of chess.

Ecological literature has adopted another of Shannon's ideas, the Shannon diversity index. Intended by Shannon to quantify entropy in strings of text, it has been used to represent the biodiversity of plant and animal species.

Shannon joined the MIT faculty in 1956 and worked at MIT until 1978, when he retired. After the breakup of the Bell System, AT&T's remaining part of Bell Laboratories was named Shannon Labs, which is now home to one of six statues of Shannon.

PERSONAL LIFE

Shannon met his wife, Mary Elizabeth "Betty" Moore, while working at Bell Laboratories, where she was employed as an analyst. They married in 1949. They had three children: Robert James, Andrew Moore, and Margarita Catherine.

Shannon also developed an abstract two-player strategy game called the Shannon switching game, sometimes known as *Bird Cage*. The game is played between two players, Short and Cut, on a graph on which two nodes are designated A and B. On each of Short's turns, he colors any existing edge. On each of Cut's turns, she deletes any edge that is not colored. The goal is for Short to build a colored path between A and B before Cut severs their connection.

In addition to being a chess player, Shannon was an avid fan of juggling, unicycles, and Pogo sticks, as part of a general enthusiasm for challenges of balance. After his retirement, he built a device that could solve a Rubik's cube. YouTube videos, long after his death, have brought new popularity to one of his most delightful innovations, the Ultimate Machine, a box equipped with a switch that, when flipped on, causes a mechanical hand to reach out and flip the switch off again before retracting back into the box.

Shannon suffered from Alzheimer's disease in his final years, and as a result he was unaware of the extent of his influence or of the digital revolution that had transpired after his retirement. He succumbed to the disease and died on February 24, 2001.

Bill Kte'pi

FURTHER READING

Gleick, James. *The Information: A History, a Theory, a Flood*. New York: Pantheon, 2011. Print. A well-known science writer's overview of the history of the information age.

Nahin, Paul J. *The Logician and the Engineer: How George Boole and Claude Shannon Created the Information Age*. Princeton: Princeton UP, 2012. Print. The role of Shannon in the birth of the modern information age.

Shannon, Claude E., and Warren Weaver. *The Mathematical Theory of Communication*. Urbana: U of Illinois P, 1949. Print. One of Shannon's key works on information theory.

STAN SHIH

Founder of Acer

Born: December 8, 1944; Lukang Township, Changhua County, Taiwan
Died: -
Primary Field: Computer science
Specialty: Computer hardware
Primary Company/Organization: Acer

INTRODUCTION

The father of Taiwan's electronics industry, Stan Shih founded Acer with his wife, Carolyn Yeh, in 1976 and turned it from a small electronics parts distributor to the fourth-largest manufacturer of personal computers (PCs) in the world. In Shih's wake, other Taiwanese companies, such as HTC and Asustek, have made waves in the computer industry, holding their own against their American and Japanese competitors.

EARLY LIFE

Shi Zhenwrong, known in the Western world as Stan Shih, was born on December 8, 1944, in Lukang Township, Changhua County, Taiwan. He was an only child raised by a single mother, his father having died in 1948. As a boy, he helped his mother sell stationery and duck eggs in two separate businesses. While the duck eggs were sold at a lower profit margin, turnover was every two to three days instead of every two to three months, and the egg business actually provided most of the Shihs' income. He studied electronics engineering at the National Chiao Tung University, earning both bachelor's and master's degrees. After school he took jobs as an electrical engineer for a few years, working on calculators and other consumer gadgets, first at Unitron Industrial Corporation and later at Qualitron Industrial Corporation (which he cofounded).

LIFE'S WORK

In 1976, Shih founded Multitech, a distributor of electronics parts, with five coworkers and his wife, Carolyn Yeh. Shih's ambitions were considerable from the start. Although the company sold mainly parts in its first years, his long-term vision was to create a global brand. Multitech did moderately well as a parts distributor and entered the personal computer market as that sector began to explode in popularity. The company released three Micro-Professor (MPF) personal computers, each of them something of an oddball: The first, MPF-I, was a tutorial computer designed for learning computer programming and was built into a case shaped like a book that also held manuals and cassettes and could be stored on a bookshelf. The MPF-II was an Apple clone with a small built-in keyboard and an unusually proportioned case. The MPF-III was ostensibly an Apple IIe clone but was made to look like a PC. Unusual as they were, the Micro-Professors sold well; indeed, the MPF-I remains in production, although it has been sold to another company.

When he founded Multitech, Shih was confident that microcomputers, not mainframes, would be the wave of the future, and his patience paid off. The Micro-Professor line was almost like an experiment—each computer radically different from the others in its design, rather than just increasing the capabilities of previous models, as the company toyed with different approaches to find the one that best suited it and its customer base. This led to the unusual choice of Multitech, manufacturer of some of the world's first Apple clones, to abandon its successful Apple clones to become a PC-compatible manufacturer—almost as though the PC appearance of the MPF-III foreshadowed the company's future.

Under Shih's leadership, Multitech focused on optimizing its supply chain and developing strong relationships with suppliers, which its first five years as a parts distributor facilitated. As a result, Multitech was able to introduce the world's second Intel 386–based PC in 1986, only a month after Compaq introduced the first. Many of the practices Shih pioneered at Multitech have been adopted as industry standards in computer manufacturing, and the spread of Multitech's cost-effective manufacturing practices was a tremendous factor in bringing computer costs down in the 1980s—and for a time accounted for the vast price differential between a PC-compatible machine and an Apple product, which helped solidify the "two-party system" of computing, rather than eventuating in one of them disappearing (as happened with the videotape format Betamax when VHS became dominant).

The following year, the company changed its name to Acer. Much of the PC manufacturing Acer did was contract manufacturing on behalf of larger companies

Stan Shih.

such as Dell and IBM. Despite his cost-saving measures, Shih was not interested in finding the least expensive way to make a computer, and he did not see cheap Chinese manufacturers as Acer's competitors. While other Taiwanese companies made components for the major Western and Japanese computer manufacturers, Shih intended to compete with them. However, the company's first sustained effort to enter the American market ended in 1999, after millions of dollars were spent trying to raise awareness of the brand, to little effect. The company restructured several times—including spinning off its manufacturing to a separate company, Wistron—and eventually reentered the American marketplace from a position of strength, acquiring Gateway (and the eMachines brand it had itself acquired) as well as others. In the meantime, just as Shih had built relationships with suppliers, so too did he build relationships with distributors in order to create a distribution chain that did not require Acer to try to beat Dell at the direct-sales game. Success in Europe was followed by success in North America, where Acer America Corporation was formed to handle Acer business for the United States and Canada.

Shih served as chair of Acer from its inception until 2004, when he retired to run a consulting firm, iD

SoftCapital Group. Among other things, iD has raised millions of dollars to help other Taiwanese companies raise their global profile. Shih has been a vocal critic of recent arrivals on the computing scene, such as the iPad

Affiliation: Acer

Acer, Inc., the Taiwanese multinational electronics corporation, is today the world's fourth-largest manufacturer of personal computers as well as the largest computer retail franchise in Taiwan. Its subsidiaries include Gateway, Packard Bell, eMachines, E-TEN, Aopen, Acer India, Acer Computer Australia, and Acer America Corporation.

Stan Shih founded Acer as Multitech in Hsinchu City, Taiwan, in 1976 with a staff of eleven, including six other cofounders, one of whom was his wife, Carolyn Yeh. A financial management student, Carolyn focused on financial operations, especially in the company's early years. Originally a parts distributor, Multitech soon entered the personal computer (PC) market with the Micro-Professor (MPF-I) in 1981. The MPF-I was a training computer to teach users machine code and assembly language, and unlike desktop computers, it was built into a book-shaped case containing a textbook, instruction manual, and two audiocassettes; the case was designed to be stored on a bookshelf. The rights to the MPF-I were sold in 1993 to Flite Electronics and remains in production.

The MPF-II followed in 1982, and like the MPF-I it differed greatly from other computers in design, although on the inside it was an Apple clone with some key differences from the Apple II (notably, keyboard and joystick differences made it impossible to play Apple games). On the outside, it was a simple box, longer than it was wide, with a small keyboard built in; a full-size keyboard was available as a peripheral, as was a dot-matrix printer and a floppy disk drive.

The MPF-III, released in 1983, was Multitech's third computer and is of historical interest because, while it, like the MPF-II, was one of the earliest Apple clones (specifically a clone of the Apple IIe), its physical design was actually based on the IBM PC. This made it the first Multitech computer with a "traditional" computer appearance, consisting of a rectangular unit including the central processing unit; a plug-in ninety-key keyboard with numeric keypad, and a composite video jack for an external display. Like the MPF-II, it was not totally compatible with Apple products. It had a CP/M emulator, allowing it to run programs designed for the CP/M operating system for Intel machines.

After the MPF-III, Multitech transitioned into manufacturing IBM PC–compatible machines and slowly became a major PC manufacturer. The company name was changed to Acer in 1987. The 1990s saw Acer's fastest growth: From 1994 to 1995, Acer passed Hewlett-Packard, Dell, and Toshiba, long powerful names in the PC-compatible market, to jump from the its position as fourteenth-largest to ninth-largest computer manufacturer. It unveiled its Aspire PC in 1995 and the following year expanded into inexpensive consumer electronics.

Acer restructured several times around the turn of the century and began acquiring some of its rivals: Gateway and the eMachines brand in 2007, E-TEN in 2008, and a 75 percent controlling interest in Packard Bell in 2008. It also acquired cloud software developer iGware, Inc., in 2011, to prepare for the coming cloud computing market.

Acer was briefly absent from the American computer market, after ending sales to the market in 1999 following significant losses from fruitless endeavors to build brand awareness. This absence ended with the Gateway acquisition, and Acer America Corporation is today headquartered in San Jose, California, serving both the United States and Canada. At the end of 2011, Acer announced plans to cut its product lines by about two-thirds. Product lines had grown to such a degree that Acer America Corporation offered 101 different models of laptop or netbook in 2011, which management blamed for consecutive losses.

Acer is one of the manufacturers offering Google's Chromebook, sold through Amazon and Best Buy. The Chromebook is a laptop running the Google Chrome operating system and designed for rapid booting and Internet browsing. Offline capabilities are limited; most computing is done through Chrome web apps. One of the advantages of the Chromebook is its price: Acer's models sell for $299 and $399.

Acer sponsors the Ferrari Formula One team (and sells a cobranded Ferrari red notebook computer), FC Internazionale Milano football, SK Gaming, and Army United FC in the Thai Premier League. It also sponsored both the 2010 Olympic Winter Games and the 2012 Olympic Summer Games.

and the MacBook Air, and has suggested that Microsoft's plan to develop a tablet is a bad decision.

Over the course of the 1990s, Shih and his wife oversaw the creation of Aspire Park in Taiwan, which shared the name of Acer's first Intel machine. Aspire Park is a community on the outskirts of Taiwan's capital city of Taipei, consisting of 425 acres of land, manufacturing facilities, apartments, single-family homes, recreational facilities, and Aspire Academy, a school teaching leadership skills to Asian executives.

Shih has served as a chairman of the Asia Business Council and is a governor of the Asian Institute of Management, a member of the Taiwan Semiconductor Manufacturing Company's board of directors, and a member of the International Advisory Panel for Malaysia's Multimedia Super Corridor. He has been recognized by numerous awards and magazine lists, including *Fortune* magazine's 25 People You Ought to Know for Doing Business in Asia in 1989, *Businessweek*'s 2004 25 Stars of Asia, and Taiwan's Ten Most Outstanding Young Persons in 1976.

PERSONAL LIFE

Shih married Carolyn Yeh, cofounder of Acer, on September 28, 1971. They have three children, and Shih's mother lives with the family. In his retirement he has been active in charitable work as well as serving as

Taiwanese president Chen Shui-bian's special representative at APEC Australia 2007, the conference of meetings among the twenty-one countries of the Asia-Pacific Economic Cooperation.

Bill Kte'pi

FURTHER READING

Dedrick, Jason, Kenneth L. Kraemer, and Tony Tsai. "Acer: An IT Company Learning to Use IT to Compete." Oct. 1999. *eScholarship, University of California*. Web. 20 Aug. 2012. Open access research article that discusses the role of Acer in the industry and Shih's smiling curve.

Garten, Jeffrey E. *The Mind of the CEO*. New York: Basic, 2001. Print. An overview of business philosophy at the corporate executive level, with Shih as one of the examples examined.

Mathews, John A. *Dragon Multinational: A New Model of Global Growth*. New York: Oxford UP, 2002. Print. Discusses Shih as a "tireless champion of nonorthdox approaches to managing global corporations from the Periphery."

Shih, Stan. *Me Too Is Not My Style*. San Jose: Acer, 2010. Print. Shih's autobiography, originally written as an internal reference manual for Acer employees and colleagues.

ALAN SHUGART

Inventor of the first floppy disk

Born: September 27, 1930; Los Angeles, California
Died: December 12, 2006; San Jose, California
Primary Field: Computer science
Specialty: Computer hardware
Primary Company/Organization: IBM

INTRODUCTION

Alan Shugart worked as a scientist for IBM from 1951 to 1968 as a member of the development team that built the first computer disk drive. First known as a memory disk, it later became most well known as the floppy disk. He next served as vice president of product development for Memorex (1969–73) and then cofounded leading floppy disk manufacturer Shugart Associates in 1973 and the pioneering hard drive manufacturer Seagate Technology in 1979. A pioneer and champion of the hard disk drive industry, he was known as the Disk King.

EARLY LIFE

Alan Field Shugart was born on September 27, 1930, in Los Angeles, California. His mother was an educator. He was raised and lived most of his life in California, developing an early love for the ocean and the relaxed, vibrant California lifestyle. He received a bachelor's degree in engineering physics from the University of Redlands in 1951 and began his career as a field service engineer at International Business Machines (IBM) the day after his college graduation. He repaired the company's accounting machines, which were operated with punch cards. Shugart would remain employed at IBM for eighteen years, from 1951 to 1969, where he developed a taste for his later renowned informal business style.

Shugart's talent and work ethic earned him numerous promotions. He soon rose through the ranks and transferred to the company's research facility in San

Jose, California. In 1955, he aided the development of the random access method of accounting and control (RAMAC), the company's first disk storage system. RAMAC made its commercial debut in 1959 with a storage capacity of five million characters of data. Shugart's early career success continued to earn recognition, and he soon found himself in a leadership role at IBM.

LIFE'S WORK

Shugart directly worked on or managed the development of many of the company's most successful products during the height of his IBM career. He rose from manager of random access memory product development to director of engineering for the Systems Development Division. Disk storage products were among the company's most profitable product lines. Shugart's IBM responsibilities included managing teams of engineers working on a variety of key company programs. Products produced under his management included the IBM 2321 data call drive and the Advanced Disk File, later known as the IBM 1301. The IBM 1301 became the basis of American Airlines' Sabre online reservation system, the first such system to be used in the United States. Shugart's engineering teams would also develop the world's first computer disk drives and portable data storage devices.

Alan Shugart.

Shugart's most renowned contribution at IBM was his leadership of the engineering team that developed the first floppy disk, then known as a memory disk. The floppy disk made its debut in 1971. It was 8 inches in diameter and had a data storage capacity of 100 kilobytes (kB). The disk was flexible (which gave rise to the "floppy" moniker), with a magnetic iron oxide coating. Computer data could be written to and later retrieved from the surface of the floppy disk. Although the floppy disk was originally designed to transfer microcodes into the disk pack file of the IBM 3330, commonly known as the Merlin, other uses were quickly discovered. Its revolutionary portable design facilitated the transfer of data between computers.

Floppy disks soon dominated the program and file storage fields. Shugart developed the 5¼-inch floppy disk and disk drive for Wang Laboratories in 1976 for use in the company's desktop computers. Sony would debut the 3½-inch hard-plastic-encased floppy disk in 1981. The 3½-inch floppy disks would grow from a 400 kB data storage capacity to a 720 kB double-density storage capacity to a 1.44 megabyte (MB) high-density storage capacity. Floppy disks were later made nearly obsolete by the development of recordable compact discs (CDs), digital versatile (sometimes inaccurately called "digital video") discs (DVDs), and computer flash drives in the early twenty-first century.

Shugart resigned from IBM in 1969 after a short, unhappy transfer to New York City. He quickly returned to his beloved California, accepting employment with Memorex. He worked as vice president of product development for that company until 1973; there, he oversaw disk drive development and production operations. He also became renowned for recruiting several hundred IBM engineers to join him in switching employment to Memorex, some of them over drinks at the popular Paddock Lounge, located next to the IBM facility.

Shugart founded Shugart Associates in 1973, which emerged as an early market leader in the manufacture of floppy disks. The company introduced an 8-inch floppy disk drive at a lower cost than others on the market. Focus on the 8-inch floppy disk drive was a calculated business risk, as the product was specifically targeted for use in the smaller computers that had just begun to appear at that time. Shugart and the company successfully gambled on their belief in the future dominance of smaller computers. He also developed the Shugart Associates Systems Interface (SASI), later known as the SCSI (for small computer system interface), which used communications prerogatives in the protocol between connected computing devices.

Shugart left the company he had founded in 1974 after a disagreement with the company's board of directors, and Xerox would later acquire Shugart Associates. Shugart worked as a private technology industry consultant, pursued business and political interests outside the industry, and spent time on his newly acquired fishing boat during his break from the corporate world. He reentered the entrepreneurial ranks in 1979, when he and Finis Conner founded Shugart Technology, later changing the name to Seagate Technology LLC. Shugart served as the new company's chief executive officer (CEO).

The California-based Seagate Technology quickly rose to prominence as the leading independent global manufacturer in the hard drive market. Although it was located just outside Silicon Valley, it was considered a Silicon Valley business. Seagate debuted a hard disk drive with a storage capacity of 5 MB. Priced at $1,500, it quickly became a best seller. The company was the also first to produce 5.25-inch hard disks. The disks quickly caught on, with numerous manufacturers producing 5.25-inch "floppies" with data storage capacities of up to 1.2 MB by the end of the 1970s.

Seagate soon branched out into the production of other computer-related products. Specialties included data management software tools and applications. Uses included information management, storage management, and network and systems management. Its first customer was the up-and-coming Apple Computer. The company proved financially successful, and Shugart's pioneering work in the field earned him a nickname as the Disk King.

An aging Shugart resigned from Seagate in 1998 at the request of the company's board of directors, but he was not done with the computer industry. After leaving Seagate, Shugart immediately established the technology start-up Al Shugart International LLC, based in Santa Barbara, California, which he oversaw until his death in 2006. He also sat on numerous boards of directors during his career, including Blue Sky Research, Fidelica Microsystems, SanDisk Corporation, Valence Technology, Inktomi, Cypress Semiconductor, Siros Technologies, Sarnoff Digital Communications, Nx-Wave Communications, and Sierra Imaging.

PERSONAL LIFE

Shugart's outside business ventures included the 1983 cofounding of Fandango with Pierre Bain. The successful five-star restaurant, which features a European atmosphere, is located in Pacific Grove on the Monterey

Affiliation: IBM

Today IBM is a transnational corporation based in Armonk, New York, and specializing in computer and information technology. IBM originated in the 1914 merger of three nineteenth-century companies to form the Computing Tabulating Recording Company. Thomas J. Watson Sr., rechristened the company International Business Machines (IBM) in 1924 and led the company to international prominence. Son Thomas J. Watson Jr., would later perform the same role. IBM is known for both its strong research and development and product sales divisions.

IBM partnered with Harvard University to develop the Mark I computer in 1944 and began independently producing computers in 1953 with the IBM 701 EDPM. The company introduced the mainframe System/360 computers with revolutionary compatible software and peripheral equipment in 1964. In 1960 the company saw another turning point, as it unbundled hardware sales from software and services; the latter had previously been included with hardware sales for no charge. The move launched a new, profitable software industry. The company also faced antitrust litigation from the U.S. Department of Justice, which was later dropped.

IBM introduced the floppy disk in 1971 and released its first personal computer (PC) for consumers in 1981. The first PC featured a Intel 8088 microprocessor and an operating system designed by Microsoft's Bill Gates. Its debut began a consumer technology revolution. IBM remains one of the world's most widely recognized and profitable global brands.

Peninsula. Shugart's political interests and commitment to citizen involvement in the political process resulted in his 1996 attempt to place his dog Ernest on the U.S. congressional ballot in Santa Cruz and his formation of the nonpartisan citizen political organization Friends of Ernest (FOE). He wrote of his experiences in *Fandango: The Story of Two Guys Who Wanted to Own a Restaurant* (1993) and *Ernest Goes to Washington (Well, Not Exactly): A True Story about the Dog Who Ran for Congress* (1998), as well as in his autobiography, *Al: The Wit and Wisdom of Al Shugart* (2002).

Shugart was married to first wife Esther Bell Marrs from 1951 to 1973. The couple had three children, Joanne, Christopher, and Teri, and four grandchildren.

He married second wife, Rita Kennedy, in 1981. He loved living by the sea in San Jose, California, and his hobbies included wine collecting and high-tech gadgets. He was a member of the National Academy of Engineering, received the 1997 Reynold B. Johnson Information Storage Systems Award (conferred by the Institute of Electrical and Electronics Engineers), and was selected as a 2005 Fellow of the Computer History Museum, as well as receiving numerous other awards and honors.

Shugart died December 12, 2006 in San Jose, California at age seventy-six of complications related to heart surgery. He was known for his trademark Hawaiian shirts, outgoing personality, unconventional nature, work ethic, honesty, colorful personality, and laid-back management style and leadership abilities, which made him popular among the engineers who worked for him. Shugart believed that entrepreneurs had to be born leaders and willing to work hard. It was reported that on the day of his death he was working from his hospital bed. He also remarked that money is a more important consideration than one's mother when founding a company. His hardworking but unstructured management style later became a hallmark of the Silicon Valley in particular and California-based computer and information technology companies in general.

Marcella Bush Trevino

FURTHER READING

Ceruzzi, Paul E. *A History of Modern Computing*. 2nd ed. Cambridge: MIT, 2012. Print. Covers the development of modern computers and the information technology field, from the first electronic digital computer through the rise and fall of the dot-com era. Includes extensive discussion of IBM's long-term role in the field.

Harwood, John. *The Interface: IBM and the Transformation of Corporate Design, 1945–1976*. Minneapolis: U of Minnesota P, 2011. Print. Explores the commercial history of the company during a critical period dominated by the design team under Eliot Noyes, including Shugart's eighteen-year employment period.

Pugh, Emerson W. *Building IBM: Shaping an Industry and Its Technology*. Cambridge: MIT, 2009. Print. Details the technological and commercial factors that led to the company's revolutionary success in the field of computer and information technology. Includes the period in which Shugart was an integral part of that success

Shugart, Alan F. *Al: The Wit and Wisdom of Al Shugart*. Brandon: Monterey Pacific, 2002. Print. Shugart's autobiography covers his life and relates business stories as well as his personal philosophy in his own words, marked by his well-known sense of humor.

BARBARA SIMONS

Former president of the Association for Computing Machinery

Born: 1941; United States
Died: -
Primary Field: Computer science
Specialty: Computer programming
Primary Company/Organization: Association for Computing Machinery

INTRODUCTION

Barbara Simons is an expert on voting technology and has served as an expert adviser to the U.S. president, the U.S. military, and other organizations regarding the security of different methods of voting. She served as president of the Association for Computing Machinery (ACM) and is involved with efforts to get more women and members of underrepresented minority groups involved in computer science.

EARLY LIFE

Barbara Simons earned her doctorate in computer science from the University of California at Berkeley; her doctoral dissertation solved a significant problem in scheduling theory.

LIFE'S WORK

Simons's early professional life was spent addressing technical issues in computing. After earning her doctorate, she began working at IBM in 1980, at the company's San Jose Research Center as a research staff member. She became a senior programmer at IBM's Applications Development Technology Institute and later became a senior technology adviser for IBM Global Services. Her career at IBM has been devoted primarily to research on scheduling theory, algorithm analysis

Barbara Simons.

and design, and compiler optimization. Her expertise in technical computing has been recognized by her designation as an ACM Fellow and her election to the presidency of that organization. She is perhaps best known nationally as an expert on voting technology and security issues involved with electronic voting systems and Internet voting.

Simons has testified before the U.S. Congress, the California legislature, and various government agencies on technology-related issues, and he has written or coauthored reports on technological issues, including Internet and other types of electronic voting. She served as a member of the National Workshop on Internet Voting in 2001 and on the Security Peer Review Group, which evaluated the Department of Defense's proposal to allow overseas U.S. voters to vote via the Internet; the conclusion of the report from this committee, coauthored by Simons, was that Internet voting still had too many security flaws to be advisable.

In 2006, Simons and coauthors David Dill and Douglas W. Jones produced a widely publicized report cataloging the many security flaws in touch-screen voting machines manufactured by Diebold, as well as the fact that Diebold was aware of these flaws and chose not to solve them. Simons has also criticized the computerized database of registered voters that each state was required to create under the 2002 Help America Vote Act, pointing out that although the databases were meant to prevent voting by those not eligible and safeguard the rights of those who were eligible, they could have the opposite effect: If the databases were not secure and not properly monitored, it would be easy for an unscrupulous person to add the names of ineligible voters or remove the names of eligible voters. Simons has published many other articles and given lectures on the state of security for electronic voting, a particularly timely issue because many local governments in the United States had recently purchased electronic voting machines, sometimes with federal assistance, in response to the 2002 Help America Vote Act and the "hanging chad" and "butterfly ballot" controversies in the presidential election of 2000. As Simons and her coauthors pointed out, such machines made it easy for election results to be manipulated, and because no record of the vote existed other than that registered electronically, it would not be possible to hold a recount or otherwise audit the election (both possibilities in elections in which paper ballots are used). In 2012, Simons and Douglas W. Jones published *Broken Ballots: Will Your Vote Count?*, a book-length study of voting technology written to be accessible to the general public and with particular focus on current issues in electronic voting in the United States.

Simons has received many awards and other honors for her work. In 1992, she was given the Norbert Wiener Award for Professional and Social Responsibility and was featured in a special edition of *Science* magazine focused on women in science. In 1993, she became a fellow of the Association for Computing Machinery. In 2005, she received the Distinguished Alumnus Award in Computer Science and Engineering from the University of California, Berkeley; she was the first woman to receive this honor. She is also involved in efforts to increase the number of women and underrepresented minorities working in computer science; her efforts in this regard include serving on the boards of the Coalition to Diversify Computing and the Berkeley Foundation for Opportunities in Information Technology, and she was a cofounder of the Reentry Program for Women and Minorities in the University of California, Berkeley's computer science department. Simons is also a Fellow of the American Academy for the Advancement of Science and serves on the Electorate Nominating Committee for the Information, Computing, and Communication Section.

Affiliation: Association for Computing Machinery

The Association for Computing Machinery (ACM), founded in 1947, is among the world's largest educational and scientific organizations, with more than one hundred thousand members from all sectors of computer sciences, including design and construction, programming, and utilization. The ACM holds more than 170 conferences annually, publishes and distributes more than fifty publications, and maintains a digital library online, including the full run of ACM publications, publications by affiliated organizations, conference proceedings, and oral history interviews. The ACM includes thirty-seven special interest groups, including both technical (Algorithms and Computation Theory, Computer Architecture, Bioinformatics) and more general foci (Computer Science Education), and offers a number of resources for K–12 students and teachers and college students and professors as well as computing professionals. The ACM also gives a number of awards recognizing achievement in computer science and technology, including the A. M. Turing Award, the Gordon Bell Prize, the Grace Murray Hopper Award, and the Eugene L. Lawler Award. ACM is also involved in public policy work, addressing issues relevant to computing such as accessibility, security and privacy, intellectual property, education, and innovation.

Barbara Simons founded the ACM's U.S. Public Policy Committee (USACM) in 1993 and served as chair or cochair of USACM for many years. She was president of ACM from 1998 to 2000, is a Fellow of ACM, and is a member of the ACM Distinguished Speakers Program, offering a lecture on issues with computerized voting machines. Simons has produced many reports on election issues as part of her work, including a report to U.S. president Bill Clinton on Internet voting in 2001, a review of the Secure Electronic Resgistration and Voting Experiment (SERVE) project for Internet voting in 2004, and a report on election auditing for the League of Women Voters. In 2012, she published a book on electronic voting, *Broken Ballots: Will Your Vote Count?*, coauthored with Douglas W. Jones, a computer scientist from the University of Iowa.

PERSONAL LIFE

Simons is retired from IBM and acts as an expert adviser and guest speaker on issues related to voting machinery and the security hazards posed by electronic voting technologies. She is divorced from James Harris Simons, a hedge fund manager, mathematician, and philanthropist. Their son, Paul, was struck by a car and killed in 1996 while riding a bike near his father's Long Island, New York, home.

Sarah Boslaugh

FURTHER READING

Hall, Thad E., R. Michael Alvarez, and Lonna Rae Atkeson, eds. *Confirming Elections: Creating Confidence and Integrity through Election Auditing*. Hampshire: Palgrave Macmillan, 2012. Print. A collection of essays addressing different issues in election auditing, a topic of particular concern since the disputed 2000 presidential election in the United States. The essays address fundamental issues in auditing and discuss historical examples, making suggestions for the future.

Herrnson, Paul S., Richard G. Niemi, Michael J. Hammer, Benjamin B. Bederson, Frederick C. Conrad, and Michael W. Traugott. *Voting Technology: The Not-so-Simple Act of Counting a Ballot*. Washington, DC: Brookings Institution, 2008. Print. A review of current issues regarding the use of technological systems for voting, by a team of interdisciplinary experts. The final chapter offers recommendations for creating a voting system to maximize the probability that each voter's true intentions will be recorded and counted.

Jefferson, David, Aviel D. Rubin, Barbara Simons, and David Wagner. "Analyzing Internet Voting Securing: An Extensive Assessment of a Proposed Internet-Based Voting System." *Communications of the ACM* 47.10 (2004): 59–64. Print. A nontechnical article about the Secure Electronic Resgistration and Voting Experiment (SERVE), an Internet voting system developed to facilitate voting in U.S. elections by nonresidential U.S. citizens, military personnel, and their families. Simons and her coauthors conclude that the SERVE system has many vulnerabilities that cannot be easily eliminated.

Jones, Douglas W., and Barbara Simons. *Broken Ballots: Will Your Vote Count?* Stanford: Stanford Center for the Study of Language and Information, 2012. Print. A history of the use of voting technology, including the types of devices used and the regulatory structures and legislation involved, with particular focus on recent concerns, including the controversies regarding the 2000 election in California and the known security risks involved with using computers to record votes.

Schwartz, John. "The 2004 Campaign: Voting: Online Ballots Canceled for Americans Overseas." *New York Times* 6 Feb. 2004: 18. Print. A news article covering the 2004 decision by the U.S. Department of Defense not to allow overseas voters to vote in U.S. elections through an overseas voting program, called the Secure Electronic Registration and Voting Experiment (SERVE), developed by the Department of Defense. The article cites the use of voting technologies in other elections and quotes Simons on the problems inherent in securing an electronic system of voting.

CHARLES SIMONYI

Microsoft Office developer

Born: September 10, 1948; Budapest, Hungary
Died: -
Primary Field: Computer science
Specialty: Computer software
Primary Company/Organization: Microsoft

INTRODUCTION

As a computer programmer and software developer, Charles Simonyi led the team that developed Microsoft Word, Excel, and other application programs. He is credited with helping to develop such basic elements of personal computing as icons, pull-down menus, and the mouse. Before he joined Microsoft, he was employed at Xerox's Palo Alto Research Center (PARC) in California, where he led in the development of a text editor and graphical user interface that made personal computing possible. Leaving Microsoft in 2002, Simonyi cofounded Intentional Software Corporation, for which he serves as chairman of the board and chief technology officer. He is also well known as a philanthropist and a space tourist, the first to make two flights.

EARLY LIFE

Charles Simonyi was born Károly Simonyi on September 10, 1948, in Budapest, Hungary. His father was a professor of electrical engineering, and through his influence Simonyi was allowed to spend time assisting an engineer who was working on one of the few computers in Hungary at that time, a Russian-made Ural II with two thousand vacuum tubes. Sixteen-year-old Simonyi was hired as a night watchman at the Central Statistical Office so that the computer could be left on overnight to conserve the vacuum tubes. It was during this period that he began writing programs, one of which brought him a job offer from a computer research facility in Copenhagen, Denmark. Because he was still seventeen when he graduated from high school, too young to be drafted by the military, he was allowed to accept the job for one year. He and his father planned for this to be Simonyi's way out of Communist-controlled Hungary.

After eighteen months in Denmark, Simonyi left for the United States, where he enrolled at the University of California, Berkeley, to study engineering and mathematics. He worked in the university computer

Charles Simonyi.

center to earn enough to pay his tuition. A program he wrote as a student led to a job with the Berkeley Computer Corporation. He was recruited in 1972, as he was completing requirements for a bachelor of science degree, to work at Xerox's Palo Alto Research Center (PARC). Assigned to a PARC team that was developing the Alto, Xerox's first personal computer, one of the projects he worked on was the development of a text editor for the Alto. He was also a graduate student in computer science at Stanford University at the time, and he decided to make the text editor project part of the research for his dissertation. In 1975, Bravo, the first text editor to implement a variety of features such as upper- and lowercase characters, underlining, boldfacing, justification, and margin setting, became operational. Bravo also allowed users to make changes, such as adding text, moving blocks of text, deleting text, and incorporating graphics into a document. Simonyi received his Ph.D. from Stanford in 1977.

LIFE'S WORK

In 1980, Simonyi met Bill Gates, and the following year he accepted an offer from Gates and moved to Seattle to start Microsoft's new-applications group. Until his arrival, Microsoft had focused on programming languages and operating systems. Simonyi brought with him the knowledge of the software he had worked on during his time with Xerox. He invented the method of writing code that Microsoft's programmers have used for more than twenty-five years. Building on the Bravo product, Simonyi and his team created the first version of Word in 1983. Features such as line breaks, boldfacing, and italics on screen and typeset-quality printing were innovations in the program. Not only was Word compatible with the MS-DOS operating system; it was also among the earliest applications to appear on IBM's OS/2 and Apple's Macintosh computers. The first version of Word for Windows was released in 1989, two years ahead of Corel's WordPerfect for Windows—an edge that helped to establish Word as the leading word-processing program. By 1994, it held a 90 percent share of the market.

Simonyi is also considered the father of the Microsoft Excel spreadsheet. Electronic spreadsheets were not new. A Harvard Business School student had invented VisiCalc (for "visible calculator") in 1978. Simonyi had insisted, upon his arrival at Microsoft in 1981, that the company procure the latest in graphical user interface (GUI) technology. Having created Bravo using GUI, Simonyi strongly believed in the future of the technology,

a belief shared by Gates. Microsoft introduced a spreadsheet program called Multiplan in 1982, which became Microsoft's best-selling application, but then Multiplan's dominance was challenged by Lotus 1-2-3. Lotus seemed to be winning the competition by 1983.

On October 25, 1983, Gates summoned Simonyi and other strategists to a retreat at the Red Lion Inn near Bellevue, Washington, to consider action. The result of the session was the concept for what became Microsoft Excel. A trademark lawsuit by a software company that had developed earlier a banking program called Excel required that the Microsoft name be used with the company's new program. In September 1985, the first version of Microsoft Excel for the Macintosh shipped. The first Windows version was released in November 1987. Lotus, like Corel, was slow to produce a Windows 1-2-3 application, and by 1988 Excel was leading the spreadsheet competition. The program was the first that allowed the user to define the appearance of the spreadsheets (fonts, character attributes, and cell formats) and the first to introduce intelligent cell recomputation, which allowed changes to cells dependent on the modified cell without recomputing the full spreadsheet. Microsoft was becoming the leading software developer for personal computers, due in large part to Simonyi's contributions. During the 1980s, as Microsoft researchers worked to develop and improve the Windows operating system, the company was financially supported by profits from Simonyi's application programs. The company's growth into the leading software developer for personal computers was due in no small part to its software applications.

By 1991, Simonyi had become chief architect of Microsoft Research, a title he held until 1999. Dissatisfied with the costs of software failure, which (according to a 2002 study by the National Institute of Standards and Technology) ran as high as $59.5 billion annually, he wanted to develop an approach to stem the waste of resources—not only in dollars but also in talent and time. The concept, which he called "intentional programming," would ultimately, he hoped, result in generic tools created by programmers that could be modified by end users according to their needs. By March 1995, his team had built a working system for using intentional programming. In September 1995, he delivered a paper, "The Death of Computer Languages," in which he described his ambition and the result of his team's research. In 2001, Microsoft began pushing developers who wrote software for Windows to adopt a new programming system, the .NET Framework. Not

Affiliation: Microsoft

Microsoft was founded as Micro-Soft in 1975. Bill Gates and Paul Allen, high school friends, started the company to write software for the MITS Altair 8800 computer. Beginning in 1980, the by then unhyphenated Microsoft partnered with IBM to provide the software package for the computers IBM manufactured. The following year, Gates hired Charles Simonyi to direct the company's new software applications program. Simonyi invented the method of writing code that Microsoft's programmers would use for the next quarter century. He also led in the development of Word, the word-processing software first introduced in 1983. Word defeated all competitors to claim 90 percent of the market for word-processing software by 1994. Microsoft Excel, the revolutionary spreadsheet program introduced in 1985, became another winner for the company and was also developed under Simonyi's leadership.

The first Windows operating system, in 1983, used the same type of graphical user interface (GUI) that Apple had pioneered, but as personal computers loaded with Windows increased in speed and numbers, Microsoft achieved market dominance. By the early 1990s, the company's success had made Gates the world's richest man. Allen, who retired in 1983, was several rungs lower on the wealth ladder, although he was numbered among the world's fifty richest men.

The company spent the next decade increasing profits and battling antitrust suits. It was not until May 2010 that Apple passed Microsoft to become the most valuable technology company in the world. Microsoft responded to the challenge by unveiling a tablet computer called Surface in June 2012. The same month, the company announced that it was spending more than $1 billion to buy Yammer, a social networking service that has been described as Facebook for businesses.

the fifth space tourist, transported to the International Space Station aboard a Soyuz rocket and spending two weeks there. He visited the International Space Station a second time in March 2009. He reportedly paid $25 million for the privilege of traveling in space.

A noted philanthropist, Simonyi has endowed three professorships: in 1995, the Simonyi Professorship of the Public Understanding of Science at Oxford University, held by his friend, evolutionary biologist Richard Dawkins from 1995 to 2008; in 1997, a Simonyi Professorship for Innovation in Teaching at Stanford University; and in 2005, the Simonyi Professorship of Mathematical Physics at the Institute for Advanced Study in Princeton, New Jersey. In January 2004, he established the Charles Simonyi Fund for Arts and Sciences. Grants have been awarded to the Seattle Symphony, the Seattle Public Library, the Metropolitan Opera, the Juilliard School, the Institute for Advanced Study, and the Large Synoptic Survey Telescope.

Simonyi's personal collection of paintings by Roy Lichtenstein and Victor Vasarely, artists whose work he believes anticipated the digital age, are showcased at Villa Simonyi, his glass-and-steel residence in Medina, Washington, designed by legendary Seattle architect Wendell Lovett. Seen frequently accompanying Martha Stewart to social events from 1993 to 2008, he married Swedish consultant Lisa Persdotter, three decades his junior, in 2008. The couple's first child, a daughter named Lilian, was born in February 2011.

Wylene Rholetter

only did this system require a less radical break from conventional techniques, but it also produced finished work. Clearly, the time was not ripe to push Simonyi's intentional programming. He left Microsoft in 2002, taking with him a patent-cross-licensing agreement that allowed him to use the concepts of his intentional-programming research but forbade him to take any of the code developed while he was employed by Microsoft.

PERSONAL LIFE

After leaving Microsoft, Simonyi founded an independent company, Intentional Software, an engineering firm that focused on realizing his vision of software less prone to errors and less expensive. His company was not his only new adventure. In April 2007, he became

FURTHER READING

Cringely, Robert X. "All IBM Stories Are True." *Accidental Empires: How the Boys if Silicon Valley Make Their Millions, Battle Foreign Competition, and Still Can't Get a Date*. New York: HarperBusiness, 1996. 119–38. Print. Focuses on the personalities at the center of computer technology. The author pays special attention to the combination of creativity, ego, flaws, and foibles that made these men extraordinary but all too human. Simonyi is covered.

Fisher, Adam. "'Very Stunning, Very Space, and Very Cool.'" *Technology Review* Jan./Feb. 2009: 58–69. Print. Presents edited extracts from interviews with five people who participated in trips into space organized by Space Adventures. Simonyi is one of the five.

Greene, Stephen G. "Software Entrepreneur Seeks to Promote Excellence through Philanthropy." *Chronicle of Philanthropy* 19 Feb. 2004: 20. Print. Profiles Simonyi, offering details on his education and his career at Microsoft. Includes a list of institutions that have benefited from his philanthropy. One color photograph.

"Out-of-This-World Software Engineering." *Fortune* 15 Nov. 2010: 33–34. Print. The article describes the founding of Intentional Software by Simonyi and his plan for transforming the way software is created. Simonyi shares his reasons for believing the transformation is necessary. Two color photographs.

Rosenberg, Scott. "Anything You Can Do, I Can Do Meta." *Technology Review* Jan./Feb. 2007: 36–48. Print. This lengthy article offers a detailed account of the early life of Simonyi as well as an account of his career at Microsoft, his vision for Intentional Software, and his plans for space travel. One color photograph.

GEORGE STIBITZ

Early developer of digital computing

Born: April 20, 1904; York, Pennsylvania
Died: January 31, 1995; Hanover, New Hampshire
Primary Field: Computer science
Specialty: Computer hardware
Primary Company/Organization: Bell Laboratories

George Stibitz.

INTRODUCTION

George Stibitz was a part of what may have been the greatest technical innovation organization of the twentieth century, Bell Laboratories. Not as well known as other innovators of the twentieth century, Stibitz conceived the first electric digital computer. The claim has been disputed by some, as similar work was being performed in Germany, Japan, and Cambridge, Massachusetts, but none was as advanced or resulted in an operating machine as early as Stibitz's 1940 Model I Complex Calculator. Stibitz designed the prototype and supervised construction of this machine, demonstrating its remote use in 1940. During World War II, he led the development of increasingly advanced computers. After the war, he continued that work until he transitioned to developing computerized solutions for medical problems and performing medical research.

EARLY LIFE

George Robert Stibitz was born in York, Pennsylvania, on April 20, 1904, to George and Mildred Stibitz; he was one of four children. At an early age, Stibitz moved with his family from Pennsylvania to Ohio. His father was a professor of theology; his mother, a former teacher of mathematics. Like other innovators of the twentieth century, such as Larry Roberts and Leonard Kleinrock, Stibitz, from an early age, showed a talent for building and designing electrical devices. In his case, it was electrical motors that captured his interest. His fascination with such devices never diminished, and he eventually entered a technical high school, Moraine Park, in Dayton, Ohio.

After graduating from high school, Stibitz went to Denison University, where he graduated in 1926 with a bachelor's degree. He received his master of science degree from Union College in upstate New York. After working for a year, Stibitz returned to school, specializing in mathematical physics at Cornell. He received his doctorate in 1930 and immediately began his employment at Bell Telephone Laboratories (Bell Labs), where he would spend the next eleven years.

LIFE'S WORK

When Stibitz began work at Bell Labs in 1930, his role was as a mathematician. The use of telephones (and consequently the development of telephone networks) at this time was growing exponentially. Even at this early stage, Bell Telephone understood that the topologies (both physical infrastructure and the logical flow) had to be designed and planned to accommodate rapidly expanding requirements. For Stibitz and his colleagues, that meant a great deal of work performing calculations to support design decisions, assisted only by desktop manual calculators.

This situation encouraged Stibitz to consider what could be done to replace the mechanical calculators with something that could perform more work, accurately, in a fraction of the time. In 1937, Stibitz had the idea that an electrical digital computer could handle large numbers of complex calculations in a fraction of the time that it currently took. He proposed his idea to management at Bell Labs but was initially turned down. Later that year, however, the decision was reversed, and Stibitz began to design his calculator. He completed the design in the following year, and in 1939 work on a prototype began, with Stibitz doing the construction in his kitchen at home with odd pieces of equipment he had acquired from Bell Labs.

The prototype worked; the next step was to enlarge and enhance it into what became known as the Model I

Affiliation: Bell Laboratories

Bell Laboratories (Bell Labs), where George Stibitz performed his most important work, can rightly be described as the most active and highly developed commercial technical development and experimentation center in the United States in the twentieth century. As significant as Stibitz's efforts in developing a digital computer were, they were far from the only advanced technology to emerge from that organization.

Bell Laboratories began in 1925, when the Western Electric and American Telephone and Telegraph (AT&T) companies separated some of their engineering and research departments to form a new entity that was owned by both companies. The main purpose of the organization, which at its peak employed almost fifteen thousand individuals working at several sites, was to design equipment required by both companies.

Through its history, Bell Labs developed many new technologies that became incorporated into communications networks. These included FAX transmissions (demonstrated at Bell Labs although not initially developed by Bell Labs), an early form of talking movies, television (in 1927), and stereo recordings (in the early 1930s). After World War II, Bell Labs also developed the transistor (to replace vacuum tubes in radios, early computers, and other electronic equipment), the laser, and fiber optics.

More than tangible products emerged from Bell Labs: The contributions made by the scientists and engineers working for Bell Labs also included methodologies, such as statistical control and best practices. The latter concept was extremely important, as it documented the best way to conduct maintenance and perform repairs, and it has been adopted by nonengineering, nontechnical businesses worldwide to streamline operations. By documenting these practices and then requiring employees to perform them as written, regardless of location, Bell Labs ensured that there would be an approach to work ad to resolving any problem that not only would be the most effective but also would ensure uniform results.

Software—including the Unix operating system and the C and C++ programming languages—was also developed at Bell Labs. Bell Labs was also responsible for advancements in information theory. Seven of its employees were awarded Nobel Prizes for their work.

In the last quarter of the twentieth century, Bell Labs saw a steady reduction of personnel. As part of the AT&T telephone conglomerate ("Ma Bell") into separate entities in 1984, Bell Labs was also divided: Bellcore (now Telcordia Technologies) was immediately split off to serve the research and development needs of local telephone exchanges, and the remainder of Bell Labs evolved into Lucent Technologies, now known as Alcatel-Lucent.

Complex Calculator, a machine about the size of a closet. By early 1940, the machine was in operation, successfully performing calculations for Stibitz and his colleagues. Problems to be solved (inputs) were handled by an operator sitting at a teletype machine who entered the values comprising the problem. The results would be returned in seconds. The Model I Complex Calculator was a dramatic improvement and represented a major advance that would make it possible for mathematicians to support network design.

There were, however, some real limitations, which would become obvious as time went on and which would contribute to an agenda in coming years for improving computers. For example, although three workstations (basically teletype machines) were connected to the calculator, only one could be used. Creating the capability to handle multiple, simultaneous users would not be possible for several years. Second, at least initially, the calculations were restricted to combinations of multiplication and division, although addition and subtraction would be introduced in later models. Finally, the machine was not programmable; it was mainly a very large and faster version of the desktop calculator. A limited degree of programmability would be introduced as computers developed.

On balance, the machines were faster than their predecessors, always accurate, and could support an ever-increasing demand for work. There was another capability, however, that would be demonstrated in dramatic fashion by Stibitz on September 11, 1940, at Dartmouth College in Hanover, New Hampshire. The Mathematical Society of America was conducting its annual meeting. In attendance were the country's most distinguished mathematicians, including John von Neumann and Norbert Wiener.

Stibitz showed the assembled group a workstation similar to those used at the Bell Labs facility in New York City. The workstation was connected to the calculator by telephone lines. Participants were invited to submit problems that would then be entered into the teletype machines, transmitted via the phone lines to the computer at the New York facility. The correct solution would be returned in seconds. Stibitz had demonstrated not only the capabilities of an electric computer but also the possibilities of remote processing.

The first model remained in use at Bell Labs until the late 1940s, and there would be successor calculating machines of greater complexity in the coming years. In addition to their increasing speed and ability to perform advanced calculations, the newer machines were designed to be more reliable and could be maintained by workers who were not necessarily advanced engineers. Stibitz, however, would not be involved in those projects. In December 1941, the United States entered World War II, and Stibitz, like many advanced engineers and scientists, would be heavily involved in war work.

Military operations required substantial mathematical expertise to calculate ballistics. There were many different types of artillery for various purposes. For crews to be able to hit their targets, firing tables that gave solutions to how to set weapons, depending on range and other factors (such as temperature), were necessary. Consulting these ballistics tables and applying the correct settings to guns and other weapons before they were fired would, one would hope, result in hitting the target on the first try. These ballistics problems were complicated by the increased use of antiaircraft artillery, which fired at objects moving at various speeds and at various altitudes.

To construct these tables, some government agencies hired large pools of junior-level mathematicians (who were called *computers* at a time when the term did not primarily denote a machine). Automating this process, however, was a priority—a project in which Stibitz became involved during the war years. Such efforts would eventually contribute to the development of early computers.

With the end of the war, Stibitz did not return to Bell Labs. For several years he worked as a consultant, performing research and experimentation with the goal of developing new computers. After that, he made a major transition in his career, becoming a member of the faculty at Dartmouth College, specializing in biotechnology, in 1964. The field focused on using computer science to investigate medical issues, such as the movement of oxygen, the movement of blood, the anatomy of brain cells, and mathematical models of capillary transport. Stibitz officially retired from Dartmouth in 1973 but remained as a researcher there until the early 1980s.

PERSONAL LIFE

In 1930, the year in which Stibitz began work at Bell Labs, he married Dorothea Lamson. Together they had two daughters.

Stibitz personally held thirty-eight patents, not including those awarded to Bell Labs for technologies to which he had contributed. Stibitz's achievements were widely recognized during his lifetime; he was presented with several awards. These included the Harry M. Goode Memorial Award (1965, with Konrad Zuse) from the American Federation of Information Processing Societies, membership in the National Academy of Engineering (1976), and the Babbage Society Medal (1982). He was inducted into the Inventors Hall of Fame in 1983. Stibitz died on January 31, 1995, in Hanover, New Hampshire, of natural causes; he was ninety years old.

Robert N. Stacy

FURTHER READING

Gertner, Jon. *The Idea Factory, Bell Labs and the Great Age of American Innovation*. New York: Penguin, 2012. Print. A well-received account not only describing the history of Bell Labs and its accomplishments but also offering a good analysis of the consequences of those inventions on today's technical and economic environments.

Grier, David Alan. "George Stibitz's Values and R. C. Archibald's Slide Rule." *Computer* 39.1 (2006): 11–13. Print. A description of Stibitz's legacy as an innovator and developer at Bell Labs.

Irvine, M. M. "Early Digital Computers at Bell Telephone Laboratories." *IEEE Annals of the History Of Computing* 23.3 (2001): 22. Print. An account of computer development at Bell Labs from 1937 (the beginning of Stibitz's efforts to develop an electronic computer) to 1958.

Stibitz, George. "Early Computers." *A History of Computing in the Twentieth Century*. Ed. N. Metropolis. New York: Academic, 1980. Print. Stibitz's own account of the rise of electronic computing to the dawn of personal computers.

BJARNE STROUSTRUP

Creator of the C++ programming language

Born: December 30, 1950; Aarhus, Denmark
Died: -
Primary Field: Computer science
Specialty: Computer software
Primary Company/Organization: Bell Laboratories

INTRODUCTION

Bjarne Stroustrup created the C++ language, the first widely used object-oriented programming language, and remains a highly influential spokesperson on issues such as the design of programming languages, education in computer science, and the philosophy of computer programming. Stroustrup also wrote an influential book on programming, helped develop standards for C++, and continues to teach, conduct research, and advise students at Texas A&M University.

EARLY LIFE

Bjarne Stroustrup was born and raised in Aarhus, Denmark, to a working-class family (his father was an upholsterer, his mother a secretary). As a child, he preferred sports to academic pursuits, foreshadowing his contrarian tendencies. He studied at the University of Aarhus, receiving his master's degree in mathematics and computer science. While in school, he also acquired a great deal of practical experience doing contract programming for business applications and later reflected

on the appeal that practical work held for him. Stroustrup then continued his studies in the United Kingdom,

Bjarne Stroustrup.

earning his Ph.D. in computer science from Cambridge University in 1979; his topic was distributed computing, and his thesis adviser was David Wheeler. While at Cambridge, Stroustrup shared office space with Jeremy Dion, Mark Pezzaro, David Harper, Neil Grey, and Bruce Croft; he also cites Roger Needham as an influence on his intellectul development. Stroustrup later became a fellow of Churchill College. After graduation from Cambridge, Stroustrup was invited to work at Bell Laboratories, which was also the professional home of Dennis Ritchie and Kenneth Thompson, who played key roles in developing the C programming language and the Unix operating system.

LIFE'S WORK

While at Cambridge University, Stroustrup became interested in distributed computing. He continued this work at Bell Labs but found that existing programming languages were inadequate to the tasks. Languages such as C were essentially linear, and Stroustrup became interested in object-oriented programming as an alternative way to organize work within a computer program. In an object-oriented language, programs are organized around classes and objects, rather than routines, and lend themselves more naturally to distributed computing.

Stroustrup worked in the AT&T Labs Research section of Bell Labs, and within this section of the Labs headed the Large-Scale Programming Research Department until leaving in 2002 to become a professor of computer science at Texas A&M University in College Station, Texas. However, he remained an AT&T Fellow until 2012, thus maintaining a connection with AT&T Labs. As of 2012, Stroustrup held the chair of computer science in the College of Engineering at Texas A&M.

Stroustrup's work on C++ grew out of his graduate work in distributed computing; as part of a project to distribute Unix over a network, he developed the "C with classes" language (the earliest name for C++), building on the C language developed by Ritchie and Thompson. Compatability with C has been cited as both a strength and a weakness of C++: On the positive side, people working in C++ have access to all the features of C and are able to put to use the large quantities of C code already written; on the negative side, the decision to keep C++ compatible with C meant that the new language had to accommodate many peculiarities of the old.

Stroustrup originally worked with an object-oriented language called Simula but decided it was too inefficient for his purposes. He also wanted to capitalize on the popularity of the C language and thus decided to extend C by adding object-oriented features to it rather than creating an entirely new language; this extended version of C was named C++. This new language became extremely popular, in part because it was easy to use, not only because many programmers were also working in the C language but also because Stroustrup wrote a textbook, *The C++ Programming Language*, which has seen several editions and made it easy for programmers to learn the new language. Stroustrup exerted considerable effort to standardize C++, in part because he was concerned that the language could degenerate into a series of "dialects" that would not be compatible.

Despite its widespread adoption and influence on other languages, C++ has also been criticized over the years. One of the most serious criticisms is that C++ allows programmers to make serious errors; Stroustrup himself has said, in essence, that while C++ has solved some of the problems with C that allow a coder to shoot himself or herself in the foot, C++ includes other features that allow a coder to blow off an entire leg. Because of its large number of features and flexibility, C++ is often perceived as overly complex and unnecessarily difficult to learn. Interestingly, Stroustrup argued, in an interview with the Massachusetts Institute of Technology's *Technology Review*, that a good computer language should help people solve problems and express their ideas and that an emphasis on the elegance of a language for its own sake is a mistake. Stroustrup emphasized in the same interview that he did not design the language with the goal of corporate efficiency in mind, but included expert features that perhaps only a small number of programmers would be able to use well; in this choice, he cites the influence of Søren Kierkegaard and the idea of valuing the exceptional individual rather than catering to the average crowd. In other interviews, he has identified C++ as a product of his own individual work; in contrast to the way many languages and computing projects are developed, C++ was not developed by a committee.

At Texas A&M, Stroustrup teaches, conducts research, and is a member of the Parasol Lab. He is involved in the development of the Standard Template Adaptive Parallel Library (STAPL), a framework to develop parallel programs in C++. He also founded the Programming Techniques, Tools, and Languages Group in 2003, within the Parasol Lab.

Stroustrup has received many honors during his career. In 1990, he was named one of America's top

Affiliation: Bell Laboratories

Bjarne Stroustrup did much of his most important work while at Bell Laboratories (Bell Labs), a research laboratory attached to telephone company AT&T. Bell Labs has gone through several changes of ownership and name since it was founded in 1925 through the merger of the AT&T engineering department and the research labs of Western Electric. Today, its parent company is Alcatel-Lucent, and it consists of eight research centers located in the United States, Belgium, China, France, Germany, India, Ireland, and South Korea. Employees work on both practical problems related to telephone service and more fundamental problems in science and technology, and they have collaborated with the U.S. government (for example, on the space program) and with other universities and research entities. Many important scientific innovations have come from the work of Bell Labs scientists, and work at the Labs has generated more than thirty-three thousand patents. Researchers at Bell Labs have received seven

Nobel Prizes (all in physics), two Draper Prizes, seven National Medals of Technology, and nine National Medals of Science.

Important scientific breakthroughs at Bell Labs include the development of the transistor (1947), which replaced mechanical relays and vacuum tubes in computers and other electronics products; practical solar cells (1954), to convert the sun's energy into electricity; the laser (1958), which has had myriad applications in scientific research and medicine; Telstar I, the first orbiting communications satellite (1962), which allowed telephone calls to be communicated wirelessly around the world; the Unix operating system and the C language (1969–72), which together facilitated the creation of large-scale computer networks and portable computer programming; and the digital signal processor, or DSP (1979), which is used in many communications devices today, including wireless phones, voice synthesizers, and digital cameras.

young scientists (a total of twelve were named) by *Fortune* magazine. In 1993, he received the Grace Murray Hopper Award from the Association for Computing Machinery (ACM) for his work on C++, and he became an ACM Fellow and a Bell Laboraties Fellow. In 1995, *Byte* magazine named him one of the twenty most influential people in the comptuer industry. In 1995, he became an AT&T Fellow. He served as an honorary professor at Xi'an Jiaoton University for the years 2002–06 and as an honorary professor in the Department of Computer Science at the University of Aarhus for the years 2010–15. In 2004, Stroustrup was awarded the Computer Entrepreneur Award from the Institute of Electrical and Electronics Engineers (IEEE) for his work on developing an object-oriented langauge and the subsequent influence of object-oriented programming on industry and business; in the same year, he became a member of the Texas Academy of Medicine, Engineering, and Science and a member of the National Academy of Engineering. In 2005, he became a Fellow of the IEEE and won the William Procter Prize for Scientific Achievement from the scientific research society Sigma Xi. In 2008, he received Dr. Dobb's Excellence in Programming Award, for individuals who have advanced software development. In 2010, he was awarded the Rigmor and Carl Holst-Knudsen Award for Scientific Research from the University of Aarhus, the oldest and

most prestigious honor in science for people associated with that university.

PERSONAL LIFE
Stroustrup is married to Marian Stroustrup; their daughter, Annemarie, was born while he was a student at Cambridge University, and their son Nicholas was born in Watchung, New Jersey, while Stroustrup was working at Bell Labs. Annemarie became a physician and, as of 2012, was a professor of pediatrics at the Mount Sinai Hospital in New York City; also as of 2012, Nicholas was a graduate student in systems biology at Harvard University in Cambridge, Massachusetts.

Sarah Boslaugh

FURTHER READING
Biancuzzi, Federico, and Shane Warden. *Masterminds of Programming: Conversations with the Creators of Major Programming Languages*. Sebastopol: O'Reilly, 2009. Print. A series of interviews with the creators of influential computer programming languages, including Stroustrup (C++), Thomas E. Kurtz (BASIC), Don Chamberlin (SQL), James Gosling (JAVA), and Larry Wall (PERL).
Pontin, Jason. "More Trouble with Programming." *Technology Review* 7 Dec. 2006: n. pag. Print. In an interview with the MIT Technology Review, Stroust-

rup discusses good and bad programs written using C++, and discusses changes that he expects to see in the practice of computer programming in the future. He also argues for the acceptance of programming as a skilled trade, rather than a simple task to be undertaken with minimal training.

Stroustrup, Bjarne. *The C++ Programming Language.* 4th ed. Boston: Pearson, 2012. Print. Stroustrup's classic manual for his programming language, updated for C++ version 11 and dense with detail at more than a thousand pages. Covers both well-known and obscure aspects of the language.

---. *The Design and Evolution of C++.* Reading: Addison-Wesley, 1995. Print. Stroustrup's account of how he designed and developed C++; will enlighten programmers about why Stroustrup made certain decisions regarding the language and provide information about how the language has been updated over the years.

---. "Viewpoint: What Should We Teach New Software Developers? Why?" *Communications of the ACM* 53.1 (2010): 40–42. Print. In an opinion piece, Stroustrup locates some of the problems with contemporary softer in the disconnect between the academy (universities) and the demands of industry, and argues that both a mastery of theory and experience in practical programming problems should be expected of those who teach and study computer science.

ROBERT TAYLOR

Early developer of the Internet

Born: February 10, 1932; Dallas, Texas
Died: -
Primary Field: Computer science
Specialty: Internet
Primary Company/Organization: Defense Advanced
Research Projects Agency

INTRODUCTION

*Robert Taylor is one of the fathers of the Internet. He
helped to created the ARPANET, a scientific- and defense-
oriented network funded by the U.S. Department of Defense. Throughout his career, Taylor, whose background
included studies in philosophy and psychology, remained
focused on the usefulness of computers as a means
of communication and extending the reach of human
thought—a remarkable perspective in the early years of
computing, when computers were considered primarily
as computational machines and when interacting with
them required stacks of punched paper cards. Through
his leadership and direction of funding, he also facilitated
development of a number of influential innovations that
changed how people interact with computers.*

EARLY LIFE

Robert Taylor was born in Dallas, Texas, in 1932 and
was adopted as an infant; his adoptive father was a
Methodist minister, and much of Taylor's young life
was marked by frequent moves, as his father was transferred from one parish to another. Taylor entered Southern Methodist University (SMU) at age sixteen; he left
the university to serve in the Navy during the Korean
War but continued his education after finishing his military commitment, enrolling at the University of Texas

(Austin) under the G.I. Bill. Taylor's original intent was
to join the ministry, but he sampled a wide range of
courses before graduating with a bachelor's degree in
experimental psychology and minors in English, mathematics, philosophy, and religion. He continued his education at the University of Texas, receiving his master's
degree in experimental psychology in 1964; as part of
his studies at this time, he became familiar with the

Robert Taylor.

work of Massachusetts Institute of Technology (MIT) professor J. C. R. Licklider, who would later play an important role in his career.

Taylor worked briefly as a high school mathematics teacher in Florida before, in 1960, accepting a position as a systems design engineer at the Martin Company. The next year, he worked briefly for ACF Electronics before accepting a position with the National Aeronautics and Space Administration (NASA) in the Office of Advanced Research and Technology; he had attracted the attention of NASA while at ACF because of a proposal he wrote for a flight-control simulation display. While working at NASA, Taylor became involved in computer science research.

LIFE'S WORK

Taylor joined the NASA Office of Advanced Research and Technology in 1962. While working at NASA, Taylor met Licklider, then the director of the Advanced Research Projects Agency (ARPA), formed in response to the Soviet success in launching the space satellite Sputnik. ARPA would later be renamed the Defense Advanced Research Projects Agency or DARPA (the name was changed back to ARPA in 1993) and was inspired by Licklider's guiding vision of interactive computing and of the computer as an extension of human thought and a medium for the exchange of knowledge, rather than simply a machine to do computations rapidly. Licklider was named head of the newly created Information Processing Techniques Office (IPTO) at ARPA; the mission of this

---

Affiliation: Defense Advanced Research Projects Agency

The Defense Advanced Research Projects Agency (DARPA) was created within the U.S. Department of Defense in 1958 as the Advanced Research Projects Agency (ARPA), in response to the perceived threat posed by the technological and scientific achievements of the Soviet Union, as marked by their successful launch of the Sputnik satellite. It became the largest agency in the United States, funding research and development, and through the 1960s was involved in many important innovations that led to the development of the Internet. In 1972, the name of ARPA was changed to DARPA, the *D* standing for Defense—a change that signaled a shift toward research with more specifically military applications. The name was changed back to ARPA in 1993 and then returned to DARPA in 1996.

---

office was to create a computer networking system that would facilitate resource sharing. Licklider left the IPTO in 1964 and was replaced by Ivan Sutherland; when Sutherland left in 1966, Taylor succeeded him as the head of IPTO. In this position, Taylor garnered further resources for IPTO and ushered in a golden age of computer science and networking research through his choice to fund visionary projects that he believed would substantially change the way computers worked and were used.

In 1966, Taylor developed the idea of a single network through which multiple computers could communicate, an idea that was realized in the Advanced Research Projects Agency Network (ARPANET). This project was born in part out of his frustration with existing capabilities for communications: For instance, although Taylor's computer could connect with computers at MIT (in Cambridge, Massachusetts), the University of California (in Berkeley, California), and the Systems Development Corporation (in Santa Monica, California), he frequently had to duplicate effort because none of those computers could communicate directly with each other. If he wanted to send an e-mail to all three computers, he had to send each e-mail separately and even had to move his chair to use a different computer to communicate with each of the distant computers.

Charles Herzfeld, ARPA's director, charged Taylor with developing a time-sharing, cooperative computer network that would provide the kind of efficient connectivity Taylor envisioned. The government had multiple interests in the creation of this netowork: Not only would it allow scientists and other researchers to share information more readily; it would also create an efficient method of communication should the United States be the victim of a nuclear attack (not an idle question during this Cold War period). Taylor recruited MIT scientist Larry Roberts, who was experienced in computer networking, to help with this project, and ARPA contracted with Bolt, Beranek, and Newman to create the physical network for the system. In 1968, Taylor and Licklider published an influential article, "The Computer as Communications Device," that expressed their vision of a unified computer network that would facilitate the creation of communities bound by common interests rather than geographical location. Although their thoughts were focused on using computers to facilitate work (for example, sharing files, finding others interested in the same topics), this attitude has also led to the creation of worldwide "virtual" communities bound together by their interest in a particular sports team, popular singer, or other leisure interest.

Work on the ARPANET led to development of the technology of packet switching, an approach to communication in which information to be transmitted across a network is not transmitted whole but instead is broken down into "packets" or chunks that are transmitted separately, then reassembled at the receiving destination. Packet switching helped the network make the most efficient use of high-speed connections between computers. The network to communicate among computers was designed so that the computers were linked through nodes (similar to the hub-and-spoke system used to organize modern air travel and the system used in the telegraph network), thus reducing the number of connections needed, rather than having each computer directly connected to all the others. The problem of facilitating communication among different types of computers was solved by having a translating computer, called an interface message processor (IMP), attached to each node. ARPA also funded research at the Stanford Research Institute, including Douglas Engelbart's work, which led to developing the computer mouse, another important piece of technology facilitating interactive computing.

Taylor assisted the U.S. military effort during the Vietnam War and was given the honorary rank of brigadier general; his work included setting up a computer center for military use in Saigon (the capital of what was then South Vietnam). However, in 1969 Taylor left ARPA and joined the computer science department at the University of Utah; this move was motivated in part by his frustration at pressure from the U.S. government to shape ARPA to serve military rather than general computing goals. In 1970, he began working at Xerox as manager of the computer science laboratory within the company's Palo Alto Research Center (PARC).

One focus of Taylor's work at PARC was computerizing all functions of the modern office. The PARC computer science lab produced many groundbreaking developments, facilitated in part by an unusual cooperative structure wherein many scientists worked together on a single project rather than working separately on small aspects of a larger problem. The lab also became famous for its weekly meetings in the "dealer's room," outfitted with massive white boards, where PARC scientists met to share ideas and challenge one another to create greater innovations. In 1973, scientists at PARC created the first personal workstation, called the Alto; this computer had many interactive features now basic to computing, including cut-and-paste word processing, a graphical point-and-click interface, and a WYSIWYG ("what you see is what you get") display. The laser printer, another staple of modern office life, was also developed at PARC and became a highly profitable product for Xerox.

Taylor left PARC in 1983, in part because Xerox was reducing funding for the lab, and founded the Systems Research Center (SRC) at Digital Equipment Corporation (DEC). He recruited many PARC scientists to work at SRC and moved the development of computing forward through projects such as the first electronic book, the first fault-tolerant local area network (LAN), improved networking and storage systems, and an object-oriented programming language, Modula 3, that was a predecessor to Java. In 1995, AltaVista, the first full-text and searchable index for the World Wide Web, was developed at SRC. Taylor retired in 1966 but remained a consultant for DEC, later acquired by Compaq.

PERSONAL LIFE

Taylor received the National Medal of Technology in 1999; the citation applauds his leadership in developing computer technology, including ARPANET, and his work in developing the personal computer. In 2004, Taylor received the Charles Stark Draper Prize from the National Academy of Engineering; the latter was for his work, along with three other PARC scientists, in developing the Alto. In 2010, the University of Texas Graduate School honored him as an Outstanding Alumnus and created awards in his name for graduate students in psychology and computer science.

Taylor retired in 1996. Residing in Woodside, California, he continued to work as a consultant, making occasional public appearances and giving interviews. In a 1999 interview for the *New York Times*, Taylor has received no financial rewards from the Internet boom.

Sarah Boslaugh

FURTHER READING

Hiltzik, Michael. A. *Dealers of Lightning: Xerox PARC and the Dawn of the Computer Age*. New York: HarperBusiness, 2000. Print. A popular history of the Xerox Corporation's Palo Alto Reseach Center in the 1970s and 1980s, focusing on the personalities (including Taylor's) of those working there as well as their innovations.

Markoff, John. "Robert W. Taylor: An Internet Pioneer Ponders the Next Revolution." *New York Times* 20 Dec. 1999: 38. Print. A newspaper profile of Taylor, conducted after his retirement and focusing on his career, the ideas that led to the development of the Internet, and his vision of a computer network that would facilitate sharing and the creation of virtual communities.

Salus, Peter H., ed. *The ARPANET Sourcebook: The Unpublished Foundations of the Internet*. Milton Keynes: Peer to Peer Communications, 2008. Print. A collection of important documents (papers and research reports) related to development of the AR-PANET; some are well known (such as Taylor and Licklider's 1968 paper), but many are rare and not generally available elsewhere.

Taylor, Robert, and J. C. R. Licklider. "The Computer as Communications Device." *Science and Technology* Apr. 1968: 21–41. Print. Taylor and Licklider's revolutionary paper outlining their vision of the computer as a device to facilitate communication and dealing with issues such as the costs of computing and the computer's ability to create interactive online communities.

Wu, Timothy. *The Master Switch: The Rise and Fall of Information Empires*. New York: Vintage, 2011. Print. An analysis of information empires of the recent past—such as those built around the telephone, radio, and film—and their tendency over time to be dominated by a monopoly or small cartel. Suggests that the same fate may befall the Internet.

KEN THOMPSON

Cocreator of the Unix operating system

Born: February 4, 1943; New Orleans, Louisiana
Died: -
Primary Field: Computer science
Specialty: Computer programming
Primary Company/Organization: Bell Laboratories

INTRODUCTION

A computer engineer with Bell Laboratories, Ken Thompson contributed a number of innovations to the industry, including the character-encoding set used today by the World Wide Web, the first purpose-built chess computer, and the use of regular expressions in computer applications. However, his most influential achievement was his development of the Unix operating system with Dennis Ritchie.

EARLY LIFE

Kenneth Lane Thompson was born on February 4, 1943, in New Orleans, Louisiana, to Lewis Elwood Thompson and Anna Hazel Lane Thompson. His father was a fighter pilot in the U.S. Navy, and the family moved every few years. He attended the University of California, Berkeley, studying under information theorist Elwyn Berlekamp, and earned both a bachelor of science degree (1965) and a master of science degree (1966) in electrical engineering and computer science. While at Berkeley, Thompson participated in a work-study program with General Dynamics, a government defense contractor. After graduate school, Thompson took a job with Bell Laboratories (Bell Labs), working on programming languages and operating systems.

LIFE'S WORK

Bell Labs had been formed in the 1920s by the merger of the research laboratories of Western Electric and AT&T, and it had become one of the world's most significant research laboratories. It had been especially instrumental in furthering the computer industry; the transistor was invented by a Bell Labs team in 1947, the 1950s had seen advances in computer networks, and

Ken Thompson.

just before Thompson's stint researchers at Bell Labs had invented the metal-oxide-semiconductor field-effect transistor. Thompson would contribute to Bell Labs' place in the history of computers by developing the Unix operating system in 1969, working with Dennis Ritchie.

Ritchie was a second-generation Bell Labs scientist, the son of Alistair Ritchie, who had pioneered switching circuit theory. While working on the C programming language, Ritchie collaborated with Thompson on several projects, beginning with the Multics operating system. Multics had begun as a collaborative effort between Bell Labs, General Electric (GE), and the Massachusetts Institute of Technology (MIT), intended to result in a commercial product for GE. Multics was a multiplexed operating system (hence the name) and was designed to be much more flexible and versatile than anything that had yet been developed. It was created for time-sharing systems, and GE had some thought of developing computing as a utility like telephony and electricity. (This thinking gives some indication of how abruptly the personal computer revolution began, since the first personal computers—which would make GE's idea completely unnecessary—were on the horizon, barely a decade away.)

Bell Labs pulled out of the Multics project, which continued with GE and later Honeywell, in 1969. Thompson and Ritchie moved on to other work, but they had had the chance to develop some ideas on operating systems, which led to their creation of Unix. Thompson wrote an early computer game on the Multics system: *Space Travel* (sometimes confused with *Spacewar!*, a better-known game that was released to arcades). *Space Travel* simulated travel through the solar system, and the development of Unix began when Thompson and Ritchie ported *Space Travel* from Multics to the PDP-7 computer. The code they wrote in the process became the basis for the Unix operating system, making *Space Travel* a sort of *Hobbit* to Unix's *Lord of the Rings*. The influence of Multics on Unix is so obvious in some areas that it is sometimes overestimated. The naming of commands is similar and sometimes identical— Thompson and Ritchie naturally retained the names to which they were accustomed from the work they had been doing. The name Unix, first spelled Unics, was a play on Multics. However, Unix was more of a reaction against Multics and its design flaws than a continuation of the Multics work. Thompson later described Multics as overwrought and overdesigned; Unix was designed to be simple and small, powerful but without placing an unreasonable demand on computing resources. Retained were the shell and the hierarchical file system.

The year Unix was born was also the year ARPANET, the Internet's forefather, was launched and the Apollo program landed a man on the Moon. Unix was not originally an official Bell Labs project—that is, one with actual funding. When Thompson wanted more resources in order to keep the project going, he and Ritchie interested Bell Labs in providing funding and computing resources by adding text-processing capabilities with a text-formatting program called roff. The successor to roff was troff, the first publishing software with full typesetting capability.

While working on Multics, Thompson also developed the Bon programming language, probably named for his wife Bonnie. Bon was not developed very far, but it may have lent its initial to the B programming language Thompson designed in 1969, based in part on the Basic Combined Programming Language (BCPL) developed in 1966 and used in the Unix project. Ritchie did some work on B after Thompson developed it, and it had a great influence on Ritchie's later C computer language— bridging the gap between C and earlier languages such as Forth. B remained in use through the rest of the century, mainly on Honeywell mainframes. The first open source multiuser dungeon online role-playing game (MUD), AberMUD, was written in B in 1989, although later copies of it were ported to C and run on Unix.

In 1971, Thompson developed ed, a line editor for Unix, which was one of the first Unix end-user programs and has been standard in Unix systems since. It was based on Thompson's Multics implementation of qed, an earlier line editor, and preserved the innovation Thompson had introduced: the use of regular expressions, to which Thompson had been introduced in a mathematics paper. Regular expressions are patterns that specify sets of strings, such as the vertical bar used to represent the Boolean expression *or*: "dog|cat" matches all occurrences of "dog" or "cat." Regular expressions can also be used to match variant spellings (or common misspellings or typos). Thompson's qed implementation and ed were the first editors to use regular expressions, and the popularity of Unix spread them throughout the computing world. Successors of ed include ex and vi.

Unix was rewritten in C, which Ritchie had developed based on B, in 1972. Over the course of the 1970s, Unix became extremely popular in academia, and versions of Unix and Unix-like operating systems (such as Linux and BSD) were implemented by many of the start-ups of the era, such as Sun Microsystems' Solaris operating system.

Affiliation: Bell Laboratories

Bell Laboratories (Bell Labs) was, in its most famous period, a research laboratory and think tank operated by the telephone company AT&T and home to some of the most remarkable accomplishments in the United States during the twentieth century. Although Alexander Graham Bell had previously run laboratories that were the spiritual ancestors of Bell Labs, Bell Labs was officially created as Bell Telephone Laboratories, Inc., a separate entity from AT&T, in 1925 as a joint venture between AT&T and Western Electric Research Laboratories.

It was intended to research and develop technology related to Bell System operations, especially the equipment Western Electric built for AT&T. However, Frank B. Jewett, president of research from Bell Labs' inception until 1940, also allocated a few researchers for pure research, which proved fruitful. Bell Labs researcher Clinton J. Davisson in 1937 became the first Bell Labs researcher to receive a Nobel Prize for work done at the Labs. He was awarded a share of the Nobel Prize in Physics for demonstrating matter's wave nature.

The innovations developed at Bell Labs are numerous. Television signals were transmitted in 1927. The one-time pad (OTP) cipher was developed in the 1920s, with employee Claude Shannon proving during World War II that OTP was not only unbreakable but also a model for the characteristics any unbreakable system must possess. Shannon also pioneered information theory when working at Bell Labs on behalf of the war effort. The groundwork for radio astronomy and solid-state electronics was done in the 1930s, and the vocoder was invented in 1937. One of the most famous Nobel Prizes awarded for work done at Bell Labs was awarded in 1956 to John Bardeen, Walter H. Brattain, and William Shockley for inventing the first transistors in 1947.

Information theory, particularly binary code systems, was further developed in the 1950s. The first solar cell was invented in 1954, the first transatlantic telephone cable was laid in 1956, the first computer program playing music was written in 1957, and the laser was invented (on paper) in 1958. The first continuous-light laser followed at Bell Labs only two years later, and the carbon dioxide laser in 1964.

Bell Labs scientists Arno Penzias and Robert Wilson discovered the cosmic microwave background radiation in 1965, receiving the Nobel Prize in Physics for this work in 1978. The Unix operating system was introduced in 1969, and computing became a major Bell Labs concern in the following decades: Dennis Ritchie developed the C programming language in 1970, the first fiber optics systems were introduced in 1976, and the first single-chip 32-bit microprocessor was introduced in 1980. An extension of C, the C++ programming language, was developed at Bell in 1983.

The following year, the federal government forced the breakup of AT&T after years of discussion of antitrust complaints. Bell Telephone Laboratories, Inc., became a wholly owned subsidiary of AT&T Technologies (formerly Western Electric), and Bellcore was split off as a separate entity, now known as Telcordia Technologies. Bell Telephone Laboratories was spun off in 1996 to become Lucent Technologies, which became Alcatel-Lucent after being acquired by Alcatel SA, a French corporation.

In the 1970s and 1980s, Thompson and Joseph Condon built Belle, the first purpose-built chess computer. With custom-made software, it was the most powerful chess computer of its era, winning numerous chess computer championships and confiscated at one point by the U.S. State Department to prevent it from entering the Soviet Union, which was considered a violation of restrictions on the transit of advanced technology to foreign nations. Thompson used Belle to research endgame tablebases, the computer databases of endgame position analysis that are used by computer chess engines to determine their plays.

Thompson also worked on Plan 9 from Bell Labs, a free operating system developed as a Unix successor. Work began in the 1980s, and the first edition was released in 1992 to universities; a second version was released in 1995 for commercial purposes; and the third version was released in 2000 under an open source license. The current version, released in 2002, was free. Plan 9 was used at Bell Labs for operating systems research, and it remains in development at Bell Labs and by MIT personnel. The mascot of Plan 9 is Glenda the Bunny.

In 1992, Thompson and Rob Pike developed the UTF-8 character encoding scheme, which has become the predominant encoding scheme on the World Wide Web, in use on more than half of its pages.

Thompson retired from Bell Labs on December 1, 2000, to pursue flight instruction full time. Google tempted him back, and today he is a distinguished engineer there. At Google, he developed the Go programming language with Pike and Robert Griesemer.

Development began in 2007, and the language was in use by 2010. A language designed for extremely fast compiling, it is also fairly easy to learn, relying on clean syntax and a small number of basic language concepts.

Thompson was named to the National Academy of Engineering in 1980 for his Unix work. In 1983, he and Ritchie were jointly given the Turing Award for Unix and their development of operating systems theory; his acceptance speech, "Reflections on Trusting Trust," introduced the Thompson hack, a type of backdoor attack, and is a major work in the theory of computer security. Thompson and Ritchie were honored again for their work in Unix in 1990 with the Richard W. Hamming Medal from the Institute of Electrical and Electronics Engineers (IEEE); in 1997, when they were inducted as Fellows of the Computer History Museum; in 1999, when President Bill Clinton awarded them with the National Medal of Technology and the IEEE awarded Thompson with the first Tsutomu Kanai Award; and in 2011, when they were given the Japan Prize for Information and Communications.

PERSONAL LIFE
Thompson and his wife, Bonnie, have two children. In the computer industry and hacking community, Thompson is generally known simply as ken (intentionally lowercasing his name). He cut Unix distribution tapes by hand and often included the note "Love, ken." While at Bell Labs, Thompson would sometimes work thirty hours straight without sleep.

Bill Kte'pi

FURTHER READING
Chandler, Alfred D. Jr. *Inventing the Electronic Century: The Epic Story of the Consumer Electronics and Computer Science Industries*. New York: Free Press, 2001. Print. A history of electronics told principally in the context of the history of companies rather than focusing on "great man" inventors.

Cringely, Robert X. *Accidental Empires: How the Boys of Silicon Valley Make Their Millions, Battle Foreign Competition, and Still Can't Get a Date*. New York: HarperBusiness, 1996. Print. A history of Silicon valley from before the dot-com bubble burst.

Kenney, Martin. *Understanding Silicon Valley: The Anatomy of an Entrepreneurial Region*. Stanford: Stanford Business Books, 2000. Print. An overview of Silicon Valley culture.

Rao, Arun, and Piero Scarulfi. *A History of Silicon Valley*. San Francisco: Omniware, 2011. Print. An overview of the Silicon Valley tech company culture.

Seibel, Peter. *Coders at Work: Reflections on the Craft of Programming*. New York: Apress, 2009. Print. Includes a chapter on Thompson.

JANIE TSAO

Cofounder of Linksys

Born: 1954; Taiwan
Died: -
Primary Field: Computer science
Specialty: Computer hardware
Primary Company/Organization: Linksys

INTRODUCTION
Janie Tsao, a Taiwanese immigrant to the United States, is a cofounder of Linksys, a leading manufacturer of home networking products with a line of wired and wireless products for consumers and small office or home office users. Tsao and her husband founded Linksys in April 1988 and over the next fifteen years worked to make the company a market leader. Linksys was acquired by Cisco Systems in 2003 for $500 million. Tsao, who had served as vice president of worldwide sales, marketing, and business development for the company, continued in this role for the Linksys division of Cisco until 2007. She was named Entrepreneur of the Year by, Inc. magazine in 2004.

EARLY LIFE
Janie Tsao was born in Taiwan in 1954. As a child, she remembers being singularly without ambition, dreaming only of becoming a perfect housewife and mother. She attended Tamkang University, where she majored in literature. While she was at Tamkang, she met Victor Tsao, also a student there. The two were a team from their first meeting. Shortly after Tsao graduated in with a B.A. degree in 1976, she and Victor left for the United States. In 1977, they moved to Chicago, where Victor attended graduate school at the Illinois Institute of Technology.

Janie Tsao.

Janie took a data-processing job at Sears, the beginning of her career in the field of technology. She credits her work experience in the management information system department at Sears, where she remained for eight years, with giving her a solid foundation in business. The Tsaos married and settled in California, where Victor received a master's degree in business administration from Pepperdine University in 1984. The couple's oldest son, Michael, was born the same year. A second son, Steven, was born two years later.

Returning to work five weeks after the birth of her first son, Janie worked as a systems analyst for TRW, Inc.'s Business Credit Department and as a systems manager at Carter Hawley Hale, Inc., where she was responsible for the programming computer systems at seven retail outlet divisions as well as mainframe systems. She and her husband often talked about their plans for a business of their own. They were particularly interested in ideas that would allow them to use their cultural background as an advantage. In 1988, they decided they were ready. Since her husband was the higher wage earner at the time, the plan was for him to continue with his job, contributing what he could to the family business after hours. Janie resigned from her job and launched DEW International, a company that paired American technology vendors with manufacturers in

Taiwan who could make parts that American businesses needed inexpensively.

LIFE'S WORK

The Tsaos were working long hours and carefully watching costs at DEW, creating what Victor once described as a high-tech version of a mom-and-pop Chinese restaurant, when one of their Taiwanese manufacturers had an idea for which he needed a U.S. marketer. The manufacturer had invented a means of using telephone wire to extend cables used to connect printers and personal computers (PCs) from the usual 15 feet to 100 feet. The manufacturer offered products that had the capacity to connect multiple PCs to multiple printers. The products sold well, and the Tsaos renamed their company Linksys. By 1991, both Janie and Victor were working full time at Linksys, and the company moved out of the family garage, eventually settling into a 2,000-square-foot office.

Linksys expanded slowly, moving from selling printer-to-PC connectors to PC-to-PC Ethernet hubs, cards, and cords. Small businesses and households in increasing numbers were eager to connect computers so that they could share data. By 1994, Linksys revenue had reached $6.5 million. The company was still small, but it was healthy. The frugality of the Tsaos was legendary. Victor was working 100-hour weeks, negotiating with U.S. vendors by day and Taiwanese manufacturers by night. For the first years, Victor drew no salary, and the family survived on the salary of $2,000 per month that Janie drew as vice president of business development and sales. Careful management meant that in addition to the Tsaos' initial $7,000 investment, only one bank loan had been required in 2001, and it was paid in full in less than six months.

The company's sales volume was steadily increasing. Janie successfully negotiated with large retailers CompUSA and Computer City to carry Linksys products, and she soon added another thirteen retailers. By 1992, Linksys had acquired a reputation for reliability that made it one of the top-selling brands. The company's biggest break came in 1995, when Microsoft released its Windows 95 operating system with built-in networking functions. Operating networks became simpler for small offices and homes, and the potential market for Linksys increased substantially. Still, growth remained relatively slow until 2000, when Linksys targeted the homes and small businesses that wanted to take advantage of cable and digital subscriber line (DSL) broadband connections by networking computers. Janie was traveling constantly, looking for new customers. She found a lucrative market in Canada, where no one else was supplying routers. In 2001, Linksys launched a system of wireless routers and computer cards. Although it was not first on the market with the wireless transmission that later came to be called Wi-Fi, Linksys had the advantage of name recognition. In 2001, Linksys's revenue and market share jumped to $346.7 million and 34.2 percent, respectively.

In fall 2002, Cisco Systems, a global leader in networking technology, contacted the Tsaos about acquiring Linksys. Cisco had a large share of big-business networking, but it lacked the small-business and home-office products that Linksys could supply. The Tsaos were not eager to sell, but they were realists. Most of the company's revenue came from the United States and Canada, and the company lacked the capital to expand into other markets. Competitors such as Dell, Hewlett-Packard, and Microsoft were all aiming for the same markets. In March 2003, the deal was announced. Cisco would pay $500 million in stock for the company, which, except for a small employee stock option plan, was owned by Janie, Victor, and their two sons. The deal included a provision for Linksys to be a separately operating unit and for Janie and Victor to remain with the company in executive management roles for two years.

In her role as vice president of worldwide sales, marketing, and business development for the Linksys division of Cisco, Janie continued to develop business partnerships and sales channels. She directed the adaptation of Linksys for new markets and oversaw the development of the Linksys distribution, e-commerce, and international channel market strategies and programs. She also developed a broadband strategy that included partnerships with AT&T Broadband, Verizon, Charter, AOL, Time Warner, Sprint, Telus, and British Telecom to provide high-speed Internet-sharing access via wired or wireless solutions to PC users. In May 2006, after doubling the company's revenue at the time of acquisition, Janie and Victor left their executive positions with the Linksys division of Cisco to serve as consultants to Cisco in identifying investment opportunities in its Chinese markets. By then, they had founded Miven Venture Partners, a company that provides capital for consumer-related technology start-ups in the areas of information technology, telecommunications, converged media, entertainment, and wireless. They began shifting their attention to Miven in 2007.

PERSONAL LIFE

Janie Tsao spend so much time working that she has difficulty remembering what she does in her rare free time.

Affiliation: Linksys

Linksys by Cisco (more commonly known as Linksys) is a brand of home and small-office networking products such as broadband and wireless routers, Ethernet switching devices, wireless Internet video cameras, and network storage systems. Linksys was founded as DEW International by Janie and Victor Tsao in their garage in 1988. The couple changed the name to Linksys a few years later. Beginning in 1997 and continuing over the next seven years, Linksys was named to the, Inc. 500, *Inc.* magazine's list of the five hundred fastest-growing companies. With the advent of Wi-Fi, the company experienced a more rapid growth rate, and by 2002, it claimed nearly 50 percent of the market, with revenues of $430.4 million. The company's customers included specialty stores such as Best Buy, big-box retailers such as Walmart, and Internet retailers such as Amazon. That year, Cisco came calling.

In 2003, the Tsaos sold Linksys to Cisco for $500 million in stock. The deal kept Linksys operating as a company separate from the behemoth Cisco, and the Tsaos were assured of executive positions at Linksys for two more years. They left in 2006, and in 2007 Cisco CEO John Chambers announced a long-term plan to kill the independent Linksys brand, explaining that it had been kept solely because of its power among U.S. consumers. By 2008, all Linksys products were packaged and rebranded as "Linksys by Cisco." In 2010, Cisco-Linksys had an estimated $564 million in sales and four hundred employees.

She admits to a fondness for bookstores and quiet places, particularly those that come with the sound of waves. She also heads the Tsao Family Foundation. Among other projects, she has worked with the nonprofit Center for Asian American Media to produce a series of documentaries promoting understanding and communication.

She was named Entrepreneur of the Year by the Orange County Business Association in 2000 and was the recipient of a BridgeGate 20 Award in 2002, which recognized leaders who make a measurable difference in the Southern California's information technology and new media communities. In 2004, Tsao was named Entrepreneur of the Year by, *Inc.* magazine. All these awards she shared with Victor. In 2005, however, the Anita Borg Institute for Women and Technology named Janie alone as the recipient of its Women of Vision Award for

Leadership, honoring her for her accomplishments as a business owner, innovator, colleague, and mentor. In her acceptance speech, Tsao attributed her success to persistence and passion for her work. Since leaving Cisco Systems, she has been president of Miven Venture Partners, the multistage venture and public equity investment firm that she and Victor founded to encourage entrepreneurial talent in China, California, Israel, and Vietnam.

Wylene Rholetter

FURTHER READING

Allen, Kathleen R. "Linksys: The Essence of Opportunity Recognition." *Launching New Ventures: An Entrepreneurial Approach.* 5th ed. Cincinnati: South-Western, 2008. 477–80. Print. A case study in a textbook on entrepreneurship and small business management, tracing the development of Linksys from its beginnings in the garage of Janie and Victor Tsao through its purchase by Cisco Systems.

Boudreau, John. "Technology's Women of Vision." *San Jose Mercury News* 19 Oct. 2005: n. pag. Print. This article provides brief profiles of the women recognized by the Institute for Women and Technology in the inaugural year of the Women of Vision Awards. Janie Tsao was the recipient in the leadership category.

Chuang, Tamara. "Taiwan Woman Founded Top Maker of Home-Networking Devices." *Orange County Register* 27 Nov. 2000: n. pag. Print. A feature on Janie Tsao that provides an overview of her achievements as cofounder and vice president of Linksys. It also highlights the company's best-selling products.

Mount, Ian. "The Entrepreneurs of the Year: Be Fast, Be Frugal, Be Right." *Inc. Magazine.* Jan. 2004: 64–70. Print. This article, the main feature of the issue in which it appeared, takes a close look at Jamie and Victor Tsao, who were the magazine's Entrepreneurs of the Year. Includes background on Linksys, with specific information on its revenues before it was acquired by Cisco and a time line of milestones in the history of the company.

Sidhu, Inder. *Doing Both: How Cisco Captures Today's Profit and Drives Tomorrow's Growth.* Upper Saddle River: FT Press, 2010. Print. This book is Cisco senior vice president Sidhu's explanation of how his company increased revenue, profits, and earnings per share in an unstable global economy. Provides context for and includes references to Cisco's acquisition of Linksys.

ALAN TURING

Mathematician, computer scientist, and founder of artificial intelligence

Born: June 23, 1912; Maida Vale, London, England
Died: June 7, 1954; Wilmslow, Cheshire, England, United Kingdom
Primary Field: Applied science
Specialty: Mathematics and logic
Primary Company/Organization: Government Code and Cypher School (United Kingdom)

INTRODUCTION

Known as the father computer science and artificial intelligence, Alan Turing successfully decoded the Nazi encryption device, the Enigma machine. This accomplishment is regarded by many as a deciding factor in the Allied victory in World War II. In addition, he created the Turing machine; the bombe machine; the Turing test; a blueprint for an early stored-program computer, the Automatic Computing Engine (ACE); and software that established the field of artificial intelligence.

EARLY LIFE

Alan Mathison Turing was born on June 23, 1912, in a northern suburb of London, Maida Vale. His family had long-standing links to science and scientific thought. Turing's mother, Ethel Stoney, came from a line of Irish Protestants. His father, Julius Mathison Turing, was in the Indian Civil Service. Turing's parents had met on a voyage during their travels between India and England. He and his younger brother, John, were both born soon after their parents' marriage in 1907, with Turing being born while the family was on leave in England. His father's government duties often took Turing's parents away from him during his childhood. Turing and his brother were therefore raised by relatives and friends until he was sent to various boarding schools. He finally was enrolled at Sherborne School, a college preparatory school.

Although as a student Turing was absorbed by science and mathematics (in which he got outstanding marks) and found it difficult to focus on other subjects,

Alan Turing.

he managed to pass all his classes. Inspired and motivated by his best friend and fellow mathematician Christopher Morcom, who died prematurely after contracting bovine tuberculosis, Turing was determined to be the greatest mathematician he could be. Despite his inconsistent grades at Sherbourne, Turing won a scholarship and attended King's College, Cambridge. He excelled and continued his education at Cambridge as a graduate student; he was elected Fellow of the college. In 1938, he traveled to Princeton University, where he studied mathematics, ultimately earning his Ph.D. in that field.

LIFE'S WORK

Turing's earliest groundbreaking work was his idea for the Turing machine. During his studies in Cambridge, he had encountered the work of David Hilbert on decision-making problems focusing on first-order logic. Hilbert proposed three questions to the mathematical world to prove or disprove the underlying principles of mathematics. The questions questioned whether mathematics were complete and consistent and if there existed a decidability factor in mathematics to judge whether a mathematical proposition is true or false. Although the first two parts of Hilbert's theory were quickly proven incorrect, Turing wanted to find a way to prove or disprove the third part through further exploration. He

developed the blueprints for a machine that could compute numbers infinitely.

The machine comprised a roll of never-ending tape. The tape comprised squares with 1s and squares that were blank, representing 0s. Much like a typewriter, Turing's machine was able to print or erase. Unlike a typewriter the machine worked alone. Each sequence of 0s and 1s represented a different number. Because the possibilities for sequences of 0s and 1s were infinite and the tape unending, so was the possibility of creating an infinite list of computable numbers. No matter how long was the list of numbers created by the Turing machine, there would always be other numbers, "uncomputable numbers," to add to that list. The potential for possibilities, or decisions made, was therefore infinite and undefined. Turing thus was able to answer the last part of Hilbert's decision first-order logic theory with a definite theory that disproved Hilbert's offered conclusion. Unknown to Turing, another scientist at Princeton University, Alonzo Church, had already disproved the theorem by completely different means. Church used more fundamental mathematics instead of Turing's imaginary computer. Still, Turing's design would soon become the starting point for computer programming systems. Turing wrote one of his greatest papers, "On Computable Numbers, with an Application to the *Entscheidungsproblem*," as a result of this study. The paper demonstrated that a general solution to Hilbert's problem was impossible. The results of the study are known as the Church-Turing theorem in recognition of both mathematicians' work.

In 1939, World War II began in Europe and Turing started his work at the British Government Code and Cypher School, located at a Buckinghamshire estate, Bletchley Park. There Turing was employed as a full-time cryptographer, working alongside other mathematicians to decipher the German Enigma machine. The Enigma machine was a device that converted messages into intricate codes that would keep German wartime messages secret if intercepted by the enemy. An operator would enter the desired message onto rotors. The machine would then take that message and turn it into code, or cipher, using a complex combination of variables including a plug board and rotors that continuously changed the cipher. There were thousands of possible settings that the machine's operator could change, and this made deciphering the codes extremely difficult. The operator would first send the rotor positions, then, by separate transmission, the coded message.

The French had managed to obtain an instruction manual for the Enigma machine. This top-secret information gave the Allied forces a good start on deciphering the coded messages shared between the German command and German U-boats. From the manual, the cryptanalysts were given numerous examples of encoded messages and were quickly put to work on figuring out how the rotors were wired. The French shared their information with the Polish government, and soon these two groups were leading the effort to break the Enigma for the Allies. The Poles had made headway in deciphering the Enigma machine's messages already, but their intelligence service was limited. The Polish machine used to break the Enigma code was called the bombe, in reference to the ticking noise that it made while working. The French and British governments soon adopted the bombe. The original machine could read Enigma messages at only the most basic level, it was a start.

Turing and fellow Cambridge mathematician Gordon Welchman soon saw a way to strengthen the bombe so that if a small portion of an Enigma message could be guessed using common words, then the entire message could be decoded. This guess-and-check method was similar to that Turing had employed to devise the Turing machine and compute numbers. By the end of 1939, Turing had cracked the Enigma code. Soon, German intelligence, aware of failed Nazi attacks, added more rotors to the Enigma, making previous Allied deciphering techniques useless. Turing and his team managed to persist in their decoding efforts and succeeded in decoding Enigma messages throughout the war. Turing, along with other British experts, kept up with the ever-evolving Enigma machine by producing new ways to make better guesses and in the process developed a computing program that could recognize patterns by reading a paper tape. Eventually they were able to store these patterns electronically. By cracking the Enigma machine, the mathematicians and scientists at Bletchley Park, especially Turing, saved countless Allied lives and made a significant contribution to the Allied victory in the Atlantic.

Turing received high praise for his work on the Enigma problem, and because of his skills as a cryptanalyst he was awarded an Order of the British Empire (OBE). Turing did not care much for the award and did not display it for long. However, the experience he had gained working with machine-based computing as a cryptanalyst helped in the building of the Colossus, regarded as the first programmable digital computer, capable of comparing two data streams. The Colossus was also used in decoding Axis communications during the war. Although the Colossus machine was kept top secret until a few years after the war had ended, those who had

Affiliation: Government Code and Cypher School

After the conclusion of World War I, the British government determined that it needed a more coordinated approach to peacetime code breaking. To that end, the Government Code and Cypher School (GCCS) was founded in 1919 and provided with an initial staff of between fifty and sixty specialists and clerical staff.

The GCCS was given a dual charge by government leaders. First, it was to advise all government departments regarding the security of all codes and cyphers that these departments used and to assist in their provision when necessary. Second, the GCCS was also to review and study the cypher communications methods used by foreign governments and to report on these.

During World War II, the GCCS was based at Bletchley Park in Milton Keynes, a large town located about 50 miles northwest of London. During the war, GCCS personnel worked on a large number of projects, including the Enigma machine and the Lorenz code. At the conclusion of the war, the GCCS was redesignated as the Government Communications Headquarters, the name by which it is still known today.

created it carried the knowledge gleaned from the experience to other projects.

The building of all-purpose, programmable computers became a reality after the war ended and the newest wartime technology was released to the public. Instead of returning to Cambridge, Turing decided to continue working on computers at the National Physical Laboratory in London, where he gained additional experience designing computers and programming them. One of his projects, the pilot Automatic Computing Engine (ACE), was capable of storing not only data but also programs that allowed it to process whatever data it was working with at any given time. Turing had essentially introduced the world to a program for an automatic electronic digital computer equipped with internal program storage.

After working on the ACE in London for two years, Turing returned to Cambridge to resume his duties and taught mathematics for a year. He then went to Manchester University in 1949 to work on a team dedicated to building a computer. Turing had been interested in chess from a young age and had the idea to program a machine to play chess. Although Turing never created an actual chess-playing machine, he did create model involving the idea. In 1950, Turing published a paper, "Computing Machinery and Intelligence," in which he developed his notion of the Turing test, a method to to determine whether a machine can be defined as intelligent or not. The test involves a human subject having a conversation with a computer. The subject would be positioned at a teletype machine and would type messages to another person or machine at the other end of the line. The role of the subject is to determine whether the replies originate from a computer or a human being. Turing believed that in the future it would be possible to program computers to imitate human interactions so well that they could fool an average interrogator. The idea of a program that imitates human interactions was the basis for research into artificial intelligence. The Turing test is still used today when modern programmers and engineers consider whether their programming systems are able to pass as human or human-like.

PERSONAL LIFE

Turing was an avid long-distance runner and ran with the Walton Athletic Club, a club based in Walton, Surrey. He was known for his exceptional, almost Olympic-caliber, marathon time of 3 hours, 46 minutes, and 3 seconds.

During his time at Bletchley Park, Turing had been briefly engaged to Joan Clarke. The engagement only confirmed Turing's homosexuality. In 1952, was convicted of engaging in homosexual behavior, which at the time was considered a crime of "gross indecency." The punishment required either imprisonment or chemical castration, and Turing opted for the latter. He was forced to undergo a regimen of estrogen injections. He had chosen the hormone therapy so that he could continue his scholarly pursuits. Although he continued to work on mathematical biology, particularly morphogenesis, his security clearance was revoked and he was no longer able to consult for the British government. The estrogen treatment caused Turing to suffer depression and impotence. He died on June 8, 1954; an examination revealed the cause of death to by cyanide poisoning, later determined to be a suicide. He was not quite forty-two years old.

In 1966, the Association for Computing Machinery established a prize in Turing's honor, the Turing Award, which today is held great esteem. It is granted annually to an individual who has made significant contributions to the computing community.

Stephen T. Schroth and Claire C. Turner

FURTHER READING

Copeland, B. Jack, ed. *Alan Turing's Automatic Computing Engine.* New York: Oxford UP, 2005. Print. The definitive guide to the machine that Turing envisioned and that was subsequently built, including his original proposal, a description of the obstacles, and the machine's influence.

---, ed. *The Essential Turing.* New York: Oxford UP, 2004. Print. A collection of Turing's articles, with extensive commentary by the editor, covering his early mathematics, his works on computers and thought, and his late work on mathematical biology.

Hawking, S. *God Created the Integers: The Mathematical Breakthroughs That Changed History.* Philadelphia: Running Press, 2005. Print. A chronological look at the works and mathematical proofs of seventeen breakthrough mathematicians.

Henderson, H. *Modern Mathematicians.* New York: Facts on File, 1996. Print. A collection of profiles examining different internationally famous mathematicians.

Hodges, A. *Alan Turing: The Enigma.* London: Random House, 2012. Print. Presents Turing as the man who saved the Allies from the Nazis, established the fields of computer science and artificial intelligence, and anticipated the gay liberation movement. Hodges was the first biographer to address Turing's homosexuality (in his 1983 biography).

Leavitt, D. *The Man Who Knew Too Much: Alan Turning and the Invention of the Computer.* New York: Norton, 2008. Print. Covers Turing's career and contributions in the context of his homosexuality and the conviction and "treatment" that resulted in his suicide.

Millican, Peter, and Andy Clark, eds. *Machines and Thought: The Legacy of Alan Turing.* Oxford: Clarendon, 1996. Print. A collection of essays addressing Turing's views about the possibility of designing machines that think, as well as consequences for machines doing mathematics.

Petzold, C. *The Annotated Turing: A Guided Tour through Alan Turing's Historic Paper on Computability and the Turing Machine.* Indianapolis: Wiley, 2008. Print. The seminal work of Turing, with explanatory notes and context.

Teuscher, Christof, ed. *Alan Turing: Life and Legacy of a Great Thinker.* New York: Springer, 2004. Print. Examination of the state of the disciplines in which Turing worked and Turing's own arguments fifty years after his death.

JOHN VON NEUMANN

Mathematician, game theorist, and designer of the MANIAC computer

Born: December 28, 1903; Budapest, Austria-Hungary (now Hungary)
Died: February 8, 1957; Washington, D.C.
Primary Field: Computer science
Specialty: Computer hardware
Primary Company/Organization: Institute for Advanced Study

INTRODUCTION

John von Neumann was a Hungarian American scientist who is widely accepted as the finest mathematician in modern history. Like Vannevar Bush and Albert Einstein, he did much to bridge the gap between the nineteenth and the twentieth centuries, advancing the state of his fields considerably. He was a central figure in both the Manhattan Project and the Institute for Advance Study in Princeton, two of the most significant institutions of mid-century American science.

EARLY LIFE

Neumann Janos Lajors (his Hungarian name), better known as John von Neumann, was born in Budapest on December 28, 1903, five years before his future Manhattan Project collaborator and fellow Hungarian American Edward Teller. The eldest of three brothers, he came from a wealthy Jewish family that had moved to Budapest in the 1880s. His father's family came from northern Hungary, and his father—Neumann Miksa, a banker and lawyer—was appointed to the Austro-Hungarian nobility in 1913 (acquiring the "von" in the Germanized version of the name). Young Janos was a true child prodigy, familiar with both differential and integral calculus by age eight, when he began high school

at the Lutheran school in Budapest, Fasori Evangelikus Gimnazium.

His photographic memory made learning easy for him, and although his greatest interest was in mathematics, he had a skill for languages, literature (he could recite any of his favorite passages from memory, to the end of his life, often in multiple languages), and ancient history—to the extent that in pursuits that were hobbies

John von Neumann.

to him, he often had a professional's command of the material. He was tutored in advanced calculus twice a week by Gabor Szego, and at age nineteen he published

two mathematical papers. In one of them, he provided the definition of ordinal numbers that is still used today. At twenty-two, he received a Ph.D. in mathematics from Budapest's Pazmany Peter University and a bachelor's degree in chemical engineering from Switzerland's Eidgenössische Technische Hochschule Zürich. He also minored in chemistry and experimental physics.

In his doctoral dissertation, von Neumann introduced the axiom of foundation (which dealt with the construction of sets), the method of inner models for demonstrating that axiom, and the notion of class as understood in set theory. These contributions completed the axiomatic system of set theory. Thus, von Neumann's work led to Kurt Gödel's groundbreaking first theorem of incompleteness, introduced in 1930, which stated that no consistent system of axioms can prove all arithmetical truths—they are, in other words, incomplete. A couple weeks later, von Neumann contacted Gödel to point out the inevitable implication, called the second theorem of incompleteness: No such axiomatic system can demonstrate its own consistency.

Despite his deep talents for mathematics, von Neumann's father wanted him to pursue a more practical profession. Earning an engineering degree was the Neumanns' compromise; as a result, John gained a marketable skill on which to fall back if mathematics did not work for him. It worked for him.

Affiliation: Institute for Advanced Study

The Institute for Advanced Study (IAS) is a postgraduate research center founded in 1930 in Princeton, New Jersey. It is sometimes erroneously assumed that there is a formal relationship between IAS and Princeton University, and IAS was housed in Princeton's mathematics building from 1933 to 1939. However, beyond that tenancy relationship, connections have been informal, based on proximity and collaborations. Rather than being founded by Princeton, IAS was in fact founded by brother and sister Louis Bamberger and Caroline Bamberger Fuld. Bamberger had opened a department store in 1892, and in 1929 it had become the fourth most prosperous store in the country. He sold it to Macy's that year, narrowly avoiding the market crash that precipitated the Great Depression, and divided a portion of the proceeds among his 240 employees. Of the remainder, $5 million was used to fund IAS. Bamberger was also a major donor to Community Chest, the charity that inspired the Monopoly card, and to the efforts to help Jews escape from Nazi Germany.

IAS was founded on the advice of Abraham Flexner, an education theorist and personal friend, who persuaded Bamberger and his sister that the country needed more abstract research. Flexner served as the first director of the institute, from 1930 to 1939 (although the institute did not open until 1933). He was succeeded by Frank Aydelotte (1939–47), Robert Oppenheimer (1947–66), Carl Kaysen (1966–76), Harry Woolf (1976–87), Marvin L. Goldberger (1987–91), Philip Griffiths (1991–93), Peter Goddard (2004–12), and Robbert Dijkgraaf (as of 2012).

Over the years, IAS has been home to Hungarian mathematician Paul Erdos, linguist and cognitive scientist Noam Chomsky, theoretical physicist Freeman Dyson, computer scientist Alan Turing, and many others. Part of its fame and influence comes from the pedigree of its original faculty, which included Albert Einstein, David Mitrany, Oswald Veblen, John von Neumann, and Hermann Weyl.

Today, the school has a permanent faculty of twenty-eight and awards 190 annual fellowships to visiting faculty, termed members. Programs are divided among four schools: Historical Studies, Mathematics, Natural Sciences, and Social Science. Permanent faculty members are granted lifetime tenure. The founding principle of IAS, in its commitment to pure research, is that researchers who are not assigned specific duties and tasks and whose jobs are secure will produce the best work. Physicist Richard Feynman criticized this approach, saying that even a great mind needs the discipline of required work.

LIFE'S WORK

Von Neumann taught for four years at the University of Berlin, as the youngest professor it has ever employed. He was publishing nearly one major paper per month during that time, making a name for himself far beyond central Europe. While still working at Berlin, von Neumann introduced von Neumann algebra, which he called the theory of rings of operators. He continued to develop this algebra through the 1930s and 1940s. The von Neumann algebra work led to the introduction of continuous geometry in a 1936 paper.

After teaching at the University of Berlin, in 1930, von Neumann was recruited by Princeton University. He taught mathematics there for a time and was soon selected as one of the inaugural faculty members of the Institute for Advanced Study (IAS), along with Albert Einstein and Kurt Gödel. The IAS is located in Princeton, New Jersey. Until 1939 it was housed in Princeton University's mathematics building, but it is actually an independent, privately owned research center. Faculty members do not teach courses but instead are expected to pursue their own research. The IAS was founded on the principle that the country needed a pure research center comparable to the applied research center it had in Bell Laboratories. Von Neumann worked for IAS from 1933, when it opened, until his death.

Although von Neumann did the bulk of his significant work at IAS, he also became involved with the Manhattan Project, the classified effort to develop the atomic bomb, whose feasibility was implied by Einstein's work. Von Neumann had become intrigued by the complicated mathematics of modeling explosions and became the world's authority on the mathematics of shaped charges. His association with the military led to his recruitment to the Manhattan Project, where he worked with Vannevar Bush, future IAS director Robert Oppenheimer, Enrico Fermi, Richard Feynman, and fellow Hungarian American Edward Teller. Von Neumann was one of five scientists named to the 1945 target selection committee, which chose Hiroshima and Nagasaki, Japan, as the first targets for the atomic bomb when the United States was at war with that country. Von Neumann actually voted for Kyoto. He was also one of the eyewitnesses to the first detonation of the atomic bomb, on July 16, 1945, along with other personnel at the Los Alamos installation.

After the war, Von Neumann was critical of Oppenheimer's public comments about the project, implying that Oppenheimer took credit for more than his contributions merited. He transitioned, with Edward Teller, to working on the hydrogen bomb project. In 1955, he was made a member of the U.S. Atomic Energy Commission.

During this Cold War period, von Neumann also developed and promoted the mutually assured destruction (MAD) strategy, a piece of game theory stating that so long as each side in a potential nuclear war was sufficiently frightened of the other side's retaliation, neither side would make the first strike. The MAD acronym was deliberate, and typical of von Neumann, who also designed the Mathematical Analyzer, Numerical Integrator, and Computer (MANIAC). His work on the hydrogen bomb had been conducted with the aid of computers, which had undergone a revolution in the late war

and immediate postwar years. He consulted on the Electronic Numerical Integrator and Computer (ENIAC) project, which was completed in 1948, and on the Electronic Discrete Variable Automatic Computer (EDVAC) project in 1949, developing programs for both. In the course of this consultation, he prescribed a model of computer architecture—in which data and program share space in the computer's memory—that remains in use, in contrast to early computers, which required their circuitry to be physically altered to "program" them. Von Neumann later used the ENIAC to construct the first numerical weather predictions and remained fascinated by the mathematics of weather prediction.

Much of von Neumann's work had applications discovered long after he completed it. Intrigued by the mathematics of self-replication, he did a deep mathematical analysis of it and constructed self-replicating automata with pencil and paper before the molecular structure of DNA had been discovered.

PERSONAL LIFE

Von Neumann's father died in 1929, a year before his son moved to the United States and thus too soon to see the impact John would leave on the world of science. His mother and younger brothers relocated to America with him, however, and von Neumann became a naturalized citizen of the United States in 1938.

In 1930, he married Mariette Kovesi, just before they moved to the United States. They had one child—a daughter, Marina—and divorced in 1937. The following year, von Neumann married Hungarian computer programmer Klara Dan. She became attached to the ENIAC project and later wrote the preface to von Neumman's posthumously published collection of Silliman lectures. She remarried after von Neumman's death and committed suicide in 1963. Marina von Neumann Whitman became a professor of business administration and public policy at the University of Michigan. She served on President Richard Nixon's Council of Economic Advisers from 1970 to 1973 on the Princeton board of trustees from 1980 to 1990.

A poor driver, von Neumann was known to read while driving, leading to numerous accidents and arrests, some of which were paid for by his employers. He had a loud, colorful personality, far from the introspective sort one might expect of his genius. Einstein complained about his loud music, played while the two worked in nearby offices, and new acquaintances were sometimes shocked by his love of dirty jokes, limericks, and raucous parties.

Von Neumann was diagnosed with cancer in 1955, which some have speculated was caused by his attendance at nuclear tests. The disease progressed quickly, and he died in Washington, D.C., on February 8, 1957, at age fifty-three, with military personnel stationed nearby out of concern that his medicated state might lead him to reveal still-classified military secrets.

Bill Kte'pi

FURTHER READING

Halberstam, David. *The Fifties*. New York: Ballantine, 1994. Print. Perhaps the best general overview of the 1950s, putting von Neumann's life and work in context.

MacRae, Norman. *John von Neumann*. Providence: American Mathematical Society, 1999. Print. MacRae's was the first comprehensive biography of von Neumann and remains one of the best.

Redei, Miklos, and Michael Stoltzner, eds. *John von Neumann and the Foundations of Quantum Physics*. New York: Springer, 2010. Print. The physicist's role in one of the most active and controversial areas of physics of his day.

Israel, Giorgio, and Ana Millán Gasca. *The World as a Mathematical Game: John von Neumann and Twentieth Century Science*. Boston: Birkhäuser, 2009. Print. A scientific and intellectual biography, from set theory to quantum mechanics to economics and von Neumann's theory of automata.

Rédei, Miklós, ed. *John von Neumann: Selected Letters*. Providence: American Mathematical Society, 2005. Print. Von Neumann's thoughts and outlook, in his own words.

Rédei, Miklós, and Michael Stoltzner, eds. *John von Neumann and the Foundations of Quantum Physics*. New York: Springer, 2010. Print. The physicist's role in one of the most active and controversial areas of physics of his day.

von Neumann, John. *The Computer and the Brain*. New Haven: Yale UP, 2000. Print. Collects lectures that von Neumann delivered in the 1950s.

W

TED WAITT

Cofounder of Gateway

Born: January 18, 1963; Sioux City, Iowa
Died: -
Primary Field: Computer science
Specialty: Computer hardware
Primary Company/Organization: Gateway

INTRODUCTION

Ted Waitt founded Gateway, a company that specialized in providing quality computer hardware at a low price to individual customers. Waitt made his fortune with the company, capitalizing on the fact that he entered the business at a time when the market for personal computers was booming, then left in his early thirties to pursue other interests. After leaving Gateway in 2000, Waitt became a well-known philanthropist. He returned to Gateway in 2002 to help the company through difficult times.

EARLY LIFE

Ted Waitt was born in Sioux City to a family in the cattle business. Although not an outstanding student in high school, he enrolled as a marketing major at the University of Iowa. Waitt became interested in the computer business after visiting friends who worked for Century Systems, a computer retailer, and dropped out of the university to work at Century; he was fascinated by the process of long-distance retail and would use that concept when establishing his own company. He and a colleague from Century, Mike Hammond, founded the Texas Instruments Personal Computers (TIPC) Network, which began retail operations in 1985; they renamed the business Gateway 2000 in 1987, the name signifying that Waitt wanted to work for the company only until the year 2000.

LIFE'S WORK

Waitt founded Gateway as a retail computer hardware business that specialized in providing current, quality computers at a low price to the general consumer. Gateway computers began as a family operation in many ways: The loan for Waitt's original company, TIPC Network, was secured by his grandmother, and the company was originally located on his family's cattle ranch.

Ted Waitt.

Waitt provided the vision and marketing expertise for the company, while his colleague Hammond provided the computer expertise; Waitt's brother Norman joined

---

Affiliation: Gateway

Ted Waitt founded Gateway, a company specializing in selling personal computers to individuals at a low cost, making it possible for many individuals to own their own personal computers. Gateway, originally called TIPC Network, was a family business from the start: The company began operation on Waitt's family's Iowa ranch, the company's initial financing was secured by his grandmother, and at the time of Gateway's initial public offering (IPO), 1993, members of the Waitt owned 85 percent of company stock.

Waitt emphasized the midwestern roots of the company in advertising: An early Gateway advertisement featured computers and black-and-white spotted cows, with the question "Computers from Iowa?" The black-and-white pattern was echoed in the company's logo, which included a cube marked with black and white spots similar to those on the cow, and a similar pattern was featured on the boxes used to ship Gateway computers. Feeling that consumers associated the Midwest with values like stability and hard work, Waitt believed that his customers would feel assured this his company would be around to support them and would not go out of business in a few months—as many computer companies did during the early boom period.

Gateway was noted for its low prices, and Waitt found many ways to economize, including keeping a low inventory and moving the company's operations to South Dakota, a state with neither corporate nor personal income tax. Gateway prospered during the early years of the personal computer market, surpassing Dell as the leading direct marketer of computers in 1991, with $627 million in sales; by 1993, sales had risen to $1.7 billion.

Waitt retired from the company while in his thirties in order to pursue other interests. However, the company suffered severe financial losses after his departure, due in part to the fact that the computer market had changed in ways that the company was not ready to respond to, and Waitt returned to Gateway after less than two years of retirement. He was not able to solve Gateway's problems completely, and he sold the company to Acer in 2007.

---

the company in its first year as financial manager. As the TIPC Network, Gateway began as a membership organization: Customers paid a $20 fee to join and have the privilige of purchasing discounted computer hardware from the company. This business model succeeded because of the low price for TIPC/Gateway products: Customers saved more than the membership fee through discounted purchases. Originally Gateway targeted a single specialty market: owners of Texas Instruments computers who wanted the add-ons that would allow them to run IBM software on their computers.

Gateway grew rapidly in its early years. In its first partial year of operation (September–December 1985), Gateway Computers sold $400,000 worth of computer equipment. In 1985, the company saw $1 million in sales. The company began selling complete computers in 1987 and was able to sell a complete IBM-compatible personal computer (known colloquially as a clone) for 33 percent less than a comparable model cost if ordered from Texas Instruments: $1,995 from Gateway as opposed to $3,000 from Texas Instruments. In 1992, sales reached $1 billion, and Gateway was identified as the fastest-growing company in the United States. Gateway went public in 1993, raising $150 million on its initial public offering (IPO); at this point, members of the Waitt family owned 85 percent of the company. Waitt emphasized the midwestern location of his company through ads featuring a black-and-white spotted cow and the slogan "Computers from Iowa?" Both were contrarian strategies, subtly playing on the presumed association in the American consumer's mind between the Midwest and qualities such as stability and honesty; the purpose of the strategies to set Gateway apart from the numerous other companies then in the personal computer business, many of which went out of business fairly quickly.

By 1996, Gateway was making more than $1 billion in sales per quarter and had a global workforce of more than nine thousand employees. Gateway continued to expand, entering the international computer marketplace with forty overseas stores as well as production facilities in Ireland and Malaysia. In 1998, the company changed names again, becoming simply Gateway (not Gateway 2000), and in 1999 Waitt retired from the company and left Jeffrey Weitzen in charge as president and chief operating officer.

As it evolved, Gateway used many strategies to keep costs low. The company originally operated from a building on Waitt's family's cattle ranch and did not move to an office in Sioux City until 1987. Waitt later moved the company to South Dakota to avoid paying Iowa's personal and corporate income tax. The company kept a lean inventory of parts, and PCs were assembled on demand, a strategy that also ensured that the most up-to-date components would be used. The company had a streamlined operation, paid relatively low wages, had no budget for research and development, and produced most of its advertising in house.

Gateway was innovative in including many features on its computers that have since become standard, such as CD-ROM drives; these choices were driven primarily by Waitt's instincts, which proved in line with the way the computer business was developing. After Gateway experienced serious financial losses in the second half of 2000, Waitt fired Weitzen and returned as chief executive officer (CEO). However, he retired again in 2005, unable to restore the company to its former heights. In 2007, Gateway was acquired by Acer, a computer manufacturer based in Taiwan.

Today, Waitt owns the Avalon Capital Group, a company that invests in entertainment, health care, finance, technology, and real estate companies that make innovative uses of technology. Companies in which Avalon Capital Group has invested include Vizio, Lava Supply Chain Solutions, and Fisker Automotive.

PERSONAL LIFE

Waitt is married to Joan Waitt, a businesswoman and philanthropist. The couple have four children and live in La Jolla, California.

Waitt has been engaged in a number of philanthropic ventures. In 1993, he established the Waitt Foundation, which has given more than $118 million to charitable and nonprofit organizations. The original focus of the foundation was on helping people in at-risk communities in Sioux City and the surrounding region. In 1999, the foundation moved to San Diego and broadened its charitable programs. In 2005, Waitt created two new institutes, the Waitt Institute and the Waitt Institute for Violence Prevention.

Today, the Waitt Foundation focuses on ocean conservation, supporting the creation of marine protected areas, improving fisheries management, encouraging

cooperation among nongovernmental organizations, and promoting sustainability. The Waitt Institute focuses on research and exploration; notable expeditions carried out by the Institute include a 2009 deep-sea search for the remains of Amelia Earhart's plane and a 2010 search for the Air France plane designated for Flight 447, which crashed in the Atlantic Ocean in June 2009. The Waitt Institute for Violence Protection focuses on preventing bullying and gender violence; initiatives include the documentary film *Bully* and the Sioux City Project, a five-year effort to increase awareness of violence and bullying.

Sarah Boslaugh

FURTHER READING

Booker, Katrina. "I Built This Company, I Can Save It." *Fortune* 143.9 (2001): 94–102. Print. An interview with Waitt shortly after his return to managing the company. Discusses the company's fortunes, the different management styles of Waitt and his successor Jeff Weitzen, and Waitt's plans for the future of the company.

Dessner, Michael, Greg J. Packard, and Andy Sherrell. "Waitt Institute Completes Pacific Survey Utilizing AUV Technology." *Sea Technology* 51.6 (2010): 19–24. Print. A description of the results of a collaboration among the Waitt Institute, the Woods Hole Oceanographic Institution, and Florida Atlantic Institute's Harbor Branch Oceanographic Institute to use two autonomous underwater vehicles to search for Amelia Earhart's aircraft.

Ericksen, Gregory K. *What's Luck Got to Do with It? Twelve Entrepreneurs Reveal the Secrets Behind Their Success*. Hoboken: Wiley, 1997. Print. Profiles of twelve business entrepreneurs, including Waitt, Jim McCann (1-800-FLOWERS), Jim Koch (the Boston Beer Company), William Ungar (National Envelope), and Richard M. Schulze (Best Buy).

Tiku, Nitasha, and Jason Del Ray. "Revolutionary Roads." *Inc.* 31.3 (2009): 100–01. Print. A feature article about several entrepreneurs who became successful by following unconventional paths. Waitt and Mike Hammond's launching a computer business in Iowa is one of the examples used.

LARRY WALL

Creator of the Perl programming language

Born: September 27, 1954; Los Angeles, California
Died: -
Primary Field: Computer science
Specialty: Computer programming
Primary Company/Organization: Unisys

INTRODUCTION

Larry Wall created the scripting language Perl and remains its "Benevolent Dictator for Life," overseeing its continued development.

EARLY LIFE

Larry Wall was born on September 27, 1954, in Los Angeles, California. He was the son of a pastor, and both his grandfathers were pastors as well. His family moved to Bremerton, Washington, on the Puget Sound, and he enrolled at Seattle Pacific University in 1976. He shifted majors from chemistry to music to a premedical program, and after taking some time off from school to work in the university's computer center, he earned his bachelor's degree with a self-designed major in natural and artificial languages. His intention when attending graduate school for linguistics at the University of California, Berkeley, was to find an unwritten language and create a writing system for it. Instead, he took a job with the Jet Propulsion Laboratory, part of the National Aeronautics and Space Administration, in Pasadena, California.

LIFE'S WORK

Wall later took a programming job at Unisys, where he created the Perl programming language. Unisys was formed in 1986 by the merger of two mainframe manufacturers, Sperry and Burroughs, both of which had been part of the creation of the COBOL programming language in 1960. The new name was formed from a contraction of United Information Systems. The merger made Unisys the second-largest computer company, with about 120,000 employees.

Wall began work on Perl in 1987 and released version 1.0 on December 18, 1987, distributing it through the comp.sources.misc Usenet newsgroup. Perl is a high-level general-pupose dynamic programming language, originally designed as a Unix scripting language. Like many computer terms, the name Perl was originally uncapitalized; when it was capitalized in the first edition of *Programming Perl* (1991), for the purposes of typesetting, the change was made permanent, and Perl has been capitalized since. (Perl is occasionally written as PERL in all caps, out of the mistaken belief that it is an acronym; "backronyms" such as Practical Extraction and Report Language have even been attributed to it and are sometimes used in literature about it, erroneously reported as the "full name" of the language.) *Programming Perl* was the first published documentation for the language; prior to, that documentation had simply been stored at the main page. The book—called the Camel Book by the programming community because of the Camel symbol O'Reilly Media used on the cover and subsequently trademarked for Perl-related uses—covered Perl 4.0, which was substantially similar to Perl 3, released in 1989, but renumbered for association with the book.

Wall continued to develop Perl 4 through 1993, at which point he began to develop Perl 5. It is notable that Perl 5 remains the current version, almost twenty years later, compared to the four versions released in the four

Larry Wall.

Affiliation: Unisys

Unisys is a multinational technology company based in Pennsylvania. It originated in 1986 with the merger of the Sperry Corporation and the Burroughs Corporation, both of which had long histories in the computing industry. Sperry had begun as a gyroscope and aviation equipment company, which acquired the company that developed the Universal Automatic Computer (UNIVAC). Both companies had been among the largest computer mainframe manufacturers, and they were two of the six companies involved in the development of COBOL in 1960. When Burroughs bought Sperry for $4.8 billion, the new corporation was named Unisys, for United Information Systems. Unisys was the second-largest computer company in the world, employing 120,000 workers.

The mainframe business had already peaked, although Unisys continued to accrue revenue from maintenance and support of its existing installations of mainframes, and while fellow mainframe giant IBM had focused on personal computers and had been partially responsible for the personal computer revolution of the 1980s, Unisys shifted to the server business instead. Like IBM, it also began offering high-quality information technology (IT) services, including outsourcing, technical services, and consulting.

The company prospered in the 1990s but began to decline in the mid-2000s. In 2008, it fell below the Standard and Poor's 500 minimum market capitalization of $4 billion and was removed from the list. Today, most of its revenue—more than 90 percent—comes from services rather than goods. These services are typically sold to government agencies—such as the Transportation Safety Administration, the Internal Revenue Service, and the Federal Aviation Administration—or large corporations, including Dell, Lufthansa, Lloyd's of London, and Nextel. Services include ongoing outsourced IT, business process outsourcing, help desk and end-user service outsourcing, data hosting and management, maintenance of hardware or software systems, building and installation of computer systems, cloud computing, data security, operational process planning, and miscellaneous onetime consulting jobs.

Unisys systems today are mainly used in industry. Unisys developed the first Doppler weather radar system and continues to develop such systems, as well as other weather data systems. It is very involved in shipping port management and operates the world's largest radio frequency identification (RFID) network, tracking 9 million containers on behalf of the American government. Other Unisys systems process checks or taxes, handle reservations for airlines or hotels, manage personnel and other business records, securely manage medical records, automate backups and live data replication, and manage content for newspapers, magazines, and other publishing concerns.

In 2012, Unisys launched a suite of cloud-based IT service management solutions, as well as a suite of mobility solutions to help businesses manage and support mobile devices, smart phones, tablets, and their apps. The company has made a recent commitment to cloud computing research, security issues, and social collaboration tools within the company.

---

years from 1987 to 1991. Perl 5.000, released on October 17, 1994, was a significantly overhauled version of the language, adding objects, modules, and a completely rewritten interpreter. Because modules allowed extensions of the language without needing to change the interpreter, Perl 5 has remained in active development without the need for an overhaul. The Comprehensive Perl Archive Network was established a year later as a repository for modules for the Perl community. It remains active and an integral part of the Perl programming community, with nearly twenty-five thousand modules as of 2012, representing the work of about ten thousand authors.

The 5.004 release in 1997 gave Perl more module functionality, including the CGI.pm module, which thenceforth drove Perl's popularity in CGI scripting, which is now one of its most popular uses. As of this release, Perl supported most popular operating systems, no longer just a Unix scripting language. The next major change was 64-bit support, added in Perl 5.6 in 2000. Perl 5.6 also changed the numbering scheme of Perl versions. Wall had in the interim become more deeply involved with and committed to the open source movement, which had developed considerably in the 1990s, and Perl's versioning scheme adopted the scheme in common use through the movement. Since 2002, Perl 5 has been updated roughly yearly. As of May 2012, the current release is Perl 5.16, which added the ability to emulate older versions of Perl so that older scripts could be run without needing to be rewritten.

Today, Perl is used for CGI, system administration, finance, network programming, and graphics programming, but it is flexible enough to be used in most scripting language applications. It is one of the most commonly used languages on the Internet. In some ways it is the opposite of Python, another common scripting language on the web; whereas Python is small and elegant, written by a programmer who had no concerns for practical uses, Perl is inelegant but easy to use and highly practical. Wall often says, "Easy things should be easy and hard things should be possible." Perl is influenced by Wall's education as a linguist, which sometimes affects the terminology; he refers to verbs and nouns instead of variables and functions, for instance. Perl's grammar is Turing-complete, meaning that it can simulate any other general-purpose language.

Perl is also associated with the onion logo, owned by the Perl Foundation, a pun on "pearl onion." Wall's annual addresses on Perl matters are called "State of the Onion" addresses.

Work on Perl 6 actually began in 2000, when Wall asked for suggestions for the new versions. Almost 400 documents in response to this requests for comment (or RFC) formed the first stage of Perl 6 development. Wall spent years preparing a design for Perl 6, and has presented it in a series of what he calls "apocalypses," documents that present Perl 6 specification. Originally intended only to remove the "warts" from Perl, Perl 6 has turned into a language distinct from Perl 5 and will not have backward compatibility. Damian Conway has written a series of "exegeses" that explain Wall's apocalypses. There is a source code repository at Github, as well as a set of Perl 6 development mailing lists run by perl.org and a #perl6 IRC channel. No Perl 6 implementation has yet been completed, nor has an expected release date been announced.

In addition to his Perl work, Wall wrote the rn Usenet client in 1984 for Unix systems. Even apart from its superiority to most other newsreaders, rn is notable for introducing the KILL file: a user-edited file containing any regular expression, which would mark as read any news article containing that expression. The KILL file thus allowed the user to avoid reading posts on certain specified topics or by certain specified users. The term *killfiling* has become a synonym in the Internet community for blocking a topic or user, whether in newsgroups, in logged-in message boards, in chat rooms, on instant-messenging programs, or in e-mail—it is a key element of the Internet's social sphere, and the combination of kill and search forms the main difference between social interaction online and offline.

Wall also wrote the patch program for Unix, which accesses a user-edited text file called the patch file and follows the instructions in that file in order to update other text files. It was released in 1985, and although usable with any text file, it became associated with programmers' need frequently to update, or patch, source code files to newer versions.

PERSONAL LIFE

Wall is married and attended graduate school with his wife, the linguist Gloria Wall. The couple have four children. He is well known for his sense of humor and is genuinely one of the best-liked prominent figures in the computer industry.

A devout Christian, Wall is a member of the New Life Nazarene Church. The terminology he uses in his work has been influenced by his Christianity: The name Perl is a reference to the "pearl of great price" of the Gospel of Matthew (there was already a language called PEARL, prompting Wall to change the spelling just before release), and Perl includes a function called bless. Wall has been known to speak frankly about his beliefs at conferences.

Bill Kte'pi

FURTHER READING

Burks, Alice Rowe. *Who Invented the Computer?* New York: Prometheus, 2003. Print. Includes Unisys's role in the debate over whether the ABC or ENIAC was the first computer.

DiBona, Chris, Sam Ockman, and Mark Stone. *Open Source: Voices from the Revolution.* Sebastopol: O'Reilly, 1999. Print. Coverage of the open source debate in the computer industry, including Wall's role in the discussion.

Wall, Larry, Tom Christiansen, and Jon Orwant. *Programming Perl.* Sebastopol: O'Reilly, 2000. Print. The fundamental guide to Wall's programming language, often called "the Camel book."

AN WANG

Cofounder of Wang Laboratories

Born: February 7, 1920; Shanghai, China
Died: March 24, 1990; Boston, Massachusetts
Primary Field: Computer science
Specialty: Computer hardware
Primary Company/Organization: Wang Laboratories

INTRODUCTION

An Wang was a Chinese-born naturalized American citizen who was instrumental in the development of modern computing, initially at Harvard University as a developer of core memory; then as the founder of Wang Laboratories, which created electronic calculators and a wide range of applications that used numerical controls; and finally as a significant player in development and sales of word-processing and computing hardware of various sizes.

EARLY LIFE

An Wang was the eldest of five children born to Yu Lin and Zen Wan Wang. Born near Shanghai, he learned English at home and entered school at age six, beginning in the third grade because that was the first grade available in the school where his father taught English. He developed an early interest in mathematics and science but was an otherwise indifferent student. In high school, he began building radios and studied communications engineering at Chiao-Tung University in Shanghai, remaining a year after graduation as a teaching assistant. He spent World War II in a secure inland location designing and building transmitters and radios, learning to scavenge, adapt, and economize. With government assistance, he moved to the United States and enrolled at Harvard University, where he majored in engineering and applied physics, receiving a Ph.D. in 1947 or 1948.

LIFE'S WORK

He was hired by Howard Aiken in 1948 as a postdoctoral researcher at the Harvard Computation Laboratory, where the Harvard Mark I computer had been built and the Air Force was contracting for others. Wang's assignment was to improve core memory, to find a way to store and retrieve information. Wang developed the pulse memory core, a donut-shaped ferromagnetic material that could store information that became readable when a current passed through it. The concept of core memory created by Wang was important to researchers

at the Massachusetts Institute of Technology (MIT), who expanded it into a more practical form. Wang and a coworker published a paper on the idea, Wang patented the core memory, and a long process of patent litigation began. When Harvard decided to end computer research because the field was ripe for commercial development and Harvard did not do commercial work, Wang left the university and opened Wang Laboratories in 1951 with no orders and only a few hundred dollars in capital.

Wang first custom-built magnetic shift registers. He also built magnetic tape control and numerical control devices. The company sold magnetic cores and contracted for research and development. Wang was his own sales force and spent much time at trade shows seeking business. In 1952, he got an order for a custom-designed synchronizer and counting device for a company called Laboratory for Electronics located in Cambridge, Massachusetts. At the same time, he offered IBM a license on the pending patent for the magnetic core, beginning four years of negotiations with IBM. He also had a contract with IBM to design a method for using magnetic

An Wang.

cores for memory functions in IBM's electronic calculators. In 1956, he sold the core to IBM just a few weeks before he won the patent (he later suggested that IBM had abetted a challenge to his patent).

Wang incorporated in 1955 with himself as president and treasurer. Once Wang sold the core patent, the company moved away from consulting to development and sales of its own line. The early years were a time when Wang was learning how to run a business, and he made many mistakes.

Government contracts started in the late 1950s. One development arising from an Air Force contract was an angular encoder to measure cloud cover. Wang's transistor-based encoders promoted development of automated control systems for machine tools. By the late 1950s, Wang had several types of control unit in its Weditrol (Wang Electronic Digital Control Units) element. With twenty workers, Wang produced and annually sold between sixty and eighty of the units at $700 apiece.

In 1959, wanting funds to expand, Wang signed an agreement with Warner and Swasey of Cleveland, a user of Wang's control systems for machine tools. Wang sold 25 percent of the company for a $50,000 equity investment and $100,000 in short-term loans. He soon realized his mistake, however. At roughly the same time, Wang made a second mistake, developing a semiautomated hyphenating phototypesetter (Linasec) for Compugraphic, which immediately began selling the machines on its own because Wang had allowed a clause that permitted such manufacture without payment of royalties.

In the early 1960s, Wang began establishing its own sales force, selling directly to users. The firm moved to Natick, then Tewksbury, Massachusetts. The Linasec had its first successful year in 1963, with $300,000 in sales. Doubled sales over the next two years brought Wang over the $1 million mark in 1964.

A digital logarithmic converter that Wang had invented in the mid-1960s allowed basic arithmetic functions at high speeds and relatively low cost. The Wang desktop calculators soon replaced traditional mechanical calculators. The calculators shared a processor, and the keyboards sold for more than $1,000 apiece. Schools, engineering firms, and scientific laboratories were eager customers. Wang created programmable calculators, first the LOCI in 1965 as the company's first scientific calculator and the stimulus for the desk calculator market nearly monopolized by Wang in the late 1960s. When Wang simplified the calculators and lowered their price, he moved into the business market in 1969.

Affiliation: Wang Laboratories

An Wang began his business in a single room over a Boston electrical fixtures store. In 1955, the company incorporated. By the mid-1980s the company had more than fifteen thousand workers in several buildings in Lowell, Massachusetts, and offices throughout the world. Expansion came through several sales of stock, as well as several accruals of debt. The family retained control of the firm by controlling the type of stock that allowed administrative power. In the early 1980s, growth slowed but the debt remained, so Wang relinquished some of his control in favor of standard management practices. Wang's son Frederick and other managers took greater roles in running the company, allowing Wang to develop other interests.

However, the computer industry ran into hard times, and Wang returned to a more active role in the company. The company was bringing in a billion dollars a year in 1982 and more than $3 billion in 1989, but by the early 1990s Wang had gone through Chapter 11 bankruptcy. The company's founder died of cancer in March 1990 at age seventy. In 1992, Wang was a $1.9 billion company employing 13,000 workers and listed on stock exchanges in the United States and Switzerland. It provided computer based information processing systems and networking products. In 1992, despite the $1.9 billion in sales the company lost $139 billion and entered Chapter 11. Eastman Kodak bought Wang's software business in January 1997 for $260 million. Wang was out of software. Relationships with Microsoft enabled Wang to reestablish prosperity.

In 1967, wanting to expand again, Wang went public, selling 210,000 shares on the New York Stock Exchange. By then, Wang had a reputation as the leader in electronic desktop calculators. However, the future of electronic calculators was limited. Wang recognized that the future belonged to transistors, and handheld calculators would make his machines obsolete, so he began looking for new ventures. Wang developed its first computer in 1967; the machine was a failure because Wang had sparse programming experience. In 1968, the company bought Phillip Hawkins, the state's largest supplier of data-processing services, for $7.4 million, a generous price. In 1970, the Wang 3300 debuted to little success. The fourth Wang effort, the 2200, was the first viable minicomputer for the firm.

Wang controlled the company, and the decision to retreat from the calculator market was his. Even as the company backed away and moved to computers, however, the calculators brought in profits, and 1970 was the first $25 million sales year

Between 1970 and 1975, Wang introduced word processors and computers, but earnings were unstable because of performance problems for some of the products as well as the unsettled economy in the wake of the oil crisis; Wang's business was down 70 percent. I\nN 1975, Wang was borrowing money, cutting salaries, and laying off workers.

The company rebounded in the late 1970s, after the 1976 introduction of its CRT-based word-processing minicomputer. By 1976, Wang was selling word processors that were easy for the uninitiated to use and featuring database management as well as routine business calculations. Wang moved to personal computers, taking on IBM in a David and Goliath ad campaign; by the end of 1978, Wang was leading in CRT-based word processors and small business computers. It bought other companies, including Graphic Systems (1978), InteCom (1984–86), and Informatics Professional and Legal Systems (1988). Revenues soared 61 percent annually in the years between 1979 and 1984.

Increased emphasis on research and development and the introduction of new products at cut-rate prices allowed Wang to take some of IBM's market share in the 1980s. It was a glorious run, but a decade after Wang switched from calculators to computers the computer industry went into a recession in 1985, with Wang's first decline in a decade and an income drop of 66 percent, generating a 5 percent workforce layoff of sixteen hundred workers. Critics said that Wang was too slow to enter the PC market, persisting in the minicomputer field even as the smaller and more powerful machines were making Wang's machines obsolete. Service was below standard, not as good as sales and development.

An Wang released some control, with John F. Cunningham becoming president in 1983 while Wang remained chair and chief executive officer (CEO). Cunningham was a veteran, starting with Wang in 1967, and his strength was office automation. However, other companies made the rapid technological strides that shrank Wang's market share, the company reorganized and top managers resigned under pressure, and finally in 1985, when revenues were way down, Cunningham resigned. He said later that his decision came after An Wang revealed that his son, Fred, would be the future head of the company. After Cunningham and Executive Vice President Jon A. Kropper left, Wang resumed control, and reorganizations continued along with resignations. Fred Wang moved from treasurer to president in 1986, and the company made a small profit in 1986 before losing $70 million in 1987 and $92 million in 1988. At the end of fiscal year 1989, in June, Wang posted a $424 million loss, and the company was in crisis because of its debt burden. In August that year, An Wang replaced Fred with Richard W. Miller, a former General Electric executive. Wang, Inc. at that point was more than $1 billion in debt, with $575 million in bank loans.

Miller streamlined, cut layers of bureaucracy, sold nonessential assets, and moved Wang into new markets. Rather than relying on proprietary designs and software, he moved Wang into standard PC software and Unix standard larger computers. Layoffs continued in 1990, and the company was divested of $200 million in peripheral assets such as overseas manufacturers and real estate. Then in March, An Wang died. Miller became chair and CEO. Wang continued selling nonessential businesses and cutting bank debt and annual expenses. The total was $1.25 billion, but the company still lost $715.9 million on sales of $2.5 billion. By the end of the year, the company was free of bank debt, had a contract with the U.S. State Department worth potentially more than $800 million, and had sold InteCom, its integrated voice-data switching equipment maker. The fall quarter showed the first profit in seven quarters. Wang moved into a stronger alliance with IBM, but the decline persisted through 1992, and eventually the company filed for Chapter 11 bankruptcy.

PERSONAL LIFE

An Wang married Lorraine Chiu in 1949; they would have three children, two sons and a daughter. He and Lorraine became naturalized U.S. citizens in 1955. When the company was well established, Wang became a member of the University of Massachusetts board of regents, advised several colleges, and founded the Wang Institute of Graduate Studies (1979), which provided advanced software engineering degrees.

Wang's honors included election as Fellow of the Institute of Electrical and Electronics Engineers, election as Fellow of the American Academy of Arts and Sciences, induction into the National Inventors Hall of Fame in 1988, and an honorary degree from Lowell Technological Institute. He died of cancer at the relatively young age of seventy and did not live to see his company's demise.

John H. Barnhill

FURTHER READING

"Hard Cases: Life and Death Lessons from Wang Laboratories, Snow Brands and GM." Strategic Direction 21.10 (2005): 25–27. Print. Analyzes mistakes made by companies including Wang.

International Directory of Company Histories. Vol. 6. Wang Laboratories, Inc. Detroit: St. James, 1992. Print. A dated but still useful chronology (ending in 1992) of the rise and fall of the company, including its rivalry with IBM and its eventual bankruptcy.

Kenney, Charles C. "Fall of the House of Wang." Computerworld 17 Feb. 1992: n. pag. Print. Comprehensive If brief overview of the collapse of the company.

---. Riding the Runaway Horse: The Rise and Decline of Wang Laboratories. Boston: Little, Brown, 1992. Print. A journalistic exposé that deals with the official story as well as the insider charges of infighting and micromanagement that brought Wang down.

Wang, An, and Eugene Linden. Lessons: An Autobiography. Reading: Addison-Wesley, 1986. Print. Wang's succinct version of his life story, focusing on his business but also including personal information, including his philosophy of life and business.

CHARLES WANG

Cofounder of Computer Associates International

Born: August 19, 1944; Shanghai, China
Died: -
Primary Field: Business and commerce
Specialty: Management, executives, and investors
Primary Company/Organization: CA Technologies

Charles Wang.

INTRODUCTION
Charles Wang, cofounder of the firm that evolved into CA Technologies, Inc., saw a need for third-party software for mainframe computers and helped to build the company that provided this into one of the largest global software providers. CA Technologies expanded its initial expertise and developed what became enterprise solution software, antivirus protection, and security products. As technology evolved, Wang helped CA Technologies expand its product lines from those intended for its initial corporate client base to offerings that were sold directly to consumers for use on their home computers.

EARLY LIFE
Charles B. Wang was born Wáng Jialián on August 19, 1944, in Shanghai, China. Wang's father, Kenneth, was an appellate judge in Nationalist China, and his mother, Mary, was a member of an old and distinguished family. The Wangs lived in the French Concession of Shanghai, that city's most affluent residential and shopping neighborhood. Fleeing Communist persecution, the Wangs moved to Queens, New York, when Wang was eight years old. Wang has two brothers, Anthony and Francis. The Wangs moved into a single-family house and experienced a cold reception because of racial differences between the family and their all-Caucasian neighbors. Wang was an indifferent student throughout elementary school but attended the prestigious Brooklyn Technical High School, located in the Fort Greene area of Brooklyn.

Despite Brooklyn Tech's elite reputation, Wang was unhappy there and later expressed dissatisfaction with the teaching styles of most of the faculty, who seemed to value rote memorization above creative thinking skills. As a result of this difference with his teachers, Wang received poor grades. He was, however, accepted at Queens College, which he entered in 1961.

Wang worked hard while enrolled at Queens and enjoyed much more success as a student than he had previously. In 1966, Wang earned his bachelor's degree in mathematics and sought employment in the area. Despite never having seen a computer, Wang was hired as a computer programmer at Columbia University, where he impressed his potential employers with his work ethic and strong communication skills. Over the next four years, Wang worked with a variety of computer programs at Columbia.

In 1969, while Wang was still employed at Columbia, International Business Machines Corporation (IBM), the globe's largest producer of mainframe computers, made a decision that would change Wang's life. IBM was facing regulatory pressure from the federal government for possible antitrust violations and as a result decided to separate, or "unbundle," the sale of computer software and support services from the sale of its mainframe machines. This decision created a demand for third-party software, and Wang left Columbia to join Standard Data Corporation (SDC), a provider of data-processing services, where he worked as a salesman, ultimately rising to become that company's vice president of sales. In 1976, Wang and Russell Artzt founded Computer Associates International, Inc., in order to provide software to IBM mainframe users.

LIFE'S WORK

Computer Associates began as a very small business with only a handful of products and very few connections with mainframe users. However, Wang, who had proven to be a master salesman while at SDC, was soon able to change this. One of Computer Associates' most promising products was CA-Sort, a program licensed from a Swiss firm and available from Pansophic Systems in 1976. CA-Sort is a utility program that helped mainframe users sort, merge, and copy files. CA-Sort also provides data management tools that help mainframe computers manipulate data and operate more efficiently. Wang's aggressive sales technique included making cold calls to potential clients and offering demonstrations of his product's virtues. CA-Sort, which was used primarily on IBM mainframes running on the Disc

Operating System/Virtual Storage Expanded (DOS/VSE), proved highly efficient and allowed Computer Associates to grow rapidly. By 1980, Computer Associates had merged with the Swiss firm that originated CA-Sort and was developing ancillary and complementary products such as CA-Dynam/D, CA-Dynam/FI, and CA-Dynam/T, which permitted the company to provide a consistent theme to customers.

After the success of Computer Associates' initial public offering (IPO) in 1981, Wang was able to expand his sales force rapidly and shift from telephone sales to a team that worked in the field. Wang preferred to hire sales representatives who had previous experience in sales, although few of his hires had previously sold software. This permitted Wang to focus sales representative training on the products Computer Associates offered rather than on sales techniques. During this period, Wang began his practice of purchasing existing software companies and merging their products into Computer Associates' already existing product lines. During his leadership of Computer Associates, the company purchased more than fifty other software firms. When Computer Associates purchased another company, Wang would lay off all of that group's sales representatives and management, preferring to promote only those who had risen up from within his firm. Through 1986, Wang concentrated primarily on providing systems utilities to mainframe users, and to that end he purchased a variety of companies that provided such products, including Capex Corporation, Johnson Systems, UCCEL Corporation, and Value Software. Beginning in 1985, Computer Associates began marketing CA Unicenter, an integrated set of its mainframe systems products. As a result of these mergers, Computer Associates had become the largest provider of mainframe infrastructure software and a leading vendor of security software.

Wang has often expressed his belief in "old commerce," a view that is uncommon in the technology field. This belief is one reason Computer Associates continued to pursue software contracts for mainframe users while much of the attention of the industry was elsewhere. Although unfashionable, this strategy helped Wang turn Computer Associates into a $25 billion company. Wang insisted on all Computer Associates employees embracing what he saw as the company's core mission: bringing value to customers. Wang demanded that, as much as possible, Computer Associates integrate all of its parts. Once it had become the market leader in mainframe systems products, Computer Associates continued to expand to new areas that could

Affiliation: CA Technologies

Formed by Charles B. Wang and Russell Artzt in 1976 to supply software to the owners of IBM mainframes (formerly Computer Associates International, Inc.) grew to become one of the largest software providers in the world. With annual sales in excess of $5 billion and more than thirteen thousand employees, Computer Associates focused on sales to corporate users and found ways to expand from its initial core of mainframe systems products to a full range of applications.

CA Technologies since 2010 has expanded by acquiring vendors of products that would help its clients and has learned how to package those products together to provide users with a variety of tools. Although CA Technologies has continued to thrive by making software that is sold to users of mainframe computers, the company has also enhanced its offerings. The company has embraced the cloud strategy and has adapted its practices to permit a more flexible approach to addressing clients' needs.

assist its customers. Acquisitions completed during the late 1980s included Unlimited Software, which offered office software such as a word processor and spreadsheets, and Software International, which provided application software such as financial packages and middleware. For the most part, these strategies worked. By the end of the decade, Computer Associates had become the second software company, topping $1 billion in annual sales.

Despite its many successes, by 1990 Computer Associates was heavily criticized by many Wall Street analysts. The company was seen as lacking focus, providing poor customer service, offering incongruent product lines, and failing to compete with office suite software offered by Microsoft and Lotus Development Corporation. In response, Wang increased the development of overseas markets, reformed the company's pricing system, and improved compatibility of Computer Associates products with that of other vendors. Wang also continued his pattern of acquisitions to build sales: Computer Associates purchased client-server vendor Legent Corporation, data storage giant Cheyenne Software, and job scheduler software from Platinum Technology International. By the end of the decade, Wang's moves had proven so successful that Computer Associates' stock price had improved from $1.70 in late 1990 to almost $70 by the end of 1999.

Wang did face some disappointments: A proposed $9 billion tender offer for the shares of Computer Sciences Corporation, a provider of information technology, was opposed by many in the media because of Wang's alleged ties to China, charges that derailed the purchase and deeply hurt him. In 2000, Wang was also named in a class-action lawsuit as having colluded to inflate the stock price of Computer Associates, with the company ultimately paying nearly $250 million to settle these claims. Wang, who had been granted a controversial $670 million in stock in 1999, tired of these charges and resigned as chief executive officer (CEO) in 2000 and as chairman of the board of directors in 2002.

PERSONAL LIFE
Wang has been married twice. In 1998, he appointed his second wife, Nancy Li, as Computer Associates' chief technology officer, a move that was criticized in some quarters. Wang and Li have three children, two girls and a boy, including a daughter from Li's previous marriage. The couple have worked with a variety of philanthropic causes, including the Make a Wish Foundation and the National Center for Missing and Exploited Children. Wang also helped to found an organization known as the Smile Train, which provides medical services, including surgery, to children born with cleft palates and lips. Sensitive to his status as a role model for many Asian Americans, Wang donated $50 million to the State University of New York at Stony Brook to build an Asian American cultural center. Wang also joined his brothers in honoring their father's judicial service by donating a new law school building to China's Soochow University.

In 2000, Wang purchased part of a National Hockey League (NHL) team, the New York Islanders; he became the majority owner in 2004. Wang has helped to develop properties around the Nassau Coliseum, where the Islanders play their home games, and has demonstrated a willingness to spend money on player salaries and development. Despite this, the Islanders have lagged in attendance and Wang has investigated the possibility of selling or moving the team, the lease of which expires in 2015.

Stephen T. Schroth and Kin Vong

FURTHER READING
Hamm, Steve. "Charles Wang's Messy Second Act." *Businessweek* 4156 (2009): 30. Web. 6 Aug. 2012. Describes Wang's activities in real estate development as of late 2009, noting that his history with CA has haunted him.

Maney, K. *The Maverick and His Machine: Thomas B. Watson Sr. and the Making of IBM*. Hoboken: Wiley, 2004. Print. Explores some of the challenges facing IBM as it sought to provide corporate clients with complete business solutions.

Pugh, E. W. *Building IBM: Shaping an industry and its technology*. Cambridge: MIT, 2009. Print. Explores how decisions made in the 1980s have helped to shape and form IBM, with its emphasis on providing clients "complete" business solutions and a hesitation to embrace new markets that might harm existing profit centers.

Pugh, E. W., L. R. Johnson, and J. H. Palmer. *IBM's 360 and Early 370 Systems*. Cambridge: MIT, 1991. Print. Looks at IBM's great success with early mainframe computers and how technical decisions regarding innovations opened the door for competitors to develop a customer base from IBM clients.

Tennant, D. "Why So Many People Vilify Sanjay Kumar and Not Charles Wang, the Real Perpetrator of CA's Sins." *Computerworld* 42.4 (2008): 4–5. Print. A controversial article arguing that Kumar, former CEO of CA and now serving a twelve-year sentence as a result of CA's legal woes, did not deserve his fate and that instead founder Wang instilled a culture of fraud that permeated the company.

Wang, C. B. *Techno Vision: The Executive's Survival Guide to Understanding and Managing Information Technology*. New York: McGraw-Hill, 1994. Print. Wang provides advice for business leaders regarding how best to find solutions for their organizations.

Watson, T. J., and P. Petre. *Father, Son, and Co.: My Life at IBM and Beyond*. New York: Bantam, 1990. Print. The former CEO of IBM discusses challenges IBM faced as a result of government uncertainty about how best to deal with its monopoly on the business it had created.

JOHN WARNOCK

Cofounder and cochairman of Adobe

Born: October 6, 1940; Salt Lake City, Utah
Died: -
Primary Field: Computer science
Specialty: Computer software
Primary Company/Organization: Adobe

INTRODUCTION

As founder and chief executive officer (CEO) of Adobe Systems, John Warnock has been one of the major designers of computer software. He was behind the design of the portable document format (PDF), which has transformed the sharing of computer files and, through the digitization of books, journals, and newspapers, transformed access to scholarship for academicians and general readers around the world. Warnock's success came from making the Adobe Reader for Adobe Acrobat freely available, and then charging for the "maker" program.

EARLY LIFE

John Edward Warnock was born on October 6, 1940, at Salt Lake City, Utah. He then went to the University of Utah, where he earned his bachelor's degree in mathematics and philosophy in 1961 and then his master's

John Warnock.

degree in mathematics in 1964, studying under David Evans and others. Warnock's master's thesis was about providing a theorem for a problem that had been posed by U.S. mathematician Nathan Jacobson in 1956. Warnock had to solve the Jacobson radical for row-finite matrices. His thesis was finished in 1964. Subsequently, this work, coauthored with N. E. Sexauer, was published in the *Transactions of the American Mathematical Society*.

In 1963, when he was completing his master's thesis, Warnock managed to get a summer job recapping car tires for Firestone. He was later to recall that "working there was hot, dirty and incredibly noisy" and he left after three weeks. He then managed to get a job with IBM, which trained him in Seattle and Los Angeles. He then decided to go back to the university for his doctorate. He married soon afterward and worked in the computer center at the university. Warnock completed his doctoral thesis in electrical engineering (computer science) in 1969. In this thirty-two-page work, "A Hidden Surface Algorithm for Computer Generated Halftone Pictures," he developed his own recursive subdivision algorithm (now called the Warnock algorithm) for hidden surface determination in computer graphics. Warnock initially decided to be a computer entrepreneur and moved to Vancouver, British Columbia, Canada, to work for Computer Sciences of Canada. He next worked briefly in Toronto before moving on to the Goddard Space Flight Center in Greenbelt, Maryland.

LIFE'S WORK

In 1962, Warnock moved to California to work for Evans and Sutherland, a computer graphics company that was based in Salt Lake City. It had been established by David Evans and Ivan Sutherland, both professors at the University of Utah; Evans formerly taught Warnock, and the Sutherland had moved to Salt Lake City from Harvard. They were establishing a company that was working on the Illiac IV supercomputer project, which was involved in providing the National Aeronautics and Space Administration with a flight simulator. This was later to be used as a flight simulator for aircraft pilots in training. The simulators quickly transformed computer graphics using technology that would contribute to simulation models for the military and large industrial companies.

During his time at Evans and Sutherland, Warnock, working with John Gaffney, developed a computer language that they called Design System. The company offered Warnock a promotion and a move back to Salt Lake City. Warnock and his wife wanted to remain in

California, and Warnock therefore left the firm in 1978 to work as a principal scientist at the Xerox Palo Alto Research Center (PARC). There he met Charles M. "Chuck" Geschke, originally from Cleveland, Ohio, and who had graduated from Carnegie Mellon University. Warnock had offered some of his ideas to Xerox, but Xerox did not want to invest the necessary time and money to commercialize the InterPress graphics languages. Xerox was using the languages and wanted to develop them for use by all their printers, whereas Warnock wanted to get the language widely accepted more quickly.

Warnock and Geschke decided to combine their knowledge to form a new company, Adobe Systems, Inc., which was founded on December 2, 1982. Warnock had helped develop some of the basis of the PostScript computer language at Evans and Sutherland, and this language was further developed at Adobe. Warnock wanted to popularize the program quickly so that it could be used by everybody, rather than restrict access, and he felt confident enough to publish it and offer support for other computer systems developers. This led to the file format that Warnock first called Camelot but later came to be known as the portable document format (PDF).

Camelot was launched in the spring of 1991. It allowed anybody to print an electronic document anywhere in the world, regardless of the local platform or printer used, and it would appear exactly as designed at the source. Adobe released a free program, Reader, that allowed anyone to view such documents; however, the company would charge for the programs required to adapt documents to PDF format. Updates to Reader remain freely downloadable over the Internet from Adobe's trusted site.

The PostScript technology and the use of PDF files made it easy to print text and images. It was quickly used for digital publications and then for the digitizing of print documents, including books. As the PDF system became popular, tens of thousands of books, magazines, and newspapers were digitized. The files themselves were often relatively small, which contributed to the ease of file transfer. In spite of the obvious need for such a system, Adobe Acrobat—the computer program used to create the PDF files was not initially very popular; although Warnock tried to impress executives at IBM with the importance of making documents available through his system, they were not very interested.

Warnock continued to develop and improve Acrobat, enhancing the programs by adding security features and allowing for optical character recognition—especially after Adobe managed to acquire OCR Systems, Inc., in 1992—which did add considerably to the size of the files. However, the issue of file size was evolving into an negligible one: Improvements in the Internet, as well as the availability of larger and larger hard drives on personal computers, made the need to minimize file size less and less important.

Adobe was listed on NASDAQ in 1986. Adobe's success prompted some companies to try to develop their own similar systems, but although a few became relatively popular, none achieved the widespread acceptance of PDF files. The sudden wealth in the company resulted in media coverage that may have contributed to Geschke's being kidnapped from the parking lot of the Adobe headquarters in Mountain View on the morning of May 26, 1992. A large ransom payment was handed over, but the kidnappers were followed by the Federal Bureau of Investigation, and Geschke was freed. The two kidnappers sentenced to imprisonment for life.

Under Warnock and Geschke, Adobe continued to grow with the further development of PDF and the design of Photoshop and Flash. Once PDF became the most widely used system for formatting documents, it became the basis of the digitization of vast databases, as well as several million books and journals. Some journals and newspapers are available in PDF daily, and there are an increasing number available only in PDF. Many journals also have digitized their back issues in PDF. This has resulted in PDF documents being used in scholarship and academic libraries around the world and cataloging of digitized "e-books" just as print copies are cataloged.

In 1994 Warnock oversaw the acquisition of Aldus and thus the page layout program InDesign. Over the next few years, QuarkXPress superseded PageMaker as the standard program used for publishing, and as publishers migrated from using out-of-house typesetting services to bringing these production tasks in house by using these programs ("desktop publishing"), Adobe focused developing its own desktop publishing software, InDesign. Adobe was a natural source of this software, since most printers were now using PDF file formats. The first version was released in 1999 and has been regularly updated and enhanced since. It allows publishers to control the final page content, layout, design, and export to PDF format that is ready for the printer and, increasingly, e-book and online publication.

Warnock has received a large number of awards. In 1989, he won the Software Systems Award from the

---

Affiliation: Adobe

Adobe Systems was founded in December 1982 in Mountain View, California, although its headquarters are now located in San Jose, California. Created by John Warnock and Charles Geschke, it took its name from the Adobe Creek, which ran being the houses of the two founders when they were living in Los Altos, California.

The company's first major product was PostScript. This program offered digital fonts, including TrueType fonts, which allowed for scalability. However, Adobe's most important product would be Adobe Acrobat, with the development of the languages to allow for the portable document format (PDF).

In 1992, Adobe acquired OCR Systems, Inc., and two years later it bought the Aldus Corporation. In recent years it has focused heavily on Adobe InDesign, publishing software, which took over from PageMaker, and has also made inroads into the market formerly dominated by QuarkXPress.

Adobe is a public company and in 2011 had revenues of $4.21 billion and a net income of $832 million. It employs about ten thousand people and has offices around the world.

Association for Computing Machinery (ACM). In 1995, the University of Utah recognized him with its Distinguished Alumnus Award, and in 1999 he was inducted as a Fellow of ACM. The Bodleian Library at Oxford University inducted him as a Fellow of the Computer History Museum. He and Geschke have been recipients of the annual Medal of Achievement Award of the American Electronics Association as well as the National Medal of Technology and Innovation, the highest U.S. honor awarded to engineers and inventors. As of 2012, Both Warnock and Geschke remained the cochairs of Adobe Systems.

PERSONAL LIFE

Unlike many other computer entrepreneurs who have spoken of the influence of their parents and family, Warnock has kept his personal life private. He married Marva around the time he started his doctorate at the University of Utah, where she earned her bachelor of science degree, and they had three children. The couple donated 200,000 shares of Adobe Systems, valued at $5.7 million, to the University of Utah to build the John E. and Marva M. Warnock Engineering Building, which was completed in 2007 for the University of Utah College of Engineering.

Justin Corfield

FURTHER READING

Martin, Justin, Aditya Mittal, Michelle Richaud, and N. Dominic Taboada. "Adobe Systems Incorporated." *Strategic Management Cases: Competitiveness and Globalization*. Mason: South-Western, 2012. 1–15. Print. A study of Adobe as a business, explaining its projects and its success in various fields.

Pifner, Pamela S. *Inside the Publishing Revolution: The Adobe Story*. Berkeley: Peachpit, 2003. Print. A history of Adobe, Inc., showing how Adobe Acrobat has transformed publishing around the world.

Warnock, John. "Adobe Cofounder John Warnock on the Competitive Advantages of Aesthetics and the 'Right' Technology." 20 Jan. 2010. *Knowledge@Wharton*. Web. 12 Aug. 2012. An interview in which Warton discusses the founding of Adobe and his passion for design.

Warnock, John. "John Warnock." n.d. *Programmers at Work*. Web. 12 Aug. 2012. A biographical sketch of Warnock precedes this interview with him about the history of the PostScript language, Adobe, and what accounted for his success.

Weil, David, ed. *Leaders of the Information Age*. New York: H. W. Wilson, 2003. Print. Includes a biographical article on Warnock.

PADMASREE WARRIOR

CTO of Cisco

Born: 1961; Vijayawada, India
Died: -
Primary Field: Computer science
Specialty: Computer hardware
Primary Company/Organization: Cisco Systems

INTRODUCTION

A chemical engineer by training, Warrior was chief technology officer (CTO) for Motorola and Cisco Systems and had a huge and positive impact on both companies. She is known in the technology industry for her ability to identify trends. She recognizes the need for constant development of new technology to improve business networking systems. Her analytical and pragmatic mind has helped secure Cisco Systems' place as a leader in technology.

EARLY LIFE

Padmasree Warrior was born into the Telugu culture of India in 1961. She attended high school and college in India, obtaining an undergraduate degree in chemical engineering from the Indian Institute of Technology. She then received a master's degree in chemical engineering from Cornell University. Both of her parents provided Warrior with a firm foundation in mathematics and science, supporting her self-confidence and desire to keep learning and sending her to study and work in the United States.

LIFE'S WORK

Warrior received her graduate degree in 1984 and began working for Motorola, Inc., that year. She was employed

Padmasree Warrior.

at Motorola's semiconductor plant in Arizona before she graduated from college. There she worked on improving the technology systems of the plant and made her reputation as the only female engineer in the factory. The academically minded Warrior had little intention of devoting her life to corporate technology but managed to spend twenty-three years at Motorola doing just that. She became an executive in 2003, making her the first woman in the company to achieve that level. She was promoted to senior vice president in 2005.

Warrior left Motorola on December 4, 2007, when she began working for Cisco Systems. She was one of the few Cisco employees to be handed an executive position rather than having to work up from the ground floor of the ever-expanding company. Warrior had graduated from college the year Cisco was incorporated. The company had been founded in 1984 in San Jose, California, after cofounders Sandy Lerner and Leonard Bosack perfected their new router technology while working for Stanford University. The company's first product was a smart router that allowed multiple machines, computers, and networks to work together regardless of manufacturer. Cisco sold its first router in 1986. Cisco had web-based sales before web sales were popular: Others in the new technology field needed the products Cisco offered in a world where very few networking products were available.

Since those early days, Cisco has become one of the world's largest manufacturers and distributors of Internet and computer technology selling routers, switchers, network adapters, and networking software. Cisco sells its products using the business-to-business model, the majority of sales coming from large corporations, government entities, schools, and distributors. Cisco became a public company in 1990. At that time, 251 people worked for the company.

As the Internet took off, online sales at Cisco increased along with the need for routers, switches, and corporate computer networking. By the time dot-com boom developed in the 1990s, Cisco was already well placed to corner the market. *Fortune* magazine named Cisco the second-fastest-growing company in the United States in 1992. The deregulation of the telephone industry provided Cisco the opportunity to partner with phone companies to provide customers with Internet technology for their homes and fiber optics for all their communication systems.

In order to improve their customer service and provide their customers with the latest in digital technology, Cisco began purchasing smaller technology companies from the niche markets to improve their overall product line. By 2001, Cisco had acquired more than seventy different companies and had taken on their employees in the process. Cisco's theory of "strategic acquisitions" has been the driving force behind the company's growth. The company acquires businesses that have the skills or services their current customers need in order to grow more customers.

When Warrior arrived at Cisco in 2007, therefore, it was already one of the largest and most successful companies in history. After joining Cisco, Warrior worked with the other executives and trustees to improve strategic acquisitions. Her job was to ensure the company had the best technology it could to improve

Affiliation: Cisco Systems

Sandy Lerner and Leonard Bosack met during their time working for the information technology department at Stanford University. While there, they developed router technology that allowed them to network their two departments on campus. After an initial squabble over intellectual property rights with the university, Lerner and Bosack created their own company, Cisco Systems. The company was named during a ride over the Golden Gate Bridge in San Francisco. Cisco began in 1984 and went public in 1990. That year, Cisco had 251 employees and just under $70 million in annual revenue.

Cisco developed some of the earliest networking technology for the corporate world, including Internet switches, routers, and other hardware. Cisco goods online before online shopping was widespread; its first Internet sale was in 1986. By utilizing the Internet for sales, after-service assistance, and inventory management, Cisco grew the company at an extraordinary pace, enjoying 30 percent annual growth rates for several years. Cisco went from $15 billion to $100 billion in sales in just three years.

In 1993, Cisco began its hallmark practice of buying companies, and bringing their technology and employees under the Cisco corporate umbrella to ensure that customers were provided with the latest in technology products. This practice of strategic acquisitions and vertical integration has ensured that Cisco continues to grow and dominate the technology sector. As of 2011, Cisco had more than seventy thousand employees, ninety-five field offices located around the world, and revenue of $43 billion.

sales and service. Through tireless research, watching market trends and constantly exploring new partnerships, Warrior assesses the future technology needs of customers and determines which technology partners will help Cisco reach its goals. She has thus worked to ensure that Cisco stays on the top of the technology pile and hears and responds to the needs of its corporate customers. With product integration and annual growth rates exceeding all expectations, Cisco has grown from the beginning and, as of 2012, was continuing to expand its ideas and customer base.

In her role as CTO of Cisco, Warrior created forward-thinking business models for her colleagues and coworkers. She continually improved and expanded on the company's technology affiliations and partnerships, bringing fresh ideas to an already extremely successful company. She was personally responsible for a large portion of Cisco's annual revenue through her many innovations and careful executive handling of associates. She oversaw more than twenty thousand Cisco engineers every day. In 2011, *The Huffington Post* referred to Warrior as "one of the most powerful women in Silicon Valley."

On June 26, 2012, Warrior replaced longtime Cisco chief strategist Ned Hooper, who left the company to start his own investment firm. Warrior's new responsibilities meant reducing her time with Cisco's thousands of engineers, turning her focus and energy to the company's technological future, and directing the company toward it. She often plays the role of keynote speaker for Cisco, sharing her experience and wisdom with the company's employees and affiliates. The company's website is full of Warrior's articles and blog posts; she works to keep in touch with the customer base.

In 2012, Warrior made a public announcement that she saw a "new Internet" developing with a focus on providing users with single platforms for new technology and media based on collaboration between different providers. She suggested that Cisco Systems would explore green solutions and quality platforms for video in the near future.

PERSONAL LIFE

Warrior is married to Mohandas Warrior, a successful chief executive officer for a laser manufacturing company. They have one son, Karna. Warrior sits on the board of the Joffrey Ballet and the Museum of Science and Industry. She has received rankings in all the top business and technology rating systems and holds an honorary doctorate from New York Polytechnic. She sits on

several advisory councils and boards. Warrior also enjoys sculpting, writing haiku, reading, and attending the theater. Her favorite author is P. G. Wodehouse.

Trish Popovitch

FURTHER READING

Augustin, Xavier. "Padmasree Warrior, CTO, CISCO Systems on Wikipedia." *The Global Indian* 16 Mar. 2009. Web. 8 Aug. 2012. Details Warrior's upbringing, education, and personal life and explains her desire to explore the world of technology from a pragmatic stand point.

Bosker, Bianca. "Cisco Tech Chief Outlines the Advantages of Being a Woman in Tech." *The Huffington Post* 27 Oct. 2011. Web. 8 Aug. 2012. Explains in detail Warrior's role at Cisco and her approach to business in the technology field. Provides background on Warrior as well as a color photograph.

"Cisco Corporate History." *International Directory of Company Histories*. Vol. 34. New York: St. James, 2000. Web. *Fundinguniverse*. 8 Aug. 2012. Covers how Cisco was founded, the challenges faced during the early years, the type of equipment and services the company offers, and Cisco's philosophy of strategic acquisition.

Cisco Systems. "Cisco Systems Annual Report." *Cisco. com*. 2011. Web. 8 Aug. 2012. Provides statistical data as well as a narrative on the state of the company at the end of 2011. Details growth rates, revenues, and future plans.

---. "Padmasree Warrior Biography." *Cisco.com*. 2012. Web. 8 Aug. 2012. Professional biography detailing Warrior's many awards and industry rankings. Includes information on her role a Cisco and what she brings to the strategic planning process.

Hamblen, Matt. "Q&A: CTO Says Video a Key Driver in Cisco's Strategic Decisions." *ComputerWorld* 10 May 2010. Web. 7 Aug. 2012. Covers what Warrior views as the future of technology needs. Emphasizes green technology and the many possibilities that come with voice and video in the virtual and corporate setting.

Paulson, Ed. *Inside Cisco: The Real Story of Sustained M&A Growth*. New York: Wiley, 2001. Print. A wealth of information about Cisco's origin, founders, and corporate perspective. Covers executives who made strategic changes to Cisco's way of doing business.

Sibley, Lisa. "Padmasree Warrior Replaces Ned Hooper as Cisco CTO." *Business Journal* 26 June 2012.

Web. 8 Aug. 2012. Explains changes in Cisco's executive lineup, including Warrior's replacing longtime strategy chief Ned Hooper. Includes photographs and a number of links.

Tully, Shawn. "How Cisco Mastered the Net: You Think Amazon.com Is Big? The Real Money Online Is Business-to-Business Sales, and the King of Routers Is Writing the Manual." *Fortune* 17 Aug. 1998. Web. 8 Aug. 2012. Discusses the rapid growth of the company during its early years and the use of Internet sales to expand the customer base. Marketing strategies are discussed in detail.

Warrior, Padmasree. "American's First CTO?" Interview by David Talbot. *Technology Review* 112.2 (2009): 28–29. Web. 9 Aug. 2012. Interview with Warrior when everyone thought she would be named the first CTO of the Obama administration. She discusses what she would do if the job were to become hers.

White, Bobby. "Top 50 Women to Watch in 2008." *Wall Street Journal* 10 Nov. 2008. Web. 8 Aug. 2012. An article with portrait photographs of the fifty female executives worth watching in 2008. Mentions Warrior, her work with Cisco, and her accomplishments.

THOMAS J. WATSON SR.

Former CEO of IBM

Born: February 17, 1874; Campbell, New York
Died: June 20, 1956; New York, New York
Primary Field: Computer science
Specialty: Computer hardware
Primary Company/Organization: IBM

INTRODUCTION

Thomas J. Watson Sr., was one of the first entrepreneurs in computing. He built International Business Machines, now IBM, from a maker of accounting equipment into the dominant corporation in business machines before transitioning the company to computers and inexorably moving into worldwide dominance. He gave the company its succinct motto: "Think." His forty-two years at IBM also saw the company struggle to adapt as rapidly as smaller competitors. Hamstrung by its very success, the organization's massiveness made rapid change difficult. Still, he left a business that dominated the field the one against which others were forced to measure themselves.

EARLY LIFE

Thomas J. Watson was born into a family, descended from Scots, who came to the United States from Ireland during the potato famine of the mid-nineteenth century. The family business was lumber, and Thomas was exposed to business from an early age. His father wanted him to study law after he finished school, but he decided he would be a teacher instead. After spending a day as a teacher, however, he changed his mind, deciding to enter business. His father required him to attend business school, which he did, finishing business and accounting courses at the Elmira School of Commerce and then, at age eighteen, becoming bookkeeper and sales clerk in Clarence Risley's Market in Painted Post, New York, for $6.00 per week. The sedentary office life failed to hold his attention, so he went on the road selling

Thomas J. Watson, Sr.

sewing machines and pianos. While he held their horses, he studied the techniques employed by veteran salesmen and soon overcame his initial lack of skill at sales. When he quit, the boss offered to sell him the business. Instead he went to National Cash Register in Buffalo, New York. Rising through the ranks to general sales manager, he sought to motivate his sales force and introduced the motto "Think," which would become the internationally recognized byword of IBM.

LIFE'S WORK

National Cash Register (NCR), or "The Cash," exposed Watson to John Range, the manager who gave Watson the skills he needed to become not only a salesman but also a role model, a manager of other salesmen. The first lesson was harsh. Watson was not successful at selling cash registers, and Range not only told him to stop making excuses but also gave him a first-rate tongue lashing, followed by an exploration of what sales involved. Range took Watson on the road with him, letting Watson watch as Range sold a cash register at each attempt. Soon, twenty-five-year-old Watson was NCR's top salesman. He moved up to manager of the Rochester branch and lifted the sluggish branch from near the bottom to sixth from the top. When sales slumped as a result of market saturation and competition, Watson sabotaged competitors' machines. He set up shops next to secondhand shops, used NCR's cash advantage to undercut the competition, and drove the rivals out of business in what was unethical if not illegal practice.

Watson did so well that he secured a meeting with NCR founder John Henry Patterson. Patterson had brought NCR to its peak from nothing by making better machines and establishing a sales manual. His factory incorporated floor-to-ceiling glass windows, included landscaping, and was well ahead of its time. Patterson shared automaker Henry Ford's paternalistic idea that employees would be good producers if they were healthy, well fed, and well treated. Patterson bought Watson a car and a house, and Watson rose to NCR's executive level. Watson and Patterson were among the thirty NCR executives charged with and tried for unfair business practices, generating unfavorable publicity for NCR. Watson received a jail term of one year and a fine of $5,000. He appealed and lived several months in the shadow of the open case. In 1915, the appeals court reversed the verdict, and Watson was rid of the threat of jail.

At age forty, Watson famously argued with Patterson in a meeting; Watson saw electric cash registers as the wave of the future, and Patterson wanted to stick

with mechanical cash registers. Patterson fired him on the spot. (Legend has it that he had Watson's desk carried out of the building and lit on fire, leading to the American colloquialism for being sacked.) In 1914, Watson joined the Computing Tabulating Recording Company (CTR), the company formed from Herman Hollerith's Tabulating Machine company, which had manufactured the punch card sorting and tabulating machines for the U.S. Census of 1890 but which by 1914 was close to failing and deep in debt. The company also manufactured time clocks, scales, and accounting machines

Incorporated in 1911, CTR had fewer than four hundred employees when Watson became president in May 1914. Watson improved Hollerith's tabulating machine, capitalizing on his experience at NCR making the knockoffs that looked like the opposition's product but with intentional design flaws guaranteeing them to fail and thus damaging the competitor's reputation. In 1915, he became president of CTR, and by 1917 the company was grossing $8 million, up from $4 million in 1914. In 1919, CTR marketed an electrically operated machine with an automatic card feeder and a built-in printer, and by 1920 CTR was grossing $14 million. In 1924, at age fifty, Watson became chief executive officer (CEO), merged CTR with IBM, and renamed the business as International Business Machines (IBM).

In 1929, only 2 percent of U.S. accounting business was done by machine. At the same time, Benjamin D. Wood of Columbia University was having problems marking thousands of test results by hand. He met with Watson and sold him on the idea that IBM could solve Wood's problem. Watson sent trucks full of tabulators, card punches, counters, sorters and the engineers and trainers to get Wood's staff up to speed. However, Wood was not satisfied, wanting more speed. He challenged Watson, holding the speed limit was that of light, and IBM engineers began working on the problem. Wood began working for IBM, the company's first Ph.D. When Columbia astronomer Wallace Eckert asked for IBM machines to help in lunar calculations, he persuaded Watson to set up the Thomas J. Watson Astronomical Computing Bureau at the university to provide the sequencing mechanism and mechanical multiplier that supported calculations—a primitive precursor to the electromechanical computer.

When Howard Aiken began his computer research in 1936, he knew that the 601 multipliers and sequencing mechanisms would not do, and he did not like Watson's paternalism and demanding style, but he asked for IBM's help, which Watson provided, first in the form of

Affiliation: IBM

Thomas J. Watson defined IBM. When he took over in 1914, one hundred shares cost $2,750. By 1925, that number of shares had grown to 153, with a value of $6,364. At his death, the shares would total 3,990 and be valued at $2.16 million, including cash dividends of more than $200,000. Watson himself began at $6.00 a week; by 1940, his $546,000 annual income was second only to Louis B. Mayer's $704,000. Watson forewent compensation from war contract profits during the World War II. In 1955, he received $346,590. Money was not his driving motivation; rather, he was compelled by providing technology that he believed would provide better future.

During the Great Depression, Watson not only kept IBM's plants open but also expanded his sales force. He stockpiled inventory until the demand returned, as he knew it would. At his death, the company had two hundred offices in the United States. as well as factories in ten countries and assembly plants in half a dozen others. IBM employed sixty thousand people, had gross assets of $629.5 million, and could boast a 1955 net income of $55.8 million. In eighty countries around the world, the slogan on the wall, "Think," and the way of doing business were the legacy of Watson, Sr. The foundation was in place for his son, Thomas J. Watson Jr., to make the business an overwhelming force—and for the overwhelming force to find itself struggling, because of its size, to adapt to the changing world of computing after the 1960s.

$1 million and ultimately $5 million. The Mark I computer debuted in 1944. In 1946, IBM put out the Selective Sequence Electronic Calculator (SSEC) after Watson ordered his engineers to work around the clock. The SSEC had 12,500 valves, 21,400 relays, and the ability to store eight 20-bit numbers in memory, 150 numbers on relays, and 20,000 numbers on 60 reels of punched tape. It had more power than the Electronic Numerical Integrator and Computer (ENIAC), the electronic computer that had debuted the preceding year, and was the first publicly available computer, well ahead of its competitors. It served for many years.

When J. Presper Eckert and John Mauchly asked IBM for help with their Universal Automatic Computer (UNIVAC), Watson rebuffed them and they went to Rand (by then, Sperry Rand) instead. However, Rand failed to capitalize on its advantage, and IBM made up for its initial error. IBM introduced 603 electronic calculators in 1946, but its first true electronic computer, the IBM 701, did not debut until 1952 (and still used punch cards). IBM leased twenty of these machines for $24,000 per month, and IBM was in the computer business.

Watson Sr., had become chairman of IBM's board in September, 1949. His son, Thomas J. Watson Jr., became IBM's president in January 1952 and CEO in May 1956. Another son, Arthur K. Watson, was president of IBM's international operations. Watson Sr., remained chairman until his death in 1956 at age eighty-two. Watson Sr., brought a loose collection of relatively small companies into a group that nearly monopolized the accounting machine industry but that eventually dominated the industry and successfully made the transition to computing. His style was not that of the smooth, efficient, and cold IBM stereotype; rather, he took an intensely personal, hands-on approach.

Watson inculcated in his employees the industrial "family" concept, with customers coming first, then employees, and finally owners. Customers needed new machines for new needs, and IBM found new needs for old machines. Customers deserved good value, workers were to be paid sufficiently, and owners were to reap the profits. Watson was unafraid to borrow money, and he used loans wisely in developing laboratories for creating new product lines: computers, machines that could simultaneously weigh and count items, translators, and scientific and other calculators. Also, under Watson Sr., IBM leased rather than sold. Rentals in the early 1950s brought in $100 million annually.

In 1952, the government sued IBM, alleging that the company owned 90 percent of the country's tabulating machines with a rental value of $250 million. IBM then began selling the machines, set up a separate service and parts divisions, and agreed to license its patents.

PERSONAL LIFE

Thomas J. Watson Sr., was tall, dignified in appearance, ascetic, and impeccably groomed. He was a devotee of education, the arts (including opera), sailing, and horseback riding. He regarded his immense wealth as something he was obligated to spread through public service and philanthropy.

He was president of the Old Merchants Association and hosted New York City affairs for visiting dignitaries, including kings, presidents, and others. He served as president of the International Chamber of Commerce, provided a stage worth $25,000 to the United Nations, and developed the slogan "World Peace Through World Trade." He was a trustee of Columbia University for twenty-three years, and his support helped build a laboratory and alumni activities. He received many awards and honorary degrees, was friends with Presidents Franklin D. Roosevelt and Dwight D. Eisenhower, and in 1947 received the Medal of Merit from Harry Truman, who appointed him special ambassador to the jubilee of Queen Wilhelmina of the Netherlands. The causes he supported included religious and nonsectearian organizations: He gave the Methodist Church $1 million in 1955, for example, and supported the Boy Scouts and the Masons.

When Watson died in 1956, he was survived by his wife Jeanette (née Jeanette M. Kittredge), two sons, two daughters, two sisters, and fifteen grandchildren. He had married Kittredge on April 17, 1913, in a wedding that was almost canceled because the date fell two weeks after his NCR antitrust conviction (for which he was later acquitted).

John H. Barnhill

FURTHER READING

Belden, Thomas Graham, and Marva Robins Belden. *The Lengthening Shadow: The Life of Thomas J. Watson*. Boston: Little, Brown, 1962. Print. Still valuable and interesting, despite being half a century old.

Greulich, Peter E. *The World's Greatest Salesman: An IBM Caretaker's Perspective; Looking Back*. Austin: MBI Concepts, 2011. Print. Former IBM employee Greulich documents the founder's leadership of the early IBM.

Maney, Kevin. *The Maverick and His Machine: Thomas Watson Sr., and the Making of IBM* Hoboken: Wiley, 2003. Print. The definitive biography of Watson Sr.

"Thomas J. Watson Sr." *Bloomsbury Business Library: Business Thinkers and Management Giants*. 2007. *Business Source Complete*. Web. 12 May 2012. An overview of the life and career.

Watson, Thomas J., and Peter Petre. *Father, Son and Co.: My Life at IBM and Beyond*. New York: Bantam, 2000. Print. The autobiography of the son with the biography of the father and the story of the company.

Watson, Thomas J. Jr. *A Business and Its Beliefs: The Ideas That Helped Build IBM*. New York: McGraw-Hill, 2003. Print. Originally published in 1962 and rereleased in this edition, a volume that is especially informative on the business values of the Watsons and IBM, by the man who led the company into the computer age.

Zientara, Marguerita. "History of Computing, Part 7: Thomas J. Watson Sr., the Businessman's Businessman." *Computerworld* 21 Sept. 1981: n. pag. Print. A good introduction to the personal and professional Watson. Including some telling anecdotes.

MAURICE WILKES

Creator of EDSAC

Born: June 26, 1913; Dudley, Worcestershire, England
Died: November 29, 2010; Cambridge, Cambridgeshire, England
Primary Field: Computer science
Specialty: Computer programming
Primary Company/Organization: Cambridge Computer Laboratory

INTRODUCTION

Maurice Wilkes was one of developers of the Early Delay Storage Automatic Calculator (EDSAC), which was the successor to the J. Presper Eckert with John William Mauchly's first general-purpose digital electronic computer, the Electronic Numerical Integrator and Computer (ENIAC). EDSAC was the first practical stored-program computer, the first capable of running realistic programs and achieving useful outputs. Wilks also invented microprogramming and wrote an early standard textbook in computer science. Today he is considered the father of British computing and a major figure in the international computing field.

EARLY LIFE

Sir Maurice Vincent Wilkes was born to a switchboard operator for the Earl of Dudley's private telephone network. His father encouraged Wilkes's interest in electronics. At King Edward VI's Grammar School in Stourbridge, Wilkes built a radio transmitter, which his

Maurice Wilkes.

father allowed him to use at home. Wilkes suffered from recurring bouts of asthma, but by his teens he was vigorously studying mathematics and science, increasing his knowledge of amateur radio from a subscription to *Wireless World.*

When he went to St. John's College, Cambridge, in 1931, he studied mathematics but was a spare-time student of electronics and attended engineering lectures. He held the license for the students' amateur radio station and continued building radios on his vacations so could contact ham operators throughout the world. After taking a first in mathematics, he earned a Ph.D. While at Cambridge, Wilkes was familiar with Alan Turing (they were exact contemporaries although at different colleges), whom he later studiously avoided describing as someone he disliked by saying that "you don't regard your contemporaries as great men"; Turing was, according to Wilkes, "not in any sense a team leader; he didn't know how to get things done." Wilkes also worked on the propagation of radio waves in the ionosphere and became interested in tidal motion in the atmosphere. He would publish his first book, *Oscillations of the Earth's Atmosphere*, in 1949.

LIFE'S WORK

Wilkes's attended a lecture by mathematician Douglas Hartree on (human) computing and the differential analyzer, the wheel-and-disk apparatus that solved differential equations. He built a model using parts from Meccano (a maker of toy construction sets). In 1937, Wilkes became a university "demonstrator" (essentially an associate professor) in the newly established Mathematical Laboratory (colloquially called the Maths Lab and ultimately transformed into the Computer Laboratory), located in the former anatomy school. His job was to acquire a differential analyzer to provide calculating services to university researchers. He had to suspend this academic position in 1939, however, when he was called to serve in World War II. During the war, he worked on radar with Robert Watson-Watt and John D. Cockroft and later on submarine tracking and missile and aircraft design.

After the war, Wilkes returned to head the Cambridge Maths Lab. There, his primary assignment was to explore the potential of calculating machines. In 1946, he was invited to attend a course on theory and techniques for design of electronic digital computers at the Moore School of Electrical Engineering at the University of Pennsylvania, where much of the cutting-edge work in computers was being conducted at the time: Moore was home to the J. Presper Eckert and John Mauchly's Electronic Numerical Integrator and Computer (ENIAC). Although postwar transportation was unreliable his arrival in Philadelphia delayed, Wilkes attended the latter portion of the two-month course and heard John von Neumann's report on the Electronic Discrete Variable Automatic Computer (EDVAC), which proposed delay lines as a means of storing data in computer memory. Returning to Cambridge, Wilkes began working on what would become ENIAC's successor, and in tribute to EDVAC (which was not yet built) called it the Early Delay Storage Automatic Calculator (EDSAC). Von Neumann and others had noted that computers of the future had to have memory capable of storing not only data but also programs, sets of instructions for using the data. The future machine envisioned by von Neumann would allow users to change programs written in binary numbers without having to rewire and rejigger, a tedious and time-consuming process that took days. Three groups of scientists were working simultaneously on solutions to von Neumann's challenge: a team at Manchester University, Eckert and Mauchly in Pennsylvania, and Wilkes at Cambridge.

EDSAC debuted on May 6, 1949, computing a table of square numbers. EDSAC was a room-sized machine that used three thousand vacuum tubes arrayed on twelve racks and whose memory, like that of Eckert and

Mauchly's EDVAC, was constructed of sealed tubes of mercury (mercury delay lines) that represented data as ripples in the mercury. EDSAC used thirty-two tubes of mercury, each of which had thirty-two seventeen-bit words. Delayed pulses generated by an electrically charged quartz crystal created this memory. An electrical signal became a sound wave passing through a long tube of mercury at 1,450 meters per second, and the signal was capable of traveling back and forth along the tube. Combined, these charged tubes formed an internal memory of 1,024 words. In this machine, the first load of the program was by paper tape but later uses of the program were from memory.

EDSAC performed 650 to 700 operations per second. Before EDSAC, computers such as the Moore School's ENIAC could handle only one type of problem at a time and had to be reprogrammed over several days of resetting thousands of switches and rerouting miles of cable. Although Eckert and Mauchly's computer employed a stored program before EDSAC, when it became operational EDSAC was the first electronic stored-program computer to go into regular service (Manchester's had been the first electronic stored-program computer, but it was a small prototype). EDSAC may have been slow by today's standards, but it radically decreased the time needed to do computations and thus as a practical advance was dramatic. Moreover, its status as a practical tool for students, faculty, and researchers encouraged the creation of programs and means of using EDSAC that advanced computer programming.

EDSAC quickly, from early 1950, provided the university with an advanced computing service, the first regular computing service in the world, and Wilkes and staff developed programs and collected them into a library. R. A. Fisher's paper on genetics was the first scientific paper to use computer calculations, and the calculations were enabled by EDSAC. Another highly successful British computer, the LEO, created by Joe Lyons, was a "son" of EDSAC. In 1951, Wilkes and two graduate students, David Wheeler and Stanley Gill, published *The Preparation of Programs for an Electronic Digital Computer* (1951), the first book on computer programming, in which they described this use of a library of subroutines in programming.

Wilkes was also one of the first to realize that programming required such exacting detail that the future would inevitably include a lot of debugging to find errors that kept the programs from running properly. He thus spent a considerable amount of his time fixing mistakes in his programs during EDSAC's lifetime. That life ended when it became apparent that delay lines were on the verge of obsolescence and the future lay with magnetic storage. EDSAC was scrapped, its parts cannibalized, and its paper tapes used as streamers for children's parties.

EDSAC II debuted in 1958 with both magnetic storage and the first microprogrammed control unit. It used two magnetic core memories instead of delay lines, and it was faster and easier to program. The first "bit-slice" machine, its processor was constructed of interchangeable modules. Wilkes also realized that stored programs in the computer could represent control signal sequences, a concept he named *microprogramming*. Microprogramming is a method for implementing the control logic of a computer's central processing unit, essentially managing the construction of programs via access to low-level microinstructions from a control store of

---

Affiliation: Cambridge Computer Laboratory

Maurice Wilkes came to Cambridge in 1945 with the mandate of creating a viable computer science department, although it would rest in the mathematics department and would for many years be called the Cambridge Mathematical Laboratory, or Maths Lab. He not only established the department but also created a breakthrough computer, then another, and then a minimal local area network. His concepts were foundational for computer development, and he made the department a leader with an international reputation. EDSAC and EDSAC II established standards for digital computers that allowed them to replace the electromechanical and mechanical computers of before.

In 1970, the Mathematical Laboratory was renamed the Computer Laboratory (which it really had always been) and was reorganized into to divisions: a research division and a services division, and in 2001 the Computer Laboratory was separated from the Computer Service. The former moved to a new building in West Cambridge. The university became known for the computing businesses that developed in the Lab and Cambridge's computer science courses, including Media Dynamics, Acorn, and Bromium. In 2012, a total of 188 computing companies had been founded by Cambridge staff and alumni.

microinstructions, each of which provides appropriate control signals and sequencing information.

In the 1960s Wilkes began to plan the next generation of EDSAC, but by then the computer industry was growing. Wilkes had a small government grant to spend on upgrading the Maths Lab's computer hardware. Wilkes considered machines from two companies, IBM and Ferranti. Ferranti's Atlas proved to be the best and most cost-effective choice, and it arrived (as the Titan) in 1963. EDSAC II was closed in 1965 during an emotional ceremony.

In 1965, Wilkes received a chair as profession of computer technology (his own name for the title). In the same year, he published a paper on cache memory, the first of its kind, and also introduced time sharing, which had been created at Dartmouth College and developed at the Massachusetts Institute of Technology—thus introducing workstations and inputting via teletype machines rather than punch cards or paper tape (he would later publish *Time Sharing Computer Systems* in 1975). By 1970, the Maths Lab was divided into a computer services division and a computer science/research division.

Between 1965 and his retirement in 1980, Wilkes was professor of computing technology at Cambridge. He led what had become Cambridge University's Computer Laboratory to its status as a leading research center in England. He advised British computer companies and was a founder of the British Computer Society (over which he presided between 1957 and 1960). In 1974, he was among those who collaborated on the experimental Cambridge Ring, an early local-area network. The ring was a series of computers linked by digital communications for the purpose of sharing a printer, and commercial development was done by others.

After retirement, Wilkes moved to the United States and became a research consultant in multimedia conferencing and network systems at Digital Equipment Corporation (DEC). He also served at MIT as adjunct professor of electrical engineering and computer science from 1981 to 1985. He returned to Cambridge as a consultant researcher with funding from AT&T, Oracle, and Olivetti at various times and remained active into his nineties. In 2002, after AT&T's acquisition and shutdown of Olivetti, he returned to the Computer Lab at Cambridge.

PERSONAL LIFE

In 1947, Wilkes married Nina Twyman. They had two daughters and a son. He published *Memoirs of a*

Computer Pioneer in 1985. After returning to Cambridge in 2002, he enjoyed discussions with students and colleagues and regular academic social occasions. Upon the sixtieth anniversary of EDSAC, on May 6, 2009, Wilkes gave a speech during a celebration of the event in which he noted the achievement of the EDSAC project as having opened computing to a broad range of students and researchers—highlighting his overarching focus and interests in the practical applications of computing and the ways it contributed to the success of great scientists, including Nobel laureates. His comments underscored the often little recognized contribution of Wilkes himself: not only as a computer scientist but also as a manager, teacher, and facilitator of research. He died at the age of ninety-seven, predeceased by his wife.

Wilkes was the recipient of many honors and awards over the course of his career. He became a Fellow of the Royal Society in 1956, a foreign honorary member of the American Academy of Arts and Sciences in 1974, a Fellow the Royal Academy of Engineering in 1976, and foreign associate of the American National Academy of Engineering in 1977. He received the second A. M. Turing Award from the Association for Computing Machinery (ACM) in 1967, the Faraday Medal from the Institution of Electrical Engineers in 1981, and the Harry Goode Memorial Award of the American Federation of Information Processing Societies in 1968. He was knighted in 2000.

John H. Barnhill

FURTHER READING

Hartley, David. *Maurice Wilkes: The Man and His Machine*. Computer History Museum. 11 May 2011. Web. 6 Aug. 2012. A nearly hourlong discussion at the Computer History Museum upon the sixty-second anniversary of EDSAC. Computer programmer and former Wilkes student and colleague Hartley rehearses not only his life but also his pioneering contributions to computing and his vision.

Hoffmann, Leah. "Maurice Wilkes: The Last Pioneer." *Communications of the ACM* 54.2 (2011): 19. Print. A brief obituary provides an overview of Wilkes's early life and career.

Quested, Tony. "Cambridge Technology Cluster Thriving Thanks to University Dynamism." *Business Weekly* 24 Feb. 2012: n. pag. Web. 1 May 2012. Highlights the importance of the university's technology research for businesses and emphasizes that the core is in the computing department that arose through the efforts of Wilkes and Turing.

Sabbagh, Dan. "Maurice Wilkes." *The Computer Bulletin* 41.3 (1999): 18–19. Print. An overview of the history of Wilkes and EDSAC.

Warford, J. Stanley. *Computer Systems*. Sudbury: Jones and Bartlett, 2009. Print. Chapter 12 has a page that describes various innovations with which Wilkes is credited.

Wilkes, Maurice. *Memoirs of a Computer Pioneer*. Cambridge: MIT, 1995. Print. Wilkes's memoirs, published when he was in his eighties and still quite active.

FREDERIC WILLIAMS

Coinventor of the Manchester Mark I computer

Born: June 26, 1911; Romiley, Cheshire, United Kingdom

Died: August 11, 1977; Manchester, United Kingdom

Primary Field: Computer science

Specialty: Computer hardware

Primary Company/Organization: University of Manchester

INTRODUCTION

Frederic Williams worked on a range of projects for the British government during World War II and after the war saw the possibilities in developing a computer with a digital memory using a cathode-ray tube. He designed and built the first computer with a digital memory, which was known as the Baby, at the University of Manchester. This was followed by another computer, which was manufactured for sale. Although in comparison to current machines these early computers were large and cumbersome, they were important steps in the development of computers.

EARLY LIFE

Frederic Calland Williams was born on June 26, 1911, the younger child and the only son of Frederic Williams and Ethel Alice Smith Williams. His father was a locomotive draughtsman who worked for Beyer Peacock and had married Ethel in 1909 at Leigh, Lancashire. With the family living close to the railway line, the young Freddie, as he was nicknamed, became interested in engines. He attended a small private school in the village of Romiley. When he was nine or ten, he saw a wireless set at the house of his uncle and studied it closely. When he returned home, he made one using a cigar box. For his secondary education, he went to Stockport Grammar School. In 1929, he won the Matthew Kirtley scholarship, which allowed him to go to the School of Engineering at the University of Manchester. In his class at Manchester were George Kenyon

and J. A. L. Matheson, both later knighted at the same time as Williams.

Williams graduated in 1932 with first class honors. He also won the Fairbairn Award. Remaining at the University of Manchester, he researched under Frank Roberts and gained his master of science degree in 1933, then joined the Metropolitan-Vickers Electrical Company but did not finish his two-year course. Instead, he moved to Oxford, where he studied at Magdalen College and was awarded his doctorate in 1936. In addition to conducting his studies, he coached the college rowing team. He then returned to Manchester, studying for his doctorate there, which he earned in 1939.

Frederic Williams.

LIFE'S WORK

During World War II, Williams was involved in work on radio direction finding (RDF), later known as radiolocation, or radar. The British government was establishing a chain of radar stations around the country to give warnings of approaching aircraft. However, soon the British military wanted to have some way of differentiating between their own and enemy aircraft. This led to Williams working on the Identification Friend or Foe (IFF) system. Transponders were attached to Allied aircraft; they used super-regenerative receivers that produced oscillations different from those of enemy aircraft. After trials in late 1939 and early 1940, it was possible to install an IFF set at the Royal Air Force base at Leuchars for the Hudson squadron based there.

In mid-1940, Williams handed over his work on IFF to B. V. Bowden (later Lord Bowden) and went to work wuth A. D. Blumlein, who came up with the idea of an operational amplifier. For much of the rest of the war, Williams was based at Malvern, where he worked at the Telecommunications Research Establishment (later renamed the Royal Signals and Radar Establishment). At the end of the war, Williams was a principal scientific officer.

In 1946, Williams was appointed the Edward Stocks Massey Chair of Electrotechnics at the Victoria University of Manchester. He had also been appointed as the editor of Volumes 19 and 20 of the Radiation Laboratory Series. The former was on waveforms and the latter on electrical time measurements. For his work on these publications, Williams in November 1945 visited the Radiation Laboratory at the Massachusetts Institute of Technology in Cambridge, Massachusetts, where he heard about the idea of storing binary digits on cathode-ray tubes. He returned to the United States in June 1946 and went again to the Radiation Laboratory, where he learned more about the use of cathode-ray tubes.

After returning to England in July 1946, Williams set about making his own cathode-ray tube. Based at the University of Manchester from December 1946, he had considerable financial support with M. H. A. Newman, the Fielden Professor of Pure Mathematics, having been awarded £35,000 in 1946 to help with computer development. Williams also had the help of Tom Kilburn, Geoff Tootill, and others.

After a large number of experiments, Williams managed to devise a system of storing binary digits on the screen of a cathode-ray tube. In 1974, he was to write, "I never was, never have been, and never will be a mathematician. I did not even know there was any

> ## Affiliation: University of Manchester
>
> Frederic Williams studied at the Victoria University of Manchester as an undergraduate from 1929, and he worked there as an assistant lecturer from 1936 to 1939. After World War II, he returned there, remaining with the university until his death. Because his computers were made at Manchester, they were called the Manchester Small-Scale Experimental Machine (SSEM) and the Manchester Automatic Digital Computer.
>
> Photographs exist of the early computers Williams designed, but the machines themselves have not survived. However, a working replica of the Manchester Small-Scale Experimental Computer was made and is part of a major exhibit at the Museum of Science and Industry in Manchester.
>
> The University of Manchester—formed in 2004 from a merger between the Victoria University of Manchester (founded in 1851) and the University of Manchester Institute of Science and Technology (founded in 1824)—has had a long tradition of academic excellence and is one of the most respected institutions of higher education in the United Kingdom, with twenty-five Nobel laureates among its past or present staff and students—the third highest in the country after Cambridge and Oxford.

system of numbers other than the scale of ten...." By December 1947, the design of the computer was under way, and the initial one, reported in *Nature* on August 3, 1948, was able to store, on a single cathode-ray tube, thirty-two words each of thirty-two digits. This became known as the Manchester Small-Scale Experimental Machine (SSEM), nicknamed Baby.

The development of Baby represented was a major advance. Previous digital computers had not managed to store their work. What Williams had managed to do was to make a cathode-ray tube that stored digits as a charge pattern on the screen, and this was to form the basis of the first stored-program digital computer. This work continued through 1948 and early 1949. A second prototype machine, the Manchester Automatic Digital Computer (MADC), became known as the Manchester Mark I. The Ferranti company then produced a commercial version known as the Ferranti Mark 1, and soon there were twenty of these computers. In 1957, Williams became the first to win the Benjamin Franklin Medal, given by the Royal Society of Arts.

Following the success of Baby and its progeny, Williams gathered together some computer specialists and started to work on new designs for an induction motor. This team managed to produce a spherical motor, a log motor, and a phase change motor. However, although these were able to be made in the laboratory, they could not be produced commercially at this stage. Subsequently, Williams designed an automatic transmission for a motor car and installed one in his car, which he drove for one or two years. The first Clifford Steadman Prize was awarded to him by the Institution of Mechanical Engineers for his description of how this transmission worked.

Williams received a large number of other honors for his work. The Order of the British Empire was conferred on him in 1945, and he was made a Commander of the Order of the British Empire in 1961. In 1976, just before his death, he was made a Knight Bachelor in the Queen's Birthday Honours List.

PERSONAL LIFE

Williams spent most of his life living in the county of Cheshire, working in Manchester. In 1938 in Cheshire, he married Gladys Ward, daughter of Thomas Ward, a builder from his home village of Romiley. They had two children, Frederic and Susan. Williams and his wife settled at Spinney End, at The Village, Prestbury, Cheshire. Williams was interested in philosophy and from 1968 was a director of Granada Television Ltd. He played golf, a sport he had developed as a student and one he enjoyed for the rest of his life.

In the mid-1970s, Williams became increasingly ill, and he was not able to attend the ceremony at Buckingham Palace during which knighthood was conferred on him in 1976. He died on August 11, 1977, in a hospital in Manchester. His funeral service was held at Prestbury Parish Church on August 15, and his body was subsequently cremated at the Macclesfield Crematorium, where his ashes were interred.

There had been a tradition in the Williams family for the oldest son to be called Frederic (without the *k*), but Williams named his son Frederick. He was educated at Shrewsbury School, St. John's College at Cambridge, and the University of Bristol. From 1964 until 1967 he was a lecturer in civil engineering at Ahmadu Bello University, Nigeria, and then was a lecturer at the University of Birmingham from 1967 until 1975. He became a professor of civil engineering at the University of Wales Institute of Science and Technology in Cardiff, working as a consultant to the United States' National Aeronautics and Space Administration.

Justin Corfield

FURTHER READING

Copeland, B. Jack. *Colossus: The Secrets of Bletchley Park's Codebreaking Computers*. Oxford: Oxford UP, 2006. Print. A study of the computing machines used during World War II and the early designs made by Williams.

Kilburn, T., and L. S. Piggott. "Frederic Calland Williams, 26 June 1911–11 August 1977," *Biographical Memoirs of Fellows of the Royal Society* Vol. 24 (November 1978), pp. 583-604. Print. A long and comprehensive account of the scientific career of Sir Williams by some of his collaborators.

Laithwaite, Eric Roberts. *An Inventor in the Garden of Eden*. Cambridge: Cambridge UP, 1994. Print. An autobiography of a scientist who worked as a demonstrator for Williams at Manchester.

O'Regan, Gerard. *A Brief History of Computing*. New York: Springer, 2012. Print. An overview of the early computers including those designed by Williams.

"Obituary: Sir Frederic Williams; Major Developments in Computers." *The Times* 18 Aug. 1977: 14. Print. An overview of Williams's life and a tribute to his achievements.

Piggott, L. S. "Williams, Sir Frederic Calland (1911–1977)." *Oxford Dictionary of National Biography*. New York: Oxford UP, 2004. Web. 10 Aug. 2012. A detailed biographical essay.

Watson-Watt, Sir Robert Alexander. *Three Steps to Victory*. London: Odhams Press, 1957. Print. An account that contains details of the early work of Williams.

Williams, F. C., T. Kilburn, and G. E. Thomas. "Universal High-Speed Digital Computers: A Magnetic Store." *Proceedings of the Institution of Electrical Engineers* 99 (1952). Print. A seminal paper on digital storage.

NIKLAUS WIRTH

Designer of the Pascal programming language

Born: February 15, 1934; Winterthur, Switzerland
Died: -
Primary Field: Computer science
Specialty: Computer programming
Primary Company/Organization: Eidgenössische
    Technische Hochschule Zürich

INTRODUCTION

Although famous as the originator of the Pascal programming language, Niklaus Wirth went beyond this achievement, developing the ALGOL-W and Modula 2 languages. He is also an educator and philosopher concerning programs and programming practices, adamant that increasing complexity is not synonymous with sophistication. He is thus opposed to the increasing, and what he considers to be needless, complexity found in certain programming languages such as C++. He is credited with developing the principles of structured programming, which examines a problem and organizes it into smaller units, providing a basis for writing code. According to Wirth, programming is a holistic process and should not focus merely on the coding but also how design determines how an application should be built.

EARLY LIFE

Niklaus Emil Wirth was born in Winterthur, Switzerland, on February 15, 1934. His parents were Walter, a professor of geography, and Hedwig Wirth. As a child, he built and flew model planes, later claiming that because of his limited budget, he had to be careful to construct the simplest and most easily repairable models, an experience that would inform his views on programming.

Wirth's undergraduate education was at Eidgenössische Technische Hochschule Zürich (ETH Zürich), where he would later become part of the faculty. After graduating in 1958 with a degree in electrical engineering, he moved to North America, where he stayed for several years. Wirth received his master's degree in 1960 from Laval University, located near Quebec City in Quebec, Canada. Wirth then moved west, to the University of California at Berkeley, where he received his doctorate in 1963.

Wirth's first faculty position was at Stanford University, at its Computer Science Department, where he taught until 1968. He then accepted a position at his old school, ETH Zürich. It was there that Wirth would embark on his career as a developer of programming languages and lead teacher of the discipline of computer programming.

LIFE'S WORK

By the time Wirth returned to ETH Zürich, he had already given a great deal of thought to software languages: what was desirable and what ought to be avoided. Among the languages available at the time, there were two that had reached a position of dominance, at least in academic programming. One of these was Fortran (which stood for "formula translating"), developed by IBM for scientific work, and the other was ALGOL (for "algorithmic language"). When Wirth was at Stanford, ALGOL had gone through at least two major revisions: ALGOL 58 and ALGOL 60. The latter was released in 1960 and had several vocal partisans, among them Wirth. Wirth was convinced of the superiority of ALGOL 60 over Fortran, and in the late 1960s, when he

Niklaus Wirth.

decided to develop a language that would teach students good programming skills and principles, he based it largely on the ALGOL 60 model. Students at Stanford later recalled the vehemence with which Wirth discussed the superiority of ALGOL over Fortran.

Only in the rarest of cases are programming languages created from scratch. Several languages currently in use are based on predecessor languages such as C++ (which is built on C) or Kristen Nygaard's Simula (which, like Wirth's language, was based on ALGOL 60). Simula had introduced the concept of object-oriented programming and also influenced Wirth, although an object-oriented version, Object Pascal, would not be developed until 1985 and he would not be the one to develop it. Wirth notes that two current programming languages, Java and C#, have characteristics (in terms of simplicity) inherited from his languages, Pascal and Modula 2.

When Wirth began serious development of his new language, he had already developed one, ALGOL-W, that was an extension of ALGOL 60. The purpose of this new language was not to be a development tool; rather, its purpose was to teach students how to program using the principles that Wirth believed were being neglected or represented innovations that would improve the results of coding. These principles included his idea of structured programming, drilling down and decomposing a problem into ever smaller steps and organizing instruction sets based on this granular approach. Wirth would also incorporate other aspects of his philosophy into the new language, including simplicity, discipline (in the sense of using standard methods and not inventing new and possibly undocumented extensions), and the good design of planning and execution and not merely the syntax and values for entering commands.

Wirth's new language, released in 1970, was called Pascal for the seventeenth-century French mathematician Blaise Pascal. It was never meant to become a practical programming language like its predecessor ALGOL. It became so popular, however, and had such a wide range of capabilities, while being easy to use (and to design with), that by the end of the 1970s, Pascal was widely used. Apple was among the companies that used Pascal, notably for the Apple Lisa, Apple II, and Apple III computers and later for many applications for the Apple Macintosh. The Motorola 68000 processor in Apple computers used, as its assembly language, a version of Pascal. Pascal is still used for developing some Windows programs (Object Pascal) as well as some video games. Wirth believes that Pascal was

Affiliation: Eidgenössische Technische Hochschule Zürich

The Eidgenössische Technische Hochschule Zürich (ETH Zürich) is a government-sponsored university in Switzerland, founded in 1854. As the name implies, it concentrates on science and technology, including architecture, mathematics, and engineering. In 2012, enrollment exceeded seventeen thousand students, with thirty-seven thousand students enrolled in its doctoral programs. Like technological centers such as the Massachusetts Institute of Technology (MIT), ETH Zürich has supported study and research resulting in commercial applications, forming an important part of the institution's mandate. According to the school, at least 240 commercial spin-offs from research and development began there.

ETH Zürich's position as one of the best technical universities in the world was established during the course of the twentieth century. Among the school's teachers, graduates, and researchers are twenty-one Nobel laureates in physics, chemistry, and medicine. In addition to Niklaus Wirth, famous members of the faculty include Albert Einstein and John von Neumann.

always better received in academic than in commercial environments.

From 1979 through 1981, Wirth developed another major programming language, Modula-2. In the 1980s he worked at both the Xerox Palo Alto Research Center (PARC) and Stanford in developing languages and expanding their capabilities as well as suggesting modifications to hardware. In 1985, an object-oriented version of Pascal was introduced, providing the capabilities of object orientation to his original language. In 1988, Wirth began work on Oberon, an object-oriented language based closely on his earlier work on Modula (which, in turn, had been based on Pascal).

One of Wirth's significant, if little known, contributions, is the Alt key that appears on computer keyboards. In working with the early Digital Equipment Corporation's PDP-1, Wirth wanted to add input capability that would allow the operator a greater range of commands based on pressing multiple keys (such as Ctrl-Alt-Delete) simultaneously. The result was the addition of the Alt key, which is now located to the left of the space bar.

PERSONAL LIFE

Wirth not only was active as a researcher and as the world's foremost developer of computer languages but also was engaged in other aspects of life at ETH Zürich. He chaired the institution's computer science department twice, the first time from 1982 to 1984 and later from 1988 to 1990. Wirth retired from ETH Zürich in 1999 but remained active as a writer and researcher.

Wirth has received many honors, the most prestigious being the A. M. Turing Award from the Association for Computing Machinery (ACM) in 1984. He was presented with the Emanuel R. Piore Award from the Institute of Electrical and Electronics Engineers (IEEE). Wirth subsequently received other awards from IEEE and ACM and was presented with honorary degrees from the University of York and the Lausanne (Switzerland) Institute of Technology.

Wirth is married. He and his wife, Nani, have three children.

Robert N. Stacy

FURTHER READING

Wirth, Niklaus. "A Brief History Of Software Engineering." *IEEE Annals of the History of Computing* 30.3 (2008): 32–39. *Academic Search Complete*. Web. 12 July 2012. In this article, Wirth provides a history of software development and consequences from his own perspective as one of the foremost programming language developers of the twentieth century.

---. "Good Ideas, Through the Looking Glass." *Computer* 39.1 (2006): 28–39. *Academic Search Complete*. Web. 12 July 2012. A survey of the current state of the art, discussing the effects of hardware development as well as environment and economic factors that influence programming.

---. "Program Development by Stepwise Refinement." *Communications of the ACM* 14.4 (1971): 221–27. Print. Wirth explains how program development is done. Written the year after Pascal was released, the article describes the basic principles of structured programming and draws the critical distinction between programming, a holistic process, and simply coding (entering the code that makes the program work).

BEATRICE WORSLEY

Programmer and professor of computer science

Born: October 18, 1921; Querétaro, Mexico
Died: May 8, 1972; Waterloo, Ontario, Canada
Primary Field: Computer science
Specialty: Computer software
Primary Company/Organization: University of Toronto

INTRODUCTION

Beatrice Worsley has been recognized as Canada's first female computer scientist. She worked with Henry Wallman, a member of the Radiation Laboratory at the Massachusetts Institute of Technology, on her master's thesis and studied at Cambridge University with Douglas Hartree, who developed numerical analysis, and Alan Turing, who is often called the father of computer science and artificial intelligence. Worsley built a differential analyzer and a mechanical analog computer, and she collaborated on a compiler for the Ferranti Mark I, the world's first commercially available, general-purpose computer. In 1952, she became one of the first women to receive a Ph.D. in computer science.

EARLY LIFE

Beatrice Helen Worsley was born in Querétaro, Mexico, on October 18, 1921, the second child and only daughter of Joel and Beatrice Marie Worsley. Her father, born into a working-class family in Manchester, England, moved to Mexico to work in the textile mill his wife's grandparents had founded in the 1850s. Because the Worsley children were isolated from the community for their safety, their mother home-schooled them until 1929, when the family moved to Toronto, Canada. Worsley attended Brown Public School until 1934, when she entered the Bishop Strachan School, founded in 1867 as an Anglican alternative to the city's numerous Catholic schools. In 1939, she graduated with honors and awards in mathematics and science, including the Governor-General's Award for the highest overall grades.

That year, Worsley entered Trinity College at the University of Toronto. Again, she excelled academically, specializing in applied mathematics. She graduated in 1944 with a bachelor's degree in mathematics and physics. World War II was at its height, and soon after graduation, she enlisted in the Women's Royal Canadian Naval Service, known as the WRENS. Probationary Sublieutenant Beatrice Worsley reported on April 5, 1944, to the HMCS *Conestoga* base in Galt (now Cambridge), Ontario, the basic training center for WRENS from across Canada. On September 9, she was transferred to the Naval Research Establishment in Halifax, Nova Scotia, for harbor defense research. She was demobilized on August 11, 1946. The next month, she began graduate studies at the Massachusetts Institute of Technology (MIT), where Henry Wallman, a member of MIT's Radiation Laboratory (where the first worldwide radio navigation system was developed), served as her thesis director. In 1947, she returned to Canada and worked briefly in Ottawa at the National Research Council of Canada and for a more extended period as a project assistant at the University of Toronto Computation Centre. In 1949, she resumed her graduate studies in mathematical physics at Newnham College, University of Cambridge, where her dissertation was directed by Douglas Hartree, who built a mechanical computer for solving differential equations. Worsley was awarded a Ph.D. from Cambridge in 1952.

Beatrice Worsley.

LIFE'S WORK

Worsley, for unknown reasons, returned to Canada in 1951 and completed writing her dissertation there. Hartree came to Canada to award her degree a year later. Before she had her Ph.D. in hand, she had returned to work at the University of Toronto Computation Centre. Her strength lay in adapting scientific problems to be solved using transcoding (data conversion) and the Ferut, Worsley's name for the Mark I general-purpose computer built by the Ferranti firm and purchased by the University of Toronto. As the Ferut was installed at the Computation Centre during the spring and summer of 1952, Worsley found herself operating the console. The Ferut was a tricky computer to learn to program. Worsley and a colleague were responsible for teaching methods of programming to computer novices, including actuaries, scientists, and graduate students. Fewer than 30 percent could master the lessons, which contained both theoretical and practical components. As the only computing facility in Canada, the Computation Centre needed to simplify the programming cycle for remote users. Worsley and J. N. Patterson Hume, an assistant professor from the physics department, were asked to create an automatic coding system for the Ferut. They called their project Transcode and wrote the compiler within a year. Transcode worked. Basic lessons could be taught in two hours, and the time for returning calculations was cut from weeks to days. Both Worsley and Hume wrote articles that appeared in the *Journal of the ACM* and *Physics in Canada* announcing Transcode and describing the new and effective tool for physicists and other scientists. By 1958, when an IBM 650 replaced the ancient Ferut, Transcode had benefited hundreds of faculty and students and dozens of research groups across Canada.

Most of the seventeen papers Worsley published between 1952 and 1964 focused on Transcode and the Ferut. Other articles stemmed from her Cambridge work on self-consistent field calculations. In September 1955, the Pure Physics Division of the National Research Council (NRC) and the Computation Centre launched a joint project to develop the Hartree-Fock formulations for digital computers and calculate specific atomic wave functions. Working with J. F. Hart of the National Research Council, Worsley coded the routines for the Ferut. Hartree consulted on the project until his death in 1958, and the general scheme Worsley used can be found in his 1957 text *The Calculation of Atomic Structures*. By 1960, Worsley was spending more time teaching than engaging in research. With each upgrade

Affiliation: University of Toronto Computation Centre

In September 1947, a small grant from Canada's National Research Council (NRC) provided the funds to open the Computation Centre at the University of Toronto, one of the few computer research and development programs in North America in the 1940s. The grant covered the costs of two IBM punch card calculators and the salaries for two project assistants. Calvin C. "Kelly" Gotlieb, a member of the physics department, managed the center, and Beatrice Worsley, who had recently earned a master's degree from the Massachusetts Institute of Technology, and J. Perham Stanley, a graduate student, were hired as assistants. After training on the new machines, Gotlieb, Worsley, and Stanley tabulated a function for Atomic Energy Canada. This and similar tasks helped raise awareness and interest in electronic computing research in Canada.

Soon the center was involved in the design and construction of Canada's first computer, the University of Toronto Electronic Computer (UTEC), a parallel-processing machine designed by a team of professors and graduate students. The Canadian Defense Research Board and the NRC shared the development costs. The purpose was to create a single large computing resource to be shared nationally among government, military, and university research groups. The UTEC project, burdened by tube failures and mechanical reliability issues, was abandoned when the university ordered the Ferranti Mark 1 early in 1952. Worsley named the machine Ferut (standing for Ferranti computer at the University of Toronto).

The Ferut, which filled a large room and contained hundreds of vacuum tubes, was the first electronic computer in Canada. Worsley and Hume created software that allowed scientists to bypass the complicated Ferut machine code and to program their own applications instead. The two became the first computer programmers in Canada. Together they developed Transcode, one of the first compilers (computer language translators) and a forerunner of all modern computer programming languages. The Ferut computer was in operation until 1958, when it was replaced by an IBM 650 and later by a transistorized IBM 7090, a machine that was five hundred times faster than its predecessors. The 7090 for years was the only large-scale computer in Canada. In 1964, the university established a graduate department of computer science, the first in Canada.

Despite her Ph.D. from a prestigious university, an impressive publication record, and valuable research, it was not until 1960 that Worsley was promoted to assistant professor, and it took another four years and the creation of a graduate department of computer science before she was promoted to associate professor. In 1965, Worsley accepted a position at the Computing Centre at Queen's University in Kingston, Ontario. Queen's hired Worsley to help launch and manage its new Computer Centre with the IBM 1620, but her teaching responsibilities were heavier than they had been in Toronto.

The courses she taught were heavily grounded in numerical analysis, covered programming techniques using Fortran and WATFOR (the popular student-oriented Fortran compiler written at the University of Waterloo in the mid-1960s), and included material on the mathematical principles of computing. Added to the teaching were numerous administrative responsibilities, all without even an assistant professor's title. As computer science adviser to the Computing Centre, she was charged with selecting books and journals for the center's library, coordinating the programming staff, advising local high school teachers on computer issues, arranging seminars, and authorizing computer time. It is hardly surprising that there was no time for research and few rewards. It was not until 1968, when a master's program was created at Queen's along with a new Department of Computing and Information Science, that Worsley was given a joint appointment and promoted to associate professor in the new department.

In September 1971, Worsley was granted her first sabbatical year since she had arrived at Queen's. She planned to spend the year at the Department of Applied Analysis and Computer Science at the University of Waterloo in Waterloo, Ontario, Canada. Her purpose in going to Waterloo was to study assembler coding as it related to computer architecture. A logical assumption is that she wanted to return to her early research interests. However, her research would remain incomplete. She died in May 1972.

PERSONAL LIFE

In an early interview, Worsley indicated that she was interested in music generally and in playing the piano

in the computer, her course load increased. University extension courses in the mid-1950s became graduate courses when the IBM 650 was installed at the Computation Centre in 1958. By the time the discipline of computer science was emerging as a distinct field, Worsley was teaching undergraduates as well.

particularly and that she enjoyed photography. Little else is known of her private life. A shy, reserved woman by all accounts, she appeared content to make her work her life. An early member of the Association for Computing Machinery, she joined special-interest groups on university computing and information retrieval in the 1960s. Worsley also served as the Toronto region correspondent for the *Quarterly Bulletin* of the Computing and Data Processing Society of Canada from 1962 to 1965 and as the director of the national executive in 1968 (now renamed the Canadian Information Processing Society), and technical editor for the *Quarterly Bulletin* from 1970 to 1971.

On May 8, 1972, while in Waterloo on sabbatical, Beatrice Worsley suffered a fatal heart attack. She was survived by her brother Charles. She left her estate to the University of Cambridge. It was used to found the Lundgren Fund, in honor of Helge Lundgren. The Lundgren Research Award is presented to Ph.D. students, not ordinarily residents of the United Kingdom, who have completed at least four terms at Cambridge University and are engaged in research in a scientific subject, which can include mathematics. Preference is given to candidates who work in the computer laboratory or whose research has been "interrupted by national service or personal misfortune." Lundgren's identity remains a mystery, as do Worsley's reasons for leaving her estate to Cambridge.

Wylene Rholetter

FURTHER READING
Campbell, Scott M. "Beatrice Helen Worsley: Canada's Female Computer Pioneer." *IEEE Annals of the History of Computing* 25.4 (2003): 51-62. Print. This is a lengthy, richly detailed biographical essay on Worsley was written by a graduate student at the University of Waterloo who had access to Worsley's notes from high school through her twenty-year teaching career, archived at Queen's University, and to Alva Worsley, wife of Beatrice Worsley's brother Charles.

Ensmenger, Nathan L. *The Computer Boys Take Over: Computers, Programmers, and the Politics of Technical Expertise*. Cambridge: MIT, 2010. Print. This book describes the computer programmers, systems analysts, and data-processing managers, many of them anonymous, who were the first generation to build their careers around the technology of electronic computing. Worsley merits a brief reference. Some of the "computer boys" were not boys.

Friedland, Martin Lawrence. *The University of Toronto: A History*. Toronto: U of Toronto P, 2002. Print. Recounts the history of the University of Toronto from its beginnings as King's College in 1827 through the beginning of the twenty-first century. Includes information on the Computer Centre and Worsley's work there as one of the first computer programmers in Canada.

Misa, Thomas J., ed. *Gender Codes: Why Women Are Leaving Computing*. New York: Wiley-IEEE Computer Society Press, 2010. Print. Worsley is among the women programmers, systems analysts, managers, and IT executives of the 1960s and 1970s whose achievements are mentioned. The accomplishments of women of this period are contrasted to the diminishing number of women entering computer science in the twenty-first century.

STEVE WOZNIAK

Cofounder of Apple

Born: August 11, 1950; San Jose, California
Died: -
Primary Field: Computer science
Specialty: Computer hardware
Primary Company/Organization: Apple

INTRODUCTION

From childhood, Steve Wozniak loved electronics and practical jokes. He was adept at building computers and using them to entertain and to solve problems.

His friend Steve Jobs was a natural seller of ideas, and they formed an ideal partnership for creating the revolutionary Apple computer. When Wozniak gave up his active role in the company and Jobs was forced out, Apple floundered but was revitalized after Jobs's return in the late 1990s. Wozniak devoted his post-Apple years to philanthropic causes in San Jose, establishing the Technology Museum of Innovation and the Children's Discovery Museum and contributing to the Cleveland Ballet. He also remained active in the electronics industry, helping to develop such diverse items as the first programmable universal television remote control and wireless GPS equipment. He worked to get computers into schools and remains active in the battle against the infringement of electronic freedom and in providing legal counsel for computer hackers. In 2009, he became chief scientist for the Salt Lake City–based company Fusion-io.

EARLY LIFE

Stephan Gary Wozniak, also known as "Woz," was born on August 11, 1950, in San Jose, California. As an electrical engineer, his father, Jerry, encouraged his son's love of electronics from an early age. His mother, Margaret, was a homemaker, devoting her time to raising her children, who also included Leslie and Mark. Wozniak was shy and loved to read. In the fourth grade, he discovered that he loved mathematics. The following year, he discovered ham radios and learned Morse code. By the time he was eleven, Wozniak was writing computer games. At the age of thirteen, he won an award at the Bay Area Science Fair for his 10-bit parallel digital computer.

Wozniak began taking electronics classes in high school and was hired by an electronics company to program its computers using Fortran. With a grant from the National Science Foundation, he also took mathematics classes at local colleges. Despite a love of practical jokes that caused him to be suspended for a short

Steve Wozniak.

time, Wozniak graduated from Homestead High with honors in 1968. During a year attending the University of Colorado, he spent much of his time on computers. Returning to California, he attended a local college in Sunnyvale and got a job programming and running diagnostics on computers at Tenet, Inc. He and his friend Bill Fernandez spent their spare time designing a computer that they dubbed Cream Soda. His junior year found Wozniak attending the University of California, Berkeley.

LIFE'S WORK

By 1973, Wozniak was working at Hewlett-Packard in Palo Alto, California, which placed him in an ideal position for the upcoming computer revolution. He renewed his friendship with Steve Jobs, a high school computer geek serving an internship at Hewlett-Packard. In March 1975, the two friends attended the first meeting of the Homebrew Computer Club in Menlo Park, California. Although Jobs was five years younger, he and Wozniak found that their interest in computers outweighed the age difference. Homebrew was one of many such clubs that had sprung up in response to the release of the Altair computer kit, which allowed computer hobbyists to build their own computers. The club gave members a venue for sharing their developing knowledge. An electronics whiz, Wozniak was convinced that he could build his own computer now that the price of parts had begun to drop. After saving his money, he managed to complete his computer by January 1976.

Wozniak's computer, which became the Apple I, would be considered primitive by today's standards, but it was revolutionary for its time. It was sold without a case, a power supply, a monitor, or a keyboard. By that time, Bill Gates and Paul Allen were already selling their operating system, MS-DOS. At the National Computer Conference, an enterprising but less than honest member of Homebrew stole discarded Microsoft tapes from the garbage and carried them back to Homebrew, where they were freely distributed and used. On February 3, 1976, an open letter from Gates decrying the piracy appeared in the club's newsletter and in other publications regularly perused by hobbyists. Together, Wozniak and Jobs designed the Blue Box, a device that allowed them to bypass telephone charges. It made them a small profit but could have resulted in jail time.

While Wozniak worked at Hewlett-Packard, Jobs continued to live at home, earning money by writing computer games for Atari. In their spare time, the friends played with game development. Atari subsequently asked them to design *Breakout*, a spin-off of Atari's popular *Pong* game. Wozniak was responsible for circuitry, problem-solving, and diagram writing. They designed the game to use only 43 chips, at a time when most games were using more than 120 chips.

Despite the drawbacks of the Apple I, Jobs was astute enough to understand its potential to make money. He convinced Wozniak that they should start their own company and begin selling it, but Wozniak was initially hesitant to leave the financial safety of his job at Hewlett-Packard. He agreed to go into business with Jobs, however, and Apple was founded on April 1, 1976. Wozniak steadily improved his computer design, working mostly in the garage at the home of Jobs's parents. Within a year, the Apple II was introduced. Wozniak said later that both Apple I and Apple II were created for fun rather than profit.

In October 1976, Wozniak finally yielded to persuasion and left Hewlett-Packard to devote his efforts to Apple. In January 1977, after Mike Markkula, the marketing guru whom Jobs and Wozniak had hired to guide them through the early days, invested $250,000 in the company, it was incorporated as Apple Computer, Inc., and was relocated to Cupertino. As Apple continued to expand, it eventually needed an entire campus in Silicon Valley to house its operations.

Selling for $1,298, the Apple II was the first computer that did not need to be assembled after purchase. Using the BASIC programming language and a printed circuit board, it also contained its own keyboard, power supply, speakers, graphics, and game paddles and had 4K of memory, a user's manual, and a demonstration cassette. However, it was still dependent on a television monitor and on a cassette recorder and tapes. By 1979, however, Apple computers contained floppy disk drives for storing data. As Apple grew, Wozniak had less time to spend on computer design. Since most development work was done by teams of developers, Wozniak took on a public relations role.

The Apple III was introduced in 1980 as a rival to IBM personal computers. It was expensive at $2,995, and sales were disappointing. It was discontinued at the end of the following year. After time off to complete his education, Wozniak returned to work at Apple in 1982, but he chose to work as an engineer rather than as an executive. Although bitter infighting seemed to be tearing the company apart, Wozniak attempted to remain above the fray. Released in 1983, the Lisa (the Mac XL) was the most user-friendly computer released to that time, containing folders, pull-down menus, and an entire megabyte

Affiliation: Apple

Built out of an abiding interest in computers, the Apple computer was born at the home of cofounder Steve Jobs. Both Steve Wozniak and Jobs believed that computers should be fun as well as useful. Founded on April Fool's Day 1976 and given the name of a fruit, Apple became a name to be reckoned with in the music industry as well as the computer business. Ronald Wayne, a third cofounder, was unwilling to take the financial risk and sold his share of the company to Jobs and Wozniak.

When Apple went public in December 1980, Wozniak's shares were estimated at $88 million. Wozniak was outranked by cofounder Steve Jobs, whose shares were reportedly worth $165 million. Before going public, Wozniak set up what he called the Woz Plan to sell $2 million in stock to Apple employees and give them a chance to garner huge profits from Apple's success. Within the first month of the company's going public, shares doubled.

By 1983, Apple was listed as a Fortune 500 company. Two years later, Wozniak and Jobs were awarded the National Medal of Technology. By 1987, both Wozniak and Jobs had left the company they had founded, and it began to flounder without Jobs's innovative flair and Wozniak's technical genius. It was not until Jobs returned as CEO in 1997 that Apple resumed it upward trend.

of random access memory (RAM). At $9,995, however, it was beyond the means of the average home user.

Wozniak gave up his active role in Apple in 1987. Along with a fellow Apple engineer, he founded CL-9 (Cloud 9), concentrating on creating a universal infrared remote control, which became the first programmable remote control in history. Wozniak continued to serve as a consultant for Apple, but his friendship with Jobs steadily unraveled. They remained in contact until Jobs's death in 2011 but were never again close friends. Wozniak remained a nominal employee of Apple, however, and continued to receive an annual salary.

PERSONAL LIFE

Wozniak has been married several times. He met Alice Robertson when she called in to his Dial-a-Joke telephone line. They married on January 11, 2006, but divorced four years later. He retained two-thirds of his Apple stock, with the other third going to his ex-wife.

Wozniak subsequently became involved with Candi Clark, who worked for Apple as an accountant. He and Clark married on June 14, 1981, in the backyard of his parents' home, with Emmylou Harris as the featured entertainer. He subsequently built a lavish home for his family in Silicon Valley. His child-friendly home, which he named the Castle, was located on twenty-six acres and included a manufactured waterfall and a carousel. Wozniak lost the Castle when the couple divorced in 1987. He bought a nearby home where he spent $1 million creating a cave for his three children, Jesse, Sara, and Gary. Wozniak was married a third time, to Suzanne Mulkern, an old high school friend and the mother of three children, in 1990; they divorced in 2004. He married Janet Hill in 2008.

On February 7, 1981, with Wozniak at the controls, a plane carrying him, his fiancée (Clark), Clark's brother, and his girlfriend crashed, causing Wozniak to suffer a short-term memory loss and leading to a reevaluation of his life. Wozniak decided to return to Berkeley to resume work on a degree. After a year of taking classes, Berkeley officials allowed him to use his continuing work at Apple for course credit. He finally graduated in 1986 and delivered the commencement speech at his graduation.

The 1980s also saw Wozniak realize his dream of combining computers with his love of music. He created Unuson (United Us in Song), using $1 million of his own money, to put together a 1981 music festival that brought together artists such as The Police, Pat Benatar, Fleetwood Mac, and Emmylou Harris. This and a second festival the following year lost money, but the second festival drew a larger audience.

Elizabeth Rholetter Purdy

FURTHER READING

Carlton, Jim. *Apple: The Inside Story of Intrigue, Egomania, and Business Blunders*. New York: Random House, 1997. Print. Chronicles the founding and the management debacles that make up Apple's history. Includes notes, a bibliography, and an index.

Deutschman, Alan. "Thanks for the Future." *Time* 7 Nov. 2011: 8–13. Print. Published as part of a special commemorative issue on Jobs's death, the article presents an excellent overview of the founding of Apple. Illustrated.

Gillies, James, and Robert Cailliau. *How the Web Was Born: The Story of the World Wide Web*. New York: Oxford UP, 2000. Print. A detailed examination of the development of the Internet and the World Wide Web, with emphasis on the roles played by key individuals. Includes a time line, a comprehensive bibliography, and an index.

Kendall, Martha E. *Steve Wozniak ... Inventor of the Apple Computer*. New York: Walker, 1994. Print. Written for young adults, this book traces Wozniak's personal life and the development of Apple. Includes illustrations, a glossary, and an index.

Levy, Steven. *The Perfect Thing: How the iPod Shuffles Commerce, Culture, and Coolness*. New York: Simon, 2006. Print. Places Apple's innovative iPod in the context of contemporary culture. Illustrated.

Linzmayer, Owen W. *Apple Confidential: The Real Story of Apple Computer*. San Francisco: No Starch, 1999. Print. Written by a journalist who covered Apple from its beginnings, the book uses both interviews and archival material to develop a portrait of the computer giant. Includes illustrations, time lines for various Apple products, and an Index.

Moritz, Michael. *The Little Kingdom: The Private Story of Apple Computer*. New York: Morrow, 1984. Print. Uses interviews, newspaper articles, and personal photographs and papers to examine the early days of Apple. Includes an index.

Wozniak, Steve, with Gina Smith. *iWoz: From Computer Geek to Cult Icon; How I Invented the Personal Computer, coFounded Apple, and Had Fun Doing It*. New York: Norton, 2006. Print. Highly readable firsthand account of the founding of Apple and Wozniak's role in the computer revolution. Illustrated.

Z

KONRAD ZUSE

Creator of Z23 and Plankalkül

Born: January 22, 1910; Berlin, Germany
Died: December 18, 1995; Hunfeld, Germany
Primary Field: Computer science
Specialty: Computer programming
Primary Company/Organization: Zuse KG

INTRODUCTION

*Computer pioneer Konrad Zuse went unnoticed for
several years because he was working in Germany
during the Third Reich, in the 1930s and early 1940s.
During that time, he invented the first program-controlled Turing-complete computer, the first high-level
programming language, and the first commercial computer, but his work was not discovered outside Germany until the end of World War II, when IBM (which had
worked with the German government before the war)
optioned his patents.*

EARLY LIFE

Konrad Zuse was born on January 22, 1910, in Berlin,
in what was then the German Empire (formed by the
unification of Germany in 1871 and succeeded by a republic after the Revolution of November 1918). While
he was an infant, his family relocated to East Prussia,
and Zuse attended school at the Collegium Hosianum,
a famous Jesuit school. (Collegiums offer education at
both the secondary and higher education levels.)

In 1928, Zuse began university in the Technische
Hochschule Berlin-Charlottenburg (the Berlin Institute
of Technology). He graduated in 1935 with a degree in
civil engineering. At the university he was introduced
to vacuum tubes and Boolean operations. He worked as
an advertisement designer for the Ford Motor Company

and a design engineer at the Henschel aircraft factory,
but he was perpetually bored, a problem he had had in
school as well.

LIFE'S WORK

Tinkering on his own time, Zuse built a machine to perform some of his dullest tasks, calculations he found
laborious and routine calculations. The Z1 was the first

Konrad Zuse.

such machine that Zuse built, a floating-point mechanical calculator that could be fed instructions with perforated 35-millimeter film. It was made up of thirty thousand mechanical parts and suffered for it, because Zuse lacked the capability at home to constructed such a complex device with real mechanical precision. He followed the Z1, in 1936, with the Z2, but this time he was given money to build it: He had been drafted by the military in 1939 and was able to obtain government funding to sponsor his computer project. The mechanical memory system was the same, but he replaced the mechanical logic circuits with electrical relays meant for telephones.

Zuse founded Zuse Apparatebau to manufacture his computers in 1941, beginning with the Z3. The Z3 was an electromechanical computer like the Z2 and was the first programmable automatic computing machine. It was Turing-complete, the first machine considered a complete computing machine from a modern perspective. The German Aircraft Research Institute used it to perform statistical analyses of aircraft. It used two thousand relays operating at a clock frequency of about 10 hertz, and, as in the previous Z computers, programs and data were stored on punched 35-millimeter film. The Z3 project was highly classified by the German government, but because his project was not considered important to the war effort, Zuse was denied funding to use fully electronic switches instead of relays; most of his relays were scavenged from discarded goods. Unlike other computers—even some later computers—the Z3 did not need to be rewired in order to be reprogrammed, since its programs were stored on external media. Even the Colossus code-breaking computers of the British government—which were very important to the war effort and funded accordingly—and the Electronic Numerical Integrator and Computer (ENIAC), completed in the United States after the war, had to be reprogrammed by moving around leads and switches, lacking Zuse's basic but groundbreaking innovation of external media.

The German government commissioned two computing machines from Zuse in 1940 for use in guided missiles. The S1 and S2 were the result, devices that calculated and enacted aerodynamic

Affiliation: Zuse KG

Zuse KG was founded by German computer scientist Konrad Zuse in 1949. Zuse had more or less taught himself to make simple computers in the 1930s in order to automate the drudgery of the routine calculations required in his work as an aircraft design engineer. When World War II started, he was drafted into the military and was able to secure military funding to pursue some of his machines, including the Z3, an electromechanical computer that was the first automated programmable computing machine. The programmability was especially innovative; it preceded more famous early computers such as the Electronic Numerical Integrator and Computer (ENIAC), the Universal Automatic Computer (UNIVAC), and the Colossus code breakers, which had to be rewired and reconfigured in order to be programmed, whereas the Z3 stored its programs on external media (punched film) so that all the user had to do was insert a new program. The innovation would be discovered independently in the United States; because of the war, Zuse's early work was almost entirely unknown outside Germany (and even, for the most part, inside Germany).

After the war, Germany was in such disarray that it was difficult for him to continue with his work, much less find funding. However, IBM had optioned his patents in 1946, which provided him with some capital, and the Swiss university Eidgenössische Technische Hochschule Zürich (ETH Zürich) eventually ordered a Z4, the computer he had been developing when the war ended. The influx of money was enough for him to found Zuse KG and complete the relay-based electromechanical Z4, which refined the design of the Z3 and was delivered in 1950.

The Z4 was only the second computer in the world to be sold and the only computer to precede it, the Binary Automatic Computer (BINAC), did not work after it was delivered. The Z4 worked, and remained in use until 1959, by which point it had become obsolete. It is on display at the Deutsches Museum in Munich. The Z4 was followed by the Ferranti Mark 1 five months later, and the UNIVAC I five months after that—the computer industry had officially been born.

During the 1960s, Zuse KG continued to manufacture computers, continuing with the Z* numbering Zuse had introduced, up to Z43. The company's innovation continued: Z22 was the first computer to use magnetic storage for memory. In 1967, Zuse KG was suffering financially and was sold to Siemens, a multinational German technology company.

corrections to radio-controlled flying bombs. They were the predecessors of the modern cruise missile and were seized by Soviet occupying forces at the end of the war.

Zuse began work on a Z4, which was saved from the destruction of the Z1, Z2, and Z3 when an Allied attack destroyed Zuse's factory. However, when the war ended, it was too difficult to get funding, and the project was put on hold in 1949. Finally, in 1949 he founded Zuse KG, his postwar computer company, which finished the Z4 before moving to other work.

While working on the Z4, Zuse came up with another time-saving innovation: the first high-level programming language. A high-level programming language is one that, unlike assembly language, more closely resembles natural or mathematical language and is more intuitive to use and to understand while reading, which makes proofreading and debugging easier. Zuse called his language Plankalkül ("plan calculus"), which resembles relational algebra and relied on statements, subroutines, conditional statements, arrays, and other features of modern programming languages. Zuse wrote a book on the language, but it was never published, nor was the language released to the public; the war and his subsequent work with Zuse KG interrupted him, and before long Fortran had been developed at IBM to serve the same purpose. (ALGOL was also developed in Europe, where it was more popular.) Zuse expressed hope that Plankalkül would someday have its moment in the sun but never developed a compiler or interpreter for it; a compiler was eventually developed in 2000, years after Zuse's death.

The reason computing continued to evolve despite Zuse rather than because of him was that World War II had thrown up a wall between Germany and the rest of the world's scientific community. This happened to some extent among the Allied nations—because so many computing projects were classified, little information was shared among them, and Tommy Flowers, the developer of the United Kingdom's Colossus computers, did not receive due credit for years—but the situation was much worse with regard to Germany's relationship with the greater scientific community.

Zuse's innovations in the computer industry continued after Zuse KG was formed, although he remained less well known than less accomplished computer scientists. In 1955, he completed the Z22, the first computer to use magnetic storage for memory. It was designed to be easier to program than previous computers had been, especially for solving mathematical problems (the task that had first inspired Zuse to build a computer). It was also Zuse's first computer to use vacuum tubes and was followed by the Z23, a transistorized version, in 1961. Versions of the Z22 remained in use through the 1970s.

In 1969, after Zuse KG had been sold to Siemens because of financial troubles, Zuse published *Rechnender Raum* (translated and published in 1970 as *Calculating Space* by the Massachusetts Institute of Technology), a book on his idea that the universe itself is a deterministic system being computed by a cellular automaton. The idea has attracted some physicists, who have explored and expanded on the notion ever since, most recently in Stephen Wolfram's 2002 *A New Kind of Science*.

PERSONAL LIFE

Although Zuse worked for the Third Reich, he was never a member of the Nazi Party. He married Gisela Brandes in January 1945. The couple had five children. In the late 1980s, with funding from Siemens (which had purchased his company), Zuse re-created his original machine, the Z1. He died at the age of eighty-five, on December 18, 1995, in Hunfeld, Germany. Always a hobbyist painter, he had spent his years after retirement focusing on his art. Today the German Computer Science Society awards the Konrad Zuse Medal every two years to the leading German computer scientist.

Bill Kte'pi

FURTHER READING

Ceruzzi, Paul E. *A History of Modern Computing*. Cambridge: MIT, 2012. Print. A narrative history of the computer industry from 1945 to 1995, Zuse's era.

Ensmenger, Nathan L. *The Computer Boys Take Over: Computers, Programmers, and the Politics of Technical Expertise*. Cambridge: MIT, 2010. Print. Like the Ceruzzi book, an account of the personalities and development of the computer industry, including Zuse.

Zuse, Konrad. *The Computer—My Life*. New York: Springer, 2010. Print. Zuse's history of computing and his own experiences in the industry. Written for the layperson, with an appendix of technical information for the expert.

Appendixes

TIMELINE

These milestone events below represent a concise history of the Internet, both theoretical and commercial in scope.

DATE	MILESTONE
1957	After the Soviet Union launches Sputnik 1, the United States forms the Advanced Research Projects Agency (ARPA) to create a communications network that links the country in the event that a military strike renders conventional communication useless.
1961	"Information Flow in Large Communications Nets," a paper by computer science professor Len Kleinrock, is published; it outlines packet switching, which groups together transmitted data into suitably-sized blocks.
1965	At the federally-funded MIT Lincoln Laboratory, a research center dedicated to the application of advanced technology, the first network experiment for ARPA is conducted. During the experiment, two computers interacted with each other using packet switching technology.
1969	The Advanced Research Projects Agency Network (ARPANET), considered the predecessor of the Internet, is commissioned by the Department of Defense for research into networking. To many, this marks the official "birth of the Internet."
1969	The first APRANET message—"Lo"—is sent in an attempt to spell log-in, but the system crashed.
1972	Electronic mail is introduced by Ray Tomlinson, a computer engineer from Cambridge, Massachusetts. He used the @ sign to distinguish between the sender's name and the name of the network.
1973	The term "Internet" first came into modern usage.
1973	The first international connections to the APRANET are established to the University College of London and the Norwegian Seismic Array, or NORSAR (Norway).
1974	The first Internet Service Provider (ISP) is created with the introduction of a commercial version of APRENET called Telenet.
1975	The first all-inclusive email program is introduced, providing replying, forwarding, and filing functionalities and options.
1975	Often attributed as the first personal computer (PC), the Altair 8800 is introduced and is surprisingly sold in high quantities. Because of the computer's surprising sales and because it used Microsoft's first product (Altair BASIC), the introduction of the microcomputer becomes an important milestone in the personal computer revolution.

DATE	MILESTONE
1975	The Microsoft Corporation is founded on April 4 by Bill Gates and Paul Allen to develop BASIC (Beginner's All-purpose Symbolic Instruction Code) interpreters for use in the Altair 8800 microcomputer. It marks the first of numerous high-level programming languages developed and sold by Microsoft, which came to dominate the PC market for decades.
1976	Apple Computer, Inc., which became known for their signature Macintosh personal computers in the 1980s, is founded by Steve Jobs and Steve Wozniak. In terms of market capitalization, Apple would overtake the once behemoth Microsoft Corporation in August of 2012,
1976	Approximately five years after the first email is sent, Queen Elizabeth II sends out an e-mail on ARPANET. It marks the first usage of networking technologies by an acting head of state.
1976	For $40,000, the Computer Corporation of America offers Comet, recognized as the first commercial email product or service.
1978	The first possible unsolicited email message, known as "spam," is sent by a marketing representative advertising an upcoming presentation of new computers. By 2012, the amount of spam recorded is estimated to be in the trillions.
1980	Renowned computer scientist Tim Berners-Lee writes the program "Enquire Within," the predecessor to the World Wide Web (abbreviated simply as the Web or WWW).
1981	Though the history of personal computers arguably spans back to the 1950s, IBM announces its first personal computer in August. At the time of its introduction, the IBM Personal Computer (model number 5150) is marketed as the "smallest, lowest-priced computer system" and offers read-only memory (ROM) of 40K. The success of the IBM PC establishes it as the standard in the personal computer market.
1981	Microsoft begins distributing and licensing its operating system, Microsoft DOS, or MS-DOS (with DOS an acronym for Disk Operating System).MS-DOS and similar operating systems were standard in the PC marketplace for the next fifteen years or so.
1982	Although widely criticized at first, emoticons are introduced to integrate emotion and feeling into messages.
1983	Domain Name System (DNS) is designed by Jon Postel, Paul Mockapetris, and Craig Partridge; .edu, .gov, .com, .mil, .org, .net, and .int are all created.
1984	William Gibson writes the science-fiction novel Neuromancer, coining the term cyberspace.
1984	Apple introduces the first Macintosh personal computer, successfully ushering a graphical user interface and the ubiquitous mouse into the personal computer marketplace.
1984	The number of hosts on the ARPANET surpasses 1,000.
1985	Symbolics.com becomes the first registered .com domain on the Internet. It is registered by a computer manufacturer.

DATE	MILESTONE
1986	The ARPANET/Internet exceeds an estimated 5,000 hosts, a number which would double within one year.
1987	Cisco Systems ships its first product, a multiprotocol router.
1987	An estimated 25 million PCs are sold in the United States.
1989	World.std.com becomes the first commercial provider of Internet dial-up access to the Internet.
1989	The Internet reaches an estimated 100,000 hosts.
1989	Security software company McAfee Associates is founded; Symantec Corp. releases Norton AntiVirus for the Macintosh; antivirus expert Eugene Kaspersky begins his career as an expert in computer viruses.
1991	ARPANET ends; that same year, Tim Berners-Lee creates the World Wide Web, making access to information from around the world easier and revolutionizing modern communication.
1991	The Stanford Linear Accelerator (SLAC) becomes the first web server on the Internet.
1992	The number of hosts on the Internet surpasses 1million. The World Bank goes online.
1992	Librarian Jean Armour Polly is credited with coining the term "surfing the Internet."
1993	Jim Clark and Marc Andreessen establish Netscape Communications Corp., the company responsible for the commercially successful and once dominant web browser Netscape Navigator.
1993	The World Wide Web is developed within CERN, or the European Organization for Nuclear Research, which houses and maintains the largest particle physics laboratory in the world.
1994	The business plan for commerce company Amazon.com is written by Jeff Bezos. Amazon.com would go on to become the largest online retailer in the world.
1994	Online pizza ordering is available through the Hut online, the web portal for the Pizza Hut restaurant chain.
1995	Yahoo! Inc. is founded in Santa Clara, California, and offers Internet users a bevy of services and products, including a web search engine, email services, mapping, and more.
1996	The WWW browser war, with Netscape and Microsoft being the two main contenders, ushers in a new age of software development in which new products are released quarterly.
1997	The term "web log" is coined; it is later shortened to "blog."
1998	Internet behemoth Google Inc., which set out to collate all the information in the world in its founding mission statement, begins operations in Menlo Park, California.

DATE	MILESTONE
1999	Programmer Shawn Fanning creates Napster, opening the realm of peer-to-peer file sharing and sparking a copyright war in the music industry.
1999	It is reported that Internet traffic doubles every 100 days.
2000	Approximately 20 million websites exist on the Internet, a number which doubled in under a year
2001	Supported by a nonprofit foundation, Wikipedia is launched.
2004	The dominant social media service Facebook is launched; by 2009, the service boasts over an estimated 200 million active users.
2005	The video-sharing site YouTube.com launches; one year later, the site is purchased by Google for an estimated $1.65 billion.
2006	There are an estimated 92 million web sites online.
2006	The microblogging platform Twitter is founded in San Francisco, California; as of 2012, the social networking service has a reported 500 million active users.
2007	Developed as a program to service Apple's numerous personal devices, iTunes surpasses 1 billion downloads.
2009	According to world stats, an estimated 1.114 billion people are using the Internet.
2010	iPad announced by Steve Jobs in San Francisco at the Yerba Buena Center for the Arts
2010	MetroPCS becomes the first to offer 4G LTE service.
2011	Apple launches the iCloud storage and computing service, which allows users to store data on remote computer servers. The iCloud currently has over 150 million users.
2011	The Amazon Kindle Fire is introduced.
2012	Siri voice control for the iPod 4S is introduced.
2012	Facebook goes public with an IPO of $104 billion ($38 per share), closing at $38.23 on the first day of trading.

BIBLIOGRAPHY

Abella, Alex. *Soldiers of Reason: The Rand Corporation and the Rise of the American Empire*. Orlando: Harcourt, 2008. Print. A general history of the RAND corporation with special emphasis on its ties to and contract work for the US government, especially the Department of Defense. The extent of RAND's influence on government decision making in the areas of international policy and the military is covered.

Allen, Paul. *Idea Man: A Memoir by the Co-founder of Microsoft*. New York: Penguin, 2011. Print. Allen's autobiography, at times controversial, with the focus on the founding of Microsoft. Illustrated.

Babbage, Charles. *The Writings of Charles Babbage*. New York: Halcyon Classics, 2009. Print. Reprints Babbage's work on his attempt at building the first computer.

Baer, Ralph H. *Videogames: In the Beginning*. Springfield: Rolenta, 2005. Print. Baer's own account of the Magnavox Odyssey and the first generation of video games, of the patent infringement cases in which he testified, and of his later work.

Bagnall, B. *Commodore: A Company on the Edge*. 2nd ed. Winnipeg: Variant, 2010. Print. Account of how the superior programming of Atari and Commodore computers failed to result in the expected market success because of high turnover and poor decisions.

Beyer, Kurt. *Grace Hopper and the Invention of the Information Age*. Cambridge: MIT, 2009. Print. Focuses on Hopper's role in the development of computers using material gathered from interviews with Hopper's colleagues. Includes illustrations, a notes section, and an index.

Biancuzzi, Federico, and Shane Warden. *Masterminds of Programming: Conversations with the Creators of Major Programming Languages*. Sebastopol: O'Reilly, 2009. Print. A series of interviews with the creators of influential computer programming languages, including Stroustrup (C++), Thomas E. Kurtz (BASIC), Don Chamberlin (SQL), James Gosling (JAVA), and Larry Wall (PERL).

Bissell, T. *Extra Lives: Why Video Games Matter*. New York: Vintage, 2010. Print. Explores the popularity of video games, investigating the aesthetic and psychological appeal of many of the most popular games.

Boden, Margaret. *Mind as Machine: A History of Cognitive Science*. New York: Oxford UP, 2006. Print. A comprehensive, perhaps definitive, history of the development and achievements of cognitive science, with Newell's work discussed in the larger context of the discipline as a whole.

Burks, Alice Rowe. *Who Invented the Computer?* New York: Prometheus, 2003. Print. Includes Unisys's role in the debate over whether the ABC or ENIAC was the first computer.

Ceruzzi, Paul E. *A History of Modern Computing*. 2nd ed. Cambridge: MIT, 2012. Print. A narrative history of the computer industry from 1945 to 1995, including Cray in chapters headed "From Mainframe to Minicomputer" and "The Go-Go Years."

Christakis, N. A., and J. H. Fowler. *Connected: The Surprising Power of Our Social Networks and How They Shape Our Lives*. Boston: Little, Brown, 2009. Print. Looks at how collaboration and participation in social networking enhance an individual's effectiveness.

Christian, Brian. *The Most Human Human: What Talking with Computers Teaches Us about What It Means to Be Alive*. New York: Doubleday, 2011. Print. A popular book about the differences between human and artificial intelligence, focusing on the 2009 Turing Test (a competition in which programmers strove to build computers that could interact with a user so well that the user could not tell if he or she was interacting with a human being or a computer), but with consideration also of what Deep Blue meant to the debate surrounding human versus artificial intelligence.

Connor, J. A. *Pascal's Wager: The Man Who Played Dice with God*. New York: HarperOne, 2006. Print. Biography of Pascal that looks at his brilliant mathematical background and how his religious beliefs affected some of his explorations later in life.

Copeland, B. Jack, ed. *Alan Turing's Automatic Computing Engine*. New York: Oxford UP, 2005. Print. The definitive guide to the machine that Turing envisioned and that was subsequently built, including his original proposal, a description of the obstacles, and the machine's influence.

Dillon, Roberto. *The Golden Age of Video Games: The Birth of a Multibillion Dollar Industry*. New York: CRC, 2011. Print. A general history of video games from their early days to the rise of PC gaming and the Commodore bankruptcy.

Donovan, T. *Replay: The History of Video Games*. Lewes: Yellow Ant, 2010. Print. Looks at the commercial processes that transformed the video game from a diversion created by technophiles to a multibillion-dollar business run by multinational corporations.

Dyson, George. *Turing's Cathedral: The Origins of the Digital Universe*. New York: Pantheon, 2012. Print. A survey of the experimentation, mathematical insight, and creative endeavors leading to computers, digital television, genetics, and cosmological models based on computer code.

Edwards, Douglas. *I'm Feeling Lucky: The Confessions of Google Employee Number 59*. Boston: Mariner, 2012. Print. A memoir about working at the company.

Ensmenger, Nathan L. *The Computer Boys Take Over: Computers, Programmers, and the Politics of Technical Expertise*. Cambridge: MIT, 2010. Print. Like the Ceruzzi book, an account of the personalities and development of the computer industry, including Backus and his contemporaries.

Gertner, Jon. *The Idea Factory, Bell Labs and the Great Age of American Innovation*. New York: Penguin, 2012. Print. A well-received account not only describing the history of Bell Labs and its accomplishments but also offering a good analysis of the consequences of those inventions on today's technical and economic environments.

Girard, Bernard. *The Google Way: How One Company Is Revolutionizing Management as We Know It*. San Francisco: No Starch, 2009. Print. Focuses on Google's unique management practices.

Gleick, James. *The Information: A History, a Theory, a Flood*. New York: Pantheon, 2011. Print. A well-known science writer's overview of the history of the information age.

Greulich, Peter E. *The World's Greatest Salesman: An IBM Caretaker's Perspective; Looking Back*. Austin: MBI Concepts, 2011. Print. Former IBM employee Greulich documents the founder's leadership of the early IBM.

Hiraoka, Leslie S. *Underwriting the Internet: How Technical Advances, Financial Engineering and Entrepreneurial Genius Are Building the Information Highway*. Armonk: M. E. Sharpe, 2005. Print. A critical approach of MicroStrategy published at a time when the company was facing major problems.

Hodges, A. *Alan Turing: The Enigma*. London: Random House, 2012. Print. Presents Turing as the man who saved the Allies from the Nazis, established the fields of computer science and artificial intelligence, and anticipated the gay liberation movement. Hodges was the first biographer to address Turing's homosexuality (in his 1983 biography).

Holzner, S. *How Dell Does It: Using Speed and Innovation to Achieve Extraordinary Results*. New York: McGraw-Hill, 2006. Print. Examines how Dell uses innovations largely invented by others, improves upon them through strong implementation, and has been hugely successful in doing so.

House, C. H., and R. L. Price. *The HP Phenomenon: Innovation and Business Transformation*. Stanford: Stanford UP, 2009. Print. Explores how Hewlett-Packard's culture has allowed the company to transform itself numerous times while many of its rivals were unable to transform themselves even once, resulting in failure.

Huff, Howard R. *Into the Nano Era: Moore's Law Beyond Planar Silicon CMOS*. Berlin: Springer, 2009. Print. On the fiftieth anniversary of the creation of the integrated circuit, the question is whether Moore's law and increasing capacity/decreasing cost remain valid.

Imbibo, Anthony. *Steve Jobs: The Brilliant Mind behind Apple*. Pleasantville: Gareth Stevens, 2009. Print. Presents significant coverage of Jobs's adolescence. Contains photographs, a time line, and a bibliography.

Indovino, Shaina Carmel. *Michael Dell: From Child Entrepreneur to Computer Magnate*. Philadelphia: Mason Crest, 2012. Print. The inspirational story of Dell's rise to success.

Isaacson, Walter. *Steve Jobs*. New York: Simon, 2011. Print. Isaacson gleans information from more than forty interviews of Jobs, friends, relatives, and competitors.

Israel, Giorgio, and Ana Millán Gasca. *The World as a Mathematical Game: John von Neumann and Twentieth Century Science*. Boston: Birkhäuser, 2009. Print. A scientific and intellectual biography, from set theory to quantum mechanics to economics and von Neumann's theory of automata.

Kaiser, David. *Becoming MIT: Moments of Decision*. Cambridge: MIT, 2010. Print. A history of MIT emphasizing the developing of its pedagogic philosophies.

Lashinsky, Adam. *Inside Apple*. New York: Business Plus, 2012. Print. This journalistic interpretation contains much old information as well as much speculation, but it provides a good look at Apple.

Leavitt, D. *The Man Who Knew Too Much: Alan Turning and the Invention of the Computer*. New York: Norton, 2008. Print. Covers Turing's career and contributions in the context of his homosexuality and the conviction and "treatment" that resulted in his suicide.

Lécuyer, Christophe, and David C. Brock. *Makers of the Microchip: A Documentary History of Fairchild Semiconductor*. Cambridge: MIT, 2010. Print. An account of the development of the silicon integrated circuit at Fairchild Semiconductor Corporation in the company's first four years of business and the role of the device in the digital world.

Levy, Steven. *In the Plex: How Google Thinks, Works, and Shapes Our Lives*. New York: Simon, 2011. Print. Wired writer Levy considers the effects of Google and its corporate culture.

Levy, Steven. *The Perfect Thing: How the iPod Shuffles Commerce, Culture, and Coolness*. New York: Simon, 2006. Print. A discussion of the iPod within the context of both Apple's innovative history and twenty-first-century world culture.

Livingston, Jessica. *Founders at Work: Stories of Start-ups' Early Days*. New York: Apress, 2008. Print. Devotes a chapter to Ozzie's Iris Associates and Groove Networks.

Lohr, Steve. *Go To: The Story of the Math Majors, Bridge Players, Chess Wizards, Maverick Scientists, and Iconoclasts—The Programmers Who Created the Software Revolution*. New York: Basic, 2001. Print. Although there is no book-length biography of Backus, he is featured in the chapter on Fortran.

Malone, M. S. *Bill and Dave: How Hewlett and Packard Built the World's Greatest Company*. New York: Portfolio, 2007. Print. Concentrates on the formation of Hewlett-Packard and how the actions and leadership of its founders have continued to affect the company's culture to the present day.

Maney, K. *The Maverick and His Machine: Thomas B. Watson, Sr. and the Making of IBM*. Hoboken: Wiley, 2004. Print. Explores some of the challenges facing IBM as it sought to provide corporate clients with complete business solutions.

McKay, Sinclair. *The Secret Life of Bletchley Park: The WWII Codebreaking Centre and the Men and Women Who Worked There*. London: Aurum, 2011. Print. A history of Britain's World War II code breakers.

Meggs, Philip B., and Alston W. Purvis. *Meggs' History of Graphic Design*. New York: Wiley, 2011. Print. A comprehensive and visually rich history of graphic design, including modern web design.

Montfort, Nick, and Ian Bogost. *Racing the Beam: The Atari Video Computer System*. Cambridge: MIT, 2009. Print. A much more technically informed and literate look at Atari than provided by histories more concerned with the cultural impact or entertainment value of the games.

Moss, Frank. *The Sorcerers and Their Apprentices: How the Digital Magicians of the MIT Media Lab Are Creating the Innovative Technologies That Will Transform Their Lives*. New York: Crown Business, 2011. Print. An in-depth look at the work of the MIT Media Lab.

O'Regan, Gerard. *A Brief History of Computing*. Berlin: Springer, 2008. Print. A history of computing, written for the general reader and beginning students in computer science, including the accomplishments of Ritchie and his colleagues in creating C and Unix.

Orton, John W. *The Story of Semiconductors*. New York: Oxford UP, 2009. Print. Details the history of semiconductors and explains the science and technology behind them.

Petzold, C. *The Annotated Turing: A Guided Tour through Alan Turing's Historic Paper on Computability and the Turing Machine*. Indianapolis: Wiley, 2008. Print. The seminal work of Turing, with explanatory notes and context.

Pieraccini, Robert. *The Voice in the Machine: Building Computers That Understand Speech*. Cambridge: MIT, 2012. Print. Illustrated. Overview of the field of designing computers that are able to communicate with humans beings using natural language.

Poundstone, William. *Are You Smart Enough to Work at Google?* New York: Little, Brown, 2012. Print. Uses Google as an example of a powerful company in the new economy.

Pugh, E. W. *Building IBM: Shaping an industry and its technology*. Cambridge: MIT, 2009. Print. Explores how decisions made in the 1980s have helped to shape and form IBM, with its emphasis on providing clients "complete" business solutions and a hesitation to embrace new markets that might harm existing profit centers.

Ramsay, Morgan. *Games at Work: Stories Behind the Games People Play*. New York: Apress, 2012. Print. An interview-based history of video games, including an interview with Dabney's partner at Atari, Bushnell.

Rao, Arun, and Piero Scarulfi. *A History of Silicon Valley*. San Francisco: Omniware, 2011. Print. An overview of the Silicon Valley tech company culture.

Rasskin-Gutman, Diego. *Chess Metaphors: Artificial Intelligence and the Human Mind*. Cambridge: MIT, 2009. Print. Written by a theoretical biologist, this book discusses the cognitive task of problem solving, using the tasks presented by a chess game as a jumping-off point to examine other types of cognition. Rasskin-Gutman presents both human and artificial intelligence approaches to cognitive tasks, including the creation of a computer (Deep Blue) that could beat a human grandmaster at chess.

Saylor, Michael. *The Mobile Wave: How Mobile Intelligence Will Change Everything*. New York: Perseus, 2012. Print. Saylor's account of his belief that mobile technology will change the lives of everybody in the world.

Seibel, Peter. *Coders at Work: Reflections on the Craft of Programming*. New York: Apress, 2009. Print. A collection of fifteen interviews with influential programmers.

Sidhu, Inder. *Doing Both: How Cisco Capture's Today's Profit and Drives Tomorrow's Growth*. Upper Saddle River: FT Press, 2010. Print. Cisco senior vice president Sidhu's explanation of how his company increased revenue, profits, and earnings per share in an unstable global economy.

Smiley, Jane. *The Man Who Invented the Computer: The Biography of John Atanasoff, Digital Pioneer*. New York: Doubleday, 2010. Print. An engaging biography of Atanasoff by the acclaimed fiction writer.

Tapscott, Don, and Anthony D. Williams. *Wikinomics: How Mass Collaboration Changes Everything*. Expanded edition. New York: Portfolio Trade, 2008. Print. A business-oriented examination of the usefulness of global collaboration, with examples including Wikipedia, Linux, BMW, and Procter & Gamble. Polese is cited with regard to the usefulness of open source software for businesses.

Walter, Russ. *The Secret Guide to Computers and Tricky Living*. 31st ed. Manchester: Russell Walter, 2012. Print. Offers full coverage and instructions on various computers and affiliated hardware and software components. Also provides extensive historical background about a number of computer companies, including Gateway.

White, Pepper. *The Idea Factory: Learning to Think at MIT*. Cambridge: MIT, 2001. Print. A memoir of the unique experience of being educated at MIT.

Williams, Kathleen Broome. *Grace Hopper: Admiral of the Cyber Sea*. Annapolis: Naval Institute, 2005. Print. The focus is on Hopper's naval career. Includes an extensive bibliography and an index.

Wozniak, Steve, with Gina Smith. *iWoz: From Computer Geek to Cult Icon; How I Invented the Personal Computer, coFounded Apple, and Had Fun Doing It*. New York: Norton, 2006. Print. Highly readable firsthand account of the founding of Apple and Wozniak's role in the computer revolution. Illustrated.

Wu, Timothy. *The Master Switch: The Rise and Fall of Information Empires*. New York: Vintage, 2011. Print. An analysis of information empires of the recent past—such as those built around the telephone, radio, and film—and their tendency over time to be dominated by a monopoly or small cartel. Suggests that the same fate may befall the Internet.

Young, Jeffrey S., and William L. Simon. *iCon: Steve Jobs—The Greatest Second Act in the History of Business*. Hoboken: Wiley, 2005. Print. "Warts-and-all" biography of Jobs that is sharply critical of his more outrageous exploits and was subsequently banned from Apple stores.

Zuse, Konrad. *The Computer—My Life*. New York: Springer, 2010. Print. Zuse's history of computing and his own experiences in the industry. Written for the layperson, with an appendix of technical information for the expert.

Biographical Directory

The following list briefly summarizes the achievements of the innovators covered in this publication.

A

Howard H. Aiken: In the late 1930s, college professor Howard H. Aiken sold International Business Machines (IBM) on developing the digital computer he had designed. Although other claimants exist, Aiken, according to historians, has the strongest claim of any of the contenders to the title of inventor of the digital computer. His Automatic Sequence Controlled Calculator was the progenitor if not the prototype of the modern computer.

Frances E. Allen: Frances E. Allen, an American computer research scientist and pioneer in computing, spent nearly half a century working on compilers and high-performance computing systems. Her work led to technologies that formed the foundation for the theory of program optimization and contributed to the use of high-performance computers in weather forecasting, DNA matching, and national security-code breaking. Allen was among the first women recognized for her role in the technical aspect of computing. Her many awards include being named an IBM Fellow and winning the A. M. Turing Award; she was the first woman to be so honored with both titles.

Paul Allen: Known by the public as a cofounder of the software giant Microsoft, Paul Allen played an active role in the company until 1983, when his role ended for health reasons. Since that time, he has become a major player in a number of venues by investing in computer technologies, medical research, space and oceanic exploration, entertainment, and sports. Allen and his sister Jody founded the Paul G. Allen Family Fund to promote community projects in the Pacific Northwest. He also built the Paul G. Allen School for Global Animal Health at Washington State University. Allen owns the Seattle Seahawks football team and the Portland Trail Blazers basketball team and is part owner of the Seattle Sounders soccer team. He also owns a yacht, the Octopus which he sails annually to the Cannes Film Festival, where he hosts lavish parties for celebrities.

John Vincent Atanasoff: One of the fathers of the computer, John Vincent Atanasoff was an Iowa State College professor whose work in the 1930s and 1940s culminated in the first electronic digital computer: the Atanasoff-Berry Computer (ABC), designed with his student Clifford E. Berry. The ABC included numerous features that would become synonymous with computing, although it lacked a central processing unit (CPU). ABC's significance was not immediately recognized; it was only through a later patent case, showing that the patent sought actually derived from Atanasoff's work, that Atanasoff's seniority in the burgeoning field was established. Atanasoff was later placed in charge of designing a large-scale computer for the Naval Ordnance Laboratory and designed systems for the Navy's Operation Crossroads, a series of atomic bomb tests at Bikini Atoll.

B

Charles Babbage: Charles Babbage was the inventor of the difference and analytical engines, which became the forerunners of the modern computer. The difference engine employed the first example of computer language on record. Babbage was considered a major voice in the school of thought that sought to apply scientific methods to commerce during the Industrial Revolution, and his ideas were implemented in the development of tools and in manufacturing and engineering techniques. Although Babbage was recognized as a mathematical genius during his lifetime, his work failed to win him widespread fame. He often suffered ridicule at the hands of his contemporaries because he was so far ahead of his time. It was not until the computer age, during the last quarter of the twentieth century and nearly a century after his death, that Babbage was finally given his due as the creator of the first mechanical computer. As a result, he is now alternately known as the father, the grandfather, and the godfather of modern computing.

John Backus: John Backus's work at IBM revolutionized computer programming. In the 1950s, he assembled and led the team that developed Fortran, the first high-level programming language, one rigorous enough to remain in use today. In the course of doing so, he also introduced the first optimizing compiler, in order to encourage Fortran's adoption. Later in the same decade he introduced the Backus-Naur Form (BNF), a notation technique for context-free grammar, a meta-linguistic approach to describing languages. Such notation techniques—of which BNF remains one of the two standards—make it easier to discuss and describe programming languages. Backus used it in developing programming languages in the ALGOL family, but he continued to look for better ways to program. His function-level programming language, FP, never caught on, but his introduction of it did raise interest in functional programming as a general area of research.

Ralph H. Baer: Ralph H. Baer fled Nazi Germany to become an engineer in the United States after serving in military intelligence during World War II. Among the first to earn a degree in television engineering, he was interested in advancing the possibilities of television technology beyond passive viewing. While working for a defense contractor, he led a small team designing the first home video game console, a device intended to make home television sets interactive: the Magnavox Odyssey, soon followed by the Odyssey2, which preceded the Atari and other well-known brands, as well as including a keyboard for input at a time when personal computers were still largely unheard of. His later work included the popular handheld game Simon.

Steve Ballmer: As the chief executive officer (CEO) of software giant Microsoft Corporation since 2000, Steve Ballmer is considered one of the more influential technology executives. Microsoft initially rose to prominence on the strength of its operating systems, MS-DOS and later Microsoft Windows. Microsoft has expanded its product line from operating systems to include a suite of office productivity software, Internet search engines, gaming devices, and other products. After Bill Gates stepped down as Microsoft CEO at the end of 1999, Ballmer stepped into that role to lead Microsoft.

Clifford E. Berry: Clifford E. Berry was the cocreator of the Atanasoff-Berry Computer (ABC), the first electronic digital computer while a graduate student at Iowa State College from 1939 to 1941. Although later computers such as the Electronic Numerical Integrator and Computer (ENIAC) were better known, the ABC introduced numerous innovations critical to the advent of modern computing, including several still in use today—such as regenerative capacitor memory, parallel processing, the separation of memory and computing as distinct functions, the use of binary (base 2) arithmetic for computing, and the move away from using mechanical parts such as ratchets and gears. Little known for decades, the importance of Berry's work was recognized ten years after his death when the U.S. District Court acknowledged the primacy of the ABC.

Anita Borg: Anita Borg, an American computer scientist, is best known for her advocacy for the inclusion of women in technological and scientific fields. She founded Systers, an electronic mailing list made up of women computer professionals, and, with computer scientist Telle Whitney, founded the Grace Hopper Celebration of Women in Computing, a technical computer science conference inspired by the legacy of Navy admiral Grace Murray Hopper. Most notably, Borg founded the Institute for Women and Technology (IWT), a nonprofit research and development organization with a dual focus on increasing the number and influence of women in technology and increasing the positive effects of technology on the lives of women. She served as the first president of IWT. Shortly after her death, the institute was renamed the Anita Borg Institute for Women and Technology in her honor.

Paul Brainerd: Programmer and philanthropist Paul Brainerd is one of the cofounders of Aldus, the software company that introduced desktop publishing (a term Brainerd coined). PageMaker, Aldus's flagship product, was a software package that allowed for total manipulation of each page to be printed, from text to layout, including images, charts, and graphs. In 1985, this was a revolutionary step forward in publishing, which until that time had benefitted only slightly from word processors, machines that offered only a slight advance over typewriters, and was still dominated by typesetting. As the industry shifted from typesetting to desktop publishing, PageMaker remained the major program for more than a decade, and when Aldus was purchased by competitor Adobe, Brainerd used his share of the sale proceeds to fund the philanthropic organizations to which he later devoted his career.

Ursula Burns: Ursula Burns is an American success story. Raised by a single mother in a New York City housing project, she became the first African American woman to lead a Fortune 500 company, Xerox. Beginning as an intern in the summer of 1980, she steadily rose through the ranks at Xerox to become chief executive officer (CEO) in July 2009, succeeding Anne

Mulcahy. The transition from Mulcahy to Burns marked the first transfer of power from one female CEO to another female CEO. On May 20, 2010, Burns became chair of the company.

Vannevar Bush: American scientific researcher and electrical engineer Vannevar Bush is known for his pioneering work in the fields of analog computing, automated human memory, and information storage and retrieval. Bush served as dean of engineering and vice president of the Massachusetts Institute of Technology (MIT), president of the Carnegie Institution, and director of the U.S. government's Office of Scientific Research and Development during his lengthy career. He is known for his foresight in predicting the commercial and personal household uses of electronic devices. Bush's differential analyzer was one of the most powerful analog computers. During World War II, he emerged as a leading force behind the mobilization of the partnership between the government, scientific, and

business communities, making him an architect of what came to be known as the military-industrial complex. His groundbreaking 1945 Atlantic Monthly article "As We May Think" introduced the hypothetical information storage and retrieval machine known as the memex, which facilitated information retrieval through the use of associative linking—a theoretical forerunner of the Internet and hypertext.

Nolan Bushnell: Legendary entrepreneur Nolan Bushnell has been involved in the computer industry since its advent, working to produce hardware, software, and games that have proven highly popular over time. Bushnell has also served as a mentor, consultant, and guiding force to many young entrepreneurs, making him highly influential in several generations of technology, restaurant, and gaming pioneers. As someone who has initiated more than twenty start-up businesses, Bushnell has been one of the foremost innovators and visionaries of his generation.

C

Rod Canion: Trained as an electrical engineer and known for his soft voice, khakis, and sports shirts, Texan Rod Canion has spent much of his life defining new technologies. As a cofounder and the first chief executive officer (CEO) of the Compaq Computer Corporation, Canion led the company in breaking records during the early days of the computer revolution in the late twentieth century. Under his guidance, Compaq rose to become one of the most trusted names in home computing. The company initiated the trend in cloning the personal computer (PC) and originated the first "luggable" computer by removing the boundaries that restricted computer use to offices, allowing users to work while at home or traveling. During his time with the company, Compaq broke a number of records and set high standards for the technology companies that followed it. After being fired from the company in 1991, Canion created a new company in partnership with his old friend and Compaq cofounder Jim Harris.

Safra A. Catz: Safra A. Catz became president of Oracle Corporation, an enterprise software company, in 2004. In 2011, for the second time, she was named the company's chief financial officer as well. Generally considered the person most responsible for Oracle's financial performance, she became a member of the firm's board of directors in 2001. In 2008, she became

a member of the board of directors for HSBC Holdings plc, one of the world's largest banking and financial services organizations. Fortune magazine ranked her the eleventh most powerful woman in business in 2011, and Time included her on its 2012 list of the ten most influential women in technology. With total compensation in 2011 of more than $42 million, she topped Fortune's list of the highest-paid women in business for that year.

John T. Chambers: In the dot-com boom of the 1990s, John T. Chambers's effort to grow Cisco by promoting it as an example of e-business led to his being called an Internet evangelist and introduced as "Mr. Internet." Showing how digital technology could help improve productivity and how a company can work effectively with government to provide Internet solutions, Chambers was a visionary of the dot-com era. After the dot-com crash, eyes turned to his leadership at Cisco for guidance on how companies could refocus themselves as customer-centric organizations.

Tim Cook: Tim Cook represents the second generation of leadership in innovative businesses such as Apple and computers in general. After visionaries such as Steve Jobs created a reality to match their visions, people such as Cook—managers and nuts-and-bolts businessmen—transformed the somewhat unstable corporation into a stable venture able to adapt to changing circumstances while holding on to what made the founder's era so distinct. If Jobs and Steve Wozniak were Apple's prophets, Cook became the disciplined leader who preserved the legend.

Seymour Cray: Seymour Cray is acknowledged in the history of computer science as the father of supercomputing and the founder of the supercomputer industry.

Without him, it is quite possible that we would not have the type of computers or the electronic devices we use to this day. Joel Birnbaum famously stated that "Many of the things that high performance computers now do routinely were at the farthest edge of credibility when Seymour envisioned them." Cray led a private life away from the computer science industry until his tragic and unexpected death in 1996 as the result of a traffic accident.

D

Ted Dabney: With Nolan Bushnell, Ted Dabney cofounded both Syzygy Engineering (in 1971) and Atari, Inc. (in 1972). The latter became the first major success of the newborn video game industry. Dabney and Bushnell created the first coin-operated arcade game, Computer Space, based on Steve Russell's Spacewar! game—just as Atari's successful Pong was an adaptation of the table tennis game included with the Magnavox Odyssey home video game console. With the passage of time, Bushnell's legend has been magnified, in part through his own efforts, leaving Dabney in the shadows of the footlights.

Weili Dai: Weili Dai, born in China and educated in the United States, is the cofounder of Marvell Technology Group Ltd., a leading semiconductor manufacturer. One of the most successful female technology entrepreneurs in the world, Dai is also noted for her philanthropy and her championing of women's greater

participation in leadership and in business and technical fields.

Michael Dell: Michael Dell is one of the most successful entrepreneurs of his time, revolutionizing the manufacture and creation of the personal computer (PC) during the 1980s. While computers had previously been marketed and sold in an impersonal and distant manner, Dell made the decision to extract the middleman from the process. As a result his company, Dell Computer Corporation, served as the manufacturer and seller of the PCs it made and was able to customize products to better meet consumers' needs. This approach was highly successful, and Dell PCs became popular with corporate and higher-education users in addition to consumers. As Dell has grown, it has added product lines and services, including servers, data storage systems, and information technology support services. Dell remains one of the top sellers of PCs in the United States.

E

J. Presper Eckert: J. Presper Eckert with John William Mauchly invented the first general-purpose digital electronic computer, the Electronic Numerical Integrator and Computer, or ENIAC. They also designed the Binary Automatic Computer (BINAC). Their most notable contribution to the early development of modern computing was the Universal Automatic Computer (UNIVAC). Their business acumen was less than their technical inventiveness, and their computer company was bought by Remington Rand, which became Burroughs and eventually Unisys.

Brendan Eich: Perhaps Brendan Eich's most significant accomplishment was completing a specific assignment in about a week and a half. In that time, Eich, as a new employee at the Netscape Corporation, created a scripting language for presenting content that appeared

on the Internet. Until then, everything that users saw on their web browsers was static, essentially pages they could open, read, or leave but with which they could not interact. Eich's invention, which came to be designated as JavaScript (now officially referred to as ECMA-262), allowed developers to create interactive web pages. Content was no longer merely passive but could be developed and presented to give an Internet user a wide range of options for interacting with and manipulating it. Since that time, Eich has been in the forefront of web browser development—leading the creation of the Firefox browser, for example—and the cause of open source software, supporting open and standardized development in order to allow anyone to bring content to the web and prevent single organizations from establishing monopolies.

Larry Ellison: Larry Ellison is the cofounder and chief executive officer (CEO) of Oracle Corporation, one of the largest providers of enterprise software. Enterprise software is sold to businesses, government agencies, and other organizations and differs from that sold to individuals. Originally dominant in the database market, Oracle grew in a variety of other areas, including computer hardware systems, development software, collaboration tools, and middleware. Known for his aggressive business practices, Ellison is viewed by many as a visionary and a reliable ally. Steady growth at Oracle has permitted Ellison to become one of the most highly compensated business executives globally, and his luxurious lifestyle is not without its critics.

Douglas C. Engelbart: Douglas C. Engelbart is best known as the inventor of the computer mouse, but his life's work has focused on using computing systems to support organizations as "augmented knowledge workshops" using "online systems," the combination of tools such as e-mail, video conferencing, networking, and hypertext to advance organizations and cross-organizational efforts. He pioneered such tools to advance organizational transformation; his firsts include display editing, windows, cross-file editing, outline processing, hypermedia, and groupware. He is also the founder of the Bootstrap Institute, which is dedicated to deploying technology in service of collaboration.

Thelma Estrin: Thelma Estrin, a pioneer in biomedical engineering, used computer technology and electrical engineering to solve problems in health care and medical research. She was one of the first women to earn a Ph.D. in engineering and designed the first system for analog-digital conversion of electrical activity from the nervous system. Throughout her career as a researcher and a professor, she served as a role model for other young women who would wish to pursue careers in science, technology, engineering, or medicine. She broke the barriers of gender and religious discrimination that existed in the corporate and research professions.

F

Federico Faggin: Federico Faggin is a physicist and electrical engineer whose most notable project to date is the design of the first commercial microprocessor, the Intel 4004, in 1971, as well as other influential chips behind the computer revolution: the 8008, the 8080, and the Z80. Faggin was the guiding force during the first five years of Intel's microprocessor effort. These chips were used for a variety of purposes, especially the first home computers, including the Altair 8800 kit and the TRS-80 from RadioShack. Forty years later, his innovations are still being used in the Pentium chips that power many computers. Starting in 1981, Faggin began a life as an entrepreneur and founded several successful companies. Among his many honors are a National Medal of Technology and Innovation, presented to him in 2010 by President Barack Obama.

David Ferrucci: Despite his early decision to become a physician, David Ferrucci's lot in life was destined to deal only indirectly with medicine. Instead, he became an expert in artificial intelligence, particularly in programming computers to understand natural human language. He led the team that designed Watson, the IBM supercomputer that managed to win against two top human competitors over three days of the television game show Jeopardy! in February 2011. Watson provided a decisive victory for Ferrucci and his fellow programmers and for IBM, because it demonstrated that its ability to analyze data had implications in a variety of fields that went far beyond entertaining television audiences. Through Watson, Ferrucci was able to show that computers have the potential for improving—and possibly saving—the lives of humans as well as for improving proficiency and performance in academia and business.

Carly Fiorina: Carly Fiorina served in key leadership positions at Lucent Technologies and the Hewlett-Packard Company. While not all of her strategies proved successful, her aggressive and expansion-oriented management of both corporations kept these organizations, and Fiorina herself, in the headlines. After leaving corporate management, Fiorina served as an adviser to Republican presidential nominee John McCain in 2008 and later staged an unsuccessful run for the U.S. Senate as the 2010 Republican candidate for that office in California.

Tommy Flowers: Tommy Flowers was an English electronics engineer recruited by computer scientist Alan Turing to help with the code-breaking efforts of the British government during World War II, building on Turing's work breaking the German code known as

Enigma. In response, Flowers designed the Colossus code-breaking computer, which decrypted Nazi communiques critical to planning the 1944 D-day landings by the Allies on the beaches of Normandy. He later

continued the work he had begun before the war on electronic telephone exchanges, publishing a book on the subject in 1976.

G

Bill Gates: Bill Gates, cofounder of Microsoft, helped to redefine the world of computing. By developing MS-DOS, which became the most widely used operating system in the 1980s, Gates and cofounder Paul Allen placed Microsoft in a position to become the world's leading software developer. Microsoft was at the forefront of the growth of home computing, which expanded from three hundred thousand users in 1980 to 2.9 million users in 1983. As the information superhighway, the Internet, emerged in the 1990s, Gates led Microsoft to release improved versions of Windows and related applications that allowed computer users to navigate cyberspace, communicate through e-mail, create and manage documents, calculate using spreadsheets, manage data relationally, and browse and shop online.

Charles Geschke: Charles Geschke is cofounder of Adobe Systems. In 1982, he and John Warnock founded the company that became one of the world's largest software suppliers. He led the team that designed Post-Script, the interpretive computer language that helped to start the desktop publishing revolution. Geschke made headlines in 1992, when he was kidnapped at gunpoint from the Adobe parking lot in Mountain View, California. He was rescued by agents of the Federal Bureau of Investigation (FBI) four days later. He retired as president of Adobe in 2000, but as of 2012 he still was serving as cochairman of the company's board of directors.

In 2009, President Barack Obama presented Geschke with the National Medal of Technology and Innovation, the highest honor bestowed on scientists, engineers, and inventors by the U.S. government.

James Gosling: The father of Java, James Gosling created the programming language while working at Sun Microsystems in the 1990s. Java became one of the most important programming languages of the Internet age, allowing the creation of programs that can run on a wide variety of vastly different computers without requiring separate versions to be coded for each computer setup.

Helen Greiner: Helen Greiner, a renowned roboticist and pioneer in the robot industry, is a cofounder and former president of iRobot, the largest independent robotics company in the world. During her tenure at iRobot, the company moved from a Massachusetts Institute of Technology spin-off to an international leader in the industry. With a vision of designing robots that could be put to practical use in the consumer, industrial, academic, and military markets, Greiner developed robots that possessed greater mobility and intelligence than those previously in use. She brought the same imagination and ingenuity to CyPhyWorks, the company she founded in 2009, the year following her resignation from iRobot. As chief executive officer (CEO) of CyPhyWorks, Greiner leads the company in developing unmanned aerial vehicles.

H

Wendy Hall: Wendy Hall is one of the generation of computer innovators who are building on the work of the preceding generations to continue the spread of computing to as many people as possible around the world. Her focus is on making the Internet into a universal tool capable of delivering information in multimedia and hypermedia formats. She is a pioneer in digital libraries, the development of the Semantic Web, and the emerging discipline of web science.

Mike Hammond: As the original cofounder of Gateway, Mike Hammond experienced business success at

an early age. His expertise in manufacturing and distribution operations allowed the company to rise rapidly among the competition and become one of the dominant computer manufacturers during the 1990s.

Jim Harris: Jim Harris is best known for cofounding Compaq Computer Corporation with friends Rod Canion and Bill Murto in 1981. He was a key player in the company's operations during the 1980s and left the company with cofounder Canion in 1992 to form Insource Technology, where he works today.

Bill Hewlett: Together with his longtime friend and business partner, David Packard, Bill Hewlett helped create the modern technological industry. Although quiet and self-effacing, Hewlett was known for his leadership abilities and served as president, chief executive officer (CEO), and chairman of the Hewlett-Packard Company, which he cofounded with Packard. A model for many other high-tech companies, Hewlett-Packard combined cutting-edge technology, creativity, and a progressive working environment. It has served as a model for generations of technology entrepreneurs.

Kazuo Hirai: Hirai began with Sony as a young man and has spent his entire career breaking new ground in the video gaming and networked entertainment venues. He is credited with making Sony's PlayStation 2 a must-have entertainment system for homes throughout the industrialized world and for turning video gaming into a popular activity no longer limited to young adult males. By 2006, the PlayStation Network, which connects the PlayStation 3 to the PlayStation Store and to the computers of "friends" around the world, boasted more than 20 million subscribers. When Sony appeared headed for financial disaster in 2011, Hirai was chosen as the individual most likely to turn the company around.

Betty Holberton: Betty Holberton was an early computer programmer and pioneer in the fields of computer science and information technology. During World War II, the U.S. Army chose Holberton and five other women to program the Electronic Numerical Integrator and Computer (ENIAC), the first general-purpose electronic digital computer. The ENIAC programmers worked at the University of Pennsylvania. Although best known for her work on the ENIAC, Holberton also had several notable postwar career achievements, including the design of the control console and instruction code for

the Universal Automatic Computer (UNIVAC), one of the earliest commercial computers produced by J. Presper Eckert and John W. Mauchly at Remington Rand. She is also renowned for her development of the SORT/MERGE data-sorting program and her role in the development of the COBOL and Fortran computer programming languages. The latter two programs are still in use.

Grace Hopper: At a time when women in the field of mathematics and science were anomalies, Grace Hooper was instrumental in the development of computer languages that allowed individuals without a thorough understanding of mathematics to use computers as they evolved over the course of the twentieth century. She is considered the major force in the development of the computer system used by the U.S. Navy and across-the-board military computing technologies. She foresaw that data would be stored in computers, eliminating the need for reams of paper. Her work on COBOL was a necessary precursor to the development of BASIC, which was used in the operating systems of early computers such as IBM and Apple and in the development of Microsoft Windows. For her contributions to computer programming, Hopper earned the nicknames the Grand Lady of Software, the Grandmother of COBOL, and Amazing Grace.

Feng-hsiung Hsu: Feng-hsiung Hsu is a pioneer in computer science, focusing most of his work on developing a computer that could play chess well enough to defeat a human grandmaster. Hsu and his team from IBM succeeded on May 11, 1997, when their Deep Blue computer defeated reigning world chess champion Garry Kasparov in a series of six matches, by a score of $3\frac{1}{2}$ to $2\frac{1}{2}$. Hsu went on to become the research manager of the Hardware Computing Group for Microsoft's Asia Research Center.

J

Frederick Jelinek: Frederick Jelinek was a pioneer of information theory whose work created the foundation of modern computer language translation and speech recognition technology. Jelinek and colleagues at IBM took a novel approach to computer language processing, based on the specific strengths of the computer rather than trying to imitate human thought; the statistical methods they developed proved crucial to enabling computers to transcribe, understand, and translate natural human speech.

Steve Jobs: Steve Jobs was one of the leading innovators of the information age. Throughout his career as chief executive officer (CEO) of both Apple and Pixar Animation Studios, he consistently raised the bar on industry standards in computing and digital media. Jobs's quest for innovation was coupled with his desire to create rather than follow trends, a tendency that earned him the respect of competitors and consumers alike. Jobs's charisma and ability to convince others of the importance of his ideas were a key part of his success.

Bill Joy: Second only to Bill Gates in influence was William Joy at his peak. Gates made money; Joy made technology. The day after he announced his retirement, Joy indicated that he believed he had been working the same problems for more than two decades and needed something new. In the 1970s, he moved Internet technology into the Unix operating system. His brainchild, which came later, was Java, and he pushed Sun Microsystems into developing the technology that made e-business common. However, he was not satisfied to sit on that accomplishment but instead pushed for tiny embedded computers that allowed devices to speak directly to each other, eliminating human intervention.

K

Peter Karmanos Jr.: Peter Karmanos Jr., is one of the founders of Compuware, which he has called a "blue-collar computer company." As head of Compuware, Karmanos has been involved in every aspect of the business, working as a hands-on manager and building a company that consistently generated industry-leading profits through the 1990s. After a period of complacency, the company successfully rebuilt itself in the 2000s. Karmanos also owns the Carolina Hurricanes, the Plymouth Whalers, and the Florida Everblades hockey franchises.

John G. Kemeny: John G. Kemeny, who spent his career as a mathematician, computer programming educator, and president of Dartmouth College, was coauthor of the BASIC programming language, which he and colleague Thomas Kurtz wrote and later made more powerful with True BASIC. Their invention of the first computer time-sharing system, Dartmouth Time-Sharing System (DTSS), was equally important, adapted by universities and government agencies and foreshadowing the networked environment in which we live today.

Tom Kilburn: Tom Kilburn was instrumental in developing the English computing industry after World War II. His even more lasting legacy lies in the development of computer science at the Victoria University of Manchester, to which he devoted the bulk of his career.

Jack Kilby: Integrated circuits are the foundation for modern electronics. Jack Kilby was coinventor of the integrated circuit. Kilby also patented the portable electronic calculator and a thermal printer among his sixty patents. The Australian Computer Society's Information Age magazine listed Kilby as number one in its list of top fifty innovators, ranking ahead of Steve Jobs, Bill Gates, Tim Berners-Lee, Douglas Engelbart, Gordon E. Moore, and others. According to the chairman of Texas Instruments, Tom Engibous, Kilby ranks with Henry Ford, Thomas Edison, and the Wright brothers for the significance of his contributions to the way the world's people now live.

Thomas Kurtz: Thomas Kurtz taught computer science and mathematics at Dartmouth for thirty-seven years. With John G. Kemeny, Kurtz collaborated on projects including the design and development of the Dartmouth Time-Sharing System (DTSS) and the Beginner's All-purpose Symbolic Instruction Code (BASIC). In 1974, they received the American Federation of Information Processing Societies' first Pioneer's Day award, and in 1983 they founded True BASIC, Inc., to market and promote their standardized version of BASIC.

Sandra L. Kurtzig: The first multimillion-dollar software entrepreneur was not Bill Gates of Microsoft, Marc Andreessen of Netscape, or Larry Ellison of Oracle. Rather, it was Sandra L. Kurtzig of ASK, a company she founded in 1972 to provide inventory-tracking software to manufacturing companies, which at its peak had annual sales of $450 million. Kurtzig was a key player in establishing the business-to-business software industry. She began what is now common in the industry, the creation of easy-to-use business management software for manufacturing companies.

Ken Kutaragi: Ken Kutaragi was in large part responsible for the home game console phenomenon, almost singlehandedly forcing Sony out of its complacency and into the PlayStation era. Known as the father of the PlayStation and the Gutenberg of Gaming, Kutaragi was an iconoclast who did not fit the Sony mold. When he began, video games were a relatively small market with a nerdy image; he drove the PlayStation video game system to become a major money maker for Sony.

L

Duy-Loan Le: Duy-Loan Le came to the United States as a junior high student with limited English proficiency. She worked hard and graduated as her high school valedictorian at age sixteen, graduating from the University of Texas at nineteen. As an engineer at Texas Instruments, she rose through the ranks to become a manager of wireless communications projects and the first Asian American and first woman to be elected a Senior Fellow at that company. She is also known for her dedication to family, community service, and philanthropy.

Rasmus Lerdorf: Danish programmer Rasmus Lerdorf developed the PHP scripting language in the mid-1990s. Originally developed as a set of tools to help him maintain his own web page, PHP quickly grew to become one of the most popular scripting languages, used in millions of websites and incorporated into popular platforms such as Wordpress. His later work included contributions to the MySQL database management program and the Apache HTTP Server.

Barbara Liskov: Barbara Liskov was the first woman to earn a Ph.D. from a computer science department at a U.S. university. She did not allow gender discrimination in mathematics and science to discourage her from pursuing her academic and professional goals. Liskov developed computer languages that are still used in modern software and system applications, and she attributes her success to the assistance of her many graduate students. In her esteemed position as an Institute Professor at the Massachusetts Institute of Technology (MIT), Liskov has hired women in the computer science department and mentors a new generation of women pursuing careers in science and technology.

Liu Chuanzhi: Chinese business tycoon Liu Chuanzhi is the founder of Lenovo, which by 2012 was the world's second-largest computer manufacturer. Having taken advantage of Chinese market reforms, he continues to be a pioneer of Chinese capitalism, and his management style is widely studied.

Ada Lovelace: Augusta Ada King (née Byron), the Countess of Lovelace, was an English noblewoman whose work on Charles Babbage's analytical engine constituted some of the first work in computer programming, and she is often called the first computer programmer. She was also the first to envision uses for computers beyond mathematics, which even Babbage did not do.

M

Mike Markkula: Mike Markkula is best known as the second chief executive officer (CEO) of Apple, a position he held for only two years, between 1981 and 1983. He served the company for twenty years, working as vice president of marketing and as a company director. He was chairman of Apple's board from 1985 to 1997, but his most important contribution to the company was the financing he provided during the formation of Apple in 1977, a total of $250,000 in equity investment and loans. A dozen years older than Steve Jobs and seven years senior to Steve Wozniak, Markkula, who became Apple's third employee, is often described as having provided the adult supervision the young visionaries required in the company's early years. Wozniak credits Markkula with much of Apple's success.

Mich Mathews: Hired in 1989, when Microsoft was well known in the computer industry but far from the household name it would become outside it, Mich Mathews rose through the ranks of marketing positions at Microsoft and became principally responsible for its public image in the 1990s and 2000s. She handled the transformation of founder Bill Gates's public image and focused strongly on creating subbrand identities for Microsoft properties such as Windows, Office, MSN, Bing, and the Xbox, rather than trying to create a consistent cross-brand identity.

John Mauchly: With J. Presper Eckert, John Mauchly designed the first general-purpose electronic digital computer, the Electronic Numerical Integrator and Computer (ENIAC). The team also designed the Electronic Discrete Variable Automatic Computer (EDVAC), the Binary Automatic Computer (BINAC), and the Universal Automatic Computer (UNIVAC) I, the latter the first commercial computer in the United States. Eckert-Mauchly Computer Corporation was the first computer company. The team also originated basic concepts such as programming languages, stored programs, and subroutines. Their work was vital to the development and spread of computers in the late 1940s and after.

John McCarthy: John McCarthy's research into artificial intelligence focused on formalizing commonsense knowledge and reasoning. His career spanned several important developments in the computer era. Like many early computer scientists, he was trained as a mathematician. By initiating experimentation into time sharing, he represented a shift into a new paradigm for computing, where researchers interacted with their own computer resources. His Stanford Artificial Intelligence Laboratory (SAIL) was funded in part by the Defense Advanced Research Projects Agency (DARPA) and was one of the first sites connected to the ARPANET. McCarthy's dedication to the field of artificial intelligence earned him the A. M. Turing Award in 1971, but equally impressive is the fact that sixteen researchers affiliated with SAIL have also been honored.

Scott McNealy: In 1982, Scott McNealy cofounded Sun Microsystems with Andy Bechtolsheim, Vinod Khosla, and Bill Joy, as part of the high-tech boom of Silicon Valley during the 1980s. Unlike most senior executives in Silicon Valley then and now, McNealy had a business background and little experience in computers or engineering; he had been recruited by fellow Stanford alumnus Khosla for exactly that reason.

Bob Miner: The cofounder of Oracle Corporation, which popularized and dominated the market for relational database management systems, Bob Miner met cofounder Larry Ellison while supervising him at Ampex in the 1970s. At Oracle, Miner was in charge of product development from 1977 to 1992. He retired a year later after receiving a diagnosis of cancer.

Charles H. Moore: Charles H. Moore is best known as the creator of Forth, a programming language for process control, instrumentation, and peripherals that is still in use by the National Aeronautics and Space Administration (NASA). The name originally was Fourth, but the IBM 1130 minicomputer for which Moore originally wrote the language allowed only five-character names. Moore also founded FORTH, Inc. and created colorForth when the American National Standards Institute (ANSI) codified megaForth (which Moore found to be cumbersome and unwieldy) as the standard version of Forth. Moore is an advocate of the KISS concept (keep it simple, stupid) and improved on the original Forth to make the simpler, faster, and more versatile colorForth. He is also a follower of John McCarthy, primarily involved in artificial intelligence, in contradistinction to the other school of computing, led by Doug Engelbart, which focused on how computers could enhance the human mind.

Gordon E. Moore: Chemist, entrepreneur, and philanthropist Gordon Moore was a founding father of the Silicon Valley culture. One of the so-called Traitorous Eight who left the company of Nobel laureate William Shockley to found Fairchild Semiconductor, he predicted in 1965 that the power and complexity of silicon chips would double every year for ten years, accompanied by decreases in cost. Three years after he made his famous postulation, which came to be known as Moore's law, he cofounded Intel Corporation, the world's leading manufacturer of silicon chips. After twenty-seven years at Intel, he retired and with his wife established the Gordon E. and Betty Moore Foundation, which has contributed billions of dollars to education, scientific research, and the environment.

Nathan P. Myhrvold: Nathan P. Myhrvold worked for Microsoft for thirteen years as its chief technology officer, founding Microsoft Research, the first major industrial research laboratory in more than a generation. Microsoft Research was instrumental in transforming Microsoft from a software producer with a narrow focus in the 1980s to the giant it has become in the twenty-first century, despite some notable hardware product failures. The single laboratory has since expanded to research initiatives throughout the world. After Microsoft, the former child prodigy started Intellectual Ventures and wrote the Modernist Cuisine cookbook, which has helped to revolutionize twenty-first-century cuisine.

N

Nicholas P. Negroponte: In 1985, Nicholas P. Negroponte founded the Media Lab at the Massachusetts Institute of Technology, pioneering research on human-computer interfaces. He is also a prominent futurist, one of the founders of Wired magazine, and the founder of the One Laptop Per Child Association (OLPC). Since stepping down as chair of the Media Lab, he has been involved in angel investing and running OLPC.

Allen Newell: Allen Newell is best known for his research and work in developing artificial intelligence (AI) systems from both practical and theoretical perspectives.

He developed the Soar problem-solving architecture, which survives today. Newell was instrumental in developing programs that would solve problems effectively, work that was informed by his keen awareness of not only technical issues but also the psychological factors influencing users and their methods in seeking solutions. Newell believed that whatever the scope and extent of technical advances, if they do not operate in harmony with and do not effectively extend human capabilities, they will serve no great purpose.

William C. Norris: William C. Norris was a pioneering computer executive, serving as president of Control Data Corporation (CDC) during the period when it was one of the nine largest computer companies in the United States. CDC was well known both for the speed of its computers and for its commitment to social justice. CDC under Norris's leadership came to define supercomputing and also developed a highly profitable line of peripherals and services. During the 1980s, as users turned to personal computers (PCs) rather than the mainframes for which CDC was known, the company struggled. Eventually CDC left the computer industry, unable to compete in the changing marketplace.

Robert Noyce: Robert Noyce began his career with Philco and Shockley Semiconductor Laboratory in the 1950s. He left Shockley to cofound Fairchild Semiconductor in 1957 at the age of twenty-nine. Noyce's 1959 coinvention of the integrated computer chip, also known as the microchip, was a vital technological step

in the later development of microprocessors, helping to launch a consumer revolution in the computer industry. He would receive sixteen patents related to semiconductors over the course of his career and was noted for his insight and leadership abilities. In 1968, he and Gordon Moore left Fairchild and cofounded Intel, which would eventually dominate the market for semiconductor microchip processors. He also served as an industry spokesman, cofounding of the Semiconductor Industry Association, beoming the first chief executive officer (CEO) of the nonprofit consortium of semiconductor chip manufacturers SEMATECH, and earning the nickname Mayor of Silicon Valley.

Kristen Nygaard: In the 1960s, the Norwegian computer scientist Kristen Nygaard, in collaboration with Ole-John Dahl, developed a new programming language, Simula, and a new methodology for programming, object-oriented programming, that would result in computer programs that would more closely follow the way people work. This system, based on chunks of code (objects) that could be assembled and modified in almost limitless fashion, made it possible to create programs with greater power and to reduce the time required to devise code. In the first part of the twenty-first century, object-orented programming is used in countless business applications and is the basis for developing applications on the Internet. In addition to his technical contributions, Nygaard was an active and articulate participant in his nation's political process, seeking to keep Norway's social and economic foundations intact.

O

Ed Oates: Ed Oates was one of the three founders (soon joined by a fourth employee) who left Ampex Corporation to form Software Development Laboratories, a relational database and services company that was eventually renamed the Oracle Corporation in honor of its flagship product, the world's leading relational database management system.

Kenneth H. Olsen: Kenneth H. Olsen is cofounder of Digital Equipment Corporation (DEC, or Digital). His love for engineering and his philosophy of getting the job done and giving the customer value made his company a leading competitor against IBM in computer

sales in the 1980s. He developed a management style unheard of in the 1960s, placing faith in and giving latitude to his employees. In 1992, Olsen resigned as president and chief executive officer (CEO) of the DEC, which was bought by Compaq in 1998 for $9.6 billion.

Ray Ozzie: Ray Ozzie developed the groundbreaking collaboration software Lotus Notes after developing the integrated suite Lotus Symphony. He joined Microsoft in the twenty-first century, first as its chief technical officer and then taking over the chief software architect position from Bill Gates. He left the company dissatisfied with its progress in cloud computing.

P

David Packard: David Packard worked with his long-time friend and associate William Redington "Bill" Hewlett to create the Hewlett-Packard Company. As outgoing and gregarious as his partner was quiet and self-effacing, Packard was known for his administrative and sales abilities and served as president, chief executive officer (CEO), and chairman. Packard also took a break from Hewlett-Packard to serve as the U.S. Deputy Secretary of Defense, afterward returning to the company he helped create. Well known for his deep commitment to a variety of philanthropic activities, he was awarded the Presidential Medal of Freedom in 1988.

Seymour Papert: Mathematician Seymour Papert developed the Logo programming language, a dialect of Lisp, which is used mainly to teach programming concepts. He is also a prominent theorist in the field of artificial intelligence, serving as a faculty member in of the Artificial Intelligence Laboratory at the Massachusetts Institute of Technology (MIT) from 1967 to 1981. His work has long been concerned with theories of learning and with child development, and he was instrumental in the One Laptop Per Child project, which seeks to provide low-cost educational computers to children in developing nations.

Blaise Pascal: Blaise Pascal was a French philosopher, inventor, writer, mathematician, and physicist. He created the first mechanical calculating machine and was also an important mathematician. Although he explored projective geometry, his work on probability theory still resonates with economists and computer scientists today. Pascal's name was given to a programming language as a means of honoring his many accomplishments related to computer science.

Rosalind Picard: Rosalind Picard, founder and director of the Affective Computing Group at the Massachusetts

Institute of Technology (MIT) Media Lab, wrote Affective Computing (1997), the seminal textbook in the field she helped establish. Affective computing is computing that relates to or influences emotion and other affective phenomena. Picard, professor of media arts and sciences at MIT, is also codirector of the Things That Think Consortium, an association, begun in 1995, of more than fifty companies and research groups with an interest in embedding computation into the environment and everyday objects. She also cofounded Affectiva, Inc., in 2009 to provide emotion-measurement technologies to companies, corporations, agencies, and universities. An inventor in addition to her other roles, Picard holds patents on several sensors, algorithms, and systems related to affective computing.

Hasso Plattner: Known for his many hobbies and pragmatic nature, Hasso Plattner is a German entrpreneur with a global perspective. He cofounded the world's largest software development company, SAP AG, and has more than forty years' experience in the technology industry, making him a founding member of the digital revolution. Plattner's analytical approach to business and consensus management theory are two of the main contributers to SAP's success. By providing corporate customers with real-time solutions to their business-reporting needs, Plattner and SAP have changed the way people do business.

Kim Polese: Kim Polese was product manager for one of the most influential languages in computing, Java. She cofounded Marimba, a company specializing in "push" technology, and served as chief executive officer of SpikeSource, a company specializing in supporting open source software. She has been one of the most visible women working in Silicon Valley since the 1990s and a champion for encouraging more young women to consider careers in computing, information technology, and entrepreneurship.

R

Dennis Ritchie: Dennis Ritchie was a codeveloper of the Unix operating system at Bell Laboratories and created the programming language C. Both remain widely used today, as do their descendants, including the object-oriented language C++ and the open source version of Unix, Linux.

Virginia Rometty: Virginia Rometty, a computer scientist and electrical engineer, became president and chief executive officer (CEO) of IBM on January 1, 2012, the first woman named to lead the company in its one hundred years in business. Rometty joined IBM as a systems engineer in 1981 and spent the next three decades rising through the ranks. She held a variety of positions, establishing a reputation for technological expertise and people skills that had insiders speculating about her as a possible CEO at least a decade before the historic announcement that she would lead the company. Immediately prior to being named IBM's top executive, she served as senior vice president and group executive for IBM Sales, Marketing and Strategy. She was a key player in IBM's transformation from a seller of goods into provider of technological solutions to problems in finance, insurance, health care, and transportation.

Guido van Rossum: Guido van Rossum is the creator of Python, one of the most popular scripting languages for the Internet. Originally released in 1991, Python takes its name from the comedy group Monty Python and began as a hobby. Although Python has become one of the most widely used languages in Internet applications (Google relies heavily on it), van Rossum gave no thought to its practical ends when designing it; he was more interested in principles of programming language design than in the purposes to which that language was put. He continues to develop Python today while working for Google.

S

Jean Sammet: Jean Sammet is an influential programmer who assisted in the creation of COBOL, developed FORMAC, oversaw the development of Ada, and wrote a 1969 book on the history and fundamentals of programming that is considered a classic. She was active in the computer industry in the 1960s and 1970s, holding a number of key positions in industry groups and organizing the first conference on the history of programming languages of the Association for Computing Machinery (ACM) and its Special Interest Group on Symbolic and Algebraic Manipulation. She was also the ACM's first woman president.

Lucy Sanders: Lucy Sanders is cofounder and chief executive officer (CEO) of the National Center for Women and Information Technology, a consortium of more than three hundred corporations, universities, and nonprofits that work to increase the participation of girls and women in computing and information technology. Sanders also serves as executive in residence for the Alliance for Technology, Learning, and Society at the University of Colorado at Boulder, a campuswide interdisciplinary initiative. She worked at AT&T Bell Laboratories (Bell Labs), Lucent Bell Labs, and Avaya Labs for two decades and is a Bell Labs Fellow, the highest technical accomplishment bestowed by that prestigious organization. Sanders holds several patents in the area of communications technology.

Linda S. Sanford: Linda Szabat Sanford is a senior vice president at IBM, making her one of the highest-ranking women in the company. She has spent her entire professional career at IBM and led the company's internal transformation to becoming a globally integrated enterprise organized around the on-demand principle. As an extremely visible and successful woman achieving

success at the highest levels of technology and business management, she has received many honors and serves on numerous boards, including the board of directors of the Partnership for New York City, a membership organization of top corporate leadership dedicated to enhancing the city's position as a center of finance, commerce, and innovation.

Michael Saylor: Michael Saylor was one of the key innovators who developed the system of establishing relational databases through decision support systems (DSS). This allowed him to combine information from a large number of separate databases, often held by the same company, and trace connections among them, which, in turn, could be used by executives at that company to monitor existing sales, identify successes or failures related to promotions and advertising campaigns, and then predict the possibility of improving sales through the use of the same or different strategies.

Eric Schmidt: Former chief executive of Google from 2001 to 2011, Eric Schmidt continues to serve as its executive chairman. He has a long history in the computer industry, including work at think tanks Bell Laboratoriess and Xerox Palo Alto Research Center (PARC) and a long stint at Sun Microsystems, where he was its first software manager.

Claude Shannon: Claude Shannon has been called the father of information theory. Information theory quantifies information and originated in the context of signal processing and the compression, storage, and communication of data; it has since been applied to areas as diverse as quantum computing, natural language processing, and the evolution of molecular codes. A cryptographer, mathematician, and engineer, Shannon laid much of the groundwork for digital computers and circuitry while still a graduate student at the Massachusetts Institute of Technology (MIT), and he later contributed to the code-breaking efforts of the Allies during World War II.

Stan Shih: The father of Taiwan's electronics industry, Stan Shih founded Acer with his wife, Carolyn Yeh, in 1976 and turned it from a small electronics parts distributor to the fourth-largest manufacturer of personal computers (PCs) in the world. In Shih's wake, other Taiwanese companies, such as HTC and Asustek, have made waves in the computer industry, holding their own against their American and Japanese competitors.

Alan Shugart: Alan Shugart worked as a scientist for IBM from 1951 to 1968 as a member of the development team that built the first computer disk drive. First known as a memory disk, it later became most well known as the floppy disk. He next served as vice president of product development for Memorex (1969–73) and then cofounded leading floppy disk manufacturer Shugart Associates in 1973 and the pioneering hard drive manufacturer Seagate Technology in 1979. A pioneer and champion of the hard disk drive industry, he was known as the Disk King.

Barbara Simons: Barbara Simons is an expert on voting technology and has served as an expert adviser to the U.S. president, the U.S. military, and other organizations regarding the security of different methods of voting. She served as president of the Association for Computing Machinery (ACM) and is involved with efforts to get more women and members of underrepresented minority groups involved in computer science.

Charles Simonyi: As a computer programmer and software developer, Charles Simonyi led the team that developed Microsoft Word, Excel, and other application programs. He is credited with helping to develop such basic elements of personal computing as icons, pull-down menus, and the mouse. Before he joined Microsoft, he was employed at Xerox's Palo Alto Research Center (PARC) in California, where he led in the development of a text editor and graphical user interface that made personal computing possible. Leaving Microsoft in 2002, Simonyi cofounded Intentional Software Corporation, for which he serves as chairman of the board and chief technology officer. He is also well known as a philanthropist and a space tourist, the first to make two flights.

George Stibitz: George Stibitz was a part of what may have been the greatest technical innovation organization of the twentieth century, Bell Laboratories. Not as well known as other innovators of the twentieth century, Stibitz conceived the first electric digital computer. The claim has been disputed by some, as similar work was being performed in Germany, Japan, and Cambridge, Massachusetts, but none was as advanced or resulted in an operating machine as early as Stibitz's 1940 Model I Complex Calculator. Stibitz designed the prototype and supervised construction of this machine, demonstrating its remote use in 1940. During World War II, he led the development of increasingly advanced computers. After the war, he continued that work until he transitioned to developing computerized solutions for medical problems and performing medical research.

Bjarne Stroustrup: Bjarne Stroustrup created the C++ language, the first widely used object-oriented programming language, and remains a highly influential spokesperson on issues such as the design of programming languages, education in computer science, and the philosophy of computer programming. Stroustrup also wrote an influential book on programming, helped develop standards for C++, and continues to teach, conduct research, and advise students at Texas A&M University.

T

Robert Taylor: Robert Taylor is one of the fathers of the Internet. He helped to created the ARPANET, a scientific- and defense-oriented network funded by the U.S. Department of Defense. Throughout his career, Taylor, whose background included studies in philosophy and psychology, remained focused on the usefulness of computers as a means of communication and extending the reach of human thought—a remarkable perspective in the early years of computing, when computers were considered primarily as computational machines and when interacting with them required stacks of punched paper cards.

Ken Thompson: A computer engineer with Bell Laboratories, Ken Thompson contributed a number of innovations to the industry, including the character-encoding set used today by the World Wide Web, the first purpose-built chess computer, and the use of regular expressions in computer applications. However, his most influential achievement was his development of the Unix operating system with Dennis Ritchie.

Janie Tsao: Janie Tsao, a Taiwanese immigrant to the United States, is a cofounder of Linksys, a leading manufacturer of home networking products with a line of wired and wireless products for consumers and small office or home office users. Tsao and her husband founded Linksys in April 1988 and over the next fifteen years worked to make the company a market leader. Linksys was acquired by Cisco Systems in 2003 for $500 million. Tsao, who had served as vice president of worldwide sales, marketing, and business development for the company, continued in this role for the Linksys division of Cisco until 2007. She was named Entrepreneur of the Year by, Inc. magazine in 2004.

Alan Turing: Known as the father computer science and artificial intelligence, Alan Turing successfully decoded the Nazi encryption device, the Enigma machine. This accomplishment is regarded by many as a deciding factor in the Allied victory in World War II. In addition, he created the Turing machine; the bombe machine; the Turing test; a blueprint for an early stored-program computer, the Automatic Computing Engine (ACE); and software that established the field of artificial intelligence.

V

John von Neumann: John von Neumann was a Hungarian American scientist who is widely accepted as the finest mathematician in modern history. Like Vannevar Bush and Albert Einstein, he did much to bridge the gap between the nineteenth and the twentieth centuries, advancing the state of his fields considerably. He was a central figure in both the Manhattan Project and the Institute for Advance Study in Princeton, two of the most significant institutions of mid-century American science.

W

Ted Waitt: Ted Waitt founded Gateway, a company that specialized in providing quality computer hardware at a low price to individual customers. Waitt made his fortune with the company, capitalizing on the fact that he entered the business at a time when the market for personal computers was booming, then left in his early thirties to pursue other interests. After leaving Gateway in 2000, Waitt became a well-known philanthropist. He returned to Gateway in 2002 to help the company through difficult times.

Larry Wall: Larry Wall created the scripting language Perl and remains its "Benevolent Dictator for Life," overseeing its continued development.

An Wang: An Wang was a Chinese-born naturalized American citizen who was instrumental in the development of modern computing, initially at Harvard University as a developer of core memory; then as the founder of Wang Laboratories, which created electronic calculators and a wide range of applications that used numerical controls; and finally as a significant player in development and sales of word-processing and computing hardware of various sizes.

Charles Wang: Charles Wang, cofounder of the firm that evolved into CA Technologies, Inc., saw a need for third-party software for mainframe computers and helped to build the company that provided this into one of the largest global software providers. CA Technologies expanded its initial expertise and developed what became enterprise solution software, antivirus protection, and security products. As technology evolved, Wang helped CA Technologies expand its product lines from those intended for its initial corporate client base to offerings that were sold directly to consumers for use on their home computers.

John Warnock: As founder and chief executive officer (CEO) of Adobe Systems, John Warnock has been one of the major designers of computer software. He was behind the design of the portable document format (PDF), which has transformed the sharing of computer files and, through the digitization of books, journals, and newspapers, transformed access to scholarship for academicians and general readers around the world. Warnock's success came from making the Adobe Reader for Adobe Acrobat freely available, and then charging for the "maker" program.

Padmasree Warrior: A chemical engineer by training, Warrior was chief technology officer (CTO) for Motorola and Cisco Systems and had a huge and positive impact on both companies. She is known in the technology industry for her ability to identify trends. She recognizes the need for constant development of new technology to improve business networking systems. Her analytical and pragmatic mind has helped secure Cisco Systems' place as a leader in technology.

Thomas J. Watson, Sr.: Thomas J. Watson, Sr., was one of the first entrepreneurs in computing. He built International Business Machines, now IBM, from a maker of accounting equipment into the dominant corporation in business machines before transitioning the company to computers and inexorably moving into worldwide dominance. He gave the company its succinct motto: "Think." His forty-two years at IBM also saw the company struggle to adapt as rapidly as smaller competitors. Hamstrung by its very success, the organization's massiveness made rapid change difficult. Still, he left a business that dominated the field the one against which others were forced to measure themselves.

Maurice Wilkes: Maurice Wilkes was one of developers of the Early Delay Storage Automatic Calculator (EDSAC), which was the successor to the J. Presper Eckert with John William Mauchly's first general-purpose digital electronic computer, the Electronic Numerical Integrator and Computer (ENIAC). EDSAC was the first practical stored-program computer, the first capable of running realistic programs and achieving useful outputs. Wilks also invented microprogramming and wrote an early standard textbook in computer science. Today he is considered the father of British computing and a major figure in the international computing field.

Frederic Williams: Frederic Williams worked on a range of projects for the British government during World War II and after the war saw the possibilities in developing a computer with a digital memory using a cathode-ray tube. He designed and built the first computer with a digital memory, which was known as the Baby, at the University of Manchester. This was followed by another computer, which was manufactured for sale. Although in comparison to current machines these early computers were large and cumbersome, they were important steps in the development of computers.

Niklaus Wirth: Although famous as the originator of the Pascal programming language, Niklaus Wirth went beyond this achievement, developing the ALGOL-W and Modula 2 languages. He is also an educator and philosopher concerning programs and programming practices, adamant that increasing complexity is not synonymous with sophistication. He is thus opposed to the increasing, and what he considers to be needless, complexity found in certain programming languages such as C++. He is credited with developing the principles of structured programming, which examines a problem and organizes it into smaller units, providing a basis for writing code. According to Wirth, programming is a holistic process and should not focus merely on the coding but also how design determines how an application should be built.

Beatrice Worsley: Beatrice Worsley has been recognized as Canada's first female computer scientist. She worked with Henry Wallman, a member of the Radiation Laboratory at the Massachusetts Institute of Technology, on her master's thesis and studied at Cambridge University with Douglas Hartree, who developed numerical analysis, and Alan Turing, who is often called the father of computer science and artificial intelligence. Worsley built a differential analyzer and a mechanical analog computer, and she collaborated on a compiler for the Ferranti Mark I, the world's first commercially available, general-purpose computer. In 1952, she became one of the first women to receive a Ph.D. in computer science.

Steve Wozniak: From childhood, Steve Wozniak was adept at building computers and using them to entertain and to solve problems. His friend Steve Jobs was a natural seller of ideas, and they formed an ideal partnership for creating the revolutionary Apple computer. When Wozniak gave up his active role in the company and Jobs was forced out, Apple floundered but was revitalized after Jobs's return in the late 1990s. Wozniak devoted his post-Apple years to philanthropic causes in San Jose, establishing the Technology Museum of Innovation and the Children's Discovery Museum and contributing to the Cleveland Ballet. He also created the first programmable remote control and developed GPS technology. He worked to get computers into schools and remains active in the battle against the infringement of electronic freedom and in providing legal counsel for computer hackers. In 2009, he became chief scientist for the Salt Lake City–based company Fusion-io.

Z

Konrad Zuse: Computer pioneer Konrad Zuse went unnoticed for several years because he was working in Germany during the Third Reich, in the 1930s and early 1940s. During that time, he invented the first program-controlled Turing-complete computer, the first high-level programming language, and the first commercial computer, but his work was not discovered outside Germany until the end of World War II, when IBM (which had worked with the German government before the war) optioned his patents.

Indexes

Category Index

COMPANY INDEX

Index